Behavioral Risk Management

BEHAVIORAL RISK MANAGEMENT

MANAGING THE PSYCHOLOGY THAT DRIVES DECISIONS AND INFLUENCES OPERATIONAL RISK

HERSH SHEFRIN

BEHAVIORAL RISK MANAGEMENT
Copyright © Hersh Shefrin 2016

All rights reserved. No reproduction, copy or transmission of this publication may be made without written permission. No portion of this publication may be reproduced, copied or transmitted save with written permission. In accordance with the provisions of the Copyright, Designs and Patents Act 1988, or under the terms of any licence permitting limited copying issued by the Copyright Licensing Agency, Saffron House, 6–10 Kirby Street, London EC1N 8TS.

Any person who does any unauthorized act in relation to this publication may be liable to criminal prosecution and civil claims for damages.

First published 2016 by
PALGRAVE MACMILLAN

The author has asserted their right to be identified as the author of this work in accordance with the Copyright, Designs and Patents Act 1988.

Palgrave Macmillan in the UK is an imprint of Macmillan Publishers Limited, registered in England, company number 785998, of Houndmills, Basingstoke, Hampshire, RG21 6XS.

Palgrave Macmillan in the US is a division of Nature America, Inc., One New York Plaza, Suite 4500, New York, NY 10004-1562.

Palgrave Macmillan is the global academic imprint of the above companies and has companies and representatives throughout the world.

Hardback ISBN: 978–1–137–44560–5
E-PUB ISBN: 978–1–137–44561–2
E-PDF ISBN: 978–1–137–44562–9
DOI: 10.1057/9781137445629

Distribution in the UK, Europe and the rest of the world is by Palgrave Macmillan®, a division of Macmillan Publishers Limited, registered in England, company number 785998, of Houndmills, Basingstoke, Hampshire RG21 6XS.

Library of Congress Cataloging-in-Publication Data

Shefrin, Hersh, 1948–
  Behavioral risk management : managing the psychology that drives decisions and influences operational risk / Hersh Shefrin.
    pages cm
  Includes index.
  ISBN 978–1–137–44560–5 (alk. paper)
   1. Risk management—Psychological aspects. 2. Risk perception.
 3. Decision making—Psychological aspects. I. Title.
HD61.S4435 2015
658.4903019—dc23   2015021834

A catalogue record for the book is available from the British Library.

Printed in the United States of America.

Contents

Figures and Tables   vii
Preface   xiii

1. Introduction   1

Part I

2. SP/A Theory's Focus on Three Key Emotions   19
3. Prospect Theory's Focus on Gains, Losses, and Framing   37
4. Biases and Risk   53
5. Personality and Risk   71

Part II

6. Process, Pitfalls, and Culture   85
7. Minsky, the Financial Instability Hypothesis, and Risk Management   105
8. Aspirational Pitfalls at UBS and Merrill Lynch   125
9. Cheating Issues at S&P and Moody's   141
10. Groupthink at Fannie, Freddie, and AIG   157
11. The Winner's Curse Strikes at RBS, Fortis, and ABN AMRO   173
12. Behavioral Dimension of Systemic Risk   191
13. Financial Regulation and Psychology   211
14. Risk of Fraud, Madoff, and the SEC   229
15. Risk, Return, and Individual Stocks   249
16. How Psychology Brought Down MF Global   267

17.	JPMorgan's Whale of a Risk Management Failure	281
18.	Risk Management Profiles: Con Ed, BP, and MMS	299
19.	Information Sharing Failures at Southwest Airlines, General Motors, and the Agencies That Regulate Them	319
20.	Conclusion	335

Appendix A: A Deeper Dive into SP/A Theory — 347

Appendix B: A Deeper Dive into Prospect Theory — 369

Appendix C: Integrating SP/A Theory and Prospect Theory — 385

Appendix D: A Deeper Dive into Heuristics and Biases — 409

Appendix E: A Formal Model of Organizational Risk — 435

Appendix F: Modelling FIH Issues — 445

Appendix G: Empirical Proxies of Sentiment — 453

Appendix H: A Formal Model for Identifying Failing Banks — 459

Appendix I: FIH Issues in China and Europe — 461

Notes — 469

Index — 509

Figures and Tables

Figures

2.1	Probability density functions for the future value of the positions PK and RF	22
2.2	Valuations elicited from a participant Jeff in a risk choice and valuation experiment involving undergraduates	32
2.3	Valuations elicited from a participant Tom in the same risk choice and valuation experiment involving business managers	33
4.1	Coin-flip histograms for two groups of participants in an experiment	60
6.1	Conceptual framework underlying RMP	94
7.1	Hedge finance	110
7.2	Speculative finance	111
7.3	Ponzi finance	112
7.4	Ponzi finance with short-term financing being used for longer-term assets	114
12.1	Time series of the VIX between January 2000 and September 2015	195
12.2	Trajectories for estimates of excessive optimism and overconfidence between 2002 and 2009	196
12.3	Econometric estimate of the crash probability	197
12.4	Left tail sentiment measure	197
12.5	Long-term trajectory of the Baker-Wurgler sentiment series BW	198
12.6	CAPE, Campbell and Shiller's cyclically adjusted P/E for US stocks	199
12.7	Trajectory of the Yale/Shiller crash confidence indices	200
12.8	Trajectory of the Gilchrist-Zakrajšek credit spread	200
12.9	SRISK% and leverage, at the end of March 2007	203
12.10	SRISK% and leverage, at the end of September 2007	204
12.11	SRISK% and MES, at the end of March 2008	205
12.12	SRISK% and leverage, at the end of March 2008	206

12.13	MES trajectories for select financial institutions for the period May through October of 2008	207
12.14	Absolute values of correlations between excessive optimism and MES and optimism for the period March 2007 through October 2009	208
13.1	Equation $ROE = [(EBIT - iD)(1-t)]/E$	215
13.2	Bell-shaped density function and corresponding cumulative distribution function	216
13.3	Patterns of default rates over time for double-A and B-rated bonds	217
13.4	Two density functions, one for a standard normal ($N(0,1)$), and the other for a power law	218
13.5	A vulnerability classification heuristic as a sequence of cue-defined hurdles	225
14.1	Gross value of the split-strike conversion strategy on the expiration date	232
14.2	Trajectory of cumulative monthly returns for Fairfield Sentry and for the S&P 500	234
14.3	Monthly return series for the S&P 500	235
14.4	Monthly return series for Fairfield Sentry	236
14.5	Return histograms for the monthly returns associated with Fairfield Sentry and the S&P 500 respectively	236
15.1	Linear structure associated with both the capital market line and the securities market line	250
15.2	Tim Hellman's correlations for variables expected return and risk with beta, size, B/M, and past returns	259
15.3	Correlations for variables expected return and risk with beta, size, B/M, and past returns for the group of analysts to which Tim Hellman belonged	259
15.4	Two views of the relationship between BW and expected return	262
17.1	A stylized depiction of the contingent payoffs for long positions in the two CDX contracts	284
17.2	A stylized depiction of a short HY position	285
17.3	The tripling in position size of SCP during the first three months of 2012	291
17.4	Magnitude of the losses to the portfolio during the first six months of 2012	292
A.1	Shapes of the six probability density functions (pdfs) Lopes used in her experiments	350
A.2	Illustrative pdf function $p(x)$ and its associated decumulative distribution function $D(x)$	352

A.3	How fear operates on PK	354
A.4	Functions h_s, h_p, and h	354
A.5	The probability of achieving at least $1,100 from each of the six alternatives SS, PK, U, BM, LS, RF	358
A.6	Valuations of a subject Pamela	359
A.7	Valuations of a subject Jack	359
A.8	Valuations of a subject Bill	361
A.9	Group mean valuations for WTA and WTP, for the six risky alternatives	363
A.10	Allocations and ratings scaled down by one-tenth, for the six risky alternatives	363
B.1	Shapes of three utility functions	371
B.2	Shape of the prospect theory value function	374
B.3	π-function in original prospect theory	375
B.4	w-weighting function in cumulative prospect theory	379
C.1	A graphical depiction of the information in Table C.2	388
C.2	The decumulative distributions for returns associated with Risk A and Risk B in Zeisberger's experiment	392
C.3	Graph of the SP/A L –function	399
D.1	A "fault tree" describing possible ways in which a once profitable restaurant might go out of business	410
D.2	A "fault tree" describing possible ways in which a once profitable restaurant might go out of business	412
D.3	Histogram response for subject hit rates to overconfidence trivia quiz	425
D.4	Histogram response for hit rates per question to overconfidence trivia quiz	426
D.5	Histogram response rates for Question D6 in Appendix D	426
D.6	Histogram of responses for both the prior probability and posterior probability for Question D10, the bag of chips problem, associated with the responses of a group of risk managers	433
D.7	Histogram of responses for both the prior probability and posterior probability for Question D10, the bag of chips problem, associated with the responses of a group of undergraduate finance majors	433
E.1	Elliptical confidence region for a bivariate distribution for random variables x and y	436
E.2	Impact associated with increasing the value of $xCrit$	438
G.1	Three pdfs associated with the future gross returns for the market at some specific date	455
G.2	Two different pricing kernels, one objective and one subjective	456

G.3	Output from the application of the theoretical concepts to market data from December 12, 2005	457
H.1	The analogue of Figure E.2 in Appendix E	459

TABLES

4.1	Activities and technologies associated with Question 2 in Chapter 4	57
11.1	The computation the FSA used to estimate RBS's Basel III common equity tier 1 ratio	179
11.2	The FSA's computations showing RBS's tier 1 capital	180
11.3	Details of the funding structure in which RBS used mostly short-term debt to fund €22.6b for its share of the cash portion of the deal	182
15.1	Correlations between perceived risk and specific characteristics	256
15.2	Correlations between expected return and specific characteristics	257
15.3	Impact of sentiment on pairwise correlations for judgments and characteristics	263
A.1	Payoff means and standard deviations for the six Lopes risky alternatives	350
A.2	Medians, means, standard deviations, and coefficients of variation	362
A.3	Values of SP, A, and L for the six risky alternatives when L is $L = SP + \zeta A$, where $\zeta = 900$	365
B.1	Two alternative frames for Question 3 in Chapter 3	373
B.2	Two alternatives, A' and B' that feature the same possible payoffs, $2,000 and $2,500	376
B.3	The value function v-values in a quasi-hedonic editing example involving gains using Kahneman and Tversky parameters for $v(x)$ and a weighting value $\pi(0.5) = 0.49$	380
B.4	The value function v-values in a quasi-hedonic editing example involving losses using Kahneman and Tversky parameters for $v(x)$ and a weighting value $\pi(0.5) = 0.49$	381
B.5	The computed value of v-risk showing that according to the theory, Larry rejects the risk shown in Table B.4	382
B.6	An example using the typical Kahneman-Tversky parameters illustrating quasi-hedonic editing computations	384
C.1	CPT-values and associated SP/A values for the six Lopes risks	386
C.2	Data for the Zeisberger experiment	388

C.3	Statistical information associated with the risks in the Zeisberger experiment	389
C.4	Comparison of Risk A to Risk B from the perspectives of both CPT and SP/A	390
C.5	Underlying numerical data for the L-function displayed in Figure C.3	399
C.6	Data for six subjects who participated in a series of experiments that elicited their responses to the survey questions discussed in Chapters 2, 3, and 5	401
C.7	The probability of achieving a aspiration level of $1,100	403
C.8	Sample output for a procedure in which SP/A parameters are inferred by fitting s, p, r, and ζ to the ranking and valuations of the Lopes risk alternatives	406
D.1	Average restaurant fault tree probability assignments	413
D.2	Activities and technologies associated with Question 2 in Chapter 4 and Question D1 in Appendix D	415
D.3	The results for four different groups who answered Question D1	416
D.4	The responses of four different groups to Question D2	419
D.5	A list of 18 possible events pertaining to Question D3	421
D.6	The menu of responses from which subjects chose to assess the probability attached to each life event, when responding to Question D3	421
D.7	The responses of four different groups to Question D3	422
D.8	The responses of four different groups to Question D4	423

Preface

MY INTEREST IN THE ROLE THAT PSYCHOLOGY PLAYS IN RISK MANAGEMENT goes back decades, but the events that induced me to write this book occurred after 2008. Before I get to those events, I would like to provide some historical context.

My first experience with a specific application of psychology to risk management occurred in 1978, when I worked on a consulting project for the US Department of Energy at the Lawrence Livermore National Laboratory in Livermore, California. The project theme focused on external risks that confront nuclear power facilities. By and large, the methodology for this project was rooted in traditional decision theory. However, my role was to bring in insights from what was at the time the new behavioral approach, based on insights from psychology. It was an exciting time, and I remember being at the lab describing the highlights from a working paper version of the yet to be published paper "Prospect Theory." This paper, now famous, written by psychologists Daniel Kahneman and his late colleague Amos Tversky, was specifically cited by the Nobel committee when awarding the 2002 Nobel Prize in economics to Kahneman.

Despite getting a foot in the door, it took many years for the new behavioral ideas to gain traction among both scholars and practitioners whose primary concern was risk management. During the late 1980s and early 1990s, the field was a much different discipline than it is today, and was mostly focused on issues related to insurance. From my experience speaking about behavioral topics to the Silicon Valley chapter of the Risk and Insurance Management Society (RIMS), my sense at the time was that risk managers were intrigued with behavioral insights, but had no clear sense about how to apply the ideas in practice.

During the 1990s, a new literature introduced the term "behavioral risk management" to describe the application of ideas from industrial and organizational psychology to analyze workplace risk. Prominent risk issues in this literature pertain to health and disability, which are natural topics in insurance-focused risk management. Associated behavioral issues involve interpersonal dynamics and group process.[1] In this book I seek to extend the focus of the behavioral risk management literature to address a wider set of issues.

In 1999, I saw the first sign that behavioral ideas had gained a toehold in the financial risk management community. That year, I gave a one-day behavioral finance workshop in London, organized by the conference company IIR, and one of the workshop participants was a risk manager named Luca Celati. Luca was keenly aware of the role that psychology played in trading. He went on to write the first book applying behavioral ideas to financial risk management, which he titled *The Dark Side of Risk Management*. Luca's book was published in 2005, and is full of important insights.

The year 1999 also marked the publication of my own book, *Beyond Greed and Fear*. I wrote that book primarily for financial practitioners, and the book came out during the dot-com bubble. That bubble and its subsequent collapse provided a vivid example of "sentiment risk," which is the financial risk associated with phenomena that are psychologically driven.

After 2000, I began to emphasize sentiment risk in my presentations to finance professionals. The bursting of the dot-com bubble eventually faded in memory, and in 2004 global markets moved into a euphoric period that featured high returns and low volatility. Between 2006 and 2011, I gave a series of presentations at various risk management conferences organized by the conference company International Centre for Business Information (ICBI).

In December 2006, I made a presentation at the ICBI's Ri$k Minds conference, which included the following slide highlighting the main point of my talk:

LESSON FOR RISK MANAGERS

- The risk you face is a combination of fundamental risk and sentiment.
- You ignore sentiment risk at your peril.

The conference feedback made clear that I had gotten this point across, and I remember one conference participant telling me that she shuddered when she heard me make it.

At the 2006 Ri$k Minds conference, I first met Riccardo Rebonato, who authored the book *Plight of the Fortune Tellers*, and was then chief risk officer for the Royal Bank of Scotland (RBS). Riccardo and I exchanged views about the insights psychology brings to risk management, and the degree to which it is possible to measure sentiment. I learned a lot from our exchange, and later from his book.

The 2006 conference was something of a watershed, as I began to tailor my sentiment risk message for risk managers. In April 2007, I wrote an article about sentiment risk entitled "Trader Psychology and Market Corrections" for the publication *Policy & Markets*, focusing on the biases associated with atypically low market volatility. In that article I also noted rumblings at the time that appeared to stem from growing weakness in the US subprime housing market, and other concerns such as a decline in Chinese stocks stemming from rumors about the imposition of a capital gains tax in China. In May 2007, I made a presentation at the ICBI's global derivative conference on the subject of using derivative pricing models that reflect sentiment.

In October 2007, I gave a keynote address at the Annual China Finance Conference, where I compared a bubble in Chinese equity markets that was underway at the time to the dot-com bubble that had burst several years earlier. In my keynote, I made the point that China had an opportunity to learn from the past mistakes of others how to mitigate vulnerabilty to psychological pitfalls. In Appendix I, I discuss the way in which, during the subsequent eight years, China failed to learn the associated lessons.

In June 2008, my book *Ending the Management Illusion* was published. This book analyzes the role of behavioral finance in organizational culture. Among the various cases discussed in the book are two that formed the basis for a presentation I made in July 2008 at the ICBI's Ri$k Capital conference. The first involves rogue trader Jérôme Kerviel from the French bank Société Générale. The second involves the Swiss bank UBS, which incurred major losses from its operations in securities related to US subprime mortgages. At the invitation of a former UBS wealth manager, I had given a behavioral seminar at UBS's Amsterdam office several years earlier, which led me to learn something about the bank's culture.

At the Ri$k Capital conference, my session chair, Allan Yarish, who was from Société Générale, offered some insights of his own. With respect to UBS, a conference participant (and risk manager) told me after my talk that my analysis of events at UBS was consistent with what UBS itself had reported in a self-study published the previous April. Readers will find a behavioral analysis of this report in one of this book's chapters.

The Lehman bankruptcy occurred two months after the Ri$k Capital conference, and with that event an economic downturn morphed into the global financial crisis. The world's attention was beginning to turn to what some saw as enormous failures of risk management.

Interest in the psychological dimension of risk management rose dramatically in the wake of the financial crisis, and I was positioned to speak on the topic. Since 2000, I had been teaching executive education courses in

Amsterdam at the Amsterdam Institute of Finance (AIF). Some years before, AIF had foreseen the importance of executive education programs in risk management and had partnered with New York University (NYU) to offer a Master's-level program in the area. The first cohort went through the program in 2008–2009. I had the good fortune to make a presentation to this group in June 2009. Thereafter, I continued to teach a regular module in NYU's Master of Science in Risk Management program, and in addition developed a non-Master's course for AIF. These have been great opportunities to field-test behavioral ideas with financial professionals already working as risk managers. This book reflects much of what I learned teaching these programs.

In December 2011, I gave a presentation at the Ri$k Minds conference, this time emphasizing the importance of risk culture and what might aptly be called "ending the risk management illusion." By this time, the shock of the global financial crisis had dissipated, although the aftereffects remained. Risk managers now acknowledged that they ignored sentiment at their peril. I came away from that conference with the perception that risk managers' interest in recognizing and mitigating psychological pitfalls had ramped up.

I could see increased interest at PRMIA as well. PRMIA is the Professional Risk Managers' International Association, which like GARP (Global Association of Risk Professionals), offers programs and certification for risk managers. In 2012, PRMIA held a conference to mark its ten-year anniversary, and invited me to give a keynote address on a behavioral theme. My sense from that meeting is that conference participants resonated to the importance of psychological issues, but were unsure how to deal with them in practical terms. In my talk at the conference, I noted that none of the other speakers who discussed economic and financial stability in the wake of the financial crisis mentioned the name of Hyman Minsky, whose approach I describe in this book. I found this omission striking, given that Minsky's insights appeared prophetic in the aftermath of that crisis.

I have had several opportunities to make conference presentations about Minsky's ideas. At one such conference, in 2013, the International Risk Management Conference held in Copenhagen, I was particularly struck by Ed Altman from NYU, who spoke after me, and adapted his talk to incorporate remarks I had made about Minsky's insights. At this conference I also met Shann Turnbull, whose persistence induced me to think about connections between behavioral finance and networked governance.

I also gave a keynote presentation about Minsky's ideas at ICBI's 2015 Global Derivatives & Risk Management conference. The material for the presentation came from Chapter 12 of this book, which deals with systemic risk. Discussion during the question and answer period involved an overvalued US stock market, sovereign European debt and the manner in which

Minsky's perspective was playing out in China.[2] In the months that followed that conference, events pertaining to Greek sovereign debt, the future of the euro, overvaluation of US stocks, and asset bubbles in China followed a Minsky dynamic and became front-page headlines. A discussion of these events is the subject of Appendix I.

My discussion with program managers from GARP reinforced the idea that risk managers are intrigued by behavioral ideas. At the same time, these program managers have the sense that, although GARP members might have been intrigued by speakers making behavioral presentations, they have not been able to implement behavioral insights into their day-to-day activities involving data, modeling, and regulations. My intention in writing this book is to offer a conceptual framework aimed at implementation.

A survey conducted by GARP in 2014 provides insights into the importance that their membership attaches to behavioral issues. The survey identifies risk managers' views about tasks, knowledge, and skills associated with the practice of risk management. To be sure, some of the top-ranked issues have behavioral components. For example, in respect to risk governance, communicating risk to stakeholders was accorded top priority. In respect to modeling, communicating and reporting deficiencies of Value at Risk (VaR) was accorded top priority. The communication of risk involves issues of framing, a major behavioral concept. Focusing on the deficiencies of VaR helps mitigate overconfidence, a major psychological bias.

At the same time, respondents to the GARP survey attached much less importance to issues emphasized by the behavioral approach. These issues include asset bubbles, shadow banking, and ethics, all of which feature prominently in this book. A major goal of this book is to elevate the importance of these issues in the minds of risk managers, and induce implementation changes to their processes that address them.

I have learned from the participants in my executive risk management courses what it takes to bring awareness of psychological issues relevant to the field, and what it takes to implement new behaviorally based risk management skills. Awareness comes with a combination of standard lectures and participation in the thought experiments that have guided behavioral research. New skills come from practice and experience, along the lines I outlined in *Ending the Management Illusion*, and repeat here.

I have learned from my experience as a mutual fund trustee about the practice of risk management in investment companies. In particular, chairing audit committees has given me important insights into how chief compliance officers identify and manage a variety of risks.

This book is a natural sequel to my previous books, *Beyond Greed and Fear, Behavioral Corporate* Finance, and *Ending the Management Illusion*. This book begins with the same psychological concepts as the others, and then moves to describing how those concepts apply in practice. Where this book is different is in its explicit attention to risk management issues, and to the set of events that illustrate how the psychological concepts apply. All three previous books were published before "Lehman Day," and so predated the full blown eruption of the global financial crisis. In contrast, the behavioral analysis of that crisis is a major topic of this book.

The main themes of *Ending the Management Illusion* pertain to organizational culture, process, and pitfalls. These themes are also a major part of this book, in which the aim is to focus sharply on how risk management fits into the overall framework. In this regard, there is a small amount of overlap in regard to illustrative applications, namely to BP, Southwest Airlines, and UBS. In writing about these firms here, I incorporate new material about risk management that I did not have at the time I wrote *Ending the Management Illusion*. In doing so, I build on my previous writing.

There are two important differences between what I cover in this book and what I covered in *Ending the Management Illusion*. First, in this book I add an extensive discussion about important findings from research by neuroscientists that are critical to the practice of risk management. Second, instead of distributing prescriptive advice for mitigating psychological pitfalls throughout the book, which I did in *Ending the Management Illusion*, I instead concentrate key prescriptions into a few select chapters.

In writing this book, I decided that I wanted to integrate a series of ideas I have been addressing for the last several years. In doing so, I draw on many of my previous works. For the core psychology, I drew on *Beyond Greed and Fear* and *Behavioral Corporate Finance*. For the material about the process-pitfall interaction, I drew on *Ending the Management Illusion*.

This book has several chapters that pertain to the global financial crisis. I base some of these chapters on a contribution I wrote for a collection edited by Laurence Siegel called *Insights Into the Global Financial Crisis*. I titled this contribution "How Psychological Pitfalls Created the Global Financial Crisis," and it appeared alongside a piece by Paul McCulley, entitled "The Shadow Banking System and Hyman Minsky's Economic Journey." To McCulley belongs the credit for having coined the term "shadow banking." He was also among the minority of those who appreciated the perspective of economist Minsky, whose writings in the aftermath of the financial crisis read like those of a true prophet. During the Asian currency crisis of the late 1990s, McCulley coined another term—"Minsky moment"—to describe that crisis, because it captured many of the features about which Minsky had warned. I learned a great deal from McCulley's contribution, and reading it inspired me to relate Minsky's overall perspective on the root causes of financial instability to the psychological issues on which I had focused.

In drawing on my previous work to analyze the global financial crisis, such as the contribution mentioned in the previous paragraph, I incorporated elements from a variety of sources that are documented in the endnotes. Two I would single out here are coauthored chapter contributions, one with Meir Statman, titled "Behavioral Finance in the Financial Crisis: Market Efficiency, Minsky, and Keynes," and the other with Giovanni Barone-Adesi and Loriano Mancini, titled "Systemic Risk and Sentiment."

For the chapter discussing the theme of risk, return, and individual stocks, I drew on material that appears in several of my writings, including tables and figures that appear in my article "Investors' Judgments, Asset Pricing Factors, and Sentiment."

In updating the discussion of BP from *Ending the Management Illusion*, I drew from my article "BP's Failure to Debias: Underscoring the Importance of Behavioral Corporate Finance" which is coauthored with Enrico Cervellati.

When drawing on my own previous work, I adapted wording and language where I thought it appropriate. At the same time, if changing the language seemed to offer no improvement or worse, then I left my original phrasing intact.

Several risk managers have accepted the challenge of becoming authors in order to communicate in writing the wisdom they have gained from their experiences. I already mentioned Luca Celati, the theme of whose book is behavioral risk management, and Riccardo Rebonato, whose book touches on behavioral issues. I would also mention the writings of David Koenig, whose book *Governance Reimagined* includes an explicit discussion about psychology, and David Rowe, whose regular column in the publication *Risk Analysis* identifies issues ripe for behavioral analysis. I might mention here that Koenig's book makes the connection to "networked governance structures," an approach favored by Turnbull. In the last chapter of this book, I discuss the connection between the behavioral approach and networked governance.

In their books, Celati and Rebonato both mention the Talmud, which I found quite striking, as it is the compilation of Jewish oral law. What is the connection of risk management to the Talmud? Celati mentions a Yiddish proverb that states that, although men make plans through the act of thinking, the Almighty responds by laughing. This idea is indeed consistent with a number of psychological biases discussed in the book.[3] Rebonato cites a Talmudic passage that sets limits to the degree humans should inquire about four aspects of creation: before, beyond, above, and below. He connects this passage to limits associated with four aspects of statistical inquiry, aspects that, if not recognized, also give rise to psychological biases.

The Talmudic references by Celati and Rebonato have led me to ask myself whether the Talmud has more general lessons to offer for risk management, outside of specific religious affiliation, and I think the answer is yes. The rabbis who constructed the Talmud were well aware of risk management issues. For them, violations of Jewish law encapsulated within Torah were a major risk, and it is with this perspective that they created a culture designed to limit breaches of this law.

In Judaism, the relevant risk management phrase is to "build a fence around the Torah," by which is meant developing a set of behaviors and procedures that keep people from getting right up to the edge separating actions that are permissible by law, and actions that are prohibited. Rituals, values, and behaviors were constructed with a view to achieving more than compliance, an approach that can also be applied with benefit to modern risk management.[4]

I have many people to thank in connection with this book, indeed too many to name. However, I do wish to single out a few, and to apologize to everyone else who provided advice but whose name does not appear below. It was Dennis Jullens who invited me to speak at UBS and provided me with many insights during the time he was with the firm. Mark Lawrence is the risk manager who pointed me to the UBS self-study document at the Ri$k Capital conference.

At AIF, Brenda Childers encouraged me to develop an executive risk management course to teach at AIF that focused on behavioral issues, which I did. At NYU, Manjiree Jog teamed me up with Zur Shapira to teach behavioral finance in the Master of Science in Risk Management program, and helped me shape the course to fit the needs of its students. As readers of this book will see, I learned a lot from my interactions with Zur.

I owe a debt of gratitude to the many students who have taken my behavioral risk management courses. Some were already risk managers at the time they took my course, and provided excellent feedback with many insights from their own experiences. Among them are Beth Chester and Larry Stephan, the pseudonyms of risk managers whom you will encounter as protagonists in a short story threaded through part I of this book.

I extend my appreciation to many academics and practitioners from whom I learned so much about risk management through conversation. The list is too long to enumerate, although some of those conversations were especially useful to me as I wrote this book. In this regard, I thank Mark Abbott from Guardian Life, Torben Anderson from the Copenhagen School of Business, Chris Donohue and Bill May from GARP, Bob Hirth who chairs COSO, Bob Semple (formerly) from PwC, Paul Shotton from UBS, Ard Valk from ABN AMRO, and Simona Zipursky from the World Health Organization.

The Ri$k Minds 2011 conference I mentioned earlier provided me with an opportunity to participate in a panel together with a group of risk managers, which was titled "The CRO's Challenge! Determining the Best Strategy to Balance the Human and the Financial Element to Arrive at the Optimal Risk Strategy for the Business?" For me, this was both fun and instructive, as my fellow panelists were very knowledgeable, and we had done some advance homework in preparation for the panel event. I thank Bob Stribling, Group CRO from Suncorp; Bill Dawson, CRO of Wealth, Brokerage and Retirement, Wells Fargo & Co.; Paige Wisdom, Chief Enterprise Risk Officer of Freddie Mac; Jacques Beyssade, CRO of NATIXIS; and Philip Best, CRO of Threadneedle. I also thank Richard Barfield from PwC for interviewing me for a short conference video.[5]

In writing this book, I am especially indebted to many financial professionals who read portions of the manuscript and provided constructive feedback. I took their suggestions to heart, and this book is much better as a result. Many thanks go to Luca Celati, Sanjiv Das, Tim Kuhl, Catherine Lubochinsky, Robert Mendelson, Shabnam Mousavi, Riccardo Rebonato, Elizabeth Sheedy, and Ruth Whaley.

At Palgrave Macmillan, Brian Foster initially approached me about writing this book, and did so with keen interest before leaving the firm. His successor, Laurie Harting, helped me develop a tight focus and clear message.

To my wife, Arna, I owe my thanks for her patience, support, and generosity of spirit.

CHAPTER 1

INTRODUCTION

THE PSYCHOLOGICAL DIMENSION OF MANAGING RISK IS HUGE. THOSE WITH an understanding of the underlying psychology and the skills to recognize its manifestation in practice, have the opportunity to address its implications in a systematic fashion. Those without the understanding and the skills are destined to be more hit and miss in their approach to managing risk.

The stakes associated with factoring the psychological dimension into risk management are enormous. Virtually every major risk management catastrophe in the last 15 years has psychological pitfalls at its root. The list of catastrophes includes the 2008 bankruptcy of Lehman Brothers and subsequent global financial crisis, the 2010 explosion at BP's Macondo well in the Gulf of Mexico, which many regard as the worst environmental event in US history, and the 2011 nuclear meltdown at the Fukushima Daiichi power plant.[1]

A vital critical lesson that psychology can teach to practitioners of risk management is that people's judgments and decisions about risk vary with type of circumstance. This is because psychological research in the last half century has made enormous strides in identifying the nature of these circumstances. In this regard, the research teaches us that some effects are systematic with predictable components, but at the individual level other effects are random and unpredictable. For this reason, a significant aspect of the risk to be managed is indeed psychological.

Psychological studies have documented that our attitudes to risk are not uniform. In some circumstances we are averse to risk and in other circumstances we are risk seeking. Our tolerance for risk is partly dependent on whether we perceive the possible outcomes to be gains or losses, the degree to which the probabilities attached to key outcomes are small or large, and what goals we have set for ourselves.

Studies in neuroscience have documented that our attitudes to risk are related to electrochemical activities in our brains and bodies. Just as psychology informs us about the importance attached to framing events as gains or losses, neuroscience informs us that in a stable environment, the human visual system lowers attention to objects that are motionless, even when they remain in our field of vision, to the point where they seem to disappear. However, when these objects suddenly move, a part of our brain responds,[2] quickly signaling other parts of the brain about change that is taking place. Some changes will trigger processes involving hormones, neurotransmitters, glucose, and oxygen, which can impact both perceptions of, and reactions to, risk.

By and large, the field of risk management is quantitative in nature, relying on statistical tools and simulation techniques. The psychological concepts emphasized by the behavioral approach are a complement, not a substitute, for quantitative tools. I would make the case that the most significant risk management failures in recent history have their roots in psychology, and that the practice of risk management can be improved by incorporating an explicit psychological dimension.

The Financial Crisis Inquiry Commission has characterized the financial crisis as a major failure of risk management. I agree with this characterization, and devote several chapters to explaining the psychological pitfalls that generated the crisis. Relatedly, risk management in the financial sector has come to play a dominant role in the field of risk management, and this emphasis is reflected in the number of chapters devoted to financial risk management. However, many of the same psychological issues that are present in financial firms are also present in operating companies, a fact that will become readily apparent from the chapter discussions.

I have organized the book into two main parts. The first part of the book is dedicated to introducing the core psychological issues associated with the behavioral approach. These core issues pertain to emotions, framing, personality, and judgmental errors. Discussion of many of these issues used to be confined to the pages of academic journals. However, these issues are now accessible to the general public, as researchers and other authors have sought to write for a broad readership.

Understanding a psychological concept in theory and seeing how it applies to a specific risk management issue in practice are two different tasks. This takes us to the second part of the book, which is dedicated to applying the core psychology to gain insight into major risk events that took place, mostly in the last decade. Some application chapters introduce new psychological concepts on an as-needed basis.

The practice of risk management can be greatly improved by incorporating an explicit behavioral dimension that is rooted in psychology. In this regard, improvement is a multistage process and begins with an understanding and recognition of psychological phenomena. Readers will learn that there are specific actions that organizations can undertake to incorporate understanding, recognition, and specific behavioral interventions into their practice of risk management.

Some actions are structural in nature and relate to the manner in which organizations structure their cultures and processes. Other actions are more piecemeal, and deal with hints and suggestions for making incremental improvements. It is easier to make piecemeal improvements. Of course, organizations with weak risk management cultures that only make incremental changes are likely to remain vulnerable to the impact of psychological pitfalls, but small improvements are preferable to none.

I have a "half a loaf" message to deliver. It is important to establish realistic expectations about what behavioral interventions can accomplish. Readers who expect that behavioral interventions will produce fully rational decisions are likely to be severely disappointed. Decades of psychological research have made clear that the human brain, as wonderful as it is, has its limits. The behavioral approach can help make the practice of risk management better, but in the end it will still be imperfect. Half a loaf is indeed better than none, and half a loaf is obtainable.

This book provides ideas and guidance about introducing behavioral innovations into risk management, be those innovations large or small. Readers who finish the book should develop a keen awareness of what are the main psychological issues associated with risk management, and have a strong *general* sense of how to develop behavioral interventions to reflect those issues. I say "general," because the book is not "Behavioral Risk Management for Dummies," in the sense of being a "how-to manual" that lays out specific procedures for doing so in step-by-step fashion. Rather, it has as its focus the knowledge necessary for understanding and recognizing the psychological aspects of risk taking.

There is a flow to the book in respect to this knowledge. The flow begins with a description of the main psychological issues associated with individual decisions about risk. Next is a discussion about how these issues play out in groups and organizations. This discussion focuses on an organization's operations and supporting processes such as goal setting, planning, incentives, and information sharing. The discussion describes the traits of healthy organizations that mitigate psychological vulnerabilities, but uses an example to illustrate how these traits are honored in the breach. Indeed, many of the examples in the book can be regarded as learning what not to emulate.

Recognizing what not to emulate is a critical skill. The book seeks to help readers develop these skills by intermittently posing questions during the discussion of various real cases. When readers come across these questions, I urge them to stop and reflect about what are the main issues. Doing so intellectually is the first step toward doing so in practice when emotions as well as intellect become engaged, and the challenge is to spot psychological pitfalls in order to mitigate them. In this respect, readers will discover that many of the chapters that deal with applications are rich in detail, providing opportunities to identify psychological issues that arise during complicated decision tasks.

In the remainder of this introductory chapter, I provide four examples to illustrate the flavor of what readers will find in the book. To avoid repetition, these examples are separate from the cases discussed in later chapters; however, they feature the same themes that are developed throughout the book. The examples pertain to the Fukushima Daiichi nuclear reactor site, which pertains to risk in an operating company; drug firm Bergen Brunswig's takeover of PharMerica, which pertains to risk associated with mergers and acquisitions; the Libor rate setting and currency fixing scandals, which pertains to risk in a financial firm; and risk management issues associated with global warming.

NUCLEAR MELTDOWN AT FUKUSHIMA DAIICHI

On March 11, 2011, a tsunami associated with the largest earthquake ever recorded in Japan destroyed the Fukushima Daiichi power plant and initiated the meltdown of some of its nuclear fuel rods. This event was a major disaster with ongoing long-term consequences, as Japan shut down all of its nuclear reactors and kept them down for years, switching to more expensive energy alternatives such as oil.[3]

Because the power plant at Fukushima Daiichi was built close to the ocean, and Japan has a history of experiencing earthquakes and tsunamis, the inherent risks were recognized but not fully appreciated. The question for us to ask here is what role psychology played both in managing these risks before the events of March 11, and in confronting the emergency thereafter.

According to coverage by the *Financial Times*,[4] the Tokyo Electric Power Company (TEPCO), which operated the Fukushima Daiichi plant, was prepared for a major earthquake. At the time the earthquake struck, the plant had three of its six reactors in operation. In response to the earthquake, emergency systems caused those reactors to shut down, as per design. Nuclear fission was halted, and the plant's backup electric power generators came online.

All might have been fine at Fukushima Daiichi had there not been a horrendous tsunami, whose wave front was more than 40 feet above sea level. That wave easily topped the nuclear plant's concrete sea wall, which was about 15 feet high. The rushing waters wreaked havoc on the entire facility, flooding its backup power supply. As a result, the main control room went dark, and the electricity needed to run the equipment that would keep the nuclear fuel cool began to die. Over the next weeks, this failure would lead to explosions in reactor buildings and the melting of nuclear fuel rods and leaks of radiation.

The *Financial Times* article reports that TEPCO severely underestimated the potential for a tsunami as powerful as the one that struck on March 11, and for that matter also underestimated the potential for the precipitating earthquake. Similar remarks appear in an analysis of the disaster that was published by the Carnegie Foundation.[5] In this regard, the article reports that academics, nuclear activists, and an elected official with a degree in nuclear engineering had all been critical of the TEPCO's safety assumptions, but that the firm had rejected the criticisms. Instead, TEPCO asserted that its plants were invulnerable, a claim that government bureaucrats accepted without challenge. In this regard, the Carnegie Foundation report uses the phrase "supreme overconfidence by decision makers."[6]

The *Financial Times* article describes several reasons why officials refused to listen to critics' warnings, among which was the high cost of upgrading atomic plants. The Carnegie Foundation report provides a list of possible upgrades. The list includes building dikes and seawalls to protect against a severe tsunami; installing emergency power equipment and cooling pumps in dedicated, bunkered, watertight buildings or compartments; and assuring that the seawater-supply infrastructure was robust, as the plant would require an ultimate heat sink to cool its reactors in the face of a seriously adverse event. In this regard, the international nuclear community gained considerable knowledge about the impact of flooding from an event that took place in France in 1999.[7] However, TEPCO and the regulatory agency that oversees it, the Nuclear and Industrial Safety Agency (NISA), effectively ignored the lessons.

At least two major psychological pitfalls characterize the assumptions made by TEPCO and NISA about the risks their plants faced because of earthquakes and tsunamis. The first is "unrealistic optimism," which in this case involves assigning too low a probability to unfavorable events. As readers will learn later, there are many factors that drive excessive optimism. One is "desirability," which roughly speaking amounts to "wishful thinking," and the other is "controllability," in which people are unduly optimistic about a situation because they perceive themselves to be in control. The second psychological pitfall is known as "confirmation bias," which in this case involves downplaying, if not ignoring, information that does not confirm a view currently held. The previous paragraph illustrates instances of both pitfalls at TEPCO and NISA.

A rich research program in neuroscience is providing evidence that the degree to which people are vulnerable to pitfalls depends on the presence in their bodies of specific hormones such as testosterone and cortisol, and in their brains neurotransmitters such as dopamine, which lies at the center of the mechanism that creates positive mood, especially elation and euphoria.

How might these neuroactivities been at work at TEPCO in regard to events at Fukushima Daiichi? To answer this question, I present a brief digression into the nature of testosterone and cortisol.[8] The length of this digression, several paragraphs, is intended to make a point: risk managers need to have an understanding of how hormones and neurotransmitters impact judgments and decisions about risk to complement their expertise in scenario analysis, value at risk, stress tests, power laws, and risk limits.

Testosterone and cortisol are steroid hormones that marshal a person's resources to deal with challenges. After successes in which people feel like winners, testosterone levels become elevated, while cortisol levels remain low. Later chapters discuss findings in academic research that document the role of posture, with people in high-power poses having elevated levels of testosterone and depressed levels of cortisol relative to people in lower-power poses. High-power poses and high risk-taking tend to go together, and reflect the conditions under which people are prone to experience unrealistic optimism.

Cortisol is a stress hormone that comes into play to deal with stress and the aftermath of a fight or flight situation when threats are not quickly resolved. The human stress response unfolds in a sequence of stages, of which two are quick and two are slow. The quick responses pertain to "fight or flight" when the brain's amygdala registers the existence of a crisis and transmits electrical signals to the heart and lungs to increase heart rate, blood pressure, and breathing. Adrenaline is then produced by the body's adrenal glands to produce fuel that will sustain fight or flight. It does so by initiating the breakdown of glycogen in the liver, in order to produce glucose, the sugar to fuel the fire driving fight or flight.

If the crisis lasts longer than the fight-or-flight reaction, the body's adrenal glands begin to produce cortisol. Cortisol is incredibly powerful. When it first begins to take effect, it can be invigorating, reinforcing the presence of dopamine as a challenge is faced. However, over time, elevated cortisol levels are typically damaging, and most importantly impair judgment in the midst of a siege mentality, making it difficult to stay cool at a time when alarm sirens are blaring.

The manufacture and distribution of cortisol signals the body that the crisis will not be short, and that glucose and other resources will be necessary to meet the associated threats. The body's response to the surge in cortisol is to maintain high blood pressure, keep the heart rate at its accelerated level, and slow down competitive demands for energy reserves that would normally be used for eating, reproductive activities, and growth in young people. Cortisol also calls on the body to draw on its stores of energy, converting muscle into amino acids.

Stress research has found that in addition to bodily harm, three types of situations initiate a massive stress response. They are novelty, uncertainty, and uncontrollability. The devastation at Fukushima Daiichi must have created massive stress reactions in TEPCO executives.

During the three weeks that followed the initial destruction, the company had to release radioactive steam into the atmosphere in order to prevent one of its nuclear cores from bursting. Notably, the company's handling of this issue drew loud criticism from Japan's prime minister. Thereafter, a portion of highly radioactive water that had flooded the plant's basements and service tunnels managed to leak into the sea. Next, TEPCO executives decided that they would voluntarily empty several thousand tons of lightly contaminated water from plant storage tanks into the ocean, in order to make room for more heavily contaminated water at the site. However, doing so raised loud complaints not only from local fishermen but from neighboring countries such as South Korea and China.

We can only imagine the amount of psychological stress under which TEPCO's president operated during this period. However, what we do know is that he went into his office and secluded himself for five days, and attended no meetings. For more than a week TEPCO did not disclose his incapacity.

The reaction of TEPCO's president to the stress he confronted is absolutely consistent with experiencing dramatically elevated cortisol for an extended period. Being under stress, even for an extended period, does not necessarily mean that cortisol levels will be dramatically elevated. A key issue is preparedness and the ability to take control. By being prepared, and achieving some control, cortisol elevation might be moderate, and indeed invigorating. Preparedness, or a lack thereof, can be the determining factor in whether elevated cortisol leads to an invigorated response or a response featuring impaired judgment.

Psychology played a major part in the way TEPCO judged the risks to its facilities from natural events, and the way it managed its response when those risks materialized. The events are certainly tragic, and the question becomes what we can learn about mitigating pitfalls such as unrealistic optimism and confirmation bias as well as preparing decision-makers to handle the neurological changes to their brains and bodies in different kinds of circumstances. Developing an understanding of the underlying psychology is the first step, and learning to recognize the manifestation of that psychology in a real-world environment is the second step. These are precursors to putting procedures in place to address them to the best of our ability.

Bergen Brunswig's Takeover of PharMerica

There are significant risk management issues associated with mergers and acquisitions, and I have access to a database with many examples.[9] Below is one example from the database, which first provides a chronology and then provides a discussion about the related psychology.

In January 1999, Bergen Brunswig announced that it would merge with PharMerica. At the time, Bergen Brunswig was the third-largest drug wholesaler in the United States, and PharMerica was the second-largest provider of pharmaceutical products and management services to long-term care sites.

The idea behind Bergen Brunswig's strategy was that this particular merger would provide a way for the firm to reduce health-care costs through patient-driven, disease-specific pharmaceutical care. In March, the shareholders of both firms cast their votes on whether to merge, and in April the die was cast.

Although Bergen Brunswig's executives were enthusiastic about the merger, there were some black clouds on the horizon. From the time PharMerica went public in December 1997, its earnings and stock performance disappointed analysts and shareholders alike.

Moreover, there was concern about risks associated with a recently modified Medicare reimbursement schedule, which had the potential to adversely impact prospective payments. The modifications stemmed from the Balanced Budget Act of 1997. Under this Act, Medicare shifted its method of payment from cost-based reimbursement to fix-based reimbursement. This meant that under the new system, physicians would receive fixed amounts of money to reimburse them for different types of care, instead of reimbursement amounts based on the costs they incurred.

The change was designed to control Medicare expenses that were rising rapidly because of aging baby boomers. Executives at Bergen Brunswig claimed to recognize the risks associated with the Medicare modifications, but contended that PharMerica's future earnings growth would be sufficient to offset any possible impact from the revised Medicare reimbursement structure.

The market greeted the January merger announcement with skepticism, in that the combined market value of the two firms fell after the announcement, by 21.5% on a risk-adjusted basis over the subsequent three days. A rich academic literature indicates that the market's reaction to merger and acquisition announcements is informative, with a negative reaction tending to play out unfavorably if a deal progresses. This is an important lesson for executives and board members to digest. Risk managers need be especially attentive to the market's judgment, as it signals that the managers in the acquiring firm have underestimated the risk associated with the deal. This leads acquiring firms vulnerable to overpay for targets, a phenomenon known as "the winner's curse."

Future events revealed the market's judgment about Bergen Brunswig's merger with PharMerica to have been propitious. Bergen Brunswig had partially financed the acquisition with debt. Shortly after the two firms merged, Standard & Poor's (S&P) downgraded Bergen Brunswig's credit rating from single-A-minus to triple-B-plus. S&P characterized the outlook for the merger as negative, noting that combining the two companies would present integration challenges, that PharMerica had yet to complete the integration of acquisitions it had made, and that regulatory changes were expected to reduce reimbursements for care in PharMerica's nursing home facilities.

The April lowering of Bergen's credit rating was followed by negative earnings guidance in June, when Bergen Brunswig warned that lower Medicare reimbursements would indeed hurt results at its newly acquired PharMerica unit by more than it had anticipated. Effectively, nursing homes were accepting fewer high-need patients, with the result being lower drug usage and therefore lower drug revenues. The impact was industry wide. At the end of June, S&P placed its ratings for Bergen Brunswig on CreditWatch with negative implications, noting that stock price has dropped more than 50% from its 52-week high.

During the remainder of 1999, Bergen Brunswig missed analysts' forecasts, and its stock price continued to decline. A year after acquiring PharMerica, Bergen Brunswig announced that, excluding the PharMerica acquisition, its revenues had increased by 10%.

In order to help readers develop the skills associated with understanding and recognizing key psychological issues, during the discussion of the applications I intermittently pose behaviorally focused questions. An illustrative question for the Bergen Brunswig-PharMerica merger might be the following: what psychological pitfalls might have induced Bergen Brunswig's executives to misjudge the risks of acquiring PharMerica?

At this stage, readers will only have encountered discussion of two pitfalls, namely unrealistic optimism and confirmation bias. Do these pitfalls apply here? In judging the risks of the acquisition, did Bergen Brunswig executives attach too low a probability to the impact of the change in the Medicare payments system? Did they have information at their disposal that pointed to a strong negative impact, but that they nevertheless ignored?

Making judgments is always easier with twenty-twenty hindsight. Nevertheless, at the time of the Bergen Brunswig-PharMerica merger announcement, the market's judgment was distinctly negative, virtually screaming "Don't do it!" Before the merger took effect, S&P was warning about the change in Medicare when announcing its intention to downgrade Bergen Brunswig's debt. Therefore, there are strong reasons to suspect that even in foresight, Bergen Brunswig's executives exhibited excessive optimism and confirmation bias.

LIBOR AND FOREIGN CURRENCY MANIPULATION: SISTER SCANDALS

The majority of applications in this book pertain to the financial sector, with examples such as Merrill Lynch, Fannie Mae, JPMorgan Chase, and the Royal Bank of Scotland (RBS). The next example pertains to the financial sector.

Libor is an acronym for "London interbank offer rate." The acronym applies to a series of interest rate benchmarks, published by the British Bankers' Association (BBA), for loans denominated in ten currencies and 15 maturities. The Libor benchmarks are among global finance's most important, and despite the vast size of the market for Libor-denominated securities, between 2005 and 2009 a group of banks were able to manipulate Libor rates.

It is easy to see why a trader holding a position in a security whose payoff depends on a Libor rate might want to manipulate that rate. If the position involves holding an option, then the value of that option will change when the associated Libor rate changes. For large positions, even small changes in Libor can have large implications for profits.

Manipulating Libor constitutes price fixing and is illegal. The list of major players in the Libor scandal reads like a who's who of finance: Barclays, BNP Paribas, Citigroup, Credit Agricole, Deutsche Bank, the broker iCap, JPMorgan Chase, Lloyds Banking, Rabobank, RBS, Santander, and Société Générale. In both Europe and the United States, regulatory agencies and government commissions investigated these banks, documented their misdeeds, and imposed fines and penalties.[10]

The e-mails and text messages that traders sent to each other document something of the psychological mind-sets of those involved. These messages about manipulating rates make references to exchanges of sushi, curry, and sparkling wine. In this regard, some messages include jokes, with one trader responding to another's request for rate manipulation by asking what it would be worth, and the requestor responding that he could offer some leftover sushi from the day before. Given the role that hormones such as testosterone play in risk-taking behavior, it is not surprising that traders' jokes included sexual references such as feeling like a "whore's drawers."[11]

There are many psychological issues involved in the Libor scandal. Some pertain to traders, some to regulators and investors, but for now let me single out bank executives. They need to understand and recognize the psychological forces that induce price fixing by the traders who report up the chain to them. The consequences of not doing so can be severe. Of the banks participating in the Libor rate-fixing scheme, Barclays received the most attention. In July 2012, Barclays's CEO, chief operating officer, and chairman of the board all resigned. Perhaps they knew what was going on in their organizations and adopted a "wink wink, nod nod" attitude. However, let me give them the benefit of the doubt and assume they did not know. What do executives and board members need to understand about the psychology of cheating? For rate fixing is indeed a form of cheating.

The Libor scandal had a sister scandal involving the manipulation of foreign exchange rates (Forex). A Barclays trader who participated in the Forex scandal explicitly linked the behavior to cheating in a message that read, "If you aint cheating, you aint trying."[12]

As with Libor, the Forex markets are large and difficult to fix. But a small group of traders using chatrooms managed to do so for several years, until February 2015. The traders used coordinated attacks to fix agreed upon Forex rates every day in the 30 seconds before and after 4:00 p.m. London time in what came to be known as "the 4 p.m. fix."[13] Those participating in the scandal established positions earlier in the day in the knowledge of what form the manipulation would take at 4 p.m. Besides Barclays, the banks that employed the participating traders included Citigroup, JPMorgan Chase, RBS, and UBS.

The research findings from psychology indicate that most people are predisposed to cheat. Therefore, executives and boards need to be on their guard and not complacent. Changing people's environment in a way that leads them to feel more anonymous than previously, leads people to cheat more. Even inducing the illusion of anonymity, for example by making a room a bit darker, will induce people to cheat more.

For the most part, people who cheat know that cheating is wrong. However, they give in to temptation when their impulse to cheat is stronger than their moral compass. For many, increasing anonymity increases the temptation to cheat, and for some people tips the balance that previously prevented them from cheating.

Executives and board members need to know that exercising self-control takes effort. Neurologically, exercising self-control is a mental task in which our brains need be fed enough glucose to fuel the job. However, when tired, we cheat more because we lack the fuel to fight our instincts. Only those very high in moral identity appear able to resist the temptation to cheat, even when feeling tired.

Executives and board members need to know that even cheaters value respect from their social group, also called their in-group. The text and e-mail chatter among Libor traders and Forex traders makes this evident. One can see it in the humorous references traders make to food and sex, reflecting the camaraderie among those who collaborated to cheat by fixing rates.[14] Moreover, research shows that cheating is more frequent in situations in which wealth is abundant, which of course applies to Libor-based trading and Forex trading.

Executives and board members need to know that they can introduce interventions that nudge employees to cheat less frequently. Simply brightening a room can have a positive effect. So can asking people to recall past instances of immoral behavior on their part. So too can asking people to reflect on how being caught would embarrass their loved ones, lead them to lose social standing, and damage their careers.

GLOBAL WARMING

At the end of 2104, the Intergovernmental Panel on Climate Change (IPCC) had produced five assessment reports on global warming. The fifth report was published in 2014 and paints a sobering portrait of the risks due to anthropogenic greenhouse gas (GHG) emissions that the world will face for the remainder of this century.

The IPCC reports are risk management reports. They identify groups of scenarios called Representative Concentration Pathways (RCPs). The RCPs reflect potential risks related to food security, heat stress, extreme precipitation, inland and coastal flooding, landslides, air pollution, drought, the scarcity of fresh water, a rise in sea level, and storm surges. In this regard, the IPCC assigns probability categories to events, such as virtually certain being 99% to 100%, extremely likely being 95% to 100%, very likely being 90% to 100%, and so forth. The IPCC reports also assign levels of confidence—low, medium, or high—to describe degree of agreement among scientists, and assigns high confidence to the risks identified just above.

When the IPCC speaks of risk management, it refers to mitigation, adaptation, and the response to disasters. In this regard, the reports discuss a myriad of issues, such as energy sources that do not involve GHGs, a global price for carbon, cap and trade, carbon taxes, regulation, information programs for consumers, measures to assist vulnerable low-income groups, and disaster preparedness. Implementing the associated measures is not cheap, and involves lower rates of economic growth.

A series of important agreements in 2014 provide targets for carbon emissions. The European Union agreed that by 2030 it will have reduced its emissions to 40% percent below 1990 levels. The United States and China, which are the top two carbon emitters on the globe, agreed to the following: by 2030, the growth rate of emissions in China will have declined to zero, and by 2025, the United States will have reduced emissions by between 26% and 28%.[15]

These agreements are in the right direction to reduce global GHG emissions. At the same time, they do not meet the levels that the IPCC has recommended to prevent global temperatures from rising by more than two degrees Celsius, an important benchmark associated with the initiation of climactic tipping points associated with problematic feedback processes.[16]

In the end, the world's collective response might be too little too late. Despite the enormity of the risks, movement to address global warming has been slow. At the same time, the issues are complex and involve much controversy.[17]

In the United States, there are sharply divided views about the nature of the threat and how to respond to it. Unable to obtain enough support from Congress, the Obama administration took to using the Clean Air Act of

1970 to regulate carbon emissions. Doing so initiated a series of legal challenges, although in 2014 the Supreme Court established broad conditions under which this would be acceptable.[18]

The US Congress is divided on global warming. In January 2015, the Senate voted on an amendment about climate change that stated, "[I]t is the sense of Congress that—(1) climate change is real; and (2) human activity significantly contributes to climate change." Notably, the vote was almost evenly split, with 50 Senators voting in favor and 49 opposed.

The Congressional split largely reflects the fact that the United States has a representative democracy. The Yale Project on Climate Change Communication analyzed the January 2015 vote and determined that the votes cast by individual senators effectively reflected the degree to which their constituents believe that climate change is anthropomorphic.[19] Specifically, senators from states in which a majority of constituents believe that global warming is at least partly caused by human activities were prone to vote yes on the amendment. In contrast, senators from states in which the public was close to being equally divided on the issue, or in which the majority believed that global warming is either not occurring or is naturally caused were more likely to vote no on the amendment.

In April 2015, the Yale Project reported that 63% of Americans believe that global warming is occurring, a figure that stayed relatively stable during the prior five years. The percentage of Americans who believe that the cause of global warming is mostly anthropomorphic was 52%, and also remained stable.

Do psychological issues underlie the reasons why many people fail to accept the virtually unanimous views of the climate science community on the threats posed by anthropomorphic global warming? There is good reason to suggest that excessive optimism, confirmation bias, and self-control all contribute.[20]

Relative to the IPCC perspective, those who downplay RCPs having very unfavorable outcomes are excessively optimistic.[21] As discussed in connection with Fukushima Daiichi, desirability reflecting wishful thinking is the most likely factor involved.

For those with private interests in energy based on GHG emissions, confirmation bias looms large. This group will be especially prone to attach low weight to evidence that disconfirms their view that global warming is nonexistent or is not anthropomorphic. Many industrial interests associated with the denial of climate science, and the politicians they support, fall into this group. The parallel to the Fukushima Daiichi case applies here as well.

For the public at large, self-control associated with delay of gratification looms large. Will the world reduce consumption growth now in exchange for less global warming in the future? This is a high stakes version of the famous marshmallow test asked of young children: will you choose to receive one marshmallow now, or two by waiting a few minutes?

Just as children vary in their responses to the marshmallow test, so too do adults about how to address the threat of global warming. For many, the effects of global warming are not immediately obvious, and in addition are difficult to imagine. For them, global warming is an abstract concept that registers with low impact in their overall thinking. The immediate needs of the present light up neurological circuits much more intensely than the abstract needs of the future. If choices about trade-offs are made through any kind of mental balancing, the immediate needs have a strong advantage.[22]

Might our psychological pitfalls be inducing us to make a risk management Faustian deal with the devil? Time will tell about how hot it is going to get.

Closing Thoughts

The four risk management examples discussed above introduced some of the main issues discussed in this book. Readers will see that the psychological risk management issues associated with the Libor and Forex scandals also characterize what went wrong at the ratings firms S&P and Moody's. The psychological risk management issues associated with the disaster that befell TEPCO at its Fukushima Daiichi plant also surfaced at BP with the explosion of the drilling rig Deepwater Horizon. The psychological risk management issues associated with Bergen Brunswig's acquisition of PharMerica also surfaced at RBS when it headed the consortium that acquired ABN AMRO. As for global warming, its associated risks are at a much higher order of magnitude than in the other examples. Nevertheless, the same psychological features apply.

Much of went wrong at firms such as RBS, TEPCO, and BP involves operational risk. Operational risk is where the rubber meets the road, as this is the locus of where risk is experienced. However, operations are but one of several organizational processes.

Several chapters in this book discuss risk issues associated with accounting. In the wake of accounting scandals at firms such as Enron and WorldCom, the US Congress passed the Sarbanes-Oxley Act (SOX). Section 404 of SOX requires that public companies choose an internal control framework for assessing and reporting annually on the design and operating effectiveness of their internal controls. Many firms use what is known as a COSO framework to do so. COSO stands for the Committee of Sponsoring Organizations of the Treadway Commission. COSO is a voluntary private sector initiative whose focus is effective internal control, enterprise risk management (ERM), and fraud deterrence.[23] The original COSO framework of 1992 has been replaced by a 2013 framework, which is much broader in scope than its predecessor, especially in regard to risk issues.[24]

COSO focuses on process. Notably, COSO's approach to ERM highlights the role of risk appetite and risk assessment, but does not stress the deep psychological issues discussed in this book.[25] The underlying psychology impacts the judgments and decisions made in processes such as goal setting and planning. In turn, judgments and decisions are impacted by how incentives are structured, as well as how information is shared between members of the organization. These features are part of an organization's overall culture, which encompasses other pertinent aspects such as shared values and norms, policies and procedures, governance structures, and codes of conduct.

This book touches on all of the aspects just mentioned, and does so when highlighting important psychological issues associated with risk management. The field of risk management is much too wide to accommodate a comprehensive treatment in one book. Nevertheless, I have tried to provide a book that covers the most important insights from the academic literature on behavioral decision-making that relates to the practice of risk management.

The chapters in the first part of the book introduce the main ideas, and the chapters in the latter part provide insight into how to apply those ideas to the practical world in which risk managers operate. Wherever possible, I have tried to focus on the intuition underlying the main insights, and to stay away from technical complexities. However, those interested in the technical details will be able to find additional material in the book's appendices. Serious readers might want to read the chapters in Part I before the applications in Part II, while casual readers will probably be fine moving right to the applications.

Having previewed the general approach in the book, it is time to delve into the details of what behavioral risk management entails.

PART I

CHAPTER 2

SP/A Theory's Focus on Three Key Emotions

MANAGING RISK IS ABOUT MANAGING PSYCHOLOGY. FOR RISK MANAGERS, understanding the psychology of risk has become "need to know," not "nice to know."

This chapter introduces you to critical concepts involving the role that three key emotions play in the psychology of risk. After reading this chapter, you will be able to articulate what these emotions are, describe how emotions impact the way people assess risks, choose among risky prospects, and arrive at risk valuations when trading.

Emotions lie at the heart of how we make all of our decisions, including those involving risk. In fact, the basis for the word "emotion" is "motion," in that emotion provides the mental energy we need to move into action. For example, the emotion of fear is primal and lies at the root of the "fight or flight" response. People also have other emotions, which we can easily recognize as being associated with things like hope and ambition. In fact, this chapter focuses attention on how these three emotions—fear, hope, and the feeling of ambition—interact to drive the way we make choices and judgments about risk.

People differ in the relative strength with which they experience different emotions. Some people are more fearful than others, or more hopeful than others, or more ambitious than others. The relative strength of these emotions is part of our emotional profiles. Indeed, one of the questions we want to ask is whether as a group, risk managers have different emotional profiles than other business professionals. This is an important question: the more risk managers understand about the role that interpersonal differences play in the psychology of risk, the more effective they will be when interacting with others.

Risk managers need to deal with all kinds of risks. Many financial risks are modeled using the normal distribution, at least as a first approximation. However, risk management often entails recognizing the existence of "fat tails" that are not captured by the normal distribution assumption, and the need to exchange one risk for another. Hedging and insurance can place limits on exposure to extremely unfavorable events, providing protection to limit the downside. Some risks are characterized by outcomes that fall within a narrow range most of the time, but upon occasion fall at the extremes.

Structured finance offers a risk menu from which to choose, and psychology is at the heart of how the choices in this menu are perceived and assessed with a view to making decisions. This chapter describes the role that fear, hope, and ambition play in the decisions and valuation judgments that people make when considering the risk menu before them. I have tried to provide just enough business context to help readers make sense of the ideas. I have tried to keep the details down to bare bones, in order to focus on the underlying psychology without getting overly distracted by specific applications, which will come later in the appendices for those that want to dig deeper.

You will see that many of the applications feature big personalities and considerable drama, with sharp differences between risk managers on one side and traders, portfolio managers, and CEOs on the other side. In order to set the stage for these discussions, the next section presents a short story, with just a little bit of drama, featuring differences of opinion between a risk manager and a portfolio manager.

A Risk Management Short Story

Beth Chester and Larry Stephan work for a major investment bank in New York. Larry is a senior portfolio manager who sits on a trading desk running an alternative strategies fund. Beth is a risk manager who provides analysis and support to Larry's group.

Beth received an e-mail message from Larry that has surprised her. Larry's message describes a choice he faces between two positions the firm inherited from a recent acquisition, one identified as "Peaked" (PK) and the other as "Risk Floor" (RF). Although currently both PK and RF are thinly traded and do not have reliable market prices, the firm anticipates that it will be able to close out both positions in 12 months.

Larry has agreed to accept one of the two positions and hold it for a year. The firm has indicated that it will liquidate the position Larry rejects at the earliest convenient time. Notably Larry has skin in the game: at the margin, his future compensation will be impacted by roughly 1 basis point of the value of the position.

In consultation with Beth, Larry has estimated that both positions have two important features in common. First, they share the same expected value, $1.1 billion, meaning the firm judges that on average it would be able to sell either position for $1.1 billion in 12 months. Second, both positions involve short positions in call options that cap their upsides at $2.2 billion.

In analyzing the two positions, Beth finds that PK has a higher standard deviation than RF, $442 million versus $354 million. Importantly, the two positions differ in respect to the downside. Although PK could conceivably be worthless after 12 months, RF involves a put position that limits its downside to $770 million. Technically, RF is structured as a "collar," more precociously termed a "split-strike conversion strategy." Although PK features the same maximum upside as RF, it lacks the put option protection for the downside.

Beth is well aware that Larry's compensation is performance based, and she tries to imagine herself in his shoes facing his incentives. With her training in variance-covariance-based risk modeling, she is convinced that Larry's choice is a no brainer, and that RF should be the position he selects. But she is wrong. In his e-mail message, Larry tells her that he has ranked PK over RF. She is quite mystified, because the logic seems so obvious. RF offers the same expected payoff as PK, and not only features a lower standard deviation but less exposure on the downside.

Convinced that Larry might not fully appreciate the facts associated with the contrasting risk profiles of the two alternatives, Beth puts together a simple graphic (Figure 2.1), displaying the probability density functions (pdfs) for the two positions. Reading from the left, the figure indicates that the probability that PK will be worth $0 a year from now is 1%, while the probability that RF will be worth $0 a year from now is 0. Likewise, the figure indicates that the probability that PK will be worth $726 million a year from now is 9% while the probability that RF will be worth $770 million a year from now is 31%.

Notice from Figure 2.1 that $770m serves as "floor" for RF: its value a year from now will not drop below the $770m floor. In contrast, the floor for PK is $0. At the right, RF and PK share the same "cap" of $2.2 billion: the probability that either will be worth more than $2.2b a year from now is 0.

Beth sends her figure to Larry, with a short message saying, "Before you make your final decision on the PK-RF choice, I want to be sure you've seen the associated pdfs, which highlight the difference in downside risk for the two positions. What do you think?"

A short while later, Beth reads Larry's reply, "Thanks. Your graphic clarifies a few things for me, but I'm still happier with PK." Now even more puzzled, Beth concludes that Larry needs more facts. She asks if they can set up a meeting to discuss the risk and valuation issues associated with the two positions, to which Larry agrees.

Beth prepares. Based on the difference in standard deviations, she conservatively judges that in the current market environment, the required return

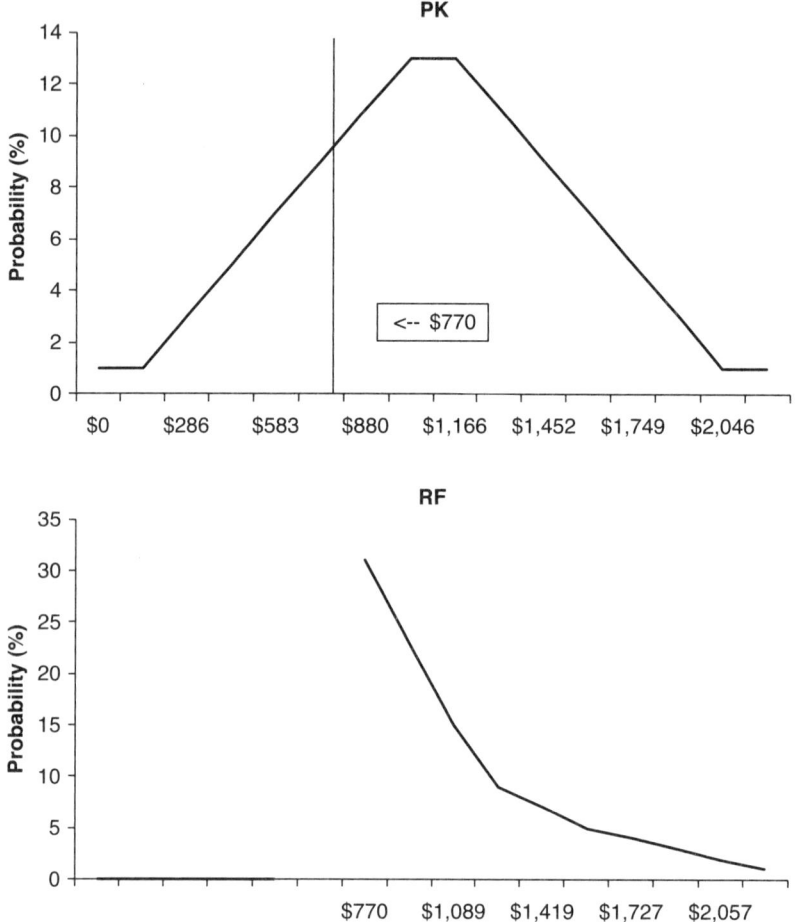

Figure 2.1 Probability density functions for the future value of the positions PK and RF being discussed by Larry and Beth.

associated with RF is 6% and for the riskier PK is 7%, a 100-basis-point differential. This leads her to conclude that the value of RF is $1.04 billion, somewhat more than the $1.03 billion she judges PK to be worth. She wonders whether the relatively small difference in valuation might be influencing Larry to underweigh the significant difference in tail risk exposure.

At their meeting, Beth asks Larry what value he assigns to the two positions today, in terms of intrinsic value. Larry's answer, "$2.25 billion for RF and $2.23 for PK," surprises her in three ways. First, he attaches a higher value to RF, even though he prefers PK. Second, his valuations are much higher than hers. Third, his valuations lie above expected value, which implies that he is risk seeking, not risk averse.

Beth's response is to ask him, with some incredulity coming through, "Larry, are you saying that you would be willing pay over $2 billion for either of these funds today?" And now Beth gets one more surprise, as Larry responds, "Not at all. Those are my ask prices. I wouldn't bid more than $1 billion for RF and $900 million for PK."

"Well," she says, "those are certainly more reasonable valuations, although we might differ a bit on the magnitudes. But frankly, I'm puzzled. You're telling me that you agree that RF has less downside risk, and that it's worth more than PK, right? To me, that seems like an open and shut case for selecting RF over PK. So why on Earth would you favor PK over RF?"

"Oh," says Larry. "That's easy to explain. I'm targeting the new position to close out at $1 billion or more 12 months from now. Conceptually, I'm thinking along the lines of value at risk, with my $1 billion target as the VaR. The probability of achieving that target with PK is about 63%. But with RF, it's only about 46%. That's a big difference. The risk of coming out below $1 billion is so much higher with RF."

As the light bulb begins to flicker in Beth's mind, she responds, "OK, I think you and I are using the word 'risk' in very different ways. But that aside, suppose that instead of PK, we had a hypothetical third position that offered a uniform density—equal probabilities—for any payoff between $0 and $2.2 billion. The hypothetical alternative also offers more than a 50% probability of hitting at least $1 billion, and it has the same expected payoff as the other two. Surely, you're not saying that you would rank it over RF!"

"Actually, I am saying that," responds Larry. "You have to pay attention to upside potential, not just downside protection. Risk isn't just about downside protection."

PSYCHOLOGY OF RISK

Beth and Larry are real people working in the financial sector, make judgments and decisions about risk. Based on the preceding short story, there is good reason to believe that psychologically, Beth and Larry are different from each other. Now, I am not suggesting that differences are bad. Instead, I am suggesting that if they were to understand their differences, they would be likely to work better together in the course of making judgments and decisions. In a nutshell, helping people like Beth and Larry is what this book is about.

Psychologists develop frameworks to analyze what makes Beth and Larry tick when they deal with risk. Part of their motivation will be external, from the incentives they face in their professional lives, and part of the motivation will be internal, driven by their own psychological makeups.

For Larry, the lion's share of his compensation is tied to bonuses that are linked to trading profits. His downside is capped at the loss of his job outcome. As a result, his compensation package naturally focuses his attention on the upside, which typically is not capped. Beth's compensation structure is different from Larry's, being linked to the efficiency with which she identifies and communicates the risk attached to different alternatives.

In the next few chapters we concentrate primarily on people's psychological responses to the incentive structures with which they are presented. Later chapters analyze the critical role played by how incentives are structured.[1]

The data upon which psychologists rely typically comes from experiments in which subjects are asked to make judgments and decisions. As it happens, in their real lives Beth and Larry have both participated in such experiments, and so their responses can provide us with important insights. Of course, they are only two individuals, and therefore we do not want to draw strong conclusions based on their responses alone. In this regard, the discussion of core psychology in the first part of this book is based on studies with many subjects.

The area now known as the psychology of risk is built on advances made by researchers working in many fields. Between the 1940s and the 1970s, economists, mathematicians, and statisticians jointly developed a systematic approach to how people make risky choices.

The economics Nobel laureates involved in this endeavor included Harry Markowitz, Herbert Simon, Maurice Allais, Milton Friedman, and Kenneth Arrow. Their work eventually motivated a group of psychologists to study the psychological underpinnings of how people make choices in the face of risk.

Some psychologists, such as Lola Lopes, whose approach is the theme of the present chapter, focused on the role played by emotions. Others, such as Daniel Kahneman and Amos Tversky, whose work I discuss in the next chapter, focused on the role played by cognition. I devote the present chapter to discussing the role of emotions and begin the discussion of cognition in the next chapter.

In the 1980s, Lopes provided a profound, powerful framework that identified the key emotions involved in the psychology of risk. Her contributions featured both strong experimental evidence and a well-structured formal theory.

Lopes did her graduate work at the University of California, San Diego, where she became interested in how poker players integrate pieces of information available to them in order to decide how much to bet. Her inquiry led her to study a variety of issues related to internal processes such as attention, perception, goal seeking, encoding, information integration, comparison, reaction time, and choice.

Lopes's research helps us understand some of the most important ways in which Beth and Larry differ from each other. Her ideas can help us describe the sense in which they think differently about what "risk" means. Her ideas can also provide us with insights into why they have different notions of what constitutes value. Most importantly, her ideas can help us understand why Beth's judgments are consistent with being averse to risk, whereas most aspects of Larry's choice and valuations are consistent with being risk seeking.

THE THREE KEY EMOTIONS

Lopes's main message is that fear, hope, and the feeling of ambition are three key emotions that impact how people make choices about risky alternatives. Her message is based on a series of experiments in which subjects rank order a series of risky alternatives such as RF and PK lying at the heart of the short story about Beth and Larry.[2]

Lopes gathered data about her subjects' attitudes to taking risk by asking them to rank alternatives in pairs. As part of her methodology, she recorded not only their responses but also their "comments" about what they were thinking when making judgments.[3] The comments are particularly illuminating for what they reveal about the psychological aspects of people's internal thought processes.

I have conducted Lopes-type experiments with my students many times over the years. Next, I provide examples of comments from undergraduate students majoring in finance who were my students and participated in these experiments. Lopes also used undergraduate students in her work. I have found undergraduate finance majors to be especially good subjects for Lopes-type experiments. They have enough aptitude and experience to understand the choices, but at the same time it is easier to get at the psychology of their thought processes because their minds are less contaminated by work experience and specialized professional training.

By analyzing rank orderings and comments, Lopes developed a framework in which she suggested that people make choices among risky alternatives by balancing three competing psychological needs:

1. the need to assuage fear by providing security
2. the need to offer hope, by providing upside potential
3. the need to succeed, by achieving a predefined aspiration level or goal

Lopes called her framework SP/A theory. Here SP/A stands for "security, potential, and aspiration."

In Lopes's framework, people rank different alternatives by comparing and balancing the way in which the alternatives provide security, upside potential, and the chance of success. She tells us that people differ in the relative strength of their emotional needs and the degree to which they set aspiration levels that reflect their ambitions.

Consider someone whose dominant emotion is fear. Lopes tells us that such a person would attach much more importance to security than to either upside potential or the chance of success. In comparing RF to PK, a fearful person would strongly favor RF as it provides much more security than PK. The probability associated with a low payoff, near zero, is itself zero with RF, but definitely positive under PK.

For someone whose dominant emotion is hope, the situation is different. According to Lopes, that person would attach more importance to upside potential than to security, and possibly to the chance of success. In comparing RF to PK, a hopeful person would strongly favor PK as it provides more potential than RF for payoffs around the mean, and about the same probabilities for payoffs in the right tail.

Lopes points out that neither fear nor hope must be dominant. She says instead that some people are "cautiously optimistic." While such people pay attention to the downside, once they are comfortable with the amount of downside protection they have selected, it is hope that then guides their choices.

In respect to aspiration there are two critical issues. The first concerns the aspiration level: how ambitious is the goal? The second concerns the relative strength attached to the chance of success. Someone who sets a moderately high aspiration level and has a strong need for success would be inclined to rank PK over RF, because PK offers a significantly higher chance of success than RF.

With these considerations in mind, consider a Lopes-type experiment involving undergraduate finance majors who were asked to make choices and valuation judgments similar to those in the short story about Beth and Larry. You can think of these students as Beth and Larry "wannabes." As you read the material below, think about the degree to which the three emotions that Lopes identified come into play.

Below are examples of comments from an experiment in which all subjects were indeed undergraduate finance majors. In the experiment, all amounts were scaled so that the expected payoffs to both RF and PK were $1,100. These names were chosen to relate to the shapes of the payoff graphs in Figure 2.1.

The first set of comments is from subjects who were explaining why they ranked RF over PK.

- I wanted to guarantee myself a solid amount of money, which I determined to be around $700. I chose the Risk Floor [RF] as my most desirable fund because the floor of it was much higher...
- I prefer to receive anything, and I almost want to be sure of this. This is why risk floor [RF] is my first choice, as it has no option of $0.
- I would rank them according to standard deviation as the mean is the same. This is how you ensure the highest risk adjusted returns.

Notice that comments of these subjects provide three different rationales for choosing RF over PK. The first subject tells us that she set an aspiration of $700, and based her ranking on the fact that receiving this amount was guaranteed with RF but not PK. The second subject has an aversion to winning $0, for which the probability is zero with RF but positive with PK. Conceivably, the "fear of not winning anything" induced this subject to rank RF over PK. The third subject applied mean-variance theory, which he learned in textbook finance. His response is in line with the kind of justification that Beth provided Larry in our short story. These three rationales are representative of the kinds of explanations that undergraduate finance majors give for ranking RF at the top of their menus.

Next consider the comments of undergraduate finance majors who ranked PK over RF:

- Peaked [PK] appears to be the most appealing to me because it holds the largest probability that I will earn about a $1,000 and my odds are for making close to that.
- I chose the "Peaked" [PK] because it is less risky... but still provides some opportunity for above average returns.
- I would personally prefer certainty..., but I also would like a reasonable chance of a decent reward...

Notice that the first subject's rationale for favoring PK is very close to the explanation provided by Larry to Beth. Notably, this subject set an explicit aspiration level of $1,000, and focused on the probability that each choice provided for receiving at least this amount.[4] The other subjects did not identify specific aspiration levels, but did attach significant importance to the achievement of above-average returns. Conceivably, the focus of the second and third subjects on earning above average returns suggests that their rankings of PK and RF were driven by hope.

Long Shots and Short Shots

Lopes made an important observation about subsistence farmers in the developing world. They often plant two kinds of crops, food crops to provide food for the table and cash crops to sell for cash in order to acquire other goods and services. Lopes tells us that food crops are relatively reliable, but have low market value. On the other hand, cash crops hold the potential to generate decent value in the market price, but at the same time are riskier.

Based upon her reading of the literature in agricultural economics, Lopes concluded that subsistence farmers manage their risks by following a safety-first approach, in which they first plant food crops, and only after judging that they have planted enough to provide for subsistence do they plant cash crops.

In the urban-centered developed world, lottery tickets often play the role of cash crops. Lopes's studies included a risky alternative with lottery-like features, which she called the "long shot." The long shot features high probabilities of very low payoffs, but a small probability of a much higher payoff than any of the other risky alternatives. On average, her subjects rated the long shot as the least attractive alternative. However, a minority of subjects gave the long shot their top rating.

Think about how SP/A theory would explain why some people would assign the long shot their top rating. By its nature, the theory focuses on the relative strength of the three key emotions and their associated needs. Certainly the phrase "high hopes" comes to mind.

Notably, from the perspective of SP/A theory, this phrase can be understood in at least two ways. The first involves the strong need for potential. The desire for potential by itself suggests a general willingness to take risk. The second way to understand the phrase is having high and powerful ambition. This second way is more nuanced than the first. Someone who is strong in fear and strong in ambition would be inclined to be generally conservative in their risk behavior, except in circumstances that provide a decent chance of success in achieving aspiration.

A long shot is a risk featuring low probabilities of receiving very large payoffs, but high probabilities of receiving small payoffs. For traders and risk managers, purchasing protection against default using credit default swaps typically amounts to taking a long shot. In an experimental setting, both Beth and Larry were asked to rank a long shot (LS) against RF and PK, when all three risks shared the same expected payoff. Both of them rated LS at the bottom.

In addition to studying how people rate long shots, Lopes also studied how they rate alternatives, which she called "short shots" (SS), that are polar opposites to long shots (LS). A short shot is a risk featuring high probabilities of receiving moderately high payoffs, and low probabilities of receiving low payoffs, but zero probabilities of receiving very high payoffs. Unlike the graph of the probabilities for RF displayed in Figure 2.1, which slopes downward from the minimum possible payoff of $770 to the maximum possible payoff of $2,200, the graph of the SS-probabilities slopes upward from $0 to $1,430. (For a visual comparison, see Figure A.1 in Appendix A). Notably, Lopes structured SS to feature a lower maximum payoff than other alternatives such as RF, PK, and LS, but the same expected payoff. For traders and risk managers, an example of a short shot is a covered call position, in which the call is just slightly out of the money.

If you view SS relative to RF and PK through the lens of SP/A theory, you can see that it does not provide as much security or potential as the other alternatives. In this regard, Lopes found that her subjects, who were general undergraduates, rated SS below RF and PK. However, when I conducted the Lopes-type experiments with both undergraduate finance majors and business professionals, I found that many of them rated SS at or near the top. For example, Larry ranked it higher than RF, but below PK. Beth actually rated SS above RF.

How would SP/A theory explain the difference? Certainly not through security or potential, so the explanation would have to come through aspiration. For moderate aspiration levels around the expected payoff, SS typically offers significantly higher values of A than the other alternatives. Therefore, if the chance of success is important, SS can be viewed attractively.

ASSESSING EMOTIONS ASSOCIATED WITH SP/A: ARE RISK MANAGERS DIFFERENT?

As a first pass to identifying the strength of the three needs that are central to the Lopes framework, consider a short survey that is designed to elicit people's self-perception about what is important to them. Below are five survey questions to elicit a person's self-perception about the relative strengths of their emotional needs based on fear, hope, and aspiration, in respect to ranking risky alternatives. Each question asks for a response on a scale of 1 to 7, the degree to which the person believes that each of the following four statements apply to him or her. Here a "1" would mean "does not apply to me at all" and "7" would mean "always applies to me."

1. When I am in a situation where the outcome is uncertain, the emotion I feel the most intensely is fear.
2. When I am in a situation where the outcome is uncertain, the emotion I feel the most intensely is hope.
3. When I am in a situation where the outcome is uncertain, I usually feel cautiously hopeful.
4. When I am in a situation where the outcome is uncertain, I usually have a target outcome in mind that defines success for me.
5. When I am in a situation where the outcome is uncertain, I would be willing to increase the odds of achieving an extremely unfavorable outcome, if doing so would increase the chances of achieving my goal.

Larry and Beth answered these questions. Remember that Larry ranked PK over RF, while Beth ranked RF over PK. Let us begin with Larry's responses. Larry gave a 2 as his response to the first question: he is low in fear. He gave a 5 to the second question, indicating that he is pretty high in hope. His response of 5 to the third question indicates that he views himself as cautiously optimistic. He also gave a 5 to the fourth question asking if he set a specific aspiration level, and he gave a 6 to the fifth question, which elicits the importance he attaches to his chances of his being successful.

Beth's response to the first question is the same as Larry's response. However, she does not perceive herself as being strongly driven by hope. Nevertheless, she does perceive herself as strongly cautiously hopeful. In respect to ambition, she tells us that she is extremely strong at setting targets, but is reluctant to take risk for the sake of increasing her chances of success. In other words, the third need does not dominate her psychological makeup in the way that it does for Larry.

People do not become risk managers randomly, but by choice, and their psychological profiles might have something to do with their choices. The same is true for CEOs and entrepreneurs.

In my research with professionals using short surveys such as the one described above, I have found that there are subtle differences between some risk managers and others. Notably, some risk managers describe themselves as being entrepreneurial while others do not. Relative to others, on average, nonentrepreneurial risk managers are more fearful, less hopeful, the most inclined to avoid unfavorable outcomes, the most inclined to favor small risks, and feel the most pain when a prespecified goal goes unmet. They are the least willing to accept large downside exposure in order to try and meet a prespecified goal.

Entrepreneurial risk managers are distinctly different breed from their nonentrepreneurial counterparts. Less fearful and more hopeful, they are much more inclined to focus on making choices that maximize the probability of achieving their goals.

At the same time, my research indicates that CEOs are the most hopeful of all groups, the most apt to set prespecified goals, and the most likely to try to achieve highly favorable outcomes. These differences are features that figure prominently in situations that risk managers will be called upon to manage. A major point of this book is that, because risk managers often advise CEOs, whose psychological profiles typically differ from theirs, they will be better equipped to carry out their functions if they have a systematic framework to help them diagnose the differences.

VALUATION PSYCHOLOGY

Most models of choice and valuation for risky prospects involve the concept of expected payoff, where expected payoff is a weighted sum in which the weights are probabilities. For example, consider a risk based on the toss of a fair coin, which pays $2 if tails comes up and $4 if heads comes up. This risk has an expected payoff of $3 = 50% × $2 + 50% × $4.

Lopes tells us that fear and hope induce people to assess the above risk associated with the toss of the fair coin as if the coin were unfair. In this respect, fear induces people to assess this risk by overweighing the probability of a tail, thereby reducing the expected payoff below $3. By the same token, hope induces people to assess this risk by overweighing the probability of a head, thereby increasing the expected payoff above $3.

As we saw above, Larry is both more hopeful and more ambitious than Beth, and in our short story, Larry's valuations provided Beth with four surprises. First, his ask prices were more than twice his corresponding bid prices. Second, his ask prices were above expected values, thereby reflecting negative risk premiums. Third, his bid prices were considerably lower than hers. Fourth, his valuations for RF were higher than for PK, using both bid and ask prices, even though his preferred choice was PK.

For Beth, valuation was straightforward in principle, and followed the principles she learned in textbooks. She assessed what expected return each position warranted based on its respective risk, and then discounted the expected payoff of each at its required return. Liquidity issues aside, she saw no reason for a major difference in bid and ask prices, let alone ask prices that reflected risk seeking. Although she did realize that Larry's required returns were higher than hers, she reasoned that the gaps might reflect different assessments of systematic risk, which is certainly an issue they could discuss. But the two items that baffled her most were the risk-seeking nature in Larry's ask prices, and the inverse relationship between his choice and his valuation.

In her communications with Larry, Beth was learning that psychology leads people, including investment professionals, to arrive at valuation judgments that are at odds with textbook theory. Many psychological studies have found that people commonly attach higher values to objects already in their possession, as opposed to the same objects not yet in their possession. Economist Richard Thaler coined the term "endowment effect" to describe this phenomenon, noting that people increase their valuation of objects once they take ownership and the objects become part of their endowments.[5]

The rest of this section describes some of the insights that come from running experiments involving valuation tasks when confronting Lopes-type risk choices. Be forewarned that the data typically display great variation in the ratio of ask-to-bid prices. Most often, between 25% and 35% of experimental subjects set the same bid and ask prices for the Lopes risks. The rest set different bid and ask prices. For undergraduate finance majors, ask-to-bid ratios are typically 1.25, and for investment professionals ratios often exceed 2. Risk managers take note: ratios are often higher for riskier choices than safer choices.

Comments of undergraduate finance majors provide insight into the intuition underlying the valuation process. Figures 2.2 provides valuations elicited from a participant we shall call Jeff in an experiment involving undergraduates where the alternatives were called "funds" and included RF, "Short Shot" (SS), PK, and "Long Shot" (LS), The bid price is a willingness to pay (WTP) and the ask price was a willingness to accept (WTA).

Consider the comments from Jeff, who gave PK his top rank, with SS next, and then RF. Jeff's valuations are displayed in Figure 2.2.

I judged my minimum WTA by the probability I would get in return while considering what the other likely scenarios are. For example, I predict that with Short Shot I would receive at least 1,000 but assume it would be higher. Therefore, I would not accept anything less than 1,000 for the fund. I used this thought process for the other funds as well.

The fact that I would be paying for this fund gears me towards a lower WTP for each of the funds. I want to pay less than what is most probable for me to make in return.... For those funds that seem more appealing to me, I raised the WTP because the odds seem more favorable that I would make a large return.

Jeff's comments make clear that he views aspirational probability as especially important for valuation. What makes this point of great interest is that high aspirations typically drive a substantial wedge between his bid prices (WTP) and his ask prices (WTA). The higher the aspirations, the lower will be WTP and the higher will be WTA. The only atypical feature of Jeff's valuations pertains to LS, where his WTP exceeds his WTA.

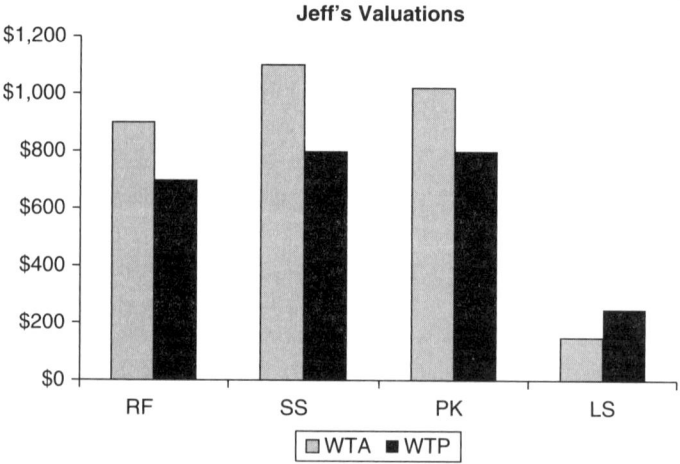

Figure 2.2 Valuations elicited from a participant Jeff in a risk choice and valuation experiment involving undergraduates, where the alternatives (RF, SS, etc.) were called "funds." Here, the bid price is a willingness to pay (WTP) and the ask price is willingness to accept (WTA).

"Preference reversal" is the phenomenon of ranking alternative X over alternative Y, and yet attaching a higher valuation to Y than to X. In this regard, this student assigned a higher WTA valuation to SS than to PK, even though he gave PK his top ranking. That is, Jeff exhibited preference reversal, and his comments suggest that his focus on aspiration is a key reason why this is the case.

Consider next the comments from a similar experiment involving executives, rather than undergraduate finance majors. Below are comments from an executive we will call Tom. Tom's valuations are displayed in Figure 2.3. In the first comment, Tom explains his thought process in rank ordering risky alternatives: he ranked SS at the top, followed by PK and RF.

> I added probabilities to earn more than $1,100, calculated the probability to earn less than $500, and made a ranking to avoid a high risk of no gain at all while keeping good chances of earning significantly more than $1,000.

Considered from the perspective of SP/A theory, Tom's remark about wanting to avoid "no gain at all" suggests some fear, and therefore a high need for security. His focus on earning significantly more than $1,000 suggests that he has an aspiration level of $1,000. Tom explains how he arrived at some of his WTA-evaluations.

> Risk floor: min. selling price is $1,200, because there is a 50% chance to earn more.

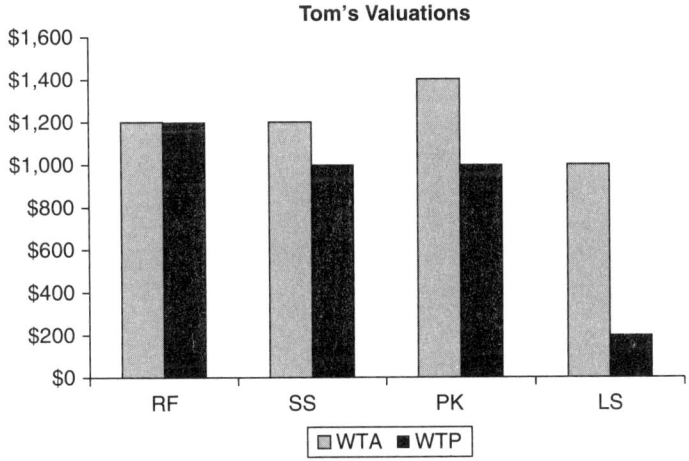

Figure 2.3 Valuations elicited from a participant Tom in the same risk choice and valuation experiment discussed earlier, but involving business managers, where the alternatives (RF, SS, etc.) were called "funds." Here, the bid price is willingness to pay (WTP) and the ask price is willingness to accept (WTA).

Short shot: min. selling price is $1,200, because there is a 65% chance to earn more than $1,000 and a low risk to lose everything.

Peaked: min. selling price is $1,400 because there is a 35% chance to earn more than $1,300, a 60% chance to earn more than $1,000, and a low risk to lose everything.

Tom's judgments are intriguing. He explicitly focuses on chances of success, meaning probabilities of receiving at least some aspirational amount. Moreover, he assigned $1,400, which was his highest WTA, to his third-ranked Peaked, but only $1,200 to his top-ranked short shot. This is a clear case of preference reversal. Relatedly, notice that Tom explicitly identifies specific amounts that are consistent with the concept of aspiration. However, unlike the theory, which takes the aspiration point as common across alternatives, such aspiration levels appear to differ across alternatives in Tom's evaluation process. Certainly, variable aspiration levels can give rise to preference reversal.

Although the comments made by Jeff and Tom offer insights about valuation thought process, they are only two anecdotes. Valuation data display great variation, and discerning reliable patterns in the valuation data that link to fear, hope, and aspiration is much more difficult than discerning patterns in the rankings data. Moreover, because the valuation data displays so much variability, there is reason to believe that the process for valuation is a much less structured task than the process for assessing rank.

Keep in mind that ranking involves comparisons between two or more risky alternatives, thereby focusing attention on a common aspiration level. However, valuation is typically done one alternative at a time, thereby making it easier for people to apply different aspiration levels to different alternatives.

Because valuation is complex, risk managers have their work cut out for them. In my studies with business professionals, I have found that the valuations of risk managers are typically more prudent, meaning lower, than the valuations of others. On average, risk managers assign the highest valuation to the short shot SS, with successively lower valuations for PK and RF. Moreover, most group average WTA valuations feature negative risk premiums.

In addition, for all groups, the indirect returns implied by WTP valuations are dramatically different from the direct returns, meaning the required return subjects explicitly attach to risky alternatives they are considering. This means that most subjects do not form valuations by discounting expected cash flows at required rates of return. The magnitudes of ask-to-bid ratios indicate that people use different thought processes to conduct valuation than they do to arrive at required returns. It is not clear why. Focusing on required returns directly might be more of an intellectual task than arriving at valuations. By this I mean that the valuation task might activate stronger emotions than assessing required returns.

Finally, by looking at Figures 2.2 and 2.3, you can see that ask-to-bid ratios for LS are significantly higher than for other alternatives. This turns out to be typical. People are reluctant to pay much for long shots. However, once they own them, they require a lot in compensation to part with them.

CLOSING THOUGHTS

Fear, hope, and the feeling of ambition are three key emotions that underlie how people rank risky alternatives and attach valuations to them. These emotions give rise to needs, which people seek to meet by providing themselves with security, potential, and the chance of success. Notably, people differ psychologically in the relative strength of these emotions and their associated needs. As we shall see throughout the book, risk managers will be better able to carry out their functions if they understand the ways in which people differ psychologically, and develop strategies for dealing with these differences.

CHAPTER 3

PROSPECT THEORY'S FOCUS ON GAINS, LOSSES, AND FRAMING

PEOPLE MAKE DECISIONS ABOUT WHICH RISKS TO ASSUME BASED BOTH ON how they feel and how they think. When the Nobel committee announced in 2002 that psychologist Daniel Kahneman would be a Nobel laureate, they singled out work he had done with his late colleague Amos Tversky. Together, Kahneman and Tversky developed a framework they called "prospect theory," which provides great insight into the cognitive aspects associated with the psychology of risk.[1]

Prospect theory brings together an important set of ideas that were developed by economists, mathematicians, statisticians, and of course psychologists. Among the economists were three Nobel laureates: Maurice Allais, Milton Friedman, and Harry Markowitz. All three had pointed out important aspects of the way that people make decisions about risk. Allais identified issues with the manner in which people mentally process probabilities, especially when probabilities are very small or risk is absent. Friedman, writing with the famous statistician Leonard J. Savage, analyzed why people seek risk in buying lottery tickets while they avoid risk by purchasing insurance policies. Markowitz analyzed the same issue and focused attention on people's notion of "customary wealth," and how taking risk leads to changes when measured against customary wealth.

Kahneman and Tversky proposed prospect theory as a framework that integrates the insights of these three economists, and ties them to psychology. Building on Markowitz, prospect theory stipulates that people interpret events through the lens of gains and losses relative to some "reference point." Building on Friedman and Savage, prospect theory stipulates that in some circumstances people are risk averse, whereas in other circumstances people are risk seeking. Building on Allais, prospect theory stipulates that people overweigh small probabilities relative to larger ones, and overweigh the perception of no risk over just a little risk. These three features are the main cognitive issues emphasized by prospect theory, to which the title of this chapter refers.

As we shall see in the wide range of risk management applications discussed in this book, the three features are absolutely fundamental to the way people make judgments and decisions about risk.

Kahneman and Tversky developed prospect theory experimentally. I have replicated prospect theory experiments with many different types of subjects, including our protagonists Beth and Larry from the previous chapter. These experiments are quite easy to explain, and amazingly powerful in how they inform our understanding. This chapter follows risk manager Beth and portfolio manager/trader Larry as they participate in the experiments, describes their behavior and relates it to other subjects. If the experimental questions are new to you, you might want to try answering them along with Beth and Larry.

When it comes to understanding the psychology of risk, prospect theory is a game changer. When it broke onto the scene, it taught us that people's attitude to risk is much more complex that we had previously thought. Prospect theory introduced us to critical new concepts, with three of the important ones being "loss aversion," "framing," and "the fourfold risk pattern." This chapter explains what these terms mean and describes some of the experiments that led to their development.

The experiments are centered on a series of question, which you will encounter below. For those of you who lack the patience to read about experiments, you can skip the details and just focus on the punch lines, which are the following: people naturally assess outcomes in terms of changes, losses loom larger than gains, people appear to be risk seeking or risk averse according to circumstances, and their behavior is sensitive to how decision tasks are framed. Nevertheless, be aware that it is in the experiments that you will find the true nuggets of wisdom.

Loss Aversion

The experimental evidence associated with prospect theory tells us that when people evaluate alternative risks, they focus on gains and losses relative to a reference point. This is what they do: what they *do not* do is translate what the gains and losses to do their overall wealth. Therefore, someone facing a risk of either gaining $1,000 or losing $1,000, and whose wealth is currently $100,000, does not focus explicitly on whether their wealth will end up being either $101,000 or $99,000. Instead, they isolate the value of their wealth from the information upon which they make their choices,

GAINS, LOSSES, AND FRAMING 39

namely the prospect of either gaining $1,000 or losing $1,000. Therefore, their choices tend to be relatively insensitive to their wealth levels, and so a person might behave the same regardless of whether their wealth is $100,000 or $500,000.

Prospect theory also tells us that psychologically, most people experience losses more acutely than gains of the same magnitude. This concept goes by the name "loss aversion." Following are two experimental questions that speak to this concept, and which Beth and Larry answered.

Question 1: Imagine that you are given the opportunity to play a fifty-fifty risky alternative whose outcome will be determined by the toss of a coin. If the coin toss comes up tails, you lose $500. If the coin toss comes up heads, you win $5,000. You can choose to accept the risky alternative or you can choose to reject the risky alternative. Would you accept or reject the fifty-fifty risky alternative where you either lose $500 or win $5,000?

Question 1 is designed to uncover which people are so averse to losing $500 that even the prospect of winning ten times that amount, in a fifty-fifty bet, leaves them unwilling to accept the risk.

Both Beth and Larry answered that they would accept this risk. Among the undergraduate and graduate students, most say they would accept the risk, while about 10% to 15% reject the risk. Most professionals also accept the risk. The next question elicits how comfortable people are taking the risk.

Question 2: Imagine a fifty-fifty risky alternative where you lose $500 if the coin toss comes up tails, but win a different amount if the coin toss comes up heads. What is the lowest amount you would have to win in this risky alternative and yet still accept the risky alternative? For example, if you accepted the fifty-fifty risky alternative between winning $5,000 and losing $500, would you still be willing to accept if the risky alternative was between winning $2,500 and losing $500? If you answer yes, would you still be willing to accept if the risky alternative was between winning $1,250 and losing $500? In other words, think about how low your win would have to be before you were indifferent between accepting and rejecting the opportunity to face the risky alternative. For you, what would be the lowest acceptable winning amount that would induce you to accept the risk?

Winning or losing $500 on a fifty-fifty coin toss is an actuarially fair bet. The expected payoff is zero. A person who demands more than a $500 gain in order to take the risk is averse to the risk. A person who demands a $500 gain exactly is neutral to the risk. A person who is willing to accept less than a $500 gain is risk seeking in respect to the risk.

Larry's response to Question 2 is $1,000, and Beth's response is $2,500. Because Beth's response is 2.5 times as great as Larry's response, prospect theory would lead us to conclude that Beth is 2.5 times more averse to losing $500 than Larry. By dividing their responses to Question 2 by $500, we could assign a coefficient of risk aversion of 2.0 to Larry and 5.0 to Beth.

For Larry, losses loom twice as large as gains. For Beth, losses loom five times as large as gains. This lesson is important because, as prospect theory emphasizes, in this type of problem people are averse to taking risk because they are averse to taking a loss. Beth and Larry participated in this experiment as part of a large group of about 40 business professionals. For their group, the mean coefficient of loss aversion was 3.8, and the median coefficient of loss aversion was 2.0.

Median coefficients of loss aversion generally tend to be considerably lower than mean coefficients, indicating that the significant presence of skewness. In responses to Question 2 from surveys I have administered to almost a thousand people, the mean coefficient of loss aversion was 5.2, and the median was 2.3. The surveys responses come from a global cross section that includes risk managers, portfolio managers, financial executives, graduate students, and undergraduate finance majors. In all of these groups, median coefficients of loss aversion are lower than mean coefficients of loss aversion, reflecting significant positive skewness in the response pattern.

Varying Risk Attitude According to Circumstances

The experimental evidence associated with prospect theory tells us that in circumstances that feature possible gains, but no possible losses, people are generally inclined to be risk averse. However, in circumstances that feature possible losses, but no possible gains, people are generally inclined to be risk seeking.

With this feature in mind, consider the next question that Beth and Larry were asked, and see if you can guess how each answered. The decision task in the next question is a little more complex than the tasks in Questions 1 and 2. Here Beth and Larry are presented with two concurrent choices. Concurrent decisions involve choices made at about the same time, and in which the risky outcomes play out simultaneously.

Question 3: Imagine that you face the following pair of concurrent decision tasks. Think of making your choices at about 9:00 a.m., with the outcome to both decisions being determined at 1:00 p.m. Imagine that it is almost 9:00 a.m. First examine both decisions, and then decide which option you would choose for the first task and which option you would choose for the second task.

> First task: Choose between
>   A: a sure gain of $2,400
>   B: a 25% chance of gaining $10,000 and a 75% chance of gaining nothing

Second task: Choose between
C: a sure loss of $7,500
D: a 75% chance of losing $10,000 and a 25% chance of losing nothing

Beth and Larry both chose the combination A&D. The choice of A over B reflects risk aversion because in order to avoid risk, the decision-maker is willing to give up $100 in expected payoff (the difference between the expected payoff of $2,500 in B and $2,400 in A). The choice of D over C reflects risk seeking, because the decision-maker is willing to accept the risk of D, even though D features the same expected payoff as the sure outcome C.[2]

Within Beth and Larry's group of 40 people, 82% chose A, 79% chose D, and 65% chose the combination A&D. In my experience, the frequency with which members of Beth and Larry's group chose A and D is a bit high relative to the general averages. Based on a general sample of over a thousand responses, 65% chose A, 70% chose D, and 43% chose the combination A&D. However, my experience with groups similarly composed to the one that included Beth and Larry—that feature a mix of professionals with different business functions but a serious interest in risk management—72% chose A, 78% chose D, and 56% chose the combination A&D. These groups tend to be a bit more extreme in their responses.

Undergraduate finance majors provide responses that are representative of the general averages, and their comments provide important insight into the thought processes underlying choice patterns in Question 3. Here are examples from two students, John and Alan, who chose combination A&D.

> *John*: I would prefer the guaranteed $2400 rather than having a 75% of getting nothing, as the guaranteed sum is quite a lot. On the other hand, I feel as though I'd take the riskier bet because in my mind there isn't much difference between losing $7,500 and $10000, either one would be disappointing. Thus, the 25% chance that I lose nothing seems appealing, though I understand the two scenarios are basically two sides of the same coin.
>
> *Alan*: For the first decision, I would choice option A over option B because I believe that a sure gain of 2,400 is better than a 25% chance of winning 10,000 and a 75% chance of winning nothing. I'm the type of guy who does like to take risk but I'm not greedy and 2,400 dollars is enough money for me for the position I am in currently. However, for the second decision, I would have to go with option D. I say this because I would rather take the risk of owing 2,500 more dollars than just giving someone 7,500 no matter what. Even though the odds are still not in your favor, I believe it is better to take the risk.

Most people do respond to experimental Question 3 as if they were risk averse when only gains are involved and risk seeking when only losses are involved. However, the relative frequencies of these responses are highly variable across different groups. Risk managers would be wise to remember that a sizeable minority, if not majority, do not choose the combination A&D. Some insight into the thought processes of people making other choices can be discerned from the following comments by two undergraduate finance majors, Christine and Kenneth.

> *Christine*: I would choose option B and C. In doing this, the most I could lose is $7,500 but I also have the chance to make $2,500. I am willing to take this risk to avoid a loss in general as opposed to taking option A and C which would guarantee me a loss of $5,100. I also don't like the idea of having two scenarios left up to chance. The first risk is the appropriate amount of risk for me.
>
> *Kenneth*: For the first scenario, the expected value of taking the bet is higher than the non-risky alternative. I also tend to be a gambler at heart, so this option sounds more fun. For the second decision, the expected value for both decisions is equal, and once again, I like to gamble, so I would take the bet.

These students are purposeful and thoughtful about their choices. Their considered responses caution us to be careful about overgeneralizing about people being risk averse in the domain of gains and risk seeking in the domain of losses.

FRAMING AND CONCURRENT CHOICE

Prospect theory has two more important framing lessons for us that pertain to the concurrent decision tasks in Question 3. Here is the first: in contemplating the choice between C and D, were Beth and Larry to "make peace" with their losses, then they would effectively think about C and D differently. In this regard, they might view C as no change, meaning the status quo, and B as a risk between incurring a $7,500 gain and a $2,500 loss. There is good reason to believe that in this frame, loss aversion would induce both to choose C instead of D. To be sure, if C were viewed as a $2,500 gain, and D were viewed as a risk between receiving a payoff of $0 or a payoff of $10,000, then Beth and Larry's choice of A over B already tells us that they would choose the reframed C instead of the reframed D. After all, the reframed decision task is now equivalent to the choice between A and B, except that the payoff in A is now $2,500 instead of $2,400.

To set the stage for the second framing issue, think about how you would expect Beth and Larry to answer the following question.

Question 4: Imagine that you are facing two concurrent decision tasks. In the first task, you have to decide between a sure outcome and a risky alternative. In the second task, you have to decide whether to accept an unconditional offer of $100 or reject the offer of $100. The "unconditional offer" means that there are "no strings attached" to accepting the $100. How would you behave in the second task? Would you accept or reject the unconditional offer of $100?

Beth, Larry, and almost everyone else answer this question by accepting the unconditional offer of $100. Those who reject the $100 typically do so because they do not trust the statement that the offer is unconditional.

Now here is the point about framing: in Question 3, people who choose the combination A&D act as if they are rejecting the risk in Question 4. To see why, think concretely about what the combination of A&D entails. Combining the $2,400 gain from A with the risky alternatives –$10,000 and $0 in D leads to net outcomes of –$7,600 and $2,400 respectively. Moreover, these two events occur with probability 75% for the $7,600 loss and 25% for the $2,400 gain.

Now consider the net outcomes to B&C, one of the alternatives to A&D. Combining the –$7,500 loss from C with the risky alternatives $10,000 and $0 in B leads to net outcomes of –$7,500 and $2,500 respectively. Moreover, these two events occur with probability 75% for the $7,500 loss and 25% for the $2,500 gain.

Both combinations A&D and B&C involve two outcomes, one loss and one gain. In addition, B&C offers the same probabilities as A&D, with the higher probability to the loss in each case. However, B&C offers $100 more than A&D, no matter whether the outcome is a gain or a loss.

The combination B&C is said to *stochastically dominate* combination A&D. This type of dominance is technically called "first order stochastic dominance."

Anyone who accepts the premise that "more is better than less" should avoid choosing stochastically dominated risks. However, Beth, Larry, and the majority of their colleagues, along with many business people and students around the world choose the stochastically dominated A&D over the "better" B&C.

Upon hearing this explanation, most people who participate in the experiment are clear to say that they were not aware of A&D being stochastically dominated when they made their choice and that had they been aware, they would have chosen differently. Of course: this is another of prospect theory's lessons. The manner in which a decision task is described can matter for the decision. The framing in Question 3 is *opaque*. In contrast, displaying the net amounts and corresponding probabilities for the combined choices is more *transparent*.[3]

Quasi-hedonic Editing: The Framing of Prior Gains and Losses

Prospect theory emphasizes the importance of framing, meaning how the elements of the choice menu are described. Next is another example that illustrates the importance of framing.

Our portfolio manager Larry has already told us that he is loss averse, and would reject an even bet between a $500 gain and a $500 loss. When we ask him if he would reject bets with lower amounts, such as $225 or $450, he gives us the following answer: "I would reject the risk, for a 50/50 split, the risk is not worth the reward. I will admit that the lower the amount goes, the more inclined I am to take a shot. At $20, I would do it as the risk of losing $20 has minimal psychological impact."

Framing matters. As it happens, Larry will accept an even bet between a $450 gain and a $450 loss if we put the issue to him more narrowly. To be specific, we ask Larry the following:

Question 5: Imagine that you previously took a risk and have just come out with a $1,500 gain. Now you have a new opportunity to take an even bet between a $450 gain and a $450 loss. Do you accept or reject the new risk?

Larry responded that he would accept this risk, and explained his thought process as follows: "Being I was already 'in the money' $1,500, the potential subtraction of my unrealized gain of $450 doesn't really affect me emotionally in any way as I feel I was playing with house money and either way, there is no personal direct out of pocket cost for me to potentially bear."

Richard Thaler and Eric Johnson provided a systematic analysis of how people's choices about risk would be impacted by prior gains and losses.[4] In respect to gains, Thaler and Johnson hypothesized that people would indeed perceive the prior gain as "house money" and be willing to accept an even bet that they would otherwise decline. The caveat is that the potential loss in the even bet be less than $1,500.

Framing matters. As it happens, were the situation to involve a $750 prior loss instead of a $1,500 prior gain, Larry would reject an even risk for a gain or loss of $225. Such a question would read:

Question 6: Imagine that you have taken a risk with the outcome being that you have just lost $750. Now you have a new opportunity to take an even bet between a $225 gain and a $225 loss. Do you accept or reject the new risk?

Larry explains: "Being I just lost $750 and downtrodden about that, I would lock in my total losses at $750 and forgo the 50/50 chance of winning back $225 or further losing an additional $225. The emotional pain of losing almost $975 bothers me much more than any pleasure I may garner from reducing my already established loss from $750 to $525."

GAINS, LOSSES, AND FRAMING   45

Framing matters. What might seem like an innocuous change in wording leads Larry to accept the even bet for $225 instead of rejecting it. In the changed wording, Larry chooses between "accepting a guaranteed loss of $750" and accepting "a fifty-fifty risk of losing $525 or losing $975." The revised wording changes neither the amounts nor the probabilities. Both versions of the wording have the exact same financial consequences. What is going on?!

Now Larry actually noticed the differences in his own responses. More than that, he himself commented on having rejected the risk after a prior $750 loss, while having accepted the risk when framed as in the preceding paragraph. Larry tells us, "It is funny, but I am well aware that this logic seems to contradict my other response. I think it may be because knowing I already lost $750, I've accepted and reset to $0 and there is no appeal to do a 50/50 bet for $225 at that point."

Larry's behavior pattern highlights the important psychological role that framing plays. In this regard, think of prospect theory as describing how people use mental sets of scales to evaluate alternative risks. When comparing two alternative risks, all the components making up a single alternative go onto one side of the scale. The person then compares the weights of the two alternatives and chooses the heavier one. Prospect theory emphasizes that the way in which an alternative is framed influences what our minds place onto the scales.

PROBABILITY MAGNITUDES

Prospect theory tells us that the magnitudes of probabilities matter in the way that people make decisions about risk. Many people make a sharp distinction in their minds between a very low risk and no risk. By the same token, they make a sharp distinction between almost certain and absolutely certain. At the same time, many treat two probabilities that are close to zero as being almost the same, and two probabilities close to unity as being almost the same. As a result, behavior might not follow the patterns that were described above.

To understand how the magnitudes of probabilities can affect behavior, consider Question 7, which is Beth and Larry's next task.

Question 7: Suppose that you face a choice between two situations, designated E and F.

> E: $2,000 with probability 90%
> $0 with probability of 10%
> F: $4,000 with probability 45%
> $0 with probability 55%

Which would you choose, E or F?

Next, consider how you would choose if the probability of achieving a positive gain were much smaller. Specifically, suppose that you face a choice between two situations, designated G and H.

G: $2,000 with probability .002
    $0 with probability .998
H: $4,000 with probability .001
    $0 with probability .999

Which would you choose, G or H?

Both Beth and Larry chose the safer choice, E, and the riskier choice, H. This is the most common response, and about half of their experimental group made the same choice. As a point of comparison, about three-quarters of undergraduate finance majors make the same choice.

In choosing E over F, Beth and Larry prefer the near certainty of a $2,000 gain over a much riskier $4,000 gain. In this regard, the two risks offer the same expected payoffs. Likewise, G and H offer the same expected payoffs, and the amounts are the same as in the choice between E and F. However, the probabilities of any positive gain in both G and H are very small. People like Beth and Larry, who choose H over G and also E over F, treat the probabilities of .001 and .002 as virtually the same. In doing so, they base their choice on amounts, and H offers twice the gain as G, which leads them to choose H.

People who choose H over G in Question 7 are making the risk-seeking choice. The thing is that G and H are risks involving only gains, and so this finding is opposite to the behavior pattern whereby people facing decisions involving only gains make risk-averse choices. Prospect theory tells us that the manner in which people behave when facing only gains depends on the magnitude of probabilities. For decision tasks like A versus B in Question 3, where the probabilities of receiving (nonzero) gains lies in the middle range, most people do indeed make risk-averse choices. However, when small probabilities of receiving gains are involved, as in Question 7, people flip, and are prone to making risk-seeking choices.

The experimental findings associated with prospect theory indicate that people's choices similarly flip for decision tasks featuring only losses. For example, when confronted with a choice between accepting a $40 loss and facing a 0.1% chance of incurring a $40,000 loss, most people prefer the sure loss.

There are four combinations of gain/loss and moderate/extreme probabilities. With four combinations and two choices of risk attitude per combination, there are 16 possible ways to fill the four boxes. If the assignment of risk attitudes to combinations were purely random, then the relative frequency for any particular fourfold combination assignment would be 1/16, or 6.25%.

Taken together, prospect theory tells us that people exhibit a specific *four-fold* behavior pattern when facing risk. For risks featuring only gains, people tend to make risk-averse choices when probabilities of nonzero gains are moderate, and risk-seeking choices when probabilities of gains are small. For risks featuring only losses, people tend to make risk-seeking choices when probabilities of nonzero gains are moderate, and risk-averse choices when probabilities of gains are small.

A word of caution for risk managers: remember not to overgeneralize. Very few people behave in accordance with prospect theory's specific fourfold pattern. Approximately 75% of responses conform to either two or three of the four patterns. For undergraduate finance majors, about 38% fit three of the four patterns. However, there is usually variation from group to group. For the group that included Beth and Larry, 25% did so.[5] Prospect theory's fourfold pattern is a statement about propensity of choice in a population, but is only a starting point at the level of the individual.

PSYCHOLOGICAL PRINCIPLES UNDERLYING PROSPECT THEORY

Prospect theory emphasizes the importance of particular psychological principles. The first involves the limitations of our cognitive abilities, if you like, the bounds to our rationality. You can see the bounds in the way that people answer Question 3, with many choosing combination A&D when the task is framed opaquely, even though they would have preferred combination B&C were the task framed more transparently. The way people think about analyzing Question 3 makes clear that we are inclined to approach the complexity of task sequences in piecemeal fashion, and that by doing so we are vulnerable to rejecting alternatives that are better for us.

Prospect theory emphasizes that what registers in our brains when we contemplate alternative decisions are changes, not final positions. In his Nobel lecture, Kahneman articulated this point by describing how we react to immersing our hands in three buckets of water, each of a different temperature, under different circumstances.[6] Kahneman asks us to imagine three buckets of water arranged by temperature from left to right, with cold on the left, tepid in the middle, and hot on the right. To begin, a person immerses her left hand in the cold water and her right hand in the hot water. Her initial reaction is to feel the extremes, but over time, those initial sensations wane as her mind adjusts to the new circumstances. Once her initial sensations wane, she then immerses both hands into the middle bucket, and what happens? The left hand feels hot and the right hand feels cold, even though both hands are now experiencing the same tepid water. Kahneman's point is that our brains are registering changes, not final position, which is why prospect theory focuses on gains and losses.

Prospect theory tells us our attitudes toward risk are driven by a principle known as "psychophysics." This principle states that incremental responses to repeated applications of the same stimulus decline in magnitude as we adapt to the stimulus. For example, psychophysics leads us to experience the first $1 gain more intensely than the second: going from $0 to $1 elicits a stronger feeling than going from $1 to $2. Correspondingly, the first $1 loss feels worse than the second. The same property applies to probabilities. Starting from probability 0%, our minds give more weight to the first 1% increase in probability than to the second increase of 1%. Correspondingly, starting from probability 100%, our minds give more weight to the first 1% decrease in probability than to the second.

If you ask how prospect theory explains the fourfold risk behavior pattern, the answer is simple: our minds are wired to focus on changes and obey the principle of psychophysics. Of course, the fourfold pattern applies to risky alternatives that do not involve mixtures of gains and losses.

For risks that feature mixed gains and losses, loss aversion comes into play. Prospect theory explains loss aversion by appealing to evolutionary forces. For our ancestors who long ago lived in forests and were potential prey, being inattentive to losses (from predators) was more important than a few extra nuts and berries.

For the most part, prospect theory emphasizes cognitive issues over emotional issues, meaning how we think more than how we feel. However, when Kahneman and Tversky first developed prospect theory, they thought that when people experience outcomes cognitively, the sensation reflects the degree to which they feel regret. In this respect, larger losses generate greater regret.

In the end, regret did not enter prospect theory formally, but Kahneman and Tversky pointed out that the experience of regret can be an important aspect of taking risk. They tell us that regret is the sensation we experience when we engage in Monday morning quarterbacking after the risk has resolved and we learn the outcome. Monday morning quarterbacking means pondering whether we might have behaved differently if given the opportunity to repeat the decision. We feel regret when the outcome turned out to be unfavorable, and we can easily imagine having chosen a different decision, one that in hindsight most likely would have turned out better.

In these circumstances, the ease of imagining having behaved differently drives the extent of regret experienced. Regret is low when someone pursues what for him or her is conventional behavior, because if the outcome is unfavorable, it is difficult to imagine having decided to behave differently on this particular occasion. However, someone who typically behaves conventionally, but one time departs from convention and experiences an unfavorable outcome, is very vulnerable to experiencing regret. Given the deviation from past policy, it is just too easy to ask "What was I thinking?"

STAKE SIZE AND INDIVIDUAL DIFFERENCES

Despite the fact that prospect theory captures "average" responses of people making decisions involving risk, many individuals do not actually behave in accordance with the precepts of prospect theory. This is why I make a point of providing statistics about response rates to various questions. In this respect, consider how Beth and Larry responded to the following question:

Question 8: Consider a decision task featuring a choice between two alternatives M and N with the same expected payoffs.

   M = a sure loss of $500
   N = a fifty-fifty risk where you will either lose $1,000 or lose $0

If you were asked which risk you would you choose, what would you say?

Although there is some variability in the way in which people respond to this question, the most frequent choice is the risky alternative, N. About 50% of undergraduate finance majors and 75% of graduate students choose N. This choice pattern appears to apply to about two-thirds of the population at the stakes specified in Question 8.

For the group containing our protagonists Beth and Larry, 68% chose N. Notably, Beth chose N, but Larry chose to accept the sure loss, M. Beth explains, "I don't like the concept of sure losses and am willing to take the 50/50 risk to avoid loss altogether." In contrast, Larry explains, "It seems much more appealing to me to lose $500 than it is for a 50/50 chance to lose either $1,000 or $0. For me, the emotional pain of losing the additional $500 is much more intense than the pleasure I would receive if I didn't lose anything at all."

Someone who behaves in accordance with prospect theory will indeed choose the risky prospect, N. Moreover, according to prospect theory, this person would choose N even if the stakes were larger or smaller than the amounts specified in Question 8. In some versions of the experiment, I tested the impact of stake size by asking subjects to indicate whether they would have responded differently had the stakes been larger by a factor of 10 and 100 respectively, and smaller by factors of 1/10 and 1/100 respectively. There is considerable variation in the comments people provide. Here are two comments:

- I would rather take the sure loss. If the stakes were larger by 10 or 100 I would take the loss. If the stakes decreased by 1/10 or 1/100 I would flip the coin.
- I would choose to take the chance to lose $1000, since the odds are 50–50, I feel like I have a good chance of losing $0, which is the optimal situation. If the factors were increased, I would probably not choose the same, because I would risk losing a larger amount of money. If the odds were decreased, I would not change my answer, because I would be risking less money in the process.

As with Beth and Larry, these respondents made opposite choices. However, they did agree that as the size of stakes increase, they are less willing to take the risk. I do have to say that this is not always the case. Some people say that they would behave the same way no matter what the stake size. Therefore, risk managers who apply prospect theory need to be judicious because one story does not fit all.

HATING TO LOSE: AVERSION TO A SURE LOSS

You might have noticed that the previous chapter on SP/A theory mostly dealt with gains rather than losses. Losses only came up in the discussion of WTP, where a loss is incurred if the payoff turns out to be less than WTP, the amount the decision-maker paid to play. For example, someone who pays $870 to take a chance on the risky alternative RF, but receives back $770 will have lost $100.

The original papers about SP/A theory that were cited in the previous chapter suggest treating the zero net gain/loss point as an aspiration level. Viewed this way, losses are framed in the same way as in prospect theory, namely negative payoffs. Therefore, the SP/A framework can be applied to losses in the same way as it applies to gains. In this respect, "high hopes" can lead to a person's being risk seeking in the domain of losses.

Certainly hope can induce a decision-maker to mimic unrealistic optimism about breaking even, and so too can the importance people attach to the aspiration of breaking even. In this context, the A in SP/A is the probability of avoiding a loss, and if A carries a strong weight relative to SP, then strong aspiration can induce someone to seek risk in the domain of losses.

One of the experiments that tested SP/A theory asked subjects to interpret outcomes as losses instead of gains. For example, in RF (discussed in the previous chapter), an outcome of $770 in the revised condition meant that the subject would lose $770, not gain $770.

Think back to the two alternatives, RF and PK, which are depicted in Figure 2.1. If you remember the original discussion about what happens with gains, a subject who is strong in fear, weak in hope, and whose aspiration is $770, will typically rank RF over PK. Why? Because fear will induce him to overweigh the most unfavorable outcomes that are possible with PK, underweigh the most favorable outcomes under PK, and find the certainty of receiving at least $770 under RF to be irresistible.

Now in the revised experiment, a person who is strong in fear and weak in hope, but with a reference point of $0 loss will think about ranking RF and PK totally differently. In the reinterpreted setting, the worst possible outcome, a $2,200 loss, is the same for both alternatives. However, RF offers no opportunity to reach the aspiration point of zero loss, whereas PK does.

Therefore, if reaching zero loss aspiration is important, a subject will rank PK over RF.

When the payoffs are interpreted as losses instead of gains, SP/A theory suggests that the result will be a reversal in rankings. This means that the LS, which is ranked at the bottom in the original experiment involving gains, emerges as the top alternative in the experiment involving losses. Of course, the reason is that LS offers the highest probability of a zero loss. Consistent with risk seeking in the domain of losses, the top ranking of LS occurs despite the fact that the possible loss under the LS is the most unfavorable among all the other risky alternatives.

The SP/A experimental data on losses also featured a lot more variability in orderings among subjects than was the case in the original experiment involving gains.[7] Risk managers take note: greater variability calls for greater caution in applying the frameworks to explain the behavior or real people.

"Aversion to a sure loss" is the name that Kahneman and Tversky gave to behavior in which a person is willing to take an actuarially unfavorable bet in the hope of beating the odds and breaking even.

It is easy to confuse the terms "loss aversion" and "aversion to a sure loss" because they both pertain to loss and to aversion. However, they are not the same. Loss aversion concerns the fact that losses loom larger than gains, so that the pain of loss induces people to reject actuarially fair risks featuring mixed gains and losses. Aversion to a sure loss states that the pain of loss induces people to be risk seeking in order to try and avert a sure loss.

If you look back at all of the experimental questions in this chapter that feature losses, you will see that the risky alternatives all offer the chance of breaking even. However, what happens if the risky alternative allows for the possibility of a lower loss than the guaranteed loss, but no chance to break even? Will people still be risk seeking? SP/A theory predicts that if the aspiration level is breaking even, then only very hopeful people will be risk seeking. Prospect theory predicts that when the probabilities attached to nonzero losses are moderate, people are willing to be risk seeking if the odds are sufficiently favorable. What happens in practice? To find out, consider how people, such as Beth and Larry, would respond to the following question:

Question 9: Consider the following decision task, which features a choice between two alternatives, O and P, with the same expected payoff (–$500).

O = a sure loss of $500
P = a 2:1 risk where you will either lose $1,000 with probability 1/3 or lose $250 with probability 2/3

Given that you had to choose between these two risks, which you would you choose?

The most frequent choice is the risky alternative P. Notably, Larry chose P, but Beth chose to accept the sure loss O. In Beth and Larry's group, 65% chose P. About 60% of undergraduate finance majors and 70% of graduate students chose P.

Larry, who in Question 8 accepted the sure loss, M, chose P in this problem. He explains, "The odds seem to be in my favor to take the 2:1 risk to lower my losses. Either I can take a guaranteed/sure loss of $500 or take a 66.67% chance of the loss being reduced to $250 and a 33.33% chance of doubling the loss from $500 to $1,000. Based upon the 2/3 odds of lowering my losses by 50%, I indicated I would take the additional risk over the sure loss."

Beth, who earlier took the risky alternative N, chose O in this problem. She explains, "I am going to lose money no matter what and would rather cap losses and not risk having them extended even with these probabilities."

Closing Thoughts

Prospect theory is a rich framework that informs us about important psychological influences on people's decisions about which risks to take. As we shall see from the applications discussed throughout this book, loss aversion, the fourfold risk pattern, aversion to a sure loss, and framing effects loom large. Risk managers absolutely need to understand these principles.

Prospect theory emphasizes cognitive issues, while SP/A theory emphasizes emotional issues. Both theories are important, and both tell us part of the story about the role psychology plays. Moreover, cognition and emotion are interlinked concepts.

Just as Appendix A provides the formal modeling details for SP/A theory, Appendix B provides the formal modeling details for prospect theory, and Appendix C discusses a model for integrating SP/A theory and prospect theory.

A final message for risk managers: when it comes to the psychology of risk, one size does not fit all. Risk managers who apply psychological theories cavalierly risk overreliance on the stereotypic behavior associated with prospect theory especially. Yes, prospect theory stipulates that people interpret events through the lens of gains and losses relative to some "reference point." Yes, prospect theory stipulates that in some circumstances people display risk-averse behavior, whereas in other circumstances people display risk-seeking behavior. Yes, prospect theory stipulates that people overweigh small probabilities relative to larger ones, and overweigh the perception of no risk over just a little risk. However, locating individual people who display all of prospect theory's features is more difficult than it seems. Just do not forget that individual differences are also an important part of the behavioral story.

CHAPTER 4

BIASES AND RISK

IDENTIFYING AND QUANTIFYING RISK ARE TWO OF THE MOST IMPORTANT activities in which risk managers engage. Research in psychology over the last four decades has taught us that these activities are extremely vulnerable to judgmental biases. People overestimate some risks and underestimate, if not overlook, others. What are the major biases that risk managers need to understand in order to exhibit expertise? And what can be done to help mitigate these biases?

After reading this chapter, you will be able to provide answers to these questions. You will be able to articulate what are the most important biases that impact people's judgments of risk, and describe ways of mitigating these biases.

The preceding chapters have focused on psychological theories about how people make decisions about risk. That discussion focused on choice when underlying probabilities were known. This focus enabled us to abstract from the very difficult question of how risks are assessed.

Risk managers who write about risk management, such as Luca Celati (author of *The Dark Side of Risk Management*) and Ricardo Rebonato (author of *The Plight of the Fortune Tellers*), emphasize that risk managers will be much better at assessing routine risks than the risks associated with rare events and highly complex situations. They tell us that the frequentist approach to probability will apply to routine events, but that rare events are likely to require some kind of Bayesian approach.[1]

In order to communicate the main concepts in this chapter, I use a lot of examples. The examples are widespread. Some pertain to the restaurant industry, some to energy and the environment, some to financial risk, some to life events, and some to medical risks. As in previous chapters, I draw on material upon which psychologists have based a series of experiments.

The number of specifically identified psychological biases currently number well over 100. This is far too many to discuss carefully within a single chapter. Instead, the chapter focuses on what I suggest to be the most important half dozen or so.

Here is a capsule summary of these biases, for those interested: people tend to misjudge risks when they rely too heavily on information that is readily available. Their intuitive judgments of risky events is based on the degree to which they understand specific risks and dread the outcomes. As a result, perceived risk is often at odds with expert judgments about risk. People rely too heavily on stereotypes, which leads them to have poor intuition about the nature of randomness. They tend to be excessively optimistic on average. Relatedly, people tend to be overconfident and underestimate risk. They place excessive weight on evidence that confirms their views and insufficient weight on evidence that disconfirms their views. People are inclined to underestimate the degree to which they can control risks. Finally, they have poor intuition about how to use Bayes' rule, one of the pillar concepts of probability theory.

The summary points described in the preceding paragraph comprise the main messages of this chapter. As noted in previous chapters, psychologists have documented the phenomena associated with these messages through experiments. Knowledge of the experiments is not necessary for having a basic understanding of the concepts discussed here; however, for those who want a deeper appreciation of the concepts, it is a good idea to learn how the experiments were structured and what general findings emerged.

AVAILABILITY BIAS

Most people base their judgments of risk on information that is most readily available. As a result, they render themselves vulnerable to overweighing information that is easily available and underweighing information that is less readily available. Psychologists Amos Tversky and Daniel Kahneman describe this behavior pattern as "availability bias."[2]

Here is an example of availability bias. Opening a restaurant is risky. A 2003 television commercial run by American Express pointed out that 90% of restaurants fail during their first year of operation. The commercial aired on the NBC reality program *Restaurant: A Reality Show*. Thereafter, the 90% figure came to be repeated many times in the media.[3]

The initial American Express commercial and the subsequent mentioning of the 90% figures in media reports made that figure highly available. But was it right? As it happens, the answer is no. The ease with which the figure was easily recalled had instilled a bias in the general population. A more accurate figure was reported in a 2005 study published in the *Cornell Hotel and Restaurant Administration Quarterly*.

The study documented that failure rates for eating and drinking establishments rank at the top among all retail businesses, and that actual failure rates for the first year are much lower than the American Express figure. The authors of the Cornell study found failure rates to be approximately 27% for independent restaurants and 24% for chain restaurants. Failure rates for the first three years are approximately 61% for independent restaurants and 57% for chain restaurants. When pressed by the study authors as to the source of the 90% figure, American Express responded that they could not provide an explanation for how the figure was generated.[4]

Both Beth and Larry, our short story protagonists from Chapter 2, participated in an experiment that involved a question relating to availability bias. The question reads as follows:

Question 1: Consider the danger of death or injury in the United States stemming from four sources, all involving water:

1. shark attacks
2. hurricanes
3. rip currents
4. floods

Which item in the above list presents the greatest danger to people?

Most people rank hurricanes and floods as the top two dangers. Risk manager Beth and portfolio manager Larry, conform to this pattern. Beth gave her top rank to floods, and Larry gave his top rank to hurricanes. In a group of 133 people who share similar interests in risk management as Beth and Larry, 38% ranked flood danger at the top and 32% ranked hurricane danger at the top. Notably, a distant 17% ranked rip current danger at the top, and only 12% ranked shark attack danger at the top.

How do these judgments stack up against historical frequencies? Data from the National Oceanic and Atmospheric Administration (NOOA) indicates that between 2004 and 2014, the number of flood-related deaths was 75 per year. By contrast, NOOA reports that for the same period, hurricane deaths per year have been 108. The big surprise is for rip currents. According to NOAA, rip currents caused 46 deaths per year. Notably, 64 people died in rip currents in 2013. However, the United States Lifesaving Association estimates that the annual number of deaths due to rip currents exceeds 100, placing it above floods and close to hurricanes. As for deaths from shark attacks, on average there are 16 shark attacks per year, with one fatality every two years.

The most interesting feature of the general response pattern is the low response rate for rip currents. Hurricanes and floods are more dramatic events. When they occur, they are newsworthy and gain a lot of media coverage. Therefore, deaths from hurricanes and floods tend to be highly salient, because information about them is readily available in the media. A similar remark applies to shark attacks.

In contrast, deaths from rip currents do not garner a lot of media attention. We rarely read stories appearing, say, in the Associated Press, that begin, Four swimmers drowned yesterday in two days of treacherous ocean currents at beaches in Long Island and New York City.

Availability bias leads to the underestimation of the risk posed by rip currents, as reflected in the responses above, because of a lack of salience. Events that are not salient are less easily recalled from people's memories than events that are salient. Events that are easily recalled are said to be mentally *available*.

By their nature, rare events tend not to be salient. "Out of sight, out of mind" is a risk that availability bias poses for risk managers, and others, in making judgments about the risks associated with rare events. The issue is important, and is discussed further in Appendix D.

PERCEIVED RISKS

Risk managers do not always see eye to eye with others when it comes to rating risks. Psychologist Paul Slovic has helped identify where and why the judgments of risk experts differ from those of nonexperts. Understanding these differences, and being able to articulate them, is a critical skill that risk managers need to have.[5]

Slovic studied a wide-ranging set of risks. Some were well known, concrete, and closely associated with everyday activities such as driving motor vehicles, smoking, and the consumption of alcoholic beverages. Others were associated with sports and recreation activities, such as skiing, mountain climbing, and football in high school and college. These too were generally familiar to most people. Yet other risks were more abstract and less familiar, such as those associated with railroads and nuclear power.

Slovic tells us that when risk managers assess these types of risks, they tend to focus on variables such as expected death rates, much as I did earlier in this chapter when discussing risks associated with water-related events. However, he points out that nonexperts rely on intuitive assessments of risk called *risk perceptions*, which can be very different from the judgments of experts.

In order to appreciate the insights Slovic offers, imagine that you are asked the following question:

Question 2: Consider the activities and technologies displayed in Table 4.1. On a scale of 1–10, rate these activities and technologies in terms of how risky you perceive them to be for the general population in the United States, how well you feel you understand each of the risks in the table, and the

Table 4.1 Activities and technologies associated with Question 2 in Chapter 4

Possible Risk Events

1	Mountain climbing	15	Bicycles
2	Fire fighting	16	Surgery
3	General aviation	17	Prescription antibiotics
4	Motorcycles	18	Skiing
5	Smoking	19	Commercial aviation
6	Food preservatives	20	Hunting
7	Power mowers	21	X-rays
8	Police work	22	Handguns
9	Large construction	23	Spray cans
10	Swimming	24	Vaccinations
11	Alcoholic beverages	25	Nuclear power
12	Pesticides	26	Home appliances
13	High school and college football	27	Railroads
14	Contraceptives	28	Electric power

degree to which you would dread the consequences attached to each, with 10 representing the highest level of dread.

Slovic found that experts and nonexperts appear to rate risks using different considerations. Experts focus heavily on annual death rates when assessing risk. In contrast, nonexperts' risk perceptions are driven by two factors, one Slovic calls *dread risk* and the second he calls *unknown risk*.

Dread risk encompasses dread and an additional set of considerations such as perceived lack of control, fatal consequences, catastrophic potential, and inequitable distribution of costs and benefits. Slovic suggests that nuclear power would rate highly on dread risk. In this regard, serious events that occurred at Three Mile Island, Chernobyl, and Fukushima Daiichi spring to mind.

Unknown risk pertains to lack of familiarity, such as whether the activity or technology is new, unobservable, unknown, and delayed in generating harmful consequences. Slovic suggests that some biotechnology activities would rate highly on unknown risk. In this regard, genetic modifications to food come to mind.

Because risk managers take different considerations into account, and weigh these considerations differently than the general public, risk managers can judge risk differently from the general public. Writing in 1987, Slovic used nuclear power as an example of such a difference. At the time, he pointed out that the general public viewed nuclear power as being much riskier than did risk experts. He suggested that the reason for the difference could be traced both to dread risk and unknown risk, both of which loomed large in the public's mind. In contrast, actual deaths directly attributable to nuclear power were small, even given incidents such as those that occurred at Three Mile Island in 1979 and Chernobyl in 1986.

Almost 30 years later, little has changed in regard to the basis for assessing risks associated with nuclear power. The World Nuclear Association (WNA), representing the nuclear industry, makes the case that after six decades of experience nuclear power is safe. In regard to the accidents at Three Mile Island, Chernobyl, and Fukushima Daiichi, the WNA points out that the first was contained without harm to anyone, the second involved an intense fire without provision for containment, and the third severely tested the containment and allowed some release of radioactivity. Compared to other risks, the WNA website describes the risk of accident as low and the consequences of an accident or terrorist attack as minimal.[6]

In contrast, the consumer group US Public Interest Research Group (PIRG) describes nuclear power as a risk not worth taking. The group characterizes nuclear power plants as dangerous, unproven, and potentially catastrophic. It draws attention to the threat of radiation, mentioning stored spent fuel rods awaiting disposal, earthquakes, and the proximity of some plant sites to groundwater that supplies drinking water to large populations.[7] The reaction of the German public to the 2011 events at Fukushima Daiichi was so negative that in 2011, the German government announced a new policy in which it would close all of its nuclear power plants by 2022. The announcement reflected a reversal of government policy, which had called for expanding the role of nuclear power. This reversal illustrates the point that subjective risk perceptions can substantially differ from those of technical experts. Reaction in other European countries was mixed. For example, France decided to continue its reliance on nuclear power, Poland to increase its dependence, and Switzerland to reduce its dependence eventually to zero.[8]

Dread risk is complex. Perceived control is an important issue. In this regard, psychometric research has found that people are willing to tolerate voluntary risks, for example, from skiing, 1,000 times as great as risks related to nonvoluntary activities, for example, from food preservatives.

Unknown risk is important because people naturally have a fear of the unknown. This relates to aversion to ambiguity, where the ambiguity in question pertains to not knowing the probabilities associated with risks being encountered. The accident at Three Mile Island generated a massive public reaction despite there only being relatively minor damage. However, people's fear of the unknown, of a real nuclear meltdown with potential for great catastrophe, was very strong.

In a separate study from 2000 with colleagues Melissa Finucane, C. K. Mertz, James Flynn, and Teresa Satterfield, Slovic reports that biases are related to gender and race. Specifically, white males are less prone than any other group to rate risks as very high. These authors point out that they find no gender effect for nonwhites, suggesting that the behavior pattern is not biological. Instead their analysis supports the idea that white males perceive situations to be less risky because they generally have more power and control, benefit more from many technologies and institutions, are less vulnerable to discrimination, and as a result see the world as less dangerous.[9]

Slovic warns that risk managers need to pay attention to judgments of risk by the general public, even though these might exhibit bias. This is not just because public perceptions impact public behavior, thereby affecting the interests of risk managers' direct constituencies. It is also because the public might actually be sensitive to possible blind spots impacting risk managers' judgments. For example, risk managers' focus might be narrowly constrained by availability bias.

Slovic speaks of "signal potential" or "informativeness," by which he means concerns about "tip of the iceberg" effects. For example, the accident at Three Mile Island generated fear that significant aftershocks might follow the initial incident, the magnitudes of which could potentially be very large. The events at Fukushima that followed the initial tsunami incident come to mind. The actual Fukushima scenario appears to have been well outside the scenarios for which risk managers had planned.

Representativeness

Generating scenarios, arriving at judgments of probability, and making predictions are challenging tasks for which people rely on heuristics. One class of heuristics is based on a principle known as "representativeness," which involves assessing how close a specific item fits the stereotype of a class of objects.

Closely fitting the stereotype is synonymous with being representative of the class. Kahneman and Tversky, who introduced representativeness as a concept, apply it to judgments about how likely a person with a given set of characteristics is to work in a particular type of job or occupation. At the heart of this application is the following question: how closely does a person with this set of characteristics fit the stereotype of someone who does this type of job? The heuristic effectively identifies "highly likely" with "closely fitting the stereotype."[10]

Consider an example. Risk managers often need to generate hypothetical scenarios of how the future might unfold, and to attach probabilities to these scenarios. Therefore, consider a scenario-generation task for tosses of a fair coin.

Question 3: Imagine that you have a fair coin in your hand and get ready to record a sequence of 15 imaginary coin flips. If you imagine that a coin flip comes out as heads, write down an H, and if you imagine that a coin flip comes out as tails, write down a T. Next, pull out a real coin and flip it 15 times. After each flip, record whether it was an H or a T.

People whose intuition about coin flips derives from representativeness tend to generate imagined sequences that are biased relative to real coin flip sequences. This is because our intuition about independent flips of a fair coin is that the "representative sequence" will feature frequent alternation between heads and tails, so that along the imagined sequence the proportion of flips that come up heads does not stray too far from 50%. This intuition appears to be rooted in "the law of large numbers," which says that for long sequences, the probability is close to unity that the percentage of flips will be very close to 50%.

Notably, for short sequences, it is actually typical for the percentage of heads to deviate from 50%. Tversky and Kahneman facetiously coined the term "law of small numbers" to describe the mistaken belief that "the law of large numbers" would apply to short sequences in the same way that it applies to long sequences. The upshot is that people who believe in the law of small numbers expect more frequent alternation between heads and tails than is true for real coin flips. Therefore, they expect more runs (coin toss sequences featuring the same side of the coin) and shorter runs than what typically occurs when real coins are flipped.

I conducted the Question 3 experiment with 37 finance professionals. Figure 4.1 displays the histograms for both the imagined coin flips and the corresponding real coin flips. The two histograms are generally similar. However, the histogram for the real coin flips has fewer runs of length 1 than the corresponding histogram for imaginary coin flips. This feature is indicative of the law of small numbers.

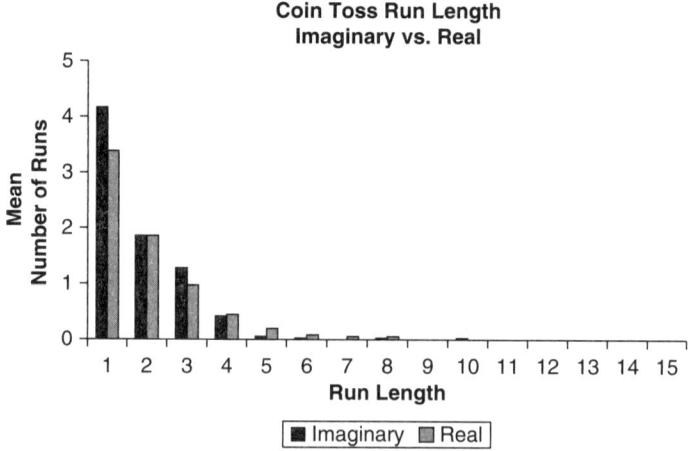

Figure 4.1 This figure displays coin-flip histograms for two groups of participants in an experiment. One group flipped and recorded the outcomes of a real coin in 15 consecutive tosses, and the second group recorded what they imagined as the outcome of 15 consecutive tosses.

The theoretical expected number of runs is 7.5, half the sequence length. In this regard, I would also mention that the mean number of runs in the imaginary flips was 9.1, and for the real flips it was 8.1.

Belief in the law of small numbers induces people to succumb to the bias known as "gambler's fallacy." Gambler's fallacy is the phenomenon of predicting unwarranted reversals. Here is an example. Suppose a fair coin is flipped five times in a row, and produces heads each time. What is the probability that the sixth flip will result in tails? The correct answer is 50%, because the coin is fair. However, a person who relies on representativeness will be asked which sequence of six flips is "more representative" of fair coin flips, one that features five heads and a tail or one that features six heads. Belief in the "law of small numbers" will incline this person to view five heads and a tail as more representative. If the person bases his judgment of relative likelihood on relative representativeness, then he will succumb to gambler's fallacy and judge tails on the sixth flip as being more likely than heads.

Representativeness does not always produce unwarranted beliefs in the reversal of a trend. In some circumstances, representativeness can produce the opposite: unwarranted belief in continuation of a trend. This bias is known as the "hot hand fallacy." The term "hot hand" derives from basketball and refers to a player having a hot hand when they appear to be unusually accurate in making baskets during a particular game.

With the hot hand fallacy, people do not assume that the underlying probabilities stay the same over time, as is the case with a fair coin. Instead, they allow for the possibility that the probabilities change, and make inferences about those changes based on what they observe. Therefore, if they observe that a particular player is hot during a specific game, they will be inclined to judge that the player's accuracy is temporarily improved.

Statistical analyses of the records from professional basketball games has been somewhat mixed about whether players do develop hot hands. The first study, by psychologists Tom Gilovich, Robert Vallone, and Tversky concluded that accuracy rates for players tended to be constant over time.[11] Newer studies, which are based on richer data than the original study, have concluded that there is weak evidence of a hot hand effect. However, it is not large: a study by Andrew Bocskocsky, John Ezekowitz, and Carolyn Stein estimates the increase in hit rate to be between 1.2% and 2.4%.[12]

OPTIMISM

Psychologist Neil Weinstein conducted the first systematic study of optimism bias using an experiment about personal risks. A person who is unrealistically optimistic overestimates the probability with which they will experience favorable events, and underestimates the probabilities with which they will experience unfavorable events.[13]

Weinstein first found evidence of unrealistic optimism by testing undergraduate students in respect to life events. An example of a favorable life event is being recognized for a prestigious reward. An example of an unfavorable event is contracting a serious disease. See Table D.5 in Appendix D for additional information. The type of question Weinstein posed to his subjects was as follows:

Question 4: For each event, compared to other people in your group—same sex as you—what do you think are the chances that the following will happen to you in the future? The choices range from much less than average, to average, to much more than average.

In an unbiased group, the expected mean response to all of these questions is "average." However, Weinstein's main finding was that the mean response for favorable events was above average, and the mean response for unfavorable events was below average. That is, the responses are consistent with unrealistic optimism, albeit with individual differences. In this regard, see the discussion of Larry and Beth's responses in Appendix D.

The drivers of unrealistic optimism are varied. Weinstein identified four particular factors that are positively associated with unrealistic optimism. The four factors are controllability, desirability, familiarity, and representativeness. People tend to be more optimistic about situations in which they perceive themselves to exert a reasonable degree of control. They engage in wishful thinking and are more optimistic about outcomes they want to happen. They are more optimistic about situations with which they are familiar than unfamiliar, and they are more optimistic about favorable events when they view themselves as representative of the type of person to whom the event happens.

OVERCONFIDENCE

Psychologist Stuart Oskamp identified the degree to which people are prone to be overconfident. In this respect, people who know less than they believe they know are overconfident about their knowledge. People who are less capable in performing a task than they believe themselves to be are overconfident about their ability. The bottom line from years of research is that overconfidence about both knowledge and ability are highly prevalent, but not universal.[14]

Overconfidence typically leads people to underestimate risk, and that is perhaps the most important point about overconfidence that risk managers need to know. A good way to understand why overconfidence has this effect is to consider how overconfidence about knowledge is tested. Subjects are provided with difficult factual questions to answer, and asked for their best response together with a 90% confidence interval response. The interval response consists of a low answer and a high answer, with the range set so that the subject feels 90% confident that the correct answer lies within the confidence interval. Notably, responses need to be from memory alone, without consulting external information sources.

An example of a difficult question to answer is the following:

Question 5: In miles, what is the length of the Colorado River? Provide three estimates, your best estimate, a low estimate, and a high estimate. Specify your low and high estimates so that you are 90% confident that the correct answer lies between your low estimate and your high estimate.[15]

A person who is well calibrated and answers many such questions should expect correct answers to lie in their respective confidence intervals about 90% of the time. However, in practice, people set confidence intervals that are too narrow. As a result the percentage of correct answers that lie within people's confidence intervals is typically far less than 90%. Beth and Larry were typical in this regard, with additional details provided in Appendix D.

Part of risk assessment is establishing confidence intervals for specified probabilities. People who set such confidence intervals too narrowly underestimate risk.

CONFIRMATION BIAS

The applications in this book illustrate situations in which risk managers found it difficult to persuade others to accept what on the face of it are compelling facts, evidence, and arguments. A person who stubbornly holds onto their beliefs in the face of disconfirming evidence is said to display confirmation bias. Psychologist Peter Wason developed an experiment to identify the underlying thought processes when people consider evidence in respect to evaluating a position such as whether or not a particular statement is true. In this respect, Wason used the following question to identify the bias:[16]

Question 6: Imagine that you are presented with four cards placed flat on a table in front of you. There is a letter appearing on one side of the card and a number on the other side of the card. You see the following on the four cards: a, b, 2, and 3.

      a   b   2   3

Your task is to test the following hypothesis about these four cards: "Any card having a vowel on one side has an even number on the other side." In particular, select those cards, and only those cards, that will determine whether the statement is true. That is, select the *minimum number of cards* that will enable you to determine whether or not the statement is true. Of the four cards, which would you turn over?

The "position" experimental subjects are asked to evaluate is the statement that any card of these four specific cards that has a vowel on one side has an even number on the other side. The correct way to evaluate whether the statement is true or false is to begin with the presumption "innocent until proven guilty," or "assumed true until proven false." The evidence for a guilty verdict is turning a card over and finding that its contents do not satisfy the condition that there is a vowel on one side and an even number on the other side.

If you were to turn over *all* four cards and find that none of these cards produces a guilty verdict, then you would rightly conclude that the statement is true. However, not every card need be capable of producing a guilty verdict, and if a card is incapable of producing a guilty verdict, then there is no point in turning it over. Therefore, to choose the minimum number of cards required to check whether or not the statement is true, you should only turn over those cards that have the potential to generate a guilty verdict.

The cards that are capable of generating a guilty verdict are the "a" and the "3." The card with the "a" has a vowel on one side. If you turn over that card and the number on the other side is odd, then you need go no farther: the statement is false. If you turn over the card with the number "3" and find a vowel on the other side, you have a guilty verdict: the statement is false.

Turning over the card with a "b" cannot produce a guilty verdict because the statement is silent about cards with consonants. Turning over the card with the "2" cannot produce a guilty verdict. This is because finding a vowel is consistent with the statement, and finding a consonant is irrelevant to the statement, which as I just indicated is silent about cards with consonants.

Wason conjectured that many people would be inclined to turn over the card with the "2" even though doing so does not help them accomplish the evaluation task. However, he suggested that people are prone to overweigh "confirming" evidence, meaning evidence that supports a position they are considering, and by the same token underweigh "disconfirming" evidence. He called the phenomenon "confirmatory bias," and today we simply call it "confirmation bias."

Our protagonists Beth and Larry responded to Question 6 differently from each other. Beth chose "a&3," the correct response, while Larry chose "a&2," the response reflecting confirmation bias. In the group that included Beth and Larry, 10% chose correctly and 59% chose "a&2."

GROUPTHINK

At the collective level, confirmation bias goes by the name of *groupthink*. Groupthink typically occurs when a group places the goal of achieving consensus ahead of making effective decisions. Groups that exhibit groupthink are prone to stifle their members' individual creativity and independent thinking. Doing so retards effective problem solving and decision-making, largely because groupthink suppresses the desire to present and debate alternatives. Instead, group members come to understand that group cohesion is a primary issue, and that expressing unpopular opinions threatens that cohesion. In consequence, groups affected by groupthink overlook realistic alternatives and make poor choices.

There are several factors that can make a group vulnerable to groupthink. First, a group might have an outspoken leader who discourages dissent.[17] An outspoken leader makes clear what he or she wants to do and wants to hear. By nature people are self-interested, and for most, their self-interest will lead them to look for ways to offer support for what the leader wants to do. The leader wants to hear "yes," not "yes, but" and certainly not "no."

There are other reasons, besides having an outspoken leader who does not tolerate dissent, that produce groupthink. The group might be composed of members with similar backgrounds. As a result, confirmation bias and availability bias combine to limit discussion of issues and perspectives.

A group might have cohesion as an important value. As a result, group members will be inclined to sacrifice alternative views for fear that it will reduce that cohesion. The urge to conform might be especially strong among group members, leading them to conform to judgments expressed by the majority.[18] The group might have no clear rules or defined processes for decision-making. As a result, strong personalities might come to dominate decision-making, as those with weaker personalities are either intimidated or incapable of raising their voices in an articulated way. Finally, the group might be isolated from outsiders. As a result, availability bias limits their perspective on issues relevant to the outlook of its members and the factors that drive group decisions.

Groupthink has a special implication when it comes to the risk choices made by the organization. It leads to "polarization," a phenomenon whereby the group dynamics amplify the risk attitudes of the group members, whatever they may be. For example, if group members are moderately risk seeking in their attitudes, groupthink will lead the group to be very risk seeking. A similar statement applies when the group is moderately risk averse: polarization leads the group decision to be very risk averse, a topic to be explored in Chapter 6.

Regardless of the source of groupthink behavior, polarization occurs because group members seek to reinforce each other's judgments and proposals. For example, a group member might propose a risk seeking strategy. Then others chime in offering reasons for why this would be a good idea. As the reasons for taking risk mount, the strength of the evidence on the table increases, and members come to feel comfortable with even more risk.

In the end, the group chooses to be more risk seeking than any of its members initially felt as individuals. Moreover, the deliberations leave them with a sense of confidence and acceptance that doing so charts a wise course.

Groupthink dynamics also cause group members to refrain from sharing important information with each other. This issue is especially important when critical information is distributed across the group, rather than consolidated in a single location. The issues are the same. A group member will typically only disclose information in his or her possession if doing so supports a direction in which the group is moving, thereby inducing the affirmation of others in the group. Information running counter to that direction is withheld. The same is true for information that is unfavorable, if disclosing that information will lead the discloser to be viewed in a less favorable light.

ILLUSION OF CONTROL

Control is an important issue for how people make judgments about risk. In the preceding discussion about risk perception, I described evidence that white males who are business professionals are more inclined to rate risk as being lower than others. In this section, I report the results of an experiment that tests whether people overestimate the amount of control they have in risky situations.

The experiment was designed by psychologist Ellen Langer, and has two versions, the first of which is as follows: imagine that you are offered the opportunity to participate in a baseball pool. The pool works as follows. The operator of a baseball pool at your workplace places in front of you two identical piles. Each pile contains 227 different baseball cards, face up so that you can see the identities of the various baseball players. The operator of the pool asks you to look through the pile closest to you, select one card, and show it to her. After you have done so, the organizer looks through the second (identical) pile, locates the twin of the card you selected, and deposits the twin into a brown cardboard carton. In order to participate, you pay $1 to the operator for each card you select. If the operator manages to sell all the cards, there will be 227 cards in the operator's carton, of which one will be yours. The operator will then draw exactly one card from the carton. The owner of the winning card receives a $50 prize.[19]

Suppose that the organizer does indeed manage to find buyers for all of the baseball cards in the pile, but the drawing has yet to take place. Just before the drawing, the operator approaches you to say that someone who really wanted to participate cannot, because all the cards have been sold. She asks you what amount you would be willing to accept in exchange for the card you drew.

Question 7: What is the minimum amount you would ask, to give up your card? That is the question you face.

In the second version of her experiment, Langer makes the following change. Instead of laying out the cards in front of you and asking you to select one, she instead flips through the pile, selects one herself, and hands it to you. The rest of this version of the experiment proceeds exactly the same as the first version. In particular, the organizer will ask you at the end to specify the minimum amount you would ask, to give up your card?

Langer found that subjects who selected the cards themselves responded with a mean valuation of $8.67. In contrast, subjects to whom the organizer handed the card, responded with a mean valuation of $1.96. The question arises as to whether a subject is 4.5 times more likely to win the $50 because they selected the card themselves as opposed to having it selected by organizer. Of course, the outcome is completely determined by chance, and the odds of winning are exactly the same in the two versions of the experiment.

Langer interpreted the difference in valuations as stemming from subjects' beliefs about how much control they exercised over the outcome of the random draw. She concluded that subjects who themselves selected the card reported higher valuations because they were subject to the illusion of control, believing they exercised more control over the outcome than they actually did.

Of course, both mean valuations are far higher than the expected value attached to the risk. The expected value of a 1 in 227 chance of winning $50 is $0.22. However, as we learned in Chapter 2, the combination of high hopes and high aspirations that are deemed important gives rise to high WTA values. The illusion of control simply adds one more layer to this complicated process.

BAYESIAN AVOIDANCE

Risk managers are responsible for updating their probabilistic judgments of risk as new information arrives. In theory, Bayes' rule provides the formal basis for these updates. Bayes' rule is especially important for making probability judgments in the face of limited data, such as for rare events.

In practice, I submit that most people not only avoid using Bayes' rule but are incapable of describing it. I dare say that this statement applies to risk managers, despite it being covered and discussed in many books about probability and statistics.

In Appendix D, you will find a series of problems whose solution requires the application of Bayes' rule, along with a discussion about the degree to which people make probabilistic judgments that are inconsistent with Bayes' rule. In the remainder of this section, I present one of these problems and suggest an intuitive way to think about how to be a Bayesian.

Question 8: Consider breast cancer screening using mammography that is conducted in your region. You know the following information about women in this region:

- The probability that a woman has breast cancer is 1%.
- If a woman has breast cancer, the probability that she tests positive is 90%.
- If a woman does not have breast cancer, the probability that she nevertheless tests positive is 9%.

A woman tests positive. She wants to know from you what the chances are she has breast cancer. In light of the test result, which we will call a "signal," what would you tell her about her risk of having breast cancer?[20]

The principle behind Bayes' rule is simple. Begin with what is called the prior probability and then scale it by what is called the likelihood ratio. The likelihood ratio measures the strength of the signal as a "smoking gun." In Question 8, we are interested in the probability that a woman has breast cancer, given the signal that her mammogram test is positive.

Coming up with an answer requires two pieces of data. The first piece of data is what is called "the prior probability." This is just the probability we would assign to the woman having breast cancer if we did not have the results of her mammogram. In this case, the "prior probability" is 1%. The second piece of data is "the likelihood ratio," measuring the strength of the smoking gun. The likelihood ratio is used to adjust the prior probability to reflect the information in the signal. If the likelihood ratio for the mammogram problem were 15, then we would multiply the 1% by 15 to arrive at a probability of 15% that the woman has breast cancer, given her positive mammogram test.

Appendix D describes how to calculate the likelihood ratio, which for Question 8 turns out to be 9.2. Therefore, the probability we are after to answer Question 8 is actually 9.2%.

Even though using Bayes' rule is unintuitive for most, in practice people can learn to be decent intuitive Bayesians. They only need remember that what is required is multiplying two numbers together, one being the unconditional probability of the event of interest, and the second being the likelihood ratio measuring the strength of the smoking gun. A little experience can go a long way in getting the feel for what are reasonable values for both.

CLOSING THOUGHTS

The landscape associated with judgments of risk is loaded with psychological land mines. Even risk perceptions and judgments by experts are prone to a wide spectrum of psychological influences. Concepts such as dread, familiarity, availability, overconfidence, confirmation bias, illusion of control, representativeness, and optimism loom large. Almost all of the professionals I have surveyed are unable to explain, let alone apply, Bayes' rule, and Bayes' rule is one of the foundation pillars of probability theory.

Mitigating susceptibility to bias is a gargantuan task. There is little evidence to suggest that debiasing on one's own is likely to prove fruitful. Making inroads along the debiasing dimension requires group effort and can only take place in the right kind of social environment. It is cultural, and risk management culture is a consistent theme in the rest of the book.

CHAPTER 5

PERSONALITY AND RISK

PEOPLE WITH DIFFERENT PERSONALITIES HAVE DIFFERENT TENDENCIES WHEN it comes to risk taking. Not surprisingly, these tendencies relate to fear, hope, and the pain of loss, factors lying at the heart of Chapters 2 and 3. This chapter describes what managers of all stripes can begin to infer about behavior from their understanding of people's personalities.

Entrepreneurial characteristics are part of personality. Risk managers routinely interact with traders and executives who characterize themselves as entrepreneurs. To be sure, some risk managers also characterize themselves as entrepreneurs. This chapter discusses the role that entrepreneurship behavior plays in risk taking, and what factors distinguish entrepreneurs from nonentrepreneurs.

There is an important message for risk managers in this chapter. Be judicious about applying theory to practice. Be careful not to be dogmatic. As we shall see, no single theory explains all behavior. It is easy to allow ourselves to take theories to their extremes. And it can also be dangerous.

That is why risk managers who seek to understand the psychological aspects of risk taking will need to know how to synthesize different approaches. Such a synthesis involves bringing together strands from different psychological frameworks, from personality traits, and from the roles people play within organizations. Therefore, risk managers should understand and be familiar with several theoretical frameworks. This means having a working knowledge familiarity of the nuances associated with emotion, cognition, judgmental biases, and other personality traits. In this regard, the chapter provides a "toolkit" for analyzing how personality traits and risk-taking styles impact choice.

For those interested in more detail, Appendix C describes a model for synthesizing SP/A theory and prospect theory, the frameworks developed in Chapters 2 and 3. Because these theories are sometimes in conflict when it comes to predictions, risk managers who use them will benefit from having a nuanced understanding of how to apply these theories.

RISK MANAGEMENT STYLES

David Ingram and Elijah Bush describe a personality-based risk management approach that has been applied to the insurance industry.[1] This approach is built on a framework known as "plural rationality theory" and features decision-makers being categorized by four specific risk management styles. In the remainder of the book, I use the phrase "PRM styles" where PRM stands for "plural risk management" or when the context is clear simply "risk styles."

Ingram and Bush suggest that an organization will tend to gravitate toward one of these risk styles at any particular time, even though all four styles might be represented within the organization by its various members. They also suggest that members of organizations should be aware of becoming locked into a style that becomes inappropriate when circumstances change. The first style is known as "conservator." The major focus of conservators is avoiding loss. Viewed from the perspective of prospect theory, conservators have high coefficients of loss aversion, meaning that they experience losses much more acutely than gains of comparable magnitude. Viewed from the perspective of SP/A theory, conservators set their aspiration levels at the point of zero loss and attach high weight to the probability of achieving an outcome in the domain of gains. They also have fear as a dominant emotion. As a result, conservators exhibit loss controlling behavior, focusing attention on identifying exposure to events they would frame as losses, and seek ways to avoid experiencing these losses wherever possible. Viewed from the perspective of biases, conservators are vulnerable to the hot hand fallacy, particularly in respect to successive and growing unfavorable outcomes. As a result, conservators favor protection such as risk limits to protect against unfavorable outcomes. The conservator style is particularly appropriate for the managing of left-tail risks, which are acute and severe.

The second style is known as "maximizer." Maximizers are focused on accepting risk to achieve gains, provided they judge that the rewards compensate for the risks. Financial firms adopting this style are focused on quantifying the magnitudes of risk premiums, while operating companies tend to focus on positive net present value projects having high discount rates. Viewed from the perspective of prospect theory, maximizers have low coefficients of loss aversion. Viewed from the perspective of SP/A theory, maximizers have hope as their dominant emotion, set high aspiration levels, and attach importance to achieving aspiration. Viewed from the perspective of biases, Ingram and Bush's portrayal of maximizers also suggests that they are vulnerable to gambler's fallacy. As a result, maximizers are inclined to have a mean-reverting view of circumstances, with unfavorable events being temporary. To this extent, they are inclined to bet unduly on reversals. Maximizers who are vulnerable to behavioral biases can expose themselves unduly to extreme negative tail risk.

The third style is known as "managers." Managers carefully balance risks and rewards, basing their decisions on cost/ benefit analysis and risk/reward analysis. Organizations dominated by this style are prone to practice enterprise risk management (ERM), typically employing experts to help them maintain a dual focus. First, they seek to identify the risks that offer the best rewards. Second, they seek manage these risks to keep their organization safe. In a population composed of both conservators and maximizers, managers seek to balance the concerns of both groups, plotting a very careful course between them. This compromise view involves adopting maximizers' mean-reverting view for normal, moderate risks, but favoring risk limits favored by conservators to protect against tail events. Viewed from the perspective of SP/A theory, managers are cautiously hopeful.

The fourth style is known as "pragmatists." Unlike the first three styles, in which decision-makers are comfortable making probability assessments, pragmatists are less confident about making probability judgments and more inclined to adopt an uncertainty perspective rather than a risk perspective. Psychologically they use decision weights, a concept formally explained in Appendix B, instead of probability weights, with overweighting in the tails. As a result, pragmatists seek strategies in which they can stay limber and flexible, adjusting exposure as their environment changes. Moreover, they seek to avoid concentrated exposures, instead choosing a variety of different positions that they intuitively judge to be relatively independent. In this respect, they seek diversification, yet lack confidence in the kinds of quantitative models that generate precise recommendations.

Jeff Bezos: Entrepreneur

Risk managers need to understand the behavioral tendencies of entrepreneurs, for entrepreneurs are most often the decision-makers taking risks. Jeff Bezos, the founder of Amazon.com, is one of the greatest entrepreneurs of our age. He is also a realist, and when speaking of Amazon's success, acknowledges being lucky, given the low odds of a given start-up turning out to be a success. With a touch of humor, he describes his success at Amazon as consisting of half good timing, half luck, with the remainder being brains. It is safe to conclude that Bezos's PRM style is not conservator, but which of the other three categories best captures his style? We need to know a bit more in order to provide a reasoned response.

Bezos is correct in his realism. Survival rates of private firms are only around 34% over the first ten years of the firm's life. In fact, the average return to all private equity is actually similar to that of the public market equity index. However, the risk is higher. Therefore, most entrepreneurs appear to make suboptimal financial choices. Entrepreneurs accept lower median lifetime earnings than similarly skilled wage earners, and earn low risk-adjusted returns. In addition, they hold poorly diversified portfolios, concentrating their wealth in their own private businesses. As a prototypical entrepreneur whose risk profile is highly concentrated, it is safe to rule out that Bezos has a "manager" style.

Bezos makes an important connection between optimism and risk taking. He tells us that most people have the misconception that entrepreneurs are risk loving. Instead, he suggests that successful entrepreneurs hate risk, and as a result focus on identifying and eliminating risks. By doing so, they continuously modify their strategies, until they reach a point where they can be genuinely optimistic. If we had to choose between the two remaining PRM styles, maximizer and pragmatist, strategy modification would lead us to lean toward classifying Bezos as a pragmatist.

Founding Amazon was a big move. Expanding its business model from online bookseller to general online merchant was a big move. Bezos's September 2013 purchase of the renowned *Washington Post* was a big move. As you read the risk management applications that come later in the book, you will see that many of the key decision-makers are willing to take big risks. We will have a much better understanding of how they approach risk if we have a framework for characterizing the personalities of these decision-makers, and are able to relate their personality traits to SP/A theory and prospect theory. This chapter provides a conceptual framework for doing so.

Optimism and Entrepreneurial Risk Taking

Duke University academics Manju Puri and David Robinson have studied the question of whether entrepreneurs are more optimistic and less risk averse than nonentrepreneurs. Their research has uncovered findings that are striking. First, entrepreneurs are indeed more optimistic and less risk averse than the rest of the population. Second, these traits are separable in that the correlation between risk tolerance and optimism is low. Third, entrepreneurs tend to have long planning horizons, good health practices, and strong family ties. In respect to planning, entrepreneurs are almost three times more likely to indicate that they never intend to retire. Moreover, people who do not plan to retire work about 3% longer per week.

What exactly is optimism? Psychologists have identified two separate concepts of optimism. One is unrealistic optimism, which was discussed in Chapter 4. The other is called "dispositional optimism," which is about having a positive general outlook in life. In my studies, I find evidence that the two concepts are positively related, but weakly so, when measured by the correlation between dispositional optimism and the favorable-unfavorable probability differential.

A school of thought, known as "positive psychology," focuses attention on how psychological mind-sets relate to performance.[2] In this regard, we know from research that optimism is important in a wide range of settings. For example, optimistic cancer patients face lower mortality risk. Optimists experience faster recovery after coronary artery bypass surgery than pessimists do. They adjust more smoothly to major life transitions like going to college or failure to achieve a desired pregnancy.

According to the school of positive psychology, dispositional optimism is generally a good thing. Still, one can have too much of a good thing. In this regard, the Puri-Robinson article devotes a section to the relationship between optimism and prudent decision-making. Puri and Robinson test whether mild optimism is more likely to correlate with positive behaviors, but extreme optimism is more likely to correlate with negative behaviors associated with unrealistic optimism. Notably, they find that mild optimists have prudent financial habits, whereas extreme optimists do not. For example, mild optimists pay off their entire credit card balance each month, whereas extreme optimists do not.

In their analysis of entrepreneurs, Puri and Robinson do not actually measure optimism bias directly. Instead, they infer it from self-reported estimates of own life expectancy in the *Survey of Consumer Finances*. According to Puri and Robinson, an optimistic person provides a forecast of his or her life span that is longer than the forecast provided by actuarial tables based on underlying demographics.

Puri and Robinson report that their measure of optimism correlates with beliefs about future economic conditions. In this regard, respondents to the *Survey of Consumer Finances* who report that they think economic conditions will improve over the next five years are statistically much more optimistic according to the life expectancy measure than those who think conditions will stay the same or deteriorate.

DIMENSIONS OF PERSONALITY

Many of the risk management applications in this book discuss the personalities of the people who made the decisions. Readers will have an opportunity to decide for themselves the extent to which personality differences played a role in the decisions that got made and the outcomes that resulted.

Personality has many dimensions, and in this section I have selected a few from the academic psychology literature that are relevant for entrepreneurial risk taking. The list features dispositional optimism, desirability of control, social anxiousness, self-monitoring behavior, life satisfaction, and affect.[3]

By applying psychological surveys, psychologists measure the degree to which people have rosy outlooks on life, need to be in control, are anxious in social settings, are sensitive to their own feelings and the feelings of others, are satisfied with their overall lives, and are happy. Below you will find brief descriptions of each concept and an illustration of the type of survey questions used to measure traits.

Dispositional optimism: Puri and Robinson tell us that entrepreneurs have a rosier look on life than nonentrepreneurs. The survey question I like to use to measure optimism consists of eight questions, the responses of which fall on a five-point scale where 1 means "strongly disagree" and 5 means "strongly agree." Representative questions are "I'm always optimistic about my future," and "I hardly ever expect things to go my way."

Desire for Control: In Chapter 4, I introduced the concept "illusion of control," in which people believe they have more control than they do. Illusion of control is related to, but distinct from, how important it is to be in control, meaning the desire for control.

The entrepreneurs in the Puri-Robinson study own some or all of at least one privately owned business and are full time self-employed. In my research, I have studied whether people who classify themselves as entrepreneurs feel a need to exert more control over their working environment than nonentrepreneurs. Put somewhat differently, the question is whether entrepreneurs possess a strong need for control that leads them to choose a career in which they seek to meet that need. My main research finding is that desire for control is much stronger for entrepreneurs than nonentrepreneurs, with the difference being stronger than with any other trait under discussion.

The survey instrument to measure desire for control consists of 20 questions. Two representative questions are "I prefer a job where I have a lot of control over what I do and when I do it," and "I would prefer to be a leader than a follower." The range of possible responses varies from 1 to 7, where 1 means "The statement does not apply to me at all," and 7 means "The statement always applies to me." For 15 of the questions, 7 is associated with the strongest desire for control, while for 5 of the questions, 1 is associated with the strongest desire for control.

Social Anxiousness and Self-Monitoring: These psychological attributes relate to the finding that entrepreneurs marry at a higher rate than nonentrepreneurs and have more children. This finding suggests that entrepreneurs like people. In this regard, two psychological instruments relate to interpersonal relationships. The first involves social anxiousness, the degree to which people are uncomfortable in social situations. The second involves self-monitoring.

The survey instrument used to study social anxiousness features 15 questions. Two of the questions are "I often feel nervous even in casual get-togethers," and "I get nervous when I speak to someone in a position of authority." Responses are on a 5-point scale, where 1 means "Not at all characteristic," and 5 means "Extremely characteristic." A lower score signals less social anxiety, and therefore I prefer to use a negative transformation of the variable so that it measures "social comfort."

Self-monitoring involves being sensitive to social cues, and being able to adapt to those cues. The self-monitoring survey features questions such as the following: "I am often able to read people's true emotions correctly through their eyes." "In social situations, I have the ability to alter my behavior if I feel something else is called for." The range of possible responses comprises a 6-point scale from "Always false" to "Always true."

Affect and Well-Being: Are entrepreneurs happier than nonentrepreneurs? What makes this question especially interesting is that entrepreneurs work more than nonentrepreneurs and earn lower risk-adjusted returns on their investments. To investigate happiness and life satisfaction, I use two survey instruments.

The affect survey asks respondents to indicate how frequently they experience a variety of emotional states such as "interested," "distressed," and "excited." Responses are on a 5-point scale, in which 1 means "very slightly or not at all," and 5 means "extremely." Some states connote negative affect and some connote positive affect. A score of zero connotes neutral overall affect.

The life satisfaction survey asks respondents 25 true/false questions such as "I always seem to have something pleasant to look forward to," and "Often I get irritated at little annoyances." Of the 25 questions, 11 relate to feelings of positive life satisfaction and 14 to negative feelings.

Profiles of Silicon Valley entrepreneurs: Silicon Valley is the world's leading location for venture capital. The size of Silicon Valley venture capital investment is about four times larger than the second leading area (New England), and is about ten times larger than either China or Germany.

In my own research, I have had opportunities to test the degree to which Puri and Robinson's findings apply to Silicon Valley entrepreneurs. My research suggests that these entrepreneurs are quite optimistic and in addition have a much stronger desire for control than nonentrepreneurs. Silicon Valley entrepreneurs have higher levels of affect and well-being than nonentrepreneurs. In addition, their reported levels of social comfort and social monitoring are higher than for nonentrepreneurs. Collectively, these findings are consistent with entrepreneurs having a higher marriage rate and larger families than non-entrepreneurs.[4]

PERSONALITY AND SP/A THEORY'S THREE KEY EMOTIONS

Viewed from a PRM style perspective, there is good reason to believe that entrepreneurs are more likely to be managers or maximizers than they are conservators or pragmatists. Viewed from a personality trait perspective, there is reason to believe that entrepreneurs are also likely to rank more highly on optimism and the desire for control than others. Next, we turn to the question of how these features correspond to the factors emphasized by SP/A theory and prospect theory: fear, hope, aspiration, loss aversion, and the 4x4 risk behavior pattern. This section focuses on SP/A theory.

Remember that SP/A is an acronym for security, potential, and aspiration. Security meets the need to alleviate fear, potential meets the need for hope, and reaching aspiration meets the need to achieve a goal. In Chapter 2, I pointed out that fear induces people to act as if they are pessimistic and that hope induces people to act as if they are optimistic. As a general matter, optimism is negatively correlated with fear and positively correlated with hope. For the group that included Beth and Larry, the correlation between fear and optimism is -0.46—the negative sign is in line with the prediction—and the correlation between hope and optimism is 0.6. In regard to aspiration, the correlation between optimism and "pain experienced from missing a goal" was -0.4. That is, optimists are less susceptible to feeling deep disappointment when they fail to meet their goals.

Notably, other than optimism and desire for control, none of the other personality traits is strongly related to the SP/A emotions. Therefore, although the other personality traits are part of the pattern that differentiates entrepreneurs from nonentrepreneurs, when it comes to risk taking, only optimism and desire for control are germane.

Beth and Larry's group included a mix of CEOs, entrepreneurial risk managers, nonentrepreneurial risk managers, and other business professionals. Virtually all CEOs identify themselves as entrepreneurs.

Levels of optimism in Beth and Larry's group were similar across subgroups, except for nonentrepreneurial risk managers: they were the least optimistic. Nonentrepreneurial risk managers were also the most prone to report pain associated with missing a goal. In contrast, entrepreneurial risk managers lie at the other end of the spectrum, a finding in line with the earlier discussion about entrepreneurs. Interestingly, both subgroups of risk managers were highest in affect and well-being. One striking finding was that the CEOs and the nonentrepreneurial risk managers were highest in desire for control. This feature can provide the backdrop for a battle of wills in the face of differing opinions.

LOSS AVERSION, SP/A, AND RISK TAKING

In the PRM style classification, high loss aversion is what sets conservators apart from others. Consider next the degree to which the coefficient of loss aversion is related to the kinds of risk choices that people make, at least in respect to the way they answer experimental questions. This section discusses this issue, as well as the impact of the three key emotions.

Think back to Question 3 from Chapter 3 in which people were asked to choose between a sure $2,400 gain and a 25% chance to gain $10,000 ($0 otherwise). In the group that included Beth and Larry, 81% chose the sure outcome, which means that 19% went for the risk. Now 19% is not small; it's one in five. Moreover, in my overall sample, 35% go for the risk. That is one in three, which means that we need to be careful in cavalierly proclaiming that people make risk-averse choices in the domain of gains when not facing lottery-like probabilities.

What distinguishes those who go for the risk and those who take the sure $2,400? My data suggest that the coefficient of loss aversion, whose value was inferred from the answer to Question 2 in Chapter 3, is a key factor.

Recall that on average, the mean coefficient of loss aversion is 5.2, and its median counterpart is 2.3. The coefficient of loss aversion for those accepting the sure $2,400 is 5.5, whereas for those accepting the risk, it is 3.8. Intuitively, this feels sensible. People who really dislike losses are prone to be more conservative in their choices than those who do a better job of stomaching losses. I should mention that, although in theory the coefficient of loss aversion plays no role at all in choices among risks that involve only gains, it nevertheless has predictive power in practice.[5]

What about the other side of the coin, where the risks involve only losses? Recall that Question 3 in Chapter 3 discussed a choice between accepting a sure $7,500 loss and taking a risk with a 25% chance to lose nothing, but a 75% chance to lose $10,000. Here those accepting a sure loss have a distinctly higher coefficient of loss aversion than those taking the risk.[6] These findings suggest a general pattern, namely that those who are less loss averse are more prone to take risk than those who are more loss averse.[7]

Loss aversion is a strong differentiator when it comes to explaining exceptions to the general risk patterns that characterize prospect theory. Parenthetically I would also mention that the SP/A emotions also appear to differentiate those choosing the sure loss from those choosing risk. Those choosing to accept the sure loss appear to be distinctly higher in fear and lower in hope. In my data, this pattern is common across different groups.

Question 7 in Chapter 3 focuses on situations involving gains only, where the tendency is for people to make risk-averse choices when the probability of receiving a positive gain is moderate, but become risk seeking when that probability is small. In my data, about 75% of undergraduate finance majors behave this way, while for business professionals the corresponding percentage is 47%, a bit under half.

As it happens, loss aversion plays a role in differentiating those who display the prototypical pattern when answering Question 7 from those who not.

In respect to undergraduate finance majors, mean loss aversion for those who conform to the prototypical pattern is distinctly lower than for all others. The same statement applies to business professionals.[8]

My data suggest that SP/A variables described in Chapter 2 are also germane to how people make the choices under discussion. In respect to undergraduate finance majors, mean levels for cautious hope and for establishing target outcomes are higher for those who conform to the prototypical pattern in Question 7 than for others. To this point, those who conform also feel the pain of missing a goal much less acutely than others. Moreover, those who switch contend that they are much more willing to take risks if meeting a goal is not an issue, either because achieving the goal is guaranteed or because achieving the goal is impossible. For business professionals, all effects are similar, with the exception of the cautious hope effect, which reverses.[9]

Similar remarks about loss aversion and SP/A characteristics apply to quasi-hedonic editing. When comparing those undergraduate finance majors who conform to the prototypical quasi-hedonic pattern, loss aversion is lower for those who switch from accepting a sure gain to taking a risk (after a prior gain) and higher for those who switch from taking a risk in the domain of losses to accepting a sure loss (after a prior loss).[10]

Survey Questions to Probe for Style

The Appendices in this book provide models for analyzing how emotions and cognitive factors impact decisions about risk. These models can be quite complex. However, it is possible to elicit information about these factors using survey questions. You will already have encountered some of the questions in the preceding chapters. This section presents some additional questions to help identify different people's risk management styles.

In respect to prospect theory, Question 2 in Chapter 3, which elicits information about loss aversion, can be easily generalized to probe how people view risks that feature only gains, and risks that feature only losses. For gains, one might ask a person to consider a fifty-fifty chance of winning either $1,000 or $0. The question to be posed then asks what would be the smallest dollar amount that the person would consider in lieu of the risk. This amount is called the certainty equivalent. The larger the certainty equivalent, the more averse to risk is the person. A similar question can be asked to elicit certainty equivalents for the same amounts, but with those amounts interpreted as losses.

In respect to SP/A theory, Chapter 2 presented a set of five questions to elicit information about the three key emotions. These five questions are part of a longer list of 17 survey questions to elicit information about the emotional profile associated with the SP/A framework.

Instructions for taking the survey are as follows: below you will find a series of statements. Please read each statement carefully and on a scale of 1 to 7, respond by expressing the extent to which you believe the statement applies to you. Here a "1" denotes "the statement does not apply to me at all," and a "7" denotes "the statement always applies to me."[11]

The first five questions mentioned above are followed by a group of six questions, and then another group of six questions. This next group of questions probes for the signature of the three key SP/A emotions on people's thought processes when facing risk.

6. When I am in a situation where the outcome is uncertain, my major concern is avoiding as unfavorable an outcome as possible.
7. When I am in a situation where the outcome is uncertain, my major concern is to achieve as favorable an outcome as possible.
8. I am comfortable taking a risk where there is a small but reasonable chance of an extremely favorable outcome as long as the downside is not too unfavorable.
9. I am comfortable taking a risk where there is a small but reasonable chance of an extremely favorable outcome even if the downside is quite unfavorable.
10. I prefer taking small risks to large risks because the downside looms much larger for me than the upside.
11. I prefer taking large risks to small risks because the upside looms much larger for me than the downside.

Each of the above questions relates to the impact on risky choice associated with the strength of the emotion of fear relative to the emotion of hope. For Beth and Larry, it turns out that the question on which they most differed was number 10. Larry's response was a strong 6, and Beth's response was a weak 2. In this regard, if you recall the discussion from Chapter 2, Beth gave her top rank to the SS, while Larry gave his top rank to PK. In the group that included Beth and Larry, Question 10 similarly differentiated those whose ranking of SS and PK was the same as Beth's from those whose ranking was the same as Larry's.[12]

The next group of questions pertains to the manner in which aspiration is manifest within a person's thought process about risk. The questions are as follows:

12. When I am in a situation where the outcome is uncertain, my major concern is to maximize the odds of my achieving an outcome that I would characterize as success.
13. When I am in a situation where the outcome is uncertain, I would be willing to take a little more risk on the downside if doing so would increase the chances of achieving my goal.

14. When I am in a situation where the outcome is uncertain, I would be willing to lower the odds of achieving an extremely favorable outcome, if doing so would increase the chances of achieving my goal.
15. When I am in a situation where the outcome is uncertain, I would be willing to increase the odds of achieving an extremely unfavorable outcome, if doing so would increase the chances of achieving my goal.
16. When I am in a situation that can only turn out well, I am willing to take more risk than usual.
17. When I am in a situation that can only turn out badly, I am willing to take more risk than usual.

For the group that included Beth and Larry, Questions 12 and 15 were key discriminators between those whose top choice was SS and those whose top choice was PK. The average response to Question 12 for those who gave their top ranking to SS was 5.8, while the average response for those who gave their top ranking to PK was 5.2.

As for Question 15, the mean response for those who ranked SS at the top was 3.5, while for those who ranked PK at the top was 4.2. Beth and Larry also differed significantly in their responses to Question 15, which asks about willingness to accept downside exposure in order to achieve a target. Beth's response was a weak 2, while Larry's response was a strong 6.

Closing Thoughts

This chapter describes survey instruments to identify personality traits and relate these to the emotional and cognitive features that underlie the psychology of risk. The point of the chapter is to say that personality is important, and that it exerts its influence through the factors that make up SP/A theory, prospect theory, susceptibility to cognitive biases. Readers interested in an integrative modeling approach to some of the deep structural issues pertaining to the psychology of choice will find additional information in Appendix C.

This is the point at which we move from focusing on core psychology to focusing on real-world risk management applications. The rest of the book applies psychology to the study of big issues, occasionally with big personalities. There are still new psychological concepts to come, but these enter on an as-needed basis, in order to help us better understand specific risk management issues. For the most part, we now say goodbye to Beth and Larry, whose responses to experimental questions provide important insights into how fear, hope, aspiration, loss aversion, framing, and reliance on heuristics impact their judgments and decisions about risk. But do not be surprised if Beth and Larry occasionally come to mind as those insights play out in real-world events discussed in later chapters.

Part II

CHAPTER 6

PROCESS, PITFALLS, AND CULTURE

RISK MANAGERS NEED TO UNDERSTAND MORE THAN THE PSYCHOLOGY impacting individual behavior. They also need to understand how these issues play out in organizations, and the important role of organizational culture.

Organization decision-making takes place through processes. Organizations have processes for goal setting, strategic planning, compensation, communication, and operations. All of these processes are vulnerable to being infected by psychological features associated with SP/A theory, prospect theory, problematic personality traits, and judgmental biases.

To analyze the impact of psychological features impact on organizations, I favor the use of a process-pitfall framework that builds on a concept known as "open-book management" (OBM). For over 20 years, OBM has been a widespread movement that has been chronicled in the media for its impact on many industries.[1] The "book" in open-book management refers to the financial statements associated with managerial accounting. The "open" refers to building organizational processes in such a way that financial information is shared and used efficiently across the organization.

The major processes central to OBM are standards, planning, incentives, information sharing, and operations. The main pitfalls in the process-pitfall framework are the concepts discussed in the earlier chapters, along with a few more that are introduced in later chapters. For the most part, risks materialize through actions taken during operations; however, operational risk often has its roots in judgments and decisions associated with the other processes.

The process-pitfall framework applies to the broad range of judgments and decisions made within organizations, including the way they conduct risk management. This chapter presents the general ideas underlying the process-pitfall approach, which are then applied to a specific example involving the Ebola outbreak in 2014. In order to focus attention on the role of risk management, the discussion about general processes and pitfalls is followed by the presentation of frameworks for managing organizational risk.

The concept of culture runs through the entire discussion in this chapter. OBM provides a framework for analyzing the values that an organization espouses, the manner in which it communicates its values internally and externally, the degree to which members of an organization express those values, and the impact of those values on behavior in respect to organizational judgments and decisions. Risk management culture is an important dimension of organization culture, and deals with an organization's values in respect to taking risk.

PROCESS AND CULTURE

OBM emphasizes four specific processes in addition to those associated with production operations. This section discusses these processes, along with the role these processes play in organizational culture. OBM was developed in the private sector. However, as will become clear later in the chapter, these processes apply to all kinds of organizations besides profit-making firms, such as regulatory bodies and government agencies.

Standards are quantitative goals that define aspirational levels. Standards provide the metrics and benchmarks against which performance is judged. Some standards relate to risk, as we shall see in many of the applications discussed in this book. OBM emphasizes training in financial literacy, so that the workforce understands what standards measure and how they relate to performance. In for-profit organizations, standards are related to profitability, as reflected in financial statements. However, not-for-profit organizations often have multiple objectives that are loosely defined, and not reflected within financial statements. In this regard, the important point for not-for-profits is to develop measurable standards and have ways to track performance relative to standards, as opposed to focusing on financial statements per se.

Planning is an activity that combines the setting of standards, the selection of a strategy, and the forecasting of outcomes. OBM emphasizes that planning should involve the entire organization in order that everyone participates in developing standards to which they can commit and be evaluated. Most importantly, OBM-style planning asks members of an organization to think carefully about how they will operationalize the organization's strategy in order to carry out the plan to which they will agree.

Incentives comprise a mix of financial compensation and nonfinancial rewards such as power, prestige, and recognition. Base salaries, bonus plans, and stock and option plans are key ingredients of incentive packages. OBM-style incentives link all rewards to performance relative to the standards established during the planning phase. In addition, profitability and value are critical components of compensation. For this reason, compensation parameters are established as part of planning.

Information sharing takes place at all times within the organization, but especially during manufacturing operations when it produces the goods and/or services that it delivers to its customers. OBM-style information sharing is regular and routine, seeking to share as much relevant information about ongoing performance relative to the standards embedded within the plan. Information sharing, when it is effective, keeps salient ongoing performance relative to standards as well as indications of where accountability lies within the organization, both for superior performance and inferior performance. Information sharing based around standards also serves to reduce delays in identifying problems and seeking solutions. Information sharing around incentives makes clear, on a regular and consistent basis, what is valued within the organization.

OBM processes are interlinked and provide the infrastructure through which an organization expresses its culture. An organization with a strong culture establishes standards to reflect its values and develops its plans around its standards. Standards need to be associated with reasonable goals and operationalized through metrics. Through its planning, such an organization incorporates incentives to motivate its workforce by rewarding them appropriately for performance judged to meet or exceed its standards and plans. By investing in training, an organization helps its personnel understand how their behavior ultimately impacts compensation. Through the way it engages in information sharing, an organization reminds and reinforces its workforce about its values, its standards, and its performance relative to its values, standards, and plans.

Companies that are run along open-book lines are implicitly structured to mitigate groupthink. They especially do so during their planning process by encouraging devil's advocacy to challenge planning assumptions.[2] This mind-set starts at the top of the organization, as senior executives actively support debate within the company, and group leaders refrain from expressing their opinions or ideas until most group members have had an opportunity to express opinions.

Groups are especially vulnerable to groupthink when they rely on consensus and do not have preset rules and processes for decision-making. Therefore, mitigating groupthink in the presence of disagreement requires that a group establish and follow rules for making collective choices.

Open-book companies also recognize that there is a natural tendency for group members to refrain from sharing information and to limit the number of alternatives they consider. This is especially the case in large groups. Therefore, when groups are large, open-book companies tend to use breakout sessions with subgroups to engage in brainstorming before the whole group convenes to discuss a complex issue.

Compensation structures are immensely important to the practice of risk management. Practitioners of OBM emphasize the importance of aligning incentives across the organization as closely as is feasible. In practice, there are circumstances in which this is possible, but not always. As discussed below, line managers and risk managers often need to be compensated differently in order for both to be effective at their jobs. This state of affairs can produce important tensions, as we shall see in some of the applications that arise in later chapters.

By their nature, open-book organizations practice "enterprise risk management." Those that do it well will be on their guard to detect and address within themselves the psychological pitfalls described in earlier chapters. The most important pitfalls include excessive optimism, overconfidence, confirmation bias, aversion to a sure loss, and regret aversion.

Excessive optimism involves overweighting the probabilities of favorable outcomes relative to unfavorable outcomes. Overconfidence typically leads to the underweighting of probabilities of rare events. Confirmation bias leads to errors in conditioning probabilities on available information. Aversion to a sure loss involves risk-seeking behavior in an attempt to avert a sure loss. Regret aversion leads people to be unduly timid, out of a concern that if the decision turns out badly, they will experience strong negative emotions due to second-guessing of the decision. As discussed later, regret aversion can have an organizational manifestation, as unfavorable outcomes from decisions can lead key decision-makers not just to feel badly but also to be passed over for promotion or fired. This issue is discussed later in the chapter and also in Appendix E.

The fact that standards reflect aspirations suggests that the psychological issues emphasized by SP/A theory can be germane. In this regard, management scholars James March and Zur Shapira developed an organizational framework with two aspirational focal points, a lower one they label "survival" and a higher one they label "aspiration."[3] Not to be confusing about terminology, but just to be clear, it can be said that, viewed through the lens of SP/A theory, both lower and higher focal points are actually aspiration points, only one is very low.

The "dual focal point" framework describes how risk-taking behavior varies according to which focal point is operative. Based on the framework, when an organization's resources place it exactly at its operative focal point, the organization will seek to take as little risk as possible. However, risk taking will increase with the absolute distance between the firm's resources and its operative focal point. In the case when resources lie above the operative focal point, the firm increases risk taking gradually in reaction to increases in its resources; but risk taking is distinctly higher whenever resources lie below aspiration and the aspirational focal point is operative.

Between survival and aspiration lies a gray zone, in which organizations will struggle about which focal point will be operative. A focus on "survival" will lead to a conservative risk exposure, whereas a focus on "aspiration" will lead to an aggressive risk exposure.

EBOLA OUTBREAK OF 2014

To illustrate the process-pitfall framework, consider how the World Health Organization (the WHO) handled the Ebola outbreak of 2014. Notably, because the WHO (read as "the W H O") is a United Nations body, not a for-profit firm, this example will serve to emphasize the generality of the process-pitfall approach.

Ebola is an untreatable, contagious, and often fatal disease. The first incident of the 2014 outbreak actually took place in December 2013, when a one-year-old boy from Meliandou, Guinea, contracted the disease and died. Shortly thereafter, members of his family also died, along with a nurse, doctor, and other health workers who treated them. Within several months, the outbreak spread to three contiguous African countries: Liberia, Sierra Leone, and Guinea. The health-care system in West Africa is extremely limited. It was not until mid-March 2014 that hospitals and public health services alerted Guinea's Ministry of Health that an Ebola outbreak was underway.[4]

This section uses the tools developed above to analyze how the WHO managed the risks associated with the outbreak. The WHO is headquartered in Geneva, with its Regional Office for Africa located in Brazzaville, Congo. Organizationally, its structure was decentralized, with the regional offices having considerable decision power.

That March, the WHO began to monitor the situation, and on March 30 reported that there were 112 suspected and confirmed Ebola cases in Guinea, including 70 deaths. The WHO also reported that Liberia had two confirmed cases, and Sierra Leone two suspected deaths. It classified the outbreak as being Level 2 on a 3-point scale.

Médecins sans Frontières (MSF), also known as Doctors without Borders, is a highly respected international organization that provides medical services to countries in the developing world. Unlike the WHO, which is a large bureaucratic organization with a broad mission for developing health policy and systems around the world, MSF has a much more narrowly focused mission, providing beds and medical personnel to treat patients in disadvantaged areas.

In March, as part of an emergency response to help stop the outbreak, MSF sent 60 fieldworkers to Guinea, to join a team of 24 health-care professionals already there. At the time, MSF warned that the spread of this epidemic was "unprecedented." It contrasted the situation at that time with past outbreaks, which were "contained and involved more remote locations," whereas the geography of the current outbreak was "worrisome" because transmission rates would be much higher.

In the latter part of March, the MSF's judgment of the outbreak sharply contrasted with that of officials at the WHO in Geneva. The WHO's view was that the outbreak was still relatively small, and it noted that past outbreaks had never numbered more than a few hundred. In this regard, WHO officials were certainly familiar with past outbreaks of Ebola. At the end of March, when the MSF issued a press release with dire warnings about a large-scale outbreak, the WHO tweeted that there was no need for the MSF to exaggerate.

There is a serious question of whether there was managerial confusion at the WHO, a decentralized organization that was already challenged by budget cuts and competing demands to put out other fires.[5] The WHO's head, Margaret Chan, viewed the role of the Geneva headquarters as serving the needs of the regions, each of which has its own special needs and interests.[6]

Before becoming head of WHO, Chan had been a public health administrator in Hong Kong when in 2003 severe acute respiratory syndrome (SARS) broke out in China. In that episode, Chan acted boldly in attempting to limit the spread of the disease, but was heavily criticized for her decisions.

The WHO's governance and culture were an important part of the Ebola narrative. Under Chan's leadership, the WHO had delegated leadership of the early response to its regional representatives on the ground in West Africa. However, the WHO had reduced that region's budget for epidemic preparedness and response by 50% over the previous five years. Therefore, it was natural for Geneva to request assistance from the US Centers for Disease Control and Prevention (CDC), which it did in March. However, CDC personnel sent out to help were held up by the regional office in Brazzaville. An article that appeared in the *New York Times* suggested that regional office officials might have been keen to show they were capable of addressing the outbreak on their own.[7]

An important part of the Ebola narrative is that the epidemic occurred in three adjacent countries with porous borders. This meant that, although people infected with Ebola migrated with ease between those countries, the health systems of those countries stopped at the borders.

Communication between countries appears to have problematic at this time. The WHO's Guinea office and the country's Ministry of Health endeavored to take blood samples and collect case histories. They recorded suspected cases, but the information they generated never reached the government team that was doing surveillance in Sierra Leone. The epidemiologist on the team who helped draft the report gave a presentation to officials from both Guinea's Ministry of Health and the WHO. Guinea's director of disease control admitted to receiving the report, but contends he did not read it. He pointed out that he relied on the WHO for sharing information among the three countries, as there were language differences that acted as barriers.[8] Officials in Sierra Leone, both at the WHO and at the country's center for disease prevention and control, claim they never received the report from Guinea.

At the end of June, MSF's director of operations stated that the epidemic had gotten out of control, with a tangible risk of spreading to other areas, requiring a major deployment of resources. However, it was not until August that a WHO emergency committee determined that the Ebola outbreak was not only an extraordinary event but a public health risk to other countries. It declared the outbreak to be a Public Health Emergency of International Concern, and reallocated its resources to focus much more intently on addressing the impact. The emergency coordinator for MSF responded to the WHO's declaration by saying that the effort came too late: with an Ebola outbreak, being a step ahead is critical, and the effort was now two steps behind.

In late July, the WHO developed a $103 million response plan through December in conjunction with the governments of Guinea, Liberia, and Sierra Leone. However, at the same time, the WHO reported a funding gap of $71 million.

Between March and August 2014, the number of Ebola cases mushroomed from a few hundred into the thousands. At the end of August 2014, the WHO reported that counting all confirmed, probable, and suspected cases in Guinea, Liberia, and Sierra Leone, there were 3,052 cases, including 1,546 deaths, since the epidemic had begun. They also noted that 120 health-care workers had died during the outbreak. In October, more than 5,000 people had died from the disease, and the WHO was projecting that by the end of 2014, there would be 5,000 to 10,000 Ebola cases per week in Guinea, Liberia, and Sierra Leone.

In October 2014, the WHO also issued an internal self-study report, admitting to having responded much too slowly to the outbreak, effectively acknowledging the missed opportunities. The report noted that the agency's experts failed to grasp that traditional infectious disease containment methods would not be effective in a region with porous borders and poorly functioning health-care systems. The *Associated Press* obtained a copy of the report and published a short excerpt that read, "Nearly everyone involved in the outbreak response failed to see some fairly plain writing on the wall.... A perfect storm was brewing, ready to burst open in full force."[9]

A year after the MSF raised the alarm, the public health effort to reduce the incidence of Ebola gained traction, and the rate of new cases dropped dramatically. In July 2015, the total number of cases stood at around 28,000, with about 11,300 deaths. During the period May through July 2015, the number of new cases per week in Guinea and Sierra Leone varied between 10 and 20, and in Liberia it was fewer than 5.[10]

Asking the Right Questions about Pitfalls and Processes

Analyzing situations is critical to the process-pitfall process and that typically begins with a series of questions. Below are some examples of questions that relate to the Ebola outbreak and the WHO's reaction in March 2014, along with some brief sample answers. This situational question-and-answer format can help you think about how to apply the framework to analyze decisions involving the management of risk.

Did the WHO set clear numerical standards for dealing with the outbreak? Was the initial outbreak of Ebola on the radar of the WHO Geneva-based headquarters, and how concretely did the WHO plan for an epidemic of the size and scope of the outbreak? Given the broad-based mission of the WHO, did the providers of its funds incentivize activities associated with epidemic preparedness or, instead, activities for which outcomes are more salient? Did the decision-makers responsible for cutting budgets understand the associated risks that were in consequence created? How effectively did WHO personnel share information with each other?

The Ebola chronology described above provides some partial answers to these questions. In respect to standards, recall that in March 2014 when MSF was marshaling resources to send to West Africa, the WHO stated that although the Ebola outbreak was serious, as a risk it was "relatively small, still." In respect to planning, the WHO's October 2014 internal report suggests that no clear plan for dealing with a potential epidemic was developed. In this regard, it was not until August that a WHO emergency committee determined that the Ebola outbreak was not only an "extraordinary event" but a public health risk to other countries. Only then did it declare the outbreak to be a Public Health Emergency of International Concern. In terms of incentives, given an environment of budget cuts and competing demands, it might have been natural for the WHO's personnel to characterize the outbreak as being low risk. In terms of information sharing, the communication between countries was lacking, with a team from the WHO's office in Guinea collecting data and writing a report but never sending it to officials outside of their own territory.

Pitfalls are the other half of the process-pitfall dichotomy. Here are some questions about pitfalls to consider in connection with the Ebola outbreak, and the WHO's reaction in March 2014.

When the WHO classified the outbreak as a Level 2 on a 3-point scale, was it being excessively optimistic? When the bureaucracy at the WHO's regional office delayed a team dispatched from the United States to lend support, was that office exhibiting overconfidence about its own ability? When the WHO dismissed the MSF's characterization of the outbreak as an exaggeration, were they exhibiting confirmation bias? In the light of the criticism Chan received when she aggressively attempted to limit the spread of SARS, was her initial slow response in dealing with the Ebola outbreak a reflection of regret aversion, of "once burned, twice shy?"

The answers to these pitfall questions are judgment calls. Reasonable people might disagree about their answers. However, the process-pitfall framework provides a structure for asking the right questions about the factors driving an organization's decisions about risk. In this regard, it is worth keeping in mind that the WHO is designed primarily to focus on health policy and systems rather than to provide rapid response to complex outbreaks, such as occurred with Ebola in 2014. The skills and processes needed for rapid response are different from those needed to develop policy and systems.

Risk Management Structure and Culture

An OBM-style approach to risk management focuses on an organization's standards for risk, how these standards are embedded within the organization's planning and budgeting, how the organization trains its workforce about risk, how compensation plans and nonfinancial rewards reflect risk, and how information about risk exposure is shared across the organization.

There is a rich academic literature about safety culture. Economist Elizabeth Sheedy and psychologist Barbara Griffin have surveyed this literature and are the first to produce a synthesis approach for characterizing an organization's "risk management profile," which I will refer to as RMP.[11] In the next paragraph, I briefly describe Sheedy and Griffin's approach to RMP and relate it to OBM.

Figure 6.1 depicts RMP's conceptual framework. The left side of the figure refers to the structural drivers of an organization's risk management culture. Some drivers are organizational in nature, such as the kind of training programs it offers, its compensation plan, the traits of its leaders, and its governance structure. Other drivers relate to the traits of individuals within the organization, such as demographic characteristics, knowledge about risk, tolerance for risk, and attitude toward risk management. The right side of

Drivers	Risk Culture	Outcomes
Organizational	Shared views & beliefs	Organizational
Individual	Individuals' perceptions	Individual

Figure 6.1 This figure depicts the conceptual framework underlying RMP. The left side of the figure refers to the structural drivers of an organization's risk management culture. The right side of the figure refers to behavioral outcomes. In the middle of the figure is a column relating to organizational culture, which RMP depicts as a medium through which risk drivers are transformed into outcomes.

the figure refers to behavioral outcomes. Some outcomes are organizational in nature, such as the frequency and severity of unfavorable outcomes. Other outcomes relate to individuals and taking responsibility for problems that have occurred. In the middle of the figure is a column relating to organizational culture, which RMP depicts as a medium through which risk drivers are transformed into outcomes.

In the RMP framework, organizations are analyzed along three dimensions, namely risk management structure (RMS), risk management culture (RMC), and risk management behavior (RMB). Each of these has four subcategories, and so you can think of evaluating a firm's level of RMP on 12 dimensions. The next three paragraphs describe what it means for an organization to be strong on all 12 dimensions.

Members of an organization with strong risk management structures establish *effective* policies, procedures, and systems. Risk management is a skill, and so the organization seeks high-*quality* risk managers. The organization also invests in risk management *training* for its members as it is a skill. The organization's *remuneration* incorporates key performance indicators (KPIs) that include key risk indicators (KRIs) pertaining specifically to risk.

Members of an organization with a strong risk management culture perceive and acknowledge that risk management is a *valued* activity. They are *proactive* about identifying and addressing risk issues within the organization. Within the organization, there is much sharing of ideas about identifying risk and dealing with it, an issue discussed at length by Gerd Gigerenzer in his book *Risk Savvy*.[12] From a human resource perspective, the managers to whom they directly report are good *role models* for risk management behavior. The members of the organization are also on their guard when it comes to the *avoidance* of risk management, by being careful to make risk issues salient and to address policy breaches when they occur.

Members of an organization with strong risk management behaviors attach great importance to *positive* risk management practices, such as being willing to speak up in groups about risk issues and if necessary play the devil's advocate. Likewise, they attach great importance to refraining from *negative* behaviors such as assigning low priority to risk management and bending rules because of the drive to accomplish goals. When it comes to the behavior of other members, they are attentive to behaviors involving the manipulation of controls and the downplaying of the importance of risk management. They also monitor for signs of overconfidence that the organization judges that it is immune to risk.

Active devil's advocacy is an important aspect of RMP and serves to mitigate groupthink. It also induces group members to share information that they might be reluctant to disclose for fear of not appearing to be supportive. Especially germane to risk taking is that devil's advocacy mitigates the phenomenon known as "polarization," whereby group dynamics amplify the individual risk tolerance profiles of the individual members. Polarization occurs because in the course of attempting to support other group members, especially the group leader, a chain reaction generates magnification.

For intellectual tasks that feature correct answers that can be verified after the fact, groups are able to exploit a phenomenon known as "the wisdom of crowds," by seeking input from different group members and averaging that input. However, for judgmental tasks such as how much risk to take on, there is no wisdom of crowd effect, but just the opposite—polarization. That is why active, purposeful devil's advocacy is so important.

Sheedy and Griffin developed their framework as a way of empirically measuring the cultural strength of an organization and have applied their approach to analyzing banks. Their technique is based upon responses to a survey consisting of 67 questions, which is administered to a sample of employees across specific business units and business lines of each bank.[13]

Just as with OBM, applying a risk management process to an organization involves asking specific questions. For instance, in respect to the WHO's handling of the Ebola outbreak, questions using the risk management structure might be the following: Did the WHO have high-quality risk managers at its Regional African office? Were WHO personnel proactive about identifying and addressing risk issues within the organization? Did WHO personnel engage in negative behaviors such as assigning low priority to risk management?

For OBM to work, incentives, training, leadership, and governance are central to creating a risk management structure. In turn, this structure is critical to creating a risk management culture, especially when embedded within incentives and communicated as part of information sharing so that the workforce is quite clear about what the firm values. Finally, pitfalls and information sharing are central to anyone exhibiting risk management behavior.

Risk management decisions take place within the broader environment of the organization. Firms need to set standards that reflect their goals for profits and for risk. Jack Stack, one of the founders of OBM, has said that in training its workforce on how to run the business, his firm has focused on teaching them how to be both profitable and safe in the course of providing customers with good quality.[14]

Often, setting standards for both profit and risk involves trade-offs that need to be balanced. Notably, profit is much more easily quantified and communicated than risk, which creates important challenges for risk management. Different ways of approaching these kinds of issues are taken up in the next section.

KAPLAN-MIKES RISK TYPOLOGY FRAMEWORK

Robert Kaplan from Harvard University gave us the concept of a balanced scorecard. In conjunction with Annette Mikes, the two have now proposed systematic guidelines for how companies can approach risk management.[15] They have drawn their ideas from field research and organized their framework around a typology involving three risk categories, which they respectively call

1. preventable risks;
2. strategy risks; and
3. external risks.

The categorization is important, as Kaplan and Mikes make clear that each risk category calls for a different approach.

Preventable risks: There are all kinds of preventable risks, many of which relate to production operations. Preventable risks are those for which the benefits of prevention exceed the costs of prevention. For example, an electric utility might allow tree branches to grow too high, threatening to damage some of its overhead power lines. Correspondingly, a financial services firm might overeconomize on cyber security, thereby leaving itself vulnerable to being hacked. Incidentally, in the financial sector, preventable risk is often called "operational risk." Any firm that is growing quickly needs to be concerned that in expanding its sales force, it will hire account representatives "who lack the experience to evaluate their customers."[16]

Kaplan and Mikes suggest that addressing preventable risks begins with training employees, not just in detailed procedures but also on the mission statements of the organization for which they work, the value statements that make clear what it means to violate an organization's standards, and the boundaries set by the organization's culture. With these norms providing a foundation, a rules-based control model involving standard operating procedures, internal controls, and internal audit processes to assess compliance then provides the fabric for seeking to prevent risky outcomes that are preventable. In summary, preventable risks are monitored and controlled through rules, values, and standard compliance tools.

Strategy risks: These are entirely different from preventable risks. There are no obvious benefits to bearing preventable risks, except for saving the cost of mitigation. However, bearing strategy risk provides upside potential, the opportunity to generate greater rewards to the organization.

Many of the experimental questions described in the previous chapters provide subjects with the opportunity to accept or reject risks. Those who accept the risk do so for the upside potential that is offered. In the short story from Chapter 2, Larry might view his ranking of PK over RF in this vein.[17]

One of the most important tasks associated with strategy risks is identifying and quantifying what these risks comprise. Accomplishing such a task requires a risk-management system. A risk management system provides a structure for estimating the probabilities that the risks in question might materialize and improving the organization's ability to contain the risks, or respond appropriately, should they materialize.

Kaplan and Mikes discuss three different ways of managing strategy risk. The first involves using independent experts at the project level to question and challenge project leaders. The point of doing so is to introduce devil's advocacy into the analysis in order to combat psychological pitfalls such as groupthink, confirmation bias, excessive optimism, overconfidence, and aversion to a sure loss.

The second way of managing strategy risk involves facilitators. Facilitators are composed of small central risk management teams that interact with different groups within the organization. Facilitators work by collecting information from operating managers, and in doing so increase managers' awareness of risks across the organization. The perspective that facilitators provide enables decision-makers to have a fuller picture of their organization's risk profile.

The third way of managing strategy risk involves the use of embedded experts. As the term "embedded" indicates, this approach involves risk managers working side by side with the line managers, continuously monitoring and influencing the organization's risk profile. As an example of embedded risk managers, Kaplan and Mikes mention JPMorgan Private Bank, which embeds risk managers within the line organization so that they report both to line executives and to a centralized, independent risk-management function. In the story in Chapter 2, Larry is a line manager, and Beth is an embedded expert. Risk managers are charged with assessing how trades proposed by portfolio managers impact the risk of the entire investment portfolio, under both normal circumstances and in times of extreme stress. By virtue of being in face-to-face contact with line managers, risk managers have the opportunity to challenge the assumptions portfolio managers make and encourage them to consider a variety of possible scenarios.

Notably, all three ways of managing strategy risk require processes in which managers openly discuss risks and either seek cost-effective ways to reduce the probabilities of unfavorable events or else mitigate the consequences of these events.

External risks: Kaplan and Mikes tell us that external risks are not preventable. Besides natural disasters with immediate impact, there are geopolitical and environmental changes with long-term impact, and competitive risks with medium-term impact. Instead of focusing on prevention, an organization's management can only focus on identifying external risks with the purpose of mitigating their impact. As with strategy risks, addressing external risks requires processes in which managers openly discuss risks and either seek cost-effective ways to reduce the probabilities of unfavorable events or else mitigate the consequences of these events.

Questions of moral hazard, in which being insured induces people to take on more risk, are irrelevant for external events, as these are nonpreventable. Therefore, organizations can use insurance or hedging to mitigate some risks. Airlines can use futures contracts to manage their cost of fuel. Manufacturers in earthquake-prone areas can make capital investments to reinforce the physical resilience of their critical facilities to major quakes. However, many external risk events require a different analytic approach either because their probability of occurrence is very low or because managers find it difficult to envision them during their normal strategy processes.

Kaplan and Mikes suggest three techniques for addressing external risk: tail-risk tests, scenario planning, and war-gaming. Tail-risk stress testing typically relies on formal models that organizations can use to assess major changes in one or two specific variables. The tail-risk effects in question are taken to be both major and immediate, with the exact timing being unclear.

Scenario planning is a systematic process for defining plausible boundaries for future trajectories. Scenarios typically involve major changes in several variables. This tool is suited for long-range analysis, typically five to ten years out.

War-gaming uses a form of role play to assess an organization's vulnerability to disruption within the next one or two years.[18] Examples of the type of events being studied are disruptive technologies and changes in competitors' strategies. Business continuity plans can be regarded as contingency plans associated with disruptive physical events. In a war game, the organization tasks three or four teams to develop plausible threats that would constitute serious disruptions. These set the stage for discussions about possible responses by the organization.

Kaplan and Mikes provide many examples of strategy risk and external risks to illustrate different facets of their approach. The firm Jet Propulsion Laboratory (JPL), which has been responsible for many space missions, frequently addresses strategy risk through risk review board meetings in which technical experts intellectually confront project engineers.

Hydro One, a Canadian electricity company makes use of facilitators to address strategy risk. Every year, its chief risk officer runs workshops in which employees from all levels and functions identify and rank what they perceive to be the principal risks to their organization. Workshop participants rate the risks, and their judgments are linked to budgeting decisions, in which projects that efficiently reduce risk are viewed favorably. Establishing risk as an explicit criterion for evaluation induces line managers to be forthcoming about the risk profiles in the projects they propose, instead of downplaying them as the natural tendency of most.

At Hydro One, workshop participants rate risks on a scale of 1 to 5, in terms of impact, the likelihood of occurrence, and the strength of existing controls. They then discuss their rankings with each other and develop a consensus view. In addition, they recommend action plans and inject accountability by designating an "owner" for each major risk.

A framework known as the "Simons approach to risk management" also uses a scale of 1 to 5 to focus on three sources of risk, namely growth, culture, and information management.[19] Each source can be thought of as featuring three dimensions. For growth, the dimensions are pressure for performance, rate of expansion, and inexperience of key employees. For culture, the dimensions are rewards for entrepreneurial risk taking, excessive resistance to bad news, and level of internal competition. For information management, the dimensions are transaction complexity and velocity, gaps in diagnostic performance measurement, and degree of decentralized decision-making. A score of 1 means close to no risk exposure and a score of 5 means very high risk exposure. With nine dimensions overall, the maximum risk exposure score from an unweighted sum is 45.

The Simons approach uses a simple diagnostic heuristic. An organizational score that is 20 or below prompts the following question: is the organization is playing it too safe and not taking enough strategy risk? A score between 21 and 34 signals that managers need to exercise caution and be attentive to whether any of the three risks have high scores along two of its three dimensions. A score above 34 signals danger, and managers are urged to develop strategies for addressing risks.

From a risk typology perspective, the WHO effectively deals with preventable risks associated with public health, such as working to make vaccines available to populations in developing countries, and external risks such as the outbreak of Ebola. The issue with external risks is not about prevention, but how to respond to them in order to limit the damage. In respect to the Ebola outbreak, the question to ask is whether the WHO engaged in serious scenario planning and war-gaming for this type of event. This question is about preparedness. Given the budgetary issues the organization faced, and the early response they displayed, there is reason to suspect that they did not.

INCENTIVES AND RISK TAKING

When it comes to risk management, incentives are a big issue. To be sure, the structuring of incentives already receives major emphasis by both OBM and RMS. However, linking risk management to overall value creation by the organization is especially complex in the presence of vulnerability to psychological pitfalls, different personality types, and the need to incentivize executives, line managers, and risk managers differently.

This section introduces some of the basic ideas for analyzing the role of risk in the setting of incentives. Appendix E elaborates on the basic points.

In his book *Risk Taking: A Managerial Perspective*, Zur Shapira describes a conceptual framework to represent how organizations establish incentives for risk taking and to elucidate why some organizations take on inappropriate amounts of strategy risk, either too little or too much.[20] Shapira's framework implicitly provides us with a way of describing what the risk management function accomplishes and the role that risk management plays in the setting of budgets. Budget setting is often where sparks fly in organizations as organizational members compete for resources and project approval.

Shapira's framework features an organization assessing a project proposal and arriving at a figure of merit, such as the estimated value of the project if adopted. Based on the estimated value, an organization then makes a decision about whether or not to adopt the project. In general, the project will involve risk, and so if adopted, the actual value might be quite different from the organization's estimated value. Typically the adoption criterion for accepting projects involves figures of merit clearing a particular threshold called a "hurdle rate." The collection of all projects approved and their associated expenditure levels comprise the organization's budget.

Imagine that the organization establishes a standard for judging, after the fact, whether or not a project turns out to have been a success or a failure. Given the dichotomous choice, accept or reject, the organization will view projects as eventually falling into four broad categories, based on the combination of choice and outcome. Consider each category in turn.

First, the organization might accept a project that turns out to be a success. Shapira calls this possibility selecting a "winner." Second, the organization might accept a project that turns out to be a failure. Shapira calls this possibility "a white elephant." Third, the organization might reject the project and subsequently learn that it would have been a failure. Shapira calls this possibility "good judgment." Fourth, the organization might reject the project and subsequently learn that it would have been a success. Shapira calls this possibility "a missed opportunity."

Assessing the risks associated with individual projects and how these risks aggregate into the risk profile for the enterprise as a whole is the task of risk management. At the enterprise level, standards for success and hurdle rates combine to determine the probabilities attached to the four categories described above. In theory, risk managers provide this information to decision-makers, who in turn make the budgeting choices about which projects to adopt and which to reject.

Ideally, hurdle rates are set and projects are adopted in order to create maximum value for the organization. However, decision-makers make their choices in line with their own personality traits and the manner in which the organization has structured their incentives. The challenge is to establish incentives so that risks are properly evaluated and decisions made to create as much value for the organization as possible.

It is natural to expect that decision-makers will be rewarded for adopting winners and penalized for adopting white elephants. In some cases, they might also be rewarded for displaying good judgment, but be penalized for missed opportunities. Notably, if the penalty for selecting a white elephant looms relatively large, but the penalty for missed opportunities looms relatively small, decision-makers' interests will typically lead them to be conservative when facing risk. That is, they will be inclined to adopt projects only when the probability of success is very high. However, if decision-makers are rewarded handsomely for winners and are not sufficiently penalized for white elephants, they will prone to take excessive risk.

Decision-makers interpret organizational incentives through the lens of their own personality traits. Loss aversion, fear, and regret aversion induce decision-makers toward being more conservative than they otherwise might be. In this respect, think about how you would expect someone with a "conservator" risk style to behave. High aspirations, strong hope, excessive optimism, and overconfidence induce them to be more aggressive than they would be otherwise. In this respect, think about how you would expect someone with "maximizer" risk style to behave.

Designing incentives might require taking account of personality traits. In this regard, compensation packages designed for decision-makers characterized by high coefficients of loss aversion, strong fear, and significant regret aversion would need to overweigh rewards for winners relative to white elephants. For decision-makers characterized by high aspirations, strong hope, excessive optimism, and overconfidence, the reverse would be true.

Tolerance for white elephants is partly cultural. Business cultures that are intolerant of white elephants are not conducive to creating many successful new companies. Since 1975, the countries that now make up the eurozone have created just one company, Inditex, that qualifies as being among the world's 500 largest. By way of contrast, in the same period, California has produced 26. In 2012, the top 50 companies founded in Silicon Valley generated revenues that exceeded 50% of India's GDP, and 6% of US GDP. Silicon Valley companies account for 12% of all US patents and initial public offerings (IPOs). Apple, Cisco Systems, eBay, Google, Hewlett-Packard, Intel, Microsoft, Genentech, Oracle, Yahoo, LinkedIn, and Twitter were all created in Silicon Valley, and that is a short list.[21]

In Silicon Valley, entrepreneurs whose start-ups became white elephants often receive funding for new ventures. This is because Silicon Valley investors view white elephants as potential learning opportunities for what not to do in the future. As a result, entrepreneurs are willing to take higher risks than they would in a more punitive environment, where a single white elephant is enough to brand them as a failure for life.

Reputation is part of reward, and how it enters into decisions can be complex. Some decision-makers will make conservative choices for fear of being stigmatized by white elephants. Other decision-makers will be able to find scapegoats to blame for white elephants and be more aggressive. Senior executives might be willing to cut budgets for risk management if they are able to fault others in the organization when unfavorable events occur.

In addition to resources, risk management takes time, and in some cases can interfere with decision-makers' authority to act quickly or independently. Therefore, incentive issues might arise in the sense that line management decision-makers need to be incentivized to use risk management, for example, by using bonus payments as rewards or clawbacks as penalties.

In the presence of information asymmetries, line managers and risk managers typically face different incentives, an issue that Appendix E discusses in further detail. To be sure, the amount of emphasis to place on profit and loss (P&L) outcomes can be challenging. From a dual focal point perspective, incentives if not psychology can induce line managers to have aspiration as a focal point, while risk managers have survival as a focal point. In addition, academic studies by Edward Deci and Richard Ryan find that for creative tasks, excessive focus on financial outcomes can be distracting and reduce the quality of decisions.

Sheedy and Griffin find through their survey that banks whose incentive systems rank high in emphasizing P&L are associated with excessive risk taking.[22] In this regard, remember that psychologically, being below aspiration or in the domain of losses activates neurological mechanisms for risk-seeking behavior. Addressing this issue requires awareness, discipline, and a deft touch.

High hopes and aversion to a sure loss are particularly pronounced among rogue traders. The current official rogue trading record holder is Jérôme Kerviel, whose actions caused French bank Société Générale (SocGen) to lose €4.9 billion ($7.3 billion). Kerviel maintains that his bosses knew about his highly risky trades, and implicitly approved them.[23] If he is correct, then SocGen had an incentive problem whereby Kerviel's managers benefitted from his successes, but blamed him when his trading went sour.

Closing Thoughts

The management of risk within organizations is embedded within its overall processes and culture. A systematic approach to organizational risk management requires a clear sense of how to categorize risks and put processes in place to deal with them intelligently. As Goldilocks learned, some bowls of porridge are too hot and others are too cold.[24] Because of psychological pitfalls, some organizations are prone to taking excessive risk, and other organizations are prone to taking insufficient risk. Risk management is a delicate and challenging exercise.

CHAPTER 7

Minsky, the Financial Instability Hypothesis, and Risk Management

AT THIS POINT WE TURN OUR ATTENTION TO RISK MANAGEMENT IN THE financial sector. The next several chapters apply the concepts developed to analyze the psychological dimension of risk management at major financial institutions that were at the heart of the global financial crisis. This chapter sets the stage by providing a general framework for understanding financial instability from a macroprudential perspective, in which macroprudential is understood as referring to the welfare of the financial system as a whole. To do so, the chapter presents the insights of acclaimed economist Hyman Minsky, who died in 1996. Minsky's study and analysis of the causes and consequences of financial fragility, financial crises and economic instability are unparalleled.[1]

The global financial crisis that erupted in 2008 was without question a "Minsky moment."[2] Many of his early predictions unfolded almost exactly in this crisis, and it is because of these insights that risk managers in particular need to understand his ideas.

During his entire academic career, Minsky told us that financial crises are inevitable. In fact, he railed against political leaders and the economists who advise them for raising false hopes. History keeps on proving him correct.

Minsky told us that, rather than trying to avoid financial crises entirely, we need to take steps to make financial crises less severe. For risk managers, this is a major takeaway, because their judgments and decisions will impact the magnitude of future crises. The actions of some will magnify these crises, while the actions of others will mitigate these crises.

This chapter describes Minsky's worldview in nine components.[3] The first eight components pertain to the factors that cause instability and are interconnected. Minsky used the term "financial instability hypothesis" (FIH) to describe these ideas. The ninth component pertains to his policy recommendations, which he called reforms. These can mitigate the amplitude of financial crises and soften the negative fallout that they bring. In the remainder of the book, I shall use FIH as a shorthand term to refer to all nine components.

By now, most of the details associated with the unfolding of the global financial crisis are well understood. To illustrate key points, I will describe how Minsky's general insights about general financial crises apply to the global financial crisis that fully erupted in 2008.[4] In doing so, I remind readers not to view his perspective with twenty-twenty hindsight. Minsky died in 1996, more than a decade before the global financial crisis. Yet no other perspective is as cogent in identifying how and why the global financial crisis happened, and how future crises can and will develop.

Psychological issues lie at the heart of the issues Minsky emphasized. Because behavioral economics was not well developed during the time Minsky developed his ideas, his discussion of psychological concepts is rudimentary. Minsky suggested that euphoria drives the actions that generate financial fragility, crisis, and instability. For this reason, this chapter covers the neurological basis for euphoria. However, I hasten to add that other psychological issues besides euphoria are critical drivers of the actions that produce financial instability.

EUPHORIA AND HORMONES

Minsky tells us that it is during times of euphoria that we see the acceleration of financial innovations that lay the groundwork for financial instability. Notably, euphoria reflects optimism, confidence, and positive sentiment, all features emphasized by John Maynard Keynes in his discussion of economic booms and busts. However, euphoria has an important neurological basis, and it is crucial that risk managers understand it.

Neuroscientist and former Wall Street trader John Coates tells us that feelings of euphoria are associated with elevated levels of testosterone.[5] Coates admits to having been euphoric during bubbles during his trading days at Goldman Sachs. He describes his fellow traders as having been euphoric and delusional during the dot-com era as they experienced feelings of omnipotence.

Testosterone is a steroid hormone, as are estrogen and cortisol. Testosterone and cortisol play critical roles in both risk taking and competition, and in the experience of triumph and exuberance. Coates emphasizes that there is a feedback loop between brain and body, in which the brain reacts to new information by instructing the body to increase testosterone, which subsequently feeds back to the brain, altering brain chemistry itself. He suggests that this feedback mechanism serves to coordinate our complex internal processes and get us focused on dealing with the situation at hand. In contrast, cortisol is a stress hormone, which increases in the face of a threat.

Both testosterone and cortisol can stay elevated, even after the events that initiated the increases have passed. Coates speaks of a "winner effect" when testosterone levels remain elevated after success. On a winning streak, increased testosterone levels tend to induce increased risk taking and additional victories produce increased testosterone.[6] However, excessive testosterone is too much of a good thing, because it transforms risk-taking behavior into reckless behavior. As for cortisol, by its nature it stays elevated after the initial threat, keeping people on their guard.

Coates urges us to think of the mind and body as an integrated system. He tells us that prolonged elevation of testosterone and cortisol is problematic, impairing mental processes and reasoning skills that are interwoven into the brain's motor circuits. This means that reasoning and actions are structurally intertwined. Emotions are what we feel when our brains are urging us to do something. However, our brains are not perfect. If our hormones are out of balance, our brains can, and often do, induce us to take inappropriate actions such as being reckless. Neuroscientist Susan Greenfield suggests that the portion of the prefrontal cortex that normally checks reckless behavior does not receive sufficient amounts of dopamine to overcome the impact of very high testosterone.[7]

What happens in a bubble? Do professional traders recognize the bubble and bet on the way up, planning to exit in time before the inevitable crash? Or do they mindlessly bet on the bubble as if it is a permanent state of affairs? Coates suggests that elevated levels of testosterone lead them to bet as if the bubble is permanent.

Let us see how euphoria plays out in Minsky's financial instability dynamic.

LEVERAGE

Excessive leverage is one of the key focal points in Minsky's analysis, and it plays a major role in the Minsky models discussed in Appendix F. For banks, net worth to total liabilities reflects the size of the capital cushion. Smaller equity cushions leave banks more vulnerable to failing during times of economic stress. For households, higher debt-to-income ratios make it more difficult for them to service that debt during times of economic stress. Therefore, a negative economic shock of a specific magnitude is more apt to induce a financial crisis when capital cushions for banks are low and household debt is high.

Minsky tells us that between 1950 and 1960, average asset-to-equity-ratios for banks trended downward from about 13.5 to about 11.6. However, after 1960, the ratio increased, reaching to 17.9 in 1974 and then leveling off at about 16.6 in 1978. Minsky noted this drop in bank capital with some alarm. As for household debt, he pointed out that debt-to-income grew at a steady rate until 1964, and then followed a cyclical pattern.

Traditional corporate finance textbooks suggest that firms choose their leverage in order to balance the benefits of tax shields against the expected costs of financial distress. When the expected cost of financial distress is low, firms can afford to take on high leverage. Minsky warned that during the middle phase of an economic recovery, a sense of euphoria would begin to develop that would lead to the expected costs of distress being underestimated. Therefore, firms would choose higher levels of leverage than would be rational. The same euphoria would lead households to make the same mistake. Therefore, the costs of distress would turn out to be much higher than anticipated.

In ignoring Minsky, we learned hard lessons about excessive leverage. In 1974, when Minsky was already warning about debt levels being excessive, the ratio of private sector debt to GDP stood at about 120%. So what did we do thereafter in the long lead-up to the global financial crisis?

Martin Wolf, the editor of the *Financial Times* and a Minsky devotee, documents how private sector debt in the United States grew during the period 1974 through 2012. In 2008, before the onset of the financial crisis, the ratio of private sector debt to GDP peaked at about 300%! In 2012, as the global financial crisis subsided, the ratio of private sector debt to GDP fell to 250%. I think it fair to say that Minsky would still be sounding the alarm about leverage being excessive.

FRINGE FINANCE

In 1913, the US Congress created the Federal Reserve System to provide a series of protections in which the Federal Reserve served as a lender of last resort to its member banks. These protections were intended to address the panics that had characterized the US banking system during the 19th century. However, the protections failed to prevent massive bank runs during the Great Depression. As a result, the framework was augmented in the 1930s to include federal deposit insurance in combination with regulatory oversight.

Shadow banks are financial institutions that engage in banking functions, but are not regulated in the same way as commercial banks and do not have the Federal Reserve as their lender of last resort. In 2007, a decade after Minsky died, PIMCO economist Paul McCulley coined the phrase "shadow banking," which, in McCulley (2009), he discusses in connection with Minsky's work.[8] Minsky's term for "shadow banking" was "fringe finance." His concern with fringe financial institutions was that their activities lie outside the purview of financial regulators. He suggested that as a result, fringe financial institutions take on excessive leverage and risk, with commercial banks serving as their lender of last resort.

Minsky postulated that the period between the end of World War II and 1960 was something of a golden age in respect to economic stability. However, things changed in the early 1960s when the financial system became more speculative. He points out that between 1960 and 1974, business lending by finance companies, the commercial paper market, REITs and nonmember commercial banks—all examples of fringe finance—grew relative to other entities making up the financial system.

Minsky suggests that the shift to fringe finance made finance more fragile and the economy less stable. The period between 1960 and 1975 featured higher inflation and higher unemployment than the corresponding 15 years between 1945 and 1960. Moreover, as fringe banking institutions grew, they became customers of banks that were part of the Federal Reserve system, often establishing lines of credit. As a result, member banks, especially the large money market banks, became de facto lenders of last resort.

In ignoring Minsky, we learned hard lessons about fringe finance, alias shadow banking. The Financial Crisis Inquiry Commission (FCIC) points out that during the three decades that preceded the financial crisis, the shadow banking system grew to the point of becoming comparable in size to the traditional banking system. Examples of such shadow banking activities include the repo lending market, off-balance-sheet entities, and use of over-the-counter derivatives.

The FCIC notes that shadow banking institutions achieved this growth by taking on short-term debt, just as Minsky had said. And just as Minsky had complained, the FCIC complained that this structure lacked the protective structure that had been put in place during the first half of the 20th Century.

PONZI FINANCE

Minsky emphasized the important role that financial innovation plays in creating economic instability. In this regard, he told us that financial innovation was especially dangerous when it involved an excessive amount of what he called "Ponzi finance." Ponzi finance is short-term lending by financial institutions against long-term assets, in which repayment of both interest and principal depends heavily on asset price appreciation rather than the generation of cash flows.

Just as a Ponzi scheme collapses without sufficient cash inflows from new investors, Ponzi finance collapses without sufficient price appreciation for the asset being financed. Minsky distinguished Ponzi finance from "hedge finance" and "speculative finance." In hedge finance, the maturity of the liability matches the maturity of the asset underlying the debt. In speculative finance, the maturity of the liability is less than the maturity of the asset, and the cash flows from the asset are sufficient to cover interest payments, but the debt needs to be rolled over in order for the cash flows from the asset to cover remaining interest and price appreciation necessary for full repayment of principal.

Minsky told us that debtors and bankers who are engaged in speculative and Ponzi finance expect borrowers to make their payment commitments by refinancing or increasing debts, or selling off other financial assets. He emphasized, in the strongest possible terms, that the proportions of hedge, speculative, and Ponzi finance in an economy are a major determinant of that economy's stability. In this regard, he specifically cautioned that the existence of a large component of positions financed in a speculative or a Ponzi manner is a necessary condition for financial instability.

Risk managers need to pay close attention to Minsky's financing classification system, and to use it as a basis for assessing risk. An easy way to see the difference between hedge, speculative, and Ponzi finance is to consider an example in which the financing structure is fixed, and then to vary the cash flows of the asset being financed. In the example, the interest rate is 10% per year, and a $1,000 loan features interest only of $100 per year, with the principal returned when the loan matures after seven years.

Figure 7.1 illustrates hedge finance, in which the expected cash flows from the asset being financed are exactly the same as the cash flows associated with the loan. Cash flows and appreciation are depicted by the heights of

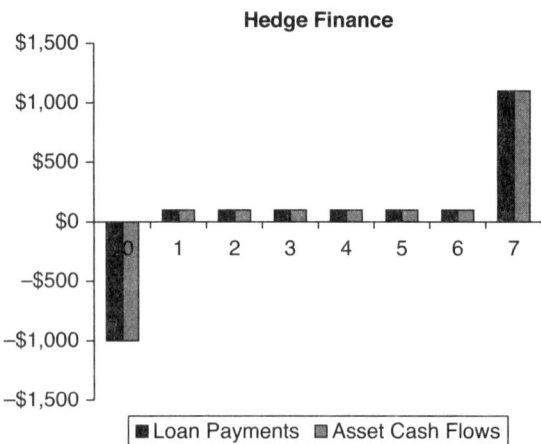

Figure 7.1 This figure illustrates hedge finance, in which the expected cash flows from the asset being financed are exactly the same as the cash flows associated with the loan. Cash flows and appreciation are depicted by the heights of the vertical bars. In hedge finance, the expected cash flows from the asset are sufficient to cover repayment of principal when the loan matures, with the expectation being that no asset appreciation is required to repay principal in full.

the vertical bars. In the figure, the expected cash flows from the asset are sufficient to cover repayment of principal when the loan matures, with the expectation that no asset appreciation is required to repay principal in full.

Figure 7.2 illustrates speculative finance, whereby the asset's expected cash flows are sufficient to cover interest payments during the term of the loan. However, the expected cash flows from the asset at the time the loan matures are not expected to cover repayment of principal in full. Instead the expectation is that asset appreciation will be required to supplement the actual cash flows in order that the principal be repaid.

Figure 7.3 illustrates Ponzi finance. Here expected cash flows from the asset are insufficient to cover interest payments as well as repayment of principal. Instead, the expectation is that sufficient appreciation in the value of the asset will be required to cover both. Therefore, the principal repayment for the Ponzi finance loan, corresponding to the sum of the expected asset cash flow and required appreciation, will be higher than the corresponding principal repayments depicted in Figures 7.1 and 7.2.

The amount of appreciation depicted in Figure 7.3 will exactly cover required principal and interest over the life of the loan. In Minsky's dynamic, during the bubble phase of a boom, the expected amount of appreciation might well be more than the minimum required to cover the loan obligations. However, during the later phases of the bubble, the overpricing of the asset will lead expected appreciation to fall below the amount required to cover the terms of the loan. Indeed, expected appreciation might well be negative during the latter stage of a bubble.

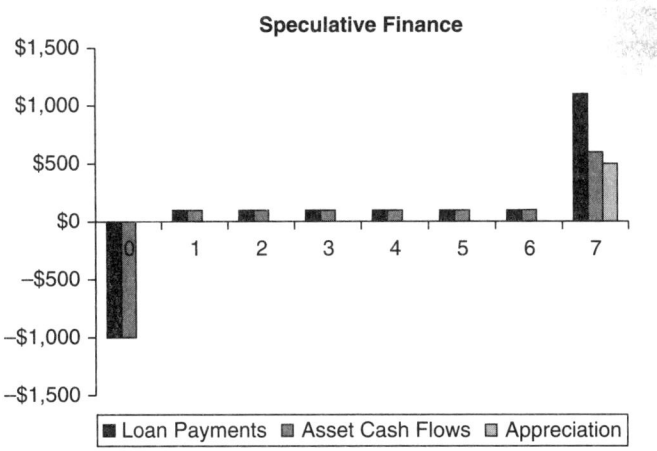

Figure 7.2 This figure illustrates speculative finance, whereby the asset's expected cash flows are sufficient to cover interest payments during the term of the loan, but not full repayment of principal. Instead asset appreciation is required to supplement the actual cash flows in order that the principal be repaid in full.

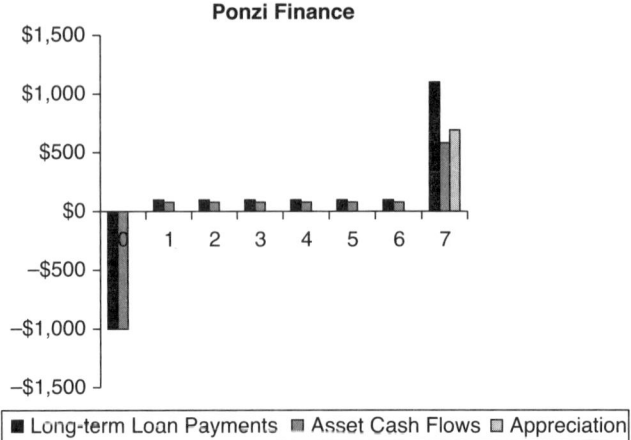

Figure 7.3 This figure illustrates Ponzi finance where expected cash flows from the asset are insufficient to cover interest payments as well as repayment of principal. Instead, sufficient appreciation in the value of the asset is required to cover both.

In ignoring Minsky, we learned very hard lessons about speculative and Ponzi finance. The FCIC documents that approximately 70% of subprime mortgage borrowers used innovative products such as hybrid adjustable-rate mortgages (ARMs) featuring low "teaser" rates that last for the first two or three years, which then adjust periodically thereafter.

The most popular Alt-A products included perfect examples of Ponzi finance, namely interest-only mortgages and what are called payment-option ARMs. An option ARM allows borrowers to choose how much they pay each month, with a provision called negative amortization for increasing the principal that is due. Notably, if the balance becomes large enough, an option ARM loan converts to a fixed-rate mortgage, often with a much higher monthly payment. In 2003, option ARMs comprised 2% of mortgages. By 2006, this figure had jumped to 20%.

According to the FCIC, many ARMs were structured to fail, but for rising real estate prices that would bail out most of the borrowers. Of course, this is the nature of Ponzi finance. The testimony of Jamie Dimon, CEO of JPMorgan, to the FCIC nicely summarizes the consequence of shifting from hedge finance to Ponzi finance: "In mortgage underwriting, somehow we just missed, you know, that home prices don't go up forever and that it's not sufficient to have stated income."

FINANCIAL INNOVATION AND ASSET VALUES

Minsky argued that during the evolution of a boom, the financial sector uses innovation as a tool to increase leverage and risk. Moreover, the shift from hedge finance to speculative and Ponzi finance fuels the creation of price bubbles for particular assets. In turn, asset price bubbles generate a feedback effect, because they temporarily support additional reliance on Ponzi finance and short-term lending for the financing of long-term assets. This dynamic exacerbates the bubble during a period of monetary expansion, with the bubble eventually bursting when monetary expansion gives way to monetary contraction. A major danger of Ponzi finance is that the bursting of bubbles leads to defaults and weakness in the balance sheets of lending institutions.

The preceding paragraph provides a capsule summary of how financial innovation and asset-pricing bubbles evolve during an economic expansion and eventually make the economy more fragile. Next consider some of the details.

As Minsky reminds us, a positively sloped term structure creates opportunities for profit by borrowing short term and investing long term. Minsky's thesis is that the profit opportunities from borrowing short and investing long typically begin when the financial structure is relatively robust. At this stage, liquidity is plentiful because hedge finance predominates and perceived risk associated with cash flows is relatively low. In an atmosphere of relative confidence, with no strong urge for a flight to safety, short-term rates will be lower than long-term rates. These conditions are conducive to a shift from hedge finance to speculative and Ponzi finance.

The shift to speculative and Ponzi finance will take place through financial innovation. For a number of reasons, it will also be gradual. Economic agents will have to adjust their risk limits in the wake of the previous bust portion of the boom and bust cycle. It takes time to develop new innovative financial products. It takes time to build institutions capable of accepting the liabilities of economic agents, and issuing new securities, the value of which investors can trust. It takes time for investors to gain confidence that they will be able to find refinancing, which they need to do in order to borrow short term and invest long term.

The gradual shift in speculative and Ponzi finance during the early and middle stages of a boom will place upward pressure on the long-term assets being acquired, thereby generating capital gains. These gains provide support for further shifts toward speculative and Ponzi finance. Notably, the proportions of speculative and Ponzi finance characterizing the balance sheets of banks will trend upward.

The shift toward speculative and Ponzi finance is endogenous, and it leads the economy to become more fragile. An economy that is fragile is more vulnerable to a financial crisis emanating from a negative macroshock than is an economy that is robust. When a negative shock is large enough to produce a financial crisis, the process described above goes into reverse.

Risk managers take note: Minsky warned against using short-term financing to fund long-term assets during the early phase of a boom. Doing so, he cautioned, involves exposure to interest rate risk, as interest rates tend to rise during the latter stages of a boom. However, he also warned that borrowers expose themselves to rollover risk, as banks stop lending during runs. Figure 7.4 illustrates Ponzi finance with short-term financing being used for longer-term assets. It is that double spike in the middle of the figure, the principal due in need of being refinanced, which captures rollover risk.

In the aftermath of a crisis, bankers and businessmen, especially those who have been burned, are much more reluctant to engage in speculative and Ponzi financing. The bust portion of the "boom and bust cycle" begins. Perceived valuation risk soars, leading to a sharp drop in the prices of securities reflecting speculative and Ponzi finance. Liquidity dries up.

The bust accentuates the balance sheet weakness of lending institutions, as the market value of their assets declines. Displaying a form of aversion to a sure loss, institutions tend to resist marking assets to market, thereby masking the intrinsic value of their capital cushions from financial markets. In resisting, they take a risk hoping that future increases in the market value of nonperforming assets will alleviate the need for markdowns. Therefore, speculative and Ponzi-like forces continue to operate within the institutions during economic busts, but in a different way than during booms, as the institutions curtail their lending.

In ignoring Minsky's insights, we learned the hard way about the downside of financial innovation and its role in fueling asset-pricing bubbles. The FCIC report documents how between 2003 and 2007, house prices rose 27% in what proved to be a national housing bubble. This bubble was financed

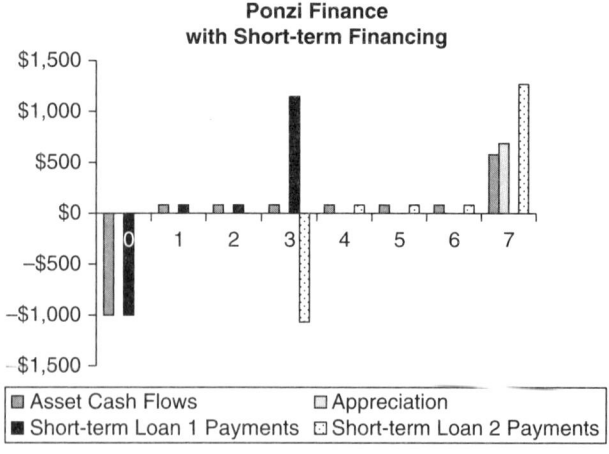

Figure 7.4 This figure illustrates Ponzi finance with short-term financing being used for longer-term assets. The double spike in the middle of the figure represents principal coming due which is in need of being refinanced.

by the creation of $4 trillion in mortgage-backed securities. In respect to innovation, the FCIC tells us that the financial sector issued approximately $700 billion in collateralized debt obligations (CDOs) that included mortgage-backed securities as collateral.

The FCIC tells us that hybrid ARMs became the workhorse of securitization, because they made mortgage payments affordable, at least temporarily, as home prices rose faster than incomes. The FCIC also tells us that in respect to the housing price bubble, ARMs and CDOs were not new instruments per se; however, there was great innovation in the use to which they were put.

New Era Thinking

Minsky tells us that during an economic boom with rising asset values, people concoct new era explanations, consistent with free market ideology, to justify the inflated asset prices. By people, he means central bankers, government officials, bankers, businessmen, and economists. Their beliefs about a new era having arrived allows them to enter a period of euphoria and to ignore any warnings about speculative and Ponzi finance making the financial system fragile and the economy prone to becoming unstable. In this regard, euphoria corresponds to excessive optimism and overconfidence, while the refusal to reject new era thinking as risk builds corresponds to confirmation bias.

Just to be clear: Minsky's insistence that the shift toward speculative and Ponzi finance during a boom is endogenous stems from these psychological biases. If the "people" described in the previous paragraph were fully rational, they would avoid destabilizing the economy and producing financial crises.

Minsky argues that during an investment boom, the demand for financing puts upward pressure on interest rates. Such increases eliminate profit opportunities, or, if you like, risk premiums. As a result, the growth in investment activity eventually tails off, and the economy slows, thereby shattering the views of those holding new era thinking.

In ignoring Minsky, we learned the hard way that people succumb to new era thinking. In this regard, the FCIC quotes a hedge fund manager, Mark Klipsch, of Orix Credit Corp., who in 2005 expressed his concern about irrationality in the housing market being explained away by people who were saying, "It's different this time." The backdrop for his remark involved news reports from 2005 that highlighted weakening in the housing market. Specifically, home sales had begun to fall, and Fitch Ratings were reporting increases in mortgage delinquencies. Klipsch made his remark at the American Securitization Forum, a securities trade group, telling participants that investors were "over optimistic" about the market, and using the phrase "I see a lot of irrationality." When Klipsch used the phrase "It's different this time," which the FCIC described as "a rationale commonly heard before previous collapses," he stated that he was unnerved.

Regulatory Failure

Minsky argued that the financial sector is politically more agile and powerful than the regulators who oversee it, which is why the financial sector ultimately wins the regulatory game. In respect to new era thinking, he suggests that during booms free market ideology permeates the mind-sets of regulators. In this regard, he was very concerned that the Fed has historically overfocused on monetary policy at the expense of overseeing the quality of lending in financial markets. This focus, he suggested, would lead regulators to fail at their task. A particular concern of his was that regulators would fail to monitor the degree of Ponzi finance in the financial system.

Minsky drew attention to disingenuous behavior by conservatives, who he said used free market rhetoric, while "their corporate clients" lobbied to have legislation passed institutionalizing their market power. He spoke of bankers and businessmen recoiling in horror at the thought of having to face competition in their industries, as changes in technology and institutions blurred the boundaries that once separated distinct lines of business. He spoke of corporate executives who paid "lip service to free enterprise" when extolling the tenets of Adam Smith, yet striving to maintain and legitimize their state mandated market power, which Smith abhorred.

In respect to central banks, Minsky described the manner in which they regulated profit-seeking banks as a "game." The game he described featured the central bank setting interest rates and reserve requirements, while the banks engaged in financial innovation intended to circumvent regulations. His point was that, although the central bank controlled the rate of growth of the monetary base, the banking and financial structure determined the efficacious use of that base.

Is the game played fairly? Minsky called it "an unfair game." He told us that it was unfair because of a disparity involving incentives and, I would add, the power of resources. In his view, bureaucrats at central banks have much less at stake than "entrepreneurs of the banking community." He speaks of bureaucrats routinely being surprised by financial markets, and the banking community winning the game. And in winning the game, he tells us that they destabilize the economy and inflict losses on those who cannot protect themselves from unemployment and inflation.

"Money supply blinders" are what Minsky contended central banks wear. He proposed that they take off those blinders and focus their attention on the composition of bank portfolios, the way those portfolio change, and how they affect the stability of the economy. Minsky noted that central banks tend to ignore the erosion of bank equity, the growth of liability management banking, and the increased use of covert liabilities until it is too late. Only when financial markets begin to break down do these issues move to the center of central bank bureaucrats' radar screens. Then the Federal Reserve responds in its role as lender of last resort and injects reserves into the banking system to refinance banks in order to prevent the financial system from collapsing.

In ignoring Minsky, we learned very hard lessons about regulatory failure. In its report, the FCIC asks, "Where were the regulators?" They tell us that in the years before the crisis, declining underwriting standards and new mortgage products had actually been on regulators' radar screens. However, the delay in taking action stemmed from disagreements among the agencies and the preference for minimal regulatory interference articulated by Alan Greenspan, who was Fed chair at the time.

In describing Greenspan's mind-set, the FCIC report quotes him as saying, "Those of us who support market capitalism in its more competitive forms might argue that unfettered markets create a degree of wealth that fosters a more civilized existence. I have always found that insight compelling." As part of a May 2005 speech, Greenspan articulated a core element of his ideology when he stated that "private regulation generally has proved far better at constraining excessive risk-taking than has government regulation."[9]

Risk managers, take note. The FCIC report tells us that during the 1990s, regulators began to rely extensively on banks' own internal risk management systems. In 1999, Greenspan described this "risk-focused" approach as providing constructive feedback that the bank can use to enhance further the quality of its risk management systems.

Corroborating Minsky's contention about the regulatory game being unfair, former housing and urban development secretary Henry Cisneros made the following remark to the FCIC about the Office of Federal Housing Enterprise Oversight (OFHEO): "OFHEO was puny compared to what Fannie Mae and Freddie Mac could muster in their intelligence, their Ivy League educations, their rocket scientists in their place, their lobbyists, their ability to work the Hill."

In 2006, Ben Bernanke replaced Greenspan as Fed chair. In a letter to the FCIC, Bernanke wrote that in 2006, members of the Federal Open Market Committee (FOMC) and its staff could not develop a consensus on whether house prices were overvalued. The consensus they did reach was that a major spillover from the housing market to financial institutions was a moderate probability event. Indeed, two months after the FOMC meeting, an internal memo written by economists at the Fed acknowledged the possibility that housing prices were overvalued. However, the memo downplayed the severity of any downturn.

Runs on Financial Institutions and Markets

Economic booms do not last forever, and booms themselves tend to generate increases in interest rates, which eventually bring booms to an end. If leverage and Ponzi finance have been strong during the boom, Minsky tells us that the bust that follows will feature runs on financial institutions and markets for short-term debt such as commercial paper.

The "boom financial industry" during the early 1970s consisted of REITs, securities backed by real estate that were free of corporate income tax as long as dividend payouts were at least 90%. These REITs were used to finance construction projects, and were highly leveraged with short-term debt. Therefore, they featured rollover risk, and their valuations were sensitive to interest rates.

These REITs qualified as Ponzi finance. This is because the assets associated with REITs did not generate cash flow while the construction projects were underway, and yet income accrued. This means that REIT investors expected to receive a cash dividend stream, despite the absence of project cash flow. Hence, REITs needed to borrow in order to pay dividends. They did so by issuing commercial paper.

In 1974, a combination of interest rate increases, construction delays, and a glut of finished apartments proved disastrous for REITs. Their capital fell so dramatically that they found it difficult to sell commercial paper. Between 1973 and 1974, REIT commercial paper fell by 75%. This effectively amounted to a run on REIT commercial paper.

REITs turned to commercial banks for funding and were able to raise short-term financing. In practical terms, commercial banks served as the REITs' lender of last resort. Although there was effectively a REIT speculative bubble, the actions of the bank prevented a sudden crash. However, by lending to REITs, banks ended up with much weaker balance sheets and were more fragile going forward.

In ignoring Minsky, we learned hard lessons about runs on commercial paper. Three decades after the 1974 run, the market for commercial paper experienced another set of runs, also related to real estate.

The FCIC documents that the more recent episode involved subprime and Alt-A mortgage-backed securities, which were largely funded using short-term lending in the commercial paper and repo market. In the lead-up to the global financial crisis, independent mortgage originators did not have access to deposits. Therefore, they typically relied on lines of credit extended by banks and money borrowed in the repo market to finance new mortgages. These loans were increasingly collateralized by highly rated mortgage securities that in turn were backed by increasingly risky loans.

During the summer of 2007, the values of some highly rated mortgage securities declined precipitously. Hedge funds run out of investment bank Bear Stearns were heavily invested in those securities, and as a result the funds imploded. Investors started to become very nervous, and in late July there was a run on asset-backed commercial paper (ABCP). Very soon thereafter, panic ensued in the markets for short-term funding. The panic was widespread, and even impacted securities not exposed to risky mortgages. For the remainder of 2007, volume in the ABCP market declined by a third. A year later, after the Lehman bankruptcy in September 2008, the commercial paper market experienced a second run.

TOO BIG TO FAIL

Large busts threaten the existence of many large financial institutions and other large firms, some of which require large-scale government assistance in order to survive. Moreover, some of those institutions are beneficiaries of this assistance precisely because they are too big to fail. Minsky called this approach "contingency socialism," pointing out that many financial institutions will wind up with weakened balance sheets as a result of the bust.

Minsky complained that large corporations carry an "implied public guarantee" on their debts, which amounts to a contingency liability. As a result, large corporations and large banks enjoy a significant financing bias, which provides them with favorable rates but also an incentive to hold riskier assets than they would otherwise. Minsky notes that these assets are often securities issued by fringe institutions, for which commercial banks are lenders of last resort. In consequence, the normal impact of economic downturns on commercial bank balance sheets becomes amplified.

The state of affairs just described leads to systemic risk in the financial system, with the clear possibility of a domino effect from the failure of large financial firms. Minsky warned that a domino effect would cause a serious disruption to the financing hierarchy. Moreover, he pointed out that nature of the fragility would be nontransparent and therefore difficult to discern. The source of the opaqueness, he suggested, would be the layered structure of the financing hierarchy along with the creation of new financial strategies that made credit available by tapping pools of liquidity.

By ignoring Minsky, we learned the hard way about the cost of allowing firms to become too big to fail. The FCIC documents that between 1998 and 2007, the combined assets of the five largest banks in the United States more than tripled, from $2.2 trillion to $6.8 trillion.

Just as Minsky warned, the fragility of the financial system was opaque to policymakers, regulators, and financial executives. None appears to have understood how dangerously exposed were major firms and markets to the potential contagion from a decline in housing prices.

In March 2008, the shares of Bear Stearns collapsed in price, which led to its acquisition by JPMorgan. The acquisition was undertaken at an emergency meeting with the support of the US Treasury and the Federal Reserve, which provided guarantees to ensure that Bear Stearns would be acquired, as it was regarded as being too big to fail. In September 2008, government-sponsored enterprises (GSEs) Fannie Mae and Freddie Mac went into conservatorship, and the shares of Lehman Brothers came under heavy pressure. Lehman was too big to fail. This we learned the hard way, because it did fail, and what had been a normal downturn gave way to the worst recession since the Great Depression, along with a global financial crisis. The government did not repeat the mistake with other firms too big to fail, and made sure to rescue them: AIG, Citigroup, and General Motors serve as examples.

Psychology might have played an important role in the government's decision not to rescue Lehman. Treasury secretary Hank Paulson became sensitive to criticism from free market advocates for having provided public funds to rescue Bear-Stearns, Fannie Mae, and Freddie Mac. Paulson, Bernanke, and Timothy Geithner, who headed the Federal Reserve Bank of New York, were the three key government figures who responded to the developing financial fragility. To Bernanke and Geithner, Paulson complained that he was being called "Mr. Bailout," and would not support the use of taxpayer money or liquidity provided by the Federal Reserve to rescue Lehman.[10] His sensitivity to this issue quickly changed in the wake of Lehman failure, as several days later the Federal Reserve made an $85 billion loan to AIG in exchange for assuming 80% ownership.

MINSKY'S POLICY RECOMMENDATIONS

Minsky proposed a series of reforms to make the economy more stable and the financial sector less fragile. These reforms break down into four categories:

1. fiscal
2. employment
3. industrial
4. financial

Although he claimed to be less confident about the efficacy of these reforms than he was about the causes of financial fragility, it is worthwhile discussing his ideas and relating them to events associated with the global financial crisis.

In respect to *fiscal policy*, Minsky advocated running a large enough public sector so that fiscal deficits could offset dramatic decreases in aggregate demand in the private sector. At the same time, he cautioned against the public sector becoming too large. He also recommended that corporate income tax be abolished, because he thought that the tax deductibility of interest encourages excessive leverage.

The key issue about fiscal policy reform involves the public sector being large enough to provide sufficient stimulus in the wake of a financial crisis and economic downturn. As it happens, the amount of fiscal stimulus that followed the financial crisis of 2008 was insufficient.

Economist Paul Krugman consistently complained that the stimulus program was too small.[11] He tells us that it was all in the math, and that math involved Keynesian multiplier equations (discussed in Appendix F). In January 2009, the Congressional Budget Office forecast that during the next two years, the US economy would perform 6.8% below its potential. Krugman tells us that the magnitude of this gap corresponds to $2.1 trillion of lost output. Given the forecast, the question to be asked is how much should the stimulus package be to bring the economy back up to potential quickly, and what form should the stimulus package take?

The ratio of the forecasted gap to the size of stimulus is a multiplier. Macroeconomic analysis provides an estimate of what this multiplier will be, based on such variables as savings rates, tax rates, and the breakdown of the stimulus package into government spending and tax cuts. Krugman places the theoretical multiplier at 1.5.

The Obama administration's stimulus package was about $775 billion. Multiply that by 1.5 and we get $1.16 trillion, which is only 55% of the $2.1 trillion gap. Moreover, tax cuts have a lower multiplier than government spending. Because 40% of the stimulus package consisted of tax cuts, even 55% was optimistic. The stimulus package needed to have been at least double the size that it was. As a result, the recovery of the US economy was anemic.

The size of the stimulus program was the product of the US political system. Some feared the potential consequences of a larger stimulus program. Conservatives expressed concern that more stimulus would lead to inflation, thereby hindering rather than facilitating economic recovery. They were concerned that expectations of higher inflation would lead to higher bond prices, which would make it more expensive for the Treasury to borrow. This view was even held by some of the most influential economists in the Obama administration. Notably, others on the opposite side of the political spectrum argued that austerity was the best way to heal the economy, especially the political movement that came to be known as the Tea Party.

In the end the stimulus turned out to be no better than half strength. As a result, government policy relied heavily on monetary stimulus for increasing output and employment. As discussed below, the Fed did comply, with a massive quantitative easing program that left short-term interest rates near zero. Had the inflation rate been moderate, the real interest rate might have been substantially negative. However, inflation was also low, and so the real interest rate might have been too high to provide the necessary stimulus, as household spending continued to be low as a result of deleveraging. The economy might have been stuck in a situation similar to what Keynes called a "liquidity trap," with the Fed unable to lower real interest rates to a level that would induce sufficient private sector spending in the economy.[12]

I think that it is safe to say that Minsky would have judged Krugman's perspective on stimulus to have been close to his own.

In respect to *employment policy*, Minsky advocated having public employment programs in place to keep employment from plummeting. Born in 1919, Minsky's teen years were spent during the Great Depression. The strategies developed by the administration of Franklin Roosevelt provided him with an approach for addressing unemployment. That approach was the collection of New Deal programs: the Civilian Conservation Corps, the National Youth Administration, and the Works Progress Administration. He wanted the government to be the "employer of last resort," just as the Fed is the "lender of last resort."

I think it is safe to say that the response to the financial crisis of 2008 and associated Great Recession did not feature any initiatives along these lines. Unemployment rates fell very slowly during the subsequent recovery.

In respect to *industrial policy*, Minsky advocated having measures in place to keep systemically important firms from becoming too big to fail.

I think it is safe to say that there has been no systematic effort to prevent large firms, deemed too big to fail, from becoming larger. In the past, the Glass-Steagall Act served as an obstacle to banks becoming large. In the late 1990s, the dismantling of Glass-Steagall enabled the merger of Travelers Group and Citicorp, resulting in the creation of what became the world's largest financial services firm.

The CEO of Citicorp, Sandy Weill, had lobbied hard to have Glass-Steagall dismantled. Indeed, he was reported to have hung a portrait of himself in his office that was etched with the phrase "The Shatterer of Glass-Steagall."[13]

It is all the more amazing, therefore, that in 2012 Weill called for the breakup of banks that were too big to fail. Here is what he said, precisely: "What we should probably do is go and split up investment banking from banking... Have banks do something that's not going to risk the taxpayer dollars, that's not too big to fail." In this regard, Weill mentioned overleveraging and a lack of transparency as having been major contributors to the problems faced by banks in the run-up to the financial crisis. He went on to say that in the wake of the crisis, the banking system stopped innovating and came to be distrusted by the public.

In 2014, the Fed set a rule mandated by the Dodd-Frank Act, to prohibit financial mergers that lead the size of the merged entity to exceed 10% of all liabilities in the financial system. However, the rule does not require that financial firms that are already that large become smaller, and does not prevent them from becoming that large through organic growth.

Despite the importance of the 2008 bailouts, both in the United States and in Europe, to prevent the collapse of the global financial system, public policy has instituted measures to make bailouts of financial firms more difficult. Dodd-Frank implemented provisions in this vein, which curtailed but did not eliminate the government's ability to rescue financial firms.[14] In July 2015, Republicans introduced legislation to eliminate the provisions in Dodd-Frank that permit taxpayer-funded bailouts.[15] The month before, a Federal judge ruled that the government overreached in rescuing AIG.[16]

I think that it is safe to say that Minsky would have judged Weill's comments from 2012 as reflecting his perspective, and the Fed's 2014 rule as being much too meek. Limiting the government's rescue ability for financial firms might reduce the incentives these firms have to take on high risk, in the belief that they will be bailed out in a crisis. At the same time, keep in mind Minsky's warning that psychological pitfalls render financial crises inevitable, and therefore the failure to rescue will make crises that much worse—as we saw with the Lehman bankruptcy in 2008.

In respect to *financial policy*, Minsky advocated having the Fed play a more active role in financing at the discount window, so as to keep tabs on the growth in speculative and Ponzi financing. Notably, he recommended that the Fed place regulation on the same level as monetary policy.

In April 2012, Fed chair Bernanke gave a speech in which he described one of the major lessons he learned from the financial crisis, namely that the Fed needed to place regulation on an equal footing with monetary policy.[17] Although the speech makes no mention of Minsky, this was exactly what Minsky had advocated decades earlier.

The FCIC report tells us that in the report of a "lessons learned" analysis after the crisis, the New York Fed acknowledged its mistaken belief that "markets will always self-correct." The report concluded that "[a] deference to the self-correcting property of markets inhibited supervisors from imposing prescriptive views on banks."[18]

Based on his study of failed monetary policy during the Great Depression, Bernanke directed a program of quantitative easing at the Fed in which the monetary base grew to a record level. In doing so, the central bank purchased many of the troubled assets that sat on banks' balance sheets.

Amazingly, the Fed bought assets not just from commercial banks but from shadow banks too.[19]

In 2014, Janet Yellen took over from Bernanke as Fed chair. Unlike her two predecessors, Yellen was willing to use Minsky's name and discuss his ideas. This she did in 2009, when she was president and CEO of the Twelfth District Federal Reserve Bank, at San Francisco.[20] In July 2014, she began to warn about some US stocks being "substantially stretched."

I think it is fair to say that Minsky would have regarded the change in Fed policy as being positive.

Closing Thoughts

In its focus on the root causes of financial system fragility and economic instability, Minsky's FIH provides one of the most comprehensive conceptual frameworks for analyzing macroprudential regulation. The psychological basis for the framework involves euphoria and its influence on the risks associated with excessive leverage, speculative and Ponzi finance, and reliance on short-term financing.

The next few chapters examine how all the psychological concepts developed earlier in the book impacted some of the key parties to the global financial crisis. Included in the list of parties are investors and investment banks such as UBS and Merrill Lynch, rating agencies such as S&P and Moody's, financial firms that guaranteed mortgage defaults, such as Fannie Mae and AIG, banks that engaged in aggressive acquisitions such as RBS and Fortis, and regulatory agencies such as the Securities and Exchange Commission (SEC).

What the parties mentioned above have in common is that they were major players in the global financial crisis that assessed financial risk, succumbed to major psychological pitfalls, and made serious value-destructive decisions. In respect to the safety and soundness of individual financial institutions, this being the microprudential perspective, we want to learn from the experiences of each of these parties, in order to provide insights about constructing better regulatory practices. The FIH provides the broad overview for how systemic risk is generated across financial markets and the economy. The chapters that follow focus attention on the details of what occurred in each organization and the extent to which the individual experiences reflect the issues emphasized by the FIH.

CHAPTER 8

Aspirational Pitfalls at UBS and Merrill Lynch

When it comes to the global financial crisis, the devil lies in the details. This chapter reviews the histories of two investment banks, UBS and Merrill Lynch, identifying the psychological issues that drove the decisions they made which promoted financial fragility and subsequent economic instability.[1] Both banks participated actively in the market for CDOs constructed with mortgage-backed securities. Both banks practiced risk management poorly, and both banks incurred large losses as a result. What happened within these organizations that permitted this magnitude of errors?

In April 2008, five months before the Lehman bankruptcy, UBS released the results of a self-study to analyze what had gone wrong. This document is amazing in several respects. Most importantly, it describes internal decisions at the bank, including some of the flawed thought processes that were at work. However, it is also notable in its degree of disclosure, and for that the bank's CEO at the time, Marcel Ospel, and Investment Bank Group CEO Marcel Rohner are to be commended. I drew heavily on the self-study for this chapter.[2]

Merrill Lynch did not release the results of their own self-study. The main source material describing events and decisions at Merrill Lynch instead comes from the FCIC report and the work of journalists. Although the character of the various source documents is quite varied, what they describe about the activities undertaken at the two banks is remarkably similar.

To present these two cases, I use a layered framework to analyze the psychological issues at UBS and Merrill from the early 2000s through the beginning of the crisis. The overarching framework is the pitfall-process structure, which focuses on the manner in which psychological pitfalls infected banking processes. For both banks, the discussion identifies the psychological issues that were highly problematic in respect to how they conducted planning, set standards, incentivized their workforce, and shared information across the organization.

Additional layers in the analysis of the chronologies at UBS and Merrill feature the frameworks developed to analyze risk management structure, culture, and behavior; risk typology; dual focal points; risk styles; and the FIH.

UBS

UBS is a Swiss bank with headquarters in Zurich and Basel, having three main businesses that serve private, institutional, and corporate clients worldwide. Its businesses comprise wealth management businesses, asset management, and investment banking. UBS has a presence in major financial centers throughout the world and employs about 60,000 people. It has offices in more than 50 countries, with about 35% of its employees working in the Americas, 36% in Switzerland, and the remainder in the rest of Europe, the Middle East and Africa, and in the Asian Pacific.

In their self-study report, UBS tell us that their focus was on the root causes of the losses, which they sought to understand in order to improve their processes. The bad news about losses began to spill out at the end of 2007, when the bank announced that it would write off $18 billion of failed investments involving the subprime housing market in the United States. This was only the beginning. By mid-2008, the write-offs had increased to more than $50 billion, and in October 2008, the Swiss central bank announced its intention to take $60 billion of toxic assets off UBS's balance sheet and inject $6 billion of equity capital.

Planning at UBS

In 2005, Peter Wuffli was the UBS Investment Bank CEO. Wuffli, who had previously been a principal with McKinsey, engaged the consulting firm Oliver Wyman to develop a new strategic plan for the bank. Oliver Wyman had a long track record of expertise in risk management that dated back to the 1990s, particularly in credit risk management. The end result was a five-year strategic plan for the period 2006–2010. This plan set a goal of increasing revenue significantly and allowed for costs to rise accordingly.

In its review, Oliver Wyman compared UBS's past performance with that of its chief competitors, noting that UBS's performance trailed those of its competitors. The review noted that the biggest competitive gap was in fixed income, stating that since 2002 UBS's position in fixed income had declined relative to its leading competitors, with revenue growth having weakened significantly since 2004.

To close the competitive gap, Oliver Wyman recommended a series of strategic and tactical initiatives involving product expansion. The recommendations focused attention on a series of areas, of which mortgage-backed security (MBS) subprime and ARM products were highlighted for their revenue-generating potential. Notably, the review made no mention of risk capacity issues associated with the recommended product expansion.

When reading about the events described in the UBS example, it is clear that there are many psychological issues at play behind the decisions made. Given how Oliver Wyman has framed the situation for UBS, which elements of SP/A theory and the dual focal point framework appear to be especially salient? Does the emphasis in the review on closing the gap between UBS and the market leader induce UBS to establish top industry performance as its aspiration? Viewed from the perspective of prospect theory, did Oliver Wyman's framing induce UBS to set its reference point so that it viewed itself psychologically as being in the domain of losses?

If the answers to these questions are yes, then it seems to me that SP/A theory, the dual focal point framework, and prospect theory all point in the same direction. SP/A theory stipulates that when people set high aspirations and regard the achievement of their aspirations as very important, then they are inclined to take risks. From the perspective of the dual focal point approach, UBS's position lay between its survival point and the top industry position. With the top position as its aspiration and operative reference point, it would have been psychologically set to accept a lot of risk going forward. Prospect theory indicates that when people view themselves as being in the domain of losses, they are inclined to be risk seeking. In this regard, risk seeking means more than simply taking risk. It means being willing to accept a risk that is actuarially unfair, hoping to beat the odds that events will turn out favorably.

Standards for Risk at UBS

Standards for risk management include targets and goals that relate to accounting controls and include position limits and other risk-control mechanisms. UBS's self-study report tells us how the bank approached risk in respect to its new strategy.

To construct CDOs, UBS purchased MBSs, which were pools of mortgages already sliced and diced into risk tranches. These MBSs were warehoused, meaning held in inventory, while UBS engaged in the CDO production process. Production entailed further pooling equivalently rated tranches from different MBSs, and then engaging in further slicing and dicing of the newly created pools. This process, which included putting together the appropriate legal documentation, took time. From the time UBS acquired the MBSs until it sold them, the bank exposed itself to valuation risk in respect to the contents of its warehouse. Notably, UBS executed part of its strategy through a hedge fund subsidiary, Dillon Read Capital Management, an arrangement that figured into the risk it faced.

UBS's internal report tells us the bank judged that its risk profile would not change substantially, at least in 2006. The report further tells us that the bank did not institute operational limits on the CDO warehouse. In addition, it did not institute umbrella operational limits across the combination of the investment bank and Dillon Read, thus limiting overall exposure to securities, derivatives, and loans associated with the subprime sector.

Was this behavior rational, or did UBS irrationally ignore risk for psychological reasons? Notice that, although Oliver Wyman's review specifically identified subprime as providing significant revenue growth opportunities, it did not consider the implications for UBS's risk capacity. Did UBS not regard the implications for risk as important? If UBS was already induced to be risk seeking, then risk as an issue might have already been significantly downgraded as a priority.

CDOs are akin to families of mutual funds that hold bonds instead of stocks. Each member of the fund family, or tranche, holds bonds with a different degree of priority in the event of default from the priority of other tranches in the family. Investors pay lower prices for riskier tranches. Holders of the senior tranche are the most protected, but the existence of a "super-senior" tranche is also possible. If the CDO contains leverage, meaning that the issuer of the CDO borrowed money to purchase assets for the CDO, then some party must stand ready to absorb the losses once the holders of even the senior tranche receive no cash flows. Holders of the super-senior tranche play this role. Instead of paying to participate in the CDO, they receive payments that are analogous to insurance premiums.

As we shall see, UBS's investment banking unit did not ignore risk. They simply underestimated it. The investment banking unit did hold super-senior positions, and relied on rating agencies such as Moody's and S&P, to judge the risk of those positions. The self-study report mentions that in its VaR-based analysis, market risk control (MRC) relied on the triple-A rating of the super-senior positions to determine the volatility sensitivities they applied to super-senior positions. The report notes that until the third quarter of 2007, the five-year time series demonstrated very low levels of volatility sensitivities. In consequence, even unhedged super-senior positions contributed little to VaR-based results.

At various points in the book, the point will be made that statistical methodologies such as VaR or volatility sensitivities are not designed to take into account exceptionally adverse events. A decade earlier, for instance, overreliance on such measures contributed to the demise of hedge fund Long Term

Capital Management (LTCM), and lightning struck twice as UBS was a major investor in LTCM.

As is now well known, the triple-A ratings assigned to CDO tranches were highly flawed, and anybody who relied on ratings exclusively would have seriously underestimated the risk they faced. Notably, these ratings were readily available, and the self-study report makes clear that the investment bank's reliance on ratings was virtually exclusive. Think about how the total reliance on ratings was a manifestation of availability bias. This bias occurs when people depend on information that is readily available, but do not actively search for additional information that is less available.

As an indication of availability bias, consider that in analyzing the positions held by the bank, MRC did not carefully scrutinize—their term was "look through"—the CDO structure to analyze risks attached to the underlying collateral. Among the list of items MRC would have done well to examine on a regular basis, but instead overlooked, were Fair Isaac Corporation (FICO) scores, whether lien status was first or second, and the year in which the assets backing the securities had been sourced. Most importantly, MRC did not distinguish a CDO from an asset-backed security (ABS). This was particularly important as ABSs with a particular rating were of much higher quality than CDOs with the same rating.

According to the self-study, UBS made no attempt to develop a risk factor loss structure to capture more meaningful attributes related to the US housing market generally, such as defaults, loan to value ratios, or other similar attributes to statistically shock the existing portfolio.

Was it rational for UBS to make no attempt to investigate key statistics related to the US housing market, such as loan to value (LTVs), percentage of loans that featured 100% financing, limited-documentation loans, and default rates? Between 2001 and 2006, the following occurred: the LTVs of newly originated mortgages rose from 80% to 90%; the percentage of loans that were 100% financed climbed from 3% to 33%; and limited-documentation loans almost doubled, rising from 27% to 46%. These trends strongly suggest increasing risk during this period.[3]

With respect to the FIH, it is safe to characterize many of the subprime mortgages as Ponzi finance.[4] Was Ponzi finance as a concept part of the dialogue at UBS? The discussion in the self-study report strongly suggests the answer to be no. Nothing in the report appears to suggest that risk managers raised FIH-type questions about how to classify the securities that were part of their operations.

The self-study notes that UBS's CDO desk underestimated risk, in that it considered a super-senior position to be fully hedged if 2%–4% of the position was protected. In this regard, UBS erroneously judged that its hedged super-senior positions featured an associated VaR that was effectively zero.

To its surprise, by the end of 2007, the hedged positions contributed approximately 63% of total super-senior losses. It also had unhedged super-senior positions. These were retained for the purpose of executing future trades. However, these trades never materialized, and at the end of 2007, they contributed approximately 27% of total super-senior losses.

Unwarranted disappointment is the hallmark of excessive optimism, and unwarranted surprise is the hallmark of overconfidence. By every indication, UBS's investment banking group displayed excessive optimism and overconfidence.

Members of an organization with a strong RMC perceive and acknowledge that risk management is a valued activity. They are proactive about identifying and addressing risk issues within the organization, and from a human resource perspective, the managers to whom they directly report are good role models for risk management behavior.

To address the role model issue, consider which "risk style" was operative among key risk managers at UBS at the time. Given the decisions UBS made about risk limits, does "manager" come to mind as their style? Remember that the manager style seeks to balance the aggressive posture of maximizers against the prudence of conservators.

The absence of risk limits, the overreliance on credit ratings, and insufficient hedging of super-senior positions makes clear that UBS did not impart a strong "manager" risk style to their investment banking group. This was not a group that acted as if it were proactive about identifying and addressing risk issues within the organization, were averse to ambiguity about the probabilities they faced, and were concerned about concentrated positions. This was a group that instead behaved as if its risk style were "maximizer" and subject to severe psychological pitfalls.

INFORMATION SHARING AT UBS

The self-study report speaks of "complex and incomplete risk reporting." It tells us that instead of presenting a holistic picture of the risk situation of a particular business, the investment banking group instead siloed the risk.

Daniel Kahneman and Amos Tversky present strong evidence about the importance of framing when facing decision tasks involving risk. In particular, they draw our attention to decision-makers' reliance on mental accounting, which can leave them susceptible to narrow framing and opaque framing.

Framing is a critical part of risk management, and the report criticizes MRC for its poor communications with senior management. The report is particularly critical of MRC for not routinely putting numbers into the context of market fundamentals and the broad economy. As a result, when subprime positions began to deteriorate in value, MRC's silo-based thinking led them to assume, mistakenly, that the values of their other ABS positions would not be impacted.

According to the self-study report, MRC too frequently shared information that was overly complex and often out of date. Examples of what went wrong involved risk managers netting long and short positions, thereby obscuring the manner in which positions were structured, and not making the inventory of super-senior positions clear.

Information sharing takes place as part of group deliberations about which decisions to take. In the RMP framework, strong risk management behaviors include being willing to speak up in groups about risk issues and, if necessary, play the devil's advocate. The self-study report indicated that members of the investment bank senior management did not sufficiently challenge each other in relation to the development of their various businesses. The report singles out the fixed income strategy, in particular, for not having been subjected to critical challenge. The criticism was not just because the strategy did so poorly, but because it involved substantial investment in systems and in human and financial resources that the growth plans entailed.

Housing prices in the United States peaked in February 2006. During the first and second quarters of 2007, UBS began to experience losses on its inventories of MBS. However, the risk management team did not implement additional risk methodologies. The losses did not go unnoticed by senior management, who queried the CDO desk about those losses. In response, the CDO desk did provide what the self-study report calls "a relatively pessimistic outlook" for certain aspects of the subprime market. However, despite the pessimistic assessment, the MBS CDO business substantially added to its mezzanine residential MBS holdings. Moreover, the CDO desk prepared a paper to support the significant limit increase requests.

Was this a case of denial? Underweighting evidence that does not confirm a view being held is the essence of confirmation bias, and groupthink is collective confirmation bias.

INCENTIVES AND GOVERNANCE AT UBS

In theory, compensation provides managers with incentives to maximize the value of their firms. Incentive compensation frameworks (beyond base salary) often rely on a combination of (1) a bonus plan that relates to the short term and (2) equity-based compensation that relates to the long term.

A company with strong risk management structures establishes compensation programs that incorporate KRIs, meaning KPIs pertaining to risk. The self-study report tells us that UBS's compensation structure generally made little recognition of risk issues and did not adjust for other qualitative factors. This is just one more way in which the bank exhibited a weak RMS.

Keep in mind that fundamental value is based on discounted cash flow, where the discount rate reflects risk as well as the time value of money. Higher risk leads to a higher discount rate and, therefore, to lower discounted cash flows. UBS's compensation structure barely took risk issues into consideration and made little to no adjustment for risk. Therefore, employees had no direct incentive to focus on risk when making decisions, including decisions about positions involving subprime mortgages and their associated derivatives. Failing to attach sufficient importance to risk in the compensation structure was UBS's first major flaw in structuring incentives.

The self-study report tells us that UBS's remuneration structure, including bonuses, emphasized short-term P&L results over longer-term performance. This was a second flaw. To be sure, the compensation structure did feature an equity component, which did provide some indirect incentive to avoid risks that were detrimental to long-term value. The bonus focus, however, dominated. Bonus payments for successful and senior fixed-income traders, including those in businesses holding subprime positions, were significant. Particularly noteworthy is that UBS based bonuses on gross revenue after personnel costs, but did not take formal account of the quality or sustainability of earnings.

Finally, the self-study report indicates that the bank's reward system did not distinguish between whether returns were generated on the basis of skill or instead were based on routines such as exploiting UBS's comparatively low cost of funding in what were essentially carry trades. This was a third flaw in UBS's compensation system. No special arrangements were made for employees working in the businesses that held subprime positions.

MERRILL LYNCH

When you consider the three individual components of risk management, namely structure, culture, and behavior, UBS struggled with many of these classic risk management strategies. Keep this in mind as we now move on to a discussion about Merrill Lynch, the biggest player in the market for CDOs constructed with mortgage-related securities.

In November 2008, Merrill Lynch's described itself on its website as "a world leader in wealth management, capital markets and advisory companies with offices in 40 countries and territories and total client assets of approximately $1.5 trillion." The firm's customers are private clients, small businesses, and institutions and corporations. In terms of businesses, Merrill organized its activities into two interrelated segments, called respectively (1) Global Markets & Investment Banking and (2) Global Wealth Management. In November 2008, the firm's workforce comprised about 70,000 employees.

For most of its history, Merrill Lynch was among the best-known brokerage firms in the world, widely recognized for its use of a bull as its logo to denote bullishness. However, Merrill had also become one of the five major houses that collectively came to be known as "Wall Street." The other four were Goldman Sachs, Morgan Stanley, Lehman Brothers, and Bear Stearns. Only Goldman and Morgan Stanley survived the financial crisis as independent firms. In September 2008, Merrill Lynch sold itself to Bank of America in order to avoid bankruptcy.

Like UBS, Merrill did both wealth management and investment banking. Like UBS, Merrill's financial performance deteriorated in 2007. In October 2007, Merrill announced the largest loss in its history, $2.3 billion, which reflected a $7.9 billion write-down from its exposure to CDOs constructed with mortgage-related securities. During the first nine months of 2008, the firm recorded net losses of $14.7 billion on its CDO positions. Through October 2008, approximately $260 billion of Merrill's asset-backed CDOs had begun to default.

As was the case with UBS, these losses reflect Merrill's having had ineffective measures in place that failed to address psychological biases in its processes. As you read the chronology below, think about whether Merrill suffered from the same psychological biases that afflicted UBS or whether different biases were involved. Doing so will help you form your opinion about whether Merrill merited a passing grade on any of the three individual components for RMS, RMC, and RMB.

Planning at Merrill

To place Merrill's planning mistakes in context, we need to consider its financial situation before 2005. Merrill's performance was positive but well below those of its chief competitors, especially Goldman Sachs and Lehman Brothers. Its CEO from 2002 to 2008, Stanley O'Neal, constantly compared himself to Goldman and Lehman, and was less than pleased by the comparison. One of his former direct reports said that being in his office the day Goldman reported its earnings was not a good idea.[5]

In July 2004, Merrill reported that its second-quarter net income rose 10%, noting that its revenue was nearly flat. Notably, net revenue in the global markets and investment banking segment fell 7.3% percent. In a prepared statement, O'Neal stated, "We navigated through a progressively more challenging business environment during the second quarter."

Just a few months before, Lehman had been reporting outstanding performance for its investment banking, capital markets, and client services businesses, with record first-quarter income, net income rising by 39% from the prior year, and net revenue up by 84%, with Europe and Asia up by 57%.

Clearly Lehman's business environment was not as challenging as that of Merrill.[6]

In interviewing former Merrill executives, the *New York Times* learned just how envious was Merrill of Lehman's performance. In their planning process, as they contrasted their own weak investment banking performance with the strong performance at Lehman, they focused on Lehman's ability to profit from the market for mortgages and mortgage-based products.[7]

Like other investment banks, Merrill had a mortgage desk and did CDOs. In 2002, Merrill ranked in fifteenth place for doing CDO deals. During its planning, the firm decided to ramp up in a way that would catapult them from fifteenth place to first, a feat they accomplished by 2007. They planned to do so by becoming heavily involved in the entire supply chain: this meant becoming involved in originating mortgage loans, administering the associated paperwork, packaging mortgages into CDOs, and then selling the CDOs to investors.

To put its strategy into place, Merrill made a series of acquisitions. In the two years between January 2005 and January 2007, the firm acquired a dozen residential or commercial mortgage-related companies or assets. It made purchases around the world for commercial properties, a loan servicing operation, and a mortgage lender. Its largest acquisition was the domestic subprime lender First Franklin, which meant that it would concentrate its strategy in the riskiest segment of the housing market, where the probability of default by borrowers was highest.

Standards for Risk at Merrill

When O'Neal took over as CEO, the culture of the organization could be described as having a high coefficient of loss aversion, in the sense of not being able to "stomach" large losses.[8] In implementing a more aggressive CDO strategy, O'Neal needed to change the organization's standards for risk. He did this in a variety of ways, beginning with the firm's VaR. Merrill employees at the time recall his being angry that VaR was too low and needed to be increased.[9]

Merrill's desk was headed by a trader named Jeff Kronthal. Kronthal shared O'Neal's view that Merrill's standards for risk were excessively conservative and that its risk limits were unnecessarily constraining. At the same time, Kronthal was much more concerned about mortgage security-related left-tail risk than O'Neal, especially when it came to the bank's own exposure as opposed to the exposure faced by its customers.

Where O'Neal was anxious for Merrill to accept increased left-tail exposure, Kronthal was reticent. In mid-2006, Kronthal ensured that Merrill's total exposure to MBSs in its CDO warehouse was in the range $5 billion to $6 billion, an amount that was manageable and did not expose the firm to undue risk. Yet there were tensions. Kronthal reported to Dow Kim, who was in charge of all fixed income. O'Neal maintained constant pressure on Kim for not generating as much profit as Lehman or Goldman.[10] In turn, Kim pressured Kronthal.

Kronthal felt squeezed from Kim above and from below by the head of his CDO desk, Chris Ricciardi. Before joining Merrill, while at Prudential, Ricciardi was part of a group that had first constructed CDOs using securitized pools of mortgages. Where Kronthal was cautious, Ricciardi was aggressive. Ricciardi also had strong support from Kim and O'Neal.

In 2006, Merrill swamped the competition, originating $38.9 billion in mortgage-related CDOs. In contrast, second-ranked Morgan Stanley did just $21.3 billion. All told, Merrill's CDO machine earned more than $1 billion in fees between 2003 and 2006. However, Ricciardi left Merrill in 2006. Kim and O'Neal wanted to replace him with someone having the same aggressive posture. After Ricciardi left, Kim instructed the rest of the team to do "whatever it takes" not just to maintain market share but also to achieve the number one ranking.[11]

Shortly thereafter, Kronthal made a presentation outlining the risks to Merrill's fixed income desks and suggesting that they be less aggressive about mortgage-related securities, not more. Shortly thereafter, O'Neal fired Kronthal and his entire team.[12]

According to the FCIC report, CDO activity intensified in the second half of 2006 and into 2007, despite the fact that housing prices had peaked in February 2006. The FCIC described the market as having become "self-fueling," suggesting that senior executives at banks like Merrill did not accept, or perhaps understand, the inherent risks. Moreover, although mezzanine tranches were being purchased by other CDOs, and equity tranches were being sold to hedge funds, senior CDO tranches were being retained by the firms that arranged the securities. Was this is an activity that Kronthal would have put standards in place to prohibit? What does this suggest about the effectiveness of policies and procedures (RMS), whether there was care to make risk issues salient and to address policy breaches when they occur (RMC), and whether there was monitoring for signs of overconfidence that the organization judges that it is immune to risk (RMB)?

The FCIC describes this period as "the madness." Merrill, and some other banks, moved into synthetic CDOs, which were constructed not from MBSs per se, but from credit default swaps on mortgage instruments. Synthetic CDOs made it easier for investment banks and CDO managers to create CDOs more quickly, which they did. As it turned out, these banks also retained much of the risk of those synthetic CDOs by keeping the super-senior and triple-A tranches. Ask yourself whether "madness" behavior conforms to Merrill decision-makers having elevated levels of testosterone, in accordance with euphoria and the "winner model."

As for mezzanine tranches, the arrangers sold these to other CDOs. The FCIC tells us that there appeared to have been "a Streetwide gentleman's agreement: you buy my BBB tranche and I'll buy yours."[13]

According to the FCIC, Merrill continued its CDO activity in the face of signals the market was weakening. Up until the end of 2005, Merrill had effectively hedged itself against mortgage defaults by purchasing credit default swaps from American International Group (AIG). AIG had already insured $9.9 billion of Merrill's CDOs. However, at the end of 2005, AIG became less willing to provide this protection, explicitly stating that it had concerns about the mortgage market. During the spring of 2006, AIG actually stopped insuring even the very safest, super-senior CDO tranches. In response, Merrill switched to the monoline insurance companies as a substitute.

In the summer of 2006, the bank's management noticed that its biggest competitor in underwriting CDOs, which happened to be Citigroup, had chosen to take more super-senior tranches of CDOs onto its own balance sheet at razor-thin margins. Doing so meant that in effect, it was subsidizing returns for investors in the BBB-rated and equity tranches. How did Merrill respond? In a phrase, they raced Citigroup to the bottom, by increasing the size of their CDO warehouse and super-senior positions without insurance from either AIG or the monolines.

The FCIC tells us that in September 2006, Merrill did not pull back on its CDO activities, even when one of its own analysts issued a report with the warning that exposure to subprime loans could result in a sudden decrease in earnings, as demand for mortgages assets could quickly decline. Similarly, Merrill's $1.3 billion acquisition of subprime lender had puzzled analysts because the market for subprime loans was declining at the time.

Can you think of any particular psychological bias that might have induced Merrill to downplay negative information about subprime? Would you say that something similar occurred at UBS?

Information Sharing at Merrill

Poor information sharing accentuated Merrill's inadequate risk management practices. Indeed, senior Merrill's senior management actively worked to downplay concerns about excessive risk. The key personnel in this regard were Ahmass Fakahany and Osman Semerci. Fakahany oversaw risk management at Merrill, and loosened internal controls. Semerci ran the firm's bond unit and oversaw its mortgage operation.

Fakahany modified the role of risk management in Merrill's organizational structure. The structure had featured a risk manager with access to the board, who occupied a front office position on the trading floor. This manager had been reporting directly to the chief financial officer (CFO). The reporting arrangement allowed the CFO to balance the risk management perspective against traders' perspectives, which tended to be more aggressive. The new structure removed risk management from the trading floor and demoted the position so that there was no longer a direct reporting line to the CFO. Notably, doing so is exactly the opposite of what the risk typology framework recommends about using embedded risk managers to address strategy risk.[14]

Semerci's mandate was to increase Merrill's subprime mortgage operations, and in this regard he was successful. Under Semerci, Merrill's holding of subprime mortgages rose from a range of $5–8 billion in July 2006 to $55 billion in July 2007.

Former Merrill executives describe Semerci as an intimidating person who silenced anyone who warned about the risks the firm was taking. He was reported to have walked the floors holding a pen and a clipboard, taking notes on what he did not like. In respect to information sharing, he is alleged to have chastised traders who communicated their concerns to risk management officials. The *New York Times* quotes an anonymous former Merrill executive who stated: "There was no dissent…so information never really traveled."[15]

O'Neal structured information sharing at Merrill so that executives would communicate only with him about their businesses, not with each other. According to journalists Bethany McLean and Jeo Nocera, O'Neal was "intolerant of dissent," "quick to take offense," and as a result his executives trembled if they needed to deliver bad news to him, as he was prone to kill the messenger. McLean and Nocera also tell us that O'Neal rarely asked for input when making a decision and did not tolerate being challenged, once he had made the decision.[16]

O'Neal finally got the information he needed, but not until September 2007 when markets weakened and it was much too late for Merrill to change course. He got the information from a risk manager, John Breit, who Fakahany had taken off the trading floor and demoted in the restructuring of the risk management function.[17] O'Neal called in Breit to ask for his perspective. Breit gave him a general idea about the magnitude of the losses (at least $6 billion), told him that the mortgage desk did not grasp the underlying issues, that VaR did not capture the risk, that the underlying credit quality was wrong, and that the protection which Merrill had bought from the monolines was useless because the monolines were going to be insolvent. This time, O'Neal did not kill the messenger.

INCENTIVES AT MERRILL

In theory, compensation provides managers with incentives to maximize the value of their firms. Compensation frameworks often rely on a combination of a bonus plan that relates to the short term, and equity-based compensation that relates to the long term. Incentives and KRIs are important risk management structures. As you read the discussion below, think about what the information implies about the strength of the structures at Merrill.

Did Merrill pay CEO Stanley O'Neal for performance? It certainly paid him well when the firm did well. Moreover, its board did fire him when losses began to mount. However, overall O'Neal made out well. He received $70 million in compensation over the four years he was CEO, and his severance package was worth $161 million.

Like UBS, Merrill's compensation systems emphasized short-term profitability and underemphasized risky decisions that destroy value. McLean and Nocera tell us that Semerci's bonus was based on the production of CDOs. There is an important general issue here involving misalignment of incentives in the financial sector. The economic theory of looting explains how poorly structured incentives can lead senior executives to extract large private value by bankrupting their organizations through excessive risk taking.[18] William Black, former financial regulator and now academic, applies looting theory to explain the root causes of the savings and loan (S&L) crisis in the United States during the 1980s. He emphasizes that when executives extract value by bankrupting their organizations, they rapidly grow the assets of their firms.[19]

In looting theory, a key problem with incentives involves limited downside risk to executive compensation, combined with large short-term upside and the absence of clawbacks associated with subsequent losses. In regard to Merrill Lynch, O'Neal eventually fired Semerci, who did not return his bonus. As emphasized by Black, Merrill's assets grew rapidly during Semerci's tenure.[20]

Academics routinely criticize CEO compensation for being insufficiently variable with performance. This might have been the case at Merrill Lynch. That being said, my sense is that simply structuring better compensation packages would not have prevented Merrill from taking the value destructive decisions that it did. The value-destroying decisions stemmed not from conflicts of interest so much as from psychological excesses associated with high reference points, excessive optimism, overconfidence, opaque framing, and confirmation bias.

Incentives failed to prevent Merrill Lynch from making bad judgments about mortgage-related risk and choosing positions that exposed it to unwarranted risk. In this they were not alone, as many financial institutions behaved similarly. At the market level, the failure of incentives upstream in the mortgage process allowed unaffiliated mortgage brokers downstream to originate very risky subprime mortgages but not hold the risk themselves, instead passing it upstream to large financial institutions.

Nobody went to jail for decisions leading to the global financial crisis. Many are surprised, as they perceive fraud to have been committed in promoting very risky securities as being safe. Some have called for bringing criminal cases against executives, and not just the banks they worked for. Doing so would certainly send a signal about incentives. By the same token, not doing so also sends a signal—perhaps the wrong signal.[21]

CLOSING THOUGHTS

There are two striking similarities between the psychological issues that drove risk taking at UBS and Merrill Lynch. The first involves the early stages of their chronologies, when both firms viewed themselves as mediocre relative to their top competitors. In this respect, both aspired for the top ranking. From the perspective of SP/A theory, both established high aspiration levels and attached great importance to achieving aspiration. Viewed through the lenses of SP/A theory and the dual focal point framework, high aspirations relative to where they were induced them to take high risk.

The second similarity involves groupthink, which was prevalent at both firms. It was particularly pronounced at Merrill, where intimidation was used like a club. To be sure, neither firm had strong risk management structures, cultures, and behaviors; however, Merrill seemed intent on decimating its risk management infrastructure.

In addition to high aspirations and groupthink, processes at UBS and Merrill were plagued by excessive optimism and overconfidence about housing prices and mortgage default rates. These biases represent the state of euphoria that is emphasized by the FIH, and what behavioral finance describes as "market sentiment." Viewed through the lens of the FIH, the combination of high aspirations, groupthink, and biases such as excessive optimism and overconfidence led UBS and Merrill to be active players in the markets for speculative and Ponzi finance.

CHAPTER 9

CHEATING ISSUES AT S&P AND MOODY'S

IN THE EARLY 2000S, THERE WERE THREE MAJOR RATING FIRMS IN THE United States: S&P, Moody's, and Fitch. Rating agencies have reputational capital to protect: the opinions they express only have value if people believe those opinions are accurate indicators of creditworthiness. Therefore, in the lead-up to the global financial crisis, how in the world could two of these firms, S&P and Moody's, have assigned triple-A ratings to many mortgage-related securities that plummeted in value when the housing bubble burst?[1]

To understand how problematic decisions were made at both S&P and Moody's, this chapter provides a historical account of the two rating firms and their role in the lead-up to the financial crisis. To make psychological sense of the associated events, we apply psychological concepts developed earlier in the book. In this regard, we want to understand the psychological dimension at three levels: at the level of individual decision-makers, at the level of the organization, and at the level of the overall financial system.

At the level of individual decision-makers, we want to apply SP/A theory, prospect theory, personality, and biases. Doing so helps identify the roles possibly played by fear, hope, aspiration, the framing of gains and losses, risk styles, and a host of pitfalls. Moody's and S&P are not amorphous decision bodies, and real people made real decisions to take on real risks.

At the level of the organization, we want to view the chronology of events through the lenses of process-pitfall, the dual focal point framework, and risk management structure, culture, and behavior. Doing so enables us to understand how issues pertaining to individual psychology became manifest within organizational dynamics.

At the level of the financial system, we want to apply the FIH to relate events at the ratings firms to financial innovation, Ponzi finance, and asset-pricing bubbles.[2]

The last part of the chapter introduces some new psychological concepts that relate to self-control and cheating.

Rating Firms: History and Context

Moody's is a publicly traded company. In 2011, approximately 70% its revenues were generated by ratings. In calendar year 2011, Moody's was an international company with aggregate sales of $2.3 billion, assets of $2.9 billion, and operating income of just under $1 billion.[3]

S&P is part of the publishing firm McGraw-Hill. In this regard, S&P's ratings business is embedded within the larger S&P financial information enterprise that compiles and publishes financial indexes such as the well-known S&P 500 index. In 2011, S&P's ratings unit had revenues of $1.8 billion. Like Moody's, S&P is an international business, and roughly half of their revenue from ratings comes from outside the United States.

The story of Moody's began in 1909 when John Moody began publishing a manual that rated bonds issued by railroad companies, which he sold to investors who bought bonds. In 1916, the Poor's Publishing Company began issuing ratings, and in 1922, so did the Standard Statistics Company. In 1941, Standard Statistics and Poor's Publishing merged to form Standard and Poor's (S&P).

At present, it is common practice for the organizations that issue bonds to pay the rating firms to provide ratings. Some suggest that this arrangement involves a conflict of interest, as competitive pressures might lead ratings firms to provide ratings that are unduly optimistic, with the purpose of securing more business. In this regard, it is worth remembering that early on it was investors, not issuers, who paid the ratings firms.

During the 1930s, regulators of commercial banks began requiring that these banks only value their holdings of investment-grade bonds at par. Bonds that were below investment grade needed to be marked to market. This requirement was the beginning of a game changer for the rating agencies, as it was they who determined whether or not a bond was investment grade. After the SEC was created in 1934, federal bank regulators required that regulated banks only hold investment grade bonds in their portfolios. This requirement served to induce banks' investments to appear more prudent, and the delegation of authority from the regulators to the ratings firms conferred enormous power on these firms. Their opinions effectively became the rule of law.

Over time, state regulators of insurance firms, federal regulators of pension plans, and the SEC as regulator of securities firms all followed suit in relying on rating firms' opinions. During the late 1960s and the early 1970s, ratings firms transitioned from an "investor pays" business model to an "issuer pays" model. This change opened the door to the possibility of issuers "gaming the system," possibly making side payments in exchange for favorable ratings. Despite the possibility, before 2000, no major media coverage arose suggesting that this was a cause for concern.

In the early 2000s, there were three major ratings firms—S&P, Moody's, and Fitch—and a handful of about seven other smaller ratings firms. All three of the big players, and a few of the smaller players were designated by the SEC as "nationally recognized statistical rating organizations" (NRSRO). Only ratings from NRSRO firms could be used in the determination of the capital associated with the capital requirements of securities firms (the net capital of broker-dealers).

Moody's and S&P entered the 2000s as part of an effective oligopoly made possible by their NRSRO designations and the mandates conferred by the regulators. Neither the firms nor the NRSRO system attracted much attention until the Enron bankruptcy, which occurred despite Enron's bond ratings having been investment grade until the five days that preceded the event.

The ensuing public attention on rating firms resulted in passage of the Credit Rating Agency Reform Act (CRARA) of 2006. The CRARA instructed the SEC to be transparent about designating new NRSROs, but insisted that the SEC refrain from interfering with the business models used by existing NRSROs.

By this time housing prices had peaked, and much damage had already been done in ratings of CDO tranches constructed with mortgage-related instruments. Before 2000, there was little evidence of these firms having seriously biased their bond ratings in the face of competing with each other. However, the situation changed dramatically during the housing bubble.

The FCIC report tells us that in 2006, $600 billion worth of subprime mortgages were originated, comprising just under 25% of the mortgage market. Before 2004, that percentage had not exceeded 11%. By 2009, of the mortgages originated between 2005 and 2007 that were initially rated triple-A, less than 10% of those that were either Alt-A or subprime were impaired. However, for triple-A rated tranches of CDOs it was another story, as by 2009 more than 50% were impaired. For ratings that were double-A and below, by 2009 most were impaired.

In February 2013, the Department of Justice filed suit against McGraw-Hill arguing that its ratings of residential mortgage-backed securities (RMBS) and CDOs underestimated default risk, and thereby damaged investors who relied on its ratings.[4] An attorney representing S&P suggested that the Justice Department suit lacked merit because there was no evidence that issuers explicitly demanded fraudulently high ratings.[5] In February 2015, S&P settled with the Justice Department and agreed to pay a record level fine of $1.37 billion. Although the Justice Department had initially sought an admission of wrongdoing from S&P, in the end it relented. As you read the chronology below, you can form your own opinion about this aspect of the resolution.

Together with several states, the Justice Department also indicated that it was contemplating filing suit against Moody's. In the discussion below, I mostly focus on S&P, and then at the end of the chapter relate the issues to Moody's.[6]

OPERATING FRAMEWORK AT S&P

To understand how the disconnect between ratings and credit quality materialized, consider the judgment and decision framework at S&P. S&P's Structured Finance Department establishes the ratings of RMBS and CDOs. In respect to RMBS, S&P's starting point for an RMBS rating process occurs when the RMBS issuer of a mortgage-related security contacts S&P to discuss a particular security. In doing so, the issuer e-mails the relevant statistical information on the underlying mortgage pool, the size of which varies from several hundred to several thousand. An S&P quantitative analyst then evaluates the proposal using a system S&P calls LEVELS, an acronym for Loan Evaluation & Estimate of Loss System. LEVELS generates summary information for both the pool and the tranches associated with the proposal.

The quantitative analyst submits the results from LEVELS for sign-off to a committee of analysts. Subject to possible modifications, the proposal is then passed to a lead rating analyst responsible for preparing a confidential report for presentation to an RMBS rating committee as well as a document to become public information once the deal gets closed. The main committee members are the chair and a second senior analyst, who sign off after they are satisfied. The lead rating analyst then sends a letter to the RMBS issuer with the rating results for the different tranches and permission to publish the information on the RMBS closing date. S&P then publishes the ratings on its own website.

S&P's process for CDOs is similar to that for RMBS. The default probability associated with each CDO tranche is required to meet a designated minimum that is rating specific. To evaluate a CDO, S&P uses what they call their "CDO Evaluator." The rating on the underlying asset is the main input for the CDO Evaluator and the most important factor for determining the rating of the CDO's tranches. The results of the evaluation are then placed into a Ratings Analysis Methodology Profile (RAMP).

For cash CDOs, a cash flow analysis using a procedure called Genesis was also conducted, leading to a report called a "Quantitative Ramp" (Q-Ramp). The Q-Ramp indicates whether the estimated CDO cash flows appear to be sufficient to satisfy the obligations to the investors holding the various tranches.

In doing so, S&P methodology involves the expected (or scenario) number of defaults for each tranche (SDR) not exceeding a corresponding breakeven default counterpart (BDR). The BDR for a tranche is the maximum number of defaults on the underlying CDO securities consistent with the CDO tranche fulfilling its promised cash flow. The primary inputs for determining the SDR are the underlying cash flows associated with the CDO's collateral and the default correlations across the various members of the associated pool. For a cash CDO to pass the Q-ramp, the SDR for every tranche has to meet its BDR threshold.

In the lead-up to the financial crisis, the CDO rating committee consisted of three members. As with RBMS, the lead analyst would present a proposal to the committee, based on RAMP and Q-Ramp. Although the committee would typically offer comments, which the lead analyst would take up with the issuer, it was rare for the committee to revisit a proposal. On the CDO closing date, S&P prepared a letter, similar to what they did with RMBS.

Typically, it is the investment banks representing the arranging entities that are S&P's Structured Finance Department's main customers. In this regard, rating fees are typically passed through to the investors who purchased the tranches. In the lead-up to the financial crisis, S&P's fee for rating a nonprime RMBS was $150,000, for a cash CDO up to $500,000, and for a synthetic CDO up to $750,000. After issuing a rating, S&P continued to monitor the rated security, and in the case of CDOs charged $50,000 for providing surveillance.

The Structured Finance Department was an important profit center for S&P, which in turn was an important profit center for McGraw-Hill. In this regard, fees from rating RMBS and CDOs were a significant contributor.

START OF A RACE TO THE BOTTOM

There is a good argument to be made that when it came to mortgage-related securities, S&P and Moody's engaged in a race to the bottom.[7] That race might have begun in earnest in August 2004 when Moody's introduced a new credit-rating model. One of the main innovations of the new model was relaxing a condition that penalized concentrated risk, a so-called "undiversification penalty." Relaxing this condition permitted Moody's to increase their ability to provide top ratings for mortgage-related securities.

According to Douglas Lucas, who was head of CDO research at UBS Securities LLC in New York, Moody's responded to pressure from Wall Street. Lucas is quoted as having said, "I know people lobbied Moody's to accommodate more concentrated residential mortgage risk in CDOs, and Moody's obliged."[8]

One week later, S&P moved to revise its own methods. Consider S&P against the backdrop of its parent organization, McGraw-Hill Companies. According to reports that appeared in the *Wall Street Journal*, CEO and

Chairman Harold McGraw established unrealistic profit goals for his organization.[9] The suggestion was that because McGraw-Hill had been suffering financially in other areas, it exerted pressure on S&P to expand by 15% to 20% a year. McGraw-Hill's financial services unit, which includes S&P, generated 75% of McGraw-Hill's total operating profit in 2007, up from 42% in 2000. In 2007, the ratings business generated a third of McGraw-Hill's revenue.

With respect to the last paragraph, keep in mind that SP/A theory tells us that setting high aspirations and attaching great importance to achieving success predisposes people to take high risk. Likewise, the dual focal point framework tells us that when an organization's resources lie below its aspirations, but well above its survival point, then it will be inclined to take high risk.

The complaint that the Justice Department filed against McGraw-Hill provides much detail about judgment and decision-making within S&P's Structured Finance Department. Below I summarize some of the highlights, and ask readers to reflect on the information with a critical eye.

Decision-Making in Structured Finance at S&P

Personalities are important. Between June 1999 and 2007, the Structured Finance Department's executive managing director at S&P was Joanne Rose, and she also led its Structured Finance Leadership Team (SFLT). Reporting to Rose was the head of the Global CDO group that rated CDOs (Richard Gugliada from 1999 to 2005 and then Patrice Jordan from 2005 to 2007), Frank Raiter, who until 2005 headed the RMBS group; Thomas Gillis, who headed the Criteria and Research group; and Gale Scott, who until 2008 headed the commercial mortgage-backed security (CMBS) group. One additional name to mention is David Tesher, a key decision-maker reporting to the head of the Global CDO group. During the spring of 2004, most of these individuals deliberated the making of an important change in the way in which Structured Finance assigned ratings.

At the heart of the change were two concepts, which they respectively called "market insight" and "rating implications." Market insight involved directly soliciting information about ratings from interested parties, namely investors in the product, investment bankers, and issuers, to obtain a 360-degree perspective.

Up until that point, S&P did not consult with their clients about what rating they would assign. Neither did the firm follow a rating process that explicitly took into account the implications of their ratings for S&P's market share and profitability. But now there was a proposal on the table to make changes.

Not everyone at the meeting favored the changes. Raiter, the head of RMBS at the time, e-mailed Gillis, complaining that rating implications had little to do with the search for truth, and saying that he was troubled by the implications of what "market insight" implied, asking if this meant that they would review proposed criteria changes with investors, issuers, and investment bankers? His e-mail went unanswered.

What might we conclude about the strength of RMB at S&P? In thinking about this question, remember that members of an organization with strong RMB attach great importance to active devil's advocacy and resistance to the bending of rules for the sake of accomplishing goals.

In July 2004, Rose and Gillis circulated a memo effectively adopting all the proposals to which Raiter had objected. A month later, Scott, who headed CMBS, e-mailed Gugliada, the head of Global CDO, cc'ing Jordan, Gillis, and Tesher, saying, "We are meeting with your group this week to discuss adjusting criteria for rating CDO's of real-estate assets this week because of the ongoing threat of losing deals."

Gugliada, who was a member of the SFLT, replied to Scott saying, "SFLT is aware of the competitive threats that Moody's is taking in CDOs and has authorized us to take certain actions." Gugliada also wrote, "OK with me to revise criteria." Notably, in November 2005, on its website, S&P claimed that its internal rules prohibited it from sacrificing its impartiality for commercial interest. The CDO Strategic Plan from January 2006 speaks of using criteria and analytical tools to meet the interests of players in the market to "ensure that S&P will continue to be the one agency rating the largest share of transactions." The document explicitly states, "Criteria is one of the key competitive elements among the main rating agencies."

ADJUSTMENT, LIMITATION, AND DELAY IN THE RATING OF RMBS AND CDOs

Over the next three years, S&P engaged in a number of practices to implement its rating implications/market insight approach. In respect to RMBS, it was strategic in its decision to update the database it used in LEVELS, with the version at the time being labeled 5.6. The data used in 2004 was at least five years old and employed default probabilities based on a sample size of 166,000 mortgage loans that were exclusively first-lien, fixed rate, and prime. Of course, these default probabilities were too low to apply to many Alt-A and subprime mortgage loans, which grew rapidly during 2004 through 2007.

As it happens, by 2002, S&P had acquired a much richer database with a sample size of 642,000 residential loans that had been originated between 1971 and 2001. Moreover, the new data featured much riskier loans than the data then in use. In mid-2004, S&P built an experimental version of LEVELS, version 6.0, which incorporated the new data. It announced on its website that it was planning to release the new version at the end of 2004, to be applied to all new deals beginning in January 2005.

Version 6.0 produced default probabilities for Alt-A and subprime that were higher than those produced by version 5.6. The result was lower support levels for triple-A tranches from subordinated tranches, and lower loss coverage as measured, say, by the ratio of collateral value to senior-note obligations. The implication of switching to version 6.0 was lower ratings for Alt-A and subprime MBS, and therefore less profit potential to issuers, all else being the same. Market insight would reveal grumpy clients with the rating implication being the incentive for them to shop for higher ratings from competitors.

S&P did not implement version 6.0 in January 2005. At a meeting in February 2005, Raiter proposed moving to version 6.0 as planned, as it provided a more accurate assessment of loss coverage. He then received an e-mail explaining that doing so would have negative rating implications. In fact, S&P never adopted LEVELS 6.0 with the new data. The firm simply updated the earlier versions with an eye to staying competitive with Moody's on support levels. A sanitized version of LEVELS 6.0 was eventually reset for release in March 2007.

For CDO deals, S&P used its CDO Evaluator strategically in order to achieve market share goals, through adjustment, limitation, and delay. In mid-2004, S&P had the dominant market share for noninvestment-grade cash CDOs, but a smaller market share for investment-grade synthetic CDOs. At this time, S&P analysts in the CDO group became aware that their assumptions were inconsistent with historical data.

With a rating implications mind-set, they sought to revise the CDO Evaluator to preserve market share in noninvestment-grade CDOs and increase market share in the investment-grade synthetic CDOs. Achieving both goals with reasonable assumptions turned out to be easier said than done. The CDO group experimented with a version of the Evaluator they called E3, which they planned for release in July 2005; the current version was E2.4.3.

By this time Jordan had replaced Gugliada as head of Global CDO. That July, Bear Stearns sent an e-mail to Jordan and her team saying that the switch from E2.4.3 to E3 would eliminate a competitive advantage for S&P relative to Moody's and Fitch. The e-mail was forwarded to Rose, along with similar negative insight from the market, and the rollout of E3 was subsequently delayed so that, in Jordan's words, it could be "toned down."

On its website, S&P promoted itself as having an integrated perspective because its surveillance group monitored the assets forming the collateral in the CDOs it rated. Apparently, the degree of integration was far from complete.

Between March and October 2007, S&P failed to adjust CDO Evaluator inputs for nonprime RMBS to reflect increased credit risk. In the autumn of 2006, the surveillance group noticed severe deterioration in the performance of nonprime RMBS. Specifically, losses to recent 2006 vintage RMBS in the first six to ten months of a 30-year loan were unprecedented. Members of surveillance communicated this information in person to new issue analysts. However, fearing negative rating implications, the analysts were reluctant to incorporate the information into their models, which prompted one member of the surveillance group to complain that analysts were using an approach in which the "end justifies the means." In consequence, this particular member of the surveillance group was not invited to subsequent meetings, an action that speaks to weak risk management behaviors.

To continue the chronology, a tension now developed within Structured Finance. Many in surveillance wanted to begin the process of downgrading in response to rising defaults. However, Gillis intervened to prevent downgrades of subprime RMBS out of concern that doing so would spill over to the risk assessment of CDO tranches that had those RMBS as collateral. At the end of one contentious meeting, the decision was reached to monitor internally, but not to do downgrades. The argument was that although delinquencies might be high, losses were low. In the follow-up to address the issue of facing credit deterioration, a new committee was convened, comprised of a majority who were not from surveillance, with the purpose of minimizing downgrades in the face of negative information.

By February 2007, there was general agreement that the housing bubble had burst, and the surveillance group recommended placing all recent vintage RMBS on Credit Watch. By April 2007, credit quality had seriously deteriorated. SD stands for "serious delinquency" and CS stands for "credit support." At this time, the average SD versus CS ratio for subprime exceeded 100%, meaning that severe delinquencies exceeded available credit support for hundreds of Alt-A and subprime RMBS tranches. The issue was spillover from subprime to the rest of the market, and at S&P Structured Finance, there was resistance to recognizing spillover.

At the time, analysts were complaining about what they were being asked to do. In one e-mail, an S&P analytical staffer e-mailed another to say that a new structured finance deal was "ridiculous," expressing the opinion that "we should not be rating it." The recipient of the e-mail replied, writing "we rate every deal" and adding that "it could be structured by cows and we would rate it."

The situation just described features the leaders at S&P Structured Finance being resistant to recognizing spillover, despite the opposing views of the analysts who were working in the trenches. What is important here? Is it the existence of a difference of opinion? Is it a failure to share information? Is it that analysts were improperly incentivized? Is it that the leaders at S&P Structured Finance were improperly incentivized? Is it that these leaders exhibited a very strong case of confirmation bias? Or is it something else entirely?

From a process-pitfall perspective, pitfalls infected every single process. The standards set were excessive, which induced risk-taking behavior by key decision-makers. This carried through to planning and to incentives. Information sharing came to exhibit intentional groupthink as a strategic choice. For that matter, the decision to have weak risk management structures, culture, and behaviors appears to have had a strong strategic flavor, in the sense of being purposeful. All of this was compounded by S&P's competitive dynamic with Moody's, and it is to Moody's that we now turn.

SIMILAR EVENTS AT MOODY'S

The FCIC report provides a view of how the same general events described above played out at Moody's. During the critical period 2004 through 2007, the deals Moody's rated rose from 220 to 717, having peaked at 749 in 2006. The value of those deals rose from $90 billion in 2004 to $326 billion in 2007, having peaked at $337 billion in 2006. Between 2000 and 2006, the revenues of Moody's Investors Service from structured products, including MBSs and CDOs, rose from 33% of Moody's Corporation's revenues to 44%.

The FCIC report faulted Moody's during this time period for having failed to account properly for the lower underwriting standards in mortgages and the possibility of a dramatic decline in home prices.

To be fair, before the bubble burst, financial professionals of all stripes experienced difficulty anticipating the decline in house prices. According to Jay Siegel, a former Moody's team managing director, in 2005 "Moody's position was that there was not a...national housing bubble....There may have been [state level] components of this real estate drop that the statistics would have covered, but the 38% national drop, staying down over this short but multiple-year period, is more stressful than the statistics call for."[10] A similar view was expressed by Roger Stein, a Moody's managing director, who put it this way: "Overall, the model has to contemplate events for which there is no data."[11]

Issues about rare left-tail events and the absence of data arose in earlier chapters. This is partly because statistical techniques that rely on historical data are much less reliable. Some risk managers advocate using Bayesian models to describe risk in these situations. Others note that conceptually, it is "uncertainty" rather than "risk" that describes the situation in question.

In this regard, Appendix C describes a formal framework for analyzing uncertainty as opposed to risk.

The failure to account for lower credit quality is another matter. It was not until late 2006, by which time Moody's had rated nearly 19,000 subprime securities, that the firm developed a model to account for the layered risks associated with these securities. Of all mortgage-backed securities Moody's had rated triple-A in 2006, it wound up downgrading 73% to below investment grade.

Moody's former managing director Jerome Fons made the following statements to the FCIC about deliberations at the firm on this issue: "I sat on this high level Structured Credit committee, which you'd think would be dealing with such issues [of declining mortgage-underwriting standards], and never once was it raised to this group or put on our agenda that the decline in quality that was going into pools, the impact possibly on ratings, other things.... We talked about everything but, you know, the elephant sitting on the table."[12] Only in late 2008 did Moody's replace its key CDO assumptions about asset correlations with a value that was two to three times higher than used before the crisis.

What psychological pitfall might explain why the Moody's group ignored the elephant sitting on the table? Hint: for someone holding the view that there was an unspoken issue, the presence of an elephant is disconfirming information. Moreover, in a group of like-minded individuals who value esprit de corps, ignoring the problem gives rise to mutual support.

Some Moody's employees told the FCIC that after going public, the firm's culture changed, whereby it increased the emphasis placed on revenues and market share. The FCIC report tells us that between 2000 and 2006, Moody's revenues increased from $602 million to $2 billion, and its profit margin correspondingly increased from 26% to 37%.

In 2006, the rating of asset-backed CDOs contributed more than 10% of the revenue from structured finance. At the same time, increases in staffing did not seem to parallel increases in the CDO group's workload, let alone the revenues generated by the group. Gary Witt, a former team managing director at Moody's who covered derivatives, told the FCIC: "We were underresourced, you know, we were always playing catch-up." Witt applied the phrases "penny-pinching" and "stingy" to describe the firm's management being reluctant to pay for experienced employees. He went on to say, "The problem of recruiting and retaining good staff was insoluble. Investment banks often hired away our best people. As far as I can remember, we were never allocated funds to make counter offers.... We had almost no ability to do meaningful research."

Mark Froeba, a former Moody's senior vice president told the FCIC, "When I joined Moody's in late 1997, an analyst's worst fear was that we would contribute to the assignment of a rating that was wrong. When I left Moody's, an analyst's worst fear was that he would do something, or she, that would allow him or her to be singled out for jeopardizing Moody's market share."

The FCIC quotes an internal memo from Moody's chief credit officer, Andrew Kimball, recognizing potential conflicts generated by the firm's focus on market share and short-term profitability. His memo begins by noting that Moody's has put safeguards in place to deter teams from lowering standards in order to achieve market share. However, the memo goes on to identify two areas of vulnerability. The first is that committees make rating decisions, with committees' incentives being tied to market share. The second is that, although Moody's has established methodologies in place that constrain what teams can do, nevertheless the methodologies provide teams with the latitude to pursue market share objectives.

Kimball's memo adds the following: "Organizations often interpret past successes as evidencing their competence and the adequacy of their procedures rather than a run of good luck.... [O]ur 24 years of success rating RMBS [residential mortgage–backed securities] may have induced managers to merely fine-tune the existing system—to make it more efficient, more profitable, cheaper, more versatile. Fine-tuning rarely raises the probability of success."[13] What biases might Kimball be suggesting in his remarks? If you think back to Chapter 4, illusion of control and overconfidence might come to mind.

Psychology and Competitive Bidding

Together, S&P and Moody's engaged in a race to the bottom in their competition to rate RMBS and CDOs. The classic game known as "dollar auction" underlies this type of behavior. This is a game I have played with my classes many times. My students loved when I opened up my wallet and removed a bill. Here is how dollar auction works.

I place a $20 bill before the class that I proceed to auction off to the highest bidder, who pays the amount of his or her final bid. The auction is oral, and the opening bid must be $1. Bidders can increase the most recent bid by either $1 or $2, but these are the only two choices. In addition, at the conclusion of the auction, the second-highest bidder must pay the amount of his or her bid, but in exchange receives nothing.

Usually this game begins with a buzz as people enter bids and the bids advance. At a stage when the bids have reached $14 or so, most bidders cease participating and only two bidders remain. Eventually one of the participants, let us say a male, enters a bid of $19. The second-highest bidder, let us say a female, now contemplates paying either $17 or $18 but receiving nothing in return. If she bids $20, and wins the auction, then she will net $0 instead of losing at least $17. And typically she does.

The male bidder now has a particularly uncomfortable choice. He can stop bidding and lose $19 or he can increase his bid to $21, and if he wins, lose only $1. Typically, that is what he does. Now she faces the same type of uncomfortable choice as he did, and typically she chooses to increase her bid to $22. The ensuing escalation typically results in guaranteed losses for both, as the bids go above $30, and then $40, and then $50 or more. The players may not have planned for it to work out this way, but the competitive pressure leads them to race each other to the bottom.

Ask yourself what leads people to escalate to the point where they are far worse off at the end of the game than they would have been had they dropped out when the bid reached $20? What leads them act so myopically? Is it their competitive juices? Are their hormone levels elevated to the point where they are not thinking clearly, but instead are in fight mode rather than flight mode? Are they risk seeking in the domain of losses, betting that the other bidder will drop out first, and soon at that?

PSYCHOLOGY AND CHEATING

S&P and Moody's did not just engage in a competitive race to the bottom. They did so by assigning ratings to financial securities that were excessively positive. Some might call this cheating.

Most people are predisposed to cheat when circumstances permit. That is what the academic evidence tells us. Moreover, it is easy to structure environments that will induce most people to cheat. When we provide people with the illusion of anonymity, by inducing them to think that they are less likely to be caught cheating, then they cheat more. Amazingly, people do not even need to be told that their identities are hidden. Simply making the room a bit darker or providing people with sunglasses will induce more cheating.[14]

The temptation to cheat is strong. Not everyone gives in. However, for most it is not easy because exercising self-control takes effort. In an experiment designed to make some people tired at a time when they face the temptation to cheat, we learn that being tired is associated with a higher incidence of cheating. Subjects who were induced to feel tired also appear to have been less aware of moral issues. However, those subjects who were identified as high in moral identity were able to resist the temptation to cheat, even when feeling depleted.[15]

To understand the psychology that underlies cheating behavior, we need to understand self-control. To understand the nature of self-control, we turn to the most famous psychological experiment about self-control, namely psychologist Walter Mischel's "marshmallow test."[16] In Mischel's experiment, young children were provided with a choice between accepting an immediate reward of a favorite treat, such as a marshmallow, or delaying gratification by waiting for several minutes and instead receiving two treats.

Mischel's experiment revealed a great deal about the techniques and tactics that children use to exercise self-control. Mischel tells us to think of our brains as having two systems, one "hot," representing the drives generated by our emotions, and the other "cool," representing the influence of reasoned thought. He identified the hot system as being associated with the older part of the brain, the limbic system, which we share in common with other forms of life. In contrast, he identified the cool system with the prefrontal cortex, which is uniquely human.

Mischel's findings apply to adults, not just to small children. In remarkable research, he tracked the children in his experiment as they got older, and discovered that those who were able to delay gratification in his experiment turned out to be generally more successful later in life.

Research in neuroscience is helping us understand the neurological basis for self-control. When the prefrontal cortex processes information about a contemplated action, that processing involves a region called the ventromedial prefrontal cortex (vmPFC). This part of the brain is particularly receptive to suggestions from the hot system. In people who are able to exercise self-control, another region of the prefrontal cortex, called the dorsolateral prefrontal cortex (DLPFC) becomes highly engaged.[17]

Mischel's original marshmallow test focused on children facing temptation in a room by themselves. Today we know that his findings about self-control apply to adults, not just small children; apply to how people exercise self-control in social settings, not just individual settings; and apply to cheating, not just delaying gratification to obtain a few more sweets.

Recent psychological research tells us that people crave respect from their social groups, or, if you like, their in-groups.[18] Notably, when some in-group members engage in observable cheating, the incidence of cheating by other in-group members increases.[19] Cheating and power are connected, especially when finance is involved: increased power is associated with increased cheating.[20] Cheating tends to be more frequent in situations in which wealth is amply abundant.[21]

Sometimes, there are ways to reduce the incidence of cheating. In other words, people can be nudged to cheat less. People who contemplate cheating generally respond to incentives and psychological cues. Increasing the perceived likelihood of being caught appears to reduce the frequency of cheating. Simply brightening a room can have a positive effect. Moreover, people are less inclined to cheat after they have been asked to recall past instances of immoral behavior on their part.[22]

Disappointment, however, awaits those who hope that stronger criminal sanctions will reduce incidents of cheating, such as price fixing. Executives contemplating price fixing and a host of other unethical business practices are often undeterred by strong legal measures.[23] What does give them pause for thought is the possibility of strong social sanctions associated with embarrassment to family, loss of social standing, and damage to careers. US Supreme Court Justice Louis Brandeis once remarked, "Publicity is justly commended as a remedy for social and industrial diseases. Sunlight is said to be the best of disinfectants; electric light the most efficient policeman."[24]

Certainly, S&P learned about publicity when facing the Justice Department suit. S&P paid a record fine, but did not acknowledge wrongdoing. Setting aside this issue for a moment, consider the critical role that S&P certainly played in the FIH dynamic. According to the FIH, during an economic boom financial innovation involving a shift toward more speculative and Ponzi finance fuels asset-pricing bubbles and sows the seed of financial instability. By weakening its criteria, S&P signaled to markets that securities that could be classified as speculative and Ponzi finance were very safe, in some cases as safe as Treasury securities. As we read in the last chapter, UBS relied on those ratings as being an accurate reflection of the underlying risk, and in consequence took heavy positions in RMBS. UBS was hardly alone.

CLOSING THOUGHTS

Rating firms rate risks. They have processes to gather information about risk, analyze the information, form judgments, and decide what to communicate to their clients and the market. Unlike UBS and Merrill Lynch, which are investment banks with trading desks, the business of rating firms is to make judgments about risk and communicate their opinions.

Despite their different tasks, the rating agencies succumbed to the same psychological issues as UBS and Merrill. Notably, high aspirations and groupthink were prevalent at S&P and Moody's, as were excessive optimism and overconfidence in respect to housing prices and mortgage default rates.

From a macroprudential perspective, it is important to recognize that because of the reliance that investors such as UBS placed on ratings, the practices at S&P and Moody's fueled market sentiment. Viewed through the lens of the FIH, these practices were major drivers of the buildup of speculative and Ponzi finance in the economy.

CHAPTER 10

GROUPTHINK AT FANNIE, FREDDIE, AND AIG

FANNIE MAE, FREDDIE MAC, AND AIG SPECIALIZE IN TAKING TAIL RISK, meaning the risk associated with rare, unfavorable events. During the housing bubble, all three accepted the risks of homeowners en masse defaulting on their mortgages. In the end, all paid dearly for taking bets that threatened their survival. Were they simply unlucky? Were they misled by rating agencies? Or, did they suffer from psychological pitfalls of their own?

For Fannie, Freddie, and AIG, shaping and taking risk is the essence of their businesses. Risk is their stock in trade, and therefore risk management within these firms is essential. This chapter develops the chronologies associated with these firms in the lead-up to and aftermath of the global financial crisis.

As the chronologies unfold, we want to determine whether the same psychological issues that surfaced in the previous two chapters were prevalent at Fannie, Freddie, and AIG. Analyzing the chronologies involves using the major psychological frameworks to raise the right questions about processes and pitfalls in general, and risk management structures, cultures, and behaviors in particular. From a macroprudential perspective, we will want to ask what role Fannie, Freddie, and AIG played in contributing to market sentiment, financial innovation, shifts in speculative and Ponzi finance, and subsequent financial instability.

BACKGROUND BRIEF ON FANNIE AND FREDDIE

Fannie Mae is a mnemonic for FNMA, which in turn is the acronym for the Federal National Mortgage Association. Fannie Mae dates back to the Great Depression, when in 1938 it was created as a government corporation, chartered by the Reconstruction Finance Corporation, and part of the federal budget. Its purpose was to provide liquidity to the mortgage market by purchasing loans that had been insured by the Federal Housing Administration.[1]

Fannie Mae remained as a wholly owned government corporation until 1968, when it became a government-sponsored entity (GSE), chartered by Congress. Under the new arrangement, it was both government sponsored and a publicly traded private corporation. In its new corporate form, Fannie Mae continued to purchase federally insured mortgages.

Fannie Mae purchased mortgages originated by nondepository institutions. Therefore, they did not purchase mortgages that were originated by thrifts. For this reason, the savings and loan industry asked Congress to charter another GSE to serve the thrift institutions. This Congress did, in 1970, when it chartered the Federal Home Loan Mortgage Corporation (FHLMC), which came to be called Freddie Mac.

The legislation that created Freddie Mac altered the GSE landscape by permitting both GSEs to participate in the market for conventional mortgages, meaning those that were not federally insured.[2] However, GSEs were restricted from purchasing loans that exceeded a certain size, the so-called "conforming loan limit." Both did so. For the next decade, Fannie Mae purchased mortgages for its portfolio. In 1981, it began issuing MBSs. Freddie Mac had begun securitizing the bulk of the mortgages from its inception.

When Fannie Mae purchased mortgages for its portfolio, it funded those mortgages by borrowing. It made money from the spread, meaning the difference between the return it received from the mortgages it held and the interest rate it paid on its debt. Fannie held these mortgages on its balance sheet, and assumed several risks in doing so, namely credit risk, interest rate risk, and the risk associated with the management and operations of holding the assets.

The GSE's securitization business involves securitizing mortgages into MBSs and guaranteeing these mortgages against default risk. Historically, MBSs were structured as undivided interest in a pool of mortgage loans. In this case, securitization is effectively a "swap" transaction, in which the mortgages are not actually held on the GSEs' balance sheets. What the swap accomplishes is a shift in interest rate risk from the GSE to the holder of the MBS, who then earns the associated return. The GSE guaranteeing the MBS continues to bear the credit risk and the associated management and operations risk. In return, the GSE receives a fee called a guarantee fee (or "g-fee"), the magnitude of which depends on a series of factors such as the volume of mortgages, the lender, and the underlying risk of the mortgage pool.

Despite the GSE acronym, Fannie Mae and Freddie Mac lacked the full-faith-and-credit government guarantee. Nevertheless, the government had a history of rescuing another GSE (the Farm Credit System in 1985). Therefore, the market perceived that the US government would stand behind Fannie

Mae and Freddie Mac in a crisis. For this reason, the securities they issued generally traded at narrow spreads above Treasuries, which amplified the spreads they earned. Shares of Fannie Mae and Freddie Mac traded on the New York Stock Exchange (NYSE) and generated high returns between 1981 and 2006: a dollar investment in either at the end of 2006 was worth roughly ten times more than had it been invested in the NYSE Composite index.

Fannie Mae's 1968 charter required it to maintain a portion of its mortgage portfolio to help serve the low-to-moderate income segment of the housing market. A similar statement applies to Freddie Mac, so that both GSEs were required to support affordable housing, effectively promoting policies that increased homeownership rates in the United States.

Notably, although the 1968 language specified that Fannie Mae support affordable housing, it also stipulated that it earn a "reasonable economic return." The language was sharpened in the 1992 Federal Housing Enterprises Financial Safety and Soundness Act to say that, while the return should be reasonable, it can be less than the next best alternative, or to use the language of the Act, "less than the return earned on other activities." The 1992 Act also identified mortgage goals for three specific groups, namely those with low and moderate incomes, those with very low incomes, and those residing in underserved areas. In 2004, Department of Housing and Urban Development (HUD) added the requirement that a fraction of each goal be met with home-purchase mortgages, as distinguished from refinancing.

Decisions and Consequences: The GSEs during the Housing Bubble

As you will remember, Moody's and S&P raced each other to the bottom by relaxing the criteria upon which they based their ratings. Against the backdrop of this race, Fannie and Freddie had a history of being judicious when setting standards for which loans that they would purchase from originating institutions. Standards, also known as criteria, for assessing risk of default included the borrower's FICO score, LTV ratio of the property, ratio of borrower's debt-to-income, the appraised value of the property, and the type of mortgage. For example, the GSEs generally set limits for the maximum LTV on loans that they would purchase. The charter acts for both specify that loans with an LTV ratio exceeding 80% percent must feature either private mortgage insurance or some form of protection against default.

During the mid-1990s, both Fannie Mae and Freddie Mac adopted automated underwriting systems to ensure that the mortgages they purchased would meet their criteria. Yet, there was slippage, as the GSEs did slide down the slippery slope of relaxed underwriting standards. Beginning around 1997, Fannie Mae purchased home mortgages with an LTV that exceeded 95%.

In 1997, those purchases comprised 3.3% of Fannie's total purchases of home loans. By 2000, the figure had increased to 4.4%. For Freddie Mac, the corresponding figures were 1.1% in 1997 and 6.1% in 2000.

In 2003, Fannie Mae and Freddie Mac's market share was approximately 57% of all mortgages purchased. At about this time, the two GSEs hit a turning point. Both were discovered to have violated accounting rules, and as a result faced corrections and fines. Their regulator was the OFHEO. In December 2003, Freddie agreed to pay a $125 million penalty and to correct not only its processes for internal controls, accounting, and governance but also its risk management. In September 2004, OFHEO discovered violations of accounting rules at Fannie, and in 2006 announced that the firm had overstated earnings from 1998 through 2002 by $11 billion.

In both cases, OFHEO contended that executives had engaged in accounting manipulation in order to increase their compensation. This effort took place against the backdrop of inept accounting that brings to mind the Keystone Cops. Amazingly, Freddie Mac's outside auditor noted that the firm's CFO had little understanding of financial accounting, generally accepted accounting principles (GAAP), and disclosure rules. Moreover, the CFO was heavily involved in the transactions that led to the firm's needing to restate its financials. At Fannie Mae, the head of internal audit had no experience or even formal training as an auditor. Fannie Mae's controller was not a certified public accountant.[3]

Executives who engage in accounting fraud to increase their compensation effectively cheat, and as you might have read in the earlier discussion of rating agencies, there is an important psychological dimension to cheating. Extreme cheating for firms such as the GSEs involves control fraud, whereby executives use a combination of growth and accounting manipulation to compensate themselves handsomely even as they take high-risk actions that are likely to destroy their firms in the long run. In this regard, there is a distinction to be made between cheating and looting. Accounting fraud is cheating, and when combined with high executive compensation is looting.

Between 2003 and 2006, as the housing bubble expanded, the GSE's management was highly distracted by the need to deal with accounting issues. Both firms engaged in expensive multiyear efforts to restate their financials and rebuild their internal controls. Senior officials at both GSEs were replaced: the list included CEOs and CFOs. The distraction came at an inopportune time, as competition for the securitization business from Wall Street heated up and the GSEs began to lose market share. By 2006, GSE market share had dropped to 37% from the 57% it held in 2003. On the other side of the coin, subprime private label MBSs and Alt-A MBSs grew rapidly: both were about 30 times greater in 2005 than they had been in 2001.

The changing nature of the mortgage market placed Fannie and Freddie in very uncomfortable circumstances. Countrywide Financial was the largest originator of mortgages in the United States, and Fannie's biggest source of mortgages. When Countrywide began loosening its underwriting criteria, Fannie did not purchase the new mortgages. As a result, while Countrywide sold 72% of its loans to Fannie in 2003, it only sold 45% in 2004 and 32% in 2005.

On June 27, 2005, Fannie Mae held an important strategic planning meeting, at which Thomas Lund, Fannie's head of single-family lending made a presentation to fellow senior officers. According to the FCIC, he told them, "The risk in the environment has accelerated dramatically." His list of increased risk factors included "proliferation of higher risk alternative mortgage products, growing concern about housing bubbles, growing concerns about borrowers taking on increased risks and higher debt, [and] aggressive risk layering."[4]

According to the FCIC report, Lund told his colleagues, "We face two stark choices: stay the course [or] meet the market where the market is." Staying the course entailed maintaining criteria and risk exposure. Meeting the market meant weakening criteria and increasing risk exposure.[5]

Here we have an important process-pitfall issue. From a process perspective, Lund framed Fannie's choice as part of a planning session. As for the pitfall, given its having lost market share, the two stark choices Lund outlined effectively amounted to accepting that loss (staying the course) or accepting the higher risks he identified (meeting the market where the market is).

In outlining the two choices, Lund drew his colleagues' attention to the significant obstacles Fannie would face if it chose to meet the market. He pointed to Fannie's lack of capability and infrastructure for structuring the types of riskier mortgage-backed securities that were being offered by its Wall Street competitors. He mentioned his concern that Fannie was unfamiliar with the new credit risks. He mentioned his concern that the expected rewards would not justify the associated risk. He mentioned his concern about regulatory issues associated with particular products.

At this meeting and others, Lund recommended that Fannie Mae study whether the current market changes appeared to be transitory or permanent. He also recommended to the board that Fannie dedicate resources to develop the capability to compete no matter what the mortgage environment might be. Lund told the FCIC that in 2005, the board adopted his recommendation that for the time being, Fannie would "stay the course" but develop capabilities to compete with Wall Street in nonprime mortgages.

The pressure was on. Citibank was the second-largest seller of mortgages to Fannie. In July 2005, executives from Citibank made a presentation to Fannie's board, warning them about another type of risk, the risk of becoming marginalized. In making their argument, Citibank proposed that Fannie begin to guarantee nontraditional products such as Alt-A and subprime mortgages. Not surprisingly, this proposal would benefit Citibank, which was a major originator of such mortgages, and it did. Over the next two years, Citibank increased its sales to Fannie Mae by approximately 25%.

In terms of the choice menu Lund had outlined, Fannie had begun to meet the market. By the end of 2005, the trend toward purchasing riskier loans was clear. Fannie's holdings of Alt-A loans at the end of 2005 were $181 billion, up from $147 billion in 2004 and $138 billion in 2003. Its holdings of interest-only mortgages were $75 billion, up from $12 billion in 2003. Its holdings of loans without full documentation, so called "liar loans," were $278 billion, up from $200 billion in 2003. Of course, there was overlap across these groups, but the pattern is clear.

Fannie CEO at the time, Dan Mudd, told the FCIC that it was a matter of relevance, saying, "If you're not relevant, you're unprofitable, and you're not serving the mission. And there was danger to profitability. I'm speaking more long term than in any given quarter or any given year. So this was a real strategic rethinking."[6]

Where was Fannie's resource position at the time relative to its survival point and its aspiration point? According to the dual focus point framework, Fannie might have been in the gray zone, in which its risk taking perspective could go either way depending on which focal point was operational.

At the end of 2005, Fannie had a total of $40 billion in capital. Its regulator, OFHEO, did not suggest that this level was inadequate. However in 2008, the Federal Housing Finance Agency (FHFA), which was OFHEO's successor, concluded that Fannie's capital was actually too low for the risk exposure it chose after 2004. Part of the issue about capital involved Fannie's financial statements having described risk exposure in a way that made it difficult to identify the firm's exposure to subprime. In particular, between 2005 and 2007, Fannie defined a "subprime" loan as one that was originated by a company or a part of a company that specialized in subprime loans. Doing so enabled Fannie to claim that its holdings of subprime loans constituted less than 1% of its business volume in 2005–2007, even as it reported that during this period, 5% of its conventional, single-family loans were to borrowers whose FICO scores were less than 620.

In January 2006, Fannie's board approved a strategic initiative to increase its penetration into subprime. The firm hired a new chief risk officer (CRO), Enrico Dallavecchia, whom board chair Stephen Ashley described as not having been hired to serve as "a business dampener." Which risk style might best capture what Ashley was looking for in a risk manager? By the process of elimination, I would suggest a manager, but one inclined to establish generous risk limits. I would certainly rule out conservator and pragmatist, and hope to rule out maximizer. Indeed, the chronology below does not support Dallavecchia being a maximizer.

That year, 2006, Fannie acquired $516 billion of loans, of which 13% had combined LTV ratios that exceeded 95%, 28% that lacked full documentation, and 15% that were interest only. In addition, Fannie purchased $36 billion of subprime and $12 billion of Alt-A non-GSE MBSs. Before housing prices began to decline, the strategic plan to increase risk and market share without raising new capital resulted in Fannie earning higher net income and generating higher compensation for its senior executives.

Might high and growing executive compensation during the housing price bubble have established psychological aspiration points or reference points for Fannie's executives? In 2005 and 2006, CEO Mudd's compensation totaled $24.4 million, and interim CFO Robert Levin's compensation totaled $15.5 million.

Like Fannie, Freddie also enlarged its portfolios with limited capital. In this regard, a drama played out at Freddie that might sound reminiscent of other events discussed elsewhere in the book. In 2005, the firm's CEO, Richard Syron, fired its CRO, David Andrukonis. According to the FCIC, Syron explained that one of the reasons for his firing Andrukonis was the CRO's having expressed his concern about the relaxation of underwriting standards in the firm's mission to meet its goals.

Freddie's chief counsel at the time, Robert Bostrom, points out that the role of CRO and chief counsel are similar. Both tend to be naysayers at management committee meetings. Bostrom notes that CEOs have to deal with many constituencies and many priorities. In Bostrom's view, the CRO's voice is, and can only be, one of many at the table.

In any event, Anurag Saksena, who replaced Andrukonis as CRO, told the FCIC staff that he too had argued for increased capital to compensate for the increased risk exposure. Notably, Syron did not make Saksena part of the senior management team. Instead, Freddie expanded its activities, purchasing and guaranteeing higher risk mortgages, lowering its underwriting standards, and increasing the use of credit policy waivers and exceptions. In 2006, it offered its newer alternative products to a broader range of customers, with these products comprising approximately 24% of that year's purchases. As with Fannie, Freddie Mac's plan to increase its risk and market share, but not its capital, did not lead to OFHEO expressing concerns.

The firing of Andrukonis and the decision to exclude his replacement, Saksena, from the senior management team is consistent with the idea that Freddie's risk management profile was weak, especially in respect to culture and behavior. Warning signs go up when there is insufficient tolerance for devil's advocacy, especially with respect to risk.

In 2004, Fannie Mae and Freddie Mac significantly increased their purchases of private label mortgage securities. Before 2004, Fannie's holding of private label securities did not exceed $50 billion at any one time. However, in 2004, those holdings more than doubled and constituted just under 3% of their overall portfolio. Private label mortgage securities were larger for Freddie Mac, comprising close to 9% of its portfolio.

By 2007, housing prices had peaked and mortgage debt growth had slowed. During the board meeting held in April 2007, Lund characterized the dislocation in the housing market as an opportunity for Fannie to reclaim market share, and at the May meeting, Lund suggested that Fannie could increase its share from 37% of the market in 2006 to 60% in 2007. At the time, Fannie was actively purchasing subprime non-GSE securities, and billions of Alt-A mortgages.

In June of that year, Fannie prepared its five-year strategic plan, which they titled "Deepen Segments—Develop Breadth." The plan called for an increase in mortgage credit risk, with deeper exposure to the credit pool. The plan also forecast increases in revenue and earnings during each of the following five years.

Fannie's senior executives told the board that the firm's risk management function would be able to act on the plan. However, CRO Dallavecchia disagreed with the view that Fannie had both the will and the resources to change its culture in order to support taking on more credit risk. For one thing, the plan called for a 16% reduction in his budget. Even more importantly, Dallavecchia was concerned about the caliber of Fannie's internal controls. According to the FCIC, he e-mailed Chief Operating Officer Michael Williams to say that the firm had "one of the weakest control processes that he "ever witnessed in [his] career... [and] was not even close to having proper control processes for credit, market and operational risk." He went on to say that the firm had reverted "back to the old days of scraping on controls... to reduce expenses," adding that given the circumstances, either "people don't care about the [risk] function or they don't get it."[7]

There is an important question of whether Fannie Mae properly priced the risk it assumed to guarantee mortgages against default. Did it misprice the protection it sold in order to increase its market share? At the heart of the issue was the fact that the magnitudes of the risk premiums implicit in its guarantee fees were less than the magnitudes implied by the firm's models.

Mark Winer was head of Fannie's Business, Analysis and Decisions Group. He had the responsibility for the models used to set fees, and raised the concern that Fannie's prices for guaranteeing Alt-A mortgages were too low. Todd Hempstead was senior vice president at Fannie in charge of their Western region. He told the FCIC that Fannie undercharged for guarantees in order to increase market share.

Robert Levin was Fannie's chief business officer and interim CFO. Winer told the FCIC that Levin disagreed with his contention about Alt-A guarantee pricing, and said to him, "Can you show me why you think you're right and everyone else is wrong?" Mudd, Fannie's CEO, acknowledged that there was a difference between the fees implied by their models and the fees they actually charged. He told the FCIC that scarcity of historical data for many of the loans caused the model's output to be unreliable.

By the end of 2007, as housing prices declined and defaults rose, the damage to the GSEs' balance sheets was apparent. In its 2007 Form 10-K, Fannie acknowledged the credit losses, forecast that they would increase with time, pointed to the lower credit quality of the mortgages it guaranteed in 2006 and 2007 relative to previous years, and noted that the average management and guarantee fees on 2007 issuances were insufficient to keep pace with the increase in expected default costs associated with their commitments. As subprime delinquencies increased, both GSEs also incurred significant losses on their private label holdings. Indeed, the GSEs' total capital was small compared to these losses.

As the housing market deteriorated, major mortgage lenders such as Countrywide Financial and IndyMac Bank became insolvent. The market capitalization of the GSEs reflected these events. Between the end of 2007 and the third quarter of 2008, Fannie Mae's market capitalization declined from $39 billion to $1.6 billion. Freddie Mac's market capitalization declined from $22 billion to $1.1 billion.

The cost of credit default swap protection on Fannie Mae five-year debt also increased significantly. In December 2006, the price of protection was 6.3 basis points, but in March 2008 it rose to almost 88 basis points. Despite the longstanding perception that the federal government was standing behind the GSEs' debt obligations, spreads over Treasury yields on their debt rose from 40 basis points to approximately 100 basis points. Moreover, lenders became willing only to lend to the GSEs on a very short-term basis, signaling the beginning of a run, as faith in the implicit government guarantee began to wane.

The FHFA had authority to place Fannie Mae and Freddie Mac into conservatorship, and in September 2008 did so. In its announcement, the FHFA mentioned a host of factors pertaining to safety and soundness such as current capitalization, current market conditions, the financial performance and condition of each company, the inability of the companies to fund themselves according to normal practices and prices, and the critical importance of each company in supporting the residential mortgage market. Also cited was Fannie's practice of charging guarantee fees that were less than the fees implied by their models, in an effort to compete more aggressively against Wall Street and Freddie Mac with the purpose of growing market share.

Background Brief on AIG

AIG is the largest insurance organization in the world. Headquartered in New York, AIG offers products in property casualty insurance, life insurance and retirement services, mortgage insurance, and aircraft leasing. It services more than 88 million clients with a network of over 64,000 people in 90 countries.

AIG was founded in 1919 by an American, Cornelius Vander Starr, in Shanghai. The firm expanded globally and through acquisition began to operate in the United States during the 1950s. In the 1960s, the firm adopted the name American International Group (AIG) and became a publicly traded company. In 1968, Starr picked Maurice (Hank) Greenberg as his successor, who held the position until 2005 and was replaced by Martin Sullivan. Greenberg was effectively forced to step down as the result of an investigation of questionable accounting practices at the firm by then-New York Attorney General Eliot Spitzer.

During the 1970s, AIG focused on products for the energy, transportation, entertainment industries. During the 1980s, the firm acquired United Guaranty Corporation and began offering mortgage insurance.

In 1987, AIG created a financial products division (AIGFP).[8] AIGFP generated income by assuming various parties' counterparty risks in transactions such as interest rate swaps. It was able to do so because its parent AIG had a triple-A rating and a large balance sheet. AIGFP was highly profitable during its first 15 years and, by 2001, was generating 15% of AIG's profit.

AIGFP entered the market for credit default swaps (CDSs) in 1998 by insuring against the default risk of corporate bonds issued by investment-grade public corporations. The default risk associated with these bonds as a group was relatively low. Although insuring corporate debt remained AIGFP's key business, over time the company also began to insure risks associated with credit card debt, student loans, auto loans, pools of prime mortgages, and eventually, pools of subprime mortgages.

Decision-Making and Consequences:
AIG during the Housing Bubble

AIGFP's main role in the global financial crisis involved its trades in the market for CDSs associated with subprime mortgages. Effectively, AIG performed a similar function as Fannie Mae and Freddie Mac, but for the issuers of private label mortgage-related securities such as Merrill and Lehman, by guaranteeing mortgages in case of defaults by homeowners.

Unlike Fannie and Freddie, AIGFP developed misgivings about subprime before the dangerous period that began in 2006. However, these misgivings were not the product of strong processes at AIGFP. Rather the misgivings stemmed from individual intuition, and one of the individuals was an executive named Gene Park, who was managing director and head of North American Structured Credit at AIGFP.

When the Federal Reserve began to increase short-term interest rates in June 2004, the volume of prime mortgage lending fell by 50%. At the same time, the volume of subprime mortgage lending increased dramatically. As a result, the composition of mortgage pools that AIGFP was insuring shifted over the next 18 months. However, AIGFP's processes did not detect the shift.

In 2005, Park asked AIGFP consultant and Yale academic Gary Gorton about what would qualify as a reasonable proportion of subprime in the collateral pool associated with the "multisector" CDOs on which AIG was selling CDSs. Gorton replied that the pool should contain less than 10% subprime and Alt-A mortgages. As a result, Park asked Adam Budnick, another AIG employee, to verify the actual figures. According to the FCIC report, Budnick double-checked and returned to say, "I can't believe it. You know, it's like 80 or 90%." Park told the FCIC that he wondered whether AIGFP might be in a "horrendous business" from which they should exit.

The second individual at AIGFP who became concerned with subprime exposure was Andrew Forster. In July 2005, Forster e-mailed Alan Frost, who was AIG's salesman primarily responsible for the firm's CDS business. According to the FCIC report, the e-mail contained the following passage:

> We are taking on a huge amount of sub prime [sic] mortgage exposure here.... Everyone we have talked to says they are worried about deals with huge amounts [of high-risk mortgage] exposure yet I regularly see deals with 80% [high-risk mortgage] concentrations currently. Are these really the same risk as other deals?[9]

AIGFP's mischaracterization of the mortgage pools it effectively insured for default risk reflects very weak risk management structures. The astonished reactions of Budnick and Park suggest that the risks in question were not strategic, but instead preventable.

Because of Park and Forster's misgivings, an AIGFP group analyzed the issue over a series of weeks. They talked to bank analysts and other experts. They asked themselves whether it made sense for AIG to continue to write protection on subprime and Alt-A mortgage markets. According to the FCIC, some in the group recognized that, although some of the underlying mortgages were structured to fail, rising housing prices would serve to bail them out.

Gorton told the FCIC that he participated in a meeting with AIG and a Bear Stearns analyst. He recalls the analyst having been so optimistic about housing prices, that he and his colleagues concluded that the analyst "must be on drugs or something." In mentioning optimism, Gorton explicitly raises an important psychological issue. Viewed through the lens of the FIH, the term "euphoria" would seem to apply here. In this regard, AIGFP certainly appears to have shifted its risk exposure from hedge finance to speculative and Ponzi finance during a euphoric period.

Unlike Fannie and Freddie, the AIGFP group understood the risk posed by a decline in the housing market. Park told the FCIC, "We weren't getting paid enough money to take that risk.... I'm not going to opine on whether there's a train on its way. I just know that I'm not getting paid enough to stand on these tracks."

AIGFP was headed by Joseph Cassano. His predecessor at the helm of AIGFP was Tom Savage, a trained mathematician who understood the models used by AIGFP traders to price the risks they were assuming. Savage encouraged debates about the models AIGFP was using and the trades being made. In contrast to Savage, Cassano stifled debate and intimidated those who expressed views he did not share.[10]

Cassano was not a trained mathematician. His academic background was in political science, and he spent most of his career in the back office doing operations. At AIGFP, his reputation was someone who had a crude feel for financial risk and a strong tendency to bully people who challenged him.[11] When the issue of a shift toward taking more subprime mortgage risk eventually made its way onto a formal agenda, Cassano, pointing to the triple-A ratings from Moody's and S&P, dismissed any concerns as overblown. Needless to say, bullying behavior by a group leader and the dismissing of concerns of those who report to him is a telltale sign of groupthink.

Nevertheless, by February 2006, Park and others managed to persuade Cassano and Frost that AIGFP should stop writing CDS protection on subprime mortgage–backed securities. At the time, AIG had almost $80 billion worth of CDOs on its books from AIGFP's deals. Yet even after February 2006, somehow, AIGFP continued to work on deals that were in the pipeline. Between September 2005 and July 2006, they completed 37 deals, one involving a CDO backed by 93% subprime assets.

Despite its huge exposure to subprime, AIG never hedged more than a small fraction amounting to $150 million. This led some of AIG's counterparties to use the CDS market to bet on AIG's ability to fulfill its contracts. In particular, Goldman Sachs purchased large amounts of CDS protection on AIG.

In August 2007, in a conference call to investors, Cassano made the following statement: "It is hard for us, without being flippant, to even see a scenario within any kind of realm of reason that would see us losing $1 on any of those transactions." Cassano apparently based his statement on the fact that the subprime mortgages that were beginning to default had originated in 2006 and 2007, which were riskier years for mortgage issuance than

2004 and 2005 when AIGFP had not been scrutinizing the subprime and Alt-A proportion of the pools on which it was effectively providing default protection. In this regard, he appears to have been excessively optimistic and overconfident.

Notably, by June 2007, AIGFP had written five times the $16 billion of multisector swaps as it held at the end of 2005. These swaps contained collateral calls if the market value of the referenced securities were to decline. The collateral calls proved to be disastrous for AIG.

Park told the FCIC that neither he nor most of his AIG colleagues knew about these collateral calls at the time. Park said that he and his group only focused on credit risk associated with having guaranteed mortgages taken out by subprime and Alt-A borrowers who then defaulted in large numbers.

In contrast to Park, Cassano told the FCIC that he was aware of the potential for calls. In this respect, AIG's 2005 filings with the SEC mentioned the risk of collateral calls if AIG's credit rating as a firm were to be downgraded. In fact, when Greenberg stepped down as CEO that year, the credit ratings downgraded AIG's rating from triple-A to double-A. The downgrade triggered provisions in some of AIGFP's CDSs, requiring AIG proper to turn over $1 billion in collateral to counterparties.

The contrast between Cassano's knowledge of the collateral call provisions and Park's ignorance of their existence is indicative of a severe weakness in the process for sharing information at AIGFP.

In August 2007, as subprime assets plummeted in value along with housing prices, Goldman Sachs demanded $1.5 billion in collateral from AIG. By October, it had posted nearly $2 billion. Other counterparties were also beginning to make demands for collateral. In November, AIGFP reported that its CDS portfolio lost $352 million, and in December, Cassano placed the figure at $1.1 billion.

Within AIG there was great uncertainty about the value of AIGFP's portfolio. Cassano did not share information with AIG's internal auditor, who complained that Cassano refused to allow AIGFP's transactions to be properly audited. The internal auditor described Cassano as "high handed," a term strongly suggestive of overconfidence.[12]

In February 2008, AIG announced that it had posted $5.3 billion in collateral, along with estimated losses of $11.5 billion. That month, CEO Sullivan announced that Cassano would step down, effective March 31. However, AIG retained Cassano as a consultant and paid him $1 million a month. This amount can be compared to Cassano's compensation of $43.6 million in salary and bonuses in 2006, and $24.2 million in 2007.

AIG's credit rating was downgraded further in September 2008 from AA to A. The downgrade was a disaster for AIG, because it triggered calls for collateral that AIG lacked the liquidity to meet. On September 16, the Federal

Reserve Board announced that it would take a nearly 80% equity stake in AIG and would provide an $85 billion loan. In the end, AIG required a $182 billion in assistance from the US government. The rescue of AIG was a defining moment in the unfolding of the global financial crisis.

AIGFP incentives did balance long-term against short-term results. To its credit, AIGFP required that employees leave 50% of their bonuses in the firm, a policy that skewed their incentive toward the long run. As for Cassano, he left almost all of his compensation in the firm. Clearly, he had a strong financial incentive to maximize the long-term value of AIG.

Ben Bernanke, who was Fed Chair at the time of the AIG rescue, made very harsh comments about the manner in which AIG had been run. He said that no other episode that occurred during the lead-up to the financial crisis made him more angry than AIG having exploited a huge gap in the regulatory system to bypass having oversight of its financial products division.[13] In expressing this view, he was comparing AIG's regular insurance business, which has regular oversight and appropriate requirements for capital and liquidity, with its insurance-like CDS trades at AIGFP, which had no regulatory oversight and no requirements for capital and liquidity.

Greenberg was known for being a diligent monitor, and his successors lacked the deep understanding he had of the company. Perhaps his needing to step down as CEO of AIG in 2005 was a factor in poor oversight of AIGFP. We will never know for sure. However, for the six-month period preceding the bailout, the firm had neither a full-time CFO nor a chief risk assessment officer, and it was engaged in a search for both. As a result, in the period leading up to the bailout, the executives of the eighteenth-largest firm in the world had no clear sense of their firm's exposure to subprime mortgage risk.

Closing Thoughts

Fannie Mae, Freddie Mac, and AIG bore an inordinate amount of default risk associated with subprime mortgages. All three firms would have failed, but for being rescued by US government action. The chronologies make clear that all three firms featured weak risk management structures, cultures, and behaviors.

Like UBS, Merrill Lynch, S&P, and Moody's, Fannie and Freddie Mac established high aspirations to which their senior executives accorded great importance. As with the senior executives at UBS, Merrill Lynch, S&P, and Moody's, the senior executives at Fannie and Freddie Mac displayed little tolerance for devil's advocacy on the part of risk managers. At the same time, there were some notable differences between AIG and the two GSEs in terms of when they recognized the dangers posed by subprime risk and how they compensated executives.

Reflecting back on the previous three chapters, the evidence is growing that excessively high aspirations in combination with groupthink are common themes that characterized the psychological issues that impacted many of the firms that played major roles in the global financial crisis. So too were excessive optimism and overconfidence, two key components of market sentiment. The presence of these psychological pitfalls at the highest levels of management have the potential to foster conflicts between CEOs and CROs, as evidenced by events at Freddie Mac, and if you will recall from Chapter 8 also at Merrill Lynch.[14]

From a macroprudential perspective, by being willing to accept subprime default risk in the early to middle phase of the housing bubble, Fannie Mae, Freddie Mac and AIG provided the mortgage industry and Wall Street with the comfort they needed to engage in speculative and Ponzi finance-based financial innovations that fueled an asset bubble. The FIH tells us that the combination of financial instability and too big to fail leads to contingency socialism. The experiences of Fannie Mae, Freddie Mac, and AIG make this point in no uncertain terms.

CHAPTER 11

THE WINNER'S CURSE STRIKES AT RBS, FORTIS, AND ABN AMRO

THE YEAR BEFORE THE FINANCIAL CRISIS ERUPTED, RBS LED A CONSORTIUM to acquire the Dutch bank ABN AMRO. The end result proved to be a disaster for RBS, ABN AMRO, and at least one other party. Sir Philip Hampton, who became CEO of RBS in the aftermath of the acquisition, described the initiative as "the wrong price, the wrong way to pay, at the wrong time and the wrong deal."[1] In other words, the outcome was not just a matter of bad luck but, as we shall see, a series of flawed decisions that were psychologically driven. Given that the acquisition set a record for bank takeover, the case is especially interesting.

At the time of the ABN AMRO acquisition, Riccardo Rebonato was chief risk officer at RBS. In the second edition of his book *Plight of the Fortune Tellers*, Rebonato explains that, although he anticipated some kind of oncoming financial storm before the crisis, he misjudged where that storm would first materialize. In particular, he indicates that he simply missed the warning signs that the storm would erupt in structured credit products linked to US subprime mortgages.

Because of hindsight bias, it is easy to think that it should have been simple to spot where the storm would break, if break at all. However, as previously pointed out, most market professionals failed to anticipate the eruption in structured credit products linked to US subprime mortgages. Indeed that feature illustrates an important aspect of the FIH dynamic, as it is that failure that propels the economy along its path to instability.

With that we now turn our attention to what lessons can be learned from the acquisition of ABN AMRO.

BACKGROUND BRIEF ON ABN AMRO AND ITS APPEAL TO RBS

ABN AMRO is the product of a 1991 merger between two Dutch banks, Algemene Bank Nederland (ABN) and AMRO Bank. In 2000, Rijkman Groenink became CEO of ABN AMRO and formulated new goals to turn the bank into a top performer. Yet between 2003 and 2006, ABN AMRO's profit per share had only gone up 19% when the top five European banks had doubled profit per share. At the time, ABN AMRO was eighth largest in size.

In March 2006, Barclays was the United Kingdom's second-largest bank and 50% larger than ABN AMRO. It had been striving to generate half its profit outside of the United Kingdom, but trailed its main rivals, RBS and HSBC. It was at that time that Barclays CEO John Varley and Groenink began discussing the idea of merging the two banks. That November, Barclays's governors decided that ABN AMRO would be an attractive acquisition for them.

ABN AMRO owned a US bank, LaSalle. In March 2007, RBS contacted ABN AMRO to indicate interest in purchasing LaSalle, but hinted that it had other goals in mind. Notably, the RBS board had analyzed a possible deal with ABN AMRO and concluded that their bank did not have to do the deal. The board also decided that it would walk away from a deal if the price for ABN AMRO were to become excessive.

Although RBS's primary interest in ABN AMRO was its American subsidiary LaSalle, it was also interested in some of its other businesses. For example, RBS concluded that if they could acquire ABN AMRO's global clients and wholesale banking business as providing a geographic network and broad client base, then they could accelerate their own investment banking and wholesale strategy. RBS was also interested in ABN AMRO's global payments system and its international retail banking operations, specifically because its branch networks in Asia and the Middle East would provide opportunities for growth.

RBS estimated that in addition to becoming the third-largest business in the world for corporate and institutional banking and markets, the incorporation of ABN AMRO's business into its own Global Banking and Markets (GBM) division would lead it to rank first in the United Kingdom and Continental Europe, and fifth in the United States. Moreover, the combined firm would rank first globally in respect to number of product lines, such as global securitizations and all international bonds. By shooting for a number one ranking, RBS might have set itself a very high aspirational bar.

THE THRILL OF THE CHASE

On March 20, 2007, Barclays and ABN AMRO announced the principles of a potential combination. On April 23, they made public the terms of their agreement: a €66B valuation featuring the exchange of 3.125 Barclay shares per share of ABN AMRO.[2]

During the next month, April, a group from Merrill Lynch approached RBS and two other banks, Spanish bank Santander and Belgian bank Fortis, about forming a consortium that would engage in a takeover of ABN AMRO and an associated carveout. In the carveout, Fortis would take ABN AMRO's retail, private banking, and asset management groups. RBS would take the American subsidiary LaSalle, along with global transaction services and corporate banking. Santander would take the Brazilian assets and the Italian bank Antonveneta (which ABN AMRO had recently purchased).

For RBS, LaSalle was a particularly attractive opportunity. RBS already had a US business, Citizens. Combining LaSalle with Citizens would lead RBS to become the fifth-largest bank in the United States by asset size. In this regard, RBS estimated that globally the combined business would be the third largest by fixed income revenue in the corporate and institutional banking business.

At the time, the CEO of RBS was Sir Fred Goodwin. Under his leadership, RBS had already achieved the successful acquisition of British bank NatWest. And so it was that under his leadership a consortium made up of RBS, Santander, and Fortis made a move to outbid Barclays for ABN AMRO.

On April 29, 2007, a due diligence team from the consortium visited ABN AMRO's headquarters in Amsterdam. ABN AMRO made available materials consisting of two lever-arch files and information contained on a CD, along with information on LaSalle.

This was the extent of the information that the consortium would have in its possession as the basis for preparing an offer. In consequence, RBS and its consortium partners could not determine the quality of the assets in ABN AMRO's structured credit portfolios, the valuation of those positions, and whether there were any significant deficiencies in its key risk management practices. Nevertheless, the RBS Board requested and received assurance from the firm's executives that for the majority of due diligence "work streams," there were "no show stoppers." Given the paucity of information available to the due diligence team, might the "no show stoppers" judgment reflect any specific psychological biases? The issue here is overconfidence: how much confidence the acquirers should have in judging the risk of proceeding.

RBS's initial interest in ABN AMRO was primarily to acquire LaSalle. However, a week before the due diligence team's visit to Amsterdam, ABN AMRO announced that it would sell LaSalle to Bank of America. Surprised but undeterred, the consortium spent a week reviewing the due diligence findings. On May 5, the consortium submitted a bid for LaSalle. Notably, this proposal was conditional on the completion of a proposed public offer for all of ABN AMRO at a price of €38.40 per ABN AMRO share. However, ABN AMRO concluded that Bank of America's offer for LaSalle was superior to the consortium's offer, and it rejected the consortium's proposal.

The decision to sell LaSalle to Bank of America presented RBS with an opportunity to reconsider its bid. Despite the ostensible importance of LaSalle for doing the deal, RBS had already begun to assess the acquisition without LaSalle. Indeed, without LaSalle, RBS executives concluded that the synergy for their bank had decreased from €2.9b to €1.7b.

Despite the changing landscape, the consortium maintained its offer of €38.40 per ABN AMRO share, despite the exclusion of LaSalle. They did so with the understanding that RBS would receive the proceeds of the LaSalle sale to Bank of America, and made the formal offer in late July 2007. Might any psychological biases have led the consortium members not to have decreased their offer after ABN AMRO's sale of LaSalle to Bank of America? Confirmation bias is a strong candidate, as RBS had reduced their estimate of the synergy associated with the acquisition, but not their acquisition price.

In any event, the key terms of the consortium offer included

1. €35.60 in cash plus 0.296 RBS ordinary shares for each ABN AMRO ordinary share;
2. valuation at €38.40 per ABN AMRO ordinary share, with a total value of €71.1b; and
3. an increase in the amount to be paid in cash from €56.2b in the May offer to €66.1b, with proportionally, the percentage paid in cash increasing from 79% to 93%.

The increase in cash payment reflected the cash proceeds from the LaSalle sale. Given that these proceeds would accrue to RBS, RBS decided to use a combination of those proceeds and bridge finance to fund its cash obligations for the deal. The bridge finance was short term, with a weighted average maturity of six months. Overall, more than half of the cash needed to complete the deal was funded by debt with a term of one year or less.

In late 2007, a run on ABCP marked the first phase of the market's recognition that there were problems with US subprime mortgages. To be sure, RBS executives noticed—and indeed sought—legal advice about whether these events represented material changes in respect to their published offer. The consortium had published its formal offer on July 20, 2007. Apart from any of the consortium members being unable to obtain approval from their shareholders, the only way that the consortium could have withdrawn after July 20 was to exercise clauses in their offer document.

One clause in the offer was termed the Material Adverse Change (MAC) condition and the other was the Regulatory Approvals (RA) condition.

On August 10, the RBS board contemplated using the MAC to reduce the consortium's offer price, but in the end decided against doing so and chose to hold a shareholder vote to approve the deal, for which 95% of the votes were cast in favor. Given the change in market conditions and the kinds of risk that financing the acquisition with a lot of short-term debt posed, might any specific psychological bias have made RBS reluctant to have been more aggressive in respect to reducing the offer price or making more of an effort to withdraw from the deal? As with the reaction to the loss of Lasalle, confirmation bias is a strong candidate, with RBS downplaying information that did not support the decision they had reached to proceed with the acquisition.

On October 10, 2007, the consortium declared its offer unconditional, and the acquisition was completed on October 17. At €71.1b, this set a new world record for bank takeovers.

The sale of LaSalle to Bank of America was also settled that October, and ABN AMRO recognized a gain of €7.17b.

Barclays share price increased on completion of the deal. The *Guardian* reported that Barclays experienced a lucky escape.[3]

RBS POSTACQUISITION

Months before when RBS's board was analyzing the deal, they concluded that execution risk would likely be high, as would integration costs. In this regard, they noted that integration would be more difficult than previous transactions such as NatWest. However, RBS planned to use the same integration team for ABN AMRO as they had with NatWest, a fact that provided reassurance to the Financial Services Authority (FSA), RBS's regulator in the United Kingdom.

RBS was the largest member of the consortium. Although its share of the consortium deal was only 38.3%, the structure of the acquisition gave RBS a controlling position, and for this reason it was required to consolidate ABN AMRO in full for both regulatory and accounting purposes.

Notably, RBS's 38.3% share of the acquisition was equivalent to approximately 61% of its reported tier 1 capital at year end 2006. In other words, this was a highly concentrated bet on RBS's part, in that it left the bank with a very thin capital cushion. Although CEO Sir Fred Goodwin had denied that doing the deal would cause RBS to have to raise more capital, in June 2008 RBS undertook a £12b rights issue. In July, RBS shares fell because of their exposure to the mortgage meltdown, through its Citizens unit and the associated sale of an insurance unit.

In 2008, credit trading losses of £12.2b were a significant portion of the losses incurred by the bank as a whole, and exceeded the £7.1b losses recognized due to impairment on loans and advances. Things went from bad to worse as the financial crisis erupted in full after the Lehman bankruptcy.

On October 7, 2008, approximately a year after the consortium had acquired ABN AMRO, RBS received Emergency Liquidity Assistance (ELA) from the Bank of England. The UK government announced a recapitalization package, with RBS being one of three major UK banks to obtain capital through this scheme.

Goodwin resigned as CEO, characterized the acquisition of ABN AMRO as "a bad mistake," and lost his knighthood.[4]

For RBS, ABN AMRO might have been the straw that broke the camel's back. The FSA report investigating the failure of RBS tells us that many of the factors that led to the bank's failure were already present before the consortium acquired ABN AMRO. In this respect, RBS's core capital ratio was already low. Acquiring ABN AMRO simply took its core capital position to a tipping point. Moreover, a significant proportion of RBS's losses were from assets the bank originally held: it was not assets acquired as part of ABN AMRO that made the difference between success and failure.

A *Financial Times* postmortem of RBS's position made four interesting points.[5] The first point was that RBS made similar decisions as its competitors, but took those decisions to extremes. The second point was that Goodwin was an optimist by nature and that having been proved right many times in his life led him to expect that his winning streak would continue. The third point was that the incentive packages in the banking industry induced RBS's management to focus on increasing revenue, profits, assets, and leverage instead of focusing on capital, liquidity, and asset quality. The fourth point was that with 17 directors, the board was too big and was vulnerable to groupthink.

THE FSA'S TAKE ON RBS'S RISK MANAGEMENT

According to the FSA report, there were four ways in which the acquisition of ABN AMRO contributed to RBS's vulnerability and, ultimately, its failure. All four are core issues for risk management in financial institutions. This section dives into these issues, as the devil lies in the details, and for risk managers this is where the rubber meets the road. From a behavioral risk management perspective, the overarching question to ask is whether the unfavorable outcomes described below stemmed from overconfidence and confirmation bias, or were instead unfavorable outcomes from risks that had been properly assessed and prudently taken. The risk typology framework provides a good basis for identifying whether the risk RBS faced through its role in the acquisition was preventable, systematic, or external.

Capital Position, Liquidity Risk, and Risk Exposure

Consider RBS's capital position just before the acquisition. At mid-year 2007, RBS had the lowest tier 1 ratio among its peers. In this regard, the FSA estimated that at year end 2007, RBS's Basel III common equity tier 1 ratio would have been 1.97%. Table 11.1 displays the data underlying the calculation, with the tier ratio appearing on the last line.

What the ABN AMRO deal did was to increase RBS's exposure to structured credit and leveraged finance assets, and monoline insurers whose business is to guarantee mortgage products against default. Exposure to these assets was highly risky and ended up creating major losses. In this regard, the ABN AMRO assets experienced proportionately larger write-downs on high-grade super-senior CDOs.

Relative to ABN AMRO, RBS had more exposure to RMBS, CMBS, and monoline insurance. However, the acquisition effectively quadrupled RBS's off balance sheet liquidity risk from conduits (special purpose vehicles) associated with ABCP. RBS's investment banking division, GBM, which had

Table 11.1 This table displays the computation the FSA used to estimate that at year end 2007, RBS's Basel III common equity tier 1 ratio would have been 1.97%, with the tier ratio appearing on the last line

Estimates of a proxy Basel III common equity tier 1 measure for RBS, as of December 31 2007	
£bn	
Gross core tier 1 capital (net of prudential filters)	79.8
Of which: minority interest in core tier 1	−39.1
Gross core tier 1 capital attributable to RBS shareholders (net of prudential filters)	40.8
Recognition of minority interest equity	35.1
Regulatory adjustments	
Deduction of excess minority interest equity attributable to third-party owners	−4.5
Deduction of intangible assets	−52.5
Deduction of material holdings	−2.9
Adjustments for prudential filters	−0.6
Net common equity tier 1 (including partial recognition of minority interests)	15.4
Net common equity tier 1 (excluding minority interests)	6.5
Basel I risk-weighted assets (RWAs)	609
Market risk and counterparty risk changes	155.6
Add securitization exposures weighted 1250%	18.1
Basel III RWAs (Review Team estimate)	782.6
Common equity tier 1 attributable to RBS shareholders/estimated RWAs	0.83%
Basel III common equity tier 1 capital ratio (Review Team estimate)	1.97%

been its most rapidly growing area, absorbed many of the ABN AMRO assets that were assigned to RBS.

In addition, the acquisition led RBS's trading book assets to almost double from year end 2006 to year end 2007. In terms of risk-weighted assets (RWAs), trading book assets carry low risk weights. Nevertheless, the acquisition had implications for RBS's capital cushion. Even assuming a 5.25% target core tier 1 ratio (compared to the 2% minimum), the low risk weights associated with trading assets implied that RBS only held £2.3b of core tier 1 capital to

Table 11.2 This table displays the FSA's computations showing that the low risk weights associated with trading assets implied that RBS's only held £2.3b of core tier 1 capital to cover potential trading losses from the roughly £470b on its balance sheet

RBS's banking book and trading book assets and RWAs from end-2004 to end-2008

£bn			Basel I		Basel II
	31/12/2004	31/12/2005	31/12/2006	31/12/2007	15 31/12/2008
Banking book assets	392.9	444	459.4	1140.9	1338
Trading book assets	186.4	200	243.5	470.9	1018.3
Total assets of the United Kingdom regulatory consolidation group (including ABN AMRO from end-2007)	579.4	644.1	702.9	1611.8	2356.3
Banking book RWAs	306.7	354.8	378	564.8	551.4
Trading book RWAs	17.1	16.2	22.3	44.2	107.5
Operational RWAs					36.9
Total RWAs	323.8	371	400.3	609	695.8
Amount of core tier 1 capital that would have been held against banking and trading book assets, using RBS's target core tier 1 capital ratio of 5.25% (5.25% × RWAs)					
Banking book	16.1	18.6	19.8	29.7	28.9
Trading book	0.9	0.9	1.2	2.3	5.6
Operational risk	0	0	0	0	1.9
Total core tier 1 capital	17	19.5	21	32	36.5

cover potential trading losses from the roughly £470b on its balance sheet. For details, see Table 11.2. As it happened, in 2008, RBS incurred losses of £12.2b in the credit market portion of its total trading book.

Prior to the acquisition, RBS already depended on short-term funding. Therefore, RBS was vulnerable to a liquidity shock in the short-term market, which the acquisition of ABN AMRO exacerbated.

As the events of 2008 unfolded, RBS's lenders began to express serious concerns about the quality of its assets, as well as its capital and liquidity positions. Of course, it is such concerns that turn into runs on a financial institution. At the end of June 2008, £8.6b of liquidity from RBS's and ABN AMRO's own-sponsored conduits had been drawn but not yet repaid. The highest drawn balance for each of the two banks' own-sponsored conduits peaked at different points during the six months between January and June 2008.

The maximum amount drawn was £10.2b, with £8.5b being from ABN AMRO's own-sponsored conduits. As markets became more turbulent in early 2008, RBS's Strategic Asset Unit (SAU) began to absorb and manage many of ABN AMRO's assets, alongside assets originated by RBS. In both 2007 and 2008, RBS recognized losses of £3.2b and £7.8b respectively on assets that had been absorbed into the SAU. In both years, RBS used a 2:1 ratio to split the losses between the assets that had been originated by RBS and by ABN AMRO, with RBS assets bearing the greater losses.

RISK IMPLICATIONS OF RBS'S DECISION TO FUND ACQUISITION PRIMARILY WITH SHORT-TERM DEBT

Recall that RBS decided to use mostly short-term debt to fund €22.6b for its share of the cash portion of the deal. Of the €22.6b, €12.3b was through debt with a maturity of one year or less. Table 11.3 provides details of the funding structure. As a result, the bank anticipated that the acquisition would lead its core tier 1 capital ratio to decline from 5.07% in December 2006 to 4.65% in December 2007. Of course, such a reduction would leave it with less of a buffer to face negative shocks. Notably, before the acquisition RBS conducted a scenario analysis, or stress test, to assess whether its total capital ratio would remain above its minimum requirements, even in a market crisis.

RBS had raised €12.3b in short-term funds, with the expectation that it would pay down some of this amount promptly from the proceeds of the sale of LaSalle. Although €10.9b cash was due to RBS following the sale of LaSalle in October 2007, these funds ended up being retained in the Netherlands longer than RBS initially expected, thereby exerting an unexpected need for liquidity.

Table 11.3 This table provides details of the funding structure in which RBS used mostly short-term debt to fund €22.6b for its share of the cash portion of the deal

	€m	
Issue of new ordinary shares	4,281	
TOTAL equity component	4,281	
Preference shares	4,567	19%
Other tier 1 securities	1,557	7%
Senior funding	9,941	42%
Bridge funding	7,400	32%
TOTAL cash component	23,465	100%
Cash funding required	22,600	
Cash funding surplus as of September 26, 2007	865	

The effect of goodwill on its capital cushion was also significant. RBS recognized £23.9b goodwill on the acquisition of ABN AMRO, of which £6.3b was due to its own share of the ABN AMRO business and £17.6b to the share of the ABN AMRO businesses attributable to minority interests. Therefore, when at year end 2007 RBS took a goodwill charge on its balance sheet, the result was to reduce its capital.

After the ABN AMRO acquisition, RBS relied more heavily on short-term borrowing than many of its peers. In addition, some of its counterparties reduced the amount they were willing to lend to RBS and ABN AMRO as a combined entity, thereby reducing RBS's borrowing capacity in those markets.

RISK IMPLICATIONS ASSOCIATED WITH ABN AMRO'S BASEL II APPLICATION

In December 2007, RBS's Supervision Team became aware that ABN AMRO had not yet received permission to use its own internal ratings based (IRB) models to calculate their respective credit risk capital requirements. Before the acquisition, RBS assumed that ABN AMRO's application to use its own IRB models would be approved. But in December, RBS came to understand that ABN AMRO was actually not well placed to move to a Basel II standardized approach. In this connection, RSB's regulator, the FSA, allowed ABN AMRO to calculate RWAs on a Basel I basis for consolidated capital purposes, provided that it received written confirmation from De Nederlandsche Bank (DNB) that the latter agreed with ABN AMRO's approach to implementing Basel II.

Under the Capital Requirements Directive, RBS and ABN AMRO were required to move to Basel II. On January 1, 2008, both banks applied for permission to use their own IRB models to calculate their respective credit risk capital requirements. However, the acquisition raised questions about how the postacquisition consolidated firm would comply with Basel II.

In fact, in early 2008, ABN AMRO and DNB, the central bank, agreed that ABN AMRO would withdraw its application and continue to report capital on the basis of Basel I. And so in March 2008, ABN AMRO withdrew its application to move to an IRB approach and therefore did not receive approval from DNB for its models.

Notably, ABN AMRO had not made contingency plans to move to the Basel II standardized approach, that being the alternative approach for firms that had not received permission to use model-based approaches. This approach involved revised minimum ratios of 9% for tier 1 capital and 12.5% for total capital along with the requirement that capital deductions would be treated in the same manner as under Basel II.

The Basel I basis produced a higher capital figure than the figure implied by the Basel II IRB model-based approach. The higher capital requirement placed additional strain on RBS's capital, and at the end of March 2008 the bank fell below individual capital guidance. The FSA, which had accommodated the uneven approach through July 2008, carried out detailed work to establish an appropriate level of conservatism. At the end of the process, the FSA required ABN AMRO to calculate its capital requirements based on Basel I RWAs using an additional 30%, which it did.

Risks Generated by RBS's Decision to Lead the Consortium

By virtue of being the largest of the three consortium members, RBS was required to consolidate the whole of ABN AMRO. Doing so forced RBS to bear a disproportionate share of effort in dealing with the inherent complexity of the transaction structure, the complex financial reporting that followed the acquisition, and a series of information-sharing difficulties with Dutch parties with which it was working. All of these issues represented transaction risk, which RBS did not communicate well to the markets; and markets do not like negative surprises.

RBS's pro forma financial statements did not fully capture RBS's role during the transition phase of the acquisition. Instead, the pro forma statements applied the future development of RBS once it had integrated its share of ABN AMRO. This had the effect of obscuring RBS's true financial position from the market. It also obscured the overall exposures of the consortium members and ABN AMRO not only from the markets but also from the regulatory authorities.

From late 2007, the opacity of the public information released by RBS led to concern in the markets about the effects of the acquisition. Markets were especially concerned about the quality of the assets and obligations that RBS had assumed as leader of the consortium. In this respect, its leadership role made RBS responsible for the whole of ABN AMRO during the restructuring phase, not just its portion. As a result, RBS faced greater downside risk exposure than its consortium partners.

Because the capital contributed in respect to consortium partners' interest in ABN AMRO, RBS recognized significant minority interests in its capital resources. This effect of doing so was to overstate the amount of capital that was available to the combined entity in order to absorb losses. In addition, when it consolidated ABN AMRO, RBS had to recognize goodwill and other intangible assets that had increased because of the acquisition: of £23.9b in goodwill, £17.6b was attributable to minority interests. Amortizing this goodwill in 2008 gave rise to significant losses for RBS.

Given the market turmoil in 2008, and subsequent reappraisals of business forecasts, RBS determined that its investment banking division GBM could no longer support any goodwill. In addition, significant write-downs were needed elsewhere in the organization. The total loss recorded at year end 2008, as a consequence of impairment to goodwill related to the acquisition, was £30.1b. This proved to be the largest contributor to RBS's £40.7b operating loss in 2008.

These write-downs did not actually impact RBS's tier 1 or total capital resources, because RBS had deducted goodwill from its regulatory capital. In addition, much of the goodwill write-down (£14.5b) related to Fortis's minority interest in ABN AMRO. As the global financial crisis erupted, RBS's consortium partner Fortis came close to collapse. In consequence, the Dutch government nationalized ABN AMRO and Fortis Nederland as part of a €16.8b bailout. At this time, the restructuring was not yet complete, and there was concern in the markets that RBS would have to meet Fortis's obligations under the terms of the acquisition. There were also concerns that the Fortis crisis would cause other collateral damage to RBS.

HORMONES AND MALE COMPETITION

Neuroscientist John Coates tells us that hormones play an important role in risk taking, especially when it involves male competition.[6] He points out that when two men enter a competition, their testosterone levels rise, leading to increased muscle mass and the ability of blood to carry oxygen. The elevated testosterone levels also enhance appetite for taking risk.

Competitions tend to produce winners and losers. Much of the testosterone tends to stay in a winner's system, while a loser's testosterone will fall off quickly. Therefore, in the next round of competition, the winner will begin with an already elevated level of testosterone. This typically leads him to begin with an advantage over his next opponent, an effect that continues to reinforce itself.

Coates speculates that repeat winners will find that their testosterone levels will climb above a certain peak, which will lead them to make reckless decisions. For example, in the animal world, repeat winners will go out in the open too much. They will pick too many fights. They will neglect parenting duties. And they will patrol areas that are too large. In the language of behavioral decision-making, they will become overconfident in the extreme. This dynamic, when applied to financial markets, suggests that traders with elevated testosterone levels become insensitive to price, rendering them vulnerable to misdiagnosing asset-pricing bubbles.

Acquisition and Male Competition

Fortis was too small to have acquired ABN AMRO on its own. Nevertheless, decision-makers at Fortis took personal delight in participating in the consortium that took over ABN AMRO. In fact, there were scores to settle. As you read the discussion below, ask yourself whether male competition played an important role in risk taking at Fortis and ABN AMRO in respect to acquisitions.

Ten years before the consortium acquired ABN AMRO, Fortis board chair Count Maurice Lippens found himself in competition with ABN AMRO's CEO Groenink over who would acquire the Belgian Generale Bank (GB). Although GB eventually accepted the Fortis offer, Groenink's active bidding caused Fortis to pay a significantly higher price than it had hoped. In addition, Fortis CEO Jean-Paul Votron had previously worked at ABN AMRO and had unsuccessfully sought to be appointed to the bank's board.

In the context of SP/A theory, how might these events have influenced Lippens and Votron's decision that Fortis participate in the acquisition of ABN AMRO? Might their past interactions have induced them to view the acquisition as an ambitious aspiration to which they attached great importance? This is important because according to SP/A theory, answers of yes indicate that in circumstances such as these, people are inclined to take high risk. For Fortis, a key risk was biting off more than it could chew because it was too small to manage a bank as large as ABN AMRO.

In the end, Fortis did bite off more than it could chew. Like RBS, Fortis was forced to raise new capital. In June 2008, Fortis announced that it was raising another €8.3 billion of capital by selling assets, placing shares, and scrapping its interim dividend. A month later, Votron resigned. Do you think that Fortis's having bitten off more than it could chew is consistent with Coates's male competition paradigm involving the impact of elevated testosterone levels?

Between the time ABN AMRO bid for GB and the time it sold itself to the consortium, Groenink had taken his bank on an eventful journey. When Groenink took over as CEO in 2000, ABN AMRO emphasized its corporate business division, with credit analysis as a core competency. However, under his leadership, traditional credit activities disappeared from the agenda. Instead, investment banking deals became more of a priority. Still, Groenink failed to provide the bank with a clear strategic direction. In August 2001, it was difficult to tell the degree to which the bank was prioritizing wholesale, retail, or asset management, its three main businesses.

The Netherlands follows what is known as a "dual board" or "two-tier" system in which corporations are governed by two separate boards of directors. The two boards are respectively called the "management board" and the "supervisory board." The two boards work together to run the corporation. The management board oversees day-to-day operations. Its responsibilities are tactical, and major decisions it makes require the approval of the supervisory board. The supervisory board is elected by shareholders, and is responsible for the corporation's long-term strategy.

Having processes for good communication between the two boards is essential for effective decision-making. The boards share information about a variety of important functions, which include risk management, business development, and variances between actual performance and planned performance.

The two ABN AMRO boards consisted of 12 governors and 8 managing directors. Groenink chaired the management board. Under his leadership, ABN AMRO sought to sharpen its corporate strategy by developing a second European market for the bank, one with a retail focus. Their plan was do so by creating a merger of equals, sometime in the 2002–2003 time frame. To this end, they considered several candidates, which they rejected because of a size mismatch. Barclays and Fortis were larger than ABN AMRO, while Unicredito and SocGen were smaller.

Three years passed, but none of the attempts at merger worked out. Although the supervisory board was unhappy about the situation, its members took no action to replace Groenink as CEO. By this time, Groenink had come to understand that ABM AMRO's size made a merger of equals difficult. Moreover, its size created ambiguity about whether in an acquisition the bank would be an acquirer or a target or, using more colorful language, whether it would be predator or prey.

For this reason it is important that in 2004, Groenink suggested for the first time that ABN AMRO might become a target. The trigger event appears to have been a bribery issue in the United States, which led to a cease and desist order that limited ABN AMRO's ability to engage in mergers and acquisitions (M&A).

The year 2005 was fateful. Groenink met RBS's chair Goodwin for the first time, and the two discussed the general pros and cons of a merger between their banks. Groenink also met with John Varley, who headed Barclays, to discuss possible merger issues. ABN AMRO acquired the Italian bank Antonveneta in what was a hostile takeover. In this regard, although ABN AMRO's strategy called for it to acquire a bank that was in the top three of Italian banks, Antonveneta was number eight. ABN AMRO funded the acquisition with a rights issue and anticipated a short-term decline in earnings as a result.

In July 2005, the ABN AMRO boards met at Petra to review and assess the bank's strategy. The tone at this meeting featured a sense of urgency because past targets had not been met. The general sense was that ABN AMRO needed to create much more value if they aspired to be among the top five European banks, and they saw that value creation required that they be an integrated bank.

Coming out of ABN AMRO's Petra meeting was the "Petra Plan." This plan called for the bank to divide itself into ten business units and focused on the identification of clients who could benefit from the network of activities they offered. To accomplish this goal, the bank expanded the management board, which was now overseen by the CEO and the CFO. However, there was concern among supervisory board members that the new matrix structure was overly complex. Viewed from a process-pitfall perspective, the key process involved here was planning, and the supervisory board might have been concerned that the management board was excessively optimistic and overconfident about the new structure.

In 2005, ABN AMRO was among the least efficient banks in its sector. Its new CFO promised that the bank would strive to improve efficiency and work toward becoming one of the 25 most efficient banks. Failing to do so would clearly delegate the bank into the category of prey, and Groenink had already had preliminary discussions with Barclays's CEO Varley about a possible merger.

In March 2006, Varley and Groenink met to continue their discussions. Barclays was the second-largest bank in the United Kingdom, and 50% larger than ABN AMRO. As was mentioned above, Barclays sought to generate half its profit outside of the United Kingdom, but lagged its rivals RBS and HSBC on that score.

With these merger discussions underway, ABN AMRO was experiencing difficulty in successfully implementing its Petra Plan. In June 2006, estimates for ABN AMRO's second-quarter results were poor. Profits were up by 8%, but costs were up by 11%. The CEO and CFO were not sure why this was the case, but suspected that it was the new complex structure, which featured insufficient accountability. In this regard, remember that the Supervisory Board had been skeptical about the Petra Plan.

In June 2006, the two ABN AMRO boards met to assess the state of the bank. In 2006, ABN AMRO was a €40b bank. However, its goal was to become a €100b bank by 2012, in order to rank among the top five. Yet, its current situation was hardly stellar. Antonveneta cost more than expected. Its US operations were not as productive as they had hoped, and the new organizational matrix was proving to be costly.

In the context of male competition, it is better to be predator than prey. Despite the fact that the supervisory board did not want to become an M&A target, the bank had no money left for more acquisitions, and it reluctantly accepted the idea that if it was to grow, it would need to combine with a larger party, which would leave it as the junior partner in a combination. The boards made the decision to sell their US bank LaSalle. Groenink would seek a white knight such as ING, Barclays, or Unicredito.[7]

Then in February 2007, one of ABN AMRO's major shareholders, the hedge fund TCI, sent a letter to Groenink asking that a series of items be placed on the ballot for the next shareholder meeting. At the top of the list was a measure to break up the bank, as TCI believed that its parts were worth more than the whole.[8] ABN AMRO challenged TCI's proposal in court, but had to wait for a ruling.[9]

In March 2007, there were hints of male competition heating up. RBS called to express interest in buying LaSalle, and it hinted at more. Rumors about ING and ABN AMRO began to circulate and were reflected in higher prices for shares of ABN AMRO.[10]

A combined Barclays and ABN AMRO would be the second-largest bank in Europe. Groenink forged ahead with Barclays and told them that they needed to move quickly. In this regard, Groenink preferred a combination with Barclays to a combination with RBS, because a deal with Barclays would leave ABN AMRO intact. Prey who are captured prefer not being dismembered. On March 19, Barclays announced that it was in exclusive preliminary discussions with ABN AMRO concerning a potential merger. This announcement triggered RBS to consider an acquisition more seriously.

On March 20, Barclays and ABN AMRO announced the principles of a deal: €66b in total and 3.125 Barclay shares per share of ABN AMRO. At about that time, ABN AMRO announced that it planned to sell LaSalle to Bank of America. However, in May, a Dutch court found in favor of TCI, thereby preventing both the sale of LaSalle without ABN AMRO shareholder approval and the deal with Barclays.

In April 2007, the consortium began to form, as Merrill Lynch helped RBS, Santander, and Fortis discover that each was interested in obtaining different pieces of ABN AMRO. Fortis wanted ABN AMRO's retail, private banking, and asset management businesses; RBS wanted its American subsidiary LaSalle, global transaction services, and corporate banking; and

Santander wanted its Brazilian business and Antonveneta. The newly formed consortium engaged Merrill Lynch as its investment banker to secure funding, if necessary.

On July 13, 2007, the Dutch Supreme Court overturned the provisional injunction that had earlier been issued, and ruled that ABN AMRO could sell LaSalle without shareholder approval. This decision enabled Bank of America to proceed with its acquisition of LaSalle.

Of course, from the earlier part of the chapter you know how the rest of the story unfolded. The RBS-led consortium battled Barclays in a competition that Goodwin, Lippens, and Votron very badly wanted to win. As Coates tells us, intense male competition involves hormone changes that can induce competitors to take excessive risk. In their desire to win, RBS and Fortis did take excessive risk, not only in acquiring ABN AMRO but in the way they funded the acquisition, and as the chapter recounts, they lost those bets and experienced the winner's curse.

CLOSING THOUGHTS

The events surrounding the acquisition suggest that the same psychological phenomena that operated on decision-makers at US financial institutions were also at work in Europe. Once again, the excessive aspirations and groupthink were clearly in evidence. Of course, the list of pertinent phenomena also includes unrealistic optimism and overconfidence, two of the key ingredients of market sentiment.

There is no way to tell how the acquisition of ABN AMRO would have turned out if the global financial crisis would have been less severe. Nevertheless, in line with the FIH's portrayal of what happens in a boom—excessive leverage, weak regulatory oversight, overreliance on short-term financing, and runs on financial institutions as the boom ends—all figured into the saga of the acquisition, as did contingency socialism. Indeed, almost seven years after the UK government rescued RBS, it began to sell its 80% stake in the bank, at a loss. In February 2015, RBS reported its seventh consecutive annual loss. In doing so, it announced its intention to dismantle its investment bank and to scale back its global presence.[11]

CHAPTER 12

BEHAVIORAL DIMENSION OF SYSTEMIC RISK

SYSTEMIC RISK AND SENTIMENT ARE CORE CONCEPTS OF THE FIH. A FINANCIAL firm is systemically risky when it is too big to fail in a financial crisis, and as a result contingency socialism comes into play as it is rescued by government action. According to the FIH, the route to contingency socialism features the occurrence of euphoria during an economic expansion. Euphoria is the leading edge of sentiment. This chapter discusses empirical aspects of analyzing the coevolution of systemic risk and sentiment over time.

Most of the financial firms discussed in the preceding four chapters required some form of rescue to survive during the global financial crisis. UBS, Fannie Mae, Freddie Mac, AIG, RBS, ABN AMRO, and Fortis all needed direct government assistance to survive. Merrill Lynch survived, only by being acquired by Bank of America.

As the preceding four chapters note, euphoria is part of a broad set of psychological features that underlie the decisions leading to financial fragility and economic instability. Very high aspirations, groupthink, excessive optimism, and overconfidence were strongly evident in every one of the preceding four chapters. Those chapters documented the presence of these phenomena along with the details of how the phenomena were manifest in the risk-taking behavior at specific firms, including those mentioned above.

Sentiment is the collective manifestation in market prices of the psychological phenomena mentioned in the preceding paragraph. Excessive optimism and overconfidence about home prices and defaults led to bubbles, not just in the markets for houses and mortgages but also in credit markets and equity markets.

According to the FIH, there is an important lead-lag relationship between sentiment and the recognition of the buildup in systemic risk. In the FIH dynamic, the emergence of euphoria leads financial firms to take on excessive leverage, the shadow banking system to expand, and financial innovation involving speculative and Ponzi finance to accelerate, which in turn fuels asset-pricing bubbles. Most importantly, the FIH also tells us that as a result of new era thinking, financial firms, investors, and regulators will overlook that these changes are symptoms of increased financial fragility. In consequence, financial regulation will be ineffective.

Eventually the recognition of systemic risk will come, but only when the euphoria dissipates and the associated downshift in sentiment leads to runs on short-term instruments in financial markets, and then contingency socialism as a financial crisis erupts. The upshot is that according to the FIH, the recognition that systemic risk is building in the system is delayed, and occurs as a tipping point once the euphoria has waned

This chapter traces the coevolution of sentiment and systemic risk before and during the eruption of the global financial crisis. In doing so, the chapter discussion draws on the cases described in the previous four chapters. Doing so allows us to compare what was taking place internally within these financial firms with what markets were indicating about how systemically risky these firms were at different points in time. To provide additional context, this chapter also discusses other firms that were central to the crisis, such as Lehman Brothers, Bear Stearns, JPMorgan, Citigroup, Washington Mutual (WaMu), and Wachovia.

Below you will find that the chapter is organized around three questions. How can the systemic risk of a financial firm be measured? How can sentiment be measured? How did sentiment and systemic risk coevolve before and during the financial crisis?

MEASURING THE SYSTEMIC RISK OF FINANCIAL FIRMS

The FCIC describes systemic risk as "a precipitous drop in asset prices, resulting in collateral calls and reduced liquidity."[1] In its report, the FCIC concluded that "dramatic failures of corporate governance and risk management at many systemically important financial institutions were a key cause of this crisis."[2]

The eruption of the global financial crisis created "a systemic event" that led the equity values of many financial firms to plummet. What makes a financial firm systemically important is that the value of its equity, its capital cushion, is highly sensitive to the occurrence of a systemic event. Firms such as RBS, Fortis, Merrill Lynch, and Fannie Mae illustrate the point. None had enough capital to sustain the losses it incurred when the financial crisis erupted in 2008.

This chapter analyzes systemic risk using two variables, marginal expected shortfall (MES) and Systemic RISK (SRISK), which are computed using only publicly available market data. These variables, which are described below, are computed for global financial firms and reported by New York University's Volatility Lab (V-Lab) website: V-Lab is one of the best sources and most easily accessible sites for this type of information.[3] V-Lab provides real-time evidence, measurement, and the modeling of market dynamics for researchers, regulators, and practitioners.[4]

MES is the expected equity loss per dollar *conditional* on the occurrence of a systemic event.[5] In practice, a short-term systemic event is a decline of 2% or more in the value of the market portfolio on a given day. A long-run systemic event is a decline of 40% or more during a six-month period. The default is to treat MES as short run and to be explicit when speaking of the long run.

There are four components for the computation of a firm's MES.[6] The first is an estimate of the market return, conditional on that return falling below −2%. The second component is the standard deviation of the daily return of the firm's stock. This measures total volatility, which is why the third component is the correlation of that return with the daily return of the market. Multiplying these three terms together provides the basis for computing MES. However, because a firm's connectedness to the financial system might be different in a crisis than it is under normal conditions, there is a fourth component, which adjusts for the special nature of extreme left-tail events. Therefore, the methodology for computing MES is based on both correlation with the market return and tail expectations of a standardized innovations distribution.

The V-Lab methodology identifies the presence of a capital shortfall SRISK whenever a firm's equity falls below 8% of its total market capitalization (the sum of its equity and debt).[7] When equity exceeds the 8% ratio, the firm is said to have surplus capital. Surplus capital can be expressed as $E - 0.08(D+E)$, or equivalently $0.92E - 0.08D$, where E denotes equity and D denotes debt. Of course, firms fail when their equity falls to zero, and so E is never negative.

Capital surplus is a dollar amount. V-Lab computes a firm's expected surplus, conditional on the occurrence of a systemic event. When expected surplus is negative, the firm is expected to face a capital shortfall. V-Lab also aggregates the expected capital surplus amounts across firms to compute the expected surplus for the market as a whole.

Because firms vary in size, their contribution to systemic risk will vary. V-Lab reports a variable SRISK% for each firm, which measures the percentage contribution of a firm to the market's expected capital shortfall. Values for SRISK% are computed on a daily basis and used to rank firms on the basis of being systemically risky. The firm with the highest SRISK% is given the number one ranking.

MES provides the basis for computing the expected capital shortfall of a firm should a financial crisis occur. A firm whose total capital shortfall in a crisis is high, especially as a percentage of overall financial sector capital shortfall, not only suffers a major loss but is a major contributor to a crisis. Because a firm with a large capital shortfall will have difficulty raising equity in a crisis, the firm will likely require an infusion of taxpayer money to survive, or else will fail, thereby injecting additional stress into the financial system.

The MES approach is market based in that it reflects the premise that the market will recognize which firms will perform poorly in a crisis. The premise is based upon the belief that the equity holders of a firm that is systemically risky will be aware that they are likely to suffer major losses in a financial crisis, and as a result reduce their positions if a crisis becomes more likely.

Measuring Sentiment

Sentiment pertains to incorrect probability beliefs associated with market events, especially returns.

In probabilistic terms, excessive optimism pertains to overestimating the probabilities of favorable events and underestimating the probability of unfavorable events. As a result, excessive optimism implies upward bias when computing expected value. In the period that preceded the global financial crisis, investors who expected that long-term housing prices would continue to increase much faster than the entire economy were excessively optimistic. The preceding chapters described how during this period, UBS, Merrill Lynch, S&P, Moody's, Fannie Mae, and Freddie Mac, were all excessively optimistic about housing prices.

Overconfidence comes in several forms. One of these forms involves setting confidence intervals that are too narrow. Overconfidence about return distributions implies underestimating future volatility, as measured by return standard deviation. Figure 12.1 depicts the time series of the VIX between January 2000 and September 2015. Notice the low values between 2004 and 2007, indicating that during this period, investors forecast low future volatility. Contrast these low values with their counterparts in 2008 and 2009 as the financial crisis erupted. This contrast suggests investor overconfidence in the years just prior to the financial crisis.

A systemic event is associated with the left tail of the return distribution and corresponds to a crash. When the probability that the market attaches to the future return being −20% or worse is lower than the probability associated with our econometric estimate, we say that the market displays "excessive crash confidence" and measure crash confidence as the log difference

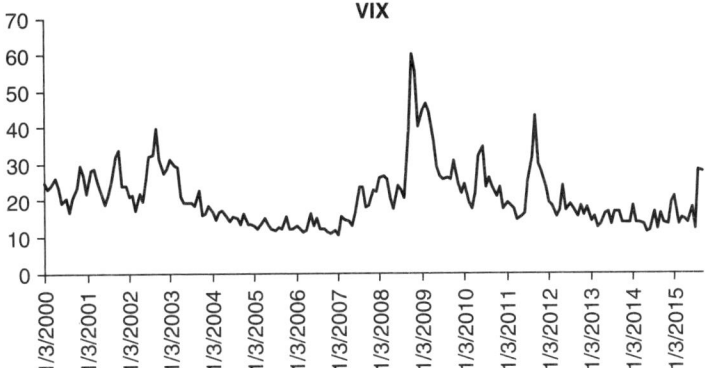

Figure 12.1 This figure depicts the time series of the VIX between January 2000 and September 2015. The low values between 2004 and 2007 indicate that during this period, investors forecast low future volatility, which contrasts with the value of the VIX in 2008 and 2009 as the financial crisis erupted.

between the two probabilities. Excessive crash confidence can be regarded as a special case of excessive optimism.

The discussion in earlier chapters described the key determinants of excessive optimism, namely desirability, control, familiarity, and representativeness (which in particular underlies the hot hand fallacy). Anchoring and adjustment is one of the key determinants of overconfidence linked to confidence intervals that are too narrow.

My fellow economists Giovanni Barone-Adesi and Loriano Mancini and I codeveloped a technique for extracting aggregate probabilistic biases from market data.[8] The basis for our technique involves the computation and comparison of two stochastic processes. The first process is an econometric estimate of future returns for the S&P 500, using past returns and interest rates as data, and relying on GARCH estimation. The second process extracts the market's beliefs (in the aggregate) of future returns for the S&P 500, using index option data and a statistical technique called filtered historical simulation. Appendix G provides additional discussion about the technique used to estimate aggregate probabilistic biases from market data.

In our study, options and stock data cover the period January 2002 to October 2009, and so encompass the lead-up to and eruption of the global financial crisis.[9] For this period, we studied the manner in which market beliefs about future returns differ from our best econometric estimates of future returns. In this regard, we focused on three specific variables: expected return, return standard deviation, and the probability attached to a 20% decline in the market. Notice that the methodology provides an econometric estimate for the probability of a systemic event.

When the market expected return for the S&P 500 exceeds our econometric estimate, we say that the market is excessively optimistic, and measure excessive optimism by the difference between the two. When the market's return standard deviation is less than our econometric estimate, we say that the market is overconfident, and measure overconfidence as the difference between the two. When the market attaches a probability to the occurrence of a crash that is lower than the econometric estimate, we say that the market displays excessive crash confidence.

Figure 12.2 displays the trajectories for excessive optimism and overconfidence between 2002 and 2009. Notably, recessions served as bookends for this period. During the economic expansion between 2004 and 2007, both excessive optimism and overconfidence trended upward.

Figure 12.3 displays the econometric estimate of the crash probability. Notice that this probability followed a U-shape from 2002 through the beginning of 2008, in which it declined during the expansion and rose during the recessions. Notably, the crash probability was high and volatile during the financial crisis. Figure 12.4 displays the left tail sentiment measure, which shows the degree to which the market misestimated this probability. Notice that during the expansion, the market seriously underestimated the crash probability, but overestimated it during the recessions. During the financial crisis, the extent of overestimation is consistent with panic.

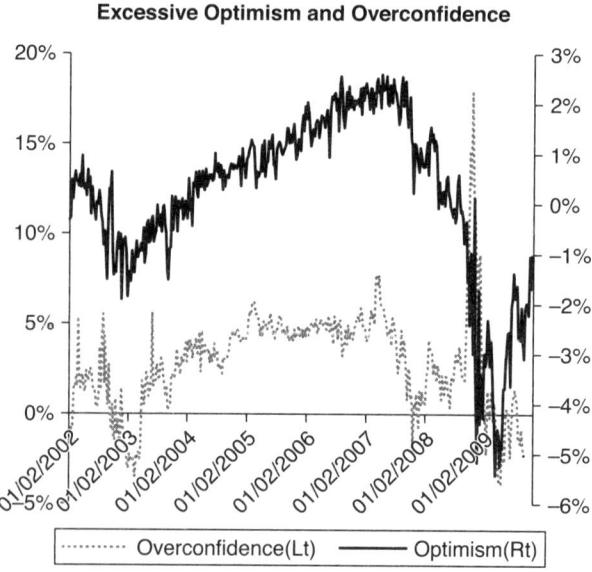

Figure 12.2 This figure displays the trajectories for estimates of excessive optimism and overconfidence between 2002 and 2009, which were extracted from index options data. The period is bracketed by recessions at both ends, and during the intervening economic expansion both excessive optimism and overconfidence trended upwards.

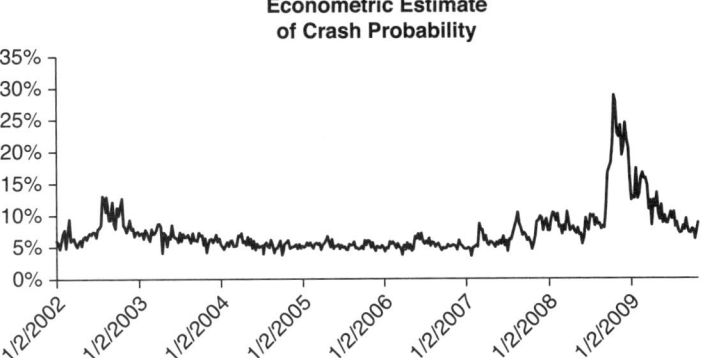

Figure 12.3 This figure displays the econometric estimate of the crash probability. The crash probability followed a U-shape from 2002 through the beginning of 2008, in which it declined during the expansion and rose during the recessions. The crash probability was high and volatile during the financial crisis.

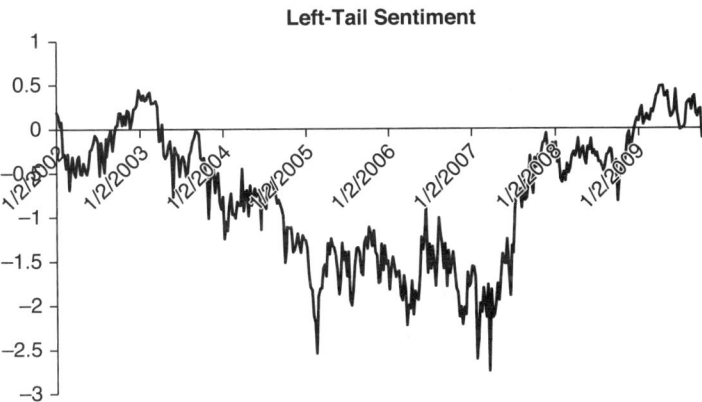

Figure 12.4 This figure displays the left tail sentiment measure, which shows the degree to which the market overestimated the probability of a crash. During the expansion, the market significantly underestimated the crash probability (reflected by negative overestimation), but overestimated it during the recessions. During the financial crisis, the extent of overestimation is consistent with panic.

OTHER INDICATORS OF SENTIMENT

To gain perspective on sentiment, it is important to consider a range of indicators pertaining to sentiment. Economists Malcolm Baker and Jeffrey Wurgler developed one of the most widely used sentiment indicators, henceforth called BW.[10] Appendix G discusses the data used to construct BW. Baker and Wurgler suggest interpreting BW as measuring "optimism or pessimism about stocks in general."[11]

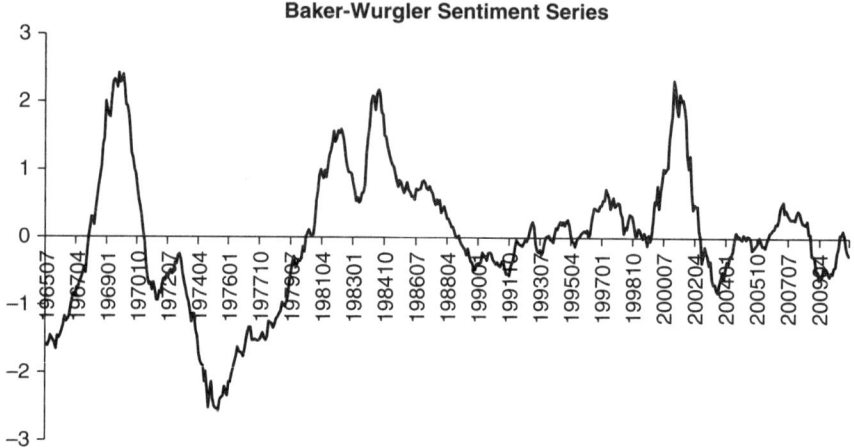

Figure 12.5 This figure displays the long-term trajectory of the Baker-Wurgler sentiment series BW. BW was especially high during the 1960s, the early 1980s, and the late 1990s. BW hit its trough during the 1970s.

Figure 12.5 displays the long-term trajectory of BW. Notice that BW was especially high during the 1960s (the Nifty Fifty period), the early 1980s (beginning of the long bull stock market), and the late 1990s (dot-com bubble). BW hit its trough during the 1970s when oil prices quadrupled, economic growth was weak, and inflation was high. For the period 2002 through 2009, the trajectory of BW is very similar to the trajectory in Figure 12.2 for excessive optimism. Not surprisingly, the two series are highly correlated.

Another important indicator of sentiment is the price-to-earnings (P/E) ratio developed by economists John Campbell and Robert Shiller.[12] Campbell and Shiller's P/E for US stocks features a stock price index P being divided by an average of earnings over the prior ten years. They call this the cyclically adjusted price-earnings ratio (CAPE). Here both price and earnings are adjusted for inflation. One of their key findings is that subsequent ten-year returns to stocks are negatively and statistically related to P/E. See Figure 12.6, which displays both P/E and long-term interest rates.

Campbell and Shiller suggest when investors become "irrationally exuberant," prices rise relative to earnings in an unwarranted manner. As a result, future returns are low because current prices are too high.[13] Notice that for the period 2002 through 2009, P/E followed a trajectory similar to both excessive optimism and BW.

In 1984, Shiller began collecting questionnaire survey data on the behavior of US investors. That project now continues as the Investor Behavior

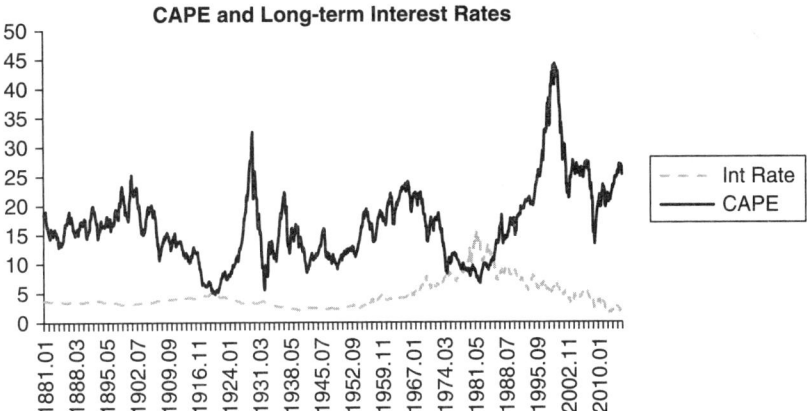

Figure 12.6 This figure displays CAPE, Campbell and Shiller's cyclically adjusted P/E for US stocks, that features a stock price index P being divided by an average of earnings over the prior ten years. The figure displays the trajectories for both P/E and long-term interest rates for the period January 1881 through August 2015.

Project at Yale University (IBP), under his direction, and collects data from both the United States and Japan. There are four IBP confidence indexes. These respectively measure confidence that the market is fairly valued, confidence that there will be no crash in the next six months, confidence that the market will go up in the next 12 months, and confidence that the market will reverse in the short term (buying-on-dips).

Here we focus on crash confidence, which measures the percentage of the population who attach little probability to a stock market crash in the next six months.[14] Figure 12.7 depicts the trajectory of the crash confidence index. Notice that the crash confidence index follows a trajectory that is inversely related to left-tail sentiment portrayed in Figure 12.4.

Crash confidence relates to left-tail risk, as do credit spreads. A credit spread measure developed by Simon Gilchrist and Egon Zakrajšek measures the component of the corporate bond market default premium index that is not related to firm-specific information on expected defaults. Figure 12.8 depicts the trajectory of this component, called the "excess bond premium." The excess bond premium is typically negative during economic expansions, but turns positive before and during declines in economic activity. A rise in the excess bond premium represents a reduction in the effective risk-bearing capacity of the financial sector and, as a result, a contraction in the supply of credit with significant adverse consequences for the macroeconomy. Notice that the bond premium index follows a similar trajectory to left-tail sentiment.

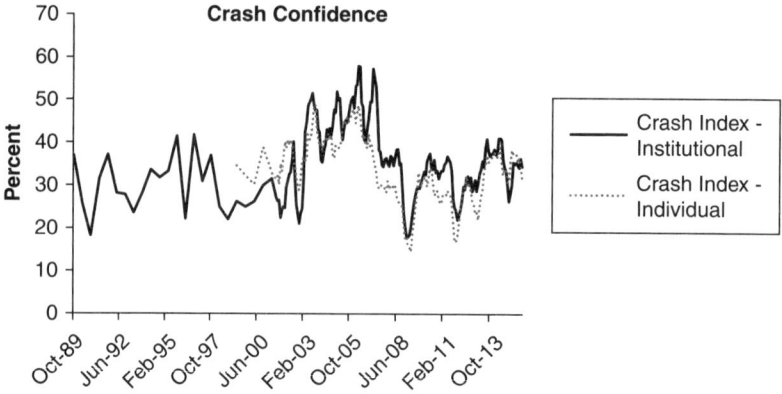

Figure 12.7 This figure displays the trajectory of the Yale/Shiller crash confidence indices for both institutional investors and individual investors, October 1989 through August 2015.

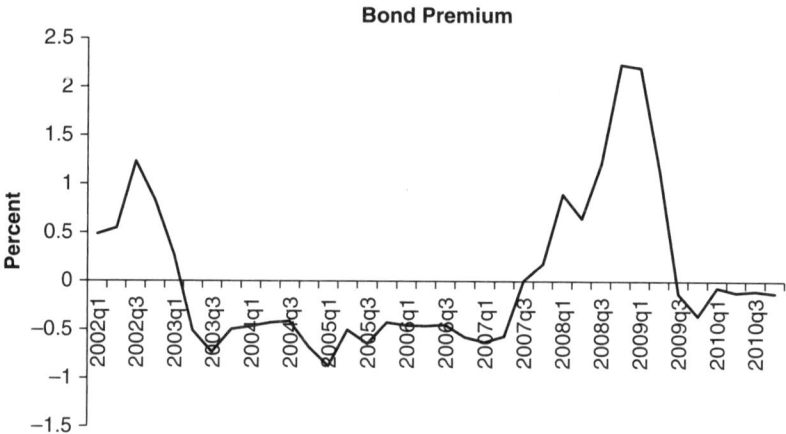

Figure 12.8 This figure displays the trajectory of the Gilchrist-Zakrajšek credit spread, called the "excess bond premium," measuring the component of the corporate bond market default premium index that is not related to firm-specific information on expected defaults.

There is a bottom line here: the various aspects of sentiment all roughly align, be they derived from option markets, equity markets, bond markets, and investor surveys.

TRAJECTORIES OF SENTIMENT AND SYSTEMIC RISK AS EUPHORIA WAXED AND WANED

This section describes the coevolution of sentiment and systemic risk during the euphoric period that preceded the eruption of the financial crisis.

Figure 12.2 show us that between January 2004 and February 2007, the values of optimism and overconfidence both rose. Figure 12.7 indicates that crash confidence trended upward, meaning that investors grew less concerned about an imminent crash. Figure 12.6 indicates that P/E stabilized around 25, a level historically associated with major market declines. Figure 12.7 also depicts the trajectory of interest rates. Notably, the risk premium (difference between expected return and the risk-free rate) gradually declined.

Housing prices continued to climb at about 10% per year, and peaked in early 2006. Defaults on subprime mortgages increased in the first quarter of 2007. Notably, both optimism and overconfidence were strongly correlated with the level of housing prices.

In respect to systemic risk, the V-Lab data, which begin in 2000, suggest that in 2005 and 2006 financial firms' leverage was relatively stable and did not rise dramatically, even when optimism and overconfidence increased.[15] Only in March 2007 did both MES and leverage begin to deteriorate, with the deterioration becoming ever more severe as the crisis unfolded.

The V-Lab systemic risk measures are based on market prices. The fact that these measures were stable during the ascent of optimism, overconfidence, and left-tail sentiment suggests that the market overlooked the rise in risk of systemically important firms. This feature is exactly in line with the FIH.

Just take a moment to reflect back on what the previous chapters described about what was happening between 2004 and 2007 at Fannie Mae, Freddie Mac, AIG, Merrill, and UBS. In 2004, Fannie Mae and Freddie Mac significantly increased their purchases of private label mortgage securities. In 2005, AIG learned that the proportion of subprime in the collateral pool on which it was selling CDS protection was not the reasonable 10%, but between 80% and 90%. Between January 2005 and January 2007, Merrill Lynch became the largest seller of mortgage-based CDOs, and UBS ramped up its CDO business during the same period.

Some people took notice. In October 2005, the head of the Office of the Comptroller of the Currency (OCC), John Dugan, gave a speech that warned about Ponzi finance in the mortgage market. Although he did not use the term "Ponzi finance," the following excerpt makes clear that is what he is describing: "Recent studies show that a significant number of borrowers are frequently choosing to pay the minimum amount possible, a payment amount that typically falls short of the interest accruing on the loan.... Because such minimum payments fall considerably short of the total interest accruing each month, the unpaid interest is added to the loan principal, and negative amortization occurs.... Of course, the borrower might be able to refinance, but what if interest rates have increased substantially, or house prices have dropped below the value of the loan? That would put the borrower in a far more difficult position."[16]

Back then, what was the market missing? It certainly missed the shift toward speculative and Ponzi finance that Dugan identified, which according to the FIH markets and regulators are prone to discount. Therefore, the market missed the shift and associated buildup of systemic risk during this period. Between 2004 and 2007, the MES for Merrill fluctuated between 2 and 5 with no discernable trend. The same statement roughly applies to AIG, Fannie Mae, and other firms that figured prominently in the financial crisis to follow, such as Bear Stearns and Lehman Brothers.[17]

Between March and September 2007, the euphoria began to wane, but gradually. Overconfidence declined, but optimism continued to increase. This finding is especially interesting because, as discussed in previous chapters, the FCIC uses the term "madness" to characterize investment decisions during the first part of 2007. They do so because, despite housing prices having peaked in early 2006 and subprime mortgage default rates beginning to rise, some financial firms such as Citigroup, Merrill Lynch, and UBS continued to increase their exposure to subprime mortgages.

The crash confidence index peaked at the end of February 2007 and subsequently declined sharply. A run on commercial paper took place between August and December 2007, as bad news about defaults on subprime mortgages intensified. During this time, optimism and overconfidence both declined, temporarily dipping below zero in November.

V-Lab provides data to monitor leverage, MES, expected capital shortfall, and SRISK% with its implied systemic risk ranking. Keep in mind that MES is the expected equity loss per dollar invested in a particular financial firm if the overall market decline corresponds to a systemic event. The empirical approach underlying the analysis at V-Lab recognizes a bidirectional effect, in that firms having the highest MES are likely those that contribute the most to the market declining. Therefore, firms having the highest MES are the most important candidates for being characterized as systemically risky.

At V-Lab, leverage is measured as the ratio of assets over equity, measured in terms of market value A firm whose equity comprises 8% of their assets has a leverage ratio of 12.5. Recall that V-Lab treats 8% as the threshold value for the presence of a capital shortfall.

"The madness" period included March 2007, which featured some indications of weakness in the subprime housing sector. According to V-Lab, the SRISK% rankings at the time placed Morgan Stanley at the top, followed by Merrill Lynch, Goldman Sachs, Fannie Mae, and Freddie Mac. Together, these five firms represented 57% of the market's expected capital shortfall. Goldman Sachs had the lowest leverage in this group, at 10, while Freddie Mac had the highest, at 21.[18]

For the rest of the chapter, we dig down into the numbers. In March 2007, the mean leverage for the top five was 13.8. At the time, Lehman ranked number seven and had leverage of 16. Bear Stearns ranked number nine and had leverage of 22. Wachovia ranked 37, with a leverage of 7. AIG ranked number 92, with leverage of 6. Figure 12.9 displays both SRISK% and leverage for these firms.

Between March and August 2007, a distinct shift in sentiment took place. Overconfidence steadily decreased from 6.25% to 3.7%, even though the S&P 500 rose by 3.7%, and optimism was quite stable at about 2% until July, when it dipped to 1.2%. In this respect, the IBP crash confidence index plummeted from 55% to 34%, and the BW index exhibited no discernible trend.

Between March and August, leverage began to increase for almost all of the firms mentioned above. Bear Stearns and Lehman were the first firms to fall during the crisis to come. For Bear Stearns, the increase was marked: from an initial level of 22, its leverage moved to 31. Lehman's leverage went from 16 to 20.

Underlying the changes in leverage were shifts in sentiment, particularly overconfidence, which impacted the value of collateral and financing arrangements. The FCIC report tells us that investment banks such as Bear Stearns relied heavily on triple-A-rated private mortgage-backed securities (PMBS) as collateral for raising short-term financing through repurchase agreements (repos). PMBS comprised roughly one-third of Bear Stearns's collateral. Once concerns about mortgage defaults began to rise, sentiment

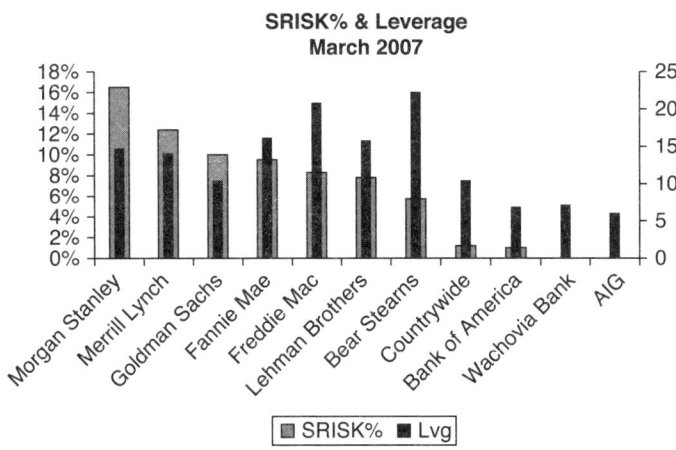

Figure 12.9 This figure displays SRISK% and leverage, at the end of March 2007, for a select set of financial firms appearing on the horizontal axis. SRISK% measures the percentage contribution an individual firm makes to overall systemic risk. Leverage is measured as assets over equity.

about PMBS quickly became negative, and investment banks lost much of their ability to borrow short term. The FCIC staff "showed that the loss of the PMBS market was the single event that was crippling for Bear, because it eliminated a major portion of the firm's liquidity pool."[19]

The sharp drop in overconfidence between March and August preceded one of two runs on ABCP during the financial crisis. The first took place between August and December 2007. As subprime mortgage defaults rose, financial firms that issued commercial paper in order to raise funds to purchase MBSs suddenly found themselves unable to do so. The run extended to financial firms issuing commercial paper not backed by mortgage assets. This suggests investor panic. During the run, optimism and overconfidence both fell sharply, falling to about –2% in mid-October before climbing back to positive territory near zero for the remainder of the run.

At the end of September 2007, the top five in the systemic risk ranking had shifted from March. Citigroup rose to the top, followed by Morgan Stanley, Merrill Lynch, Goldman Sachs, and JPMorgan. Of the future casualties, Lehman had moved into the number six position, followed by Fannie Mae, Freddie Mac, Bear Stearns, and Wachovia. AIG had moved up to number 66. Figure 12.10 displays SRISK% and leverage for these firms.

The movements in sentiment coincided with concerns that were not reflected in the S&P 500, which continued to trend upward until December 2007. During this period, sentiment was statistically related to conditions in the housing market. Between March and December 2007, the house price index declined at a 10% rate. Between 2002 and 2009, the house price index was highly correlated with optimism, overconfidence, and crash confidence.[20]

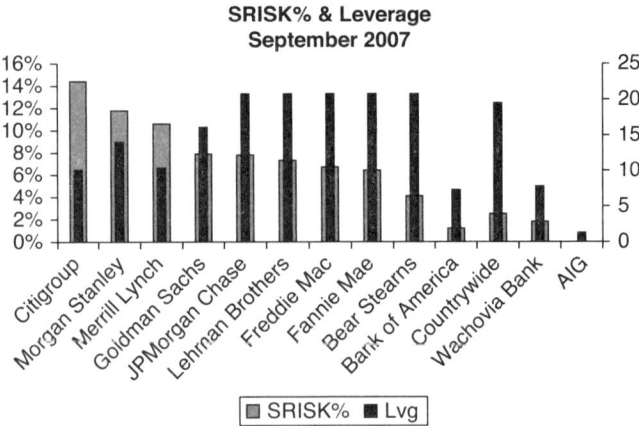

Figure 12.10 This figure displays SRISK% and leverage, at the end of September 2007, for a select set of financial firms appearing on the horizontal axis. SRISK% measures the percentage contribution an individual firm makes to overall systemic risk. Leverage is measured as assets over equity.

Sentiment and Systemic Risk during 2008 and 2009

December 2007 marked the beginning of an 18-month recession. Optimism and overconfidence briefly rebounded in January to 1% and 4% respectively before beginning a volatile decline back to negative territory. By mid-March, optimism was near zero, and overconfidence was at 2%.

At the end of December 2007, Bank of America's V-Lab systemic risk ranking was eight, and its leverage was 11. Countrywide's ranking was 16, and its leverage was 39. In January 2008, Bank of America announced that it would buy Countrywide Financial for $4.1 billion. In March 2008, Bank of America ranked number 3 in systemic risk, behind Citigroup and Merrill Lynch. Should this change in ranking have raised any red flags?

Absolutely: that March was precipitous. Bear Stearns would have failed that month, but for an emergency loan provided by the Federal Reserve Bank of New York and the firm's agreeing to be acquired by JPMorgan Chase.

Recall that MES measures the sensitivity of a financial firm's systemic risk to a short-term systemic event in which the S&P 500 declines by at least 2%. Figure 12.11 displays data for the firms described earlier, but sorted by MES. Not surprisingly, Bear Stearns is at the top, followed by Lehman Brothers.[21]

At long last, the market was finally beginning to recognize the systemic risk buildup. Bear Stearns's March MES increased to 47% in March 2008 from about 5% in February. Interestingly, its February value for MES was higher than for some banks, such as Goldman Sachs and JPMorgan, both of

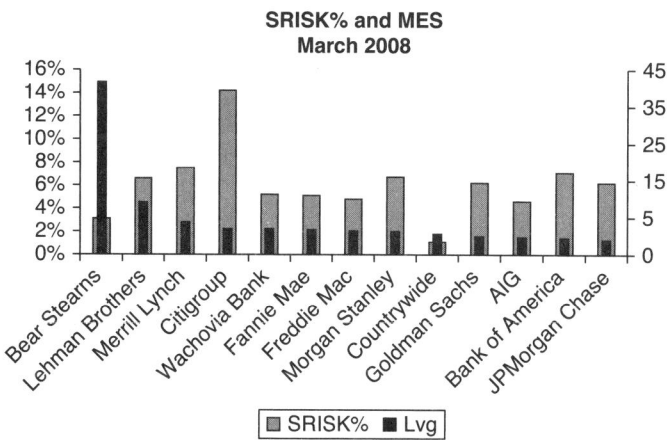

Figure 12.11 This figure displays SRISK% and MES, at the end of March 2008, for a select set of financial firms appearing on the horizontal axis. SRISK% measures the percentage contribution an individual firm makes to overall systemic risk. MES is marginal expected shortfall, and measures the sensitivity of a firm's capital to declines in the overall market.

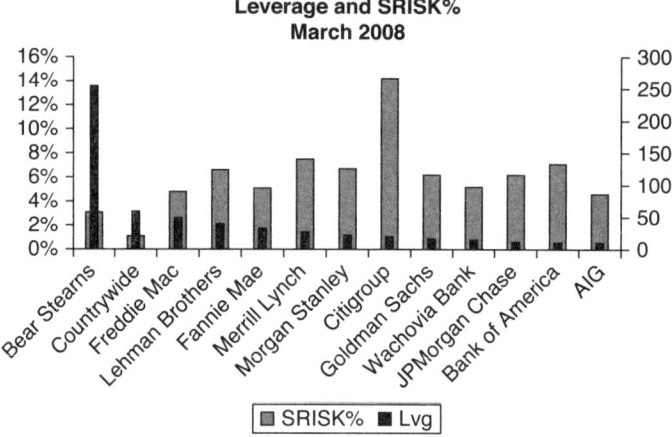

Figure 12.12 This figure displays SRISK% and leverage, at the end of March 2008, for a select set of financial firms appearing on the horizontal axis. SRISK% measures the percentage contribution an individual firm makes to overall systemic risk. Leverage is measured as assets over equity.

whose MES values were in the range of 3% to 4%, but not as high as Lehman Brothers and Merrill Lynch whose MES values exceeded 5%.

Figure 12.12 displays the March-end leverage and SRISK% values for the key firms discussed above. The most striking feature in the figure is Bear Stearns's leverage peaking at 254! Notice too that by this time Freddie Mac's leverage had increased to 49, and Fannie Mae's leverage had increased to 32. Lehman's leverage stood at 39.

By May 2008, optimism and overconfidence had both fallen to near zero. At this time, JPMorgan Chase completed its acquisition of Bear Stearns. JPMorgan Chase's leverage increased to 11 from its March 2007 value of 8. Of course, 11 was a lot less than the leverage levels at the time of Freddie, Fannie, and Lehman.

At the end of June, Freddie Mac's leverage increased to 83, and Fannie Mae's leverage increased to 45. Lehman's leverage increased to 46. Clearly these firms had extremely thin capital cushions. How sensitive were these firms' cushions to a systemic event?

Figure 12.13 provides an answer, displaying the MES trajectories for select financial institutions for the period May through October. The data are ordered according to the MES values in August, several weeks before the Lehman bankruptcy. As you can see, in August Fannie Mae, Freddie Mac, and Lehman headed the list, closely followed by AIG, Merrill Lynch, and Wachovia.[22]

At the end of August, the systemic risk ranking SRISK% placed Citigroup at the top, followed by Bank of America and JPMorgan. In this regard, keep in mind that SRISK% reflects the firm's size, while MES is the more

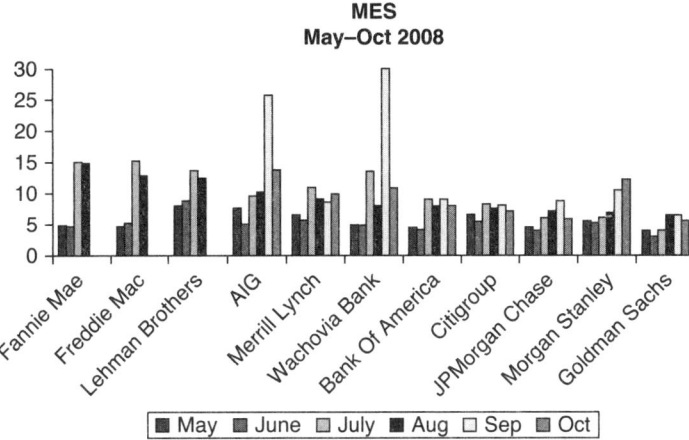

Figure 12.13 This figure displays the MES trajectories for select financial institutions for the period May through October of 2008. The data are ordered according to the MES values in August, several weeks before the Lehman bankruptcy.

appropriate indicator for measuring vulnerability to a systemic event. You can see from Figure 12.13 that Lehman's MES rose above 12% in the two months before its bankruptcy in September 2008. Yes, the market was finally recognizing Lehman's systemic risk.

How did systemic risk and sentiment evolve in the year or so after Lehman's bankruptcy? Let us begin with sentiment. Optimism plummeted after Lehman's bankruptcy and the government rescue of AIG, when it became negative, which is to say that the market became excessively pessimistic. Notably, overconfidence soared to almost 8%, which implies that investors seriously underestimated future volatility! AIG's September MES increased dramatically to 25% from already high values of 10% in July and August.

Looking at Figure 12.13, you can see that it displays no values for Fannie, Freddie, and Lehman after August, thereby reflecting Lehman's September bankruptcy and the two GSEs being taken into conservatorship.

By the end of September, the market had turned from being optimistic to being pessimistic (by over 1%). AIG's MES had soared to 25.8%. Citigroup, Merrill Lynch, Morgan Stanley, and even JPMorgan Chase all had MES values above 8%. Goldman Sachs stood out as an exception, with an MES of 6.5%. At this time, Wachovia became a casualty of the Lehman bankruptcy, and in October was acquired by Wells Fargo. Based on total assets, Wachovia had been the fourth-largest bank holding company and one of the largest providers of financial services in the United States.

Rounding out the discussion, here briefly is how the leverage-MES story played out in the year that followed. During the period through October 2009, leverage levels continued to soar. Morgan Stanley's leverage peaked at 52 in October 2008. It was unclear whether Morgan Stanley would survive, and the firm sought protection by registering as a holding company with the Federal Reserve. AIG's leverage peaked at 143 in February 2009. Citigroup's leverage peaked at 122 in March.

MES levels were also elevated between September 2008 and March 2009, and for most of the surviving firms began to decline toward the end of the sample period. AIG was an exception, as its MES, which had fallen to 5.53% in May 2009, rose again in the summer to 11%.

Between February and May 2009, the Federal Reserve, together with the Office of the Comptroller of the Currency and the Federal Deposit Insurance Corporation conducted a set of stress tests on 19 major bank holding companies. These tests were part of a program called the Supervisory Capital Assessment Program (SCAP). These tests were conducted to determine whether the capital buffers were sufficient to withstand losses and sustain lending, in the event that the economic downturn proved to be more severe than was anticipated at the time. The results of SCAP established which banks had adequate capital, and for those that did not, what were the magnitudes of their shortfalls. Bank of America topped the list, with a shortfall of $34 billion. At that time, Bank of America also topped V-Lab's systemic risk chart based on SRISK%.

During the euphoric period, correlations between sentiment and MES are virtually zero. However, as the euphoria wanes and sentiment declines, the market's recognition of systemic risk will increase, with sentiment and MES becoming negatively correlated. How strong were theses correlations? Figure 12.14 displays the absolute values of correlations between excessive optimism and MES for the period March 2007 through October 2009.[23]

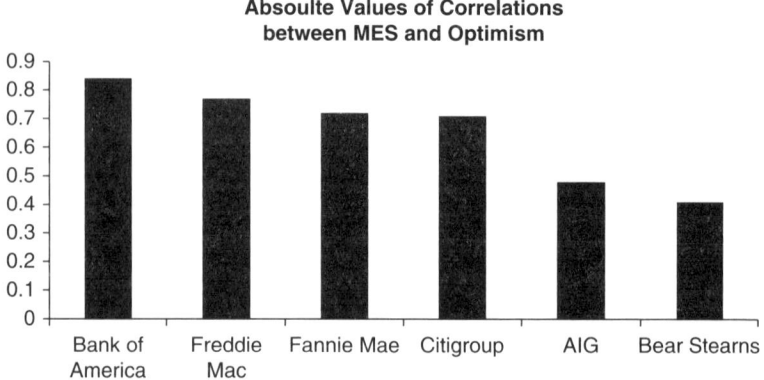

Figure 12.14 The figure displays the absolute values of correlations between excessive optimism and MES and optimism for the period March 2007 through October 2009. The sign of all correlations was negative.

CLOSING THOUGHTS

In respect to the global financial crisis, what did the market know and when did it know it? The FIH tells us that systemic risk builds during the euphoric period as financial innovation leads to higher proportions of speculative and Ponzi finance. However, because of new era thinking, markets do not recognize this buildup and ignore the shift toward speculative and Ponzi finance until the euphoria begins to wane. The global financial crisis conformed to this pattern.

Systemic risk rankings do not measure total risk, but risk conditional on the occurrence of a systemic event. Systemic risk rankings are important only to the extent that the probability of a systemic event occurring is sufficiently high. The econometric techniques discussed in the chapter provide estimates of how this probability varies over time.

CHAPTER 13

FINANCIAL REGULATION AND PSYCHOLOGY

REGULATION OF THE FINANCIAL SYSTEM WILL NEVER BE PERFECT, AND SO a key question facing regulators is how to mitigate the imperfections. Finance is complex, and complex systems fail in complex ways. This chapter analyzes key psychological phenomena impacting the process of regulating the financial system.

There are several reasons why microprudential regulation focuses so much attention on financial firms' capital cushions. Regulators, as representatives of the tax-paying public, care about capital cushions because of contingency socialism. Financial firms that are solvent, and either too big to fail or too interconnected to fail, will typically be rescued with taxpayers' money when facing the serious possibility of failure. Firms with sizable capital cushions are less prone to the threat of failure, partly because they are less immune to unfavorable events, and partly because their managers are less likely to choose excessively risky projects. Regulators have the task of monitoring the financial system to limit taxpayers' exposure to having to pick up the bill when things go financially wrong.

Regulators focus on the magnitude of capital cushions because shareholders of financial firms prefer thin capital cushions. When things go well, thin capital means there are fewer equity dollars over which to divide the spoils. When things go poorly, thin capital means that shareholders have less to lose, as taxpayers absorb all remaining losses after their capital has been depleted. In contrast, regulators theoretically have an interest in fatter capital cushions for three main reasons.

The first reason is to provide more of a buffer before bad news makes a financial firm insolvent. The second reason is because managers of firms with fatter capital cushions have more to lose if they make poor decisions. As William Black points out, ever present is the potential for control fraud through strategies featuring high risk and growth.[1] The third reason is that systemic events generate negative macroeconomic shocks by disrupting the amount of credit available to the economy, and multiplier effects that then magnify the shocks to lower aggregate economic activity and increase unemployment.

Regulators, acting through the central bank, do not rescue all financial firms that incur financial distress. Typically, regulators only come to the aid of financial firms that are solvent, but are dealing with liquidity issues because they need to raise cash to avoid a run, but can only do so by selling at fire sale prices. Therefore, central banks purchase assets from these firms, seeking to make a profit themselves, but mainly attempting to provide distressed financial firms with enough cash to fend off runs.

All of this is fine in theory. However, the global financial crisis made clear that what sounds fine in theory did not turn out all that well in practice. Surprise is the hallmark of overconfidence, and the global financial crisis surprised most everyone. Therefore, let us see what we can learn from the surprises, in order to generate some important behavioral takeaways.

AS THE REGULATORY WORLD TURNS

Among the trove of documents that the FCIC released to the public was a document known as the Beim report.[2] This report was commissioned in the wake of the global financial crisis by Federal Reserve Bank of New York President William Dudley. Dudley wanted to know why the New York Fed failed to identify the warning signs, and what it could do to improve. He intended the report to be completely confidential. However, the Beim report inadvertently found its way into the public domain.

The "Beim" in the Beim report is finance academic David Beim of Columbia University. Dudley had given him unlimited access to produce his report. Beim found that the New York Fed had a problematic culture. Fed examiners feared contradicting their bosses. Deliberations required consensus, which served to water down conclusions. As a result, the institution was not only risk averse but deferential to those banks it supervised. In this regard, Beim described the situation he observed at the New York Fed as regulatory capture: the tail was wagging the dog. Beim recommended that if the New York Fed wanted to improve itself, it needed to hire expert examiners who did not fear voicing their opinions, but were instead encouraged to do so. From a process-pitfall point of view, Beim was clearly suggesting that the New York Fed's information-sharing processes were infected by groupthink, and therefore were weak in respect to risk management behavior.

After Beim submitted his report, the New York Fed did make some organizational changes. However, changing the culture of a large institution is no easy task. The tendency to seek consensus and to mute those with dissenting views and nondeferential attitudes continued. Supervisors would criticize dissenters for disrupting the New York Fed's esprit de corps by being insufficiently relational, and, of course, dissenters could always be fired for not compromising their views. Beim described the dynamic at work in the period leading up to the financial crisis. He discovered that there were lengthy presentations to Fed officials and meetings on the topic. However, these meetings did not conclude with action items to address the information in question.

The situation at the United Kingdom at the time was similar in important ways. In 2005 and 2006, when Bank of England examiners met with financial firms in the City of London, the firms acknowledged significant imbalances in credit flows, excessively low risk premiums, and excessively high exposure to those risks. When examiners would ask whether the firms planned to reduce those exposures, the response would be no, as doing so when others were not was tantamount to economic suicide.

The bankers' response brings to mind a quip by Charles Prince, then CEO of Citigroup, about the need to keep dancing as long as the music is playing. It was July 2007 when Prince made this comment, responding to a question from the *Financial Times* about the fear of downturn in global financial markets that might be triggered by the turmoil in the US subprime mortgage market. In this regard, the *Financial Times* made the point of using the phrase "cheap credit-fuelled buy-out boom" to describe the financial climate at the time.[3]

Were the City of London bankers and Prince exhibiting short-term irrational responses in a dollar auction kind of game, or were their responses rational when viewed in the context of their incentives at the time? The answer really does depend on how their incentives were structured. Academic theory can help us understand the nature of competitive time pressures that produce this outcome. The theory also provides insight into how to use bonuses as "carrots" to incentivize money managers to rely on risk management and how to use clawbacks as "sticks" to punish manipulative behavior that gets detected.[4]

There is a moral to the stories about the New York Fed and the Bank of England. Regulatory culture matters. Psychology can inject itself to create huge gaps between theory and practice. This is not to say that theory is useless. Theory is useful, but only part of the story. The remainder of the chapter introduces the theory, and then moves on to other important parts of the story.

ASSETS, LIABILITIES, AND VALUE-AT-RISK IN THEORY

To understand why all is fine in theory, we need to begin with some theory. The following textbook formula defines the concept of a firm's return on equity (ROE), and allows us to investigate the relationship between ROE and leverage:

$$ROE = [(EBIT - iD)(1 - t)]/E.$$

In the formula, the symbol *EBIT* denotes a firm's earnings before income and tax, *E* denotes shareholder equity, *D* denotes debt, *t* denotes the corporate tax rate, and *i* denotes the interest rate it pays to its lenders. The formula is easy to understand. Because interest is tax deductible, the difference *EBIT-iD* provides the earnings base upon which corporate tax is computed. When this base is multiplied by *(1-t)*, the remainder *(EBIT-iD)(1-t)* is earnings after tax, also known as "earnings" or "net income." Dividing earnings by shareholder equity constitutes *ROE*.

To analyze the impact of the capital cushion on *ROE*, notice that the formula for *ROE* is a linear equation in *EBIT* with slope of *(1-t)/E* and intercept of *–iD(1-t)/E*. A thinner capital cushion means a lower value of *E*, relative to the other variables. Reducing the value of *E* increases the slope and lowers the intercept. In favorable times, when *EBIT* is high, a lower capital cushion *E* results in *ROE* being higher than it would be for a higher capital cushion, as the effect of the slope will dominate the effect of the intercept for large enough *E*. But in unfavorable times, when *EBIT* is low, if not negative, the higher slope and more negative intercept combine to make *ROE* lower than it would be for a higher capital cushion.[5] Figure 13.1 illustrates, with two values for *EBIT* marked, unfavorable (*U*) and favorable (*F*).

In very unfavorable times, *EBIT* becomes negative, and the associated losses reduce shareholder equity. If times are sufficiently unfavorable, these losses can wipe out all of shareholder equity. For a financial firm, such losses mean insolvency. In respect to risk, the formula for *ROE* indicates that the key drivers are statistical properties of *EBIT*, the capital structure variables *E* and *D*, and the interest rate *i*.

Notably, a sequence of unfavorable *EBIT* events causes the *ROE* line in Figure 13.1 to get steeper progressively, thereby causing the magnification factor on *ROE* to intensify. Continuing bad news about *EBIT* becomes even worse news for *ROE*.

In respect to risk of losses, the questions are how large and how likely. VaR is structured as a tool to answer these questions, based on how risky are the assets (as reflected in the statistical properties of *EBIT*), and the capital structure variables *E*, *D*, and *i*.

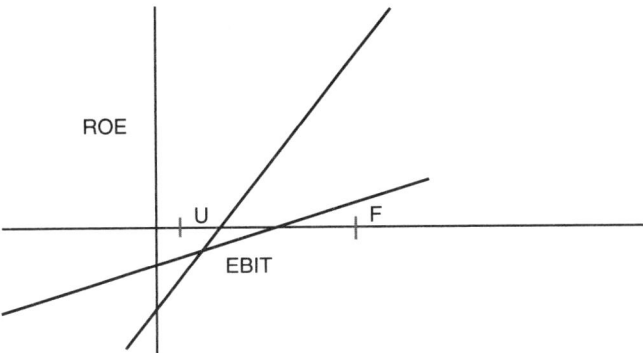

Figure 13.1 This figure displays the equation *ROE* = *[(EBIT − iD)(1−t)]/E*. Here *EBIT* denotes a firm's earnings before income and tax, *E* denotes shareholder equity, *D* denotes debt, *t* denotes the corporate tax rate, and *i* denotes the interest rate the firm pays to its lenders. *ROE* is a linear equation in *EBIT* with slope of *(1−t)/E* and intercept of *−iD(1−t)/E*. illustrates, with two values for *EBIT* marked, unfavorable (*U*) and favorable (*F*).

Because future EBIT is a random variable, the formula determining the expected value of *ROE* (*Exp(ROE)*) is

Exp(ROE) = *−iD(1 − t)/E + (1 − t)/E Exp(EBIT)*,

where *Exp(EBIT)* is the expected value of *EBIT*. From this formula it is easy to see that unless *Exp(EBIT)* is very small, lowering the capital cushion (by increasing *1/E*) raises *Exp(ROE)*. Moreover, the standard deviation of *ROE* is *(1−t)/E* times the standard deviation of *EBIT*. Therefore, thinner capital increases *ROE*-tail risk, by magnifying *EBIT*-tail risk.

The statistical properties of *EBIT* are determined by the firm's assets. For a financial firm, these properties reflect the spectrum of its exposures to credit risk, the equity markets, and derivative positions. In theory, if we specify a target VaR and associated loss probability p_L, but keep the asset side of the balance sheet fixed, then we can seek a debt-to-equity ratio *D/E* that produces the target VaR. A value of *D/E* that is too low will produce a probability for the target VaR that is too high, while a value of *D/E* that is too high will produce a probability for the target VaR that is too low.

Figure 13.2 illustrates the main issues under discussion. The figure depicts the bell-shaped density function and corresponding cumulative distribution function for a normally distributed random variable *z* with mean 0 and standard deviation 1. A realization of *z* generates the realized value of *EBIT*, which is assumed to satisfy the equation *z* = *2.5 + 2z*. Shareholder equity is assumed to be 5, and debt is assumed to be 45, so that leverage = assets/equity = 50/5 = 10. The tax rate is assumed to be 35%, and the interest rate at which the firm can borrow is assumed to be 3%. Net income (*NI*) and

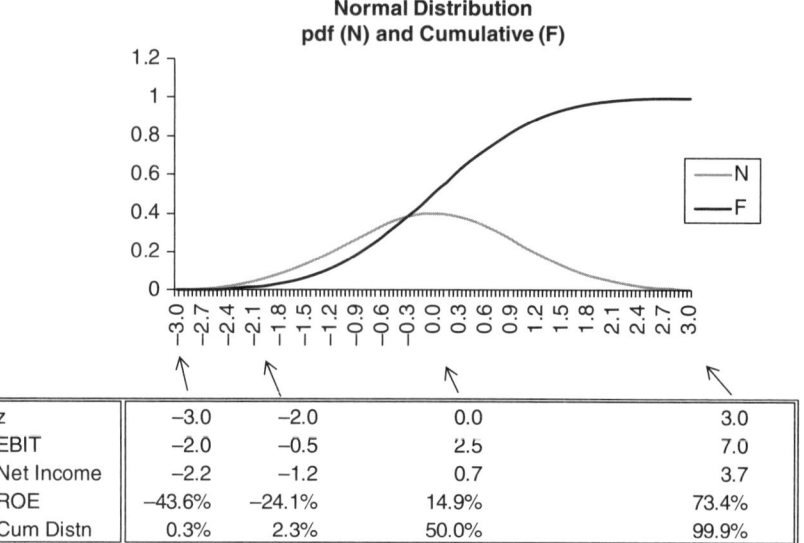

Figure 13.2 This figure depicts the bell-shaped density function and corresponding cumulative distribution function for a normally distributed random variable z with mean 0 and standard deviation 1. A realization of z generates the realized value of *EBIT*, which is assumed to satisfy the equation *EBIT* = 2.5 + 2z.

ROE are assumed to obey the formulas described above. In Figure 13.2, the probability associated with the target VaR is assumed to be 2.3%, which corresponds to an *ROE* of −24.1%.

An alternative to lowering the loss probability associated with a target VaR is to change the asset mix in order to reduce *EBIT*-risk. If the statistical effect of lowering *EBIT*-risk is about the same as increasing the capital cushion, then lower *EBIT*-risk can offset the need for a higher capital cushion. Therefore, in theory, regulators who settle on a target VaR they deem to be appropriate, will be able to match the required capital cushion to the riskiness of the firm's assets.

Assets, Liabilities, and Value-at-Risk in Practice

Assessing *EBIT*-risk in practice and then inferring the appropriate capital cushion is a nontrivial exercise. There is no perfect way of accomplishing these tasks, and so everyone must rely on heuristics to make the effort. By their nature, heuristics are imperfect, which is an important reason why there is so much debate about what are reasonable expectations for risk managers.

Between 2006 and 2008, Riccardo Rebonato made a series of presentations describing his general views on risk management.[6] He began by reminding his audience that risk managers' main task is to inform senior managers about daily volatility associated with their firm's chosen strategy. Part of this task, he said, involves highlighting adverse, but plausible, scenarios for the performance of the strategy. In this regard, he warned risk managers about recognizing the conditions under which risk management techniques such as VaR can be reliably based on frequencies derived from historical data.

The term "frequentist" refers to the approach to statistical modeling that heavily relies on historical data, and features an implicit assumption that the features of these data are germane to assessing future risk. "Frequentist" statistical techniques typically involve three stages. The first stage involves investigating the kinds of realizations that would emanate from alternative probability distributions, such as Poisson, Brownian motion, binomial, and power law. The second stage is collecting data. The third stage consists of analyzing historical data by seeking a statistical model that best fits the data.

In his presentations, Rebonato explained that this approach works well when market conditions change slowly, when data is collected frequently, when the forecast horizon is relatively short, and when the focus of attention is on moderate rather than high percentiles. However, he warned about placing too much reliance on this approach when these conditions are not met and the situation conforms to what some call "fundamental uncertainty."

Financial firms hold portfolios with securities featuring different levels of credit risk. Figure 13.3 displays the patterns of default rates over time for double-A- and B-rated bonds.[7] Default patterns for other ratings lie in between these two. Most importantly, rates of default for bonds rated A and above tended to be quite low for long tranquil periods, but were punctuated by exceptional periods featuring many more defaults.

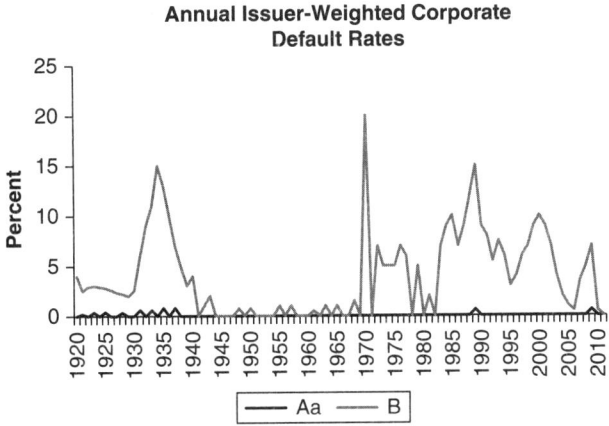

Figure 13.3 This figure displays the patterns of default rates over time for double-A and B-rated bonds.

Rebonato warned risk managers to be careful about using the same methodology to analyze exceptional events as normal (meaning typical) events. In technical terms, he warned about erroneously invoking the conclusion of the central limit theorem (CLT) that arithmetic means will be normally distributed. The main issue is that the tails, meaning probabilities attached to exceptional events, can be much fatter than those associated with the normal distribution.

Figure 13.4 is a log-log display of the probability density functions for losses emanating from two probability distributions. A log-log graph features percentage changes on both axes rather than absolute changes. Incremental movements to the right along the horizontal axis feature increased percentage losses, and incremental movements along the vertical axis feature increased percentage probability. As marked in Figure 13.4, one distribution is standard normal N(0,1), and the other follows a power law in which probability density is a scaled power function. Notice that the shape for the normal is strictly concave, whereas for the power law it is linear. This means that as percentage losses mount, percentage probabilities fall like a rock under the normal distribution, but fall much more gradually under the power law distribution. In particular, notice that tail event losses depicted on the far right feature much higher probability (log-likelihood) under the power law than under the normal.

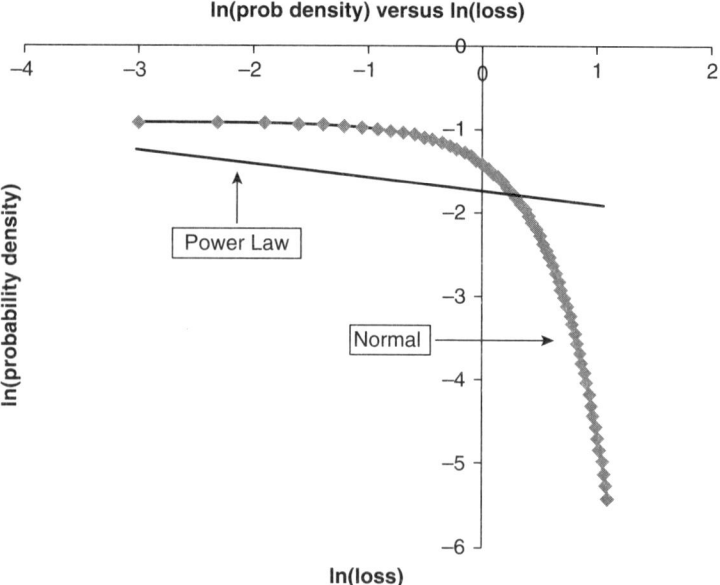

Figure 13.4 This figure displays two density functions, one for a standard normal (N(0,1)), and the other for a power law in which probability density is a scaled power function. The shape for the normal is strictly concave, whereas for the power law it is linear.

The conditions in which the CLT applies, requires a particular degree of independence of the variables being summed. Rebonato warns about using information from tranquil periods to draw strong inferences about probabilities associated with exceptional events. In financial markets, the presence of systemic risk implies that this independence condition fails, and instead exceptional events display serial codependence.

Rebonato's advice to risk managers is to partition their return data into two subsets, those associated with periods deemed as "normal" (or typical), and those with periods deemed as "exceptional." For normal returns, he argues that the appropriate methodology to employ is frequentist. However, Rebonato suggests using Bayesian methodology for the exceptional periods, constructing the prior carefully and focusing on the entire posterior, not just its central moment.

The point of being Bayesian when analyzing exceptional periods is to establish a quantitative representation for how much confidence to have in predicting various probabilities associated with those periods. Bear in mind that VaR in combination with normally distributed returns involves a structure about the degree to which extreme losses will exceed VaR. Under a power law distribution, the likelihood of very severe losses can be much higher than implied by a normal distribution—that being the point of Figure 13.4.

Basel Accord Heuristics

The task faced by regulators is at least one step removed from the risk managers operating within the financial firms being regulated. When it comes to assessing the risks associated with firms' assets and capital structures, their task is especially challenging.

Regulatory judgments are bound to be heuristic based, and so we need to ask about the nature of the heuristics employed. Which heuristics do regulators use to judge whether capital cushions are sufficient, given the risk of the associated assets?

The heuristic underlying the Basel Accord of 1988, which came to be known as Basel I, involved the partitioning of assets into four risk classes. Each class had an associated risk weight, where lower weights reflected less risk. The class of assets that were regarded as being effectively risk-free had a risk weight of zero. Sovereign debt is an example. Retail mortgages were assigned a risk weight of 50%, and corporate loans were assigned a weight of 100%. Basel I stipulated that a financial firm's capital be at least 8% of its RWA values.

The nature of the Basel I heuristic provided an incentive for financial firms to game the system in two ways. The first was by tilting their portfolios toward the riskiest assets in a given risk class. The second was to shift risky assets off their balance sheets through special purpose vehicles that engaged in securitization. For regulatory purposes, the special purpose vehicles were treated as sales; however, financial firms stood behind these entities, guaranteeing liquidity, and therefore maintained much of the risk exposure.

As a result, the Basel I framework was replaced by a more complex set of heuristics that came to be known as Basel II, which was finalized in 2004 and set for adoption in 2007. The Basel II Accord involved three pillars. Pillar 1 pertained to minimum capital requirements. Pillar 2 pertained to guidelines on regulatory intervention for national supervisors. Pillar 3 created new information disclosure standards for banks.

Basel II's pillar 1 allowed firms to use their own rating systems to arrive at a risk assessment. This is the so-called advanced internal ratings-based approach, or A-IRB. The intent of A-IRB was to align regulatory capital more closely with underlying risk exposure by reducing opportunities to game the system. Financial firms lacking the resources to operate in-house models had the option of using what was called the "standardized approach"; for an example, see the discussion about ABN AMRO in Chapter 12. This was a more granular version of Basel I with risk categories based upon external credit ratings provided by commercial rating agencies, with a minimum capital cushion that is 12% of RWA.

A-IRB consisted of three steps. In the first step, financial firms partition their assets into a discrete set of rating grades. In the second step, firms form judgments of the mean default probability (PD) associated with each rating grade. In the third step, firms identify a capital cushion such that the probability that stressed losses will not exceed the firm's capital in a one-year period is equal to 99.9%. This confidence level corresponds to a loss exceeding VaR occurring once in a thousand years. Notably, Basel II's A–IRB VaR approach extended Basel I's focus on credit risk to include market risk as well as the risk of losses on off-balance sheet assets.

During the financial crisis, roughly two-thirds of losses attributed to counterparty credit risk were due to mark-to-market losses due to from credit valuation adjustments (CVA). Only about one-third of losses were due to actual defaults. Under Basel II, the risk of counterparty default and credit migration risk were addressed but not mark-to-market losses from CVA.

In retrospect, Basel II failed to achieve any of its stated objectives. Indeed, the Basel Committee's own forecasts were for financial firms to experience large capital reductions relative to Basel I levels for banks employing the A-IRB approach. In particular, the forecast from their 2006 Quantitative Impact Study, which was based on surveys, featured an average reduction in overall capital requirements of 15.5%, and a median reduction in Tier 1 capital of 31%. Likewise in the United States, in 2003 the Federal Deposit Insurance Corporation (FDIC) reported that average capital levels in American banks that adopted A-IRB would decline by between 18% and 29% for most, and by more than 40% for some.

In early 1999 when the Basel Committee was formulating its first draft accord of Basel II, financial firms were reporting large losses on Russian government bonds that were entirely unanticipated by the VaR models they had been using. For example, Bankers Trust reported that on five days during this period, its trading account losses exceeded its one-day 99% daily VaR calculation. Statistically, a loss larger than VaR should only be expected one day out of a hundred. Similarly, JPMorgan reported daily trading results that were below average far more often than its market risk models had predicted. In December 1998, an International Monetary Fund (IMF) report criticized the stable market price assumptions inherent in VaR models, which do not capture the reality of what Rebonato calls "exceptionable" market events.

Basel II's successor, Basel III, was published in December 2010, and features an interim set of regulations known as Basel 2.5. The new framework involves more complexity and stronger regulatory constraints than its predecessors. To give you an idea, following is a short list of highlights.

Basel III increases the percentage of risk-weighted assets financial firms must hold as Tier I capital to 6% from the 4% specified in Basel II. Basel III introduces a minimum 3% leverage ratio and two required liquidity ratios.[8] Relative to Basel II, the new framework assigns higher risk weights to securitizations such as CDOs of asset-backed securities. Rather than use a standardized approach for securitizations, Basel III allows financial firms to use a comprehensive risk measure (CRM) for specific and incremental risk associated with their correlation books. The framework makes adjustments for CVA, introduces an incremental risk charge (IRC) to capture trading book losses due to default and migrations, and includes a new stressed VaR measure.[9]

Financial firms responded to the publication of the Basel 2.5 and Basel III regulations with confusion and criticism. For example, Basel III requires that some financial firms face five separate VaR calculations instead of Basel II's standardized measure or VAR-based market risk charge. Financial firms complain that these separate charges inadvertently increase operational risk, because of the need to communicate across a mosaic of internal systems that differ in respect to data, algorithms, and reporting. They also complain that the separate charges reduce their ability to diversify, and that the new framework forces them to use overly complex risk management tools that they would not choose to use on their own. On the other side, some analysts pointed out that the complexity of the new rules makes it easier for financial firms to exploit loopholes.[10]

COMPLEXITY AND VESTED INTERESTS

As Basel III takes the financial system down the path of ever-increasing complexity, it is worth pausing to ask why this is happening. The short answer is that financial firms want the combination of thin capital cushions and government backing in order to institute what Minsky called contingency socialism. But there is a longer answer.

Economists Anat Admati and Martin Hellwig have forcefully argued that capital cushions for financial firms can be between 20% and 30%, as they historically were, without causing major damage to the economy.[11] However, capital cushions that high would reduce the amount of value that financial firms extract from taxpayers.

The FIH postulates a power asymmetry between regulators and those being regulated, including the possibility of regulatory capture. There is good reason to believe that this asymmetry is why we ended up with the fiasco of Basel II.[12] Long forgotten are the lobbying efforts of the Institute of International Finance (IIF), the International Swaps and Derivatives Association (ISDA), and the Group of Thirty, all of whom campaigned hard for the version of Basel II that finally emerged.[13]

In 2013, Andy Haldane was executive director of financial stability at the Bank of England. In conjunction with his Bank colleague Vasileios Madouros, Haldane documents the surge in resources devoted to regulating the financial sector.[14] In 1980, the ratio of regulatory personnel to people employed in the UK financial sector was approximately 1 in 11,000. In 2011, that ratio had declined to 1 in 300, and reporting requirements increased by two orders of magnitude. For the United States, in 1935 the ratio of Federal regulators to banks supervised was 1 in 9. In 2011, the ratio was 3 regulators per bank, and reporting requirements almost quadrupled.

The official document listing the details of Basel III is 616 pages long, almost double the 347 pages taken to describe Basel II, which in turn is about 100 times longer than the 30-page document describing Basel I. For a midsize European bank, approximately 200 full-time positions are needed to comply with Basel III. Given that Europe has around 350 banks with total assets over €1bn, compliance with Basel III will require 70,000 full-time jobs.

Haldane emphasizes that besides increased headcount and page length, what is a real cause for concern is increased complexity. For a large bank with complex operations, the increased granularity in moving from Basel I to Basel III has resulted in an explosion of the number of estimated risk weights, from a handful to several million. Across its book, meaning its balance sheet assets, such a bank needs to estimate several thousand default probability and loss-given-default parameters.

The computation of capital requirement from these varied and complicated estimates raises the challenge to yet another level. Think about the challenges of computing VaR based on these risk models, which for large financial firms typically include several thousand risk factors. Think about the need to estimate a huge covariance matrix, and the huge amount of data required to do the job. Although the amount of computation will be huge, it is less clear that the end result will be something in which regulators can have much confidence. There is vast opportunity for inconsistency in going from bank to bank, and the associated opacity makes it easier for financial firms to engage in regulatory arbitrage.

All of this leads Haldane and Madouros to ask whether it is possible to find a way of regulating banks in which less is more?

FAST AND FRUGAL HEURISTICS

How good are experts at making numerical predictions from quantitative data? Psychologist Robyn Dawes studied this question and came up with three conclusions.[15]

Dawes's first conclusion is that what principally distinguishes experts from nonexperts is that experts know which input variables are especially important for the prediction task, and these are usually few in number. His second conclusion is that once experts reveal what are the most important prediction inputs, nonexperts can use linear prediction models based on these inputs to outperform the experts. The second conclusion came as a huge surprise. The reason for the outperformance stems from experts inconsistent weighting of the key variables from prediction to prediction.

Dawes's third conclusion is that when applying linear models, the most important thing is get right when using linear models are the signs of the equations' coefficients. The magnitudes of the coefficients are much less important for prediction accuracy. Even equal weighting generates decent predictions. The marginal value of using least squares estimates is small. Dawes described this finding by telling us that linear models are robust. Replacing the judgments of experts in the final stage of a prediction task with the judgments of a linear model can involve some controversy.

Dawes's findings about the robustness of linear models involving a small number of variables to capture expert judgment can be described by the phrase "less is more." Psychologist Gerd Gigerenzer developed Dawes's insights further. Under his leadership, the Center for Adaptive Behavior and Cognition (ABC Group) at the Max Planck Institute in Berlin has spent decades identifying situations in which simple heuristics are effective ways of dealing with complex decision tasks. The ABC Group pioneered the concept of heuristics that are both fast to use and frugal in their information requirements.

There are some decision tasks that can be structured as optimization problems that can be solved to obtain optimal solutions. In situations in which optimal solutions are complex and costly, it is possible that decision-makers might do just as well by using fast and frugal heuristics. Whether this is so or not depends on the specific decision task. The ABC group's research program focuses on identifying situations in which fast and frugal heuristics work. For situations in which the decision task is so complex that specifying or estimating a formal optimization problem is not practical, the use of fast and frugal heuristics can be compelling.

Fast and frugal heuristics are built on a small set of variables. When one particular variable predominates in importance, a fast and frugal heuristic will tend to be noncompensatory, meaning lexicographic. This means that a judgment or decision that is to be made will be based on only the most important variable, unless that variable produces a tie at the top among competing alternatives. In the event of a tie, the second most important variable will be used to try and break the tie, and if there is still a tie to be broken, then the third most important variable will be used, and so on.

The requirements for successfully completing academic programs are typically structured as heuristics based on clearing hurdles, known as "fast and frugal trees," where the hurdles are program requirements. Think about a particular course that is required and for which students can make but one attempt at its associated exam. Passing that exam is a hurdle to be cleared, because failing that exam means failing the program. Other program requirements might be structured with more flexibility, meaning that there are multiple ways for students to complete those requirements. Hurdle-based heuristics have a noncompensatory structure in that there is no way in which failing to meet a requirement can be compensated for with superior performance in some other part of the program.

Absent any single most important variable, fast and frugal heuristics will tend to use scoring formulas such as linear equations. Linear equations allow for trade-offs, with one variable compensating for another. There is no most important variable that predominates.

Decision tasks differ in their properties, and specific heuristics that work well for one task might not work well for others. The general fast and frugal methodology entails matching heuristics to decision tasks for which they are appropriate.[16] In this regard, fast and frugal trees are typically used to rank order or classify alternatives. For example, given a set of symptoms, should a medial patient be diagnosed as having a heart attack? Yes or no? And here is one more that pertains to the main discussion at hand. Given information about its leverage, liquidity, and RWAs, does the probability that a specific bank fails within the next five years exceed 5%? Yes or no?

FAST AND FRUGAL HEURISTICS FOR REGULATING FINANCIAL FIRMS

The Bank of England teamed up with the ABC Group to identify fast and frugal heuristics to regulate financial firms. Their joint conclusion is that there are better, cheaper ways for estimating bank failures and setting minimum capital cushions than the Basel approach.[17] In this regard, better and cheaper does not mean the end result is foolproof; rather, it only means improving the odds of identifying problem banks.

Let us begin with a stylized fast and frugal regulatory heuristic for judging whether or not a specific bank can be classified as vulnerable to failure. The heuristic is a classification scheme with lexicographic hurdles featuring cues for leverage, risk, and liquidity. The heuristic is based on the following four specific cues:

1. balance sheet leverage ratio = tier 1 capital / assets
2. market-based capital ratio = market capitalization / RWA
3. wholesale funding level = bank deposits + senior paper + collateralized financing (via repo) + wholesale deposits + securitized debt
4. loan-to-deposit ratio = retail loans / retail deposits

Figure 13.5 illustrates the vulnerability classification heuristic as a sequence of cue-defined hurdles. The four cues are ordered, with balance sheet leverage being the most important, and the loan-to-deposit ratio being the least

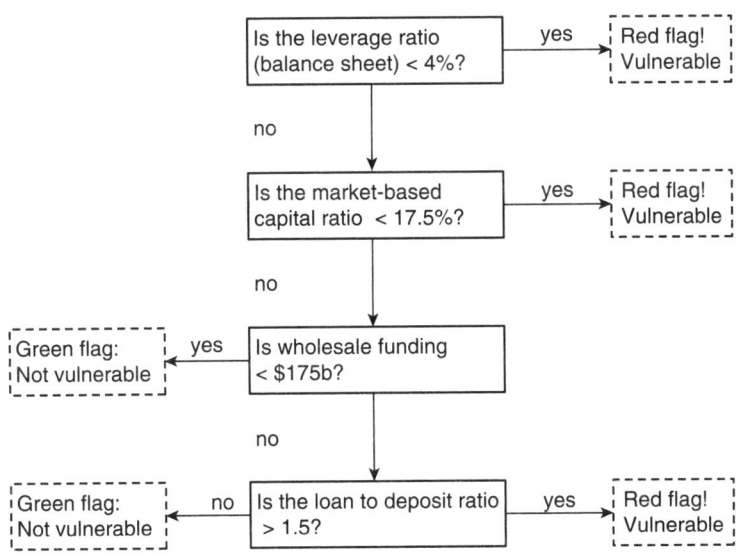

Figure 13.5 This figure illustrates a vulnerability classification heuristic as a sequence of cue-defined hurdles. The four cues are ordered, with balance sheet leverage being the most important, and the loan-to-deposit ratio being the least important. If the capital cushion as measured by book values falls below 4%, then the bank fails to clear its first hurdle, and is judged to be vulnerable to failure. If the bank's balance sheet clears the capital cushion hurdle, then the second hurdle for risk becomes operative.

important. On the one hand, if the capital cushion as measured by book values falls below 4%, then the bank fails to clear its first hurdle, and is judged to be vulnerable to failure. On the other hand, if the bank's balance sheet clears the capital cushion hurdle, then we move on to a second hurdle for risk.

On the one hand, if the market-based capital ratio is less than 17.5%, then the bank misses the risk hurdle and is judged to be vulnerable to failure. The market has spoken: market capitalization is too small relative to RWA. On the other hand, if the bank clears the risk hurdle, then we move on to the first of two liquidity hurdles.

On the one hand if wholesale funding is sufficiently small, then the bank clears the first liquidity hurdle, and is judged not vulnerable to failure. Notice that the judgment of not being vulnerable requires that the bank clear hurdles for all three criteria: leverage, risk, and liquidity. On the other hand, if the bank misses the wholesale funding hurdle, then it faces one more opportunity to be judged not vulnerable, by clearing the loan-to-deposit ratio. If it clears this hurdle, it is judged not vulnerable, but if it misses this hurdle, it is judged to be vulnerable.

Chapter 6 contains a discussion about project adoption, which is conceptually identical to the classification decision task discussed here. In the Chapter 6 framework, projects were either "successes" or "failures," and the firm had to choose an assessment threshold to decide how to classify projects as either "adopt" or "reject." In the current discussion, banks are either "sound" or "problematic" and a regulator has to choose an assessment threshold to decide how to classify banks into "not vulnerable" and "vulnerable." Appendix H provides a figure describing the formal extension of the framework developed in Chapter 6 and Appendix E to the issue of bank regulation.

As in Chapter 6, there are four categories associated with the classification of banks. They are "white elephants," in which problematic banks are classified as not vulnerable; "false warnings," in which sound banks are classified as vulnerable; "winning calls," in which sound banks are classified as not vulnerable; and "good judgment" calls, in which problematic banks are categorized as vulnerable. To illustrate how this particular fast and frugal regulatory heuristic works in practice, consider applying it at year-end 2006 to two banks that were discussed in previous chapters. As you will see, the heuristic provides a "winning call" for one bank and a "white elephant" for the other.

The first bank is UBS. At the time, it had a leverage ratio of 1.71%. Therefore, the heuristic automatically assigns it a red flag and classifies it as vulnerable to failure. The heuristic does so, in spite of UBS having had a market-based capital ratio that exceeded 17.5% and a loan-to-deposit ratio that was below 1.5. Being noncompensatory, this heuristic does not feature trade-offs between cue values, as would a heuristic that relied on a linear scoring rule. As you will recall, UBS would have failed during the global financial crisis, but for being rescued by the Swiss government, and so the heuristic produces a "good judgment" call in this case.

At year-end 2006, the regulatory heuristic would have classified Wachovia as safe. Wachovia had a leverage ratio of 5.58% and a market-based capital ratio of 20.41%. Although the bank would have missed the wholesale funding hurdle, its loan-to-deposit ratio of 1.21 would have resulted in a green flag at the fourth stage. Wachovia did fail, and so the heuristic would have registered a "white elephant." The bank failed because of its large subprime exposure; however, in line with the theme of Chapter 12, the market did not recognize the risk at year-end 2006.[18] Does this suggest that there might be room for improvement by adding one more hurdle to the heuristic in order to incorporate a Ponzi finance dimension and associated sentiment metrics?

The effectiveness of a heuristic depends on two likelihood ratios. The first is the "hit rate," which is defined as the frequency of "good judgments" over the frequency sum of "good judgments" and "white elephants." This ratio measures the probability of correctly classifying a problematic bank as vulnerable. The other likelihood ratio is the "false alarm rate," which is defined as the ratio of the frequency of "false warnings" to the frequency sum of "winning calls" and "false warnings." This ratio measures the probability of mistakenly identifying a sound bank as vulnerable.

All else equal, a high hit rate is good, as it means accurate identification of problematic banks. However, this benefit might be offset by false alarms that are set off when sound banks are also identified as vulnerable.

The Bank of England team evaluated the efficacy of performance of this particular fast and frugal approach to a very large sample of banks. They report that the heuristic had a hit rate of 82%, meaning that it correctly identified 82% of the banks that failed during the global financial crisis, and had a false alarm rate of 48%.

Are these numbers good? Is it possible to have structured a fast and frugal heuristic that would have done better on the historical data? The Bank of England team analyzed these questions by building a computer program to search through all possible fast and frugal trees, such as the one displayed in Figure 13.5, that are based on a series of 11 financial cues and associated branching threshold values.[19] The criterion they use for judging whether one heuristic is better than another is the difference (hit rate—α false alarm rate). Here α is a nonnegative parameter that weights the importance of the false alarm rate relative to the hit rate. Although the heuristic depicted in Figure 13.5 exhibits decent performance for the case in which $\alpha = 1$, there are other heuristics that perform better when the two criterion components are not equally weighted.

There are 11 very simple heuristics, which rely on just one cue. Among the single-cue heuristics, the best performing is based on leverage. Next comes wholesale funding, then loan to deposits, and then the capital market ratio. The selection of cues for the heuristic displayed in Figure 13.5 is based on this particular ordering.

Lying at the heart of the Basel framework is the risk-based capital market ratio defined by balance sheet Tier 1 capital to RWA. Notably, among the 14 single cue heuristics, this one ranks sixth from the top. As the Bank of England group notes, this is hardly impressive performance for a variable on which so much rides. Moreover, balance sheet leverage, which is based on total assets, not RWA, is superior to its RWA-based counterpart. In theory, theory and practice are equivalent, but in practice they differ, which is a sobering conclusion to reach given the enormous resources devoted to the RWA approach.

Closing Thoughts

Haldane tells us that regulators require both courage and self-confidence, because they will be called upon to correct distortions in financial markets that hold the potential to damage the economy at large. In making this statement, he also makes clear that regulators operate under imperfect information. Nevertheless, he urges regulators not to let the imperfect be the enemy of the good, because achieving good is possible by using fast and frugal heuristics in which less is more.[20]

Admati and Hellwig make a good point when they tell us that financial firms should hold much more capital than they do, thereby shifting risk back to financial firms from the taxpaying public. But the FIH tells us that what makes good economic sense does not always happen, and in many cases is unlikely to happen. The power of vested interests is very strong, and financial firms eventually win the regulatory game. Therefore, being realistic, it is better to approach regulatory issues with eyes wide open, in order to make the best of a highly imperfect situation.[21] Fast and frugal heuristics can help, but whether they come into wide use will depend on whose interests they serve, and more importantly whose interest they threaten.

CHAPTER 14

RISK OF FRAUD, MADOFF, AND THE SEC

BY ITS NATURE, THE ACT OF INVESTING EXPOSES INVESTORS TO FRAUDULENT activity by counterparties.[1] Ponzi schemes represent one type of fraud. This chapter discusses risk management issues associated with the Ponzi scheme run by Bernard Madoff, which ranks as one of the largest in history. Initial accounts placed the losses to be between $50 and $65 billion, an amount that included fabricated gains. A court-appointed trustee estimated the losses in principal to be between $17.5 and $20 billion.[2]

Madoff attracted a wide range of high-profile clients that included institutional clients such as fund of funds, foundations, and high-net-worth individuals. He did so by convincing his clients that he generated returns that were moderate in absolute terms, very high on a risk-adjusted basis, and that he rarely registered losses.

Madoff maintained his fraud by issuing fake financial statements and relying on a small short-term fund and new money to deal with redemptions. His ruse began to fall apart after the Lehman bankruptcy, when the associated abnormally high rates of redemption outpaced the assets he held. Unable to sustain his scheme in the face of these redemptions, he revealed to his wife and two sons that his apparently successful money management business was based on a Ponzi scheme. As a result, his sons turned him into the US authorities. He was tried, found guilty, and sent to prison, as was his brother, Peter. His wife divorced him, one son committed suicide, and the other died of cancer. The case continued for several years as a trustee sought to recover assets and compensate victims.[3]

There are many psychological issues associated with the Madoff Ponzi scheme.[4] Some pertain to Madoff himself, some to his individual investors, some to his professional clients, and some to the regulators who provided oversight. The most important risk management issues involve his professional clients and regulators which provide the focus of this chapter. However, before turning to the narrower and more technical risk management issues, it is worthwhile to identify what were some of the broader psychological issues.

By their nature, people have a psychological need for status. Part of Madoff's strategy was to confer status as well as manage money. He did so by providing the illusion of exclusivity, only accepting particular clients. His clients included individual investors and foundations associated with famous personalities such as Steven Spielberg, Mortimer Zuckerman, and Elie Wiesel. Their dollar losses were measured in the tens of millions.

There are good reasons to suggest that psychological forces impacted Madoff when he began his Ponzi scheme, during the time he operated it, and during the aftermath when he went to prison for it. The psychological issues associated with his beginning the Ponzi scheme most likely relate to cheating and aspirational-based risk.

There is also reason to suggest that aversion to a sure loss prevented him from closing down his scheme while it was still small. In a television interview, his ex-wife, Ruth, said the following: "I don't understand it. I don't—it's hard for me to say this, but I don't think the money was the part of it. I think he got stuck. That's what he said. And he didn't have the courage to face—face things when they might have been able to be faced on a much smaller scale."[5]

Psychological phenomena such as delusion and cognitive dissonance were also in evidence after his conviction. From prison he told a journalist that he believed that he would eventually extricate himself from it.[6]

With respect to risk management, the most interesting psychological issues by far pertain to the professionals who invested with Madoff and the regulators who provided oversight. His institutional clients included the Fairfield Greenwich Group, whose exposure was initially reported to be $7.5 billion; Banco Santander Optimal with $3.1 billion of client exposure; RBS with over $600 million of exposure; and BNP Paribas with over $475 million of exposure. These firms missed the signals that he was running a huge Ponzi scheme, and paid a major price. The psychological elements that led them to do so are the subject to which we now turn.

BARRON'S 2001 STORY ON MADOFF

In 2001, *Barron's* ran a prescient story about Madoff's operations.[7] The article describes him as an important figure on Wall Street, whose brokerage firm, Madoff Securities, played an important role in the development of NASDAQ. We learn that Bernard L. Madoff Investment Securities LLC is the third-largest brokerage firm for NYSE-listed securities, and so not surprisingly includes well-known clients such as Charles Schwab and Fidelity Investments.

The *Barron's* article informs us that in addition to brokerage, Madoff managed money for wealthy clients. In 2001, his assets under management were between $6 and $7 billion, a figure that placed him in the top three of hedge funds by size. Technically, Madoff did not organize his money management business as a hedge fund, but instead ran it as a series of managed accounts, where he managed each client's account with the same investment strategy.

Notably, Madoff's money management business was very successful, having returned compound average annual returns of 15% for more than ten years. Even more notable was that some of his large accounts funds never experienced a down year.

Madoff attributed his success to a proprietary strategy, for which he gave few details. *Barron's* contacted some of Madoff's clients, such as Fairfield Greenwich, a New York City-based hedge fund marketer mentioned above, to ask about his investment strategy. Fairfield Greenwich ran Fairfield Sentry Limited, whose investments were managed by Madoff and at the time had $3.3 billion of assets. A Fairfield partner and cofounder told *Barron's* that, Fairfield Sentry being a private fund, his firm had no inclination to discuss the fund's returns and, moreover, saw no reason why *Barron's* would be interested in exploring the question.

The *Barron's* article notes that a Madoff hedge fund offering memorandum describes his strategy as being based on a portfolio of 30 to 35 stocks in the S&P100, which are highly correlated with the index itself. In addition to holding these stocks, the memorandum mentions holding put options on these stocks along with short positions in associated call options. The article describes the combined position as a "split-stock conversion strategy."

Adding options to the stock holdings manages risk by placing a "collar" around the returns, thereby reducing the volatility of the positions. The article points out that Fairfield Sentry had experienced only four down months since inception in 1989, and had returned at least 11% every year. Options traders who were interviewed for the article expressed doubt that this record could have been produced by a split-strike conversion strategy. Indeed, one of Madoff's former investors remarked that it was naive to believe that Madoff only relied on a split-strike conversion strategy. As result, *Barron's* suggested that Madoff might be engaged in front-running his clients, which Madoff firmly denied doing.

THE SPLIT-STRIKE CONVERSION STRATEGY

Had you been a risk manager or other adviser for a Madoff client, you would have wanted to understand how the split-strike conversion strategy works, in order to evaluate Madoff's claims about the risk profile of his investment strategy in relation to the historical returns reportedly achieved. In doing so, you might have come to the conclusion that the strategy was quite simple, and much more straightforward than its intimidating name suggests. In this regard, the textbook name for the split-strike conversion strategy is a "collar." It is not fancy, and it is not especially complex. Here is an example to illustrate how it works.

Imagine an investor who purchased the S&P 500 when its value was 1000, which occurred in 1997, 1998, 2001, and 2002, and 2009. Between 1989 and 2008, the mean monthly return of the S&P 500 was 0.7%, with a standard deviation of 3.9%. This investor can construct a split-strike conversion strategy by purchasing an index put option, say with a strike price of 925, and simultaneously selling an index call option, say with a strike price of 1050. For sake of illustration, let the price (premium) of the put option be 20 and the price of the call be 40. In that case the value of the position is 980 = 1000−40 + 20.

Suppose that both options expire one month after purchase, and are European in the sense that they can only be exercised on the expiration date. If the S&P 500 were to fall below 925 on the expiration date, then the investor would exercise the put option, thereby limiting the loss to 75 = 1000−925. If the S&P 500 were to climb above 1050 on the expiration date, then the index would be called away and the investor would sell at a price of 1050, thereby limiting the gain to 50 = 1050−1000. Of course, if the value of the index lies between 925 and 1050 on the expiration date, then both options expire worthless, and the value of the position is just the value of the S&P 500 on that date.

Figure 14.1 illustrates the value of the split-strike conversion strategy on the expiration date, as a function of the value of the S&P 500 on that date.

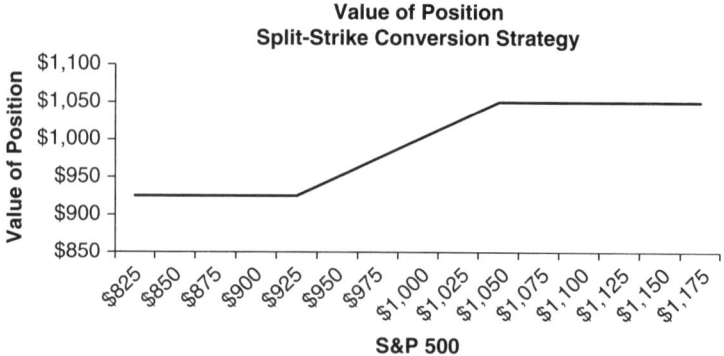

Figure 14.1 This figure illustrates the gross value of the split-strike conversion strategy on the expiration date, as a function of the value of the S&P 500 on that date. The value of the position in the figure has an upper collar of 1050 and a lower collar of 925.

Notice that the figure illustrates the collar property, as the value of the position has an upper collar of 1050 and a lower collar of 925.

On the basis of the initial value of the position, 980, the lowest possible monthly return to the position is −5.6%, and the highest possible monthly return is 7.1%. In other words, the two option positions place a collar around the strategy, limiting volatility to the band −5.6% to 7.1%. Notably, Madoff invoked this collar feature to explain how he was able to maintain a low volatility on his portfolio.

Another critical piece of any investment scheme is the costs to achieve the return. The trading costs associated with options can be significant, in the range 4% to 8% for the kinds of options Madoff purported to use. Because trading costs drag down net returns, risk managers would need to factor such costs into their analysis when doing due diligence.[8]

FAIRFIELD SENTRY

Fairfield Greenwich Advisors was heavily invested in Madoff's firm, gathering assets from clients and feeding them to Madoff to manage as a so-called "feeder fund."[9] Its apparent $7.5 billion holdings with Madoff comprised just more than half of its total assets. Fairfield Greenwich had provided capital for Madoff's program since 1989, longer than any other feeder fund.

Although Fairfield partner Jeffrey Tucker would not provide *Barron's* with any substantive comments about Madoff's strategy, Fairfield Sentry's marketing material did say that the fund used call options to increase what it called "the standstill rate of return" while providing upside potential up to the call strike price. In respect to the puts, it mentioned that these were partly funded by the sale of the calls, and were designed to provide the portfolio with downside protection.[10]

Shortly after the revelation of the Ponzi scheme, Tucker issued a statement expressing shock and saying that no indication of any potential wrongdoing had crossed their radar screen.[11] Amit Vijayvergiya was chief risk officer for Fairfield Greenwich at its subsidiary in Bermuda. A lawyer for Fairfield issued a statement to say that the firm had engaged in extensive risk monitoring of investments and dealings with Madoff's firm. The firm also indicated that investors in Fairfield Sentry, the fund it offered with the most exposure to Madoff, were aware that Madoff was running the portfolio.

From the perspective of a risk manager analyzing Fairfield Sentry as an investment, look at the return trajectory of Fairfield Sentry over its lifetime, from 1990 through October 2008. What you will see is that Fairfield Sentry earned an average compounded monthly return of 0.83%, somewhat better than the 0.69% return to the S&P 500. At first blush, this does not qualify as totally outside the bounds of credulity, but only at first blush.[12] Consider

Figure 14.2, which displays the cumulative returns to Fairfield Sentry and the S&P 500 during this period.[13] What is exceptional is the much lower volatility that Fairfield Sentry displayed relative to the S&P 500. Fairfield Sentry's monthly standard deviation was 0.7%, much smaller than the 3.9% standard deviation for the S&P 500. Figure 14.2 displays the trajectory for the monthly returns, and you can see the gray series for the S&P 500 absolutely dwarfs the black series for Fairfield Sentry.

As a risk manager, what reaction would you have to the comparable returns but much lower volatility displayed by Fairfield Sentry relative to the S&P 500, especially given the substantial trading costs Madoff charged? To be sure, the *Barron's* article from 2001 raised questions about volatility. Additional insights come from a 2001 article in the publication *MARHedge* (Managed Account Reports Hedge), whose focus was hedge fund performance.[14] The *MARHedge* article pointed out that Fairfield Sentry reported losses of no more than 55 basis points in just four of the past 139 consecutive months. Moreover, it generated consistent gross returns of about 1.5% a month, with net annual returns in the neighborhood of 15%.

MARHedge maintained a large database of more than 1,100 hedge funds. On the basis of its data, *MARHedge* reported that for the period since its inception, Fairfield Sentry ranked as the best-performing fund on a risk-adjusted basis: it featured a Sharpe ratio of 3.4 and an annual standard deviation of 3.0%. Among 423 funds that reported returns over the previous five years, Fairfield Sentry ranked tenth by risk-adjusted return, as defined by its Sharpe ratio.

MARHedge pointed out that in comparison to funds that purported to be using a similar strategy, the best known being Gateway, Fairfield Sentry

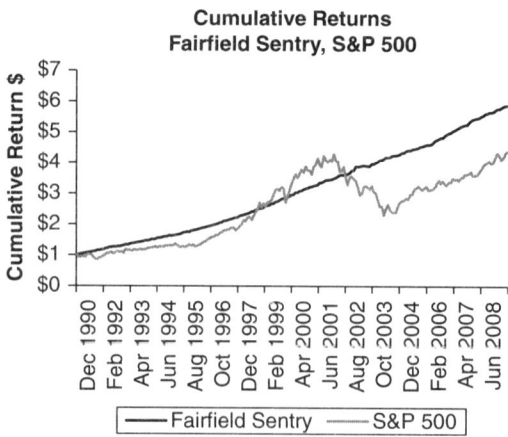

Figure 14.2 This figure displays the trajectory of cumulative monthly returns for Fairfield Sentry and for the S&P 500.

experienced far less volatility and higher returns during the same period. Given the returns, was Fairfield Sentry's volatility too good to be true?

An academic study by Carole Bernard and Phelim Boyle computed the returns to a split-strike conversion strategy for the S&P 500 over the period December 1989 through October 2008. For this purpose, they used monthly options that limited gains and losses to 5% relative to the value of the position when the option positions were established. The proceeds from rolling over the option positions were invested at the risk-free rate, and cash settlement was accomplished using these proceeds, or if need be selling some of the position. Index options on the S&P 500 were far less expensive to trade than index options on the S&P 100, which Madoff purported to use. Notably, the returns to the strategy were a bit higher on a cumulative basis than for the S&P 500 itself, displayed a bit less volatility than the S&P 500 volatility, and were much more volatile than the volatility associated with Fairfield Sentry. Moreover, Bernard and Boyle also ignore transaction costs and any price impact of the trades, and the trading costs were substantial, suggesting that Madoff's gross returns were significantly higher than the returns reported by Fairfield Sentry.

Normal return strategies featuring low volatility are exploitable. In this regard, Nomura and Neue Privat Bank together marketed access to Fairfield Sentry, but with shares that were leveraged three times. This kind of leveraging of Fairfield Sentry returns led to volatility levels similar to the market, but with large positive abnormal returns, and few negative returns. In this regard, compare the monthly return pattern in Figure 14.3 for the S&P 500 with the monthly return figure in Figure 14.4 for Fairfield Sentry. Notice the very infrequent negative returns in Figure 14.4 relative to Figure 14.3. This contrast is especially apparent in Figure 14.5, which displays the return histograms for the two series.

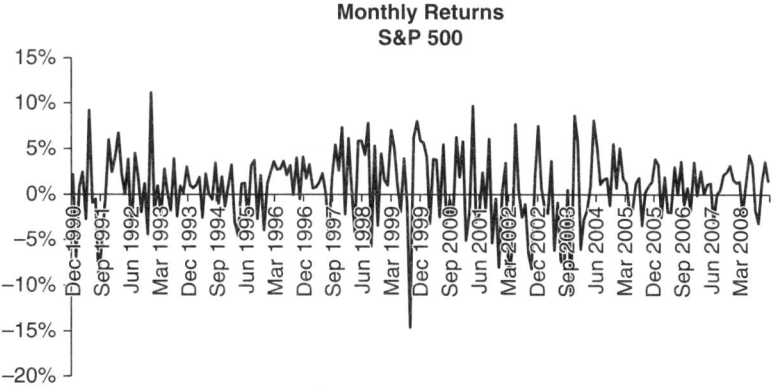

Figure 14.3 This figure displays the monthly return series for the S&P 500.

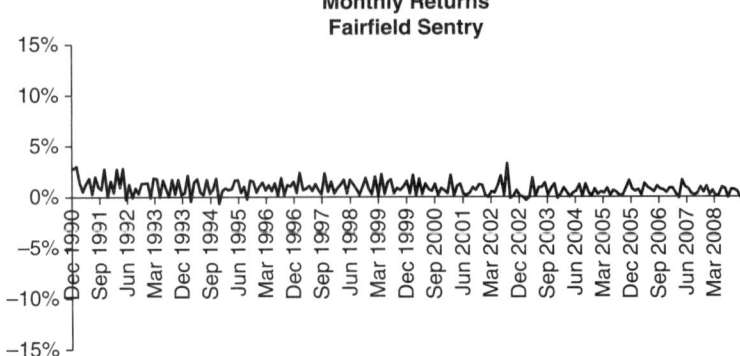

Figure 14.4 This figure displays the monthly return series for Fairfield Sentry.

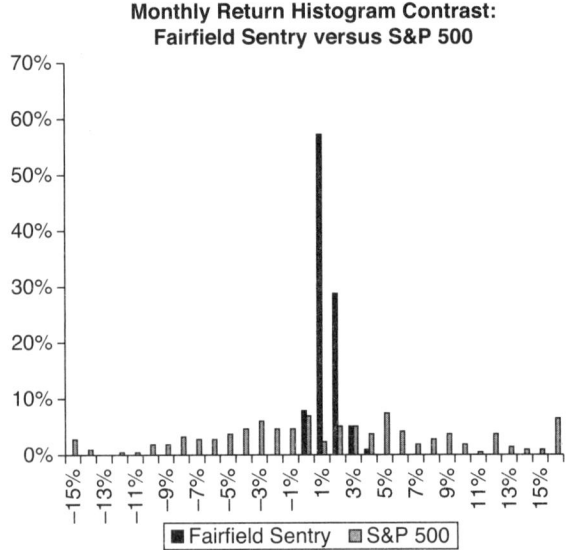

Figure 14.5 This figure displays the return histograms for the monthly returns associated with Fairfield Sentry and the S&P 500 respectively.

Are there are any psychological issues associated with crossing the zero axis into negative territory, even by minute amounts? Certainly, prospect theory suggests so, telling us that the carrier of psychological value is gain or loss relative to a reference point, with the pain of loss looming much larger than the pleasure from comparably sized gains.

The issues discussed by Bernard and Boyle are ones that a prudent risk manager would raise when doing due diligence. A 2009 report on the television program *Frontline* pointed out that Fairfield Greenwich's attorney claimed that the firm's due diligence exceeded industry standards.[15] In contrast, Sherry Cohen, who worked at the firm from 1987 to 1998 as the assistant to Walter Noel, one of the firm's founders, told *Frontline*, "I know there was no due diligence done when I worked there, no deep questions...[but instead] don't bore me with the details...and they wouldn't have gotten it anyway."

If Cohen's assessment is correct, then which biases might explain the failure of the firm to undertake appropriate due diligence? Certainly excessive optimism comes to mind. Remember that excessive optimism involves assigning probabilities to favorable events that are too high and are driven by a number of factors. In this case, desirability or wishful thinking is perhaps the strongest driver, although control, familiarity, and viewing oneself as representative of success are plausible as well.

How Madoff Responded to Issues Raised

MARHedge stated that it interviewed more than a dozen finance professionals who claimed to be knowledgeable about the split-strike conversion strategy, and all expressed views consistent with the Bernard and Boyle analysis. In addition to asking why nobody else had been able to generate similar returns using the strategy, these professionals raised questions about a number of issues related to performance, such as the following:

- Madoff's apparent ability to time the market by switching to cash from the underlying securities before market declines
- Madoff's related ability to trade large positions in the underlying stocks without impacting the market
- Madoff's pricing policy of charging only for trading commissions, and his decision not to establish a separate asset management division to offer hedge funds directly to investors in order to generate lucrative incentive fees
- Madoff's possible use of other stocks and options rather than only those in the S&P 100
- Madoff's possibly subsidizing his performance from his brokerage business and other market-making activities

Madoff did respond to questions from *MARHedge*, explaining that his fund's absolute returns were considerably lower than many other funds.[16] While not discussing details about the strategy, he indicated that his fund did well in volatile markets when the option positions were exercised, and that his strategy would perform poorly in a flat market. He agreed that market timing and stock picking were both important for his strategy to be effective. He indicated that his firm uses proprietary option pricing models. He made mention of his firm's market making ability, pointing out that he had access to market intelligence derived from significant order flow. He noted that his firm has long had a technological edge in respect to low-cost trading, but that he chose stocks that were highly liquid in order to avoid significant market impact when he needed to trade. He stressed that his strategy involved investing in Treasury securities for long periods to allow him to exploit specific market opportunities. Finally, he mentioned his firm's use of a proprietary "black box," which provides initial signals that are subject to "gut feel" override.

Madoff told *MARHedge* that other Wall Street firms could achieve similar results if they had the same operational infrastructure. He pointed out that most do not, and that he had received offers from other firms to buy his. He had rejected these offers, he said, largely because his firm employed so many members of his family. He also explained that he chose a business model in which he charged only for trading commissions and not for management fees in order to avoid conflicts with his primary business function of trading.

Apparently, Madoff's responses were convincing. Consider the professionals who ran feeder funds for Madoff's asset management operation. Feeder funds are intermediaries and distributors who collect capital from banks, hedge funds, and wealthy individuals to entrust them to fund managers. Feeder funds essentially comprise two categories. The first category consists of moderately sized firms such as Fairfield Greenwich, Tremont Capital Management, and Maxam Capital Management, all of which used Madoff's firm. The second category consists of large banks that manage funds of hedge funds, such as Santander Optimal and Union Bancaire Privée, which also used Madoff's firm.

Funds of funds promoted themselves as performing three important functions: diversification, access to star managers, and due diligence. As it happens, Madoff served as his own custodian, a practice that should have raised concerns in the due diligence process. Nevertheless, whatever due diligence was done, this practice did not generate a red light for Madoff's fund.

These were sophisticated investors. Maxam Capital Management reported a loss of $280 million on funds it had invested with Madoff. Its founder and chair, Sandra Manzke, stated that the firm would have to close as a result. Her personal wealth was mostly managed by Madoff.

In the *Frontline* documentary, Manzke states that she recognized that Madoff imposed a number of unusual conditions in his relationship with clients. For example, he insisted that his name not appear on any prospectus as a money manager. Manzke told *Frontline*, "That was always one of Bernie's conditions of getting an account."

Madoff also used as his auditor, not a large accounting firm, but a one-man accounting firm that operated in a strip mall just outside of New York City. When queried by *Frontline* about whether this practice bothered her, she replied, "Of course it bothered you.... But that was one of the conditions of doing business, that you accepted that... And part of that was his you know his proprietary trading model, the black box that he used, that he wasn't going to disclose what was in it."

Notice that Manzke's remarks are consistent with her having exhibited confirmation bias. She accepted that Madoff had a proprietary trading model that generated positive abnormal risk-adjusted returns, and downplayed evidence that might disconfirm this view, even if it bothered her.

In December 2008, Banco Santander was Europe's second-largest bank by market value, and a major Madoff victim. It was Banco Santander's Optimal unit that placed client money with Madoff. However, the network of Madoff investors was more extensive and included family members of Banco Santander chairman Emilio Botin. Botin's son and son-in-law ran M&B Capital Advisers, which directed many of their wealthy clients to Madoff.

Through M&B, private and institutional investors purchased more than €150 million in Madoff funds. Notably, Botin's son-in-law is married to Ana Patricia Botin, who succeeded Emilio as bank chair after his death in September 2014. A spokesman for Santander indicated that the bank did not have a business relationship with M&B. Similarly, M&B stated that it did not serve as a broker for Santander, and did not act as conduit for Madoff funds that were bought by its clients. We can take these statements about formal business connections as valid, but still ask whether there were any psychological issues that were germane to these sophisticated investors missing Madoff's Ponzi scheme.

In a *Wall Street Journal* interview conducted from prison, Madoff told his interviewer that he felt trapped into the fraud by others.[17] He insisted that the financial firms that distributed his funds were aware of the fraud and were complicit. He stated that his investors were sophisticated and should have realized what was going on. Perhaps Madoff is right on this point. However, being sophisticated does not rule out succumbing to cognitive biases. There is good reason to suggest that Madoff psychologically manipulated his clients, both professional and individual, so that they trusted him, relying on the affective nature of the brand he had created for himself. Sandra Manzke is a case in point.

MADOFF AND THE SEC

Notably, between 1992 and 2006 the SEC conducted five separate investigations of Madoff's operations in search of illegal activities, but failed to uncover evidence of a Ponzi scheme. They failed to do so, not because Madoff was so clever, but because their own cultural weaknesses prevented them from taking decisions that would have uncovered the Ponzi scheme. The agency's failures provide important lessons for regulators about the impact of problematic organizational structure and incentives within a major regulatory agency. As you will see, these lessons apply not just to regulators but to risk managers generally.

In 2009, the SEC's Office of Inspector General (OIG) issued a report documenting the SEC's failure to uncover Madoff's Ponzi scheme.[18] The report describes a number of issues involving the dynamics at its Northeast Regional Office (NERO) in New York City, which conducted two of the five SEC investigations of Madoff for illegal activities.

The first NERO exam took place in 2005, and occurred because an investment adviser examiner discovered a string of internal e-mails at the firm Renaissance Technologies that questioned whether Madoff was involved in illegal activity, especially front-running.

The second NERO investigation (in 2005–2006) attracted the most attention, because Boston-based financial analyst Harry Markopolos provided the SEC with a highly detailed analysis to support an allegation he made that Madoff was running a Ponzi scheme. On February 4, 2009, a contentious hearing by a House Financial Services subcommittee took place in which Markopolos testified, and the subcommittee then lambasted the SEC officials who appeared before them for having ignored the evidence Markopolos had presented to the SEC on a silver platter.

In places, Markopolos's letter reads like a cloak-and-dagger mystery thriller. Markopolos writes that "I am worried about the personal safety of myself and my family," and in the 2009 *Frontline* program, he spoke of carrying a gun to protect himself. In the substantive part of his letter, Markopolos explicitly wrote that Madoff might be front-running his clients. However, Markopolos also wrote that he attached low probability to this explanation and suggested another explanation that he regarded as highly likely: that Madoff was running a Ponzi scheme.

Markopolos's letter raises 29 specific red flags, which include all the issues discussed earlier in this chapter. He also includes new points, such as the volume of Madoff's alleged option trades being too large given the overall volume of those markets. Most importantly, he provides a cogent argument for why Madoff could not have generated the returns he reported by using a split-strike conversion strategy. He also mentions that he spoke at length with many of Madoff's clients in the United States and Europe. He tells us that many regarded Madoff as their best money manager, and that some attributed Madoff's superior risk-adjusted returns to front-running. Markopolos notes that, although front running is illegal, no Madoff client communicated their suspicions of front-running to the SEC.

The red flags effectively served as a road map to how to investigate whether Madoff was operating a Ponzi scheme. However, understanding the arguments in Markopolos's letter required specific knowledge about option trading, well beyond basic knowledge about financial institutions.

At the Congressional hearing, none of the SEC officials would explain why the agency did not act on the information Markopolos had provided. Instead they responded that, because the OIG was conducting an investigation, they were unable to provide details. This response did not sit well with subcommittee members. One member angrily stated that, although he thought that Madoff was the enemy, he was beginning to wonder whether in fact the enemy was the SEC. Linda Thomsen, then the SEC's director of enforcement, pointed out that the agency had pursued major fraud cases, including 70 Ponzi schemes, but had missed opportunities to uncover Madoff's scheme,

The puzzle was how the SEC could have missed Madoff after receiving the evidence presented to them by Markopolos. He had laid out the issues carefully, explaining what a split-strike conversion strategy entailed, as Figure 14.1 illustrates, and going on to explain why the strategy could not have produced the returns displayed in Figure 14.2. One subcommittee member likened the SEC's mistake to sitting in Fenway Park and missing first base.

As we shall see, psychological biases lie at the root of the SEC's failure to uncover Madoff's Ponzi scheme. To see which ones, consider the following chronology. Markopolos had long suspected Madoff of running a Ponzi scheme and had communicated his concerns to the SEC on three separate occasions. The 2005–2006 investigation by NERO resulted from his third initiative, which he submitted to the SEC's Boston District Office (BDO). Notably, Markopolos managed to convince the Boston office of the likelihood that Madoff was running a Ponzi scheme, and so the Boston office felt that the issue would be more efficiently handled by NERO in New York, as Madoff's operation was based in New York.

To understand what went wrong in New York, keep in mind that NERO conducted two separate investigations of Madoff, one in 2005 and the second in 2005–2006. The two investigations were conducted by different staff. The OIG tells us that the 2005 investigation was conducted by junior staff who had expertise in accounting in finance, but who might have been intimidated by Madoff's prominence in the industry. In contrast, the staff that conducted the 2005–2006 investigation, and which had the letter from Markopolos before it, possessed legal expertise, but little expertise in options trading, and no expertise in investigating Ponzi schemes.

The 2005 investigation focused on front-running, but did not investigate whether Madoff was running a Ponzi scheme. John Nee and Peter

Lamore were two of the primary SEC staff at the New York Regional Office involved in the 2005 NERO cause examination of Madoff's operations. Nee was assistant regional director. Reporting to Nee was Lamore, the Securities Compliance Examiner, who was eventually promoted to staff accountant, in part for having "reviewed all aspects of Madoff's unregistered institutional trading business."[19] Notably, it was Nee who determined that the Renaissance e-mails only raised issues related to "front-running and cherry picking."[20] When NERO received Markopolos's submission from the SEC's Boston office, they assigned it to Meaghan Cheung to direct the new investigation. Reporting to Cheung was Simona Suh, who would have the responsibility of doing most of the work. When Cheung received her new task charge, including the evidence from Markopolos, she sought out Nee and Lamore for assistance. Below you will find some of the e-mail correspondence between Lamore and Nee that pertains to Cheung's request.

E-mail messages now form a critical component of organizational communication, and it is important to understand how to identify psychological issues that are expressed through this channel. Needless to say, this statement extends well beyond regulators and risk managers, and so learning to read e-mail messages from a psychological perspective can be a critical skill.

Below you will read an e-mail exchange between Lamore and Nee about the upcoming meeting with Cheung and Suh to discuss the Markopolos submission. This meeting turned out to be an important bridge between the relatively more experienced 2005 staff and the less experienced 2005–2006 staff. The e-mail chain offers some insight about the positions of Lamore and Nee at the outset of the 2005–2006 investigation. Keep in mind that, although Markopolos's communication detailed suspicions of several illegal activities, the Ponzi scheme allegation topped his list. The first e-mail is from Lamore to Nee.

> I'm going to meet with Meaghan and Simona on Monday @ 3:00 to provide my input regarding these allegations. In short, these are basically the same allegations we have heard before. The author's motives are to make money by uncovering the alleged fraud. I think he is on a fishing expedition and doesn't have the detailed understanding of Madoff's operations that we do which refutes most of his allegations... Any thoughts?

Nee responds as follows:

> No, Pete, I don't have anything to add. I think the report speaks for itself. There is still a little mystery as to what Madoff does but a Ponzi scheme or directly trading on immediate customer order flow doesn't [appear] likely from what we've seen.

Lamore then e-mails back:

> I must admit that [I] was a bit spooked when you first forwarded me the string of e-mails between the Boston and New York SEC offices (Ponzi scheme getting ready to crash), but after having just read the "informant's" analysis I feel much better that he is incorrect.[21]

What is your sense of this e-mail exchange? Do you see evidence suggesting any specific psychological biases? Markopolos's analysis does provide a very detailed explanation as to why Madoff was either engaged in front-running or operating a Ponzi scheme. In suggesting that Markopolos's understanding was less than their own, Lamore was being very overconfident about his own abilities. Nee's rejection of both front-running and a Ponzi scheme is strongly suggestive of confirmation bias.

In retrospect, Suh told the OIG, "It's certainly true that he didn't fit the profile of a Ponzi schemer, at least...in the world that we knew then." Cheung, to whom Suh reported, told the OIG that because the SEC had conducted a recent examination of Madoff and had found only "technical violations," Madoff could not have been operating a Ponzi scheme. For this reason Cheung also rejected Markopolos's offer to assist with the investigation. Certainly confirmation bias is at work here and operating in conjunction with representativeness bias, which focuses on judgments that rely on the closeness of "profile fit."

Critically, Cheung directed the investigation to focus not on identifying a Ponzi scheme but on a completely different issue. That issue was Madoff's failure to have registered with the SEC as an investment adviser. Investment advisers having more than 15 clients are required to register as advisers with the SEC, and Madoff had not done so. Therefore, the 2005–2006 investigation team's goal became that of forcing Madoff to register as an investment adviser.

As was mentioned earlier, most of the work in the 2005–2006 investigation fell to Suh, who had no experience with Ponzi schemes. She made the following remark to the OIG: "I was told that Peter was an industry expert and I thought that if there were things that jumped out at him as things that didn't make sense, I deferred to his judgment on that point."[22] Notably, such deference lies at the heart of groupthink behavior.

In a *Wall Street Journal* interview conducted from prison, Madoff explained that his fraud persisted for so long because regulators did not verify his firm's assets at depository trusts.[23] As it happens, Suh requested and obtained Madoff's account number with the Depository Trust Company (DTC). Located in New York City, the DTC is one of the largest securities depositories in the world, providing safekeeping through electronic record-keeping of securities balances.

After providing his DTC account information to the SEC, Madoff was certain that they would uncover his Ponzi scheme in short order, and he braced himself. But it did not happen. Why? Amazingly, Suh actually initiated the verification of Madoff's positions with the DTC, but inexplicably backed off at the last moment.

Notably, Suh could have contacted the DTC early in the investigation. However, she only considered the possibility very late in the game after the process had dragged on, and only when she was focused on forcing Madoff to register as an investment adviser. She explained, "[W]e really didn't have the luxury to look at any conceivable area which might have a securities violation.... by now we're into July and, you know, we don't have an unlimited amount of time.... And, you know, for an examination that's been going on three months I don't know that that was, you know, something that we wanted to spend time on."

Regulatory agencies have limited resources to investigate issues. More resources devoted to some investigations mean fewer resources devoted to others. As one NERO staffer told the OIG, "[U]nfortunately it comes down to, sometimes, numbers, and quantity, not quality, and...I guess your supervisor gets pressure from his supervisor who gets pressure from their supervisor...and then, ultimately, maybe he is getting pressure from OCIE[24] to churn out certain numbers."[25] (OCIE is the SEC's Office of Compliance Inspections and Examinations in Washington, DC.) From a process-pitfall perspective, these statements suggest severe problems with the agency's standards and incentives.

Imagine how the SEC's two investigation teams reacted when they learned of Madoff's arrest for having conducted a Ponzi scheme. Suh told the OIG, "Well, we had the allegation so I guess—I was shocked that the allegation turned out to be so true and that the scope was so much vaster than what we had thought." Cheung testified that she "was more shocked [than someone who was not aware of the allegations] because I had investigated it."

Several days after Madoff confessed, Lamore e-mailed one of his colleagues at NERO to say, "It's been a tough couple of days for me. Although I gave the exam and follow-up investigation 110% we just didn't uncover it. I think we were very close,—*probably only 1 or 2 phone calls away from blowing it open.*"[26] The contrast between this e-mail message and Lamore's earlier one to Nee could not be sharper.

Being overconfident leads people to be surprised more often than they expect. Experiencing regret leads people to feel pain because they easily imagine having taken a course of action that turned out more favorably than what actually occurred. Based on the reactions of the two SEC teams, overconfidence and regret were both in evidence.

Culture Issues at the SEC

The two NERO investigations were the last in a chain that began in the early 1990s. And five years before NERO dismissed the Ponzi scheme allegation, *MARHedge* and *Barron's* had raised clear suspicions. What was it about SEC culture that would have prevented these articles from inducing the SEC to have moved earlier and more aggressively to test the hypothesis that Madoff was running a Ponzi scheme?

The 2005–2006 investigation had the feeling of déjà vu. Markopolos had filed a complaint with the SEC's Boston office in 2001 as well, which the BDO had forwarded to NERO. In 2001, several days after the *Barron's* article appeared, an Enforcement Branch Chief followed up with NERO regarding Markopolos's complaint, asking the director of NERO if he wanted a copy of the article. The OIG report tells us NERO decided against an investigation and rejected the BDO's request to have that decision reconsidered. The OIG report also tells us that it could find no evidence that NERO staff had reviewed the *Barron's* article. Do you think this was more of the same from a psychological perspective? What is your sense of whether these events signal a cultural weakness at the SEC?

In May 2001, OCIE's former director, Lori Richards, did review the *Barron's* article and in fact sent a copy to an associate director in OCIE. She even attached a note describing the article as "very good" and adding, "This is a great exam for us!" However, the OIG report tells us that OCIE did not open an examination.

The OIG report also tells us that they could find no record of anyone else in OCIE reviewing the *Barron's* article for several years. However, eventually SEC staff did query Madoff about the claims in the *Barron's* article, and the OIG report tells us what happened. Enforcement staff asked him about how he was able to achieve his consistently high returns. Madoff deflected their question by attacking the author of the *Barron's* article and anyone else who challenged his ability to generate those returns legitimately. He characterized Markopolos as an "idiot" (even after having been convicted and imprisoned). He attributed his ability to generate returns to a personal feel for timing the market, saying, "Some people feel the market. Some people just understand how to analyze the numbers that they're looking at."

The OIG report characterized the Enforcement staff as having been inexperienced and lacking understanding about equity and options trading. That is, they did not understand Figure 14.1, nor make an effort to generate a figure like it. Therefore, they did not perceive that Madoff was unable to provide a logical explanation for how he was able to generate the sustained return patterns displayed in Figures 14.2 and 14.4.

Alex Sadowski, former branch chief of OCIE, told the OIG that the SEC might have a cultural weakness. He described the problem as one in which examiners have suspicions of wrongdoing, miss finding evidence, and then seek to convince other Enforcement staff that their initial judgment was correct out of concern that Enforcement efforts would uncover evidence that makes them look bad. Sadowski's point might well apply to Nee and Lamore. This behavior is more self-interest than psychological bias, even though it has the feel of confirmation bias.

Sadowski used the term "culture of fear," and described an examiner displaying that fear in the following terms: "I don't want to be proven to be incompetent and so we are going to kind of—not slide this under the rug but it is just if I have already looked at something and it is not there, it is not there because I am competent and you don't need to go and look and question my judgment."[27]

As a related matter, regulators need to be especially sensitive to the issue of intimidation by the entities that they are regulating as well as by their own superiors. On this point, the OIG report quotes SEC staff as having stated,

> [I]t is easier to be more aggressive when you are examining a "penny-stock firm" rather than, for instance, Goldman Sachs...
>
> [I]n past examinations unrelated to Madoff, supervisors at the Commission appear to have been reluctant to push issues against influential people, stating:
>
> Yes. I've seen it where, you know, maybe I've been told, "Don't rock the boat so much there, because we have a good relationship with them," and "where we need to make a request for documents, they always gave it to us. So let's try to go easy." You know,... at the end of the day it turns out, yes, it is an issue, or it should be an issue.[28]

With respect to the issue of potential intimidation in the Madoff investigations, the OIG report comments on three of the five SEC investigations, including two conducted by NERO. The OIG tells us that Madoff used his stature and perceived connections to try to influence the SEC examiners and investigators. The report concludes that Madoff's stature played an ancillary role in the SEC's failure to uncover the Ponzi scheme. In the 1992 investigation, Madoff's reputation led examiners to judge that it was not necessary to look further into Madoff's operation, which induced them to curtail their efforts.

In the 2005 NERO examination, Madoff used his stature and perceived connections to intimidate the examiners, who the OIG concluded did not feel sufficiently confident to be more aggressive in their efforts, especially after they were informed by senior officials in Washington during the investigation about Madoff's reputation in the industry.

As we saw earlier, in the 2005–2006 investigation, Madoff's prominence reduced Suh's belief that Madoff could be running a Ponzi scheme. In the end, the OIG report concluded that although intimidation based on Madoff's prominence played a role, it was not the major factor that explained why the SEC missed uncovering Madoff's Ponzi scheme.[29]

For his part, Madoff used a variety of tactics to reinforce this belief and intimidate SEC staff. He dropped the names of prominent people, including an SEC commissioner. He mentioned that his name had been on the short list to head the SEC, and might be so again in the future. He became angry at times, with investigators noting that his veins were popping. And upon occasion, he belittled those who interviewed him.

Closing Thoughts

Bernard Madoff's Ponzi scheme offers many insights into the psychology of financial fraud. The narrative almost speaks for itself. In 2001, the financial media had raised enough doubts to raise serious alarms. However, the fraud persisted for seven years more, and might have continued longer, were it not for the global financial crisis.

Not all of Madoff's investors were sophisticated, but many were. They knew enough to find his statements about the split-strike conversion strategy plausible, but did not question whether the risk-return profile of his alleged performance was realistic. That they did so speaks powerfully to the importance of psychology, and why risk managers need to be ever vigilant in watching not just for signals of fraud but for the forces seeking to downplay what those signals portend. Those signals partly stem from self-interest, either from regulators who have investigated an issue and wish their judgments to go unchallenged or from investors who do suspect fraudulent activity but because they benefit from it, keep silent or downplay it.

CHAPTER 15

RISK, RETURN, AND INDIVIDUAL STOCKS

WHEN IT COMES TO INDIVIDUAL STOCKS, DEFINING RISK IS TRICKY BUSINESS. Investors can use return standard deviation for this purpose, but that definition is incomplete because it fails to take the benefits from diversification into account. They can use "beta" based on the capital asset-pricing model (CAPM), which does reflect a particular understanding about diversification, but many academic studies conclude that the CAPM does not work. They can use a multifactor model; however, there is no theory to identify exactly what the appropriate factors should be.

The absence of a widely accepted definition of what risk means for individual stocks creates challenges for the practice of risk management in investment companies. Risk managers typically rely on statistical frameworks such as variance-covariance models. However, portfolio managers might rely on risk frameworks that are different from those used by risk managers.

These differences can lead to tensions, especially when risk managers are lower in the firm hierarchy than the portfolio managers they support. It is common for the relationship between the two types of managers to become adversarial. Based on the metrics they follow, risk managers often seek to impose constraints on what portfolio managers can and cannot do. On the other side, portfolio managers can often feel that risk managers are excessively narrow in focus and lack an understanding of the portfolios they evaluate.

Even when risk managers and portfolio managers are equal in respect to seniority, the lack of a common perspective on what risk means and how it is to be measured, can lead portfolio managers to complain that risk managers lack the appropriate understanding of how to balance risk and expected return.

The tensions around making judgments about risk can also be intrapersonal as well as interpersonal, and this is both subtle and terribly important.

Judgments about risk involve not just how we think but also what we feel. How we think and what we feel are not always in unison. Therefore, judgments about risk can involve dissonance between what psychologist Walter Mischel calls our "hot system" and our "cold system," or what his fellow psychologist Daniel Kahneman calls our "System 1" and our "System 2." Often, people are not even aware of the dissonance, because the hot System 1 is so much in control.

This chapter analyzes the psychological basis for the manner in which investors form judgments about stocks and companies, focusing on investors' perspectives about risk premiums.[1] The discussion in the chapter describes evidence that contrasts the intellectual statements that investment professionals make about principles and theory with the judgments they make in practice. This is the heart of potential dissonance mentioned above. Intellectual statements tend to reflect cool System 2 thinking, often informed by textbook theory, whereas judgments tend to reflect some combination of the interaction between hot System 1 and cool System 2.

TEXTBOOK FINANCE THAT INFORMS OUR SYSTEM 2

The textbook approach to risk and return that informs our cool System 2 begins with the CAPM, and focuses on two key relationships: the capital market line and the securities market line. Both relationships can be expressed graphically and have the shape depicted in Figure 15.1. Both figures have expected return on the vertical axis, and a measure of risk on the horizontal axis.

The measure of risk on the capital market line is return standard deviation, where the return refers to the return on the market. The intercept in the capital market line corresponds to the risk-free rate of interest. This is the rate

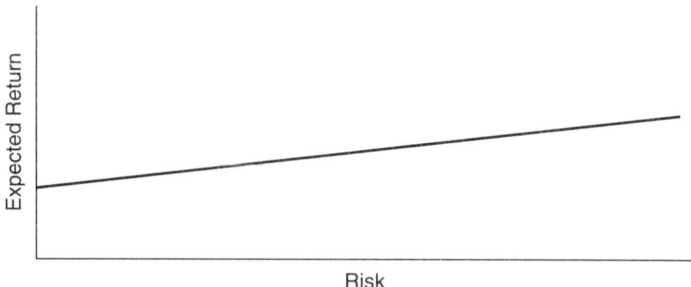

Figure 15.1 This figure displays the linear structure associated with both the capital market line and the securities market line. Both relationships have expected return on the vertical axis, and a measure of risk on the horizontal axis (return standard deviation for the capital market line and beta for the securities market line).

investors can earn without bearing any risk at all, and only reflects the time value of money. The slope of the capital market line is positive, and shows how much of a premium, measured as incremental expected return, investors require when accepting one additional standard deviation of market return.

The horizontal axis of the securities market line is CAPM-beta. The beta of a stock is the average change in the return to that stock that occurs in conjunction with a unit increase in the market return. The vertical axis measures the expected return on a given security. Therefore, in a CAPM framework, the slope of the capital market line is the market risk premium, measured as the difference between the expected return on the market portfolio and the risk-free rate.

The empirical evidence does not support the proposition that the CAPM explains risk premiums. This is not to say that textbook finance rejects the market risk premium as being irrelevant to the determination of risk premiums for individual securities. Instead, textbook finance proposes that additional factors are involved besides the market premium. These factors are associated with firm size measured by market capitalization of equity (market cap), book-to-market equity (B/M, the inverse of price-to-book ratio), and momentum as measured by past six-month returns. There is also evidence suggesting that realized returns are associated with profitability (as measured by a variant of ROE); however, this feature is not a major focus of the chapter.

In textbook finance, risk premiums are positive. Therefore, the slopes of both the capital market line and securities market line are positive. Historically, small-cap stocks have outperformed large-cap stocks, but with higher volatility. Therefore, small-cap stocks are judged to be associated with a positive risk premium. Historically, value stocks (those with relatively high B/M) have outperformed growth stocks (those with relatively low B/M). Therefore, value stocks are associated with a positive risk premium. Historically, recent winners (stocks with relatively high past six-month returns) have outperformed recent losers (stocks with relatively low past six-month returns). Therefore, momentum is associated with a positive risk premium.

Textbook finance has names for the different factor approaches. The Fama-French three-factor model explains risk premiums for stocks using factors based upon the market return, size, and B/M equity. The Carhart four-factor model adds momentum to these three. Newer models are in the process of being developed and refined in order to capture the effects from profitability and firm investment.

DISSONANCE AT A HEDGE FUND WORKSHOP

In 1999, during the frenzy of the dot.com bubble, I conducted an in-company workshop for a US hedge fund on the topic of how psychology impacts judgments of risk and return. The hedge fund is located in the New York area. The fund's director of research and chief investment officer (CIO), let me call him Cameron McDougall, emphasized the importance of having a disciplined investment process in place across all asset classes, including equity and fixed-income. In addition, McDougal was a strong believer in value investing, which provided the guiding principle for the investment process at the fund.

A key aspect of having a disciplined investment process is identifying the drivers of the judgments portfolio managers and analysts make about the risk and return associated with individual securities. As part of the workshop, I used a survey to elicit information about judgments about one-year return expectations and perceived risk. To assess judgments about the quality of the underlying companies, I used the questions from *Fortune* magazine's annual survey on corporate reputation. Begun in 1982, this survey provides the longest running and best-known basis for ranking America's most admired companies. My survey focused on eight technology companies: Dell, Novell, Hewlett-Packard, Unisys, Microsoft, Oracle, Intel, and Sun Microsystems.

By using the *Fortune* magazine questions, I was able to assess the degree to which the responses of subjects in my study were similar to the responses provided to the survey run by *Fortune*. Jumping ahead a bit, let me just say that the responses to my study questions were highly consistent with the responses to the *Fortune* study. I suggest that this consistency provides credibility to the approach discussed throughout this chapter, in that my sample sizes, both for number of participants and number of stocks, were much smaller than the corresponding sample sizes in the actual *Fortune* surveys.

The instructions in my survey asked participants to specify the return they expect for each of the eight stocks over the following 12 months, expressed as a percentage. The survey also asked participants to rate their perception of the riskiness of each stock on a scale of 0 to 10, with 0 being risk free and 10 being extremely speculative.

The *Fortune* magazine survey consists of seven questions that pertain to a company and one question that pertains to the company's stock. All answers to the *Fortune* questions are on a scale from 0 to 10. The seven questions ask about the quality of the company's management, the quality of its products, its financial soundness, the degree to which it makes wise use of corporate assets, its innovativeness, its ability to attract, develop, and keep talented people, and its responsibility to the community and the environment. The eighth question in the *Fortune* magazine survey relates to the company's stock, and asks for a rating from 0 to 10 on long-term investment value.

I constructed a composite index to measure "quality of company" by taking the unweighted average of the responses to six of the eight *Fortune* questions, and set aside the responses for financial soundness and long-term investment value. Doing so provided five variables upon which to focus attention: quality of company, financial soundness of company, long-term investment value, expected return, and perceived risk.

A value investor would expect higher returns from value stocks than growth stocks. Moreover, a value investor would most likely expect higher returns from small-cap than from large-cap stocks. The correlation between CIO McDougal's expected returns and B/M equity for the eight stocks was 0.49. The CIO's judgments about the eight stocks were consistent with those of a value investor. The correlation between McDougal's expected returns and the log-market equity for the eight stocks was −0.5. McDougal's judgments also indicated a belief in momentum: the correlation between expected return and past six-month return was 0.45. Notably, all three correlations were much stronger than the correlation between the CIO's expected return and beta, which was 0.1.

McDougal's judgments about risk were generally in line with his beliefs about expected return. He judged that value stocks were riskier than growth stocks, with the correlation coefficient between perceived risk and B/M equity being 0.75. The risk correlation for size was −0.17 and for past six-month return was 0.61.

The risk correlation for beta was −0.11, lending further support to the view that the CIO did not exhibit a strong belief in the CAPM. Nevertheless, the negative correlation coefficient by no means implies that McDougal believed the risk premium to be negative. The correlation coefficient between his judgments of risk and return were 0.67. He just did not believe that historical CAPM beta captured the essence of risk, as his −0.11 coefficient makes clear.

Now we come to the issue of dissonance. There were six core members on McDougall's team. Not all shared his perspective about risk and return. Beginning with expected returns, the judgments of three were that beta and expected return are actually negatively correlated. Only the judgments of two featured positive correlations, like McDougall's, and these were very strong. Five of the six judged that size and expected return are negatively correlated, in line with McDougal's judgment. Notably, three judged that B/M and expected return are negatively correlated, which is very much at odds with McDougall's value-investing perspective. Finally, five of the six judged that expected return and past six-month return are positively correlated.

The risk judgments of the six are somewhat mixed. Five of the six judge that beta and risk are positively correlated. Four of the six judge that size is negatively correlated with risk and that B/M is positively correlated with risk. In the main, the majority of these judgments are in line with textbook finance.

As I mentioned above, three of the six judged that beta and expected return are negatively correlated. This means that half of the group judged that the slope of the securities market line is negative, not positive as in the textbook diagrams. Possibly, this reflects the view that historical beta is not an accurate measure of risk. However, the biggest surprise was that three of the six judged that expected return and risk are negatively correlated. In other words, half of the group formed judgments that are totally opposite in direction to the precepts of textbook finance.

Before conducting the exercise, I asked the group whether they expected higher returns from riskier securities or safer securities. Virtually everyone answers the same, that they expect higher returns from riskier assets. This response is what we would expect from investment professionals whose answers are provided by their cool System 2, informed as it is by textbook finance. That half the group's judgments involve expecting higher returns from safer securities suggests that hot System 1 is at work.

I conducted the same exercise with 14 others in the firm. Not all were portfolio managers and analysts, but all felt knowledgeable enough to participate in the exercise and provide considered judgments. On average, these participants judged that expected return is negatively correlated with beta, positively correlated with size, negatively correlated with B/M, and negatively correlated with past six-month returns. The signs of these correlations are exactly opposite to those provided in textbook finance, as well as by McDougall.

In respect to risk, the judgments of the 14 others, where hot System 1 might play an active role, are more in line with textbook finance. On average, perceived risk is positively correlated with beta, negatively correlated with size, and positively correlated with B/M. The correlation of risk with past six-month return is negative, but virtually zero.

The point is that System 1 thinking about risk might naturally conform to the textbook approach that informs System 2. Therefore, any strong internal conflicts between System 1 and System 2 might involve issues that go beyond risk assessment per se, to the relationship between risk and expected return. Taken together, the judgments of the 14 others were that risk and expected return are negatively correlated, and strongly so. The mean correlation coefficient was −0.47. Three-quarters of the group judged the relationship as being negative. In contrast, for the six core members, the mean correlation was −0.1, and only half of that group judged the relationship as being negative.

General Findings from 15 Years of Workshop Data

Every year from 1999 on, I conducted similar workshops for executive education and in-company programs. These were conducted in the United States,

Europe, and Asia. In 2005, 2007, 2009, and 2014, I also conducted the workshop exercise with faculty and graduate students in finance at several European universities. The responses of these participants provided me with 15 consecutive years of data about judgments of risk and expected return.

These workshops involved 417 participants with a mean of 18 participants per workshop. The investment professionals were usually high ranking and very experienced. Examples of job titles are

- quantitative analyst, investment research, insurance firm;
- senior portfolio manager, investment bank;
- head of research, institutional asset management;
- equity analyst, investment bank; and
- senior portfolio manager, pension fund.

Prior to 2004, workshop participants were provided with copies of data downloaded from Bridge Information Systems (later Reuters), and asked to use whatever other data sources they normally would in making judgments about stocks. After 2004, participants were provided with online links to financial data (Yahoo Finance).

In late 2004, the workshop survey questions pertaining to quality of company were replaced with a single question asking about the "quality of the company" (QC). The number of stocks was increased from eight to ten, by adding eBay and Walmart. When companies were delisted from exchanges, as happened with Novell and Sun Microsystems, they were replaced with firms having similar financial characteristics. In 2013, Dell was replaced with Facebook after Dell's management announced that it wished to take the company private. In 2014, modifications were made to the composition of companies, with JPMorgan replacing Oracle and Twitter replacing Cisco.

Consider the general question of whether investment professionals perceive risk to be greater for stocks that have higher betas, are associated with smaller companies, and have higher B/M values than stocks that have lower betas, are associated with larger companies, and have lower B/M values. In other words, do the judgments that investment professionals make about risk conform to textbook finance?

In an average year, approximately 50% of the workshop participants judge that risk is positively correlated with beta, negatively correlated with size, and positively correlated with B/M. Table 15.1 displays mean correlations for the years 1999–2014. As can be seen from Table 15.1, in some years the study was conducted more than once. As a general matter, the correlation signs for beta, size, and B/M are stable across the sample. The sign for size is uniformly negative, and for B/M is mostly positive.

Table 15.1 Correlations between perceived risk and specific characteristics

This table presents the time series of mean correlations between perceived risk and the following six variables: beta, size measured by market value of equity, book-to-market equity B/M, and annualized past returns for 6 months, 12 months, and 36 months.

Risk	Beta	Size	B/M	Ret6	Ret12	Ret36
1999	0.21	−0.33	0.19	0.07	0.07	0.07
2000	0.02	0.04	−0.11	0.11	0.18	0.10
2001	0.18	−0.08	0.06	−0.13	−0.07	0.09
2002	#N/A	#N/A	#N/A	#N/A	#N/A	#N/A
2003	0.27	−0.25	−0.05	−0.04	0.02	−0.16
2004.1	0.38	−0.51	0.10	−0.02	0.28	0.00
2004.2	0.05	−0.44	0.23	−0.08	−0.04	0.04
2005	0.48	−0.47	0.29	−0.27	−0.28	0.01
2006	0.59	−0.55	0.41	−0.30	−0.20	−0.20
2007.1	0.24	−0.66	−0.25	0.40	−0.09	−0.14
2007.2	0.08	−0.53	0.01	−0.03	0.06	−0.06
2008	0.70	−0.64	0.45	−0.17	−0.15	−0.15
2009.1	0.61	−0.70	0.54	0.50	−0.69	−0.64
2009.2	0.50	−0.58	0.30	0.45	−0.48	−0.54
2010.1	0.48	−0.61	0.48	0.11	0.37	−0.52
2010.2	0.25	−0.43	0.27	−0.06	0.18	−0.18
2010.3	0.41	−0.57	0.33	−0.15	−0.07	−0.43
2011.1	0.26	−0.21	0.08	−0.01	0.09	−0.05
2011.2	0.50	−0.60	0.02	0.15	0.15	0.00
2012.1	0.47	−0.60	0.53	−0.31	−0.47	−0.31
2012.2	0.33	−0.43	0.51	−0.33	−0.43	−0.40
2013	0.31	−0.56	0.61	−0.35	0.47	−0.52
2014	0.15	−0.44	0.14	0.20	−0.12	−0.45

Table 15.1 also displays correlations for prior returns. Notice that there is more variation in sign for the prior return, than for size and B/M.

Next, consider the relationship between investors' expected returns and the six characteristic variables discussed in the previous section. When asked what they expect in principle, virtually all participants in my studies give the textbook answer that they expect higher returns from riskier securities. Are the judgments investment professionals actually make about expected return in line with their System 2 intellectual perspectives, informed as they are by textbook finance? Table 15.2 is the expected return counterpart to Table 15.1.

The key patterns in Table 15.2 are as follows. First, the correlation between expected return and beta tends to be positive for only half the sample. Second, the correlation between expected return and size is almost always positive. Investment professionals expect higher returns from larger stocks, a relationship at odds with textbook finance. Third, the correlation

Table 15.2 Correlations between expected return and specific characteristics

This table presents the time series of mean correlations between expected return and the following six variables: beta, size measured by market value of equity, book-to-market equity B/M, and annualized past returns for 6 months, 12 months, and 36 months.

ExpRet	Beta	Size	B/M	Ret6	Ret12	Ret36
1999	−0.10	0.15	−0.05	−0.05	0.02	−0.07
2000	0.01	0.16	−0.16	0.18	0.20	0.04
2001	−0.03	0.52	−0.43	0.26	−0.31	0.11
2002	0.33	0.00	0.07	0.01	0.11	0.29
2003	−0.16	0.26	−0.21	0.27	0.10	0.13
2004.1	−0.15	0.17	−0.09	0.00	−0.10	0.03
2004.2	0.07	0.17	−0.13	−0.02	−0.02	0.04
2005	0.03	0.09	−0.15	0.10	0.10	0.20
2006	0.01	0.13	−0.10	0.01	0.01	0.18
2007.1	0.07	0.11	−0.01	−0.23	0.18	0.08
2007.2	0.01	0.20	−0.12	−0.01	0.07	0.04
2008	0.11	0.11	−0.16	0.03	−0.12	0.02
2009.1	0.12	−0.08	0.10	0.11	−0.12	−0.09
2009.2	−0.11	0.14	0.02	−0.11	0.18	0.14
2010.1	−0.07	0.31	−0.27	−0.27	−0.12	0.13
2010.2	−0.13	0.30	−0.13	0.02	−0.08	0.11
2010.3	−0.31	0.42	−0.23	0.29	0.21	0.38
2011.1	0.08	0.07	0.11	0.03	0.12	−0.19
2011.2	−0.13	0.22	−0.04	0.08	0.07	−0.01
2012.1	0.04	−0.01	−0.16	0.09	0.09	0.15
2012.2	−0.10	0.22	−0.33	0.19	0.29	0.30
2013	−0.03	0.05	−0.07	0.09	−0.11	0.16
2014	−0.02	0.30	−0.30	0.17	0.28	0.48

between expected return and B/M is mostly negative. Investors expect higher returns from growth stocks than value stocks, a relationship at odds with textbook finance. These results are similar to those reported from the 1999 hedge fund workshop. Notably, the relationship between expected return and prior returns is variable in sign, but considerably more positive than negative.

JUDGMENTS OF EXPECTED RETURN AND PERCEIVED RISK: REPRESENTATIVENESS AND AFFECT

After having conducted these workshops over 15 consecutive years, I have found that the mean correlation between perceived risk and expected return has turned out to be negative for all but one group. Therefore, it seems safe to conclude that the perceived risk-expected return pattern displayed by the 1999 hedge fund group is no accident.

On average, professionals judge risk and expected return to be negatively correlated, just the opposite to the relationship depicted in textbook finance. Why should this be the case? The behavioral perspective offers two possible explanations: representativeness and affect.

As explained earlier, representativeness is a psychological principle involving reliance on stereotypes for making judgments. In an important academic article, economists Michael Solt and Meir Statman introduced the idea that investors who judge the stocks of good companies to be representative of good stocks rely on the representativeness heuristic "good stocks are stocks of good companies."[2]

Affect refers to emotional associations people make with objects, concepts, and ideas. Affect is a unitary measure of goodness, with negative affect corresponding to "bad." Psychologists suggest that we record associations of affect in our memories, which allows us to make snap judgments through pattern recognition. These associations go by the name "somatic markers." Affect and representativeness are similar in many ways, and often reinforce each other. Clearly, in the current context both concepts focus on "goodness of company."

In order to understand the way in which representativeness and affect impact judgments of risk and expected return, consider the data from a workshop I conducted in 2004. This workshop was for portfolio managers and analysts working for a company based in the United States that has been in existence for more than 50 years, has offices in over 30 countries, and offers many different funds and financial products.

Let us focus on the responses of one particular participant, whom I will call Tim Hellman. I chose Tim because his responses vividly illustrate the general pattern, and are strong across the board. His judgments for expected returns are negatively correlated with beta, positively correlated with size, negatively correlated with B/M, and negatively correlated with past six-month returns. His judgments of risk are also strongly correlated with these variables, but with opposite sign. Figure 15.2 summarizes Tim's correlations for these variables, and Figure 15.3 summarizes the correlations associated with the group's mean judgments.

The correlation between Tim's judgments for risk and expected return was −0.47. The corresponding correlation for the group mean judgments was −0.09. Clearly, Tim's judgments are in line with the group means, but are stronger.

How does representativeness help explain the thought process that might have led Tim to associate lower expected returns to riskier stocks? Begin by recalling that representativeness leads people to judge that "good stocks are stocks of good companies."

Think about what makes for a good company. According to the *Fortune* magazine corporate reputation survey, good companies are well managed, offer

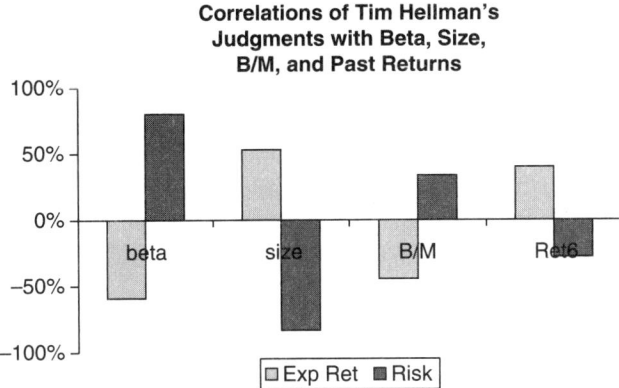

Figure 15.2 This figure displays analyst Tim Hellman's correlations for variables expected return and risk with beta, size, B/M, and past returns.

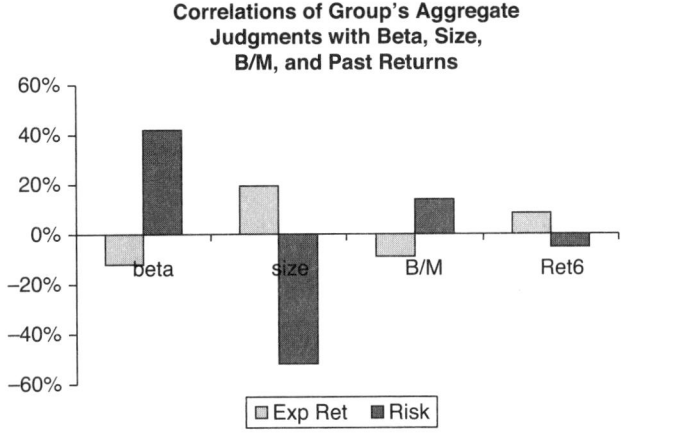

Figure 15.3 This figure displays correlations for variables expected return and risk with beta, size, B/M, and past returns for the group of analysts to which Tim Hellman belonged

high-quality products, are innovative, attract and maintain a talented workforce, are financially sound, use assets wisely, and are socially responsible.

What makes a good stock? A good stock features high returns and as little risk as possible.

In the 1999 workshop, I inferred quality of company from the responses to the *Fortune* questions. However, in the 2004 workshop, I condensed the seven traits associated with a good company into a single question about QC. Therefore, the survey provided judgments about QC and the quality of its stock (long-term investment value VLTI).

One way to test for whether investors rely on representativeness is to examine the correlation between QC and VLTI. The correlation coefficient for

Tim's judgments was 0.94, and for the mean group responses was 0.43. Tim also associated good stocks with high expected returns and low risk. The correlation coefficient between Tim's judgments for VLTI and expected return was 0.64, and for VLTI and perceived risk was −0.71. For the mean group responses, the respective correlation coefficients were 0.38 and −0.40.

Judgments of financial soundness are important both for judgments about QC and perceived risk for the stock. High-quality companies are typically thought to be financially sound. Moreover, the stocks of financially sound companies are typically regarded as safer than the stocks of companies that are not financially sound.

Tim's judgments are in line with the perspective described in the previous paragraph. The correlation between his judgments about QC and financial soundness (FS) was 0.81, while the correlation between his judgments of perceived risk and FS was −0.70. For the mean group responses, the respective correlation coefficients were 0.75 and −0.37.

In summary, representativeness will induce investors to judge that good stocks are stocks of good companies, and that good companies are financially sound. Representativeness also induces investors to judge that the stocks of financially sound companies are low in risk. In conjunction with the belief that good stocks feature high expected returns, representativeness will therefore induce investors to expect higher returns from safer stocks.

The affect heuristic ties judgments of risk and expected return to a single variable measuring "goodness." VLTI is such a measure. According to the affect heuristic, benefits such as expected return are positively related to a stock's affect, while costs such as risk are negatively associated with affect. Both Tim's responses and the mean responses for the group are consistent with the affect heuristic.

Representativeness and affect are related but different from each other. Meir Statman, a professor of behavioral finance, who is mentioned above, differentiates between two hypotheses. The first is a characteristics hypothesis in which characteristics, such as size and B/M, are the direct drivers of expected returns. The second is a sentiment hypothesis in which affect is the direct driver of expected return. Statman tests this hypothesis by using the name of a company as a proxy for affect and finding that company name is more closely associated with expected return than are characteristics.

Baker-Wurgler Sentiment

Think back to Chapter 12 which focused on the relationship between systemic risk and sentiment. Sentiment is generally understood as the aggregate bias in the overall market, and relates to the notion of market efficiency. By one definition, markets are efficient when sentiment is zero, meaning that biases at the level of the individual investor cancel each other in the aggregate. By another definition, markets are efficient when investors are unable to earn positive abnormal risk adjusted returns.

Chapter 12 introduced several sentiment indicators, one of which is the Baker-Wurgler sentiment index BW.[3] Baker and Wurgler call their index SENT, and in this regard state the following: We view investor sentiment as simply optimism or pessimism about stocks in general."[4] In this respect, think of optimism as "excessive optimism" or "unrealistic optimism" in the sense described in Chapter 5. In other words, think of BW as a bias. Notably, BW is the most widely used sentiment indicator in the academic literature. Additional details about the construction of BW are provided in Appendix G.

Figure 12.5 in Chapter 12 displays the trajectory of BW from the 1960s on, showing its highs (such as in the dot-com bubble in the late 1990s) and its lows (such as in the oil crisis 1970s). The remainder of this chapter analyzes the judgments about expected return and perceived risk over the 15 year sample through the lens of BW.

Consider whether sentiment predicts the returns to individual stocks in the sense that mean realized returns vary according to the value of sentiment in the prior month. Baker and Wurgler report that when past sentiment has been high, subsequent returns to speculative stocks, more difficult-to-arbitrage stocks, are lower than returns to safer stocks, which are easier to arbitrage. Conversely, when past sentiment has been low, subsequent returns to speculative stocks, more difficult-to-arbitrage stocks are higher than safer stocks, which are easier to arbitrage.

Consider the portion of Figure 15.4 labeled Figure 15.4a. For each date, Figure 15.4a contrasts the time series of BW and expected return (averaged over all stocks that were part of the exercise). Figure 15.4a only displays data through the end of 2010, as the BW series is only available until December 2010. The correlation between BW and average expected return is 57%.[5] Figure 15.4b displays the scatter plot depiction of these variables. For perceived risk, the corresponding correlation is only −9%.[6] The value of BW that is matched to an expected return is the one closest in time to the date the exercise was undertaken.[7]

The explanation that Baker and Wurgler provide for how sentiment impacts the cross section of realized returns involves the degree to which different stocks are easy to value and easy to arbitrage. They suggest that when sentiment increases, stocks that are difficult to value and difficult to arbitrage become overvalued relative to stocks that are easier to value and easier to arbitrage. This is an important issue, given that investors' judgments of expected return in the worksheet data are positively correlated with BW.

Baker and Wurgler identify the extent to which sentiment impacts the relationship between realized returns and characteristics such as size and B/M.

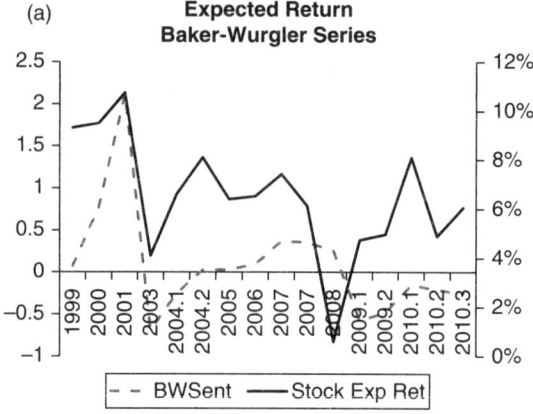

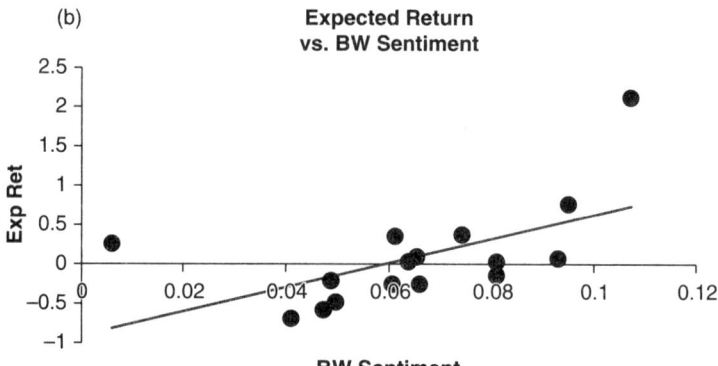

Figures 15.4 The two panels of this figure display two views of the relationship between BW and expected return, (a) a time series view and (b) a scatter plot view. For each date, Figure 15.4a contrasts the time series of BW and expected return (averaged over all stocks that were part of the exercise). Figure 15.4a only displays data through the end of 2010, as the BW series is only available until December 2010. Figure 15.4b displays the scatter plot depiction of these variables.

They report that the size effect is conditional on sentiment: when sentiment is low (below sample average), small stocks earn particularly high subsequent returns, but when sentiment is high (above average), there is no size effect at all. That is, following a month when sentiment has been negative, the correlation between realized returns and size is negative, whereas following a month when sentiment has been positive, the correlation between realized returns and size is near zero (or slightly positive).

An additional finding from the Baker-Wurgler analysis is that several characteristics that do not have any unconditional predictive power display sign-flipping predictive ability, in the hypothesized directions, after conditioning on sentiment. Specifically, when stocks are sorted into deciles by sales growth, B/M, or external financing activity, growth and distress firms tend to lie at opposing extremes, with more "stable" firms in the middle deciles.

In light of these conditional findings, consider the manner in which correlations involving judgments and characteristics vary, conditional on periods following whether BW has been positive or negative. Table 15.3 displays the results for beta, size, B/M, past six-month returns, and the percentage of investment professionals whose judgments about risk are consistent with the textbook sign patterns.

Focus on the size effect, beginning with risk. Over the period 1999–2010, the unconditional correlation between judgments of risk and size is –47%. Notably, the negative sign of this correlation is consistent with the textbook view that the stocks of small-cap firms are judged to be riskier than the stocks of large-cap firms. Following periods of positive sentiment, the correlation is –42%, which is weaker than the correlation of –53% associated with periods following negative sentiment. The stronger risk-size effect following periods of negative sentiment is consistent with the pattern for realized returns identified by Baker-Wurgler. However, the associated correlation conditional on negative sentiment does not turn positive, as is the case with realized returns.

Table 15.3 Impact of sentiment on pairwise correlations for judgments and characteristics

This table presents the time series of select mean pairwise correlations between four characteristic variables and two judgmental variables. The four characteristics are beta, size measured by market value of equity, book-to-market equity B/M, and past six-month return (annualized). The two judgmental variables are perceived risk and expected return. The table reports both unconditional and conditional values of variables. The conditioning variable is the sign of the sentiment index BW. The rightmost column of the table displays how the percentage of investors whose correlations between judgments and characteristics conform in sign to the Fama-French perspective. The conditional correlations are sorted so that the correlations for perceived risk and expected return with each characteristic are adjacent to each other. For example, the unconditional correlation between beta and perceived risk is 0.364, whereas the unconditional mean between beta and expected return is –0.059.

	Beta		Size		B/M		Ret6		% who are FF Rational
	Risk	Exp Ret	Risk	Exp Ret	Risk	Exp Ret	Risk	Exp Ret	
Unconditional Mean	36.4%	–5.9%	–46.4%	19.4%	20.4%	–11.5%	–0.5%	0.3%	7.0%
Mean if BW > 0	32.3%	–0.1%	–41.6%	16.7%	13.3%	–13.1%	–4.2%	4.6%	7.7%
Mean if BW < 0	41.8%	–13.2%	–52.6%	22.8%	29.6%	–9.4%	4.3%	–5.3%	6.1%

Over the period 1999–2010, the unconditional correlation between judgments of expected return and size is 19%. Relative to the corresponding correlation involving perceived risk, the expected return-size correlation is both weaker and of the opposite sign. The opposite sign pattern is consistent with investors' reliance on representativeness and affect-based heuristics. Following periods of positive sentiment, the expected return-size correlation is 17%, which is weaker than the correlation of 23% associated with periods following negative sentiment. Therefore, the bias associated with expected return and risk becomes stronger following periods of negative sentiment, thereby enhancing the size effect associated with risk. However, the magnitudes of the expected return-size correlations are not large enough to explain why the size effect would disappear following periods of positive sentiment.

Consider the extent to which investors' judgments about there being a size effect change over time. For judgments of risk, there is a marked BW effect on the percentage of investors who judge that risk and size are negatively correlated. Following periods of positive sentiment, 74% of investment professionals judge that risk and size are negatively correlated, and following periods of negative sentiment, 88% do so. There is no similar pattern for expected return. Following periods of positive sentiment, 32% judge that expected return and size are negatively correlated, and following periods of negative sentiment, 30% do so. These results reinforce the correlation findings reported in Table 15.3 for size.

The conditional sentiment results provide a vehicle for understanding how perceived risk and behavioral bias combine to impact realized returns. In line with the textbook view, investors' judgments that small-cap stocks are riskier than large-cap stocks on average leads realized returns for small-cap stocks to be greater than realized returns for large-cap stocks. Moreover, judgments about the risk-size interaction intensify following periods of negative sentiment, leading to a larger size effect during those periods.

However, in line with the Baker-Wurgler findings, perceived risk is not the only driver of realized returns, as judgments of expected return also exert an impact. Moreover, investors expect lower returns from small-cap stocks. As a result, investors bid down the prices of small-cap stocks to reflect their judgments about expected returns, beyond the impact associated with their judgments of risk. Following periods of negative sentiment, the bias is stronger than following periods of positive sentiment, thereby accentuating the difference in the two conditional size effects.

Table 15.3 shows that negative sentiment intensifies the correlations of perceived risk with beta and B/M, not just size. For size and B/M, the patterns are consistent with the textbook (Fama-French) perspective. For beta, the sign pattern is opposite to the textbook view. For past six-month returns, negative sentiment induces a sign pattern shift for risk, in that stocks with higher past returns are considered safer following periods of negative sentiment. For expected return, the flip in sign pattern suggests that investors believe in momentum following periods of positive sentiment and believe in reversals following periods of negative sentiment. At the same time, all correlations pertaining to prior six-month returns are small.[8]

The right-most column in Table 15.3 shows the impact of sentiment on the percentage of investors whose beliefs come closest to being rational in the textbook view. It seems fair to suggest that rationality requires judgments of both risk and expected return are positively related to beta, negatively related to size, and positively related to B/M. In addition judgments of risk and expected return are positively correlated. Table 15.3 shows that between 1999 and 2010, approximately 7% of investors satisfied the necessary conditions for rationality, with the percentage being higher following periods of positive sentiment. For the full sample period, 1999–2014, the percentage of investors who satisfied the necessary conditions for textbook rationality is in the vicinity of 10%.[9]

THOUGHTS ON AN INTEGRATED APPROACH

Cameron McDougall, the CIO of the hedge fund discussed at the beginning of the chapter, places a lot of emphasis on a disciplined investment approach. The degree to which his core team formed judgments in which risk and expected return were negatively correlated reflected his concern that the firm was in need of more discipline.

When asked whether they expect higher returns from safer or riskier securities, almost all investment professionals provide the textbook response that risk and expected return are positively correlated. However, for the majority, this cool System 2 response is at odds with their judgments in practice, which are heavily influenced by hot System 1 thinking. This means that when forming judgments, many investment professionals rely on heuristic principles that induce their judgments to be negatively correlated, and lack the discipline to cross-check their judgments and their principles. Investors who misjudge the relationship between risk and return dispose themselves to being disappointed by the returns they earn and/or surprised by the amount of risk they bear.

This internal tension between System 1 thinking and System 2 thinking is something risk managers absolutely need to understand. Most firms use a variety of risk management techniques. Examples are limits on the size of individual positions, sectors, and both gross exposures (sum of longs and short positions) and net positions (long minus short positions) exposures. While fine in theory, investment companies need to pay special attention to separating risks that bear positive risk premiums from risks that do not. And given that systematic risk, meaning the risk that brings with it rewards in the form of higher expected return, is not easy to identify, a key challenge for risk managers is to help portfolio managers and analysts understand the degree to which the principles they espouse are consistent with the judgments they render and the corresponding positions that they hold.

In April 2000, a month after the peak of the dot-com bubble, I repeated the workshop exercise with the hedge fund core portfolio managers and analysts. Over the course of eight months, their judgments had changed considerably. For example, the correlations between their judgments of expected returns at the two dates varied between −14% and 66%. The correlations between their judgments of risk at the two dates varied between −60% and 50%.

The signs of the correlations between their judgments and characteristic variables (beta, size, B/M, and prior six-month returns) also exhibited a great deal of volatility. The average number of sign flips per participant was 2.2 for both expected return and risk. That is 2.2 sign flips for 4 correlation coefficients. Moreover, for different participants, the directional effects were strong and often in opposite directions.

In a disciplined investment process, attention is focused on base rate information associated with characteristics, and then adjusted to capture singular information. When there is a lack of discipline, the tendency is for the singular information to dominate. This opens the door for wide individual variation in judgment to manifest itself.

Closing Thoughts

Risk managers in investment companies have their work cut out for them when there is no universally accepted definition of risk. In this type of situation, portfolio managers are prone to see risk managers as placing unnecessary obstacles in the path of value creation. One way in which risk managers can create value is to help portfolio managers identify the kinds of risks that are likely to bear positive risk premiums, and then to make investment decisions in which judgments and principles are aligned.

CHAPTER 16

HOW PSYCHOLOGY BROUGHT DOWN MF GLOBAL

RISK MANAGERS NEED TO UNDERSTAND MORE THAN THE PSYCHOLOGY impacting individual behavior. They also need to understand how these issues play out in organizations. Therefore, risk managers need to have an understanding of how insights from social psychology inform us about group behavior. In particular, risk managers need to understand the degree to which psychological pitfalls are mitigated or amplified by committees.

Most importantly, risk managers need to understand what constitutes normal disagreement in respect to risk appetite, and how those engaged in risk management might differ systematically from those they serve, support, and advise.

This chapter describes events at the financial firm MF Global. The "MF" derives from "Man Financial," as prior to 2007 the firm had been the brokerage division of the UK hedge fund Man Group plc. However, in 2007 the Man Group carved out MF Global through an initial public offering. As a new independent firm, MF Global was not especially profitable, and in 2008 its office experienced a $141.5 million loss from making unauthorized trading in wheat contracts. Shortly thereafter, Bernard Dan, a former CEO of the Chicago Board of Trade, took charge as CEO of MF Global.[1]

In 2010, Dan resigned, and in March 2010 was replaced by Jon Corzine, who had just lost a bid for re-election as governor of New Jersey. Within months, Corzine restored MF Global to profitability. However, 2011 proved to be an eventful year in the life of the firm, featuring drama in the conflict between the firm's CEO and its CRO.

The events at MF Global during 2011 occurred against the backdrop of the financial instability hypothesis, which tells us that the seeds of the next financial crisis are sown by its predecessor. As was mentioned in earlier chapters, the US response to the crisis featured fiscal stimulus and recapitalization of banks following stress tests. Although the magnitude of the stimulus was inadequate, it was larger than the European Union (EU) response, as Europeans responded with an austerity program and did not require that banks recapitalize to the same extent as in the United States.

Before the creation of the euro, European countries that are part of the eurozone would devalue their currencies when they experienced financial distress associated with their debt obligations. Devaluation was a preferred alternative to default. However, being part of the eurozone precluded devaluation as an alternative. In the aftermath of the financial crisis and associated slowdown in economic activity, the sovereign debt of some European countries, denominated in euros, became more risky. Greece was the first case, and was joined by others such as Ireland, Portugal, and Spain. The credit spreads on the sovereign bonds issued by these countries widened and became more volatile. This created opportunities for speculation for firms such as MF Global. For additional details on the unfolding of the European sovereign debt crisis, see Appendix I.

MF Global: A Case of Killing the Risk Management Messenger

The story of MF Global does not end happily. MF Global filed for bankruptcy on October 31, 2011. The events leading up to its bankruptcy featured a conflict between the firm's CEO, Corzine, and its CRO, Michael Roseman. This conflict was far more intense than our hypothetical short story involving portfolio manager Larry Stephan and risk manager Beth Chester. In January 2011, Corzine fired Roseman. Ultimately Roseman would have "his day in court," but that comes later, and too late to save the firm. However, first a bit more history.

As you read the chronology below, think about how the RMP framework applies to the case of MF Global. Think about what the events at MF Global suggest about the strength of its risk management structures, its risk management culture, and its risk management behaviors, both before and after Corzine joined the firm.

MF Global served farmers, hedge funds, and other customers who traded commodity contracts. It earned its revenue from trading commissions and from the spread between the rate it paid its customers for holding their cash and the rate it was able to earn by investing that cash. The firm grew through a series of global acquisitions and went public in 2007.

In February 2008, MF Global experienced an "unauthorized trading incident" in which it lost $141 million overnight on wheat contracts.[2] This event resulted in credit downgrades from two rating agencies, a sharp decline in its stock price, and deterioration in its relationships with customers. In consequence, two consulting firms were engaged to identify the cause of the incident and make recommendations to the board about preventing future similar incidents.

Because MF Global had not fully integrated the various acquisitions it made prior to its IPO, the consulting firms recommended that it implement ERM policies, enhance its risk systems, strengthen its global 24-hour risk monitoring capabilities, and hire a global CRO.

In August 2008, prior to full eruption of the financial crisis, MF Global hired Roseman as its CRO. Prior to joining MF Global, Roseman had been CRO for the Americas at Newedge, where his mandate was to elevate the firm's risk management capabilities to support its growing brokerage business. At MF Global, his mandate was to augment the firm's risk management capabilities in order to implement the consultants' recommendations and support the firm's strategic objectives. In this regard, Roseman reported to the CEO, was a member of the Executive Management team, chaired the monthly Enterprise Risk Committee meetings, and provided regular CRO reports to the board.

Under Roseman's leadership, MF Global developed a formal risk statement and adopted new delegations of authority that were approved by the board. The new approach was calibrated to the existing business and supported the strategic objectives of the firm. Notably, it encompassed all categories of risk, including market, credit, operational, capital, and liquidity risks. Roseman used the approach as the basis for a series of monthly presentations to executive management and the board about the firm's current and evolving risk exposure. The board reviewed the risk appetite statement and delegations of authority annually. This approach is consistent with sound risk management structure and culture, and with the idea that Roseman's risk style was manager.

Proprietary trading in sovereign debt was an important business line at MF Global and was a material factor role in its demise. In March 2010, MF Global held debt issued by the governments of Italy, Spain, Portugal, Ireland, and Greece, with the associated amounts being less than $500 million. As with all trading books, the firm put trading limits in place to support and control the European brokerage activity. These limits were well within the approved risk appetite, and MF Global had a process in place to adjust its limits as market conditions changed.

As was mentioned earlier, Corzine joined MF Global as its CEO in March 2010 when the firm was struggling.[3] Unfortunately for the firm, the spread between what it earned from investing its customers' cash and what it paid its customers on those accounts had declined as interest rates plummeted in the wake of the global financial crisis.

On the surface, Corzine's goal was to preserve MF Global's investment credit rating. MF Global had been struggling, and indeed had hired Corzine to turn the firm around. Credit rating agencies Moody's and S&P had both downgraded the firm, and Moody's had indicated that to preserve an investment-grade credit rating, MF Global's profit needed to be in the range of $200 to $300 million.

Corzine decided that betting on European sovereign debt, and especially Greek debt, was the right strategy to rescue the firm. This debt offered high yields because the economies of these countries had weakened considerably during the financial crisis. The high yields reflected an increase in default premiums to bondholders, compensating them for the increased risk that a government would default on its debt. Moreover, the accounting conventions allowed MF Global to book the profits on a "mark-to-market" basis from the strategy immediately, as if no default would occur in the future. Corzine described this feature as MF Global's "bridge" from its troubled present to its soon-to-be-better future.

Accounting conventions of this sort can drive risk managers crazy. Intrinsic value is determined by the risk and expected values of future cash flows, not earnings. Richard Brealey and Stewart Myers, who coauthored one of the best-known textbooks in corporate finance, were fond of telling us, earnings are not dollars you can buy beer with. Cash flows are dollars you can buy beer with.[4]

Intrinsic value is determined by the present value of the expected cash flow stream, discounted to reflect the underlying risk of those cash flows. Accounting conventions of the sort MF Global used emphasize differences in earnings and cash flow. Executives and investors who emphasize earnings over cash flows are prone to give too little emphasis to decisions that are excessively risky and value destructive.

In June and July 2010, Roseman began receiving requests from MF Global's business units to increase limits for trading positions in European sovereign debt. In response, he reviewed the positions and limits with the business heads as well as with Corzine. In those discussions, Roseman outlined the potential capital risk associated with the CDS market, along with the continued political and financial uncertainty in the relevant countries. He also raised issues pertaining to the new European Financial Stability Facility (EFSF), which had been established in May 2010 along with the forward funding schedule of the pertinent sovereigns.

Corzine and Roseman held different views about the potential sovereign default risk. Nevertheless, the outcome of the discussions within the firm resulted in an agreement to increase the total gross nominal limit across the named sovereigns from less than $500 million to $1 billion. In addition, the various parties agreed to more specific limits on holdings of sovereign debt with a series of "maturity buckets" of up to 12 months to mitigate the capital risk and keep the positions well within the EFSF's June 2013 maturity. Roseman expressed caution about the potential capital risk. Nevertheless, given the size of the limits and the ability of the firm to fund or liquidate the positions if conditions changed, he did not consider the liquidity risk of the positions to have been an issue at that point.

Corzine was no stranger to big bets in the fixed-income market. He had risen through the ranks at Goldman Sachs from being a trainee on the bond desk to become its co-CEO with Hank Paulson.[5] In 1986, as head of Goldman's government bond desk, Corzine oversaw a bet that had gone wrong. The firm had taken a position in which it established a long position in Treasuries having a coupon rate of 8.75%, together with a short position in Treasuries having a coupon rate of 9.25%. In theory, a decline in interest rates would lead the prices of the long position to increase by more than those of the short position. However, the market moved in a way that caused the value of the position to decline by at least $150 million. Corzine spent the next seven months personally involved in managing the position, and in the end market conditions stabilized in a way that allowed Goldman to emerge with a $10 million gain.[6]

Corzine described this kind of situation as a "come to Jesus moment." The partners at Goldman were astonished at how risky that bond position had been, and had difficulty understanding how the exposure was allowed to become so large. So, on the one side of the coin we have a $10 million profitable trade, and on the other we have the risk of that trade having been poorly managed initially. The importance a firm attaches to risk relative to profit can sometimes be gauged by its promotion policy. Perhaps trading profit mattered more, as in 1994 Corzine was made partner, at a time when he oversaw a hugely profitable bet on European currencies.

Fast-forward to 2010, and Corzine was using European sovereign debt to ramp up risk and profit potential at MF Global. Roseman recalled that by mid-September, the positions and limits had increased to between $1.5 and $2.0 billion. Roseman continued to express concerns about the potential capital risk associated with the larger positions, and began to sound alarms about growing liquidity risk. He also pointed out that, given the increasing materiality of the risks as they related to the board's approved risk tolerance, they needed to consult the board for approval to increase the sovereign limits. This they did, and received the board's approval.

By late October, the positions approached the range of $3.5 to $4.0 billion. On behalf of executive management, Roseman was asked to present another request to the board, this time to increase the total sovereign limit to $4.75 billion. At this point, Roseman made clear his concerns that the capital risk and liquidity risks were serious, and he described a set of unfavorable scenarios that he thought could plausibly occur. The reaction to his presentation of those scenarios was skepticism.

The firm had significantly increased its positions through repo-to-maturity (RTM) trades, and was evaluating its potential to generate profitable transactions and higher earnings. At the November 2010 board meeting, Roseman presented a detailed analysis of the potential liquidity risk stress scenarios and expressed his concern about potential margin calls from repo counterparties.

During the meeting, the board debated all of the risks Roseman had identified. In the end, some board members challenged the scenarios Roseman emphasized as not being plausible. They disagreed with him about whether the correlated liquidity risk scenarios he highlighted could occur across all counterparties and issuers at the same time. Separately and importantly, from a psychological point of view, Corzine had told the board that he would resign if they did not trust his judgment. Ultimately, the board approved the request to increase sovereign debt limits once again, conditioned on the limits being evaluated again, in early 2011.[7]

Notably, in January 2011, Roseman was notified that effective immediately, he was being replaced by a new CRO, Michael Stockman. The issue was simple: Corzine's strategy involved MF Global purchasing high-yield European sovereign debt and accepting the risk of default, betting that a collective EU would find a way to prevent an actual default. In his role as CRO, Roseman voiced the opinion that these bets on European sovereign debt were far too risky.

On October 24, 2011, Moody's downgraded MF Global's debt so that it was just above junk status. In its commentary it pointed out that MF Global's weak core profitability led the firm to take on excessive exposure to European sovereign debt. Because the company's earnings had been buoyed up through revenue recognition from its sovereign debt trading, once that trading peaked, its earnings plummeted. Earnings and the firm's stock price both declined sharply in late October 2011.

MF Global's final days began with a run by its customers and creditors, creating a need within the firm for a lot of cash to meet its current obligations. It could not find enough assets to sell in order to meet those obligations and unsuccessfully sought a white knight to stay in business.

To understand what happened, recall that MF Global was a brokerage firm that managed its clients' funds in addition to its own. By no account should the firm have used clients' funds to meet its own obligations. Yet, in the days before its bankruptcy filing, the firm did exactly that. Subsequently, farmers, hedge funds, and other customers discovered that they were without at least a third of their money: at least $1.2 billion had somehow vanished from the firm.

How did it happen? In the commodity brokerage business, customers' accounts are supposed to be segregated from the brokerage firm's own accounts and therefore sacrosanct. There were warnings within the firm about problems. Two former back office employees mentioned the existence of a report that had been produced early on MF Global's final day of business, October 28, showing a deficiency in customer cash accounts. Nevertheless, despite the warning, MF Global continued to transfer customer money without fully disclosing the potential problem to regulators.

The person who oversaw the crucial transfer of funds was the firm's treasurer, Edith O'Brien, who was based in Chicago. The amount in question was $175 million, used to replenish an overdrawn account at JPMorgan Chase in London. JPMorgan was MF Global's major lender, and it also cleared its trades.

Ordinarily, O'Brien oversaw fund transfers, normally a fairly routine task. However, in view of the source of the funds, this transfer was not routine. As it happens, JPMorgan questioned the origin of the funds and sought written assurances that the transfer was legitimate. Although MF Global did not provide such assurances, JPMorgan still accepted the funds, saying that it had received oral assurances.

On July 5, 2013, the *New York Times* reported that Corzine had called O'Brien directly from his New York office, telling her that finding the funds and transferring them was "the most important thing" that she could be doing that day.[8] According to the *Times* article, it was extraordinary for the CEO to have made such a call. In this regard, Corzine's attorney pointed out that nobody had asserted that Corzine actually told O'Brien to take customers' monies. Moreover, the article tells us that O'Brien seems to have been aware that what she was doing was wrong.

For sake of closure, I should mention that in March 2013, James Giddens, the trustee overseeing the return of customers' money, managed to successfully negotiate a deal with JPMorgan, which resulted in MF Global's American customers getting back about 93% of their money.

The psychological issues discussed in previous chapters played a key role in the MF Global saga. In a pertinent 2012 article that appeared in *Vanity Fair*, Burrough, Cohan, and McLean describe the chronology serving as a backdrop for describing my opinion about how these issues surfaced.

Although Corzine had co-run Goldman-Sachs, in a dispute with Paulson about merging Goldman with another firm, the board sided with Paulson and ousted Corzine from the firm. Corzine next moved to politics, and was elected senator from New Jersey. In this regard, he found himself being the "junior" senator from New Jersey, a new kid on the block in a culture based on seniority. Given his psychological traits, he found himself frustrated with his lack of control, and eventually resigned his Senate seat. He stayed in politics, becoming governor of New Jersey but failed to win re-election.

The first step in applying risk management frameworks developed earlier in the book is to use them to prompt questions. Based on the discussion about personality in Chapter 5, a natural question to ask is whether Corzine exhibited the features of an entrepreneur, meaning someone who is high in dispositional optimism and high in the desire for control. Based on the SP/A theory, a natural question to ask is whether he set very high aspirations and attached great importance to achieving success. Based on prospect theory, a natural question to ask is whether his ouster from Goldman and his failed bid to be re-elected governor of New Jersey psychologically placed him in the domain of losses. Based on risk-style analysis, a natural question to ask is whether he qualifies as a maximizer who exhibits the gambler's fallacy, meaning an unwarranted belief in reversion to the mean. Affirmative answers to these questions are all consistent with risk-seeking behavior.

To be sure, Corzine did not act alone, but rather as the leader of an organization. Therefore, we also need to analyze the organizational dynamics that permitted those risky choices that were made. Roseman, O'Brien, and the back office employees who warned about the cash transfers all played a role. The remainder of this chapter describes some of the most important psychological dynamics that permitted those risky choices to have been made at MF Global.

Stanley Milgram's Shocking Experiment

Did O'Brien transfer MF Global clients' money to JPMorgan Chase, knowing it was wrong, because she was responding to the wishes of a strong authority figure?

In a shocking experiment, psychologist Stanley Milgram demonstrated that in the face of strong authority, the majority of people can exhibit outrageous behavior that lies outside their norms. Here is how the experiment worked.

Imagine that you have responded to an advertisement about participating in an academic experiment about learning, for which you will be paid $100 simply by showing up at the Interaction Laboratory located in the Department of Psychology at a major university. At the moment, you are seated in a room in the laboratory, together with two other people. The first person introduces himself as Professor Harris. He is a middle-aged man, is wearing a grey lab coat, and you notice that he has an authoritative presence. Professor Harris then introduces you to Wallace, another participant in the experiment.

Professor Harris explains that you and Wallace are paired in the experiment, with one of you to play the role of "teacher" and the other "learner." First, you are to draw lots to decide who will have which role. You then draw lots, and your lot says "teacher," while Wallace's lot says "learner."

Next, Professor Harris brings you and Wallace into an adjoining room where there is a chair with straps and electrodes. He explains that he will place Wallace in the chair, apply the straps, and attach the electrodes. He will then provide Wallace with a long list of "word pairs" to read over, study, and remember as best as possible. Professor Harris explains that you, as teacher, will test Wallace's ability to remember the correct pairing of words, and administer electric shocks when incorrect answers are given.

He provides both of you an opportunity to sit in the chair and receive a sample 45-volt shock. When you do so, you feel the shock, which you find causes you some mild discomfort. Wallace has a similar reaction to you, and is then strapped into the chair and has the electrodes attached by Professor Harris.

You then return to the first room, where you are seated by a panel with a display screen and a series of 30 switches. The display screen provides a list of words you are to ask as part of the experiment, along with multiple choice alternatives to present to Wallace. Each switch in the series is labeled with a particular voltage, with the leftmost switch reading "15 volts (slight shock)" and the rightmost switch reading "450 volts (XXX)." In between there are indicators that read "Moderate Shock," "Strong Shock," "Intense Shock," "Extremely Intense Shock," and "Danger: Severe Shock." Professor Harris explains that each time you administer a shock to Wallace, you will flip a switch, starting with the lowest voltage and then choosing the switch to the immediate right of the last switch you flipped.

You then begin to present Wallace with a sequence of words and multiple choice alternatives. With each incorrect answer, you flick a switch to administer a shock. At the beginning, Wallace makes no responses after you have administered a shock. However, after you have administered a 75-volt shock, you hear a short grunt. When you administer a 120-volt shock, you hear a clear audible complaint. When you reach 150 volts, you hear Wallace pleading to be released from the experiment.

Online, you can view the real subjects in Milgram's experiment asking the authority figure that Wallace be released. The authority figure would respond, "Please continue," and the experiment would continue. When the teacher administered 285 volts, Wallace would scream in agony. Teachers would protest, many by saying that continuing was unethical, but the authority figure would respond by saying, "The experiment requires you to continue." If teachers stated that they did not want to take responsibility for flipping the next switch, the authority figure would indicate that he accepted the responsibility and ask the teachers to continue.

Milgram was shocked to discover that 65% of his subjects administered the maximum voltage, and many thought they had actually killed Wallace. In truth, the only real voltage used in the experiment was the 45-volt sample shock. Everything else was staged. Wallace was a confederate.

In experimental treatments in which teachers were themselves allowed choose the voltage levels, they only administered 83 volts on average. Only 2.5% administered the maximum 450 volts. As a result, Milgram concluded that the majority of people are prone to yield to the will of authority figures. He ran several variations of his experiment and found that people were most prone to obey when the authority figure was in close proximity, or when teachers felt they could pass on responsibility to someone else, or when the experiments was conducted under the auspices of a respected organization.

Back to O'Brien: Jon Corzine was her authority figure. He had called her directly, emphasizing the importance of what he was asking her to do. He was the CEO, and it is natural to expect that she would infer that he was taking responsibility for transferring customers' funds, even though she felt it to have been wrong. It seems reasonable to infer that she felt his authority and felt his proximity. It seems reasonable to infer that she drew these inferences, with all of this taking place in a respected organization, one of the largest commodity brokerage firms in the country.

Milgram's shocking experiment helps shed light on how normal it might have been for O'Brien to have transferred customers' funds.

Groupthink at MF Global

The discussion in Chapter 4 mentions that there are several factors that can make a group vulnerable to groupthink. First, a group might have an outspoken leader who discourages dissent. An outspoken leader makes clear what he or she wants to do and wants to hear. By nature, people are self-interested, and for most, their self-interest will lead them to look for ways to offer support for what the leader wants to do. The leader wants to hear "yes," not "yes, but" and certainly not "no."

Saying "no" to an outspoken, strong leader takes courage. CRO Roseman said "no" to CEO Corzine, who was both outspoken and intolerant of dissent. *Business Insider* described Corzine's firing of Roseman with the headline "Jon Corzine Replaced 'Risk Officer' with an 'Everything Is OK' Officer."[9]

Sometimes, the groupthink dynamic leads group members to refrain from sharing negative information or to engage in denial. Remember the warning from the two back office employees about the internal report showing a deficiency in customer cash accounts? MF Global continued to transfer customer money, but did not fully disclose the potential problem to regulators. Nor did it act on that information internally.

As was also pointed out in Chapter 4, there are additional reasons that produce groupthink. For instance, a group might be composed of members with similar backgrounds. As a result, confirmation bias and availability bias combine to limit discussion of issues and perspectives. In this regard, by hiring Stockman, Corzine chose someone who had once worked at Goldman, just like him. Notably, Representative William Posey, Republican of Florida, and member of the House subcommittee that investigated the MF Global bankruptcy, stated, "Mr. Stockman was hired to tell Mr. Corzine what he wanted to hear."[10]

HORMONES AND SELF-CONTROL

As you have read repeatedly in previous chapters, testosterone and cortisol are hormones that are critically related to behavior. Higher levels of testosterone levels are associated with aggression, dominance, and sexual behavior. Higher levels of cortisol are associated with anxiety and stress.

Neuroscientists Joe Herbert and John Coates conducted a study of professional traders to investigate how testosterone and cortisol are related to risk taking.[11] They discovered that traders' testosterone levels in the morning could be used to predict their individual profitability for the day. To their surprise, they also discovered that cortisol levels did not rise when traders lost money. However, traders' cortisol levels did rise with both the variance of trading results and the volatility of the market.

As was described in earlier chapters, testosterone plays a major role in male competition, and testosterone and risk taking are positively related. Coates likes to point out that when two men enter a competition, their testosterone levels rise, and elevated testosterone levels enhance appetite for taking risk. In the case of MF Global, CEO versus CRO amounted to male competition, with the board as judge. The choice was between risk styles: maximizer versus manager; and having initially selected Corzine to make MF Global profitable, the board chose maximizer.

The discussion in previous chapters emphasized that people tend to become risk seeking in the domain of losses. That traders' cortisol levels do not decline in response to individual losses is consistent with risk taking in the domain of losses. However, keep in mind that traders' cortisol levels do tend to rise with increased volatility of either their own trading results or market volatility.

Risk management can be an antidote to excessive testosterone and cortisol. Risk managers are charged with the responsibility of advising their firms about risk exposure. Ineffective risk management at MF Global was central to its eventual bankruptcy. Notably, that lack of effectiveness stemmed from the top of the organization, in that leaders simply overrode their own controls.

Excessive optimism, overconfidence, aversion to a sure loss, and confirmation bias all contributed strongly to Roseman's warnings going unheeded.

Risk managers take note: these are important lessons about hormone levels, both our own and those of people with whom we interact.

As you have read repeatedly in previous chapters, psychologists suggest that humans have two mental systems for making decisions. The first, called System 1, is intuitive, automatic, and operates subconsciously. The second, called System 2, is deliberative and operates at the conscious level. In his 2011 book, *Thinking, Fast and Slow*, Kahneman has described the dual system perspective, and in his 2014 book *The Marshmallow Test*, Walter Mischel has described the role of these two systems in self-control.[12]

The two systems sometimes operate in harmony, but not always. Self-control difficulties typically emerge because of a disconnection between what System 1 leads people to feel like doing, and what System 2 indicates they should be doing. Insufficient saving, obesity, and addiction all feature self-control conflicts, in which an imperfect and flawed System 2 lacks the mental resources to overrule, and in some cases oppose, the self-destructive impulses emanating from System 1.

Conscious thinking, System 2 thinking, takes effort. It is hard work compared to the relative ease with which System 1 seems to operate. That is why self-control is a challenge, where emotion appears to triumph over reason.

Hormonal issues can present senior executives, especially CEOs, with self-control challenges when it comes to risk taking. The CRO can be regarded as a surrogate System 2 to the CEO's System 1. This is an important issue for governance. Part of a board's responsibility is to monitor whether the CEO's System 1 is out of control. Some argue that creating a direct line between the risk management function and the board is a way to make this happen. Although true, there are no guarantees, as we saw with MF Global, where Roseman did have a direct line to the board.

RISKY CHOICE, INDIVIDUAL DIFFERENCES, STRUCTURE, AND CULTURE

Roseman finally had his day, not actually in court, but before a House Financial Services subcommittee. When asked why he had to leave MF Global, Roseman stated, "My views on risk certainly played a factor in that decision."[13] Indeed they did, and risk managers need to understand the degree to which people differ in respect to their choices and judgments about risk.

In terms of the four risk styles, how might you decide which one would best describe Corzine's behavior at MF Global? Would you rule out conservator right off the bat? What about Corzine's willingness to choose concentrated bets? Would that rule out his being a pragmatist? Does the strategy he chose strike you as conforming more closely to being a manager or being a maximizer?

Perhaps the association of maximizer to Corzine struck you right off the bat, without having to do the process of elimination. By the same token, Roseman's focus on ERM might have led you to associate pragmatist with his behavior.

Plausibly, the conflict between Corzine and Roseman provides an illustration of dual focal points, where Corzine had high aspiration as his focal point, and Roseman had survival as his. Psychology, compensation contracts, or both can induce risk managers and decision-makers to have different focal points. This might lead sparks to fly, but not always to explosions. At MF Global, the sparks ignited an explosion.

In terms of RMP, the explosion between Corzine and Roseman occurred because Roseman could not accept that Corzine's actions had altered the company's investment policy, which is inherent in its risk management structures, because of the degree to which risk management was valued as part of its risk management culture, and of course because of the emergence of groupthink in its actual risk management behavior.

Closing Thoughts

The case of how MF Global chose a strategy that led both to its bankruptcy and to its violating its clients' trust illustrates the importance of psychology in group dynamics. These dynamics feature several important components. First, groupthink is at the top of the list. Risk managers need to understand how groupthink can lead to polarization in respect to risk taking. Second, individual differences are central to groupthink dynamics, especially in respect to aspiration points. Risk managers need to understand the different kinds of tensions that come into play in various circumstances, especially because aspiration points can be endogenous to the underlying situation. Third, framing effects stemming from using earnings as a performance metric can be crucial for inducing risky choices, because of the role the performance metrics play in compensation plans. Finally, RMP provides a useful way of characterizing the degree to which a new CEO can alter the strength of a company's risk management structures, culture, and behavior.

CHAPTER 17

JPMORGAN'S WHALE OF A RISK MANAGEMENT FAILURE

THE DISTRESS EXPERIENCED BY ONE BANK AFTER ANOTHER DURING THE financial crisis revealed weak risk management practices. However, some banks appeared to have instituted sound risk management and were able to weather the storm without a bailout or a significant restructure. JPMorgan Chase was a bank that was viewed as a role model for best practice risk management, and its CEO, Jamie Dimon, was highly regarded.

At the onset of the crash, JPMorgan had acquired Bear Stearns, one of the first financial firms to collapse as a result of its exposure to residential subprime mortgage-backed securities. Dimon came to be regarded as JP Morgan's "ultimate chief risk officer," not just its CEO.[1] He commanded much respect both in the financial community and in Congress.

When Dimon spoke about whether some provisions in the Dodd-Frank Act were an overreach that required being scaled back, people listened, as they were listening in April 2012, when JPMorgan experienced a dramatic event that came to be dubbed "the London Whale." That incident revealed risk management at JPMorgan to be diametrically opposite to the high esteem in which it had been held. It also tarnished Dimon's reputation.

Although the London Whale incident involved a major loss to the bank, it was not so large as to threaten its existence. Nevertheless, some high-level executives were fired for their role. Criminal charges were filed. Dimon's reputation lost luster, and he lost political capital. For risk managers, the legacy of the incident will be to understand why it happened and what lessons can be learned, especially when it comes to the psychological dimension.

The risk typology framework developed by Kaplan and Mikes constitutes one of the risk management tools to be applied in this book. In their article, Kaplan and Mikes lauded JPMorgan for having pioneered the approach of embedding risk managers into the bank's operations groups. They published their article just before the London Whale incident came to light, and as a result were greatly surprised by the ensuing events.

In the aftermath, Kaplan and Mikes published a blog post in which they posed a series of important questions to their readers, and to themselves: Did JPMorgan's trading loss stem from an isolated failure of risk management, some other failure, or just plain bad luck?[2] Did the loss occur despite the bank's having established a fairly rigorous process of risk management? What kind of regulations and regulators would detect the increasing risk exposure at JPMorgan's Chief Investment Office? How costly might such regulations be?

Readers who complete this chapter will be in a position to form their own opinions about the answers to these questions and use the insights gained thereby to inform their own risk policies.

TRADING AT THE CHIEF INVESTMENT OFFICE

The locus of the London Whale incident was JPMorgan's Chief Investment Office (CIO), located in London.[3] The bank had spun off the CIO as a separate unit in 2005, with the mandate to manage the bank's excess deposits. Ina Drew was named to head the CIO, and became a key figure in the events that played out in 2012. Drew was based at JPMorgan headquarters in New York.[4]

Drew had neither a business degree nor strong quantitative skills. Nevertheless, early in her career at other banks, she was successful doing deals based on bets around interest rate moves. After JPMorgan and Chase merged in 2000, she ran the treasury department and managed low-risk trades. In contrast, the proprietary trading desk, where the bank traded its own money, was run by quants.[5]

When Dimon became CEO of JPMorgan Chase in 2004, he appointed Drew to his operating committee, a group that reported directly to him. He did so, he says, because he respected her knowledge and trusted her judgment in dealing with complex issues. Moreover, he appreciated that she was not afraid to tell him when she thought he had a bad idea.

Drew's treasury group managed risk by mostly trading US Treasury bonds and high-quality mortgages. These assets were relatively low in risk, and their value generally fluctuated with changes in interest rates. Over time, the group performed well. The Treasury positions it took in 2007 greatly increased in value as interest rates subsequently fell with the onset of the financial crisis. As the crisis broke, her group took long positions in risky collateralized loan obligations, which they deemed to be the safest of the so-called toxic assets. These positions also increased in value over time.

The CIO began as a modest operation, but grew over time. In 2006, Drew and Dimon decided together that her group would move into products that involved greater complexity and more risk. That year, the CIO commenced trading synthetic credit derivatives. In order to strengthen its operating capability, and to add the technical capability necessary to trade these more complex and riskier instruments, Drew recruited a team to trade foreign bonds and corporate bonds. To head the CIO, she hired Achilles Macris, who had worked at the bank Dresdner Kleinwort Wasserstein. Macris had a reputation for being brilliant but volatile. In turn, Macris hired Javier Martin-Artajo, a man known for his strong opinions. Macris also hired Bruno Iksil, whose personality was quieter and more reflective than the more outgoing instinctive personalities of Macris and Martin-Artajo.

From a culture and personality perspective, Drew's CIO team in London was distinctly different from her team in New York. While New York was focused on bond trading by people who were regarded as risk averse, London would be focused on the trading of credit by individuals who were much more tolerant of risk.[6] Going back to the example of Larry and Beth, our trader and risk manager from the early chapters, it is critical for management to understand how people differ from each other psychologically, and how those differences impact the risk culture of their groups. In the discussion below, you will see that, had New York better understood the London office psychology upfront, they would have been in a position to change the course of the outcome.

In 2008, the CIO began calling its credit trading activity the Synthetic Credit Portfolio (SCP), at which time, the SCP's size was about $4 billion. The key events that produced the London Whale incident began during the autumn of 2011. Iksil was the person who eventually came to be called "the London Whale"—London because he was based there, and whale because he took a "whale of a trading position."

Iksil's bet in autumn 2011 was to place $1 billion at risk using a CDS known as HY11. This CDS involved a high-yield (HY) credit index that tracked CDSs for 100 higher-risk companies. In this regard, he purchased credit protection, which would generate a profit if some of these companies defaulted on their debt.

The holder of a bond takes a long position in that bond, paying for the bond up front, and receiving interest and return of principal over time. Likewise, the seller of credit protection takes a long position in the risk, receiving coupon payments over time, but making a payout in the event of a default by the entity underlying the credit default swap. Now, because Iksil bought, not sold, credit protection using the HY11, we say that he took a short position in that security.

In terms of the terminology developed in Chapter 2, you can think of a short position in respect to the risk from purchasing credit protection as being a long shot in respect to reward. This is because the exposure features a high probability of moderate negative cash outflows (risk) from the coupon payments, and the small probability of a large cash reward, which occurs in the event of a default. Likewise, a long position in the risk of credit protection corresponds to a short shot in the reward. This is because the exposure features a high probability of moderate positive reward corresponding to the coupon payments, and the small probability of a large cash outflow (risk), which occurs in the event of a default.

Iksil hedged his short position in HY protection with a long position selling protection for investment-grade (IG) securities, using a specific CDS known as the IG9. The net position was still short, as the IG position only muted the overall exposure.

Figure 17.1 provides a stylized depiction of the contingent payoffs for long positions in the two CDX contracts. Selling protection features the receipt of coupon payment inflows, and a default is a low-probability event that triggers a large cash outflow. Per dollar of coupon value, the outflow is larger for the IG than the HY because the probability of default is lower for the IG than for the HY.

Figure 17.2 is a stylized depiction of a short HY position, partially hedged by a long position in the IG. The most likely contingent payoff involves the holder of the position receiving a large cash inflow in the event of a default by a firm that is a constituent of the HY index. Less likely contingent events are the default of a constituent firm in the IG index, both in isolation and in

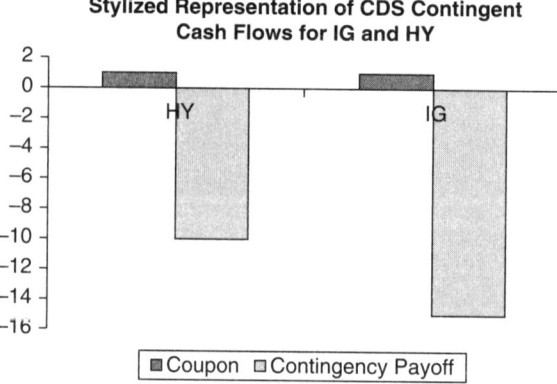

Figure 17.1 This figure provides a stylized depiction of the contingent payoffs for long positions in the two CDX contracts. Selling protection features the receipt of coupon payment inflows, and a default is a low- probability event that triggers a large cash outflow.

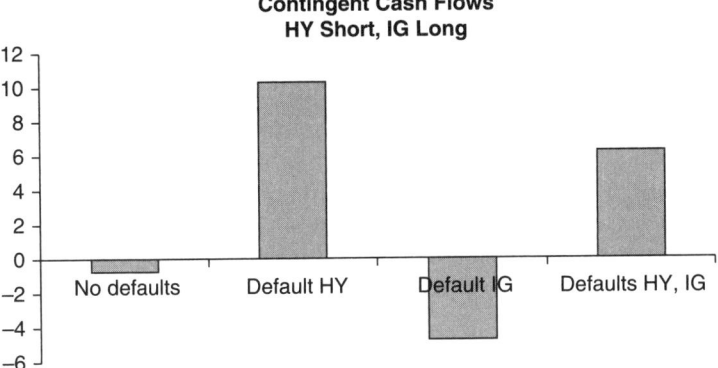

Figure 17.2 This figure provides is a stylized depiction of a short HY position, partially hedged by a long position in the IG. The most likely contingent payoff involves the holder of the position receiving a large cash inflow in the event of a default by a firm that is a constituent of the HY index.

conjunction with the default by a firm that is a constituent of the HY index. In Figure 17.2, the cash outflow associated with the absence of default indicates that the overall position is net short.

The HY11 positions expired on December 20, 2011, and generated a $400 million gain for the CIO on a $1 billion investment. They did so because, on November 29, 2011, American Airlines declared bankruptcy, and the airline was one of the 100 companies associated with HY11.

A JPMorgan Chase internal report characterized the gain as a "windfall." JPMorgan Chase's internal auditors also referred to these as "windfall gains." The revenues of the CIO contributed about 8% of JPMorgan Chase's net income for 2011.

Macris characterized the windfall gain as a great event for the CIO. For his part, Iksil stated that this kind of gain was "unprecedented" within the CIO. At the same time, several JPMorgan Chase personnel indicated that, but for that $400 million gain, the SCP would have lost money in 2011. Specifically, had American Airlines defaulted three weeks later, the SCP's short position would have already expired, and the SCP would not have reaped its "massive" profit.

Iksil's bet from the autumn of 2011 raises at least two important psychological issues. First, if the CIO would have lost money but for Iksil's bet paying off, then his bet might well have stemmed from aversion to a sure loss. Second, given that the parties characterized the outcome as a "windfall," the "house money effect" might have predisposed CIO decision-makers subsequently to seek more risk because of the prior gain.

THE PLAYING OUT OF COMPLEX OBJECTIVES

In early December 2011, Drew instructed Iksil to "recreate" the American Airlines situation, because those were the kinds of trades they wanted at the CIO: as Iksil described it, the CIO "likes cheap options."[7] This directive established the first of three goals for the CIO: to maintain default protection in order to take advantage of any large corporate defaults such as happened with American Airlines. Therefore, at the outset of 2012, although the SCP already had some long credit positions on its book, its longstanding overall position was to be net short. That is, if held to maturity, most of the SCP's credit assets would produce gains only when a referenced entity declared bankruptcy or defaulted on its debts.

In January 2012, the CIO faced a second objective, namely reducing the SCP's RWAs. The SCP is a derivatives book, and from a capital perspective, running a balanced book was very costly. In December 2011, with the size of SCP at approximately $51b, the CIO's CFO told traders that he wanted to reduce RWA by $25b.[8] That was because Drew and other senior managers were seeking to make adjustments to deal with forthcoming regulations that would impose more stringent capital requirements. In response, a CIO committee identified several alternatives for achieving this objective. In the end, and with Drew's approval, they chose a strategy whereby they would reduce risk gradually over time, and estimated the associated losses of implementing this strategy would be approximately $100 million. The criterion they used to make their choice was to minimize expected loss.

Toward the end of January 2012, the CIO found itself with a third, unexpected, objective: stemming a series of dramatic losses in the SCP. These losses stemmed from two sources. The first source was a default by Eastman Kodak that occurred on January 19. This event produced a loss of $50 million for the SCP. (This is the IG default event depicted in Figures 17.1 and 17.2). The second source was a credit market rally that appears to have taken the CIO by surprise, and that resulted in SCP losses of $100 million by the end of January.

Briefly, events unfolded as follows. Throughout January, the CIO was in the process of modifying the SCP in order to deal with its multiple objectives. One issue it faced was that at the end of December, it held some long positions that acted as hedges for short positions that had just expired. Normally, the CIO might have simply renewed these short positions. However, because one of its objectives was to reduce its overall RWA, and therefore net short exposure, the CIO only renewed some of the short positions. This decision left it exposed to a large cash outflow in the event of a default arising from a bankruptcy such as occurred with Kodak.

Then as economies strengthened in the United States and elsewhere, global credit markets rallied. The value of long credit positions increased, and the value of short credit positions fell. Defaults become less likely when interest rates fall and bond prices rise. As a result, the value of protection declines, and protection was the SCP's theme, even though the protection was hedged.

For long positions in an existing CDS, such as those whose stylized cash flows are displayed in Figure 17.1, the rally led the probabilities of the two large outflows to decline. As a result, the values of the inflow-contingent outflow combinations increased for both HY and IG. However, the CIO was short HY: the lower probability of receiving a large payoff due to a default by a constituent firm in the HY index was unfavorable for the SCP. This led the market value of the short position to decline, thereby inflicting a loss on the existing HY position.

Most importantly, HY was more sensitive to improvement in credit conditions than was the IG. Therefore, the decrease in value of the protection that they purchased was greater than the increase in value of the protection they sold. This means that the value of their net position, as depicted in Figure 17.2, declined. Macris described these events by saying that the investment grade rally "lagged" the high yield rally.[9]

During the second half of January, the SCP experienced nine straight days of losses. Under GAAP, at the close of each business day the value of derivatives, including credit derivatives, must be recorded at fair-market value, meaning "marked to market." In a January 26, 2012, e-mail, the head trader in charge of the SCP book prepared a report for CIO managers. He indicated that the SCP book had already lost $100 million and predicted further losses of $300 million.

Were the CIO executives facing the prototypical decision of whether to accept a sure loss? As you will recall, such situations predispose decision-makers to seek risk in an attempt to avoid a sure loss.

In late January, the CIO faced a choice menu that included

- closing out the short positions;
- taking no action when positions naturally expired;
- increasing its long positions; and
- taking some other action to reshape the SCP.

Macris, as head of the CIO's International Office, communicated his views to Martin-Artajo, who headed its equity and credit trading operation: the SCP book was no longer needed to hedge tail risk and should be reshaped, primarily to put a stop to the losses.

At the end of January, Martin-Artajo was receiving e-mails from Iksil advising that they should just "take the pain fast" and "let it go." However, Martin-Artajo was also receiving communications from Macris that he did not want to lose money from unwinding the book, and indeed would be "angry" if losses materialized.[10] Facing conflicting messages from above and below, Martin-Artajo rejected Iksil's advice and explicitly instructed him to stop losing money.

What were the key psychological issues that differentiated the key players at this stage? Iksil's advice to "take the pain fast...and let it go" amounts to resisting aversion to a sure loss. Macris's reaction of being "angry" if losses materialized reflects aversion to a sure loss. Faced with contrasting recommendations, power usually determines the ultimate choice. Moreover, the presence of a strong leader typically fosters the conditions for risk polarization: when individual members of a group are somewhat inclined to taking risk, groupthink dynamics amplify the inclination, as the group members seek to support the direction favored by the leader.

By the end of January, the CIO had three objectives: bet on bankruptcies, reduce RWA, and avoid losses on the SCP. How did they think about their choices, and what did they do?

Iksil strategized that the SCP could go long on credit risk, and use the longs to offset the portfolio's shorts, and thereby reduce the CIO's overall RWA. He wrote: "We can reduce [RWA] by simply selling protection but then the pnl [profit and loss] volatility will increase potentially."[11]

Selling protection would allow the CIO to collect coupon payments, which they often referred to as "carry." It could then use this carry both to finance other credit trades and to offset losses. In addition, the CIO traders expressed the view that the CIO could use the new credit assets to reduce the SCP's RWA by balancing its long positions against its short positions. Still another benefit was that the value of the long positions would increase if the market rally continued: a decline in credit spreads signals lower default risk, and therefore the value of existing contracts with established coupon payments increases. Hence, according to the CIO's market risk officer at the time, adding longs would help balance the portfolio's losses if the credit market continued to rally.

A presentation by Iksil on January 26 to the CIO's International Senior Management Group therefore proposed not to unwind, *but to increase* the size of the SCP book by adding long positions. After that meeting, CIO traders did so, buying and selling a wide variety of HY and IG securities. The CIO adopted the Iksil trading strategy even though Iksil pointed out that the SCP had already lost $100 million, and that if events turned out unfavorably, the new strategy could produce losses of another $500 million.

At the beginning of February, Drew asked Iksil how much the book would lose if the positions were reduced. He responded "a lot," because the IG9 long positions were not liquid enough to sell easily. Over the course of February, the CIO traders increased the size of the IG9 forward position from $75 billion at the beginning of the month to $94 billion at the beginning of March. During the month of February, the credit market continued to rally, and the overall value of the SCP book continued to fall.

On February 9, 2012, the SCP book breached a risk limit called "CS01." The book at that point reported losses exceeding $128 million since the beginning of the year. Iksil stated that the only solution was to continue to finance the acquisition of HY default protection through the sale of IG protection. Altogether, CIO traders added $34 billion in notional value to the SCP book in January and February 2012. This response to the breach of CS01 displays the main symptoms of aversion to a sure loss.

INA IS FREAKING

In March 2012, the CIO traders purchased additional long positions, which further enlarged the SCP. Moreover, by the end of the month these trades had moved the SCP firmly into a net long posture. Their actions increased the portfolio's risk, breaching multiple risk limits along the way, and escalated the SCP's losses, which, by the end of the month, exceeded half a billion dollars.

There is good reason to believe that the CIO's sales of protection were so large that they drove down the price at which the IG9 traded. This caused the IG9 positions that the CIO had established earlier, to gain in value, leading the CIO to post mark-to-market gains on their long positions. As the CIO continued selling credit protection through the IG9, the price of the IG9 continued to decline, leading to a stream of associated mark-to-market gains.[12] Dimon later called this strategy "a Risk 101 mistake."

In the first part of March, the credit market was "unusually bullish," and as it continued to rally, the SCP book continued to "underperform." In response, the traders continued to increase the size of the long positions in an attempt to staunch the losses.

On March 21, Drew met with Macris and Martin-Artajo. She was given SCP trading data as of March 7, but was told nothing about the intense trading activity that had taken place over the following two weeks, which had further enlarged the SCP book. Between these dates, the SCP's notional CDX IG position increased from $22.4 billion to $52.1 billion, a $30 billion increase in two weeks.[13] This was doubling down and more.

On March 22, Drew learned of the SCP's increased positions and expressed "confusion." Her reaction to the increased positions prompted one CIO risk manager to e-mail another: "Ina is freaking—really! Call me."[14]

There is reason to suggest that these events reflect weak information sharing that stemmed from being in the domain of losses. Certainly, Drew became increasingly frustrated at the shifting numbers and capital calculations at the

SCP as the quarter drew to a close, which she felt made her look "incompetent" for being unable to calculate the SCP's RWA.

At the end of March, the SCP included at least $62b in IG index holdings, $71b in iTraxx index holdings, $22b in High Yield index holdings, and a variety of other synthetic credit derivatives. Its long position in the IG9 index alone, which most likely exceeded $62b, comprised over half the market in that index. Remember: just three months earlier, the size of the SCP had been $51b.

On March 23, 2012, Drew ordered the CIO traders to "put phones down" and stop trading. The order to stop trading prevented the CIO traders from expanding the SCP still further, but came too late to prevent the losses caused by the positions already acquired.

Aversion to a sure loss certainly impacted JPMorgan Chase's processes for planning and operations during the first three months of 2012, especially in March. However, Drew did put a stop to what effectively had become rogue trading.[15] That this was rogue trading is clear from the fact that Macris and Martin-Artajo chose to conceal from her the rapid growth in exposure between March 7 and March 21. Such concealment typified an information process that was highly infected: the reluctance to communicate bad news is another reflection of aversion to a sure loss.

The CIO's stopping its trading led the losses to increase. This is because when Drew ordered the trades to stop, the SCP book had to begin absorbing the losses that came when the IG9 price began to rise, and the CIO traders were no longer taking actions to reduce the losses that had to be booked.

The CIO's IG9 trading strategy then turned into a game of "chicken" with its counterparties, mostly hedge funds. The Iksil counterparty team took the other side of the bet, buying CDSs on the Index. They also bought protection on the underlying corporate bonds to influence the value of those as well. Their hope was that Iksil's bet on the IG9 would go down in value, because his actions had caused the spread to be artificially low. Then, they assumed, Iskil would have to run to them to buy CDSs—that is, short the IG9—to cover his rear and keep his bet even.

The situation worsened on April 6 when the *Wall Street Journal* reported that the CIO had established massive CDS positions. The article headline read: "'London Whale' Rattles Debt Market." The employee dubbed the "London Whale" was soon identified as Iksil.

Dimon finally took notice and began to monitor the situation, frequently communicating with Drew. She explained that hedge funds were attempting to squeeze the bank, but that the bank would not have to unwind the position quickly, as it was a long-term position. On April 13, during the bank's first-quarter-earnings call, an analyst used the term "tempest in the teapot nature" when inquiring about the stories in the media. Dimon reiterated the phrase in his reply, saying, "It's a complete tempest in a teapot." His use of this phrase, when juxtaposed with the size of the CIO's positions, made Dimon appear either to have a weak grasp of the situation or to be less than transparent.

Was this aversion to a sure loss on the part of Dimon or instead a failure of information sharing within JPMorgan Chase? Irrespective of the answer, Dimon now had a public relations and political challenge to face as the issue continued to gain momentum in the press and also in Congress. In congressional testimony about the issue, Dimon made the following remarks: "We made a terrible, egregious mistake. There is almost no excuse for it. We know we were sloppy. We know we were stupid. We know there was bad judgment. In hindsight, we took far too much risk. That strategy we had was badly vetted. It was badly monitored. It should never have happened."[16]

The bank developed a strategy to reduce its exposure first financially, and then politically and in the media. Figure 17.3 depicts the tripling in position size during the first three months of 2012, with its attempt to reduce RWA by increasing its long position in IG. Figure 17.4 displays the magnitude of the losses to the portfolio during the first six months of 2012.

As for Drew, pressure mounted within the bank for her dismissal. In May 2012, she resigned.

LIMIT BREACHES

When it came to risk metrics, JPMorgan claimed that these metrics were intended to act not as boundaries, but as guidelines and red flags.[17] Dimon

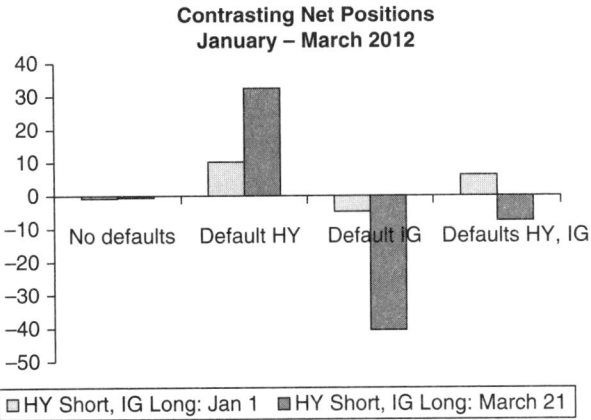

Figure 17.3 This figure depicts the tripling in position size of SCP during the first three months of 2012, with its attempt to reduce RWA by increasing its long position in IG.

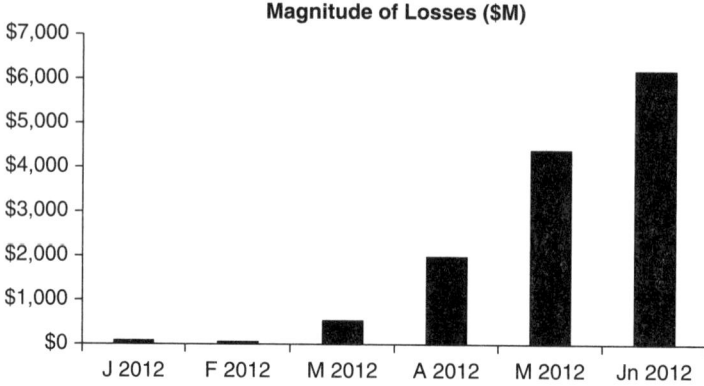

Figure 17.4 This figure displays the magnitude of the losses to the portfolio during the first six months of 2012.

stated that a breach in a risk "limit" was intended to lead to a conversation about the situation, not an automatic freeze or unwinding of positions. In fact, on January 18, 2006, CEO Dimon actually stated that VaR is a very poor number to represent risk. He also predicted that the bank's VaR would likely increase over time as it took on more aggregate risk. On April 16, 2009, in response to an analyst's inquiry during a quarterly earnings call about the rise in JPMorgan's risk gauge, Dimon responded that he does not pay much attention to VaR, as it primarily relates to hedging positions.

How did Dimon's tone and perspective play out at the CIO? By 2010, Iksil's VaR, which measures how much traders might lose in a day, was already $30 million to $40 million, and at times it surpassed $60 million. This was about as high as the level for the firm's entire investment bank, which employs 26,000 people. Does this behavior suggest any specific psychological phenomenon?

Moreover, the CIO followed Dimon's general approach to risk limits. If a risk limit was breached, CIO traders were expected to express their views about risk in the portfolio and how to address it. However, there was no charge that they immediately end the breach by reducing the portfolio's holdings.

Notably, over the course of 2011 and 2012, the SCP breached every major risk limit that the CIO had set. Nevertheless, none of the breaches led CIO personnel to conduct an analysis of whether the portfolio's trading activities were excessively risky. Instead, they repeatedly downplayed the significance, validity, and relevance of the various metrics used to quantify the risk in the SCP.

What do limit breaches tells us about the strength of JPMorgan Chase's risk management profile? Remember that members of an organization with strong risk management structures establish effective policies, procedures, and systems. A strong RMS also features high-quality risk managers. Members of an organization with a strong risk management culture are attentive to behaviors involving the manipulation of controls and downplaying the importance of risk management. They also monitor for signs of overconfidence that the organization judges that it is immune to risk.

Consider how JPMorgan Chase fared along the RMP framework's three dimensions: RMS, RMC, and RMB.

The limit "CS01" measures the expected profit or loss to a portfolio if the credit spread on a credit position widens by 1 basis point over the course of a day. From mid-August 2008 through early May 2012, the CS01 limit was $5 million.

VaR and CS01 alarms sounded in January 2012. In response to the January breaches, the CIO traders requested an increase in the CS01 risk limits to end the breaches. During the same period, as the size and volatility of its trades were growing, the bank changed its algorithms for calculating the CIO's VaR. The new model effectively understated the risk of losses from Iksil's trades: it showed an average daily VaR within the CIO of $67 million, approximately the same level that had prevailed during the fourth quarter of 2011. By the end of the quarter, the new measure indicated that risk was about half of what the old model would have indicated.

The bank's CRM sounded in early March. CSW10% measured the expected daily profit or loss to a portfolio if the credit spread widened by 10%. CSW10% sounded three weeks later. Stress loss limits sounded a week after that.

What do we know about the CIO's risk management personnel during 2011 and 2012? The CIO's chief market risk officer (CMRO) was Peter Weiland, who was described as well liked and mild mannered, but with only modest quantitative skills.[18] Weiland described his risk management role as being descriptive, not prescriptive. He viewed himself as a middleman working between the risk modelers and the traders and managers, with the objective of ensuring that risk metrics were properly calculated and communicated to decision-makers.[19] Weiland did not view his role as challenging trading decisions, as he thought that job belonged to Drew. From a risk-style perspective, Weiland was clearly not a conservator. He might have been inclined to be a manager, but by his own admission did not see his role as being to argue for the limits that would constrain the enthusiasm of maximizers like Acris.

Drew described Weiland as the CIO's CRO. However, he was not the CRO. In fact, the CIO had no CRO. The position was vacant, at least until February 2012.[20] Do you think that this might explain why Weiland viewed his responsibilities in the way he did? Regardless, CMRO Weiland did not raise concerns about the months-long breaches of the CS01 limits. Instead, his reaction, too, was to criticize the risk metric and recommend another limit increase. In a memo he wrote, "With respect to the CS01 limit, it is correct that we have been in excess for some time. This is a limit under review.... We are working on a new set of limits for synthetic credit and the current CS01 will be replaced by something more sensible and granular."

In other words, instead of acting to reduce the risk in the SCP by exiting positions, CIO risk management planned to replace the risk metric. Nevertheless, any accurate metric would have shown the same thing: the risks in the SCP were increasing dramatically.

Weiland expressed the view that the SCP was "relatively flat" and should not have triggered the breaches. The CIO changed the VaR model to end that limit breach, and yet the CRM was climbing. Weiland and others within the CIO criticized the CS01 metric in part because it did not take into account the correlations in credit spreads between positions in the SCP. For example, IG indexes typically have much lower credit spreads than HY indexes, so a market event that moves IG indexes by one basis point would likely move HY indexes by more than a basis point. The CS01 in use by the CIO assumed all of the positions moved by one basis point.

As it happens, the CIO could have chosen to use a version of the CS01 that took correlations into account. Such a metric, known as the "beta-adjusted" CS01, was already in use at JPMorgan Chase's Investment Bank in New York, but the CIO did not use it.

On March 22, 2012, the SCP breached the CIO's mark-to-market CSW10% limit. Soon after that, the bank's risk analysts discovered that the CIO differed from the bank's Quantitative Research team in how it calculated the CSW10% metric. And as with VaR and CRM, the CIO's CSW10% model produced a lower risk profile for the SCP than the bank's standard approach.[21]

On March 29, 2012, one week after the CSW10% limit was breached, the SCP's credit derivative positions caused a breach in the CIO's mark-to-market stress limits, the last of the CIO risk limits not yet exceeded, with the "oil crisis" stress test resulting in the "worst case scenario."

Stop-loss advisories are risk limits established on the basis of actual daily profit and loss reports for a portfolio. As with the CIO's VaR, the procedure used by the CIO to calculate the losses for purposes of complying with the stop-loss advisories understated the risks.

As with the CRM, CS01 and CSW10% limits, even when the stop-loss advisories were breached, the CIO made no serious effort to investigate or remediate the breaches. In contrast, JPMorgan Chase Investment Bank actively enforced its stop-loss limits.

The argument has been made that the risk metrics that were in place at the CIO were sufficient to limit, if not prevent entirely, the losses to the bank caused by the SCP, had they been heeded.[22] If the CIO stop-loss advisories had been properly calculated and respected, the CIO losses could have been mitigated well before they became international headlines.

On May 10, when JPMorgan announced the loss, Dimon said the bank had reviewed the effectiveness of the new model, deemed it "inadequate," and decided to go back to the original model. On that basis, VaR doubled to $129 million. (The bank's SEC filing showed VaR at $186 million on the last day of March.)[23]

HIDING LOSSES WITH SKEWED STATISTICS

In a subsection entitled "Hiding Losses," the US Senate Subcommittee report describes maneuvers made by the CIO in its valuation practices, beginning in late January 2012. Before then, the CIO typically established the daily value of a credit derivative by marking it at or near the daily bid-ask midpoint. Using midpoint prices enabled the CIO to comply with the requirement that it use fair-value pricing to value its derivative positions. However, later in the quarter, the CIO engaged in a "framing exercise" and modified its procedure of marking at or near the midpoint. Specifically, it began to assign its credit derivatives more favorable prices within the bid-ask spread. This modified procedure enabled the CIO to report smaller losses in its daily P&L reports that were filed internally within the bank.

The modified valuation procedures were put into practice in late January, and the process was accelerated during the next two months. By March 15, 2012, two key participants, Iksil and Julien Grout, a junior trader who reported to him, were charged with marking the SCP's positions on a daily basis. Between them, they communicated[24] about the dangers associated with the modification.[25]

Between March 12 and March 16, 2012, Grout prepared a spreadsheet that tracked the differences between the daily SCP values he reported and the values that he would have reported by using midpoint prices. According to the spreadsheet, by March 16, 2012, SCP reported year-to-date losses of $161 million. Had midpoint prices instead been used, those losses would have been higher by $432 million.[26]

Because of the modification, there were two different business lines within JPMorgan Chase, the CIO, and the Investment Bank, which assigned different values to the same credit derivative holdings. In March 2012, CIO counterparties began to learn about the price differences, and they were not happy. Several objected to the CIO's values, which led to major collateral disputes that peaked at $690 million.

In May, Ashley Bacon, the bank's Deputy CRO, directed the CIO to mark its books in the same manner as the Investment Bank (IB): the IB used an independent pricing service to identify the midpoints of the bid-ask spreads. This change in methodology did resolve the collateral valuation disputes in favor of the CIO's counterparties. It also stopped the mismarking.

In her Congressional testimony to the Senate Subcommittee, Drew stated it was not until July 2012, after she had left the bank, that she became aware of Grout's spreadsheet. She stated that she had never before seen what she called that type of "shadow P&L document."

For 2012, year-to-date CIO losses climbed from

- $719 million in March;
- to $2.1 billion in April;
- to $4 billion in May;
- to $4.4 billion in June; and then
- to $6.2 billion in December.

JPMorgan Chase transferred many SCP index positions to its Investment Bank on July 2, 2012. The total amount of losses associated with the SCP will likely never be known. In September, the CIO dismantled the rest of the SCP.

Think back to the questions posed by Kaplan and Mikes. Did JPMorgan's trading loss stem from a failure of risk management, some other failure, or simply bad luck? My view is that it was a risk management failure. Did the loss occur despite the bank's having established a fairly rigorous process of risk management? My view is that there was no rigorous risk management process in place at the CIO. The limit breaches, changing models for VaR, and skewed mark-to-market accounting are all consistent with extremely weak risk management.

THE OCC

The London Whale incident led to $920 million in penalties from regulators, including the SEC and its British counterpart, the Financial Conduct Authority (FCA). Macris and Martin-Artajo are no longer with JPMorgan. In September 2103, Martin-Artajo was indicted in Manhattan federal court for his alleged role in hiding the losses caused by Iksil's positions.[27] In addition, both Macris and Martin-Artajo continued to spar with the FCA about their exact role in the incident.[28]

It is the OCC that regulates JPMorgan Chase. The OCC wrote a Supervisory Letter outlining a series of findings and recommendations. In total, the OCC identified 20 "Matters Requiring Attention" (MRAs). These matters involved steps that required the bank to address risk, valuation, and model failures. JPMorgan did not dispute the contents of the letter. Rather, the bank outlined a series of risk management changes that it had already implemented or was planning to implement.

Among the steps that the bank took to address the MRAS was the establishment of a suite of new risk measures and limits for the CIO. According to the bank, the "CIO now has in place a total of 260 limits," including "67 redesigned VaR, stress and non-statistical limits," and new asset-class, single-name, and country-concentration limits. In addition, "29 new limits specific to the Synthetic Credit Book have been implemented to create consistency with JPMC's IB [Investment Bank] approach."[29] The new SCP limits were focused on risks inherent in credit derivatives. These measures were designed to address six dimensions of risk: directionality (exposure to spread widening), curve (long versus short), decompression (IG versus HY), off-the-run (older versus newer credit derivative index issues), tranche risk (senior versus equity tranches), and risks caused by individual corporate defaults.

At this stage, you might ask yourself the two questions posed by Kaplan and Mikes in respect to regulation. What kind of regulations and regulators would detect the increasing risk exposure at the CIO? How costly might such regulations be?

The US Senate Subcommittee report points out that, while these 260 risk limits promise to provide greater information to the bank's risk managers, it is far from clear how they will solve the CIO's risk management problems. After all, the report says, when the SCP had just five risk metrics, CIO management and risk personnel generally ignored or rationalized the breaches that took place.

Closing Thoughts

Kaplan and Mikes ask whether risk management practices at the CIO were different from risk management practices at JPMorgan's Investment Bank. The evidence indicates that they were different, and one might well ask why?

I suggest that lying at the root of this issue is the psychological insight, discussed in the first part of the book, that people are prone to combine very safe and very risky positions, sometimes in barbell fashion. This was one of psychologist Lola Lopes's major observations. Dimon and Drew's decision to set up a unit that would take very high levels of credit risk, together with its much less risky corporate bonds unit, is absolutely consistent with the traits identified by Lopes.

This kind of bifurcated strategy leads to psychological frictions, as the more risky unit tends to be run by personalities inclined to be dismissive of their more conservative colleagues, that is, until those risky positions blow up. A more subtle point is that such bifurcation fosters the conditions for rogue trading in the aftermath of losses. Were it not for rogue trading, the CIO's losses in 2012 might never have reached the level of public awareness.[30]

CHAPTER 18

Risk Management Profiles: Con Ed, BP, and MMS

Consolidated Edison (Con Ed) is a utility, and BP is an energy company. Both are large firms that face large risks. This chapter uses the risk frameworks presented previously in the book to analyze and contrast the experiences of these firms in dealing with outliers, meaning rare and extreme events. For Con Ed, the rare event was Hurricane Sandy, which in 2012 struck the Eastern seaboard, including New York. For BP, the rare event was the explosion of the drilling rig Deepwater Horizon, which took place in the Gulf of Mexico in 2010.

Con Ed is purposeful in the way in which it approaches risk management. Risk managers at the firm are familiar with the risk typology methodology described earlier in the book, and relate their approach to that methodology. It is virtually impossible to prepare fully to face an external risk like Hurricane Sandy. However, it is possible to assess the degree to which Con Ed's risk culture and structures resulted in behaviors that constituted an adequate response to the event, once it occurred.

In April 2010, a drilling accident at BP's Macondo well in the Gulf of Mexico produced the worst environmental disaster in US history, an event that dominated the daily news during the spring and summer of that year. As with Con Ed, it is virtually impossible to prepare fully for an extreme event like the explosion of Deepwater Horizon. However, it is possible to assess whether that event corresponded to an external risk and to draw inferences from BP's behavior in the period leading up to that event about its risk culture and risk structures.

This chapter uses Con Ed and BP as vehicles to discuss the impact of organizational culture and the way decisions get made about operating risk. The end of the chapter features a discussion about risk management at the regulator that oversaw BP at the time. As with companies, regulatory agencies are organizations with risk cultures and risk structures that drive the behavior of their personnel, in this case those doing the regulating.

RISK MANAGEMENT AT CON ED

Con Ed is a utility servicing New York City. In October 2012, a massive storm named Sandy struck the Northeastern United States, causing great damage. Lower Manhattan and Staten Island were inundated. Parts of the New Jersey shore were obliterated. More than 50 people died.[1]

In Con Ed's history, no other storm had generated as much disaster for its customers as Sandy. Sandy caused nearly five times as many outages as the previous record holder, Hurricane Irene, which had hit the Northeast the year before. More than a million of its customers were left without power. The storm produced widespread damage to energy-delivery systems from extensive flooding, and downed trees made it difficult for Con Ed's repair crews.

Outlier events like Hurricane Sandy put risk management activities into sharp relief. As background, we want to ask how a company like Con Ed manages risks associated with events that are more usual. In this regard, traditional energy utilities operate in comparatively stable technological and market environments, with relatively predictable customer demand. In these situations, risks stem largely from seemingly unrelated operational choices across a complex organization that accumulate gradually and can remain hidden for a long time.

Significantly, no single staff group has the knowledge to perform operational-level risk management across the many diverse functions. Therefore, firms can deploy a relatively small central risk management group to collect information from operating managers. Doing so increases managers' awareness of risks that have been taken on across the organization and provides decision-makers with a more complete picture of the company's risk profile.

In terms of the risk typology framework, Con Ed uses "facilitators." Specifically, Con Ed uses a small risk management team within its shared services unit to develop risk response assessments. Doing so requires the risk management team to gather information in the form of insights, lessons learned, do's and don'ts, and the experiences of peers about procedures related to both ordinary events and extraordinary events. Such information is typically distributed across the organization, and so is gathered through interactions with a variety of groups, such as those engaged in operations, customer outreach, environmental, health and safety, engineering, public affairs, and legal. These groups are involved in responding to the company's significant risks should they occur.

This risk management effort focuses on readiness, that is, producing materials and programs for responding to top risks. Programs featuring drills are especially important for practicing sensible behavioral response plans and procedures. Con Ed had many of these tools in place before Sandy struck. However, for extreme tail risks as unusual as Sandy, playbooks can only provide rough guidance. Situations like this are more like being soldiers in a war, where military training prepares combatants for how to improvise and adapt sensibly to conditions in the field. A successful response is shaped by using a holistic view of risk management that includes the related activities for identification, mitigation, response planning, drilled exercises, benchmarking, and knowledge sharing.

With respect to risk management structures, Con Ed works to establish effective policies, procedures, and systems. In addition, the company also appears to have invested in risk management training for its members. With respect to risk management culture, Con Ed appears to value risk management as an activity, and is *proactive* about identifying and addressing risk issues.

CON ED'S RESPONSE TO SANDY

Hurricane Sandy was a distinct outlier.[2] A report released by the National Hurricane Center on February 12, 2013, indicated that Sandy followed a meandering track, lacked the distinct eye of a hurricane, and because of unusual atmospheric occurrences was easy to underestimate and difficult to predict accurately. Despite being unusual by historical standards, there is good reason to believe that, because of global warming, storms such as Sandy might occur more frequently in the future.[3]

Within12 days of Hurricane Sandy, Con Ed managed to restore service to 98% of its customers who had been affected by the storm. For doing so, it received accolades from then-Mayor Michael Bloomberg of New York City and the Edison Electric Institute (EEI). Bloomberg called Con Ed the "best utility in America."[4] EEI named Con Ed and its sister company, Orange and Rockland Utilities (O&R), both part of Con Ed, Inc., among the winners of its 2012 Emergency Recovery Award.[5]

Con Ed's success was all the more remarkable because the firm actually lost power to its Manhattan headquarters. The power loss in Manhattan outside the low-lying downtown district came as a huge surprise, and resulted from an unexpectedly high storm surge that overwhelmed one of its main substations, which was located on East 13th Street by the East River.[6]

The substation story is remarkable. The plant had been protected by flood walls that were 12 feet high. However, the walls would have needed to be at least 14 feet to have withstood the surge from Sandy. The water flow inundated the substation's control room and caused a spectacular electrical arc.

When a day later the water had subsided from the substation, a Con Ed crew moved to dry and clean its equipment.

The East 13th Street substation was critical to restoring power. In Manhattan, the wires carrying electric power run in pairs, enclosed in ten-inch diameter pipes in which they are surrounded by thick oil.[7] These pipes must be heavily pressurized to keep out air that facilitates short circuits between the two wires. Pumps do the job of providing the pressure. However, the pumps failed when the substation lost power, and it typically takes at least 72 hours to repressurize the pipes.

On Tuesday, October 30, Con Ed Chairman and CEO Kevin Burke told the media that he expected power to be restored to all of Manhattan by Saturday, November 3. Yet, this would require the pumps to be fully operational, and at midday Wednesday, this was not the case. At this point, Con Ed's engineers took a risky shortcut. They decided that once the pumps were dry, clean, and ready to go, they would focus them on only three of their eight high-voltage lines, which was the bare minimum. Doing so speeded up the process. This left Con Ed with no margin of error. If one line failed or did not re-energize, there was no backup, and the result would be several days more of no power.

The risk paid off. Con Ed managed to restore power to Manhattan 12 hours faster than they had promised the day after the storm. The utility garnered accolades for its efficient and timely restoration of power to most of its customers.

Mayor Bloomberg was reluctant to succumb to "hindsight bias," the bias of believing in hindsight that the event that actually occurred had a much higher probability of occurrence. Of the flooding of Con Ed's East 13th Street substation, an event the utility did not anticipate, he told the press that no storm surge had previously come close to 12 feet, and that second-guessing the utility to suggest that it should have been 15 or 16 feet was unreasonable.

At the same time, Con Ed had its critics, not the least being the state's governor, Andrew Cuomo, who voiced concerns about several utilities. Under his leadership, a study was undertaken using what is known in New York State as a Moreland Commission Report, to analyze key aspects of the issues surrounding the readiness of the industry to respond to events such as Sandy.[8] As you read the list of criticisms, think about whether they are better classified as reasonable or, instead, as examples of hindsight bias.

One of main issues that threatened the utility's ability to respond to the power outages was a lack of gasoline to fuel its service vehicles. In the days following the storm, as crews moved to make repairs, gasoline supplies ran very low. Gas had to be trucked in and then pumped into Con Ed vehicles during the night so that the crews were ready to go at first light.

The Moreland Report identified a series of problems that were surfaced by the storm, and made a number of recommendations in this regard. Here are several examples.

- The gasoline shortage issue revealed that Con Ed reached out to local government on an ad-hoc basis, but had formalized steps and contacts. The Report recommended that they establish a process to interact with these agencies during nonstorm periods, with the purpose of identifying available resources and resolving issues about deploying these resources efficiently.
- Con Ed had no system for coordinating with the companies supplying natural gas to customers. As a result, there were elevated risks that turning power back on would ignite explosions. The Report recommended that Con Ed revise its Corporate Coastal Storm Plan (CCSP) to include actions to deal with widespread flooding, such as for preparing, responding, and communicating effectively with customers and other stakeholders. The Report also recommended that customers be warned that when requesting that their electricity be restored, they ensure that their gas equipment has been inspected and repaired.
- Con Ed was short of electric meter isolation devices and was forced to use older meters it had previously discontinued because they involved greater risks of fire.[9] In addition, Con Ed used an unnecessarily complex certification process to re-establish electric service. The Report recommended that Con Ed discard all of its discontinued meter isolation safety devices and replace them with the currently accepted model.
- Con Ed had an outage management system, but had never tested it for a storm remotely the size of Sandy. Both its outage management system and its damage assessment system were overwhelmed by the volume of users, and crashed. Consequently, Con Ed found itself forced to use paper forms to transmit information between the damage assessment units and engineering. More importantly, Con Ed's systems did not allow damage assessors to report their findings in real time to the control center. There was no systematic way to estimate repair times, and instead such estimates were established more by human judgments, which relied on the experience of those involved. The Report recommended that Con Ed do a better job of leveraging its available technology to improve its process for establishing estimated repair times.
- Con Ed's communication with municipalities and the public was also subject to all kinds of problems. The Report mentions that many local municipalities complained that Con Ed did not provide key information needed to make municipal decisions. The Report mentions that in some cases, there was no system to prioritize repair options. The public complained that the Con Ed's website and other communications contained inaccurate information about expected repair times. The Report contained a series of recommendations for making improvements on these issues.

- Cod Ed and O&R share a number of storm-related functions. These include weather reporting, distribution of outside resources, and other emergency management functions. The Report identifies a number of serious flaws in the resource allocation process between O&R and Con Ed that caused confusion and disorganization prior to and during Sandy. In particular, the Report identified the absence of a formalized decision-making process, and recommended that one be put in place for allocating crews and making modifications as restoration occurs.

In the aftermath of Sandy, Con Ed prepared a $1 billion plan to fortify critical infrastructure and protect its customers from major storms. A major goal of the plan is to make overhead equipment more resilient. Indeed, within a year of Sandy, the utility built new walls around substations and raised equipment, and instituted water-proofing measures for its gas and steam infrastructure.[10]

Among a host of other initiatives, Con Ed's plan also involved spending $200 million to bury 30 miles of overhead lines in 2015 and 2016, installing 70 high-tension vault switches and stronger, tree-branch resistant aerial cables. In respect to communications, the utility notes that it created a new online tool in order to improve coordination and communications with municipalities during major outages. Using this tool, municipal officials are able to obtain details about important issues such as local outages, road closures, and crew locations.[11]

How does a power utility prepare to deal with the risks associated with major storms? The Moreland Commission Report not withstanding, Con Ed tells us what they generally did to prepare for Sandy's arrival.[12] The weekend before Sandy's arrival, the company activated its Corporate Emergency Response Center, and in advance assigned thousands of company employees and field crews to work around the clock to restore power. Con Ed planners also consulted with neighboring utilities about possible impacts along the storm's path, and maintained constant communication with the New York City Office of Emergency Management and other local, state, and federal agencies. The company also encouraged customers to pay close attention to reports from local officials and company updates provided through the media.

BP and Culture

When Deepwater Horizon exploded in April 2010, 11 men died from the accident, and the United States faced the largest marine oil spill in its history. Crude oil spilled from Macondo for 87 days, contaminating approximately 68,000 square miles in the Gulf as well as 500 miles of coastline between

Louisiana and Florida. For this, the court found BP to have been grossly negligent in causing the spill, a judgment involving several billion dollars in penalties. As of July 2015, BP had paid out over $50b in connection with the Gulf oil spill.[13]

In order to provide a thorough analysis and impartial judgment of the circumstances underlying the Macondo fiasco, President Barack Obama appointed the National Commission on the BP Deepwater Horizon Oil Spill and Offshore Drilling (NCBP). In 2011, the Commission issued a number of findings. In their introductory remarks, the Commission highlighted "the importance of organizational culture and a consistent commitment to safety by industry, from the highest management levels on down."[14] The Commission also characterized the culture that needed to be changed as "a culture of complacency."

In 2008, two years before the explosion of Deepwater Horizon and three years before the publication of the Commission's report, I wrote that "BP has a systemic problem with its culture that runs deep."[15] At the time, I also pointed out that, although BP had already experienced disasters in two of the three regions of the United States in which it had operations, the shoe was yet to drop in the third region, the Gulf of Mexico.

Processes, pitfalls, and RMP provide the framework for analyzing risk management in the remainder of the chapter. Before getting to the discussion about Deepwater Horizon, it is important to understand something about BP's overall history, especially how it was managing risk when it experienced other unfavorable outcomes, such as occurred in Alaska and Texas.[16]

Alaskan Oil Spills

In March 2006, corrosion caused a leak in BP's Alaskan oil pipeline, resulting in 267,000 gallons of crude oil to be spilled onto the tundra, the largest ever on Alaska's North Slope. The spill forced BP to shut down half of its output from its Prudhoe Bay operations.

Spills are an operational risk for firms that extract and ship crude oil. An investigative panel subsequently attributed the incident to the firm's poor maintenance practices. The risk of a spill mostly comes from pipelines building up sediment through time. This sediment can eventually corrode the pipes, causing leaks and spills. Oil companies check pipelines using a technique called "pigging" that involves the injection of a cylindrical droid (the "pig") into the line. Droids equipped with sensors are known as "intelligent" pigs.

Several years before the spill, some BP employees were claiming that the company was letting equipment and critical safety systems languish at Prudhoe Bay. As a response, the company hired a panel of independent experts to examine the allegations. In their October 2001 report, the experts found systemic problems in BP's maintenance and inspection programs. According to the report, BP appeared to be attempting to sustain profits in the aging drilling field, even though production was declining. To achieve their goal, the only way seemed to be to cut costs, and cutting costs resulted in maintenance backlogs.[17] In this regard, the panel's report states that there was "a disconnect between GPB (Great Prudhoe Bay) management's stated commitment to safety and the perception of that commitment."[18]

The panel experts claimed that solving these problems was necessary to ensure mechanical integrity and operational efficiency in the long run. They warned company management that those issues could have a potential immediate safety impact or pose an environment threat. Without a systematic effort to address them, single actions could only provide temporary relief, and not be a solution in the long run.

Alaska state regulators underscored the panel's findings, claiming that BP failed to maintain its pipelines properly. During 2002, the Alaskan Department of Environmental Conservation had a dispute with BP, and to resolve it, the department asked the oil company to use intelligent pigs to probe its pipelines for leaks, along with a list of other tasks, and to pay a fine of $150,000. The company had not run an intelligent pig through its lines since 1992, which differs from the policy of its competitors, which typically pig their lines at least once every three years.[19] BP responded that it had no evidence to suggest that its pipelines had anything more than minimal sediment buildup, thus asserting there was no need to use intelligent pigs. Five days after receiving this communication, the department withdrew its requirement that BP pig its lines.

What psychological issues might be involved in the expert panel's comments about cost-cutting and safety, as well as BP's refusal to pig its lines in 2002? Aspirational risk seeking is high on the list. SP/A theory would suggest that in establishing ambitious standards for costs, BP set the stage for aspirational risk seeking. In addition, the failure to pig its lines for over a decade is consistent with excessive optimism.

In the following two years, Alaska pressured BP to comply with state laws and check its pipelines. At the same time, the company received from workers several warning regarding the danger of failing to use intelligent pigs.

Eventually, BP asked another team of outside investigators to check the warnings raised by local workers. The resulting 2004 inquiry found that pipeline corrosion and the age of the field endangered operations at Prudhoe Bay. It highlighted health, safety, and environmental concerns raised by employees who accused BP of falsifying inspection data and of pressuring workers to skip key diagnostics to cut costs. BP management was cutting maintenance costs with a "run to failure" strategy, meaning that aging equipment was used as long as possible.

BP eventually ran an intelligent pig through its lines in August 2006, only after the March spill, four years after the department asked it to do so, and fourteen years after the last probe, in 1992. The severe pipeline corrosion and leak caused BP to shut down half of its output from Prudhoe Bay.

BP's problems in Alaska continued. In September 2008, a section of a high-pressure gas line on the Slope blew apart. A 28-foot-long section of steel flew nearly 1,000 feet through the air before landing on the Alaskan tundra. Had the release caught a spark, the explosion could have been very significant. In 2009, three more accidents occurred on the same system of pipelines and gas compressor stations, including a near explosion that had the potential to destroy the entire facility.[20] On May 25, 2010, a power failure led to a leak that overwhelmed a storage tank, resulting in another major spillage, this time involving 200,000 gallons of oil.[21]

With respect to RMP, this track record suggests ineffective policies, procedures, and systems, and therefore weak risk management structures. It suggests that risk management is not a valued activity, and therefore a weak risk management culture. It suggests a willingness to bend rules because of the drive to accomplish goals, and therefore weak risk management behaviors.

TEXAS CITY EXPLOSION

In 2005, the failure of an emergency warning system at a BP refinery in Texas City, Texas, caused an explosion that killed 15 people. The Texas City facility was the second-largest refinery in the United States, but it had been built in 1934 and was poorly maintained. Two months before the accident, a consulting firm hired to examine conditions at the refinery stated, "We have never seen a site where the notion 'I could die today' was so real."[22]

The investigation that followed the 2005 accident, conducted by a panel of independent experts led by former US secretary of state James Baker, found significant process safety issues not only at the Texas City but also in the other five BP US refineries. The report concluded, "BP has not provided effective process safety leadership and has not adequately established process safety as a core value."

The investigating panel found that the explosion occurred when a tower was being filled with liquid hydrocarbons, and nobody noticed that it was being overfilled. The panel noted that workers were discouraged from talking with each other about potential safety issues, and that several workers had been on 12-hour shifts for more than a month.[23] All of this speaks volumes about BP's having weak structures, culture, and behaviors for risk management.

In evaluating conditions at BP's Texas City facility, the Occupational Safety and Health Administration (OSHA) found more than 300 safety violations, and BP agreed to pay $21 million, at the time the largest fine in OSHA history.[24] In subsequent years, a series of investigations by inspectors from OSHA found more than 700 safety violations. In 2009, OSHA proposed to sanction BP with a record fine of $87 million for failing to make safety upgrades at that Texas City refinery. The greatest part of the fine was due to the company failing to respect the previous settlement in full. Among energy companies operating in the United States, BP was the most heavily fined.[25]

Steve Arendt, a safety specialist who assisted the panel appointed by BP to investigate the company's refineries after Texas City explosion, referring to BP's management, affirmed, "They were very arrogant and proud and in denial. It is possible they were fooled by their success."[26] Notably, pride and arrogance are strong symptoms of overconfidence.

From 1995 to 2007, BP's CEO was John Browne. In the wake of accidents at its operations in Texas City and Alaska, BP's board replaced Browne with Tony Hayward, instructing him to improve safety at BP. When he was appointed in 2007, Hayward sought to reduce the complexity of the company. He restructured divisions and cut administration and support functions. In this regard, he set up a new risk management system to standardize safety practices and prevent other accidents from occurring.

Viewed through the lens of RMP, Hayward instituted the first part of RMS, namely the structures involving policies, procedures, and systems. However, in terms of behaviors, the track record of OSHA violations described above still looks poor, even in the years after Hayward became CEO, and then of course, there is Macondo and Deepwater Horizon, a topic to which we now turn.

THE MACONDO WELL

On September 2, 2009, BP announced the discovery of a very large field in the Gulf of Mexico called Tiber, estimated to hold more than 500 million barrels of recoverable oil. Extracting that oil would require deepwater drilling, a much more complex operation than drilling on land or just offshore. On the day it announced the Tiber discovery, BP's shares rose by almost 5%, indicating the importance investors attached to the announcement.

Given declining production in its established fields, such as at Prudhoe Bay, deepwater drilling was a natural candidate to drive BP's future growth. The Deepwater Horizon disaster occurred while deepwater drilling a well named Macondo, which was smaller than Tiber. In fact, drilling the smaller Macondo prospect was at the forefront of BP's strategy in the Gulf of Mexico. Although Macondo was almost 900 feet deeper than Tiber, it was only

13,000 feet below the sea bed, in contrast to 31,000 feet for the larger field.[27] BP engaged the drilling firm Transocean to drill Macondo in preparation for production, and Deepwater Horizon was the name of the drilling rig used to accomplish this task.

On April, 20, 2010, Deepwater Horizon exploded, killing 11 people and causing the worst environmental disaster in US history. To understand the setting for the disaster, and the associated risk management issues, picture Deepwater Horizon as a platform on the surface of the Gulf of Mexico. Lying 5,000 feet below the platform is the ocean floor, and lying 13,000 feet below the ocean floor sits Macondo. Descending from Deepwater Horizon into the ocean below is a pipe called a riser pipe. It carries a long drill bit that extends to the ocean floor and below. The drill bit burrows a very long borehole into the rock below the ocean floor and eventually pierces the cavity containing oil and gas trapped some distance below.

The objective of the drilling activity is to construct a production well with a series of "pipes" to carry oil and gas, with minimal leakage, from its cavity deep below the ocean to be collected at the ocean surface. Because the oil and gas are trapped at great pressure below the ocean floor, to prevent leakage it is critical that the borehole be properly lined with steel casing and cement.

Just above the ocean floor sits a critical piece of equipment called a blow-out preventer (BOP), through which the drill bit descends into the sea bed below. In case of an emergency, the BOP has "blind shear rams," which are supposed to shear the drill bit in such a way that the BOP blades remain closed, thereby preventing oil and gas from rising toward the ocean surface. In addition to the BOP, BP planned to engage the firm Halliburton to install two cement plugs to serve as barriers for oil and gas escaping from the portion of the well below the ocean floor. One plug was to be positioned in the borehole at the bottom of the well, just above the oil and gas deposit. The second plug was to be placed just below the ocean floor.

The features just described are common to the well design used by BP and the designs used by other firms such as Shell. However, to manage risk of oil and gas escaping from the well, Shell routinely includes a series of additional barriers in the borehole between the bottom of the well and the ocean floor, to serve as backups in case of leakages in the borehole at intermediate points below the ocean floor. For Shell, the BOP is redundant, what they call a "control" as opposed to a "barrier." For BP, the BOP was intended to serve as a barrier.

THE EXPLOSION AND REACTION IN WASHINGTON

In April 2010, BP was on the verge of completing the drilling stage at Macondo. It had put a cement plug in place at the bottom of the well, and was about to put a second cement plug in place just below the ocean floor, along with what is called a "lockdown sleeve." However, before it could complete this task, there was a leak of oil and gas in the well below the ocean floor. Escaping gas rose through the riser pipe to the ocean surface and ignited, creating an explosion and fire. Personnel on Deepwater Horizon attempted to activate the BOP, with the intent of preventing the oil and gas from rising above the BOP. However, the BOP did not function properly, and so oil and gas continued to pour from the well. As its blind shear rams closed, a portion of the drill pipe cross section became trapped between the ram block faces, thereby preventing the blocks from fully closing and sealing.

Among the most important pieces of safety equipment that BP was criticized for not having in place in Alaska were gas and fire detection sensors and the emergency shutoff valves that they are supposed to trigger. Similar sensors and the shutoff systems that would have been connected to them were present, but not operating in the engine room of the Deepwater Horizon rig that exploded in the Gulf of Mexico. Backstop mechanisms that should have prevented the engines from running wild apparently failed. So did the air intake valves that were supposed to close if gas enters the engine room. The engine room was not equipped with a gas alarm system that could have shut off the power.

Personnel who worked on Deepwater Horizon had complained that BP repeatedly cut corners and persevered despite warnings about safety. One worker pointed to a dichotomy in respect to safety. He stated that one day he was scolded for standing on a bucket on the rig. Yet the next day, a crane violated safety policies by operating in the face of high winds.[28]

There individual accounts of safety concerns from employees on the rig led to an interesting observation by David Michaels, assistant secretary of labor for occupational safety and health. He stated, "The way safety is measured is generally around worker injuries and days away from work, and that measure of safety is irrelevant when you are looking at the likelihood that a facility like an oil refinery could explode. This is comparable to saying that an airline is safe because the pilots and mechanics haven't been injured." In May, Congressional hearings into the explosion of Deepwater Horizon led Bart Stupak, chair of the Oversight and Investigation Committee, to point out that BP's corporate culture was characterized by excessive cost-cutting and excessive risk taking. He stated, "I am concerned that the corporate culture from BP CEO Tony Hayward down to...the leadership on exploration rigs, reflects a willingness to cut costs and take greater risks."

The Congressional investigation of the Deepwater Horizon disaster arrived at a series of specific conclusions about key aspects of BP's risk management decisions. Among them were the following. First, BP chose a risky option in installing the casing the day before the accident. Second, BP and its contractors did not run an acoustic test to check that the cement attaching the casing to the rock walls of the borehole had formed a seal to prevent gas from escaping. Third, BP did not properly secure the top of the well with a lockdown sleeve to keep it sealed tightly, so that oil and gas were able to leak out and rise to the rig at the surface. These conclusions all point to BP's having weak risk management structures in place.

THE DEVIL IN THE DETAILS: THE TESTS

In 2009, a year before the explosion of Deepwater Horizon, Andy Inglis, BP's head of exploration and production (E&P), talked about the company's expertise in working in the most challenging of deepwater fields. Inglis said, "We don't do simple things. We are prepared to work at the frontier, and manage the risks."[29] In March 2010, a month before the explosion, a JPMorgan analyst report described BP's leadership team, which included Inglis and CEO Hayward, as "confident, realistic and determined."[30]

In order to understand and assess how risks were managed at the operating level at which the critical decisions about Macondo were made, we need to dig deep into the details of what occurred on that fateful day of April 20.

Before the second cement plug and lockdown sleeve could be put in place, the well needed to be tested to ensure that the cement and steel locked together, thereby preventing any gas from leaking and causing a fire or explosion. The test is crucial. If it went successfully, BP could abandon the well temporarily until it was ready to begin production.

Normally, such a test involves the removal of approximately 300 feet of a thick drilling fluid called mud below the BOP, which is then replaced with seawater. This is because mud is used to prevent gas leaks into the well. Therefore, a test is typically conducted to ensure that the well is fully sealed, before removing too much of the mud.

In terms of the test, BP's managers wanted to remove an unusually large amount of the mud from the well, and then run the test. This would involve a deeper plug than originally envisioned. On April 16, BP requested permission from federal regulators to use a deeper plug, and received approval after 20 minutes.

BP's decision appears to have been unconventional. In July, Ronald Sepulvado, BP's manager in charge of the rig, was asked under oath by the Interior Department-Coast Guard panel if he had ever run a test in which so much mud had been removed. His reply: "No, ma'am." When asked if he had ever heard of BP doing so anywhere, his reply was the same: "No, ma'am."[31]

Robert Kaluza was BP's day-shift manager on April 20. When interviewed by BP's internal investigators as to the motivation behind removing so much mud, he is reported to have replied, "Don't know why—maybe trying to save time.... At the end of the well sometimes they think about speeding up."[32]

As it happens, the Macondo drilling project was five weeks behind schedule and over budget by $20 million. BP's altered test would help speed up a process that was costing an estimated $750,000 a day. Notably, being over budget sets the stage for increased willingness to take risks by virtue of being in the domain of losses.

Transocean workers and contractors aboard the rig indicated that they were not informed of the change in test procedure until the morning of April 20, at an 11 a.m. meeting. The change caught the Transocean crew off guard. Jimmy Harrell was the most senior Transocean worker on Deepwater Horizon that day. Harrell voiced objections to removing so much mud. Kaluza responded, "This is how it's going to be," and so Harrell agreed, albeit reluctantly. Harrell's attorney, Pat Fanning, is quoted as saying: "It was BP's well, they were paying for it. BP gave the marching orders."[33]

For the next few hours, Transocean workers removed mud from the well, and by 5 p.m. had commenced the pressure test. The test results were unusual, and Transocean workers struggled to interpret the readings. Pressure built up unexpectedly, with no clear reason as to why. Despite his earlier resistance, Harrell judged the issue to be nonproblematic. He had a valve at the top of the blowout preventer tightened, which seemed to address the issue.

However, other Transocean workers were not persuaded that the problems had been resolved. For example, Wyman Wheeler, who supervised the drilling crew for 12 hours per day, was not convinced that all signs were clear. Yet, when Wheeler's shift ended at 6 p.m. his replacement, Jason Anderson, assured both his Transocean co-workers (and his BP colleagues) that the pressure readings were normal. Anderson suggested an alternative hypothesis called "U-tubing" for the observed readings. "U-tubing" refers to cases in which the downward pressure from mud (heavy drilling fluid) located between the drill pipe and the well walls surrounding it pushes seawater back up the drill pipe.

BP managers also disagreed with each other. Donald Vidrine was the BP manager due to relieve Kaluza at 6 p.m. Despite having made the argument for removing so much mud, Kaluza was uncomfortable with the results of the test, and Vidrine was especially concerned about a surge of gas. For that reason, Vidrine decided to order a second test, somewhat different from the first. The results of the second test were especially perplexing. Gauges on the main pipe indicated nonzero pressure, which signaled a problem, although a smaller tube leading up from the well showed no pressure, a sign that the well was stable. Notably, the two pipes were connected and should have featured the same pressure. Vidrine consulted with a BP superior, Mark Hafle, in Houston, who assured Vidrine that had there been a problematic "kick" in the well, it would have already been detected. A kick means that gas had shot back through the mud.

At approximately 7:50 p.m. Vidrine instructed that a call be placed to BP engineers in Houston stating he was satisfied with the test results. His decision was taken against the backdrop of Hafle's judgment from Houston about there being no gas surge, Anderson's competing U-tubing hypothesis, a crew anxious to move to the next project, and the psychology of dealing with a project that is late and over budget. Interestingly, in his 30 years of experience on rigs, Vidrine had never seen a case of U-tubing; he had only heard about it.

Vidrine is a critical link in BP's risk management chain. He was the manager to have made the call to go ahead with the final stage of the process. On one side of the scale he heard the concerns expressed by Wheeler and Kaluza, along with the negative results from the second test. On the other side of the scale he heard Hafle's judgment and Anderson's explanation involving the U-tubing hypothesis.

Given the stakes involved, was this a sound bet? We want to be careful about hindsight bias here, in that we know Deepwater Horizon exploded. The question is whether there was enough compelling evidence to suggest that it was prudent to proceed. Or alternatively, did Vidrine display confirmation bias by applying too much weight to the information that confirmed that all was well with the well? Certainly, the legal judgment of recklessness by BP for its role in the explosion of Deepwater Horizon is consistent with confirmation bias.

From an organizational risk management perspective, there are other questions about missed signals. In the two hours between Vidrine's message to Houston and the first explosion, unfavorable signals continued to be generated. For example, electronic data reviewed by investigators after the explosion showed that the net flow of fluid from the well was negative, meaning more fluid was exiting the well than was being pumped in. Perhaps the Transocean crew missed the signals because they had become distracted by other tasks. Or they might have seen the signs, but not viewed them as abnormal. Of course, there is another possibility, namely confirmation bias.

There is one additional organizational risk management point that merits attention regarding the events that occurred on April 20. Keep in mind that the April 20 test would have been a point of high risk in the drilling process. This is because as the mud restraining any escaping gas and oil was removed, a potential escape channel opened for that gas to make its way to the ocean surface.

Given the history of the well, April 20 was a time for focusing key decision-makers on the tasks at hand, not a time for distraction. However, perhaps out of overconfidence, BP chose the distracting route. Sepulvado, the BP manager in charge of the rig, was on shore that day for a training program with his phone switched off. Transocean's Harrell, and his second-in-command, Randy Ezell, had spent much of that day hosting executives visiting the rig. The visiting executives included BP's Pat O'Bryan, who had recently been appointed vice president for drilling in the Gulf of Mexico. The agenda included commending the crew for its safety record and discussing coming maintenance. Ironically, O'Bryan was an expert in detecting gas leaks in oil wells. Yet neither he nor any of the managers mentioned in this paragraph were involved when it came time to assess the test results.

The Commission that investigated the explosion of Deepwater Horizon pointed to three recurring themes: (1) missed warning signals; (2) failure to share information; and (3) a general lack of appreciation for the risks involved. All three involve process-pitfall issues. Missed warning signals reflect confirmation bias. The failure to share information is a process weakness that usually stems from groupthink dynamics. Not appreciating the risks involved is a manifestation of overconfidence.

BUREAU OF OCEAN ENERGY MANAGEMENT, REGULATION AND ENFORCEMENT

The Bureau of Ocean Energy Management, Regulation and Enforcement (BOEMRE) is the US regulatory agency that oversees oil drilling. At the time of the Deepwater Horizon explosion, it had a different name, the Minerals Management Service (MMS).

Regulators oversee the management of operational risk at arm's length. However, MMS had a history of problems in carrying out its mandate. Prior to the spill, MMS flared into the news for misbehavior involving sex and drugs being shared by MMS staffers and energy company officials. The National Commission report specifically identifies the MMS office in Lake Charles, Louisiana, where prior to 2007 the practice of employees accepting gifts from oil and gas companies was prevalent. The report mentions that one MMS employee conducted inspections on a company's oil platforms and at the same time negotiated an employment contract with the company. This "revolving door" policy between regulators and companies sets the stage for regulatory capture.[34]

In 2008, a report by Interior inspector general Earl Devaney concluded that MMS's culture was 99.9% acceptable, but that there was a 0.1% "culture of substance abuse and promiscuity," and a "culture of ethical failure."[35] In respect to risk management, the problems ran deeper than Devaney's comments suggest.[36] The agency's resources did not keep pace with the industry's expansion into deep water drilling and its related reliance on more demanding technologies. Notably, the agency's culture shifted the attention of senior agency officials from safety to efforts to maximize revenue from leasing and production. As a result, the task fell to each individual firm to assess the risks associated with offshore activities, and demonstrate that each facility had the policies, plans, and systems in place to manage those risks.

Incentivizing regulators to emphasize revenues from leasing and production created a severe conflict of interest at MMS. Regulators who were trying to monitor risks soon learned that foxes enjoy guarding henhouses. A senior MMS official who was involved with the process told the Commission that "It was like pulling teeth.... We never got positive cooperation."

Without data and resources, a regulatory agency can find it difficult to resist arguments made by industry. When industry contended that BOPs were more reliable than the regulations recognized, warranting less frequent pressure testing, MMS conceded and halved the mandated frequency of tests. The MMS commissioned two studies on BOPs, and found that many rig operators, because they were not testing BOPs, were instead basing their assertions that the tool would work on information that appeared to be inconsistent with equipment in use.[37] Yet, MMS never revised its BOP regulations nor added verification as an independent inspection item to reflect the new information.

The Commission reported that for at least the past 15 years, every former MMS director indicated that royalty issues took most of the director's time, not offshore regulatory oversight. The commission also tells us that nobody who led MMS since the time it was created, almost 30 years before, had the knowledge required to oversee the industry. They lacked significant training and experience in petroleum engineering, petroleum geology, and significant technical expertise related to drilling safety.

Knowledge gap issues ran deep. Approximately half of MMS personnel acknowledged a lack of training. The agency neither provided formal training specific to the inspection process nor kept up with changing technology. Instead, it relied on industry representatives to explain the technology at a facility. Moreover, MMS did not establish any formal process to promote standardization, consistency, and operational efficiency. Staff complained about the agency's emphasis on the quantity rather than the quality of inspections. Clearly there were no adequate role models for either training or enforcing standards set by the agency.

BP and MMS might have been in something of a codependent relationship. In terms of Macondo, MMS focused its engineering review on the initial well design. But MMS did not assess the full set of risks associated with the procedure for capping and temporarily abandoning the well.

The National Commission made a series of recommendations about MMS, to restructure the agency to feature separate roles and responsibilities. In particular, the Commission recommended replacing MMS with three entities having clearly defined statutory authorities. One entity would be responsible for offshore safety and environmental enforcement. A second entity would be responsible for leasing and environmental science. The third entity would manage natural resource revenues.

These recommendations make sense as ways of removing conflicts of interest in the incentive systems and provide a first step toward establishing a regulatory structure with a strong RMP. However, given the issues associated with inefficient procedures and inadequate skills and training, much more is required if the goal is strong regulation.

CLOSING THOUGHTS

The Moreland Commission report on Con Ed identified several issues in the company's structure that could have been stronger and that led to some problems in the way that the company responded to Hurricane Sandy. While the findings suggested room for improvement, the behavior of the Con Ed organization is consistent with its having established a risk culture that was certainly adequate and risk structures that were quite decent.

In contrast, the report of the National Commission is quite stark in its comments about risk management, not only at BP but in the industry as a whole. In no uncertain terms, the report states, "The immediate causes of the Macondo well blowout can be traced to a series of identifiable mistakes made by BP, Halliburton, and Transocean that reveal such systematic failures in risk management that they place in doubt the safety culture of the entire industry.... Absent major crises, and given the remarkable financial returns available from deepwater reserves, the business culture succumbed to a false sense of security. The Deepwater Horizon disaster exhibits the costs of a culture of complacency.... There are recurring themes of missed warning signals, failure to share information, and a general lack of appreciation for the risks involved. In the view of the Commission, these findings highlight the importance of organizational culture and a consistent commitment to safety by industry, from the highest management levels on down."[38] In respect to MMS, the National Commission criticizes its "culture of revenue maximization."

After the release of the National Commission report, the Obama administration proposed a series of new regulations for deep water drilling off US shores. The new rules pertained to drilling well casings, the cementing of wells, and blowout preventers. The general reaction to the proposal was positive. However, William Reilly, who cochaired the National Commission, pointed out that the report emphasized cultural weaknesses in management, process design, and adherence to systems.[39]

This chapter provides a framework for evaluating cultural weaknesses, and relating those weaknesses to key concepts developed throughout the book. Despite the fact that CEO Hayward's mandate was to improve safety at BP, the Deepwater Horizon event showed that changing a firm's risk management culture is easier said than done.

CHAPTER 19

Information Sharing Failures at Southwest Airlines, General Motors, and the Agencies That Regulate Them

THE TRANSPORTATION INDUSTRY TOUCHES ALMOST EVERYONE, AS MOST people fly and drive. Therefore, risk management in the industry affects most of our lives directly. As with everywhere else, psychology impacts decisions made within the industry about risk and safety.

The odds of being killed during a flight when you fly on one of the top 39 airlines that have the best accident rates is about 1 in 20 million. If you choose an airline in the bottom 39, the odds drop to 1 in 2 million.[1] In the last decade the number of deaths per year from airline crashes has been less than 1,000. In contrast, over 30,000 people die in the United States every year in driving accidents.[2]

Southwest Airlines is not only a member of the top 39 airlines but, as this book goes to press, has not had a single fatal air crash in its history. However, in 2008 it made headline news for poor risk management procedures by allowing uninspected planes that were possibly unsafe to make regular flights. In 2014, General Motors (GM) made headline news for producing cars with ignition switches that were easy to switch off in transit, thereby causing a series of fatal accidents.

Nobody died in the Southwest "uninspected planes" incident. The number of victims associated with GM's faulty ignition switches is difficult to gauge exactly, but the number of deaths is below 200, and the number of injuries is below 100. Although the number of annual fatalities from these incidents pales in comparison to the larger statistics of those killed in car accidents, psychologically there is a big difference between accidents caused by flaws in manufacturing design, and accidents caused by nonmanufacturing-related human error. The failures at Southwest and GM attracted enormous public attention and Congressional inquiries. For GM, risk management weaknesses in handling an ignition switch mistake resulted in the largest number of deaths formally connected to an auto safety issue in the United States, since 2000. It has been the most significant safety crisis in the company's history, and triggered a criminal investigation by the Department of Justice.[3] In May 2014, GM paid a $35 million fine levied by the Department of Transportation—the maximum allowed under the law—for its failure to disclose defects and respond swiftly to the problem.

These events tarnished the reputations of both firms and cost them financially as well. Southwest incurred a $7.5 million fine from the Federal Aviation Administration (FAA). GM conducted a major recall of automobiles equipped with problematic ignition switches, and planned to take a $1.2 billion dollar charge against its earnings as a result. GM was also less than forthcoming with its regulator, the National Highway Traffic Safety Administration (NHTSA).

Psychology loomed large in the poor risk management practices at both firms. This chapter describes the decision processes at these firms, focusing on the key decision-makers and the psychological issues associated with their behavior.

What Southwest Airlines Was Doing Right

The risk management lapse at Southwest Airlines came as a surprise.[4] From a process-pitfall perspective, Southwest has generally been well run. They set sensible standards and train their employees to be financially literate. They use sophisticated planning processes, combine a mix of financial and nonfinancial incentives to create a working environment that motivates people to want to make good decisions, and excel at sharing information.

This section describes many of the things Southwest has done right. There at least two reasons for doing so. The first is to provide the backdrop against which to understand its risk management mistakes. The second is to illustrate the features of a company whose general corporate culture has been strong. In this regard, so much of the attention in this book has been on cultures that are weak.

What is especially impressive is that Southwest succeeded against the backdrop of an airline industry that is fragile and that at times has been in deep trouble. After 2001, Southwest's major competitors—United Airlines, Delta Airlines, and American Airlines—all went into bankruptcy. Eventually all three emerged to live another day, seeking to survive through mergers.

In contrast, Southwest Airlines thrived during this period, often carrying more passengers than any other airline.

Southwest succeeded both operationally and financially. Consider the annual American Customer Satisfaction Index report on airlines, hotels, and online travel agencies: in 2014, it gave the highest ratings to Southwest Airlines and JetBlue Airways in customer satisfaction, and for the third consecutive year.[5] Top performance for Southwest is not new, as other surveys such as Zagat ranked it number one in 2006, 2009, and 2010.

Southwest was jointly founded by Rollin King and Herb Kelleher, and they developed their vision of the airline in 1967. Kelleher became its legendary CEO. He hired Rita Bailey, who served as director of human resources at Southwest, and was with the firm for 25 years. Under Bailey's leadership, Southwest developed its corporate culture. A key part of the culture is being financially literate about costs. Keeping costs down is a key reason why Southwest's earnings trajectory is so impressive. Southwest is a very cost-conscious company, and has found a way to keep its cost-per-passenger-mile low, while delivering excellent customer service at the same time. It rates at or near the top when it comes to on-time arrivals, baggage handling, frequency of complaints, and canceled flights.

Planning is a key reason why Southwest has managed to be a low-cost producer. Expenses for fuel and labor are the two most important cost factors for airlines. In the past, when oil prices were low, Southwest engaged in some shrewd financial risk management by hedging its fuel prices.

In respect to incentives, Southwest ties financial rewards to its plan. If the company turns out to be profitable, all employees automatically share in the profits. Contributions to employee retirement accounts are made automatically. Executives at the level of vice president and above receive a bonus on top of profit sharing. Bonuses are linked to how well people manage within their budgets. Southwest uses stock options as well as profit sharing.

Southwest trains its employees to be financially literate. Therefore, employees understand the goals established within their budgets and understand that their goals are tied to the company's net income. They understand that if they miss their goal, they will have to deal with a profit-sharing penalty. Therefore, as the fiscal year progresses, employees keep track of where they are, where they need to be, and what they can do to impact the result, a great example of the OBM concept.

Bailey emphasizes that Southwest's culture focuses heavily on treating people in the workforce like owners. Employees receive a constant message: "You're an owner, you're what makes the business work, so you have to understand the business. This means understanding information that is relevant to the success of the business, and includes information about the competition, and about where the money goes."[6]

Southwest constantly sends messages about what it calls its three P's: pennies, planes, and people. Southwest's communications, newsletters, fliers, and messages to the workforce all seek to keep the big picture on the front burner, so that workers know what happened with business last year and know the current state of business going into current year. Southwest is a psychologically smart company. It trains its workforce to be financially literate, which allows them to monitor the company's performance and understand their stake in the outcome.

Before United Airlines's bankruptcy in 2002, both United and Southwest featured employee ownership. Like the employees at United, employees at Southwest also sacrificed pay for five years in order to build an equity stake in their company. Yet the contrast in the outcomes for those two firms is really stark.

Why did Southwest thrive when United failed? I believe that Southwest intentionally sought to develop healthy processes to mitigate pitfalls, where United did not. Employee relations at United were unhealthy. United did not treat its employees like owners, and consequently the employees did not feel like owners, even though their equity stake in the company was high.

In Bailey's view, incentives involve more than money. Ownership is not just about profit sharing because profit sharing by itself is never enough when it comes to dealing with the spectrum of human needs. She emphasizes that people need to be acknowledged as human beings. She speculates that if Southwest had profit sharing without its nurturing culture of relationships, it probably would have the same type of experience as United. Trying to address unmet psychological needs with money alone, she thinks, is doomed because money is never enough.

As evidence for her views, Bailey points out that pay at Southwest is not especially high. Yet, in the wake of September 11, 2001, employees willingly gave $2 million back to the company through payroll deductions, in order to ensure the stability of their employment. Why the willingness to be so generous? The answer is because Southwest employees truly feel like owners.

Bailey points out the need to recruit the right people. She contends that doing so is the most important part of the business, because well-run companies need to be staffed by people who have an innate interest in serving others. That might be why airline attendants on Southwest flights behave like tour guides. She asserts that there are some personal characteristics that you can buy, but simply cannot make.

Southwest's Big Mistake

In March 2007, Southwest disclosed that it failed to conduct adequate safety checks on 46 older planes in its fleet of 520 aircraft. These planes were all

Boeing 737s, which have a history of developing cracks in the fuselage. In 1988, a crack actually caused the skin of a Boeing 737 flown by Aloha Airlines to peel off in midflight, killing a flight attendant. This incident led the FAA to institute mandatory inspections.

The Boeing 737 is a workhorse, and built for short to medium-length flights. As a result, it takes off and lands at a higher rate than the planes used for longer flights. Taking off and landing involve significant changes in air pressure, and those changes stress the outer skin of the plane, putting pressure on its seams. That is why it is important to inspect those planes on a regular basis for possible cracks. Cracks are actually common, and not dangerous if minute. Larger cracks are dangerous, and can lead to the situation experienced by the Aloha Airlines aircraft.

In any event, despite all the other things it does well, somehow Southwest's maintenance processes failed. Was it a process breakdown, and if so, which process occupied center stage? Was some psychological bias at work? Was it the complexity of criteria, in that there were several directives from the FAA, not just one? Were the criteria vague about when an inspection is due, as the requirement to inspect depends on a mix of factors involving whether planes have been modified, and how many hours they have been flown? Did Southwest hire the wrong people for conducting maintenance?

The story of the failed inspections involves FAA airworthiness directives (AD) that were released in 1997, 2002, and 2004, specifying conditions that required scheduled inspections for cracks and associated repairs of "lap joints" in older 737s. As it turned out, six Southwest aircraft had developed cracks. Some were as long as four inches, although manufacturer Boeing asserts that cracks less than six inches do not compromise the structural integrity of an aircraft or compromise safety. However, the FAA asserted that Southwest flew 46 aircraft on 60,000 flights between June 2006 and March 2007 in violation of the 2004 AD.

The chronology features a fair amount of intrigue.[7] The FAA regulated Southwest out of its office in Irving, Texas. The main cast of characters at the FAA includes inspector Bobby Boutris and his supervisor, Douglas Gawadzinski. In early 2006, Boutris noticed discrepancies in Southwest's maintenance records, and wanted to raise an alarm. However, Gawadzinski prevented him from sending a formal letter to Southwest.

Bill Krivanek was head of compliance at Southwest at the time. Boutris was persistent in his criticism of Southwest's maintenance schedules, which led him and Krivanek to spar. Krivanek was resentful of Boutris's aggressive posture and sought to have Boutris reassigned. After some discussion at the FAA on the differing perspectives, a compromise was struck about what kind of information Southwest would make available to Boutris for his next inspection. That inspection began on March 15, 2007.

A few hours after Boutris arrived to examine Southwest's maintenance records, the airline alerted Gawadzinski that just the day before, it had uncovered a history of missed inspections on one hundred aircraft. Four days later, Southwest submitted a document to FAA, authored by Gawadzinski and Southwest's manager of regulatory compliance, Paul Comeau, asserting that all inspections were now complete. Previous to joining Southwest, Comeau worked at the FAA, and had a long relationship with Gawadzinski. Notably, Comeau's arrival at Southwest appeared to have initiated a warmer relationship between the airline and the FAA.

A week after his March 15 inspection, Boutris was still investigating Southwest's maintenance records. In the course of doing so, he discovered that uninspected planes were continuing to fly. Boutris complained, and for his efforts was reassigned and placed under investigation. This event led senior FAA officials to investigate the Irving, Texas, office, and after doing so to reassign Gawadzinski.

Boutris did not sit by quietly. He effectively blew the whistle. As a result, the Department of Transport (DOT) and the Office of Special Counsel looked into the issue, and in the end backed up Boutris's version of events.

Senior officials at the FAA were, of course, embarrassed. They considered fining Southwest, initially proposing a fine of $300,000. However, as time passed the officials raised the fine, first to $3 million, and then to $10.2 million. Why the increase? As it happens, the story was now attracting media attention, as well as attention from a Congressional House Panel and the DOT. The FAA was coming under scrutiny. It needed to appear to be in charge.

The FAA explained the rationale for its record-setting $10.2 million fine, noting that Southwest had misled FAA officials. Southwest defended itself, saying that it had received verbal permission to fly uninspected aircraft. Although the FAA acknowledged that Gawadzinski had indeed given verbal permission for Southwest to do so, they asserted that nevertheless, the airline knew they should not have been flying uninspected aircraft, and yet chose to do so.

Moreover, the FAA officials explained that they were upset that Southwest had reported to them that the noncompliance had stopped when in fact it had not. They also suggested tightening "ethics rules" relating to former FAA employees who take jobs with airlines. To be sure, there were ethical problems at the FAA. When the House Panel investigated the issue, they heard testimony from another FAA inspector, Douglas Peters, who had engaged in whistle-blowing. Peters told the Panel that his supervisor had threatened both his career and his wife's career if he did not pull back his attempt to save what they termed "a bunch of losers."

Southwest defended itself by explaining that it was not intentional deceit on its part, but an administrative error involving a mistaken check mark on a submission form. It reiterated that it flew with concurrence of the FAA, and had inspected 99.4% of its fleet. Southwest CEO Kelly pointed out that the airline faced a complex web of safety procedures, with modifications and upgrades, adding to the complexity. He called for streamlining. He also pointed out that Southwest had never had an accident, was proud of its safety record, and would take steps to make flying on Southwest even safer.

Eventually, Kelly would move from being defensive to issuing a public apology. When he did so, he acknowledged that the airline was not as compliant as it might have been, or for that matter as safe. He also noted that Southwest's top management had been in the dark about its inspection program. These remarks were in contrast to his initial defensiveness, when he had taken the position that the FAA was being unfair and had exaggerated the flight risks in question.

In being defensive, he missed at least two important psychological issues. The first issue was that the FAA felt embarrassed and had to act forcefully. Its reputation for protecting the flying public was in jeopardy of being tarnished. After all, in March 2007 its inspector had allowed Southwest to fly planes that had not yet been inspected. But the agency did not learn that this was the case until a year later, when Boutris blew the whistle.

The second issue involves the flying public. They were beginning to lose trust in Southwest, and trust is one of Southwest's most valuable intangible assets. Most psychological studies conclude that people misperceive risk. All the public knows is that Southwest was flying passengers around in unsafe planes whose skins could peel off in midflight, as had happened to Aloha's aircraft. The public would not understand the complexity of the inspection criteria or the relevance of crack size. In addition, Congress announced that it was launching an investigation and would hold a hearing. The issue swelled when American Airlines, which also flies a large fleet of Boeing 7373s, canceled many flights to conduct inspections, which stranded many travelers for days. Loss of trust and reputation was a bigger danger to Southwest than the FAA fine, and that was the issue that Kelly needed to address.

Some days later, Kelly did figure it out, changed his approach, and began to address the psychological issues. He openly talked about the need to regain the public's trust. He stopped criticizing the FAA and began to negotiate with them. He grounded 41 of its aircraft for reinspection, placed three employees on leave, and hired an outside consultant to analyze the company's maintenance procedures.

At the end of the story, Southwest settled in February 2009 with the FAA, and agreed to pay $7.5 million.

The psychological issues that are pertinent to this chronology do not end with the FAA and the flying public. There were also clear process-pitfall issues at Southwest.

If Kelly can be believed about top management being in the dark, then Southwest's process for information sharing had a critical flaw. Disappointment is the hallmark of excessive optimism, and large surprises are the hallmark of overconfidence. Kelly appears to have been both disappointed and surprised by the maintenance inspection event.

Given Kelly's remarks about inspection complexity, there is reason to believe that Southwest did not establish clear standards. Without standards, it is difficult to engage in effective inspection planning with a view to execution. In regard to incentives, it seems clear that Krivanek and Comeau were motivated by other considerations besides compliance. Regulatory capture is a very real phenomenon.

The compliance team might also have been overconfident by setting maintenance inspection standards that were too low, thereby underestimating the risk of failure for aircraft that flew without having been inspected. In April 2011, the ceiling on one of Southwest's 737 opened in flight, prompting a sudden loss of cabin pressure, a rapid descent, an emergency landing at a military base, and an injured flight attendant. In response, Southwest Airlines grounded 79 of its Boeing 737s planes to inspect them. But that was too close for comfort.

GENERAL MOTORS' WRONG CHOICE OF IGNITION SWITCH

Like Southwest Airlines, General Motors experienced a significant risk management failure. The core of the GM ignition switch debacle is that in 2001, one of their engineers recommended the installation of a new ignition switch design, and upon discovering the problem, sought to have it replaced. However, GM's risk management culture at the time was such that his efforts at replacement failed. Statements in GM documents from 2005 indicate that the firm decided it was too expensive to implement a fix.

Most of what is known publicly about the GM faulty ignition switch comes from former US prosecutor Anton Valukas, who was hired by GM to investigate the issue.[8] His main findings were reported by media outlets such as the *Wall Street Journal* and the *New York Times*. In addition, the *New York Times* diligently pursued the story with its own investigative journalism.[9]

Consider some of the core details in the ignition switch chronology, particularly those related to the GM employee whose decisions lie at the heart of the case. In 2001, GM engineer Raymond DeGiorgio was tasked with selecting one of two designs for an ignition switch to be placed in the automaker's new small car, the Cobalt. This decision was one of many intended to improve the brand of GM's small cars, by imbuing them with features of higher-class European models. The group responsible for communicating the strategy to engineers was known as TALC, an acronym for "touch, aroma and look."[10]

In examining the two design options, DeGiorgio selected the one that was easier to turn in order to start the engine. As it happens, this switch was so easy to turn that if the ignition key was on a key ring containing other keys, and was inadvertently bumped by a knee, it could turn off the engine while the car was in motion. Such an event created a serious risk for those driving the Cobalt, or for that matter anyone else in the Cobalt's vicinity. When the ignition to a car turns off, its *power* steering is disabled, its *power* brakes are disabled, and its airbag inflation system is disabled.

DeGiorgio did not know about these risks at the time of his decision. However, what he did know is that when GM ran tests on the ignition switch he chose, the switch performed poorly. GM subcontracted the manufacture of switches to a firm named Delphi. DeGiorgio emailed some of his GM colleagues to say that the incidence of failure was significant, and Delphi had promised to modify the switches. Improvement was not made to these switches. DeGiorgio was frustrated by his perception of the weak Cobalt switches, so he sent e-mails about his concerns to colleagues. He signed one of his e-mails "tired of the switch from hell." He sought out GM coworkers with other specialties in attempts to address the problem, including electrical engineers, supply chain managers, warranty claim managers, and test-track drivers, all to no avail. GE produced the car with the flawed switches.

Several years passed. Cobalt's ignition failures were becoming public knowledge, and the car's sales were weak. DeGeorgio came under pressure to address the problematic switch. He met regularly with Delphi personnel to seek a solution, but none was forthcoming. He turned to a high-level engineering group to see if they would approve replacing the problematic switch with a newer design that was intended for a future GM model. However, the group rejected his request. Statements in GM documents from 2005 indicate that the firm decided it was too expensive to implement a fix. Complaints about ignition failures continued to arrive, as did new test results that the Cobalt could stall while being driven. Attention by the media was intensifying. The information about this case that is publicly available to date suggests that, as with Southwest above, top-level executives were unaware of the issue.

Here is what DeGeorgio did next. In 2006, he wrote to Delphi, asking them to replace the original switch with the alternative he had rejected five years before. Very importantly, he also did not issue a new part number, the consequence of which was that the new switch and the old switch shared the same part number. Therefore, a newly produced car would have a different ignition switch than an older car, even if they were the same model. But the shared part number would make such knowledge very difficult to discover.

It was not only the Cobalt that had a faulty ignition switch. So too did the Saturn Ion. In 2004, a person named Gene Erickson was killed while a passenger in a Saturn Ion as he was traveling on a rural Texas road. The car, driven by Erikson's girlfriend, Candice Anderson, suddenly swerved into a tree, and the car's airbags did not deploy. Anderson had small traces of Xanax in her blood, pled guilty to criminally negligent homicide, and for years blamed herself for his death. Other accidents followed. According to a *New York Times* investigation, between 2004 and 2013, at least 12 victims died in ten separate accidents. With one exception, all of the accidents were single-car crashes in which the driver lost control of the vehicle and crashed into an object. In every incident, the air bags failed.

Another victim of the faulty Cobalt ignition switch was a Georgia woman named Brooke Melton. Lawyers representing her family managed to discover that older Cobalts had different ignition switches than did newer ones, despite having the same part number. In 2013, DeGiorgio would be deposed and asked by the lawyers to explain why this was the case. Under oath, he denied the replacement and denied authorizing the change. However, when presented with physical evidence, he admitted that he did see that the two switches were different. He also withheld safety information about the "switch in switch" from GM's internal investigators and from federal regulators at the NHTSA.[11]

After DeGiorgio's deposition, GM's legal department chose to settle the suit with Melton's family.[12] GM also moved to revive an internal inquiry about the problematic ignition switch, and prepared to face increased attention from lawsuits launched by the families of other victims, as well as increased scrutiny from the media.

DeGiorgio became persona non grata at GM, and the company dismissed him in June 2014 after he had worked there for 23 years. GM dismissed at least 15 people in connection with the ignition switch issue, including five attorneys. The company has not revealed whether any of those dismissed were members of the 2005 team who rejected DeGiorgio's request to replace the ignition switch.

GM's Internal Response to the Faulty Ignition Switch

There are two main cultural issues, which span a 15-year period. The first concerns the internal process weaknesses within GM's culture that prevented the company from reacting appropriately to the risk presented by the faulty ignition switch. The second is how GM interacted with those individuals outside the company in connection with the switch. This section focuses on the first issue.

In July 2014, GM CEO Mary Barra appeared before a Senate hearing to testify about the defective switch issue. During her testimony, she indicated that her company was going to fix its mistakes and emerge "a better, stronger company."[13] While the previous section focused on the role of DeGiorgio in the faulty switch chronology, this section focuses on the broader cultural issues in which GM was "poor and weak" rather than "good and strong." The *Wall Street Journal* characterized GM as having a weak corporate culture, while the *Times* described GM's culture as one that shuns accountability and features a dysfunctional bureaucracy.

The cultures of GM and Southwest were poles apart.[14] Whereas Southwest had a long record of safety, ranking high on customer satisfaction and being highly profitable, GM declared bankruptcy in 2009 during the financial crisis and received about $40 billion in government assistance. As it happens, a side benefit of the bankruptcy was to shield the firm from needing to pay accident victims for a crash that occurred prior to the bankruptcy.

At Southwest, Bailey worked to develop an ownership culture in which people readily shared information with each other in order to solve problems. In developing the architecture for Southwest's culture, Bailey poured over a book titled *The Great Game of Business* written by Jack Stack, one of the OBM's most prominent spokesmen.[15] Open-book practices provide the cultural infrastructure for sound overall management, including risk management. Conversely, companies whose practices appear weak from an open-book perspective are prone to having weak risk management.

In 2009, the *New York Times* interviewed Stack about the culture at Detroit automakers.[16] Stack expressed his opinion that the automakers would benefit by adopting an open-book approach because it would point them to their major business problems. In this regard, he noted the need to improve accountability, in line with the characterization in the *New York Times*. However, GM could have benefitted by adopting many aspects of OBM. In his book *The Great Game of Business*, Stack describes a concept he calls "leading with standards," in which managers share information about performance relative to standards in order to diagnose problems early and address them swiftly. Psychologically, leading with standards can be viewed as an attempt to combat confirmation bias, by being on the lookout for information that counters the conclusion "all is well."

Poor processes and vulnerability to pitfalls were key factors in GM's ignition switch problem, which impacted both its engineers and its lawyers. Before 2006, the engineers *framed* the problem with the switch as a "customer convenience issue," not a "safety issue." They did so, even though in 2004, Rick Wagoner, the CEO at the time, inadvertently turned off the ignition with his knee while test driving a Cobalt. Likewise, a program quality manager for the Cobalt named Joseph Taylor personally experienced moving stalls with the car, and yet did not consider them significant enough to report. He judged that all was well, or at least good enough.

In early 2006, GM lawyers and engineers met to discuss a lawsuit brought by the family of Amber Rose, the driver of a 2005 Cobalt who died when her car hit a tree and the airbags did not deploy. At the meeting, an engineer named Cathy Anderson argued that she would not have expected the airbag to deploy for the reason that the car hit the tree at an angle. The lawyers appeared to accept this argument, and did not search for another explanation such as the power having been turned off.

Was confirmation bias at work in GM's analysis of the Amber Rose crash? Perhaps, but reasonable people might disagree. However, the accident involving Candice Anderson, mentioned earlier, was another story. In 2007, lawyers and engineers met to discuss the details of the lawsuit involving that case. A GM engineer named Manuel Pearce conducted an internal investigation of the incident and concluded that the car had most likely lost power, which is why the airbags failed. In line with confirmation bias, GM acted as if Pearce's conclusion confirmed the view that all was well, or good enough, with the ignition switch. However, the company did settle the lawsuits involving Candice Anderson and the family of Amber Rose, but for years did not make Pearce's conclusions public.

In case after case, GM failed to lead with standards and as a result succumbed to confirmation bias. Consider an October 2006 Wisconsin crash that killed two teenage friends, Amy Rademaker and Natasha Weigel. In February 2007, GM received a state trooper's collision report that linked the faulty ignition switch and the air bag failure. It was seven years before a GM engineer was to read the report.

Keeping in mind that groupthink corresponds to collective confirmation bias, consider the following. At a round table to discuss nondeployment of airbags in Cobalts, which took place in 2012, a junior lawyer raised the issue of a recall. The group response to this suggestion was not welcoming. He was told that the issue had already been raised with the engineers, and left to conclude that there was nothing more that lawyers could do.

In 2006, Alan Mulally became the new CEO of Ford and soon learned that Ford's culture involved a failure to share negative information within the organization. Mulally worked hard to change this feature, and achieved a fair amount of success. Over at GM, lawyers were instructed to elevate to superiors, including the general counsel, any current or past violation of federal, state, or local law or regulation. Yet, GM's safety lawyers did not do so, even as evidence mounted about the faulty switch issue. It took years before the issue made it onto the desk of the company's chief counsel.

In July 2014, GM's general counsel, Michael Millikin, testified at a Senate hearing about faulty ignition switches. To the amazement of the senators,

Millikin told them that it was not until the February 2014 recall that he knew about there being multiple lawsuits involving cases of defective switches in which people had perished, with punitive damages being likely.

The chair of the Senate subcommittee was incredulous. Millikin did not explain how it was that GM's experienced legal team would have kept critically important information from him. He acknowledged that in the past his legal team brought safety concerns to his attention, and went on to say that in this case it just did not happen. GM subsequently dismissed five of its corporate lawyers, one of whom supervised all product liability cases.

GM's Culture and Barra's Testimony

Barra became GM's CEO in January 2014. Before that she had been executive vice president with responsibility for purchasing and the supply chain. As CEO she testified several times in 2014 before Congressional subcommittees, most notably once before the House in April and then again before the Senate in July. Her testimony sequence was strategically opposite to that of Southwest CEO Gary Kelly. He was at first defensive, and then apologetic. She was apologetic at first, and then turned defensive.

Barra was apologetic during her April appearance.[17] She expressed her sincere apologies to anyone impacted by the recall, especially to families and victims of crashes associated with faulty ignition switches. She said her company would do the right thing. In regard to crash survivors and families of crash victims, she told the subcommittee that GM had both legal and moral obligations to them. For this reason, she engaged attorney Kenneth Feinberg as a consultant. Feinberg was well known for handling large-scale compensation cases such as the BP oil spill and the terrorist attacks that took place on September 11, 2001. He would administer GM's compensation program for families of select crash victims or survivors, those affected by the faulty switch in the 2.6 million older cars that were part of the recall.

That April, Barra told subcommittee members that she was disturbed that back in 2005, a GM document indicated that cost saving was the reason for failing to replace the defective ignition switch. She called that decision unacceptable. In this regard, Barra stated that, although GM operated under a cost culture before 2009, the postbankruptcy GM operated under a customer culture. Moreover, she created the new position of vice president of global vehicle safety to oversee all safety information in the company.

However, Barra changed her tone when she testified in July.[18] Under pressure to expand its compensation program for victims, Barra established boundaries for what GM was willing to do. She was emphatic that the company would not waive the protection that its 2009 bankruptcy conferred against lawsuits. She said GM would share additional documents from its internal investigation. Under pressure from the subcommittee to dismiss Millikin, GM's general counsel who had been unaware of the entire ignition switch issue before the February recall, she insisted that he was an important part of her team, and she planned to keep him.

While Barra did characterize GM's culture as being customer focused instead of cost focused, all the evidence suggests that its culture is closed book, especially with respect to sharing information about risks. GM could benefit by Barra taking a leaf from Mulally's playbook and instituting OBM practices aimed at strengthening its RMP. In this regard, here are some important questions to consider. Were managers of engineers like DeGiorgio good role models for risk management behavior? Did GM institute establish effective policies, procedures, and systems for managing component safety? Did GM's climate encourage people to speak up in groups about risk issues and, if necessary, play the devil's advocate? The evidence suggests that the answer to all of these questions is no, but can be takeoff points for improving the company.

Interactions with the NHTSA

As we saw with the FAA in the earlier discussion about Southwest, regulatory agencies are imperfect, and there is always concern about regulatory capture. A secondary theme in the faulty switch issue is that the NHTSA was excessively passive.[19]

By way of background, the process requiring regulatory death inquiries stems from the NHTSA's failure to identify highway rollovers in Ford Explorers with Firestone tires, a problem that occurred in the 1990s and that led to 271 deaths. Congress then passed legislation that requires automobile companies to report to the NHTSA any claims in which deaths or injuries are blamed on product defects. The law also requires that the agency conduct death inquiries, eliciting information from automakers to document every automobile accident and assess the circumstances leading to each crash.

The nature of the interactions between GM and the NHTSA is complex, with the company failing to disclose information, and the agency failing to press for additional disclosure. Consider some examples.

The first example pertains to the accident involving Candice Anderson that killed Gene Erickson. Recall that GM engineer Pearce concluded that the Ion carrying Erickson had likely lost power, thereby disabling its air bags. A month after he reached that conclusion, GM told federal authorities at the NHTSA that it could not provide answers as to what had caused the crash, and in two other crash incidents involving the faulty ignition switch, the company stated that it had not assessed the cause, when in fact it had. In retrospect, the agency could have actively pursued the matter, asking that it assess the cause and report back, which it did not.

A second example involves a fatal December 2009 crash that took place in Tennessee and killed a person named Seyde Chansuthus. In that inquiry, GM told the NHTSA that attorney-client privilege prevented it from answering. Yet, at the time Ms. Chansuthus's family had not sued GM, and moreover the company had concluded a thorough investigation to determine the cause of the crash that killed her. In retrospect, the agency could have been more active in seeking answers, rather than accepting the company's argument about attorney-client privilege.

A third example involves the 2006 Wisconsin crash that killed Amy Rademaker and Natasha Weigel. GM told the NHTSA that it could not provide an answer for the cause of the crash. However, GM had sent the state trooper's report in its reply to the NHTSA. Notably, the NHTSA failed to follow through, as it is a requirement in a regulatory death inquiry that a copy of the police report is provided. The *New York Times* asked the NHTSA for a comment on the police report, and the agency's acting administrator, David Friedman, responded only by mentioning that GM's corporate culture obstructed safety. He made no specific mention of the agency's culture, but did say that it too might have been more rigorous in its actions.

A more rigorous, meaning less passive, response by the NHTSA might have led a GM recall to occur much earlier than it did, and with less hesitation. In February 2014, GM finally announced a North American recall of approximately 780,000 Chevrolet Cobalt and Pontiac G5 cars made between 2005 and 2007, citing faulty ignition switches that might cause unexpected engine shutoff that would disable airbags. However, it did so with some hesitation and was less than forthcoming about the underlying reasons, for later the same month the company expanded the recall and cited 13 deaths associated with faulty ignition switches.

A final example involves the suits filed by the family of Brooke Melton. In addition to filing the suit, their attorney also wrote to the NHTSA asking them to fine GM for not acting quickly enough once it became aware of the problem. The law requires that automobile manufacturers report safety defects to the NHTSA within five days of discovering them, with a maximum fine of $35 million for failing to do so. GM had said that its engineers did not originally think the problem was safety related because steering and brakes would still work if the engine was off. Of course, by this they meant nonpower steering and nonpower brakes. Anyone who has ever tried to steer or brake without the power features knows how much more difficult are those tasks.

In the aftermath of how it handled the GM ignition switch issue, the NHTSA appears to have learned important lessons. The agency subsequently became much more active in its interactions with automakers, leveling record civil penalties on Honda and Fiat Chrysler for recall violations.[20]

CLOSING THOUGHTS

Decision processes involving transportation safety are infused with psychological elements, both in corporations and in the regulatory agencies providing oversight. The case of Southwest Airlines teaches us that even well-run companies are not immune from poor risk management when it comes to safety. The case of General Motors teaches us not to expect strong risk management culture in companies whose overall cultures feature poor processes for setting standards, preparing plans, structuring incentives, and especially sharing information.[21] As for the regulatory agencies, if you are counting on them to counter psychological pitfalls and cultural weaknesses, do not hold your breath. They have their own problems in those areas.

CHAPTER 20

Conclusion

IF RISK MANAGEMENT WERE A GAME OF TENNIS, THEN A FOREHAND WOULD correspond to the quantitative side and a backhand would correspond to the psychological side. The cumulative message from all the applications discussed in this book is that, although risk managers tend to run around their backhands, they can develop a more balanced game.

Risk management involves risks associated with human vulnerabilities just as much as risk associated with physical phenomena and market conditions. Psychological pitfalls associated with emotions, framing effects, heuristics, and biases create major risks, and these are risks to be managed.[1] In this regard, the risk management landscape is complex. Personality and brain chemistry are part of that landscape. Individual differences are part of that landscape.

Because behavior lies at the center of operational risk, managing behavioral risk is a crucial element of risk management. Understanding and recognizing psychological pitfalls are the first steps in managing behavioral risk. Subsequent steps involve implementation, meaning the incorporation of behaviorally based actions into organizational processes, and this effort must be deliberate and purposeful.

There are two kinds of initiatives that organizations can take to incorporate behaviorally based actions to address psychological pitfalls. The first is structural, and involves building effective processes for operations, standards, planning, incentives, and information sharing. The second is incremental, and involves incorporating small modifications into existing processes, which I like to call "tips for debiasing."

Learning how to ride a bicycle or play the piano is not something that a person can easily do by just reading a book. The same goes for making structural changes to organizational processes. Succeeding at that kind of effort takes a coach, hands on training, and a lot of practice. It takes Systems 1 and 2 working together, with System 2 providing the guiding hand to imbue System 1 with good intuition and habits.[2] Learning how to make incremental changes to existing organizational processes is easier than making structural changes. That is not to say that it is easy, but with effort it is possible.

Making structural changes requires identifying the desired change in question, providing incentives to induce the change, and anticipating obstacles along the way that will likely stand in the way.[3] The first steps in making behavioral changes that address pitfalls involve understanding and recognizing those pitfalls. Understanding and recognizing are the core skills emphasized by this book. In this regard, the application chapters serve as vehicles for developing these skills. From Merrill Lynch to the WHO, and from BP to the SEC, psychological pitfalls plagued the way these organizations managed major risk challenges, and resulted in very unfavorable consequences.

There are many pitfalls that can potentially infect organizational processes. The process-pitfall framework emphasizes four as being especially important: excessive optimism, overconfidence, confirmation bias, and aversion to a sure loss. These pitfalls apply at the individual level, but become manifest at the group level through group dynamics. Groupthink is effectively collective confirmation bias. Polarization can magnify individual traits such as excessive optimism and aversion to a sure loss, while unwarranted acceptance can magnify overconfidence.

ERM is gaining traction across the corporate world as corporations move to institute CROs who bring a top-down risk perspective to their organizations. Major accounting firms now focus on providing consulting services to assist with this undertaking. Both corporations and accounting firms realize that successfully implementing ERM is a major challenge requiring a structured approach, skill, and a deft touch in executing its precepts.[4] The inclusion of a psychologically based behavioral component will be critical to ERM's success.[5]

With all of this in mind, I conclude the book by reviewing some of the major applications and re-examining some of the questions posed. Doing so enables us to extract lessons to be learned in respect to tips for debiasing, both about what not to do and what to do. In this regard, the applications serve as templates that can help guide the analysis of future risk management issues.[6]

EBOLA AND THE WHO: DOS AND DON'TS

People who underestimate the probabilities of unfavorable events are excessively optimistic. In this regard, research has identified four main drivers of excessive optimism: controllability, familiarity, desirability, and representativeness. Consider some of the questions that arose in earlier chapters about excessive optimism.

When, in early 2014, the WHO made an operational risk judgment classifying the 2014 Ebola outbreak as a Level 2 on a 3-point scale, was it being excessively optimistic? I believe that the answer to this question is yes. I also believe that the two most likely drivers for the bias were familiarity and desirability.

Why familiarity? Because the WHO had previous experience with Ebola and was therefore familiar with the disease. Why desirability? Because the WHO would find it more desirable if the outbreak were easy to contain, not difficult to contain.[7]

The discussion about the WHO also asked the following question: when the WHO dismissed the MSF's characterization of the outbreak as exaggeration, were they exhibiting confirmation bias? A person exhibits confirmation bias when he or she is prone to downplay information that runs contrary to his or her view. The early information from MSF was certainly that the 2014 outbreak was different in nature from prior outbreaks. However, this view did not accord with the WHO's excessively optimistic view, and so officials at WHO discounted the MSF characterization, to the point of tweeting that the MSF assessment was unnecessarily alarmist.[8]

For organizations, excessive optimism and confirmation bias commonly occur in connection with a phenomenon known as the planning fallacy. At the time a new project is being planned, the fallacy is that it will be completed on time and within budget, even though past projects tended to be completed late and were over budget.

It is easy to speak of don'ts: don't succumb to confirmation bias and don't be excessively optimistic. The real challenge is what to do in order to mitigate these biases. Typical advice for mitigating the planning fallacy is for decision-makers to adopt what is called the "outside view," as well as what is called the "inside view." The inside view focuses on the details of the project itself, including scenarios for how the project will unfold. In contrast, the outside view focuses on the past record of the decision-makers, especially their track records for being late or over budget.

Taking the outside view forces decision-makers to confront, squarely, past vulnerabilities to having been excessively optimistic. However, adopting the outside view also requires that information that comes from this procedure be used to modify the estimates that come from the inside view.

Human nature being what it is, some decision-makers will find themselves resisting the outside view, out of concern that doing so raises the visibility of past mistakes. This fact of life raises a governance issue, with the question being whether decision-makers have the incentive to be willing to experience the discomfort associated with the outside view. One way to deal with this issue is to establish what are called "networked governance structures," in which major decision groups within the organization have their own boards. Done correctly, such boards, by their very nature, will impose the outside view.[9]

UBS, BASEL, AND THE GLOBAL FINANCIAL CRISIS: DOS AND DON'TS

The discussion about UBS asked whether the advice it received from consulting firm Oliver Wyman about closing the gap between its position and the position of the market leader caused the bank to establish an aspiration level that would induce it to take high, if not imprudent risk? In my opinion, the answer to this question is yes, but in saying this I do not contend that seeking the top position in an industry is necessarily a mistake. It is being imprudent about the risk that is the mistake.

UBS's own self-study report tells us that in making the decision to follow the strategy recommended by Oliver Wyman, involving fixed-income securities related to US subprime residential mortgages, members of UBS's investment banking division did not assess the risk, effectively treating it as if it were unimportant. Downplaying or ignoring risk is certainly consistent with overconfidence as well as excessive optimism, and the self-study report makes clear that UBS failed to assess the quality of the underlying assets for the securities they held.

The self-study report also indicates that UBS's CDO business substantially added to its subprime positions, even in the face of an internally generated outlook for that market, which was pessimistic. This is behavior consistent with confirmation bias. Groupthink is collective confirmation bias, and in this respect, the self-study is explicit about groupthink, when concluding that members of the investment bank senior management did not sufficiently challenge each other in relation to the development of their various businesses.

Challenging each other is at the heart of constructive devil's advocacy. What is perfectly understandable is that groups that value cohesion and esprit de corps will shy away from devil's advocacy. However, if done properly, devil's advocacy need not threaten group cohesion. In this regard, the OBM approach discussed at various points in the book builds devil's advocacy into forecasting exercises, particularly for sales. Notably, dedicated teams are assigned to challenge the assumptions underlying these forecasts in a sequence of meetings, not just a one-off event.

One can think of banks like UBS on one side of a coin, and bank regulators on the other. The discussion about bank regulation in Chapter 13 focused on the role that psychology plays in complex frameworks such as the Basel Accords. Complexity is a key feature of bank regulation, and the central question is whether to match complex solutions to a complex environment or simple solutions to a complex environment. When uncertainty rather than risk best describes the decision task, the fast and frugal school of thought recommends simple solutions over complex solutions, in accordance with the maxim "less is more." The Bank of England has adopted the "less is more" position in its attitude towards the Basel accords.

Financial Sector Groupthink: Dos and Don'ts

Groupthink runs through many of the applications, making it clear that this is an issue in great need of attention. The groupthink dynamic also inhibits effective sharing of information and tends to polarize risk attitudes. In addition to the case of UBS mentioned in the previous section, consider some of the instances in previous chapters in which groupthink appears.

At Merrill Lynch, CEO Stanley O'Neal was "intolerant of dissent," "quick to take offense," and as a result his executives trembled if they needed to deliver bad news to him, as he was prone to kill the messenger. Notably, O'Neal rarely asked for input when making a decision and did not tolerate being challenged once he had made the decision.

At S&P, the head of RMBSs expressed his strong concern that adopting the strategy called "market insight" would lead the firm to review proposed criteria changes with investors, issuers, and investment bankers. His protests went unanswered, and "market insight" ultimately led S&P to race Moody's to the bottom, fueling the runaway CDO train whose crash destroyed Lehman Brothers and left the global financial system in chaos.

At AIG's financial products division, its head, Joseph Cassano, had the reputation of someone with a crude feel for financial risk but a strong tendency to bully people who challenged him. When the issue of a shift toward taking more subprime mortgage risk eventually made its way onto AIGFP's formal agenda, Cassano pointed to the triple-A ratings from Moody's and S&P, and dismissed any concerns as overblown. Ultimately, AIG required the largest government intervention in the crisis in order to survive.

At MF Global, Treasurer Edith O'Brien inappropriately used $175 million of customers' money to replenish an overdrawn MF Global account at JPMorgan Chase in London. She did so after a conversation with CEO Jon Corzine, a strong authority figure, even knowing it was the wrong thing to do. Groups with strong leaders are vulnerable to groupthink. The MF Global case effectively illustrates how weak risk management culture and weak risk management behaviors trumped the sensible risk management structures that CRO Michael Roseman put in place. In this regard, the board and CEO did not address breaches of risk limits when they were brought to their attention by the CRO, but instead fired the messenger.

At the SEC, deference was a primary factor in the reason the agency failed to investigate the complaint letter submitted by Harry Markopolos, and thereby missed identifying the Ponzi scheme run by Bernard Madoff. The person to whom most of the work in that investigation fell had no prior experience with Ponzi schemes. After the Ponzi scheme came to light, this person explained that she regarded one of her colleagues as an industry expert, and that "I thought that if there were things that jumped out at him as things that didn't make sense, I deferred to his judgment on that point."

At the Federal Reserve Bank of New York, bank examiners feared contradicting their bosses. Deliberations required consensus, which served to water down conclusions. A report, known as the Beim report, recommended that if the New York Fed wanted to improve itself, it needed to hire expert examiners who did not fear voicing their opinions, but were instead encouraged to do so.

The Beim report identifies don'ts, such as examiners fearing to contradict their bosses, and it also identifies the do's, such as explicitly encouraging examiners to voice their opinions. Devil's advocacy is important for mitigating groupthink, but it is only part of the story. Here are additional debiasing tips for dealing with groupthink.

- Develop mechanisms that encourage full participation by every member of the group. If the group is large, use smaller breakout sessions to share ideas prior to exchanges within the whole group.
- Avoid having a single alternative on the table, for which the only choices are yes and no. Instead, make it a priority to generate several plausible alternatives and to examine each in order to identify relative advantages and disadvantages.
- In evaluating alternatives, encourage group members to engage in respectful debate with a view to achieving conflict that is productive and constructive. Designate some member or members to play the role of devil's advocate.
- Bring in an outside view, by inviting experts from outside the group to share their perspectives and insights.
- Ask leaders to refrain from expressing their opinions or ideas until after all group members have had an opportunity to express their opinions.
- Institute clearly defined rules for achieving group decisions.
- Consistently apply those decision rules.

Fannie Mae and JPMorgan Chase: Do's and Don'ts

Aversion to a sure loss is the tendency to be risk seeking, hoping to beat the odds in order to avert a sure loss, thereby risking an even greater loss.

In June 2005, Fannie Mae held a strategic planning meeting, at which its head of single-family lending described two alternatives for facing its loss of market share. The choices were to stay the course and accept the lower market share, or to accept more risk by meeting the market where the market is. Fannie Mae chose to accept more risk, which is behavior consistent with aversion to a sure loss. Ultimately, the risk turned out badly, and Fannie found itself in conservatorship.

Sometimes people do beat the odds in attempting to avert a sure loss. It is just that the odds are not in their favor, and therefore they need to count on being lucky rather than being smart. More often than not, aversion to a sure loss leads people to dig themselves into deeper holes. The London Whale situation at JPMorgan Chase provides an apt illustration. Because the head of the bank's Chief Investment Office was "angry" about taking losses during the first quarter of 2012, the CIO kept on doubling down on its bets as its losses mounted, and mount they certainly did.

The don'ts in these applications are easy to state: don't be risk seeking in an effort to avert a sure loss.

What about do's? Because gains and losses are outcomes measured relative to specific reference points, aversion to a sure loss is a framing issue. This means if a decision-maker were able to reset a reference point so that all outcomes were coded as gains, then he or she would not exhibit risk-seeking behavior. A decision-maker who comes to terms with a loss—some might say, makes peace with a loss—effectively resets the reference point.

One tip for mitigating aversion to a sure loss is to look for ways to reframe the decision task to mask the loss. A technique for doing so involves asking a decision-maker to set aside recent history in their minds, pretend they were replaced by someone new and imagine themselves to be the replacement, but still face the same "gross" outcomes and associated probabilities. Doing so effectively induces them to reframe the task with a different reference point. In the new frame, the decision-maker is asked whether they would choose between a sure gain and a risky alternative instead of the sure loss and risky alternative associated with the original frame. A decision-maker who would choose the sure gain in the reframed task is induced to "not cry over spilled milk" rather than taking a bad bet.

Another tip for mitigating aversion to a sure loss is to establish a contingency plan for reacting to loss. Setting risk limits is an example, but as the JPMorgan Chase application showed us, the contingency plan needs to include living within those limits.

TEPCO, BP, AND RBS: DOS AND DON'TS

Underestimating risk involves setting confidence bands too narrowly, and therefore qualifies as overconfidence about knowledge. However, overconfidence about ability can also lead decision-makers to underestimate risk, because of misperceptions about degree of control. Either way, overconfidence typically contributes to the underestimation of risk.

At TEPCO and across the nuclear power industry in Japan, the Carnegie Foundation report justifiably used the term "supreme overconfidence" to describe attitudes about managing nuclear power risk in Japan.[10] In regard to the plant at Fukushima Daiichi, which was first commissioned in 1971, the report describes the basis of the decision to plan for a tsunami whose maximum amplitude would be no greater than 3.1 meters. The basis was a 1960 earthquake off the coast of Chile that created a tsunami of that height. Afflicted by availability bias, decision-makers paid little or no attention to the historical record featuring evidence from the last seven hundred years of at least 12 tsunamis whose maximum amplitudes were more than 10 meters. Of these, six had maximum amplitudes that exceeded 20 meters.

In a similar vein, the Headquarters for Earthquake Research Promotion, which is funded by the Japanese government, attached 99% confidence to an earthquake magnitude not exceeding 7.5, whereas the magnitude of the March 11, 2011, earthquake was 9.0. Likewise, Japan's Nuclear Safety Commission established a blackout policy with a worst-case assumption of loss of AC electric power for at most 30 minutes before reconnection to the grid. The operators at Fukushima Daiichi were totally unprepared for a long-term loss of power that resulted in a nuclear meltdown.

At BP, a year before the explosion of Deepwater Horizon, BP's head of E&P said of the company's expertise in working in the most challenging of deepwater fields, "We don't do simple things. We are prepared to work at the frontier, and manage the risks." Just a month before the explosion, a JPMorgan analyst report described BP's leadership team, which included Inglis, as "confident, realistic and determined." In my opinion, BP's leadership was not only confident but overconfident about its ability to handle operational risk.

Overconfidence appears to have been a feature of BP's culture. In this regard, a safety specialist who assisted the panel appointed by BP to investigate the company's refineries after Texas City explosion, described BP's management in the following terms: "They were very arrogant and proud and in denial. It is possible they were fooled by their success."

At RBS, the CEO who was hired to deal with the aftermath of the fallout from the acquisition of ABN AMRO described the purchase as "the wrong price, the wrong way to pay, at the wrong time and the wrong deal." Notably, RBS and its consortium partners lacked access to information that would have enabled them to determine the quality of the assets in ABN AMRO's structured credit portfolios, the valuation of those positions, and whether there were any significant deficiencies in its key risk management practices. Yet, the RBS Board requested and received assurance from the firm's executives that for the majority of due diligence work teams, there were "no show stoppers." In my opinion, given the paucity of information available to the due diligence team, the "no show stoppers" judgment reflects overconfidence about the risk of proceeding.

It is easy to say, "Don't be overconfident" of firms such as TEPCO, BP, and RBS. However, not being overconfident is easier said than done. When it comes to difficult tasks and major challenges, the psychological research finds ubiquitous evidence of overconfidence that is resistant to debiasing.

A complicating factor in mitigating overconfidence is that the phenomenon has many drivers. In this regard, three are especially important for risk management, all of which are discussed in the beginning chapters of the book. The first is perceived control, especially when technology is involved: just as with excessive optimism, decision-makers who perceive themselves to be in a situation in which they have a high degree of control are prone to be overconfident. The second is inadequate planning, which renders decision-makers vulnerable to availability bias, as we saw with TEPCO.[11] The third is the bias associated with anchoring and adjustment: setting confidence intervals by first establishing an expected value before adjusting to generate the interval boundaries tends to produce confidence intervals that are unduly narrow.

There are debiasing tips for addressing some aspects of overconfidence, such as asking people for their 99% confidence intervals when the objective is to secure 80% confidence intervals. A second tip is to incorporate safety factors, along the lines of what civil engineers do. In an insightful paper about debiasing through cognitive repair techniques, Chip Heath, Richard Larrick, and Joshua Klayman explain how engineers adjust for overconfidence in their decisions as opposed to their judgments. Essentially, civil engineers proceed in two steps. First, they use quantitative techniques to arrive at precise answers to engineering questions. Second, they add a tolerance to their estimates by multiplying by a safety factor, which is usually in the range of three to eight.[12] When tested for overconfidence, civil engineers turn out to be as overconfident as the rest of us, but they adjust for that overconfidence in their decisions, where it counts.

Notably, some of the most effective debiasing tips for mitigating overconfidence in organizations are similar to those for mitigating excessive optimism. One of the most important is to provide an outside view that complements the inside view. Organizations with effective "networked governance structures" tend to do this automatically, and if done effectively, the outside view places issues relating to perceived control, adequacy of planning, and anchoring bias into historical perspective.

The Financial Instability Hypothesis: Dos and Don'ts

The global financial crisis provides a vivid illustration of the financial instability hypothesis (FIH). The dos and don'ts pertain to the FIH components, and are challenging to implement in practice, because the dos and don'ts get flipped: people do the don'ts, but not the dos.

Among the don'ts are the following: don't take on excessive leverage, as did subprime borrowers and banks such as RBS; don't let a rise in euphoria induce financial innovation by shadow financial institutions, reflecting a shift toward speculative and Ponzi finance, which fuel asset bubbles, as happened with Merrill Lynch; don't allow regulators to justify weak regulation because of new era thinking, as happened with the Fed; and don't allow the failure of firms that are too large to fail, as happened with Lehman Brothers.

Among the dos are the following: for central banks, attach the same level of importance to financial regulation as to monetary policy, and use monetary stimulus to mitigate rising unemployment while being mindful of the implications for inflation. Among the dos for government officials are to use enough fiscal stimulus to offset declining aggregate demand in an effort to mitigate rising unemployment. In the United States, these were dos that were largely honored in the breach, and for some, such as former Fed chair Ben Bernanke, included the most important lessons learned from the global financial crisis.

Although most of the discussion about the FIH has concentrated on the United States, a discussion can be found in Appendix I of how the FIH applies to the economies of China and Europe in the wake of the global financial crisis.

Closing Remarks

By its nature, making judgments and decisions about risk involves psychology. From the figurative near meltdown of the global financial system in 2008 to the real meltdown at Fukushima Daiichi in 2011, the most dramatic adverse events after 2000 involve imperfections in human psychology. Although economic downturns and tsunamis are inevitable, there is good reason to believe that effective risk management would have kept us away from the brink of meltdown.

This book seeks to improve the practice of risk management by helping risk managers develop psychological skills to complement their quantitative skills. Instituting tips for debiasing that build on the understanding and recognition of psychological pitfalls can make risk management better. This is a realistic expectation. At the same time, expecting that doing so will eliminate vulnerability to psychological pitfalls is unrealistic. This book documents major risk management failures that occurred, mostly after 2000, and there is every reason to believe that serious risk management failures will continue to happen.

For risk managers, the challenge is not to let the perfect become the enemy of the good, and therefore to implement debiasing techniques that reduce the frequency with which risk management failures occur. My advice to organizational leaders is to think long term by developing strong organizational cultures, with associated risk management processes and behaviors.

Many debiasing techniques can also be implemented on an incremental, continuous improvement basis. One cautionary note I would add about the incremental approach is the importance of understanding that some psychological biases offset others. For example, loss aversion typically works in the opposite direction to excessive optimism. These two biases might balance out in a way that produces reasonable behavior. If so, correcting for only one bias might make things worse, not better. This is something to be mindful about.

If the world were simpler, or our capacity for decision-making better, we would not have to rely on heuristics to make judgments and choices. But the world is complex and our capabilities for making rational judgments and choices are bounded. For the most part, we will rely on heuristics, which by their nature will leave us vulnerable to bias. As in the discussion about fast and frugal trees for microprudential regulation, our challenge is to find heuristics that are sensible. We can overdo the effort to address the complexity we confront, and thereby make matters worse, not better.

Risk limits are part of a heuristic arsenal. If properly set, they can provide protection against impulses to take imprudent risk. However, risk limits are no panacea, as we saw in the JPMorgan Chase London whale case, in which such limits were honored in the breach.

Risk styles play a role in decisions about governance. Incentives are not exogenous choices, but are consciously put in place. As the cases involving MF Global, Merrill Lynch, and Freddie Mac illustrated, maximizer CEOs not wishing to be restrained by risk managers who are conservators or pragmatists, can fire their CROs, and maximizer board members might well support these terminations.

There will always be situations in which the risk styles and judgments of CEOs clash with those of CROs. Sometimes, the clash will result in compromise, and sometimes not. My hope is that adding the psychological perspective to everyone's risk management toolkit will increase the rate at which wisdom prevails.

Appendix A: A Deeper Dive into SP/A Theory

For the benefit of readers interested in a deeper discussion of Lola Lopes's SP/A framework, this Appendix discusses several topics. The most important of these is a discussion about the mathematical structure of Lopes's formal model. The model is contrasted with a heuristic approach known as "the priority heuristic," which is simpler in its informational requirements and implementation. The priority heuristic conforms to what is known as a "fast and frugal" heuristic.

The Appendix also extends the discussion to include two different types of risky alternatives. One risk involves a uniform probability distribution, and the other involves a bimodal probability distribution. Uniform probabilities are typically associated with positions in securities that are very poorly understood, but have covered call features. The second risk involves bimodality, meaning that the probability density function has a "barbell" property, with the most likely outcomes being extreme, either very unfavorable or very favorable. Positions that are bets on discrete events tend to feature this payoff pattern: either the bet pays off well because an idea "works" or the bet pays little because the idea "does not work." The next section describes the full range of alternatives that Lopes used in her experiments.

Six Risky Alternatives

Lopes used six different probability density functions in her experiments, the shapes of which are illustrated in Figure A.1. In order they are the Risk Floor (RF), Peaked (PK), Short Shot (SS), Uniform (U), Bimodal (BM), and Long Shot (LS).

The shapes depicted in Figure A.1 are probability density functions (pdfs). The horizontal axis displays possible payoffs, and the height of a bar indicates the probability with which the particular payoff will occur. For example, Figure A.1 indicates that for RF, the probability associated with a payoff of $770 is 31%. As you can easily see, RF and PK in Figure A.1 are simply scaled-down versions of RF and PK that are displayed in Figure 2.1.

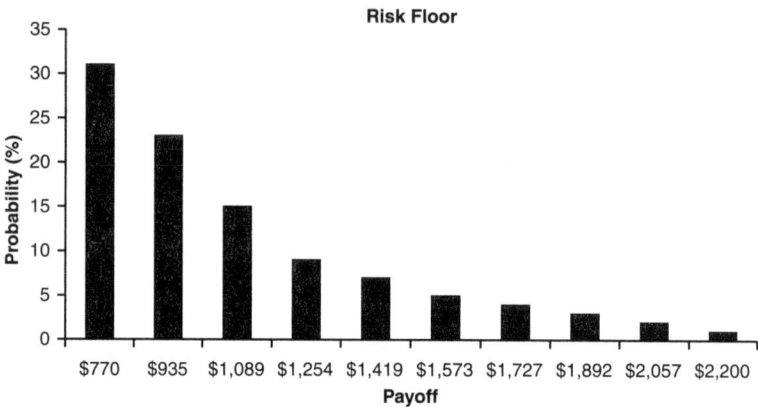
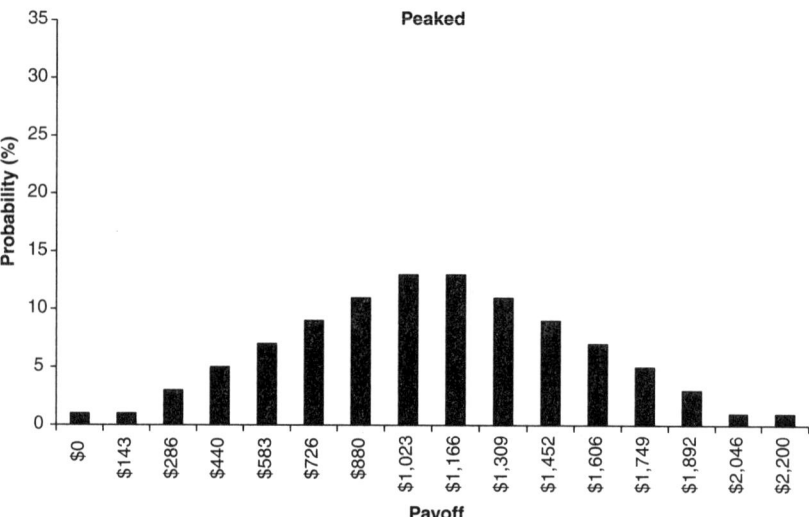
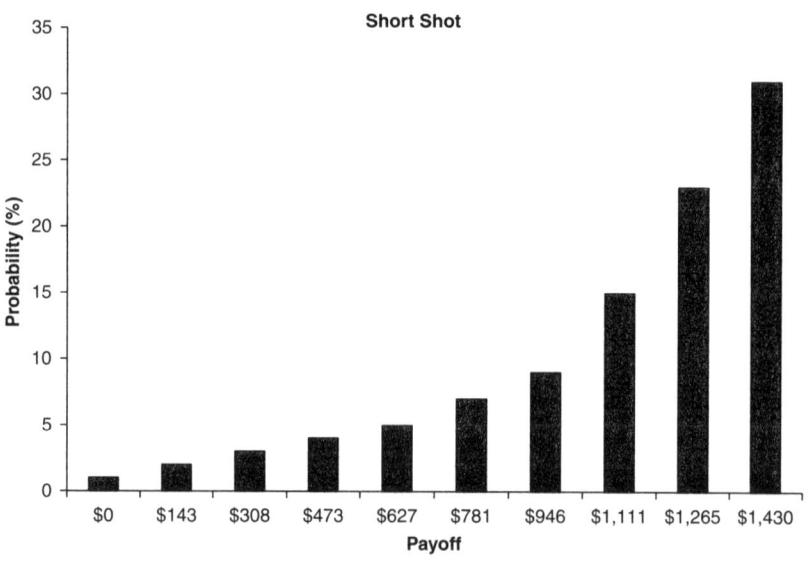

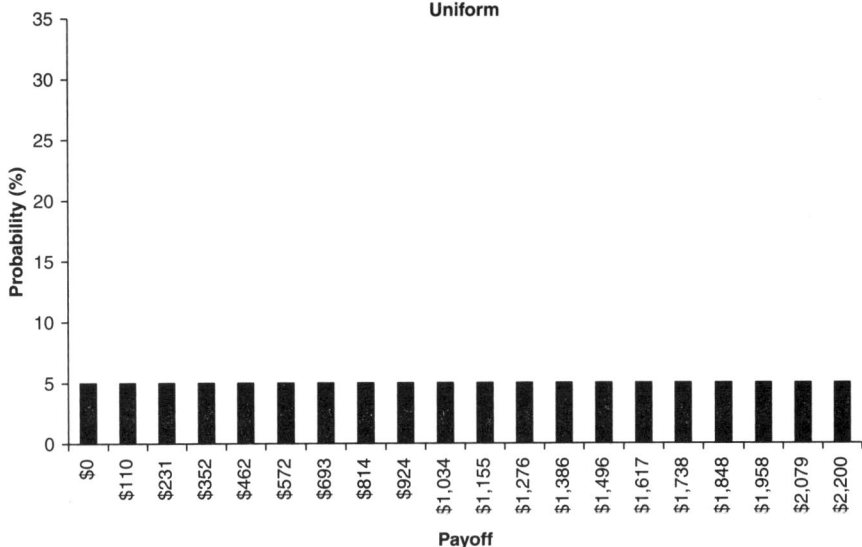

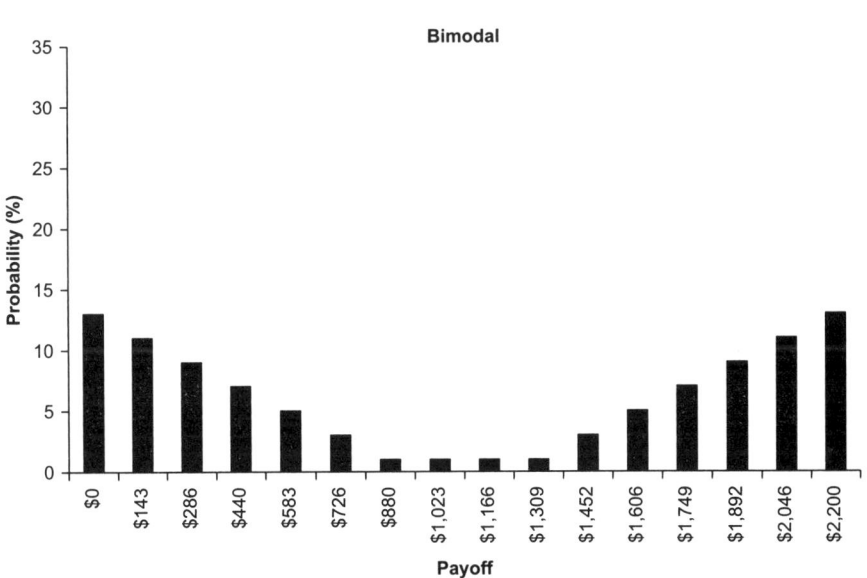

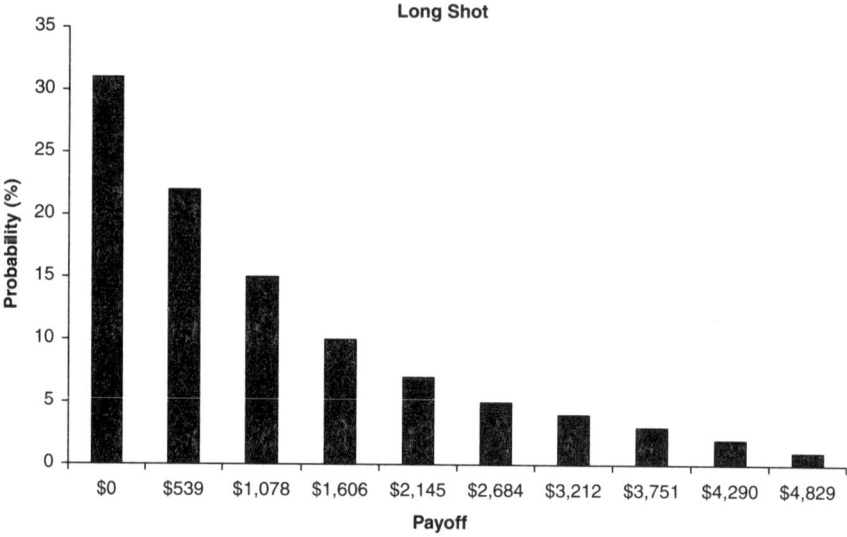

Figure A.1 This figure displays the shapes of the six probability density functions (pdfs) Lopes used in her experiments. The pdfs are respectively labelled Risk Floor (RF), Peaked (PK), Short Shot (SS), Uniform (U), Bimodal (BM), and Long Shot (LS).

Table A.1 Payoff means and standard deviations for the six Lopes risky alternatives

	Mean	**Stdev**
Risk Floor	$1,097	$354
Short Shot	$1,103	$354
Peaked	$1,093	$442
Uniform	$1,097	$666
Bimodal	$1,095	$851
Long Shot	$1,100	$1,185

Table A.1 provides payoff means and standard deviations for the six alternatives, with lower standard deviations closer to the top.

In her experiments, Lopes asked her subjects to rank order all possible pairs of alternatives, through the use of pairwise comparisons. In doing so, she found that RF most frequently emerged as the most-favored choice, and LS most frequently emerged as the least-favored top choice. She reports that the order of attractiveness is RF, PK, SS, U, BM, and LS. For completeness, I should mention that Lopes used lower stakes than those displayed in Figure A.1, with displayed payoffs ranging between $0 and $348.

In my own research, I have used experiments based on the six Lopes alternatives displayed in Figure A.1. My sample size was 315, and included risk managers, portfolio managers, business executives, PhD students in finance and economics, and undergraduate finance majors. Beth and Larry from

Chapter 2, as real people now, participated as subjects, and their responses in the short story are the identical responses they provided as subjects in the experiment.

BASICS OF HOW LOPES'S MODEL WORKS

This section describes the general features of how Lopes structured her model, along with a description of how the model can be implemented.[1] The discussion below explains how SP/A theory would capture how someone like Larry might rank PK over RF. The explanation proceeds in steps, where we imagine Larry's thought process to be as follows. In the first step, Larry examines the expected payoffs for both alternatives, which happen to be $1.1 billion.

In the second step, Larry considers the range of outcomes from both alternatives and asks himself how much he fears the occurrence of outcomes that he regards as unfavorable but possible. He then expresses his fear by being pessimistic and allowing his mind to increase the probabilities of unfavorable outcomes relative to favorable outcomes. In doing so, he scales up the probabilities of very unfavorable events and scales down the probabilities of very favorable events. The result of his emotional rescaling will be to reduce the expected payoffs from the two alternatives. The more he fears an outcome, the higher he rescales the probability of that outcome. The more fear he feels, the lower the rescaled-expected payoff. Notably, this property underlies the risk neutral probability approach used to price options and other securities.

In the third step, Larry considers the range of outcomes from both alternatives and asks himself how much hope he attaches to outcomes that he regards as favorable (and, of course, possible). He then expresses his hope by being optimistic and allowing his mind to increase the probabilities of favorable outcomes, arrived at in the second step above, relative to unfavorable outcomes. He makes the adjustment by multiplying the probabilities of extremely favorable events by a factor greater than unity, while simultaneously multiplying some other probabilities by a factor less than unity. In doing so, he increases the expected payoffs for the alternatives, from his step two computations. The more he hopes for an outcome, the more his mind increases the probability attached to that outcome. The more hope he feels, the higher the recomputed expected payoffs. In this regard, Lopes calls the net recomputed expected payoff "*SP*" because it reflects the relative needs for security and potential.

In the fourth step, Larry considers whether there is some specific outcome that he would label as "borderline successful," so that he regards all outcomes at least as good as borderline successful to qualify as "success." He then ascertains the success probabilities for both risky alternatives based on the original values before adjustment in steps 1 and 2. Lopes uses the symbol "*A*" (for aspiration) to denote success probability.

In the fifth step, Larry boils down his choice between the two alternatives by comparing their *SP*-recomputed expected payoffs and the *A* success probabilities. If one alternative has both a higher *SP* and a higher success probability *A*, then Larry's choice is easy because he values higher values of both. However, there will be some situations in which Larry will have to consider trading a lower success probability *A* for a higher *SP*-recomputed expected payoff. In such situations, Larry's choice will depend on how strong his need for success is relative to his needs for security and potential.

As we saw in the previous section, Larry attaches a very high weight to chance of success, which would incline him to rank PK over RF, unless RF offered so much more *SP* than PK that it would tip the balance. Beth, who is less ambitious than Larry, places more weight on *SP* relative to *A*. Therefore, even if she were similar to Larry in respect to fear and hope, she would be more inclined to rank RF over PK.

SP/A THEORY: MATHEMATICAL STRUCTURE

This section presents the formal structure of SP/A theory. Consider one of the risky alternatives, such as PK, whose pdf is portrayed in Figure A.1. Let x denote a random payoff and $p(x)$ the probability with which this payoff will occur under PK. PK is a discrete random variable, and the set of payoffs (x) having positive probability ($p(x)$) is finite. The decumulative probability $D(y)$ is the probability under PK that the payoff will exceed y. That is, $D(y) = \Sigma p(x)$, where the summation is over $x \geq y$. In order to recover p from D, rank order the outcomes x as $x_1, x_2, \ldots, x_n$, where $x_i < x_n$, $p(x_i) > 0$ and $\Sigma p(x_i) = 1$, where the summation is from $i = 1$ to n. Then $p(x_i) = D(x_i) - D(x_{i+1})$. Figure A.2 illustrates the functions $p(x)$ and $D(x)$.

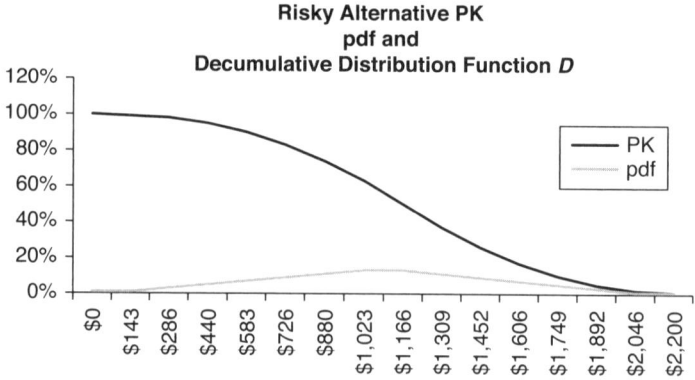

Figure A.2 This figure displays an illustrative pdf function $p(x)$ and its associated decumulative distribution function $D(x)$.

Think about how a person who is fearful might react to the information conveyed by D in Figure A.2. Fear tends to make people act as if they are pessimistic, and a pessimistic person would be inclined to treat the probability $D(y)$ as if it were lower for any $y>0$ than is actually the case. That is, a pessimist acts as if they believe that the probability $D(y)$ that the payoff will be y or better, for $y>0$, is lower than is actually the case.

Hope operates in the opposite direction. Hope tends to make people act as if they are optimistic. An optimist acts as if they believe that the probability $D(y)$ that the payoff will be y or better, for $y>0$, is higher than is actually the case.

A person who is cautiously hopeful is fearful about highly unfavorable events but hopeful about highly favorable events. Such a person treats the probability $D(y)$ as if it were lower than is actually the case, when y is highly unfavorable, and the person treats the probability $D(y)$ as if it were higher than is actually the case, when y is highly favorable.

The expected payoff $E(x)$ under this pdf is simply given by $E(x) = \Sigma p(x) x$, where the summation is over all x for which $p(x)>0$. Increased fear unambiguously reduces the expected value of x, while increased hope unambiguously increases it.

Lopes uses a simple power function $h_s(D) = D^{s+1}$ to model how fear operates on a decumulative function D, where $s \geq 0$. The case $s = 0$ denotes fear having no impact on risk. Notice that $h_s(0) = 0$, $h_s(1) = 1$, and h_s is convex between 0 and 1. Therefore $h_s(D(x)) < D(x)$ for all $0<D(x)<1$, which is the property of pessimism described above.

Lopes uses a simple power function $h_p(D) = 1-(1-D)^{p+1}$ to model how potential operates on a decumulative function D, where $p \geq 0$. The case $p = 0$ denotes hope having no impact on risk. Notice that $h_p(0) = 0$, $h_p(1) = 1$, and h_p is concave between 0 and 1. Therefore $h_p(D(x)) > D(x)$ for all $0<D(x)<1$, which is the property of optimism described above.

To model cautious hope, Lopes uses the convex combination $h(D) = rh_s(D) + (1-r)h_p(D)$, where r lies between 0 and 1. Notice that $h(0) = 0$, $h(1) = 1$, but h_p might not be uniformly convex or concave for D between 0 and 1.

Figure A.3 illustrates the functions h_s, h_p, and h. Figure A.4 illustrates how fear operates on PK, displaying the original pdf and D functions, as well as their transformations under an h function that portrays cautious hope.

SP is the expected value of x under the transformed decumulative function $h(D)$. For the case in which $s = 1$, $p = 10$, and $r = 0.9$, the value of SP for PK is $938, considerably less than $E(x)$, which is $1,100. The selection of r close to 1.0 reflects fear being much stronger than hope as an emotion. As a result, the person evaluates risks pessimistically by overweighing the probabilities of lower payoffs relative to the probabilities of higher payoffs. This is why the value of SP for PK is lower than its expected payoff. With r close to 1.0, the $h(D)$ function is dominated by the $h_s(D)$-function displayed in Figure A.4.

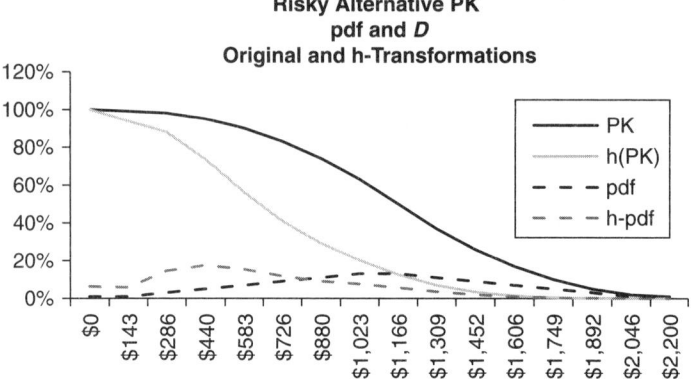

Figure A.3 This figure illustrates how fear operates on PK, displaying the original pdf and D functions, as well as their transformations under an h function that portrays cautious hope.

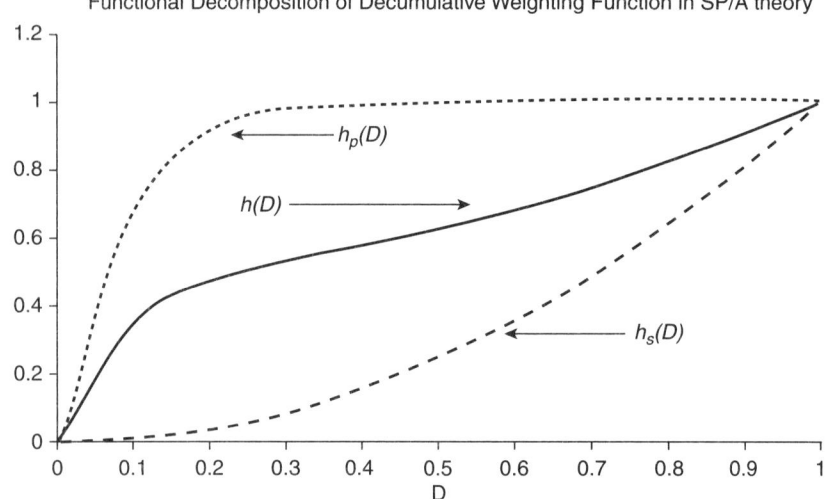

Figure A.4 This figure illustrates the functions h_s, h_p, and h.

For an aspiration level of $1,000, $A = 0.63$, meaning that PK provides the probability of receiving a payoff of $1,000 or more to be 63%. This is the actual probability, not the probability under the transformation induced by $h(D)$. In SP/A theory, fear mimics pessimism and hope mimics optimism, but only expressed through the computation of SP. SP/A theory does not hold that people are excessively optimistic or pessimistic, which is why they use the correct value for A.

In SP/A theory, each risky alternative is evaluated using a criterion function $L(SP,A)$. A particularly simple form for L is $L = SP + \zeta A$, where $\zeta \geq 0$. For this example, take $\zeta = 900$. Then $L(PK) = 938 + (900 \times 0.63) = 1,505$.

If we repeat the procedure for RF, then we would find that its *SP* value would be $998, with $L(RF) = 1,412$. Accordingly, $L(PK) > L(RF)$, which implies that PK ranks more highly than RF.

THE PRIORITY HEURISTIC

There are situations in which the complexity of the decision task becomes overwhelming. In such situations, people often resort to simple rules known as heuristics. A pertinent example is the *priority heuristic* developed by Eduard Brandstätter, Gerd Gigerenzer, and Ralph Hertwig. This heuristic provides two fairly simple rules to help a decision-maker choose among two competing risky alternatives.[2]

In cases such as this, simplicity involves oversimplification and therefore some degree of imperfection. The oversimplification associated with the priority heuristic is that only the worst and best outcomes are considered, the ones that trigger the greatest fear and hope. Moreover, the same rule applies to everyone, regardless of which emotional pole is stronger, fear or hope. In this respect, the priority heuristic is built to mimic someone who is average in respect to the relative strength of emotions, someone in the middle of the pack in respect to needs for security, potential, and aspiration. Therefore, in its strict form, the priority heuristic would not explain why Larry and Beth have opposite rankings for RF and PK.

Structurally, the priority heuristic conforms to the idea of "satisficing," which was Herbert Simon's term for deciding when an alternative being examined is good enough. The priority heuristic establishes particular criteria for deciding when choosing the safer of two alternatives is good enough. These criteria involve artificial decision thresholds for particular differences, together with a set of two tests that compare actual differences against thresholds. The tests are intended to provide one good reason for the decision-maker to choose the safer alternative.

To illustrate the priority heuristic, consider how a decision-maker would use this heuristic to choose between RF and PK for the values used in the student version of the Lopes experiment. The first test involves the difference in minimum gains possible. This test makes the safer alternative (RF) the "recommended" candidate for being selected, and then assesses whether the upside in the riskier alternative (PK) is high enough to merit taking the risk. Here the criterion for "safer" is having the higher of the two "worst possible outcomes."

Formally, for RF the minimum possible gain is $770, and for PK the minimum possible gain is $0. Therefore, the difference in minimum gains is $770. The associated decision threshold is set at 10% of the maximum gain possible (in the riskier alternative), which in this case is $220 = 0.1 \times $2,200$.

Here 10% is selected to represent a difference of one order of magnitude, based on the cultural number system being base 10. If the amount by which the difference in minimum gains (viewed as an advantage of RF over PK) is large enough, meaning greater or equal to $220, then the priority heuristic would specify RF as the choice. As the difference in minimum gains is $770, which exceeds the threshold of $220, the priority heuristic provides one good reason to choose RF over PK, and stipulates doing so.

The priority heuristic is simple and straightforward, and frugal in the information it requires about RF and PK. Because it seeks one good reason to be safe, the ranking it delivers for RF and PK coincides with Beth's assessment, but not Larry's. This is not to say that the heuristic is useless, only that it provides a useful way to think about what people focus on when dealing with complex choices about risk.

To consider a more complicated comparison, apply the priority heuristic to choose between SS and PK. This will be a bit more involved than choosing between RF and PK. For the comparison, I need to mention that Lopes constructed SS to feature a minimum possible gain of $0 with the same probability as PK (1%), as well as the same expected payoff of $1,100. In addition, she constructed SS to have the same payoff standard deviation as RF. However, the maximum gain in SS is only $1,430, which is lower than the maximum gain of $2,200 for both RF and PK.

For SS, the minimum possible gain is $0, and for PK the minimum possible gain is also $0. Therefore the difference in minimum gains is $0. Technically, neither of the two is safer according to the minimum payoff, although SS has the lower range as well as standard deviation. The associated decision threshold is set at 10% of the maximum gain possible (in the riskier alternative), which in this case is $220 = 0.1 × $2,200. If the amount by which the difference in minimum gains (viewed as an advantage of SS over PK) is large enough, meaning greater or equal to $220, then the priority heuristic would specify SS as the choice. However, the difference in minimum gains is $0, which is less than the threshold of $220. Therefore, unlike the situation involving RF and PK, the priority heuristic specifies going on to a second test.

The second test involves probabilities attached to minimum gains, and computes the difference in those probabilities (SS minus PK). The associated aspiration threshold is simply 10%, reflecting a required order of magnitude difference. Because the probability of a $0 payoff is 1% for both alternatives, the minimum probability difference is 0. The test asks whether there is enough of a probability advantage to the safer alternative (SS) to merit its selection. Because the minimum probability difference is less than the decision threshold of 10%, the answer is no.

The priority heuristic seeks two possible reasons to choose RF over PK, and two possible reasons to choose SS over PK. It comes up with a good reason to choose RF, but not SS. As it happens, in Lopes's original experiments, more people chose RF over PK than the reverse, and more chose PK over SS than the reverse. It is in this sense that I describe the priority heuristic as generating the risk choice of someone in the middle of the pack.

If you want a bit of practice with the priority heuristic, have a go at using it to rank RF and LS. In this respect, Lopes structured LS to feature a minimum gain of $0, which occurs with probability 31%, and a maximum gain of $4,829, which occurs with a probability of 1%.

The Relative Importance of Aspiration

Subjects' comments suggest that people are quite thoughtful in how they rank order risky alternatives, and that they make use of more information than what is required to implement the priority heuristic. In particular, they pay special attention to aspiration. As an example, consider the comments of an undergraduate finance major who ranked PK over RF. This subject tells us, "Peaked appears to be the most appealing to me because it holds the largest probability that I will earn about a $1,000 and my odds are for making close to that." Notably, this subject set an explicit aspiration level of $1,000, and the rationale he offers for favoring PK is very close to the explanation that Larry provided to Beth in the short story.

In general, the findings from my studies using Lopes-type experiments are similar to the findings that Lopes reports. The one notable exception is that SS ranks much more highly in my studies than in the original Lopes studies. Lopes finds that SS ranks third, below RF and PK. In my studies, SS usually ranks at the top, if not close to the top. I have found that this pattern applies equally across all my groups (risk managers, portfolio managers, undergraduate finance majors, etc.).

For someone with an aspiration to receive at least $1,100 from the six alternatives, SS offers the highest probability of doing so. As can be seen from Figure A.5 PK, U, and BM offer a 50% probability of doing so, and LS offers a 32% probability of doing so. Of course, PK offers more upside potential than SS. Looking at Figure A.1, we can see that the maximum payoff for SS is $1,430, which is less than the $2,200 associated with PK and indeed all the other alternatives. Someone with a goal of receiving anything more than $1,430 would face a 26% probability of doing so by choosing PK. Coming back to Larry, in ranking PK over SS, Larry was acting as if his aspiration is to receive much more than $1,100 from taking the risk!

The responses of experimental subjects to survey questions about fear, hope, and aspiration paint a picture of how their emotional profiles impact their risk choices for the six Lopes alternatives. The general picture that emerges from studies involving undergraduate finance majors is that relatively high scores for

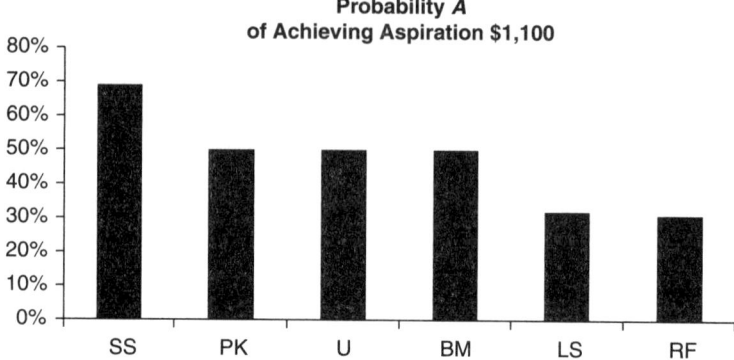

Figure A.5 This figure displays the probability of achieving at least $1,100 from each of the six alternatives SS, PK, U, BM, LS, RF.

fear are associated with the top ranking for the RF. High scores for cautious hope and being willing to trade downside exposure to reach a high goal are associated with the top ranking for PK. Low fear is associated with a top ranking for LS. Middle level scores for fear, hope, cautious hope, and aspiration are associated with the top ranking for SS. Top rankings for U and BM are rare.

INSIGHTS FROM COMMENTS ABOUT THE IMPACT OF ASPIRATION ON VALUATION

Aspiration also enters into thought processes involving valuation. Consider the remarks of an undergraduate finance major named Pamela. Her ranking from top to bottom is LS, RF, SS, PK, U, and BM. Pamela explains her top ranking for the LS is because it is "more right-skewed." Figure A.6 displays Pamela's valuations. Like Jeff, the student discussed in Chapter 2, Pamela's valuations are all in increments of $100, suggesting that she too uses a crude heuristic to adjust her valuations for risk.

Pamela makes the following comments about her thought process in arriving at WTA and WTP:

> I chose the mean values as minimum selling prices because anything below the mean would mean that the probability of gaining above that value is greater than 50% and that means it would be more likely than not that I gain a higher value.
>
> I chose the mean value as the base for the lowest variable funds and then decreased the max pay amount by $100 for each fund that increased in variance because I would pay less for the added risk associated with these funds.

Pamela makes clear that she targeted the mean payoff as the basis for determining the selling price of the safest fund, and also what heuristic she used to determine WTP for the other funds.

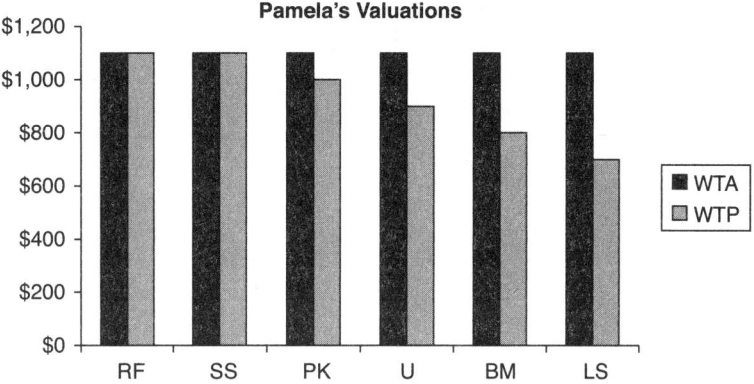

Figure A.6 This figure displays the valuations of a subject Pamela who was in the same group of undergraduates as Jeff discussed in Chapter 2.

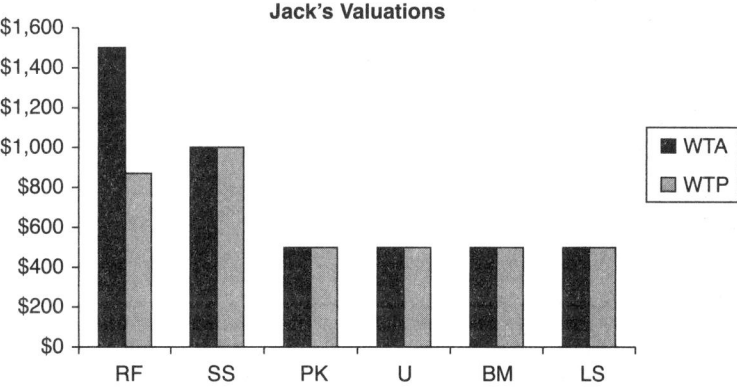

Figure A.7 This figure displays the valuations of a subject Jack who was in the same group of undergraduates as Jeff discussed in Chapter 2.

Finally, here are the considered comments of Jack, a student who was aware that paying his WTP to play involves facing the need to break even. Jack's ranking from top to bottom was RF, SS, PK, U, BM, and LS. Figure A.7 displays his valuations. The following comments describe how he came up with his judgments:

> My WTA values: I would not sell Risk Floor if I did have the option, but if I had to, I would sell it for $1,500 at the least. I think this is a great fund since it 100% ensures a payoff greater than $770, and do not want to give it up but will give it up if the buyer is willing to put up that much money (they probably would not).

Short Shot—I would be willing to sell this fund for $1,000 since I have an ensured gain (versus a 30% chance of any gain lower) and the buyer has a 70% chance to earn their payment back and more.

I would sell Peaked, Uniform, Bimodal, and Long Shot for at least $500 to ensure this much of a gain (versus a 20%, 50%, 50%, or 30% chance respectively of earning anything lower), and the buyer still has a great chance (50%, 50%, 50%, and 70%) to double back their payment back (and the buyer may be more inclined to take my sell with these odds!).

My WTP values: Risk Floor—I would be willing to pay $870, since it leaves a gain for the seller, but I still have about a 68% chance of earning back my payment.

Short Shot—I would be willing to buy this fund for $1,000 since I have a 70% chance to earn my payment back and more.

I would buy Peaked, Uniform, Bimodal, and Long Shot for at least $500 to ensure this much of a gain since I would have a chance 50%, 50%, 50%, and 70% to double my payment back."

The varied comments of undergraduate finance majors provide great insight into people's intuition for arriving at WTA and WTP valuations. Intuition appears to be a lot more complicated than discounting expected payoff at the required return. Risk managers will be much more able to be effective by understanding the varied ways in which people arrive at valuations, including themselves.

The choices, valuations, and comments of Bill, a project manager, offer a striking contrast to Tom, who was discussed in Chapter 2. Bill ranks alternatives by standard deviation, but with his top rank going to the LS, and his bottom rank going to the RF. His WTA evaluations are similarly ordered, as are his WTP-valuations, and Bill does not exhibit preference reversal.

Bill's valuations are displayed in Figure A.8. His WTA for LS is $2,100, and his WTA for RF is $1,150. His WTP valuations are all clustered in a $5 range between $1,098 and $1,103. He explained his thought process as follows:

"Rankings: My rankings were based on high variance or standard deviation in order to increase the chance of getting a higher payoff.

WTA: I want a WTA of more than the mean and depending on the upside risk.

WTP: I only want to spend money around the mean and more for the funds with a higher upside potential."

Considered from the perspective of SP/A theory, Bill's remarks suggest that he is high in the emotion of hope and therefore has a strong associated need for potential. Nevertheless, the clustering of his WTP valuations around the mean of $1,100 suggests either that the emotion of hope is not strong or that it is just counterbalanced by fear. Bill's comments make no obvious

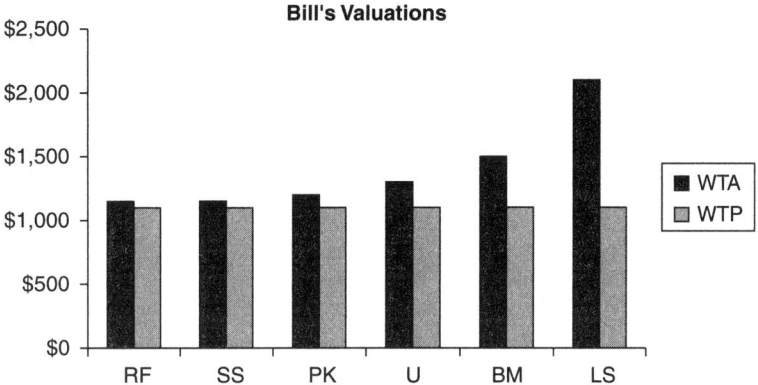

Figure A.8 This figure displays the valuations of Bill who was in the same group of managers as Tom discussed in Chapter 2.

reference to a specific aspiration level. Nevertheless, according to the theory developed below, aspiration is necessary to generate WTA/WTP ratios that differ from unity.

Behavior and comments such as these tell us that theory can be a useful guide to interpreting what people do and say. However, theory is no panacea. We need to be cautious and judicious in applying it to the judgments made by specific individuals. As Karim, a software quality consultant who participated in the experiment, remarked, "My responses to the questions were based on the probabilities shown in the graphs and described in the tasks, and sometimes were quite instinctive and not really logical."

One area in which most people's instincts appear to be at odds with logic involves the gap between the WTP price they say they are willing to pay to accept a risk, and the associated expected return they stipulate that they require in order to accept the risk. Differences between the expected return implied by WTP, the indirect measure, is typically quite different from the required expected return that is directly elicited.

For the group that included Beth and Larry, median differences between these two rates of return differed by between –6% and 5% for the four least-risky alternatives. The median differences for BM and LS were 31% and 71% respectively. For undergraduate finance majors, the median differences lay in this range across all six risks. For business people who do not include risk managers, the median differences are only small for SS and PK. Otherwise, they exceed 15%. Notably, mean differences are much larger in absolute value than their median counterparts, and standard deviations are enormous (well over 100%, with the possible exception of RF). These differences tell us that people engage in different thought processes for price than they do for expected returns. This is the nature of being "instinctive and not really logical."

GENERAL PATTERNS IN THE DATA

Table A.2 summarizes medians, means, standard deviations, and coefficients of variation for the responses of 315 subjects to questions discussed in Chapter 2 pertaining to ranking, valuation, and portfolio allocations in respect to the Lopes risk alternatives. Figures A.9 and A.10 display means graphically, with the series for ratings scaled down by one-tenth. The subjects are a mix of portfolio managers, analysts, risk managers, business professionals, PhD students studying finance, and undergraduate finance majors.

The median and mean rankings indicate that SS received the top aggregate ranking, followed by the RF, PK, U, BM, and LS. LS had the lowest aggregate rating, with a mean rating of 5.0 and a rock bottom median rating of 6.

Table A.2 Medians, means, standard deviations, and coefficients of variation for the responses of 315 subjects to questions pertaining to ranking, valuation, and portfolio allocations in respect to the Lopes risky alternatives

Ranking	Median	Mean	Standard Deviation	Coefficient of Variation
Risk floor	2	2.7	1.7	0.6
Short shot	2	2.1	1.4	0.6
Peaked	3	2.8	1.2	0.4
Uniform	4	3.7	1.2	0.3
Bimodal	5	4.3	1.4	0.3
Long shot	6	5.0	1.7	0.3
WTA				
Risk floor	1,100	1,194	541	0.5
Short shot	1,100	1,228	637	0.5
Peaked	1,100	1,189	633	0.5
Uniform	1,100	1,199	747	0.6
Bimodal	1,100	1,205	821	0.7
Long shot	1,078	1,313	1,428	1.1
Allocation				
Risk floor	25.0%	27.5%	21.3%	0.8
Short shot	25.0%	28.2%	21.3%	0.8
Peaked	15.0%	16.5%	14.8%	0.9
Uniform	10.0%	9.6%	9.8%	1.0
Bimodal	7.0%	8.2%	8.3%	1.0
Long shot	5.0%	9.9%	13.3%	1.3
WTP				
Risk floor	1,000	1,023	600	0.6
Short shot	1,000	1,029	736	0.7
Peaked	1,000	950	544	0.6
Uniform	968	929	733	0.8
Bimodal	900	901	906	1.0
Long shot	819	898	1,176	1.3

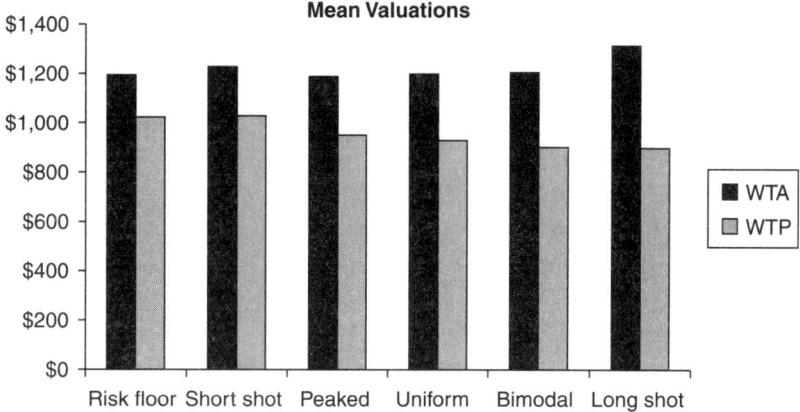

Figure A.9 This figure displays group mean valuations for WTA and WTP, for the six risky alternatives (RF, SS, PK, U, BM, LS) for a population consisting of subjects who are a mix of portfolio managers, analysts, risk managers, business professionals, and PhD students studying finance, and undergraduate finance majors.

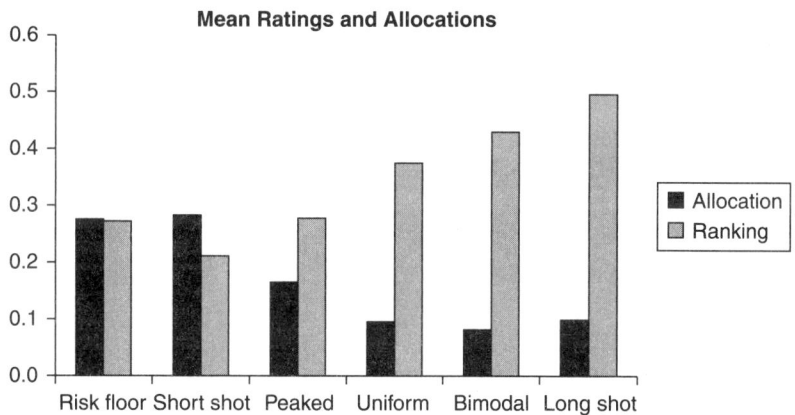

Figure A.10 This figure displays allocations and ratings scaled down by one-tenth, for the six risky alternatives (RF, SS, PK, U, BM, LS) for a population consisting of subjects who are a mix of portfolio managers, analysts, risk managers, business professionals, and PhD students studying finance, and undergraduate finance majors.

The mean and median WTP valuations are in line with the rankings. Although so too are the median WTA valuations, the mean WTA-valuations are not: BM and LS are at the top.

As for individual differences, coefficients of variation (CVs) pretty much tell the story. The CV for a random variable is the ratio of the standard deviation to the mean. For rankings, the CVs in Table A.2 range between 0.3 and around 0.6, with the riskier alternatives having the lower values. For valuations, CVs are in the range 0.5 to 1.0 with the exception of LS, which features the widest disagreement with CVs above 1.0.

Risk managers take note: the riskiest alternatives tend to feature the greatest disagreement.

While both median and mean WTP valuations are consistent with risk aversion, Table A.2 makes clear that their WTA counterparts are not. Here the median value for LS is the lone exception. As I pointed out in earlier, risk seeking WTA valuations tend to reflect high aspiration points and great importance to the achievement of aspiration. The high CVs, especially for the riskier alternatives, suggest great variation in aspiration points, and in the importance attached to achieving aspiration. Risk managers need to understand what drives their own sense of which risks are worth taking and the perspective of those whom they support and advise.

Consider the manner in which people form model portfolio allocations, with the six risky alternatives as components. The panel on the lower left of Table A.2 displays the sample statistics for portfolio allocations. The median allocations, and with the exception of LS, the means as well, are consistent with the rankings and WTP valuations. Notably, the mean allocation for LS is consistent with the mean WTA valuation for LS. The data indicate that there is a segment of people at the extreme who find LS very attractive and overweight it accordingly. Among the various groups, this tendency is especially strong among portfolio managers and analysts, and to a lesser extent among risk managers.

Risk managers take note: despite having the highest risk premium based upon WTP valuation, there is a segment of the investor population who disproportionately weight LS in their overall allocations. In this regard, consider a remark made by Marty, who classifies himself as an entrepreneur. His preferred allocation features a 40% allocation to the RF, a 20% allocation to LS, and 10% to each of the other alternatives. Marty explains, "I would spread the investment on the risk floor and long shot, because the overall amount of money to earn seems on first view more than with the others. To spread the risk I would split up the others in equal parts."

Bill, a business professional whom I quoted earlier, allocated 28% of his portfolio to LS, and only 12% combined to RF and SS. He explained, "I would spread the risk, but definitely prefer the funds with a higher upside potential." The perspectives of Bill and Marty provide insights into the thought process of those who disproportionately weight LS.

APPLYING THE SP/A MODEL TO RANKING AND VALUATION

Good models can help us understand something about how the world works. The SP/A model can help us understand something about the rank orderings

Table A.3 Values of SP, A, and L for the six risky alternatives when L is L = SP + ζA, where ζ = 900, the aspiration level is $1,000, and the other parameters for L are indicated in the discussion in this appendix

	SP	A	L
Risk floor	997.9	46%	1411.9
Short Shot	967.9	69%	1588.9
Peaked	937.6	63%	1504.6
Uniform	847.3	55%	1342.3
Bimodal	771.5	51%	1230.5
Long shot	767.0	47%	1190.0

and valuations provided by Beth and Larry. A good starting point for such an application is to examine Table A.3, which displays the values of SP, A, and L for the six risk alternatives. Here the parameter values are those used in the illustrative discussion above, with the aspiration level set at $1,000.

Keep in mind that a higher value for ζ reflects the greater importance attached to the probability of achieving aspiration, relative to lower values for ζ. Notice that with ζ set at 900, SS achieves the top ranking, and PK is ranked above RF. As for RF, it features the highest SP value. Therefore, for a sufficiently low value of ζ such as ζ = 85, RF achieves the top ranking.

If we think of Beth and Larry as actually using SP/A theory to arrive at their rank orderings, we would conclude that their ranking differences stem from their differences in the values of ζ. Larry ranks alternatives as if he uses a high value of ζ to reflect the importance he attaches to achieving aspiration. In contrast, Beth appears to rank alternatives as if ζ were low, if not zero.

Turning next to valuation, I would point out that the L-function can also be used to determine WTA and WTP for each of the risk alternatives. As an example, consider RF, which as we have just seen has an SP value of 998 and a value of A that is 46% (when the aspiration level is $1,000). Suppose that we were to model Larry's valuation process using the framework developed above. Then we would say that for ζ = 900, Larry's L-value for RF is 1,412.

Consider Larry's WTA for RF. If we were to give Larry a sure $998, which corresponds to his SP value, then with certainty he would miss reaching aspiration by $2. This means that his A value is zero, and as a result, his L value for a sure $998 is 998. However, suppose we were to boost the sure amount we give him by $2, rounding him up to the aspiration level of $1,000. In this case, his corresponding L value for the sure $1,000 jumps to 1,900! Here 1,900 is the sum of the sure 1,000 and the product of ζ and the probability of reaching aspiration (which is 100%). In consequence, Larry has no exact certainty equivalent (CE), because he strictly prefers receiving a sure $1,000 to taking RF as a risk (with its L-value of 1,412). If we were to elicit a WTA valuation from Larry, then in this situation the model predicts that he would respond with $1,000.

Determining WTP requires a different approach than the one used to determine WTA. To begin with, notice that Larry's SP value for RF is 998. This means that if aspiration was not a consideration for Larry, he would pay at most $998 for RF, because *SP* is effectively a certainty equivalent that reflects the effects of fear and hope.

If Larry does care about aspiration, then he will be willing to pay more than $998 for RF. However, $998 is just $2 shy of Larry's aspiration of $1,000. And that leads to a quandary because $1,000 is too high a WTP for RF. This is because by keeping his $1,000, instead of exchanging it for RF, Larry receives an *L*-value of 1,900, which is greater than the *L*-value he receives from RF itself. However, if Larry pays $999.99, which misses aspiration by a penny, then taking RF looks better than keeping $999.99! For this reason, Larry's WTP for RF is going to be close to $1,000.

There is an important way to think about how to express Larry's aspiration for achieving a net gain in the case in which he pays $998 for RF. In net terms, his aspiration is to receive $2, because by receiving $2 over what he pays, he receives his aspiration level of $1,000 as his gross payoff. Moreover, with RF, there is still a 46% probability that by paying $999.99, Larry will achieve at least $2 in net terms.

If we turn our attention to PK, we can see that Larry's *SP* value is $938, which is considerably further away from $1,000 than the *SP* value for RF. If Larry were to pay $938 for PK, then he would need to receive at least $62 more than he paid in order to achieve his $1,000 aspiration level. The probability that he does so is 63%. Given that our short story has Larry attaching great importance to achieving his aspiration level, it should come as no surprise that a parameter value of $\zeta = 900$ would lead Larry to set a WTP of $999.99 for PK as well. Of course, a much lower value of ζ, say $\zeta = 50$, has Larry setting $969 as his WTP for PK.

If Larry sets a very high aspiration level, and attaches great importance to reaching aspiration, then he will tend to favor high-risk alternatives like LS over safer alternatives like SS. A high value of ζ can give rise to a high "aspiration premium" ζA (over the *SP* value). However, paying an amount near the aspiration level might make the probability A of reaching aspiration much smaller in respect to WTP than WTA. With A being different for WTA and WTP, WTA/WTP will naturally differ from unity, which can also explain why the ratio WTA/WTP varies across risky alternatives.

To recapitulate the main points about applying the theory to valuation, the process of establishing WTA and WTP for alternative risks begins with the *SP* values of these risks. Greater fear lowers the value of *SP*, and greater hope raises the value of *SP*. When aspiration is unimportant, WTA = WTP = *SP*. When aspiration is important, WTA and WTP will lie above *SP*. Notably, the aspiration level itself has a "sand trap" quality that attracts WTA and

WTP, so that for a wide range of model parameter values, WTA and WTP will be equal to the aspiration level. Outside the sand trap, WTP will tend to be less than WTA because having to pay to play can lower the probability of achieving aspiration. Therefore, people become less willing to pay an "aspiration premium" when A declines, and of course, having to pay to play lowers A.

In the SP/A model developed here, WTA is the minimum of $L(SP,A)$ and the aspiration level. Therefore, the theory predicts that $L(SP,A)$ and WTA should assign similar rankings to the alternatives being evaluated, except when WTA is equal to the aspiration level. In the discussion here, I have assumed that $L(SP,A)$ takes the simple form $SP + \zeta A$. The difference WTA-SP is the "aspiration premium." WTP is similar in structure, but its associated value of A might be lower than for WTA because pay to play can reduce the probability of reaching the same aspiration level.

Appendix B: A Deeper Dive into Prospect Theory

This Appendix presents the formal structure of the model underlying prospect theory. In doing so, the Appendix presents additional experimental questions and comments from subjects that bring out important nuances.

Expected Utility

The concept of "expected utility" provides a model of rationally based choice. To explain the concept, consider the following question that is similar in form to Question 7 in Chapter 3.

Question B1: Imagine that you face a decision task in which you are to choose between

> I: a sure $2,400
> J: $10,000 with probability p
> $0 with probability $1-p$,

where the value of p has yet to be specified.

What is the lowest value for p that would place you in a position where you would "just" be willing to choose J? Another way of asking the question is what value of p would leave you exactly indifferent between choosing I and choosing J?

Consider a person who responded to Question 2 in Chapter 3, by choosing the sure $2,400 over the risky J when the probability of receiving $10,000 is 25%. Given that response, rational behavior requires better odds than that to accept the risk, meaning the p-response to Question B1 should exceed 25%.

Someone who responds to Question B1 by telling us that for him, p is 30%, would lead us to write $p(2400) = 0.3$. Technically speaking, we would say that this person assigns a "utility" of 0.3 to receiving $2,400 (in Question B1). Such a response signals a risk-averse choice: were the person to be risk neutral, then his *p(2400)* would be 0.24. In that case, risks I and J would feature the exact same expected payoffs, and were he to be risk seeking, then his *p(2400)* would be less than 0.24.

Next, consider asking the same type of question to the quantities in Question 7 in Chapter 3, where 0, 2000, and 4000 play the roles of 0, 2400, and 10,000. With these numbers, the person's risk-neutral response is *p(2000) = 0.5*. Suppose, however, that the person instead provides a risk-averse response, and sets *p(2000) = 0.6*. This information is incredibly powerful, if the person is rational. Here is why.

Suppose that the person faces two risks involving the amounts 0, 2000, and 4000. Risk 1 features respective probabilities of 20%, 35%, and 45%, and has an expected payoff of $2,500. Risk 2 features respective probabilities of 22%, 28% and 50%, and has an expected payoff of $2,560. If the person is rational, then he will choose the first risk even though the second risk features a higher expected payoff.

We know how a rational person would make his choice because we can offer him a proposition he would be just willing to accept. We ask him to consider taking the risk, learning the outcome, and then taking a second risk in lieu of the sure outcome. For example, suppose the outcome turns out to be $2,000. Then we ask him to consider exchanging the sure $2,000 for a risk of winning either $0 or $4,000, with a 60% probability of winning $4,000. Here the 60% is the utility *p(2000)* that he assigns to receiving $2,000. Because he has already told us that 60% is the probability at which he would be indifferent, he should be just willing to make the substitution.

Having made the substitution, he now faces the possibility of a two-stage risk, in which the only possible outcomes are $0 and $4,000. A little computation easily shows the probability of winning $4,000 in Risk 1 (after substitution for the $2000) is 66.0%, and probability of winning $4,000 in Risk 2 (after substitution for the $2000) is 66.8%. If he is rational, he should prefer Risk 2 over Risk 1 (after substitution), since Risk 2 (after substitution) offers a better chance of success.

The probability of winning $4,000 in Risk 1 (after substitution) is the sum of 45% and the product of 35% and 60%. This is because the person can win $4,000 in one of two ways. He can win $4,000 in the first stage of Risk 1, the probability of which is $4,000, or he can win $4,000 in the second stage, which occurs with probability 35% × 60% = 21%. Notice that the sum of 45% and 21% is just the expected utility of Risk 1: (.2 × 0 + .35 × 0.6 + .45 × 1).

The fact that the person is indifferent between the original one-stage risks and their respective two-stage counterparts implies that he can rank order all risks using expected utility. For him, better risks are risks with higher expected utility.

Utility Functions

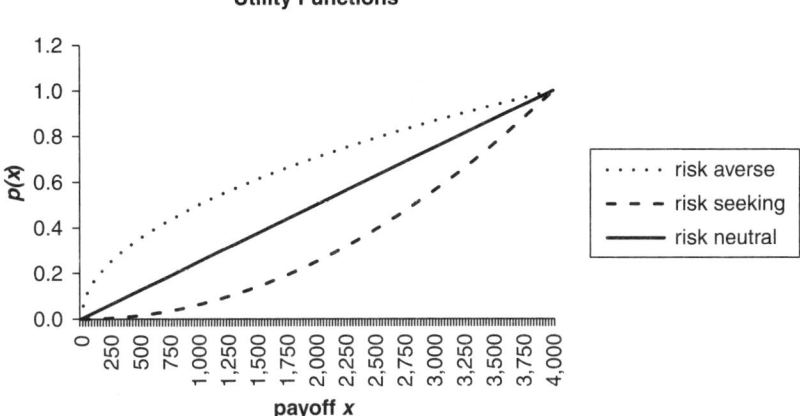

Figure B.1 This figure illustrates the shapes of three utility functions, with the argument of each function being final asset position. One function is concave pertaining to risk aversion, one is linear pertaining to risk neutrality, and one function is convex pertaining to risk seeking.

The expected utility methodology extends to risks with multiple payoffs. All that is required to make expected utility the rational criterion of choice is that a person be willing to substitute any certain amount for a second-stage risk involving the best and worst outcomes under consideration.

The shape of the utility function indicates attitude toward risk. If the person is risk neutral, his utility function $p(x)$ will be linear in the payoff x. If he is risk averse, his utility function will be concave, so that $u(x) > x$ for all x strictly between the worst and best outcomes. If he is risk seeking, his utility function will be convex, so that $u(x) < x$ for all x strictly between the worst and best outcomes. Figure B.1 illustrates.

VIOLATIONS OF RATIONALITY

Suppose the person in question is Beth. Is Beth rational? Beth's answer to Question 7 in Chapter 3 actually tells us. If Beth is rational, then we have to assume that Beth assigns a utility $p(2000)$ to receiving $2,000. Her expected utility of E is $0.9 \times p(2000)$. Her expected utility of F is 0.45. Beth's choice of E over F implies that $p(2000) > .45/.9 = 0.5$. Likewise, Beth's expected utility of G is $0.002 \times p(2000)$, and her expected utility of H is .001. Beth's choice of H over G implies that $p(2000) < .001/.002 = 0.5$.

If Beth is rational, then she cannot have it both ways. She cannot set a $p(2000)$, which is simultaneously greater than a half and less than a half. We can only conclude that Beth is not rational. Moreover, as the experimental data indicate, Beth has plenty of company.

Daniel Kahneman and Amos Tversky suggest that the driving factor behind choice behavior typified by Beth and Larry in Question 7 of Chapter 3 is that they do not mentally assign weights to probabilities that are proportional to the probabilities themselves. As a result, the ratio of weights for .45 and .9 differ from the ratio of the weights for .001 and .002, despite the fact that .45/.9 = .001/.002. In other words, viewed through the lens of prospect theory, people assign weights to probabilities that are not proportional to the probabilities themselves. Kahneman and Tversky call these weights "decision weights."

Beth's responses are actually quite normal. Actually, the word "rational" can be quite loaded, because it forces us to conclude that Beth is necessarily "irrational." For that reason, I would be inclined to use softer language and say that "Beth might not be perfectly rational." I am much more comfortable with the statement that "Beth is not an expected utility maximizer." This is a more accurate statement, and as we shall later see, leaves open other reasonable possibilities.

The comments of undergraduate finance majors make clear the underlying thought process in choosing the safer alternative E and riskier alternative H.

> *Serena*: For E and F, I prefer the odds of winning $2000 at 90% and would feel dumb if I were to choose the other option and be incorrect. For G and H, the chances are winning are so slim to begin with, that I would think the difference between .998 and .999 percent is so minimal that I would look for a $4000.
>
> *Gretchen*: Because both bets E and F have the same value, (.9 × 2000 = 1800; .45 × 4000 = 1800) I chose option one as it had a higher chance of succeeding. I chose option H because the difference between .001 and .002 in probability are so miniscule that they are irrelevant in my decision process.

Keep in mind that in responding to Question 7, many people do not choose the combination of the safer E and riskier H. The following comments of two undergraduate finance majors who chose E and G provide insight into their thought processes.

> *Alberta*: For E and F, the means are the same and I would thereby prefer the less risky alternative. For G and H, same mean, would still go for the less "risky" alternative as the probability is twice as high getting something.
>
> *Samuel*: I would choose option E because there is a higher probability that I will win money. I would choose G because I have a higher probability of winning $2000.

MODELING PROSPECT THEORY

Kahneman and Tversky have given us a formal framework to model the behavior patterns they have identified. This model has three major components. The first component is an *editing phase* that involves the manner in which decisions are framed in terms of gains and losses, relative to a reference point. The second component is a *value function* that plays the role of a utility function in expected utility theory. The third component is a *weighting function* for weighting probabilities. Consider these in turn.

Kahneman and Tversky tell us that *framing matters*. Table B.1 displays two alternative frames for Question 3 in Chapter 3. The top panel of Table B.1 presents a frame only for the individual risks (A, B, C, and D). The bottom panel provides additional information about the probabilities and payoffs associated with the four possible combination choices. Although A&D is the most frequent combination choice in the original presentation of Question 3 of Chapter 3, almost nobody chooses this combination once the information in the lower panel of Table B.1 is also presented. This is because B&C stochastically dominates A&D, a property that is more transparent when the lower panel of Table B.1 is explicitly presented.

Kahneman and Tversky tell us that when people choose risky alternatives, they attach subjective values to payoffs, with values playing a similar role to utilities in the expected utility approach. In developing their *value function*, they take as their launch point two lessons. The first lesson is loss aversion, that losses loom larger than gains of the same magnitude. The second lesson is that when the probabilities for nonzero payoffs are in the middle range, people are prone to be risk averse in the domain of gains and risk seeking in the domain of losses. To build these two features into

Table B.1 This table presents two alternative frames for Question 3 in Chapter 3. The top panel of Table A3.1 presents a frame only for the individual risks (A, B, C, and D). The bottom panel provides additional information about the probabilities and payoffs associated with the four possible combination choices

	Probability	Outcome
A	100%	2,400
B	75%	0
	25%	10,000
C	100%	-7,500
D	25%	0
	75%	-10,000
A&C	100%	-5,100
A&D	25%	2,400
	75%	-7,600
B&C	75%	-7,500
	25%	2,500
B&D	18.75%	0
	56.25%	-10,000
	6.25%	0
	18.75%	-10,000

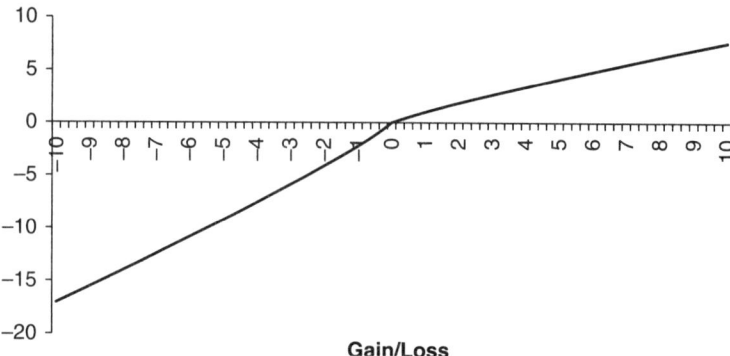

Figure B.2 This figure illustrates the shape of the prospect theory value function, with the argument of the function being gain/loss. The value function is concave in the domain of gains and convex in the domain of losses.

the value function, they import the key properties displayed in Figure B.1: concave utility to describe risk-averse behavior and convex utility to describe risk-seeking behavior.

Figure B.2 displays a typical prospect theory value function. Notice that the horizontal axis measures gains and losses, with the origin denoting a zero payoff (no gain, no loss). The value function is concave for gains to the right of the origin and convex for losses to the left of the origin. Hence, the value function is shaped like the letter S. To capture loss aversion, the value function is more steeply sloped to the left of the origin than to the right.

Kahneman and Tversky suggest a functional form for the value function $v(x)$. In the region of gains ($x \geq 0$), $v(x)$ is the function $v(x) = x^\alpha$, where α lies between 0 and 1. For losses, $v(x)$ has the form $v(x) = -\lambda(-x)^\beta$, where β lies between 0 and 1, and λ is a positive number measuring the coefficient of loss aversion. For the case of risk neutrality, $\alpha = \beta = \lambda = 1$. Based on experimental evidence, Kahneman and Tversky suggest parameter values $\alpha = \beta = 0.88$, and $\lambda = 2.25$.

The weighting function in prospect theory is a bit complex. When Kahneman and Tversky first introduced prospect theory into the academic literature, in 1979, they proposed a weighting function $\pi(p)$. Figure B.3 displays the typical shape of this weighting function. Although it is not clear from the figure, at the end points $\pi(0) = 0$ and $\pi(1) = 1$. Prospect theory holds that a person choosing among risky prospects, mentally weights probability p as $\pi(p)$. Figure B.3 contrasts $\pi(p)$ with the 45-degree line to make clear when $\pi(p) > p$ and when $\pi(p) < p$. Notice that $\pi(p) > p$ for small probabilities. In addition, notice from Figure B.3 that the slope of the weighting function is less than unity near the origin, and for that matter for a large range to the

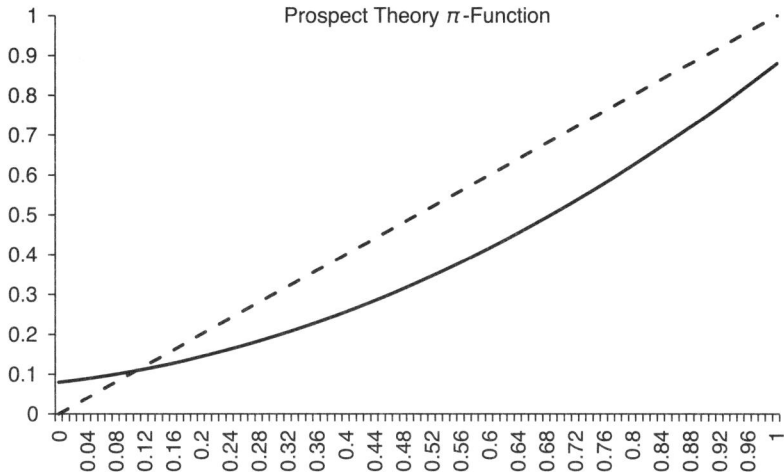

Figure B.3 This figure illustrates the π-function in original prospect theory. The argument of the π-function is probability density.

right of the origin. The relative flatness captures the idea that the ratio of decision weights is less than the ratio of the probabilities near the origin and for a large region to the right.

An important feature of the weighting function is that, unlike probabilities that sum to unity, the sum $\pi(p) + \pi(1 - p)$ need not sum to unity. The property in question is called *subcertainty*. Here is an example, involving two decision tasks, that explains how this comes about.

Question B2: Imagine that you face a decision task in which you are to choose between

K: a sure $2,400
L: $2,500 with probability 33%
   $2,400 with probability 66%
   $0 with probability 1%

Question B3: Imagine that you face a decision task in which you are to choose between

M: $2,500 with probability 33%
   $0 with probability 67%
N: $2,400 with probability 34%
   $0 with probability 36%

In Question B2, most people choose the sure K over the risky L. However, in Question B3, in which both alternatives are risky, many choose M over N. Prospect theory holds that people choose between alternatives such as

K versus L and M versus N by comparing the counterparts to expected utility and choosing the alternative that features the higher sum-product. For Question B2, the choice of L over K occurs because

$$v(2400) > (\pi(0.33) \times v(2500)) + (\pi(0.67) \times v(2400)) + (\pi(0.01) \times v(0))$$

Likewise, the choice of M over N occurs because

$$(\pi(0.33) \times v(2500)) + (\pi(0.67) \times v(0)) > (\pi(0.34) \times v(2400)) + (\pi(0.66) \times v(0))$$

where $v(0) = 0$.

As Kahneman and Tversky tell us, a little algebra shows that these two inequalities imply that $\pi(0.34) + \pi(0.66) < 1$. In this regard, notice that $\pi(0.5) < 0.5$, and therefore $\pi(0.5) + \pi(0.5) < 1$. Actually, Figure B.3 is somewhat exaggerated in respect to subcertainty. In Kahneman and Tversky's original article, $\pi(0.5)$ is approximately 0.47, significantly higher than the value displayed in Figure B.3.

As it happens, subcertainty has an implication that economists find annoying. Table B.2 provides an example featuring two alternatives, A' and B'. The two alternatives feature the same possible payoffs, $2,000 and $2,500. However, A' stochastically dominates B' because A' offers a higher probability than B' of achieving the high payoff $2,500, and correspondingly a lower probability of achieving the low payoff $2,000. Suppose we take $v(x)$ to be the function proposed by Kahneman and Tversky, and use the $\pi(p)$ function displayed in Figure B.3. Then the sum-products of $v(x)$ and $\pi(p)$, displayed as V in Table 3.2, show that $V(B') > V(A')$. That is, although A' stochastically dominates B', the values of V appear to suggest choosing B over A.

Table B.2 indicates that A' features both a higher expected payoff and a higher expected utility than B'. This is not surprising, in view of the fact that A' stochastically dominates B'. The reason why $V(B')$ exceeds $V(A')$ is that $\pi(p)$ is flatter in the region around p = 67% than the region

Table B.2 This table describes two alternatives, A' and B' that feature the same possible payoffs, $2,000 and $2,500, but for which A' stochastically dominates B'

x	v	prob A'	prob B'	πA'	πB'
2500	977.7	33.0%	28.0%	21.1%	18.3%
2000	803.4	67.0%	72.0%	48.3%	53.5%
		100.0%	100.0%	69.5%	71.8%
			V	594.9	608.8
			EU	860.9	852.2
			Ex	$2,165	$2,140

around p = 33%. Effectively, we transform A' into the inferior B' by shifting 5% probability mass from the high outcome $2,500 to the low outcome $2,000. However, because of the shape of $\pi(p)$, the shift in decision weight for $2,500 is 2.8% for the high payoff and 5.2% for the low payoff. Therefore, $\pi(p)$ downplays the "cost" of the probability shift at the high end relative to the "benefit" of the shift at the low end.

Kahneman and Tversky first suggested avoiding this problem by eliminating alternatives like B from consideration. Economists countered that this made no sense for a criterion function intended to describe choice. After years of debate, Kahneman and Tversky eventually modified the weighting function approach to accommodate the criticism, and renamed the second version of their theory "cumulative prospect theory," or CPT for short. The original formulation came to be called "original prospect theory," or OPT for short.

CPT avoids the OPT stochastic dominance conundrum because of the manner in which it generates the counterparts to probabilities. In CPT, decision weights are obtained using transformations of decumulative distribution functions. Notably, the approach is very similar to the procedure used in SP/A theory, with weighting functions similar to the inverse-S shaped h-function displayed in Figure A.5.

Imagine a risk whose payoffs features gains only. Let the possible outcomes be labeled $x_1, x_2, \ldots, x_n$ where x_1 is the least favorable outcome and x_n is the most favorable outcome. Suppose that D_i is the probability for this risk that the outcome is at least x_i. Then the CPT value V of the risk is

$$(D_1 - D_2)v(x_1) + (D_2 - D_3)v(x_2) \ldots D_n v(x_n).$$

Because $D_1 = 1$, this last expression can be rearranged to read

$$v(x_1) + D_2(v(x_2) - v(x_1)) + \ldots D_n v(x_n).$$

Notice that the CPT value of a risk is a sum product of decumulative probabilities and successive value differences, which are nonnegative. Recall from Appendix A that when one risk first order stochastically dominates the other, the first has a higher decumulative probability function. Therefore, the dominant risk will feature a higher CPT value, obtained using the last expression. Any weighting function $w(p)$, or if you like $W(D)$, that is monotone increasing will preserve this property. The weighting functions in CPT (and also SP/A theory) have this property, which is why CPT avoids the OPT stochastic dominance conundrum.

There are some technical differences between the use of transformed decumulative-CPT technique and the transformed decumulative-SP/A approach. In particular, CPT uses two different functions, $w^+(p)$ and $w^-(p)$, one for gains and the other for losses. For gains, $w^+(p)$ is applied just like $h(p)$. For losses, $w^-(p)$ is applied to the absolute value of losses.

In CPT, $w^+(p)$ and $w^-(p)$ have the same functional form, different from SP/A theory, with possibly different parameter values. The functional form in question is the ratio of $p\gamma$ to $(p^\gamma + (1-p)^\gamma)^{1/\gamma}$. Figure B.4 displays the shape of this function.

For $w^+(p)$, Tversky and Kahneman's experimental evidence suggests a parameter value $\gamma = 0.69$, and for $w^-(p)$ the evidence suggests a parameter value of $\gamma = 0.61$. I would note that for the parameter values that Kahneman and Tversky suggest, the coefficient of loss aversion inferred from Question 2 of Chapter 3 turns out to be 2.3, exactly the median value that emerges from my surveys.

As in SP/A theory, decision weights are obtained as successive differences in the transformed decumulative functions. The probabilities of the most extreme gain and loss correspond to the weighting function values respectively.

To interpret the implications of a weighting function for probabilities, think about gains. If the maximum possible gain in a set of alternatives is $10,000, then the probability of a payoff exceeding $10,000 is 0, with the associated transformed weight $w^+(0)$ also being 0.

For sake of illustration, consider a risk for a payoff of $10,000 occurs with probability 2%. The decumulative probability that the realized payoff will be *$10,000 or more* is also 2%. This is because $10,000 is the maximum gain. The decision weight attached to a gain of exactly $10,000 will be given by $w^+(0.02)$. Therefore, we obtain decision weights for the highest payoffs by working from the left side of the weighting function $w^+(p)$.

Decision weights are obtained as successive differences, which for small incremental changes correspond to the slope of the $w^+(p)$ function. Notice from Figure B.4 that the weighing function is steeply sloped at the left, flattens in the middle, and becomes steeply sloped at the right. The steep portions at the extreme ends imply that small probabilities at both extremes are typically overweighted.

Notably, for mixed gains and losses, we might never get to the extreme right of the $w^+(p)$ function when computing decision weights. This is because the decision that the payoff will actually be positive, meaning a gain, will be strictly less than unity. In other words we never get to $w^+(1)$.

Similar remarks apply to the computation of probability decision for losses. The same line of argument implies that in CPT, probabilities of extreme losses are overweighted.

An important point to notice is that with CPT, the same probability value, say 15%, might be assigned different decision weights if it appears multiple times, whether in the same risky alternative or different risky alternatives.

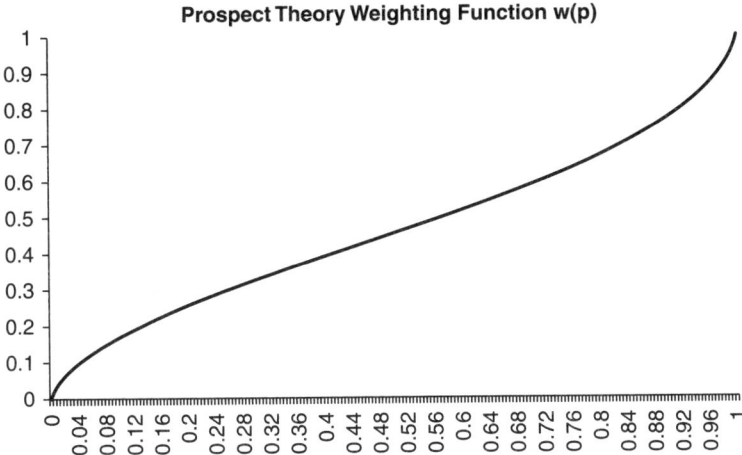

Figure B.4 This figure illustrates the w-weighting function in cumulative prospect theory. The argument of the w-function is decumulative probability.

In CPT, decision weights are sensitive to the rank ordering of the payoff. Therefore, different ranks can lead to the application of different weights, even for the same probability.

The rank-dependent approach in CPT prevents the type of situation described in Table B.2 from happening, where a stochastically dominated alternative is assigned a lower value V. This is effectively because subcertainty is eliminated in the two conditional probability distributions, one conditional on gains and the other conditional on losses. This is certainly a welcome improvement, but risk managers do need to be aware that the modification from OPT to CPT does alter the nature of decision weighting. Weights derived indirectly by applying CPT's $w^+(p)$ and $w^-(p)$ to *decumulative probabilities p* (written as D above) are much more complex than those directly specified by applying OPT's $\pi(p)$ to a *probability density p*.

QUASI-HEDONIC EDITING: PRIOR GAINS AND LOSSES

Consider next how the theory of *quasi-hedonic editing* in Chapter 3 explains behavior such as Larry's in respect to prior gains and losses. When Larry is asked outright if he would accept or reject a fifty-fifty risk of winning or losing $450, he does the following internal operation. First, he thinks about rejecting the risk. This entails receiving $0 as his dollar payoff and $v(0)$ as his psychological payoff. Hence, $v(0)$ is what Larry's mind places onto his mental scale.

Second, Larry considers the risk where his dollar payoffs are a $450 gain and a $450 loss, which have mental payoffs of $v(450)$ and $v(-450)$. The risk also features probabilities of 50% and 50% respectively, which he mentally weights. In OPT, the weights are $\pi(0.5)$ and $\pi(0.5)$ respectively, while in CPT, the weights are $w^+(0.5)$ and $w^-(0.5)$ respectively. Thaler and Johnson (1990) developed their theory before CPT, and so they used the OPT formulation. Therefore, Larry places the sum product $\pi(0.5)v(450) + \pi(0.5)v(-450)$ onto the scale. Because of loss aversion, Larry attaches greater weight to the $450 loss than the $450 gain, which tips the scales in favor of $v(0)$ so that Larry rejects the risk.

Next, consider what changes when Larry has just received a prior gain of $1,500 before being faced with the risk. According to quasi-hedonic editing, Larry's mind views the unfavorable outcome as a net gain of $1,050 resulting from having reduced his initial $1,500 gain by a subsequent $450 loss. Doing so leads him to avoid his mind's having to deal with the unpleasantness of loss aversion. In terms of prospect theory, he avoids having to invoke the coefficient of loss aversion λ into his thinking: $v(-450)$ does not make its way onto the scales. However, a subsequent gain of $450, on top of a prior gain of $1,500, is viewed as two separate gains, and mentally represented as $v(1,500) + v(450)$. Therefore, the side of Larry's scale that evaluates the risk registers the sum product $\pi(0.5)v(1,050) + \pi(0.5)[v(1,500) + v(450)]$. The side of the scale for evaluating the decision to reject the risk, and walk away with a $1,500 dollar payoff, is $v(1,500)$.

If Larry were to mentally evaluate the two consecutive gains as a net $1,950 = $1,500 + $450, his mental payoff would be $v(1,950)$, not $v(1,500) + v(450)$. Because $v(x)$ is concave in the domain of gains, $v(1,950) < v(1,500) + v(450)$. According to quasi-hedonic editing, Larry feels better by framing the two gains separately than he does by framing them as a net payoff. Therefore, the quasi-hedonic framing of this choice makes it possible that Larry would prefer to accept the risk after a prior gain. Table B.3 displays an example using Kahneman and Tversky parameters for $v(x)$ and a value $\pi(0.5) = 0.49$.

Table B.3 This table displays the value function v-values in a quasi-hedonic editing example involving gains using Kahneman and Tversky parameters for $v(x)$ and a weighting value $\pi(0.5) = 0.49$

outcome	v(outcome)
1,500	624
450	216
1,950	786
1,050	456
v(1,500)	623.7
v-risk	634.8
$\pi(0.5)$	0.49

When it comes to a prior loss, Thaler and Johnson's experimental evidence indicated that people are very sensitive to successive losses. It is as if they suffer a tortured death by a thousand cuts. Larry tells us that experiencing a loss of $225 right after a loss of $750 would lead him to be "downtrodden." Theoretically, Larry experiences the double loss as *v(–750) + v(–225)*, not *v(–975)*, even though *v(–750) + v(–225) > v(–975)* because *v(x)* is convex in the domain of losses. However, Thaler and Johnson suggest that people will experience a gain of $225 after a prior loss of $750 as *v(–750) + v(225)*, as the gain represents a "silver lining."

In evaluating whether to accept or reject a risk after a prior loss, Larry's mental calculation pits *v(–750)* on the side of the scale for rejecting the risk against the following sum product for accepting the risk: *π(0.5)[v(–750) + v(–225)] + π(0.5)[v(–750) + v(225)]*. Table B.4 displays an example using Kahneman and Tversky parameters for *v(x)* and a value *π(0.5) = 0.49*. Here Larry rejects the risk. The pain of the segregated losses is too much to bear.

The theory can also explain Larry's decision to accept the risk under the modified wording in which he asked to choose between a decision to accept a sure $750 loss and a decision to face a fifty-fifty risk between a loss of either $525 or $975. This presentation of the decision task induces a comparison of *v(–750)* for the sure loss against *π(0.5)v(–525) + π(0.5)v(–975)*. The convex shape of *v(x)* in the domain of losses provides the basis for why Larry might choose to accept the risk in this situation. Table B.5 shows that, according to the theory, he in fact does accept the risk for the same set of parameters used in Table B.4.

Quasi-hedonic editing offers important insights into behaviors such as those of Larry described above. At the same time, risk managers need to understand that all theories have limits and limitations. Consider what happens when we present Larry with a choice between a decision to accept a sure

Table B.4 This table displays the value function *v*-values in a quasi-hedonic editing example involving losses using Kahneman and Tversky parameters for *v(x)* and a weighting value *π(0.5) = 0.49*

outcome	v(outcome)
–750	–762.49
–225	–264.30
–975	–960.52
–525	–557.09
225	117.47
v(–30)	–44.9
v-risk	–51.6
π(0.5)	0.49

Table B.5 This table displays the computed value of v-risk showing that according to the theory, Larry does accept the risk for the same set of parameters used in Table B.4

outcome	v(outcome)
−750	−762.49
−225	−264.30
−975	−960.52
−525	−557.09
225	117.47
v(−30)	−44.9
v-risk	−40.4
π(0.5)	0.49

$1,500 and a decision to accept a fifty-fifty risk where he might gain $1,050 or he might gain $1,950. This is a modified presentation of the decision task described in Chapter 3 when Larry accepted the risk. The thing is that prospect theory predicts that Larry will reject the risk in the revised wording. However, he surprises us and chooses the risk.

Here is Larry's explanation for why he chooses the risk in the revised presentation of the decision task: "The reason I chose the 50/50 risk of winning $1,950 or $1,050, rather than a guaranteed $1,500 was twofold. 1) the most I could lose is a $450 opportunity loss but either way I make at least $1,050 with $0 to be paid out of pocket; and 2) the excitement to possibly win more money with no direct out of pocket personal cost means I was 'playing with house money.'"

So there it is. For the situation featuring a prior gain, Larry effectively chose to frame both versions of the problem in the same way, as a house money effect. Not everyone in Larry's experimental group behaved as Larry did. In fact, 25% of the group chose to accept the risk when it was presented as an alternative to "accepting a sure gain of $1,500," but accept the risk when it was presented as an alternative to "accepting a prior gain of $1,500." For the decision task with losses, 36% accept the risk as an alternative to "accepting a sure loss of $750," but reject the risk as an alternative to "accepting a prior loss of $750."

The lesson for these percentages, 25% and 36%, is to be cautious when applying the theory to explain, or predict, the behavior of specific individuals. The majority of people do not behave in ways that conform to the theory. What the theory does is to offer insight about aggregate responses. In this regard, about 60% of Larry's experimental group chose to be risk seeking after a prior gain, and 60% chose to be risk averse for the version of the same problem with no prior gain. For losses, 71% of the group chose to be risk averse after a prior loss, and 50% chose to be risk seeking for the version of the same problem with no prior loss.

And how about our risk manager Beth? What choices does she make? With one exception, Beth makes the same choices as Larry. The exception involves her attitude to taking risk after a loss. She tells us, "I like to cap my losers." Beth always accepts the loss, no matter which decision frame she encounters with the choices under discussion. Notably, this means that prospect theory does not explain her behavior pattern!

I am making a point here. Risk managers need to apply these theories cautiously when it comes to specific individuals. In my experience, the responses of other groups, both business professionals and students, indicate that framing effects involving losses are much stronger than for gains. Truth be told, in most large groups the effects predicted by quasi-hedonic editing when it comes to gains are sometimes weak.

The weak findings for prior gains might be because of a weak theoretical basis for the prediction. Looking back at the key inequalities, you will see that the value of $\pi(0.5)$ plays a key role in the argument. Lower values of $\pi(0.5)$ reflect greater discomfort with bearing risk. In Tables B.3 through B.5, I used an illustrative value $\pi(0.5) = 0.49$. However, instead using $\pi(0.5) = 0.48$ (or less) leads to a different implication for gains: risk aversion in both versions of the problem. In this regard, Kahneman and Tversky's illustrative function for $\pi(p)$ in their 1979 article displays a value for $\pi(p)$ that is about 0.47. This is an issue for OPT; however, it is not an issue for CPT, where subcertainty is not a factor. Using the Kahneman-Tversky parameters in a CPT formulation does imply risk seeking after a prior gain.

Table B.6 provides an example using the typical Kahneman-Tversky parameters. The example shows that for the version of the decision task known as the one-stage, in which the task description makes no reference to a prior gain, the better choice is to accept the sure $1,500. However, in the two-stage version of the decision task, in which the task description makes reference to a prior $1,500 gain, the better choice is to accept the risk.

There are reasons, other than quasi-hedonic editing, why people might choose to be risk seeking after a prior gain. Beth tells us, "I like to keep my winners running." This perspective has a different flavor than quasi-hedonic editing, and is more related to a "hot hand" effect that that is discussed in Chapter 4.

Behavior patterns also vary by professional role. In the domain of gains, when prior outcomes are not an issue, entrepreneurial risk managers are more prone to take risks than others, and CEOs are the least prone. In circumstances involving a prior gain, 75% of CEOs are prone to switch from rejecting risk to accepting risk, a rate much higher than for any other group. Other

Table B.6 This table displays an example using the typical Kahneman-Tversky parameters. The example shows that for the version of the decision task known as the one-stage, in which the task description makes no reference to a prior gain, the better choice is to accept the sure $1,500. However, in the two-stage version of the decision task, in which the task description makes reference to a prior $1,500 gain, the better choice is to accept the risk

w-prob	outcome	v(outcome)
0.454	1,500	624
0.454	450	216
0.454	1,950	786
0.546	1,050	456
	CPT	
One stage valuation		
v(1500)	623.7	
v-risk	605.5	
Two stage version		
v(1,500)	623.7	
v-risk	630.1	

business professionals are the most prone to making risk-seeking choices in the domain of losses (71% do so), the most prone to making risk-averse choices after a prior loss (86% do so), and therefore the most prone to switch between the two situations (64% do so). Risk managers need to know the degree to which they generally differ from those occupying different business roles. Along most dimensions, their behavioral tendencies lie between those of CEOs and other business professionals.

In closing, I want to offer a cautionary theoretical note. My sense is that the discussion in the previous paragraphs reflects a missing element in Thaler and Johnson (1990).[1] As far as I can tell, the article does not examine the criteria determining whether the individual chooses the risky alternative over the riskless alternative in the case of the two-stage (quasi-hedonic) frame. Instead, the argument only focuses on whether the value attached to choosing the risky alternative is higher or lower in the two-stage frame than the one-stage frame. In 1990, when the article was published, only OPT was in existence, not CPT. Therefore, OPT with parameter values reflected in Kahneman and Tversky (1979)[2] did not provide support for the Thaler-Johnson predictions about hedonic editing, in respect to both gains and losses.

Appendix C: Integrating SP/A Theory and Prospect Theory

This Appendix presents a synthesized approach to integrate the models for SP/A theory and prospect theory that were developed in Appendices A and B. The integration comes at the end of this Appendix. However, before engaging in the synthesis, we need to address a series of nuanced issues that involve where the two approaches concur, where they conflict, and where they are inconsistent. This section addresses some of the limitations of the theories.

Prospect theory tells us that people are generally loss averse, with the average coefficient of loss aversion being 2.25; that risk behavior conforms to a fourfold framework, with people being risk averse in the domain of gains and risk seeking in the domain of losses unless probabilities of nonzero outcomes are low, in which case the opposite pattern prevails; and that quasi-hedonic editing induces people to be risk seeking in the domain of gains in the face of a prior gain, but averse to risk after a prior loss.

A word of caution: the proportion of people in my data sample who satisfy each and every one of these patterns is tiny. Put differently, although the behavior patterns associated with prospect theory appear in the aggregate, they do not describe the average person any of us is likely to encounter. In this regard, for Question 3 from Chapter 3, only 43% of people choose the prototypical combination A&D, and the formal analysis developed in Appendix B implies that a person whose behavior conforms to prospect theory must choose D over C. This is because C and D have the same expected payoff, but D is riskier, and prospect theory holds that people are risk seeking in the domain of losses. However, 30% of my data sample choose C over D.

Prospect theory explanations work well for the kinds of experiments used to identify the features emphasized by prospect theory. In this regard, personality traits and emotions central to the SP/A approach take a back seat to prospect theory in respect to explaining behavior. However, consider the flip side, meaning whether prospect theory can explain behavior in the experimental conditions used to identify the features emphasized by SP/A theory.

In her work with Greg Oden, Lola Lopes examined how CPT with the parameters specified by Daniel Kahneman and Amos Tversky would rank order the risks she studied. In this respect, consider Table C.1. The second column from the left in this table displays CPT values of V used to achieve the rank ordering. Notice from the table that RF emerged as the top-ranked risk, which is consistent with the experimental evidence I discussed in Chapter 2. However, somewhat surprising is that CPT ranked LS as second. Although it takes a moment to see why, the reason is that CPT dramatically overweighs the very low probability that LS assigns to receiving a very high payoff. This is a consequence of prospect theory's inverse-S shaped weighting function with the Tversky-Kahneman parameters.

Notice too from Table C.1 that CPT placed PK in third place and SS in fourth place. Both of these rankings are at odds with the experimental evidence reported in Chapter 2.

Based on Lopes's earlier experimental work, Lopes and Oden suggest that many people set small positive numbers strictly above $0, but less than $50, as their aspiration points. They then make the point that with an aspiration point above $0, people will focus on both the probability of receiving more than $0 *and* the value of *SP* when rank ordering risks. Now consider the implications of adding $50 to all payoffs in the six risky alternatives in their experiment. Doing so makes the probability of reaching aspiration for these people equal to unity: that is, reaching aspiration is guaranteed for all risks. As a result, risk rankings in the modified payoff structure will be determined only by *SP*, not *A*, since *A* = 100% for all six risks.

Table C.1 displays an example showing how the rank orderings are impacted when the aspiration point is $1,000, the parameter ζ, which controls the importance of aspiration, is set at 900, and all payoffs are shifted up by $1,000. In this example, the *SP* and *L* functions are the same as in the example in Appendix A. As in Appendix A, with ζ = 900, SS is ranked at the top with the original payoffs. Here SS beats RF, even though it features

Table C.1 This table displays the CPT-values and associated SP/A values for the six Lopes risks (both original and shifted formulation), using the typical Kahneman-Tversky parameters

		Shift-1000				Shift-1000		
	CPT-V	CPT-V	SP	A	L	SP	A	L
Risk floor	482.9	847.7	997.9	46%	1411.9	1997.9	100%	2897.9
Short Shot	421.8	794.1	967.9	69%	1588.9	1967.9	100%	2867.9
Peaked	439.4	811.1	937.6	63%	1504.6	1937.6	100%	2837.6
Uniform	423.4	801.8	847.3	55%	1342.3	1847.3	100%	2747.3
Bimodal	411.0	794.8	771.5	51%	1230.5	1771.5	100%	2671.5
Long shot	472.7	859.5	767.0	47%	1190.0	1767.0	100%	2667.0

a lower value for SP, because it features a higher value for A. However, after all payoffs are increased by $1,000, the value of A becomes 100% for all six risks. Therefore, *SP* alone determines the rank ordering, and in consequence, RF emerges with the top ranking.

Lopes and Oden make the point that aspiration plays no role in CPT. They make this suggestion, noting that CPT only features a reference point demarcating gains and losses, but have no variable to reflect the probability of achieving aspiration. Because of the role played by the reference point in CPT, shifting all payoff amounts by a positive constant can change the coding of some payoffs from losses to gains, thereby impacting choice. However, Lopes and Oden note that when all payoff amounts are initially coded as gains, CPT predicts that such shifts do not impact choice.

In the example associated with Table C.1, the reference point is $0. Therefore, if Lopes and Oden were correct, then by comparing the second and third columns from the left in Table C.1, we should find that CPT's rank ordering of the six risks by V is not impacted by the $1,000 shift in payoffs. However, a quick CPT-calculation based on typical CPT parameters shows that it is impacted. The $1,000 shift leads to a switch in most preferred outcome from RF to LS. Notably, the decision weights are the same for the decision task with the original amounts, and the decision task with the shifted amounts. Yet the value function is applied differently, with the shift diminishing the relative advantage that the concavity of the value function accords to low payoffs. Therefore, the shift affects both CPT rankings and SP/A rankings, but in different ways.

In order to compare the predictions of SP/A theory and CPT, Lopes and Oden conducted an experiment to investigate whether people rank risks differently when payoffs are shifted up. They preceded under the false assumption in which CPT predicts that rank orderings will not be impacted by the shift, but SP/A theory predicts an impact because for some, the shift increases the values of A to 100%. The error means that the experiment does not provide a clean test. Nevertheless, it does offer a sense of how people react to the shift, and the findings can be compared to the theoretical predictions of Table C.1.

Lopes and Oden find that after the shift, the proportion of people ranking RF at the top somewhat falls. It does not fall enough to dislodge it from occupying the top position. In addition, the aggregate strength of preference for LS increases, but not enough to have it move up in the overall rankings. Lopes and Oden suggest that the reason for these effects is that with aspiration no longer a distinguishing factor, the emotion of hope induces the effect through the SP function by emphasizing the higher potential offered by the five alternatives to RF. Overall, Lopes and Oden's experimental findings are more in line with SP/A theory than with CPT, conditional on the parameter values associated with Table C.1.

As part of their "shift experiment," Lopes and Oden also investigate the impact of an upward shift when payoffs are all losses. They suggest that such a shift prevents the possibility of a $0 loss in any of the six risks. With an aspiration point of $0, this means that $A = 0$ for all six risks. Therefore, the SP function alone will determine how alternative risks are ordered. Lopes and Oden report that the biggest impact of the shift when payoffs reflect losses is to diminish the attractiveness of both LS (which receives the top rank) and RF (which receives the bottom rank). They suggest that the change in strength of preference comes about because, with aspiration no longer relevant to rankings, as $A = 0$ for all six risks, the seeking of security to address fear becomes more significant.

Directly Testing the Importance of Aspiration

Lopes and Oden make the point that CPT fails to explain their empirical findings because it ignores the role of aspiration. However, as mentioned previously, their argument contains a flaw. Therefore, consider the following experiment, based on a design by economist Stefan Zeisberger, for testing the Lopes and Oden contention.

> Imagine that you face a choice between two risky investments. The payoff structures are simple and displayed below. Each risk pays one of four possible amounts, and the probability of any specific payoff is 25%. Table C.2 displays the exact payoff amounts.

Table C.2 This table displays the data for the Zeisberger experiment

Probability	Payoff	
	Risk A	Risk B
0.25	14.0%	15.0%
0.25	1.0%	−0.5%
0.25	0.5%	−1.0%
0.25	−12.0%	−9.0%

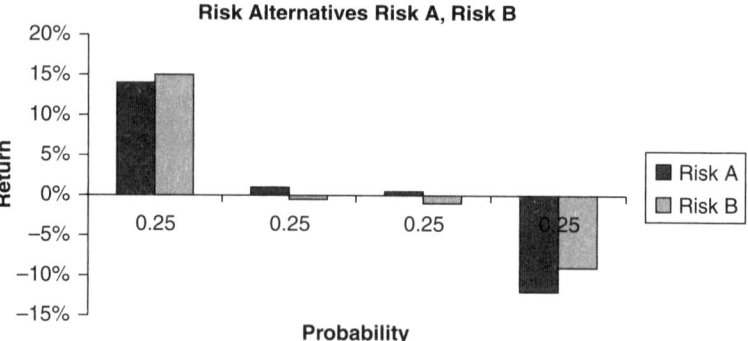

Figure C.1 This figure is a graphical depiction of the information presented in Table C.2.

Table C.3 This table displays statistical information associated with the risks in the Zeisberger experiment

Expected return	0.88%	1.13%
Standard Deviation	9.2%	8.7%
Prob{payoff < 0}	25%	75%

The graphical representation of the information presented in Table C.2 is presented in Figure C.1

Table C.3 displays statistical information associated with these risks.

Question 1: Which risk would you choose if given the opportunity, Risk A or Risk B?

Question 2: Suppose that the returns for both risks occur monthly, with the returns being independent from month to month. You will observe the monthly returns at the close of each month, and the returns will compound over the 25 months. You can only choose one of the two assets to hold for the 25 months, and you cannot switch assets or liquidate your position prematurely. Which asset would you choose, Risk A or Risk B?

Question 3: Consider now whether you had in mind a particular amount that you targeted or to which you aspired for the risk choice in Questions 1 and 2. A specific target return or aspiration is an outcome, like a goal, such that after you learned the outcome, you would have felt particularly badly that you missed achieving the goal. If you had specific target returns for either of these situations, what were they?

Table C.4 compares Risk A to Risk B from the perspectives of both CPT and SP/A. Notice from Table C.3 that Risk A has lower expected return and higher standard deviation than Risk B. When CPT is invoked to evaluate Risk A and Risk B, Risk B has the higher value of V (-0.045 for Risk A and -0.032 for Risk B). Therefore, under CPT, Risk B is valued more highly than Risk A. At the same time, the negative value for both indicates that the status quo with V-value of 0 is preferable to both risky alternatives.

SP/A theory incorporates both the value of SP and the probability A of achieving aspiration into the analysis. Table C.4 shows that Risk B has a higher SP value than Risk A. This is not surprising, as Risk B not only has a higher expected return and lower standard deviation but also has a more favorable upside and a more favorable downside. In this respect, cautious hope overweighs the extremes.

In setting up the experiment, Zeisberger treated the aspiration level as $0. In this case, the probability of achieving aspirations for Risk A is 75%, while for Risk B it is 25%. Hence, the probability of achieving at least 0% is three

Table C.4 This table comparison Risk A to Risk B from the perspectives of both CPT and SP/A. In CPT, w-weights are transformed decumulative probabilities under the CPT w-functions, and are associated with both gains and the absolute value of losses. Prob-weights are differences in w-transformed decumulative probabilities. The three columns at the right of the table display the corresponding values for SP/A theory, with h-weights being decumulative probabilities transformed under the SP/A h-function and h-prob denoting differences in successive h-transformed decumulative probabilities.

Probability	Payoff Risk A	v	Cum Probs	w Weights	Prob Weights	Payoff Risk B	v	Cum Probs	w Weights	Prob Weights	Decum Probs	h-weights	h-prob
0.25	14.0%	0.18	0.25	0.29	0.29	15.0%	0.19	0.25	0.29	0.29	1.00	1.00	0.39
0.25	1.0%	0.02	0.50	0.45	0.16	-0.5%	-0.02	0.75	0.57	0.15	0.75	0.61	0.28
0.25	0.5%	0.01	0.75	0.63	0.17	-1.0%	-0.04	0.50	0.42	0.13	0.50	0.32	0.17
0.25	-12.0%	-0.35	0.25	0.29	0.29	-9.0%	-0.27	0.25	0.29	0.29	0.25	0.15	0.15
Expected return	0.9%					1.1%							
V		-0.045					-0.032						
SP	0.041					0.042							
A	0.750					0.250							
L	0.061					0.049							

times higher in Risk A than in Risk B, and is effectively the only advantage that Risk A offers over Risk B. Notably, Risk A will have an aspirational advantage over Risk B for aspiration levels that lie above −1.5% and do not exceed 1.5%. Given an aspiration level that lies in this range, then a sufficiently high value of ζ will imply that the SP/A value of Risk A is higher than the SP/A-value of Risk B.

Zeisberger conducted several versions of an experiment involving choices between Risk A and Risk B. One version was based on questions such as the first two above, in which the choices were head-to-head. This version was conducted with 25 executive MBA students. In the single-round version (featured in Question 1), 80% of subjects chose Risk A. In the 25-round question (featured in Question 2), 56% chose Risk A. Notably, 48% chose Risk A as their answers to both questions, whereas 12% chose Risk B as their answers to both questions.

A key feature of Zeisberger's experiment involves subjects making portfolio allocation decisions between a risk-free asset and a risky asset over multiple rounds. Here there are two treatments, with the risky asset in one treatment being Risk A, with its low loss probability, and the risky asset in the other treatment being Risk B (with its high loss probability). Four versions of the portfolio allocation experiment were run, along with a robustness test with a head-to-head choice similar to the multiround decision task featured in Question 2 above. Notably, 53% of subjects chose Risk A in the head-to-head choice.

In most versions, subjects were informed about the statistical characteristics of the two risks, but in one version they needed to infer these characteristics from the investment experience itself. Using a mix of 353 undergraduate and Master's students as subjects, Zeisberger found that the mean allocation to Risk A was approximately twice the mean allocation to Risk B. He obtained this result in different versions of his experiment, where the typical experiment involved about 60 subjects. Although mean allocations differed across the various versions of his experiment, the 2:1 ratio was consistent.

Figure C.2 displays the decumulative distributions for returns associated with Risk A and Risk B when experienced over 25 rounds. The figure shows us that Risk B stochastically dominates Risk A. For example, the probability of receiving a return of at least 0% under Risk A is 58% and under Risk B is 67%. Subject to a qualification about framing, this implies that both CPT and SP/A theory would predict every subject with an aspiration point of 0% would choose Risk B.

In fact, stochastic dominance implies no matter which return we select as aspiration level, the probability of achieving that return is higher with Risk B than Risk A. Therefore, given transparent framing, in the multiround version of the decision task, everyone should have chosen Risk B.

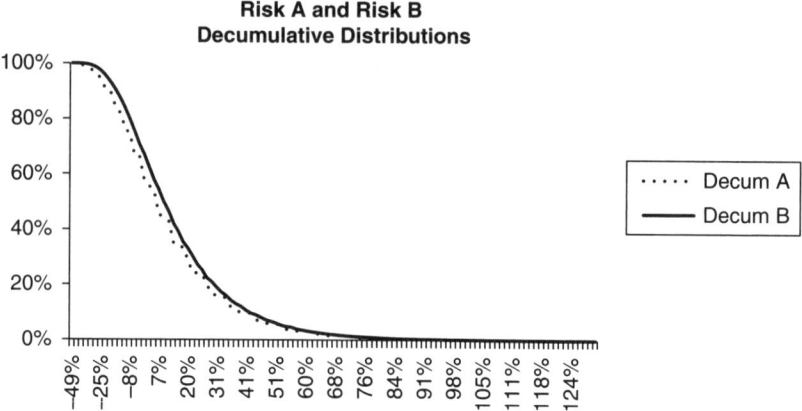

Figure C.2 This figure displays the decumulative distributions for returns associated with Risk A and Risk B in Zeisberger's experiment, when repeated over 25 rounds.

Because the above information was not presented as part of the experiment, and is opaque rather than transparent, there is good reason to suspect that some will mistakenly choose Risk A in the multiround version. In other words, there is every reason to suspect that subjects fail to understand how the information relevant to the single round aggregates over time. The behavioral term for the bias whereby people treat the multiround version in the same way as the single-round version is "myopia." When the issue at hand also involves loss aversion, the phenomenon is called "myopic loss aversion," a term introduced by economists Shlomo Benartzi and Richard Thaler.[1]

MORE INSIGHTS FROM CPT: BONDS AND DERIVATIVES

The remainder of this chapter contains a mix of mathematically oriented material and more qualitatively oriented material. To begin, consider the following example pertaining to CPT that was developed by Tversky and Kahneman.

Imagine choosing between two risks, called Risk F and Risk G, with F resembling a risk-free bond, and G resembling a risky convertible bond. Specifically, Risk F is risk free and pays $2,500 at a future date, say in 30 days. Risk G features payoff that depends on which of three events occurs during the next 12 months. Event E_L (L for low) occurs when the return on the S&P 500 turns out to be negative. If event E_L occurs, Risk G pays $0, corresponding to the bond issuer defaulting. Event E_M (M for Middle) occurs if the return on the S&P 500 lies between 0% and 30%. If event E_M occurs, Risk G pays $2,500. Event E_H (H for High) occurs if the return on the S&P 500 exceeds 30%. If event E_H occurs, Risk G pays

$7,500, corresponding to the option component of the convertible bond, when the bond converts to equity.

If given a choice between Risk F and Risk G, which you would choose, F or G?

Unlike the Kahneman-Tversky questions that we have thus far been discussing, this last question does not feature stated probabilities. You might know enough about historical returns to form a well-educated guess about the probabilities of the three events. However, Tversky and Kahneman assumed no such knowledge for the purpose of this question.

Of course, assessing risks is one of the primary responsibilities of risk managers. In this respect, exact probabilities are rarely given to us in real-world problems, and so we need to make educated judgments. We tend to draw on our experience and skills to develop a general sense of the likelihoods with which such events can be expected to occur.

As mentioned previously, in prospect theory, judgments about beliefs, even if known to be imperfect, are represented by what Tversky and Kahneman call decision weights. In CPT, these weights are also known as "capacities" and have a mathematical structure known as a "Choquet integral." The weight $W(E)$ that a person assigns to an event is "like" a probability in that it is non-negative. Moreover, just as the cumulative probability associated with an inclusive event such as "E_L or E_M or E_H" is unity, $W(E_L \text{ or } E_M \text{ or } E_H) = 1$. Moreover, $W(E_L) \leq W(E_L \text{ or } E_M)$, just as $Prob\{E_L\}$, the probability that E_L occurs, is less than or equal to $Prob\{E_L \text{ or } E_M\}$, the probability that either E_L or E_M occurs. Of course, a similar statement holds for any pair of events so selected. I should also note that CPT features two capacity functions, W^+ for gains and W^- for losses. Below I focus on the case for gains and ignore and the +-superscripts.

While the function $W(E)$ can certainly be a probability measure $Prob\{E\}$, it need not be, by which I mean that the function $W(E)$ might not satisfy all the laws of probability. For example, given that E_L and E_M are mutually exclusive, then $Prob\{E_L \text{ or } E_M\}$ must equal $Prob(E_L) + Prob\{E_M\}$. However, decision weights are not required to satisfy such a condition, and so it might happen that $W(E_L \text{ or } E_M) > W(E_L) + W(E_M)$.

Decision weights that do not conform to probabilities can change the whole game of how people face uncertain prospects when they "know" they do not know the underlying probabilities, or do not even know how probability is applicable as a concept to the situation they face.

Back to Risk F and Risk G. Here is how Tversky and Kahneman model the condition describing Risk F being ranked more highly than Risk G. The CPT value of Risk F is given by $v(2,500)$, where $v(x)$ is the prospect theory value function. The value of Risk G is the "decision-weighted average" of receiving either $v(2,500)$ or $v(7,500)$, (or $v(0)$, which is 0). CPT begins weighting at the high end, which in the case of Risk G is at $7,500.

The weight assigned to $v(7,500)$ is $W(E_H)$. The weight attached to receiving $v(2,500)$ is the marginal difference in cumulative weights, namely $W(7,500$ or $2,500) - W(7,500)$, which is $W(E_M \text{ or } E_H) - W(E_H)$. This last difference is the incremental cumulative weight that a \$2,500 gain brings when we broaden the event in which the person receives at least \$7,500 to become the event in which the person receives at least \$2,500.

According to CPT, a person for whom

$$v(7,500) > W(E_H)v(7,500) + (W(E_H \text{ or } E_M) - W(E_M))v(2,500)$$

will choose Risk F over Risk G.

Next consider a choice between two different risks, Risk J and Risk K, which can be thought of as stylized derivatives. The payoffs to both risks depend on the same three events described above for Risk F and Risk G. As you will shortly see, the payoff to Risk J corresponds to the type of "black swan barbell" strategy popularized by Nassim Taleb, while the payoff to Risk K corresponds to the payoff from an out-of-the-money index call option.

Specifically, Risk J and Risk K both pay \$0 if the return on the S&P 500 is between 0 and 30%. If the return on the S&P 500 is negative, then Risk J pays \$2,500 and Risk K pays \$0. If the return on the S&P 500 exceeds 30%, Risk J pays \$2,500 and Risk K pays \$7,500.

If given a choice between Risk J and Risk K, think about which you would choose, J or K?

According to CPT, a person for whom

$$W(E_H) v(7,500) > W(E_H \text{ or } E_M) v(2,500)$$

will choose Risk K over Risk J.

Tversky and Kahneman tell us that people choose Risk F more frequently than Risk G, and that they choose Risk K more frequently than Risk J. Here is how they analyze what this choice pattern means from the perspective of CPT. By recalling that $W(E_L \text{ or } E_M \text{ or } E_H) = 1$, and substituting $W(E_H) v(7,500)$ from the second inequality into the first, Tversky and Kahneman conclude that

$$W(E_L \text{ or } E_M \text{ or } E_H) - W(E_M \text{ or } E_H) > W(E_L \text{ or } E_H) - W(E_H).$$

To be sure, this inequality implies that $W(E)$ cannot be a probability measure, because for a probability measure, the above inequality must hold with equality. Therefore, $W(E)$ is not additive, but *subadditive*. However, the inequality also tells us that removing E_L from "E_L or E_M or E_H" has more of an impact on weight W than removing that same E_L from "E_L or E_H." This corresponds to the function $W(E)$ displaying greater sensitivity at the top extreme than in the middle range, which is in line with the CPT-weighting function, and for that matter also the SP/A-weighting function.

To gain additional insight into what subadditivity means, consider what happens when we provide probabilities. Economist and Nobel Laureate Maurice Allais proposed an example in which $Prob\{E_L\}$ = 1%, $Prob\{E_M\}$ = 89%, and $Prob\{E_H\}$ = 10%. He pointed out that in event E_M, Risk F and Risk G share a common payoff, or consequence, in that they both pay $2,500. Moreover, in event E_M, both Risk J and Risk K share a common consequence of $0. Therefore, if we begin with Risk F and Risk G, and reduce the common consequence from $2,500 to $0 for both, we will arrive at Risk J and Risk K respectively.

The impact of this last operation to an expected utility maximizer would be to reduce the amount $0.89 \times v(2,500)$ from the expected utilities of Risk F and Risk G respectively to arrive at the expected utilities for Risk J and Risk K. Therefore, an expected utility maximizer who strictly ranks Risk F over Risk G will strictly prefer Risk J over Risk K.

People whose preferences conform to CPT, with subadditive weighting functions $W(E)$, might well select both Risk F and Risk K in the two respective choice situations. CPT explains the effect by having the impact of the $2,500 shift in event E_M be lower in the transformation from Risk G to Risk K than it is from Risk F to Risk J. That is, the move away from the certainty of receiving $2,500 causes a large loss of value relative to the situation when a certain payoff was not in the choice menu.

This example underscores one of the most important features of rank-based weighting theories: the weight accorded to receiving a specific amount, say $2,500, depends not just on the probability of receiving the $2,500, but how the $2,500 ranks relative to other possible outcomes in a given risk. Between two risky alternatives, the weights can vary significantly, even when the amounts and probabilities are the same.

Rank dependence is especially important in situations involving *ambiguity*, in which people do not know what the underlying probabilities are, or even whether probability is meaningful in the frequentist sense. Nevertheless, they can still use decision weights that are structured as Choquet integrals.[2] Moreover, rank dependence provides the mechanism whereby aversion to ambiguity can manifest itself as overweighting of extreme unfavorable events in the sense of focusing on worst cases, without having to be consistent in respect to the laws of probability.

MIXED RESULTS

Both CPT and SP/A theories provide insights about important psychological issues that arise when people make decisions about risk. At the same time, neither theory offers a complete framework. CPT stresses the framing of gains and losses, loss aversion, the fourfold pattern, and quasi-hedonic issues associated with prior gains and losses. SP/A stresses emotional need—such as fear, hope, and achieving success—and how people's choices reflect their efforts to satisfy those needs.

Risk managers seeking to apply these theories need to be a bit on guard. In this section, I consider some examples to bring out important nuances. The first example pertains to how a hypothetical decision-maker with typical Tversky-Kahneman parameter values would choose between the safe A and risky B in the Kahneman-Tversky concurrent choice decision task (Question 3 of Chapter 3).

In Chapter 3, I pointed out that the majority of subjects in survey-based experiments choose A over B. Nevertheless, a quick computational check shows that a hypothetical decision-maker with the Tversky-Kahneman CPT-parameters $\alpha = 0.88$ and $\alpha = 0.69$ would actually prefer the risky B over the safe A. This is somewhat of a surprise, in that with the value of α being 0.88, the value function is concave in the domain of gains. The driving issue here is actually the weighting function, which leads the probability weight associated with receiving the highest gain of \$10,000 to be 17% higher than the associated probability. The combination of effects produced by the weighting function and concave value function with α being 0.88 provides a slight edge to B over A.

Here is a second example to bring out the nuances of applying theory to practice. Consider a decision task featuring choice from a set of two alternatives M and N with the same expected payoffs.

- M = a sure loss of \$500
- N = a fifty-fifty risk where you will either lose \$1,000 or lose \$0

If you were asked which risk you would you choose, what would you say? Although there is some variability in the way that people respond to this question, the most frequent choice is the risky alternative N. About 50% of undergraduate finance majors and 75% of graduate students choose N. For the group containing our protagonists, Beth and Larry, 68% chose N. Notably, Beth chose N, but Larry chose to accept the sure loss M.

Beth explains, "I don't like the concept of sure losses and am willing to take the 50/50 risk to avoid loss altogether." In contrast, Larry explains, "It seems much more appealing to me to lose \$500 than it is for a 50/50 chance to lose either \$1,000 or \$0. For me, the emotional pain of losing the additional \$500 is much more intense than the pleasure I would receive if I didn't lose anything at all."

When I asked people in other groups to explain their thought processes in responding to this question, I asked some of them to include a comment about whether they would have responded differently if the stakes were larger by a factor of 10 and 100 respectively, and smaller by 1/10 the size and 1/100 the size respectively. There is considerable variation in the comments people provide. Consider the following two comments:

- I would rather take the sure loss. If the stakes were larger by 10 or 100 I would take the loss. If the stakes decreased by 1/10 or 1/100 I would flip the coin.
- I would choose to take the chance to lose $1000, since the odds are 50–50, I feel like I have a good chance of losing $0, which is the optimal situation. If the factors were increased, I would probably not choose the same, because I would risk losing a larger amount of money. If the odds were decreased, I would not change my answer, because I would be risking less money in the process.

As with Beth and Larry, these respondents made opposite choices. However, they did agree that as the size of stakes increase, they are less willing to take the risk. This is not a uniform reaction: some people say that they would behave the same way no matter what the stake size.

From the perspective of CPT and SP/A theory, what are we to make of this choice mix? Given that the probabilities involved are fifty-fifty and furthest from the extremes, CPT predicts that people will always choose the risky prospect N. This choice pattern appears to work for about two-thirds of the population at these stakes, and less when the stakes are larger.

SP/A theory makes a more nuanced prediction than CPT, because it accounts for the balanced interaction among the needs for security, potential, and aspiration. Someone whose aspiration level is $0, meaning no loss, and for whom achieving this goal is very important will be prone to select N. Someone for whom the relative need for security is strongest will be prone to choose M. Therefore, SP/A theory can accommodate the mixed choice pattern for the preceding decision task, whereas CPT cannot.

Lopes and Oden implicitly view $0 as the natural aspiration level, and emphasize that when the level of the success probability A of achieving aspiration is common across all alternatives, then choice is determined by the value of SP. Such is the case when $0 is the aspiration level and no alternative offers an opportunity to reach $0.

The following decision task provides another example. This decision task features a choice between two alternatives O and P with the same expected payoff (−$500).

- O = a sure loss of $500
- P = a 2:1 risk where you will either lose $1,000 with probability 1/3 or lose $250 with probability 2/3

If you were asked which risk you would you choose, what would you say? Although there is some variability in the way in which people respond to this question, the most frequent choice is the risky alternative P. About 60% of undergraduate finance majors and 70% of graduate students choose P. For the group containing our protagonists, Beth and Larry, 65% chose P. Notably, Larry chose P, but Beth chose to accept the sure loss O.

CPT predicts that people will choose P. This is because the two alternatives feature the same expected payoff, and the person finds themselves in the domain of losses with risks that involve probabilities of moderate magnitudes. (This is easily checked using the conventional CPT-parameter values.) SP/A theory makes no definitive prediction. However, aspiration plays no role in the choice, because A = 0 under the assumption that $0 is the aspiration level. Therefore, fear would incline a person to choose the sure loss O, and hope would incline a person to choose the risky P.

Larry, who earlier had accepted the sure loss M, chose P in this problem. He explains, "The odds seem to be in my favor to take the 2:1 risk to lower my losses. Either I can take a guaranteed / sure loss of $500 or take a 66.67% chance of the loss being reduced to $250 and a 33.33% chance of doubling the loss from $500 to $1,000. Based upon the 2/3 odds of lowering my losses by 50%, I indicated I would take the additional risk over the sure loss."

Beth, who earlier took the risky alternative N, chose O in this problem. She explains, "I am going to lose money no matter what and rather cap losses and not risk having them extended even with these probabilities."

An Integrated Approach

The logical starting point for integrating CPT and SP/A theory is the editing phase of CPT. The evidence is quite overwhelming that framing is a critical issue. Both theories involve inverse-S-shaped weighting functions, and so this is an important feature that they share, as this shape is what underlies the fourfold behavior pattern. I suggest using the SP/A function for the integrated framework, as it is consistent with the principle of psychophysics, but also directly captures the strength of emotions fear and hope.

Combining the evaluation criteria of the two theories can be accomplished by redefining *SP*, whereby the CPT value $v(x)$ replaces outcome x. Doing so brings loss aversion into the integrated framework. If we label the redefined *SP* as *SP'*, then the criterion function $L(SP',A)$ will capture the impacts of fear, hope, and aspiration, alongside the gain/loss features emphasized by prospect theory.

Keep in mind that some people indicate that their willingness to be risk seeking depends on the size of stakes. When Kahneman and Tversky developed the value function $v(x)$, they adapted an idea proposed by Harry Markowitz, the founder of mean-variance analysis. Markowitz proposed a value function that is convex around the origin in the domain of losses, but is concave for large losses. This shape suggests that people are willing to be risk seeking in the domain of losses for small to moderate-size losses, but are risk averse when the possibility of large losses is involved. Using a value function with the Markowitz property will make sense for some cases.

Figure C.3 displays a graph of the L function, and Table C.5 provides underlying numerical data. Consider cells in this table that all feature the

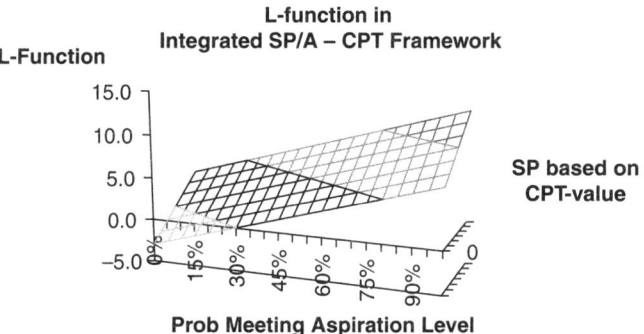

Figure C.3 This figure displays a graph of the SP/A L–function. The linear structure reflects the simplifying linearity assumption for L(SP,A).

Table C.5 This table provides underlying numerical data for the L-function displayed in Figure C.3

Aspiration-VaR Meet or Beat Probability	SP based on CPT-value function						
	−3	−2	−1	0	1	2	3
0%	−3.0	−2.0	−1.0	0.0	1.0	2.0	3.0
5%	−2.5	−1.5	−0.5	0.5	1.5	2.5	3.5
10%	−2.0	−1.0	0.0	1.0	2.0	3.0	4.0
15%	−1.5	−0.5	0.5	1.5	2.5	3.5	4.5
20%	−1.0	0.0	1.0	2.0	3.0	4.0	5.0
25%	−0.5	0.5	1.5	2.5	3.5	4.5	5.5
30%	0.0	1.0	2.0	3.0	4.0	5.0	6.0
35%	0.5	1.5	2.5	3.5	4.5	5.5	6.5
40%	1.0	2.0	3.0	4.0	5.0	6.0	7.0
45%	1.5	2.5	3.5	4.5	5.5	6.5	7.5
50%	2.0	3.0	4.0	5.0	6.0	7.0	8.0
55%	2.5	3.5	4.5	5.5	6.5	7.5	8.5
60%	3.0	4.0	5.0	6.0	7.0	8.0	9.0
65%	3.5	4.5	5.5	6.5	7.5	8.5	9.5
70%	4.0	5.0	6.0	7.0	8.0	9.0	10.0
75%	4.5	5.5	6.5	7.5	8.5	9.5	10.5
80%	5.0	6.0	7.0	8.0	9.0	10.0	11.0
85%	5.5	6.5	7.5	8.5	9.5	10.5	11.5
90%	6.0	7.0	8.0	9.0	10.0	11.0	12.0
95%	6.5	7.5	8.5	9.5	10.5	11.5	12.5
100%	7.0	8.0	9.0	10.0	11.0	12.0	13.0

same value of L, say 4.5. The points in Figure C.3 associated with a common L-value all lie on the same indifference curve. The trade-off displayed in Figure C.3 and Table C.5 involves sacrificing SP' in order to increase A. The linear structure displayed in Figure C.3 and Table C.5 reflects the simplifying linearity assumption for $L(SP,A)$. In a more general setting, $L(SP,A)$ is typically concave, but not necessarily linear.

The integrated model provides guidance for how risk managers can bring together key ideas from both CPT and SP/A theory. In practice, risk managers need a tool for identifying key aspects of the framework that is a bit less formal than the model, and yet still captures its essential features. Surveys are ideally suited to this purpose.

Rolling Up Our Sleeves and Getting to Work

A psychological theory of risk taking that integrates SP/A theory and CPT provides a broad framework for analyzing how people face risk. The survey questions discussed in the previous section provide tools for navigating the psychological lay of the land. Navigation is part art and part science, as people are systematic in some respects, but ad hoc in others.

Responses to survey questions provide risk managers with input to engage in an analysis that can be qualitative or quantitative. This section provides some examples for how the qualitative framework can be employed, and the following section focuses on a quantitative modeling analysis.

Table C.6 presents data for six subjects who participated in a series of experiments that elicited their responses to the survey questions under discussion. These subjects were part of a group of 20 experienced business people who were enrolled in an executive MBA program. Table C.6 is divided into three panels. The top panel provides information about the responses of each of the five subjects to prospect theory-motivated questions. These subjects are identified as William, Warren, Frank, Maureen, Maria, and Alfred. The middle panel provides responses to the SP/A-motivated questions. The bottom panel provides responses to the judgments elicited about the six Lopes risk alternatives. Means and standard deviations for the whole group of 20 are provided in the two columns at the far right.

The focus of this discussion is to analyze the psychological profiles and judgments of the six participants. These participants have been selected largely because of the aspiration levels they specified in connection with the portion of the survey pertaining to the Lopes risk alternatives. The range of aspiration levels is $1,000 to $1,500. As Table C.6 indicates, SS had the highest ranking. In this respect, 48% chose SS. Typically, SS and RF receive the top two rankings in most groups. For this group, 24% gave their top rank to RF, and 19% gave their top rank to LS.

Table C.6 This table presents data for six subjects who participated in a series of experiments that elicited their responses to the survey questions discussed in Chapters 2, 3, and 5

Variable	William	Warren	Frank	Maureen	Maria	Alfred	Mean	StdDev
Loss aversion	10.0	2.0	2.5	10.0	1.0	5.0	4.3	5.9
A	1	1	1	0	0	0	52.4%	51.2%
D	0	1	0	1	1	1	71.4%	46.3%
AD	0	1	0	0	0	0	33.3%	48.3%
BC	0	0	0	0	0	0	0.0%	0.0%
switched from E to H in Question 7, Chapter 3	1	1	0	0	0	0	28.6%	46.3%
quasi-hedonic in prior gains (switch)	0	1	0	0	0	0	14.3%	35.9%
quasi-hedonic in prior losses (switch)	1	0	0	0	1	0	42.9%	50.7%
1 fear	1	3	1	1	2	2	2.3	1.2
2 hope	6	4	2	2	6	3	4.7	1.7
3 cautious hope	6	6	3	3	6	4	4.8	1.4
4 target outcome	6	4	6	6	7	6	5.7	1.2
5 missing goal causes great pain	2	4	2	6	6	5	4.4	1.6
6 avoid unfavorable	6	3	1	2	3	5	3.5	1.5
7 try for most favorable	4	4	6	5	6	4	5.4	1.1
8 go for lottery if downside small	6	7	6	6	4	6	5.7	1.1
9 go for lottery even if downside not small	2	5	4	5	4	5	4.3	1.4
10 downside looms large, so take small risks	6	4	6	3	4	3	4.3	1.6
11 upside looms large, so take big risks	2	4	2	5	5	6	3.9	1.7
12 max odds success	4	4	6	6	7	6	5.3	1.2
13 willing to accept more downside risk to achieve goal	6	5	5	5	6	6	5.3	1.2
14 willing to accept less upside reward to achieve goal	6	5	5	5	6	5	4.7	1.5
15 willing to accept large downside to achieve goal	2	2	4	5	6	5	3.9	1.7
16 willing to take risks if guaranteed aspiration	6	7	5	6	7	6	5.8	1.1
17 willing to take risks if certain goal will be missed	4	1	3	3	2	2	3.2	1.9

Continued

Table C.6 Continued

	Variable	William	Warren	Frank	Maureen	Maria	Alfred	Mean	StdDev
	Aspiration level	$1,000	$1,100	$1,200	$1,300	$1,430	$1,500	$1,157	$406
Rank	1. Risk Floor	1	6	3	6	1	6	3.6	2.0
	2. Short Shot	6	1	1	5	5	5	2.8	1.6
	3. Peaked	3	2	2	4	4	4	3.0	1.2
	4. Uniform	5	4	6	2	3	3	3.6	1.6
	5. Bimodal	4	3	5	1	6	2	4.3	1.8
	6. Long Shot	2	5	4	3	2	1	3.8	1.9
WTA	1. Risk Floor	$1,100	$1,100	$1,300	$1,300	$1,400	$1,150	$1,227	$319
	2. Short Shot	$1,100	$1,200	$1,200	$1,300	$1,100	$1,150	$1,176	$382
	3. Peaked	$1,100	$1,100	$1,000	$1,400	$1,100	$1,200	$1,191	$438
	4. Uniform	$1,100	$1,100	$1,100	$1,750	$1,200	$1,300	$1,276	$419
	5. Bimodal	$1,100	$1,250	$900	$1,800	$1,100	$1,500	$1,225	$499
	6. Long Shot	$1,100	$1,400	$1,400	$1,700	$1,400	$1,800	$1,460	$652
WTP	1. Risk Floor	$1,100	$1,100	$800	$700	$700	$1,000	$914	$170
	2. Short Shot	$1,100	$1,100	$600	$700	$400	$1,000	$826	$349
	3. Peaked	$1,100	$1,100	$500	$800	$400	$1,050	$850	$343
	4. Uniform	$1,100	$1,100	$200	$900	$500	$1,100	$814	$352
	5. Bimodal	$1,100	$1,100	$400	$950	$400	$1,150	$790	$356
	6. Long Shot	$1,100	$1,100	$300	$850	$700	$1,200	$801	$392

William is the CEO of a web-centered firm who characterizes himself as an entrepreneur. Relative to the group mean, what distinguishes William is the very low response he provides for fear, and the very high responses he provides for being hopeful, cautiously hopeful, and setting a specific goal. Notably, he reports a low value in respect to feeling pain for missing a goal.

William gave his top ranking to RF, and his second top ranking to SS. In describing how he arrived at his rankings, he states, "I do not like risk that eventually pays out nothing, I like to have a certain security of getting at least something, but I am not a gambler."

We can see from Table C.6 that William identifies his aspiration level as $1,000, and all his valuations are $1,100. About his valuations, he tells us that he used a heuristic by selecting "the mean price without calculating the nearest possible fair value."

Relative to the group mean, what distinguishes Warren is the very high response he provides for being cautiously hopeful, and the low response he provides for setting a specific goal.

Warren has an aspiration level of $1,100, the expected payoff for all the alternatives. He gives his top rating to SS. Table C.7 shows that SS offers the highest probability of achieving his aspiration of $1,100. Warren's ranking judgment is consistent with Warren being average in respect to attaching importance to the achievement of his aspiration level.

Warren assigns a WTA to SS of $1,200, $100 above his aspiration level. Notably, his WTA for RF, PK, and U alternatives is his aspiration level. Theory suggests that achieving aspiration is important to Warren, in that he sets his WTA above his aspiration level. However, notice that he assigns even higher WTA values to BM and LS, thereby displaying preference reversal. Theory suggests that when Warren sees himself as holding either BM or LS, either his aspiration level increases, his hope increases, or the importance he attaches to reaching his aspiration increases.

Table C.7 This table displays the probability of achieving a aspiration level of $1,100, for each of the six Lopes risky alternatives

	Pr meet aspiration					
	RF	SS	PK	U	BM	LS
$1,000	46%	69%	63%	55%	51%	47%
$1,100	31%	69%	50%	50%	50%	32%
$1,111	31%	69%	50%	50%	50%	32%
$1,200	31%	54%	37%	45%	49%	32%
$1,300	22%	31%	37%	40%	49%	32%
$1,430	15%	31%	26%	35%	48%	32%
$1,500	15%	0%	17%	30%	45%	32%
$1,829	6%	0%	5%	20%	33%	22%

Warren's WTP-values are $1,100 for every alternative. This is consistent with the "sand trap" property associated with the aspiration level and WTP. Notice that Warren's coefficient of loss aversion is 2.0. Loss aversion lowers the value of SP below the expected payoff of $1,100. However, a high aspiration premium, when added to SP, can bring the sum of SP and the aspiration premium, which equates to WTP, back up to the aspiration level.

Next, consider the responses of Maureen, another CEO, whose aspiration level is $1,300. Maureen provides low responses in respect to experiencing the emotions of fear and hope. What differentiates Maureen from the majority of others in her group is being specific about her aspiration level. Maureen reports that missing a goal generates greater pain for her than most others in her group.

In addition, Maureen reports that her decision style involves being willing take a big risk to reach her goal. In terms of the model, this suggests a relatively high value for ζ.

Maureen gives her top ranking to BM. In this respect, Table C.7 shows that BM offers the highest probability of achieving an aspiration level of $1,300. She also assigns the highest WTA to BM, $1,800, and her WTA valuations are ordered exactly as her rankings.

She assigns her highest WTP rating to BM $950, and her WTP valuations are also ordered exactly as her rankings. Her lower WTP valuations are consistent with having a lower probability of reaching aspiration when Maureen has to pay to play. This is reinforced by Maureen's high coefficient of loss aversion, which is 10. Notice from Table C.6 that Maureen is willing to take risk in the domain of gains, but becomes risk seeking in the domain of losses.

Finally, consider Maria, whose aspiration level is stated as $1,430, but is intended to be understood as "greater than $1,430." Maria's responses for hope, cautious hope, and target are well above the group mean. What distinguishes her as well is the high score she assigns to maximizing the probability of success. In addition, she implicitly tells us that goal achievement is important to her, because she is willing to sacrifice both security and potential in order to increase the probability of reaching aspiration.

Maria assigns her top rating to RF and her second-highest rating to LS. Notably, her WTA and WTP valuations for RF and LS are equal. This equality suggests that Maria might be indifferent, or close to indifference, when it comes to these two risks. Because $1,430 is at the top of the payoff range for SS, choosing SS would lead to a probability of reaching aspiration that is 0. This fact is reflected in Maria's assigning a low rating of 5 to SS. Notice that Maria's ratings and valuations are consistent in that she does not exhibit preference reversal.

Notably, RF and LS do not have particularly high probabilities of achieving aspiration. The BM alternative offers much better odds. However, Maria provides very strong responses for hope and cautious hope, which apparently leads her to overweigh the high outcomes.

Maria has a low coefficient of loss aversion, which is consistent with her choices in the prospect theory-based questions. She also displays the quasi-hedonic editing property of becoming sensitized to a prior loss, and switching from risk-seeking behavior to risk-averse behavior in the domain of losses.

The above discussion offers a qualitative analysis of the judgments made by these five business people. A quantitative analysis is more involved. It is important to see how applying the integrated formal model works. At the same time, when it comes to examining the behavior of specific individuals, risk managers need to be cautious about being too confident about applying the model. The model is more of a tool to help guide our intuition.

APPLYING THE MODEL

Back to mathematics: bearing the preceding considerations in mind, here is what we need in the way of parameters to describe a specific individual using the integrated SP/A-CPT framework. On the CPT side, we need a parameter α to capture the concavity of the value function $v(x)$ in the domain of gains, and a parameter β to capture the convexity of the value function $v(x)$ in the domain of losses. In respect to loss aversion, we need a coefficient λ. On the SP/A side, we need a parameter s to capture the strength of the need for security, a parameter p to capture the need for potential, and a parameter ζ to capture the relative strength of the need to reach aspiration.

To try and keep the approach as straightforward as possible, here is a heuristic approach to obtaining parameter values. Below I describe a heuristic to obtain a value for α from the decision-maker's choice between the safe A and risky B in the Kahneman-Tversky concurrent choice decision task (Question 3 of Chapter 3).

Recall from the earlier discussion in this chapter that a hypothetical decision-maker with typical CPT parameter values ($\alpha = 0.88$, $\gamma = 0.69$) would choose the risky B over the safe A. A change we could make to induce the hypothetical decision-maker to choose A over B would be to lower α from 0.88 to 0.85. Doing so would give a slight edge to A over B.

As a practical matter, consider values for α that provide stronger preference between A and B, such as 0.76 and 1.0. For sake of illustration, the analysis I present below uses the heuristic that if A is chosen over B, then we set $\alpha = 0.76$, but if B is chosen over A, then we set $\alpha = 1.0$.

Similarly, we obtain a value for β from the choice between the sure loss C and the risky D. Consider using the heuristic that if D is chosen over C, then we set $\beta = 0.88$, the Tversky-Kahneman parameter value, but if C is chosen over D, then we set $\beta = 1.0$. When $\beta = 1.0$, risk aversion in the domain of losses will occur through the weighting function (fear).

In respect to λ, I propose using the imputed value reported in Table C.6, based on the response to Question 2 in Chapter 3.

Next, the SP/A parameters are inferred by fitting s, p, r, and ζ to the ranking and valuations of the Lopes risk alternatives. The idea here is to use the model to provide ballpark estimates of parameters that more or less capture, to the extent possible, the judgments people have made. Table C.8 provides sample output.

Here is an illustration using William, who you will recall is a CEO who also describes himself as an entrepreneur. By virtue of his responses to the prospect theory questions (A and C), we assign William coefficients $\alpha = 0.76$ and $\beta = 1.0$. His response to the loss-aversion question leads us to set $\lambda = 10$.

In his survey responses, William tells us that he is low in fear, but very high in hope and cautious hope. At first glance, this suggests a parameter value of

Table C.8 This table provides sample output for a procedure in which SP/A parameters are inferred by fitting s, p, r, and ζ to the ranking and valuations of the Lopes risk alternatives

		William	Warren	Frank	Maureen	Maria	Alfred
Parameters	α	0.76	0.76	0.76	1	1	1
	β	1.00	0.88	1.00	0.88	0.88	0.88
	λ	10.00	2.00	2.50	10.00	1.00	1.00
	r	0.4	0.5	0.2	0.5	0.8	0.8
	s	10	1	5.5	1	10	10
	p	2	3	0.2	2	10	10
	ζ	5	500	130	1500	1300	1300
Rank	1. Risk Floor	1	6	3	6	1	1
	2. Short Shot	6	1	1	5	4	4
	3. Peaked	3	4	4	4	5	5
	4. Uniform	4	2	2	2	6	6
	5. Bimodal	5	3	5	1	3	3
	6. Long Shot	2	5	6	3	2	2
WTA	1. Risk Floor	$1,151	$1,100	$1,200	$1,300	$1,170	$1,170
	2. Short Shot	$958	$1,100	$1,200	$1,300	$1,022	$1,022
	3. Peaked	$1,000	$1,100	$1,200	$1,300	$1,015	$1,015
	4. Uniform	$961	$1,100	$1,200	$1,300	$977	$977
	5. Bimodal	$958	$1,100	$1,200	$1,300	$1,088	$1,088
	6. Long Shot	$1,061	$1,100	$1,108	$1,300	$1,101	$1,101
WTP	1. Risk Floor	$789	$805	$835	$942	$1,111	$1,111
	2. Short Shot	$222	$488	$584	$869	$776	$776
	3. Peaked	$258	$512	$592	$862	$882	$882
	4. Uniform	$99	$283	$402	$779	$819	$819
	5. Bimodal	$57	$174	$301	$746	$795	$795
	6. Long Shot	$48	$108	$196	$784	$1,624	$1,624

q_s near 0, and a parameter value of q_p considerably larger than 0. However, assigning a high score to being cautiously hopeful might suggest high values for both s and p, with a value of 4 around 0.5. Although William tells us that he definitely sets specific targets, the fact that he does not feel pain for missing a target suggests that his need for reaching aspiration is actually low. Therefore, his combined responses suggest a low parameter value for ζ.

William assigns his top rank to RF, with LS in second place. If William were low in fear in the sense of s being near 0, but high in hope in the sense of p being considerably above 0, there would be little reason for him to assign his top rank to RF. In fact, achieving anything close to his ranking requires that William have a very high fear parameter s. The combination of parameters that produce cautious hope—that is, being simultaneously fearful about low payoffs and hopeful about high payoffs—is effectively what leads the model to favor first RF and second LS.

In respect to William top two rankings, I might mention that William commented that he is a risk taker by nature. However, having a family, he feels the need to restrain his risk-taking tendencies. Assigning the top ranking to RF and LS seems consistent with his self-categorization. As previously mentioned, in describing how he arrived at his rankings, he stated, "I do not like risk that eventually pay out nothing, I like to have a certain security of getting at least something, but I am not a gambler."

Notably, William aspiration parameter value ζ needs to be low, in that, as Table C.7 indicates, the probabilities of reaching an aspiration level of $1,000 are lowest for RF and SS.

We can see from Table C.6 that William identifies his aspiration level as $1,000, and all his valuations as being $1,100. About his valuations, he tells us that he used a heuristic by selecting "the mean price without calculating the nearest possible fair value." In this regard, the model produces values for WTA that are reasonably near $1,100, but not all equal to $1,100. The WTP values are substantially below $1,100, largely because of William's coefficient of loss aversion is very high, and he does not attach great importance to achieving aspiration.

The analysis of William judgments using the model can prompt a risk manager to ask at least two questions in a conversation with William. The questions are the following:

1. Might your aspiration level not really be $1,100, given your WTA and WTP valuations?
2. In view of your high WTP valuations, is your coefficient of loss aversion considerably less than 10?

Circling back to personality traits, the topic discussed at the beginning of the chapter, William conforms to the traits associated with being a CEO and entrepreneur. He is well above average on dispositional optimism and slightly above average in the desire for control. He is also a bit below average on well-being, as is common for people who face a lot of stress. These features serve as background context for a conversation relating to emotions, judgments, and valuations.

Readers might want to think about how the results displayed in Table C.8 can prompt questions that risk managers might ask in conversations with the other five decision-makers. In this regard, there is a general pattern in how r, s, p, and ζ vary as we move from left to right and aspiration levels rise. Notably, potential p and the importance ζ of reaching aspiration are much higher at the right. Cautious hope also strengthens, as can be seen by the higher values of both s and p, in combination with the intermediate values of r.

Appendix D: A Deeper Dive into Heuristics and Biases

This Appendix provides additional insight and detail into the experiments used to identify heuristics and biases, as described in Chapter 4. The best way to understand the experiments is to participate in them as a subject. For this reason, the discussion below is structured as if readers were subjects.

Availability Bias and Restaurant Risk

Consider the fast food chain Burger Chef. Launched in 1958 in Indianapolis by General Equipment, Burger Chef built its enterprise on technology. It equipped its franchises with automatic conveyor broilers designed to mass-produce flame-broiled patties and automated milkshakes. By 1972, Burger Chef had about 1,200 outlets, second only to McDonald's 1,600 outlets. However, McDonald's survives, while Burger Chef disappeared.

Burger Chef failed because it grew too quickly and could not manage its growth. The company which owns Hardee's, acquired Burger Chef and converted most of its locations to restaurants bearing the names of Hardee's and Carl's Jr.

In order to probe some of the risk issues associated with the restaurant business, imagine yourself to be a risk manager who has been assigned the task of assessing the various ways in which a once profitable restaurant might go out of business. For instance, one possible scenario is that revenues fall. Another possible scenario is that costs increase. Of course, both might happen, but for the purpose of this task, assume that only one happens but not the other.

In Figure D.1, you will see a "fault tree" that describes various possible ways in which this might happen, including an "all other" category at the bottom. Imagine that your task is to write down your best guess for the conditional probability attached to each branch. In practice, this undertaking would involve considerable research on the part of a risk manager. However,

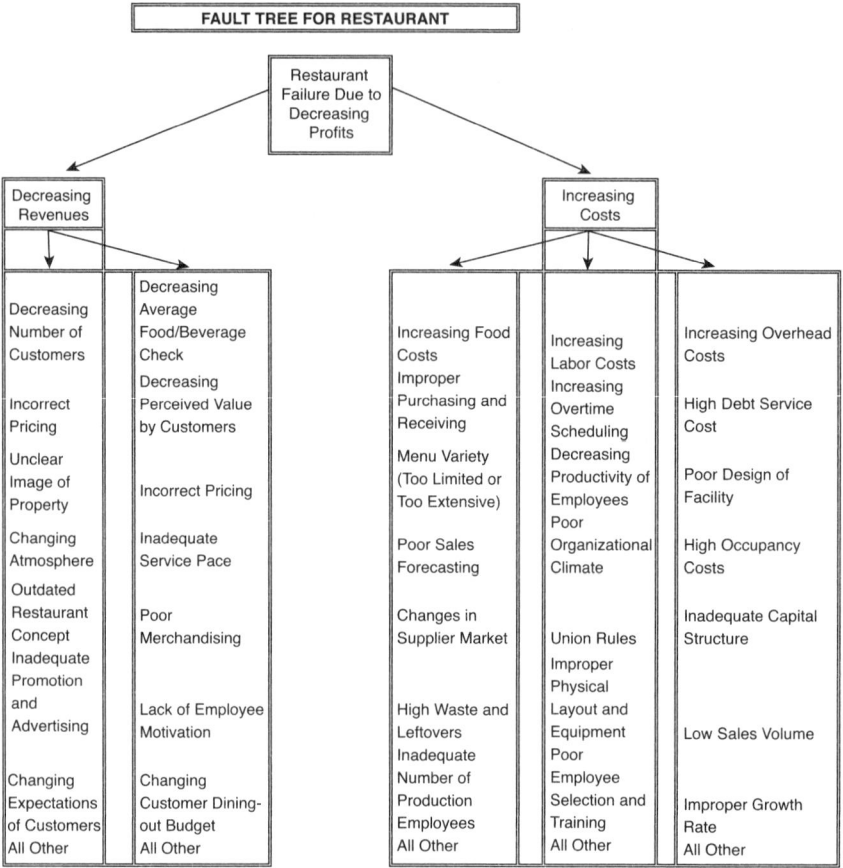

Figure D.1 This figure depicts a "fault tree" describing possible ways in which a once profitable restaurant might go out of business.

for our purposes, readers need only make their best educated guesses, and for those serious enough, jot down guesses on a sheet of paper. Most importantly, readers should do what it takes to understand the nature of the fault tree task and to become actively engaged in the exercise.

Notice that there are only two possible ways the revenues can decrease, decreasing customers and decreasing checks per customer. Assuming that both do not occur at once, the sum of the two conditional probabilities should add up to 100%. Hence, the probability you would attach to "Decreasing Number of Customers" is conditional on the restaurant failing because of "Decreasing Revenues." For example, if you assigned a 60% probability to "Decreasing Number of Customers," then you would assign a 40% probability to "Decreasing Average Food/Beverage Check."

Similarly, the probabilities under "Decreasing Number of Customers" should sum to 100%, as these probabilities are conditional on the event

"Decreasing Number of Customers." That is, the probabilities of the events beginning with "Incorrect Pricing" and ending with "All Other" should sum to 100%. Similar statements hold for all five columns in the table. Fill in the probabilities, remembering to include the probability of any reason not specifically listed in the "All Other" category.

There are many stories like that of Burger Chef. Other cases include Minnie Pearl Chicken, Steak and Ale, and Howard Johnson's. These serve as cases of once vibrant large restaurant chains that have faded from view.

There are many small, independently operated restaurants that have also been forced to close their doors. Owners of failed small restaurants frequently point to many types of reasons their establishments failed early on. Examples include inadequate financing, injudicious use of cash, poor location, and inattention to customer service.

The book *Decision Traps* by J. Edward Russo and Paul Schoemaker discusses a study at the Cornell School of Hotel Administration on restaurant fault trees such as the one displayed in Figure D.1.[1] They make a point about doing this type of analysis, and use a study based upon a somewhat more detailed fault tree, which is displayed as Figure D.2.

Readers are invited to consider how, in their role as risk managers, they would form probability judgments. In doing so, it is important not to go back and look at any prior answers based upon Figure D.1. Remember, the important thing is to do enough of this exercise to understand the nature of the task and to feel engaged. Once you have done so, please continue reading.

According to the study mentioned above, which was published in the 2005 *Cornell Hotel and Restaurant Administration Quarterly*, the most important reason why restaurants fail is lack of concept, one of the issues that appears in both fault trees (Figures D.1 and D.2). The report tells us that the lack of a documented strategy is highly problematic. Also highly problematic is the inability or unwillingness of management to establish and formalize operational standards.

The main point of asking for two fault tree assessments is not so much about concept or operational standards, as about the manner in which people assign probabilities to the "All Other" categories. Figure D.2 is more explicit about items than is Figure D.1. However, every item in Figure D.1 appears in Figure D.2. Therefore, every "All Other" category displayed in Figure D.1 contains its associated "All Other" category displayed in Figure D.2 *plus* additional items. Call the fault tree in Figure D.1 the "short tree" and the fault tree in Figure D.2 the "long tree." A risk manager who is being consistent should assign an "All Other" probability for the short tree that is greater or equal to its associated "All Other" probability for the long tree.

Table D.1 displays the average probability assignments for three different groups. The groups are (1) executive MBA students who are seasoned

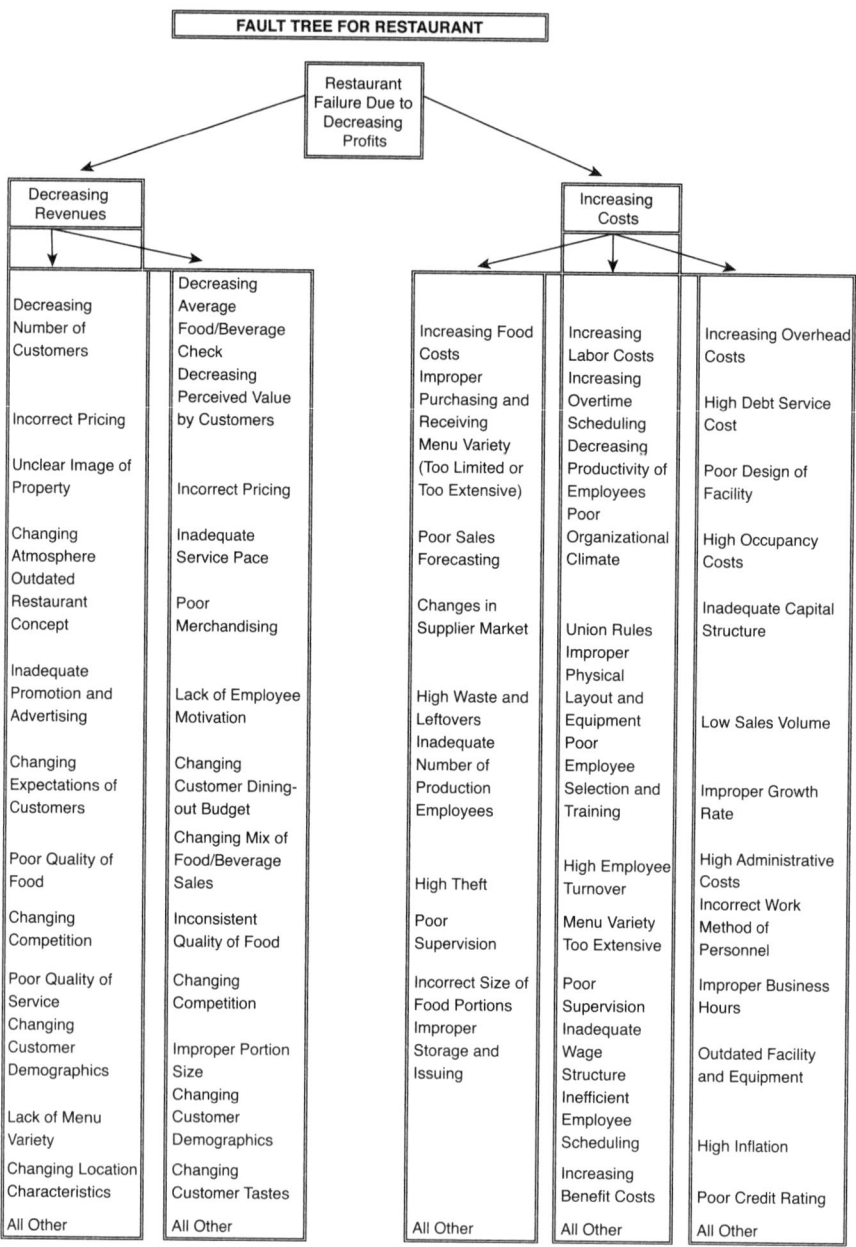

Figure D.2 This figure depicts a "fault tree" describing possible ways in which a once profitable restaurant might go out of business. The fault tree depicted in this figure includes all the possibilities explicitly mentioned in Figure D.1, and additional possibilities as well.

Table D.1 This table displays the average restaurant fault tree probability assignments for the following three different groups: (1) executive MBA students who are seasoned business people, some belonging to the C-suite; (2) undergraduate finance majors; and (3) PhD students in finance

Restaurant Failure Due to Decreasing Profits	Exec MBA			UG			Grad PhD		
	Long Tree Additional Items	Short Tree All Other	Ratio	Long Tree Additional Items	Short Tree All Other	Ratio	Long Tree Additional Items	Short Tree All Other	Ratio
Decreasing Revenues									
Decreasing Number of Customers									
All Other	47.1%	13.8%	3.4	68.2%	12.0%	5.7	48.0%	20.2%	2.4
Decreasing Average Food/Beverage Check									
All Other	37.2%	12.9%	2.9	59.9%	11.8%	5.1	47.9%	18.9%	2.5
Increasing Food Costs									
All Others	32.9%	10.9%	3.0	35.9%	10.0%	3.6	35.7%	18.4%	1.9
Increasing Labor Costs									
All Others	48.7%	12.1%	4.0	57.0%	12.2%	4.7	41.3%	20.1%	2.1
Increasing Overhead Costs									
All Other	42.5%	10.9%	3.9	51.6%	9.6%	5.4	44.5%	18.6%	2.4

business people, some belonging to the C-suite; (2) undergraduate finance majors; and (3) PhD students in finance. The ratio columns in Table D.1 display the ratios of the long tree "All Other" probability to its short tree counterpart. Notice that in all cases, the ratios are well in excess of unity. This means that the probability assigned to the short tree "All Other" categories is strictly less than its long tree counterpart, which is exactly opposite to what is required for consistency. In other words, most people get the relationship upside down. Why? And what does it mean?

Let us begin with the "why." Russo and Schoemaker suggest that the reason why people get the relationship upside down is availability bias. In the short tree version, items that are not explicitly mentioned, and therefore in the "All Other" category are out of sight and therefore out of mind if they are not immediately available in memory. As a result, people are prone to attach too low a probability to events in the "All Other" category in the short tree.

The long tree makes some of the items that belong to the "All Other" category in the short tree explicit. Doing so leads to these items being assigned higher probability in the long tree, where they are explicitly mentioned, as opposed to the short tree where they are implicit. Moreover, the added detail of the long tree might help people think of items that they overlooked when only considering the short tree. The upshot is that people assign a higher probability to the "All Other" category in the long tree, even though it is a proper subset of the "All Other" category in the short tree.

As for the "what does it mean?" the answer is the assignment of probabilities to "All Other" categories in the short tree is too low. *Out of sight really is out of mind.* The net result is the underestimation of risks that are not explicitly mentioned in the analysis.

Parenthetically, I might also mention that undergraduate finance majors, with the least real-world experience, display the greatest bias.

PERCEIVED RISK

Consider Slovic's study about risk perception discussed in Chapter 4. If you were a subject in his study, you might have been asked to answer a question such as the following:

Question D1: Consider the activities and technologies displayed in Table D.2 (which is the same as Table D.1, but repeated here for convenience).

- a. On a scale of 1 to 100, rate these activities and technologies in terms of how risky you perceive them to be for the general population in the United States. Assign a 100 to what you believe to be the riskiest activity. Low numbers should connote low risk, and high numbers high risk. Some people think about this question by guessing the average number of deaths that occur per year in connection with each category.

Table D.2 Activities and technologies associated with Question 2 in Chapter 4 and Question D1 in Appendix D

Possible Risk Events

1	Mountain climbing	15	Bicycles
2	Fire fighting	16	Surgery
3	General aviation	17	Prescription antibiotics
4	Motorcycles	18	Skiing
5	Smoking	19	Commercial aviation
6	Food preservatives	20	Hunting
7	Power mowers	21	X-rays
8	Police work	22	Handguns
9	Large construction	23	Spray cans
10	Swimming	24	Vaccinations
11	Alcoholic beverages	25	Nuclear power
12	Pesticides	26	Home appliances
13	High school and college football	27	Railroads
14	Contraceptives	28	Electric power

b. On a 10-point scale, rate each activity by how well you feel you understand the risks in the list above. If you feel you know risks extremely well, assign the item a 1. If you feel the item is virtually unknown to you, assign the item a 10.

c. On a 10-point scale, rate each activity by the degree to which you would dread the consequences attached to the item. If you feel the possibility of this item induces the highest level of dread, enter a 10. However, if you feel that there is virtually no dread attached to the possibility of this item, enter a 1.

Over a span of 15 years, I administered Question D1 above to a variety of groups such as executive MBA students and undergraduate finance majors in the United States, and business professionals and graduate students in Europe. The common finding from these responses is that dread risk looms very large as a driver of perceived risk. Unknown risk is more uneven.

To analyze these responses, I rank order the responses to each of these questions and regress the perceived risk rankings on the associated rankings for dread risk and unknown risk. For European business professionals, the regression coefficient for dread risk is 0.65. For undergraduates, the coefficient is 0.91. For European graduate students, the coefficient is 0.8. All three coefficients are statistically significant. For unknown risk, the regression coefficient is only statistically significant for European business professionals, and its magnitude is 0.48.

Slovic provides a risk ranking for the activities in Table D.2 that is based on the judgments of experts. This ranking provides the opportunity for a comparison between expert judgments and the judgments of the groups mentioned in the previous paragraph. The comparisons are based on rank orders. In this regard, I identified the activities in which a group's rank differed from the rank associated with expert judgments by at least five. If the group assigned a higher rank (greater risk) to such an activity, I inferred that the group overestimated the risk. If the group assigned a lower rank, I inferred that the group underestimated the risk.

Table D.3 summarizes the results. Notice that in respect to some activities, at least three of the four groups exhibit the same bias. Activities associated with underestimation of risks are food coloring, general aviation, pesticides, contraceptives, and spray cans. Activities associated with overestimation of risks are motorcycles, smoking, home appliances, and electric power. Entries marked NCIB signify no clearly identifiable bias.

Table D.3 This table summarizes the results for four different groups who answered Question D1

	Risk	Business Professionals, Europe	Executive MBA, United States	Undergraduate Finance Majors, United States	Graduate Students in Finance, Europe
1	Motor vehicles	NCIB	underestimate	NCIB	NCIB
2	Food coloring	underestimate	NCIB	underestimate	underestimate
3	Mountain climbing	NCIB	underestimate	NCIB	NCIB
4	Firefighting	NCIB	underestimate	NCIB	NCIB
5	General aviation	underestimate	underestimate	underestimate	underestimate
6	Motorcycles	overestimate	underestimate	overestimate	overestimate
7	Smoking	overestimate	underestimate	overestimate	overestimate
8	Food preservatives	underestimate	overestimate	underestimate	NCIB
9	Power mowers	NCIB	overestimate	underestimate	NCIB
10	Police work	NCIB	underestimate	NCIB	NCIB
11	Large construction	NCIB	underestimate	NCIB	NCIB
12	Swimming	NCIB	NCIB	NCIB	NCIB
13	Alcoholic beverages	NCIB	underestimate	NCIB	NCIB
14	Pesticides	overestimate	overestimate	NCIB	overestimate
15	High school and college football	underestimate	overestimate	NCIB	NCIB

Continued

Table D.3 Continued

	Risk	Business Professionals, Europe	Executive MBA, United States	Undergraduate Finance Majors, United States	Graduate Students in Finance, Europe
16	Contraceptives	underestimate	NA	underestimate	underestimate
17	Bicycles	overestimate	NA	underestimate	underestimate
18	Surgery	NCIB	underestimate	NCIB	NCIB
19	Prescription antibiotics	NCIB	NCIB	NCIB	NCIB
20	Skiing	NCIB	underestimate	underestimate	underestimate
21	Commercial aviation	NCIB	NA	NCIB	NCIB
22	Hunting	NCIB	underestimate	NCIB	NCIB
23	X-rays	NCIB	NCIB	NCIB	NCIB
24	Handguns	NCIB	NCIB	NCIB	NCIB
25	Spray cans	underestimate	NCIB	underestimate	underestimate
26	Vaccinations	underestimate	overestimate	NCIB	NCIB
27	Nuclear power	underestimate	underestimate	NCIB	NCIB
28	Home appliances	overestimate	overestimate	NCIB	overestimate
29	Railroads	underestimate	NA	NCIB	NCIB
30	Electric power	overestimate	overestimate	NCIB	overestimate

Nuclear power is on neither list. However, based on data collected between 2001 and 2004, both European business professionals and American business professionals underestimate the risk from nuclear power. I should mention that these data were collected before the tsunami-induced accident at Fukushima.

The overall correlation coefficients between the expert risk rankings and the perceived risk rankings are not strong. However, three of the four correlations are positive, and range from 16% to 33%. Only the rankings of the executive MBA group are negatively correlated with those of the risk experts, with the correlation coefficient being –29%.

As an independent test of the impact of gender on judgments, I examined the risk ratings of two groups in respect to gender, one a group of executive MBA students, all of whom are business professionals, and a group of undergraduate finance majors. For the executive MBA group, men perceived 75% of the activities they rated to be less risky than did women. The biggest differences were for large construction, skiing, mountain climbing, bicycles, hunting, home appliances, and railroads. Notably, men viewed nuclear power as more risky than did women. In contrast, for undergraduate finance majors, there were no discernable differences between the risk assessments of men and women. The absence of an effect for undergraduates makes sense if the effect does indeed stem from power and control.

REPRESENTATIVENESS

The following question is my adaptation of a Tversky-Kahneman experimental procedure for eliciting information on how people might rely on representativeness to make predictions. I have used this question for many years, and the results are very robust across groups.

Question D2: Santa Clara University is attempting to predict the grade point average (GPA) of some graduating students based upon their high school GPA levels. As usual, a student's GPA lies between 0 and 4. Below are some data for undergraduates at Santa Clara University, based on students who entered the university in the years 1990, 1991, and 1992. During this period, the mean high school GPA of students who entered as freshmen and graduated was 3.44 (standard deviation was 0.36). The mean college GPA of those same students was 3.08 (standard deviation 0.40). Suppose that it is your task to predict the college GPA scores of three graduating students, based solely on their high school GPA scores. The three high school GPAs are 2.2, 3.0, and 3.8. Write down your predictions for the college GPAs of these students upon graduation. Then read on.

People who rely on representativeness when answering Question D2 tend to base their predictions on stereotype. The stereotype of a good student is someone with favorable attributes in respect to intelligence, organization, diligence, good study habits, and grades. The stereotype of a poor student is someone whose comparable attributes are weak. Representativeness suggests that a student with good grades in high school will continue to have good grades in college, and likewise a student with bad grades in high school will tend to have bad grades in college. Because the question provides statistical data, high grades correspond to GPA scores well above the mean, and low GPA scores correspond to grades well below the mean.

Table D.4 displays the mean predictions for the four main groups we have been discussing. Notice that the predictions in each row of the table are quite close to each other, suggesting that people's responses to these questions are quite robust. This is especially notable given that the undergraduate finance majors are closest to having firsthand experience with predicting the grades of undergraduates.

What is common across the four groups whose results are displayed in Table D.4 is the nature of the bias in prediction. Historical data from the

Table D.4 This table summarizes the responses of four different groups to Question D2

High School GPA	UG Fin Majors	Exec MBA	Risk Managers	Finance Professionals
2.2	2.14	2.15	2.21	2.16
3	2.76	2.81	2.84	2.77
3.8	3.44	3.47	3.43	3.36

university indicates that the graduating college GPA of a student who enters college with a high school GPA of 2.2 is 2.7, which is roughly 0.5 greater than the mean prediction. For a student who enters college with a GPA of 3.8, the corresponding mean graduating college GPA is 3.3, which is roughly 0.15 lower than the mean prediction.

The differences between predicted GPA scores and actual GPA scores constitute systematic biases. People especially tend to misestimate GPA scores at the extremes, underestimating at the low end and overestimating at the high end.

The starting point for predicting college GPA scores should be the mean, which Question 8 tells us is 3.08. Were high school GPA scores to be completely irrelevant to college GPA scores, then the best prediction for all three student college GPA scores would be the mean, 3.08. If high school GPA had some small positive bearing on college GPA, then the prediction associated with 3.8 would be a little above 3.08, and the prediction associated with 2.2 would be a little below 3.08. Such a situation features strong reversion (or regression) to the mean.

When high school GPA is a strong signal for college GPA, predictions display little mean reversion, and that is the problem with the predictions in Table D.4. There is insufficient mean reversion. There are many variables that influence college GPA, and grades in high school is but one.

The data provided in Question D2 is insufficient to develop predictions based on sophisticated statistical techniques. At the same time, most people do not make use of all the statistical information that is provided, in that they tend to ignore the standard deviations. Very few compute standardized z-scores, where $z = (x-\mu)/\sigma$ measures the number of standard deviations a variable x is from its mean μ.

A high school GPA of 3.8 is exactly one standard deviation above the high school mean of 3.44. Consider the associated mean prediction of 3.44 for college GPA provided by the undergraduate finance majors. That 3.44 is 0.93 standard deviations above the college mean. Because 0.93 is less than the z-score of 1.0 associated with 3.8, we can see that undergraduate finance majors are generally aware that their predictions need to display some mean regression. However, 0.93 is only a bit below 1.0, and the degree of mean reversion is insufficient. Because the z-score for the actual GPA is 0.55, the predicted z-score is 70% higher than the actual, and that quantifies the degree of bias.

Similar remarks apply to the other two predictions as well. The larger the absolute value of the z-score for the prediction input, meaning high school GPA, the larger the bias in the z-score of the prediction. In this regard, 3.0 is 1.22 standard deviations below the mean for high school GPA, and the z-score prediction bias was 91% in absolute value. Similarly, 2.2 is 3.4 standard deviations below the mean, and the z-score prediction bias was 155% in absolute value.

The general pattern is insufficient mean reversion encapsulated in biased prediction z-scores, with the bias more pronounced at the extremes. As can be seen in Table D.4, risk managers are not much different from anyone else in this regard. As for Beth and Larry, their predictions for the GPA of 3.8 were 3.4 for Beth and 3.7 for Larry, which are significantly biased upward, as is typical. At the other end, their predictions for the GPA of 2.2 were 1.8 for Beth and 2.5 for Larry, which are significantly biased downward, as is typical. In keeping with their perspectives, Larry perceives more upside for the 3.8 and Beth perceives more downside risk for the 2.2.

UNREALISTIC (EXCESSIVE) OPTIMISM

Below is a modified version of the question that Weinstein used in his study of unrealistic optimism.

Question D3: In Table D.5, you will find a list of 18 possible events that might happen to you during your lifetime. Examine the events and answer the following: compared to other people in your group—same sex as you—what do you think are the chances that the following will happen to you in the future? The choices range from much less than average, through average, to much more than average, and are displayed in Table D.6. Please enter the number to the left of the category as your answer, not the category itself. For example, if your answer is 60% less, type 3 as your answer, not "60% less." For some of you, these events might have already happened to you in the past. If so, simply answer the question in terms of the events happening to you again in the future.

Weinstein structured his experiment to ask people to assess the likelihood of events relative to others in a group. Therefore, in a well-calibrated group, the expected mean group response for every question would theoretically be "average," corresponding to category 7 in Table D.6. Weinstein hypothesized that on the whole, people are unrealistically optimistic, which he measured by the mean responses to Question D3.

Table D.5 This table contains a list of 18 possible events pertaining to Question D3

1	Being fired from a job	10	Decayed tooth extracted
2	Your work recognized with award	11	Your achievements in newspaper
3	Having gum problems	12	Weight constant for ten years
4	Living past 80	13	Having your car stolen
5	Having a heart attack	14	Injured in auto accident
6	Tripping and breaking bone	15	In ten years, earnings greater than $2 million a year
7	Being sued by someone	16	Developing cancer
8	No night in hospital for five years	17	Not ill all winter
9	Victim of mugging	18	Deciding you chose wrong career

Table D.6 This table describes the menu of responses from which subjects chose to assess the probability attached to each life event, when responding to Question D3

1	100% less (no chance)	9	20% more
2	80% less	10	40% more
3	60% less	11	60% more
4	40% less	12	80% more
5	20% less	13	100% more
6	10% less	14	3 times average
7	average	15	5 times average
8	10% more		

Notice that some of the life events in Table D.5 are favorable, such as having one's work recognized with an award, and others are unfavorable, such as having a heart attack. A person who exhibits excessive optimism bias will attach too high a probability to favorable events and too low a probability to unfavorable events. This led Weinstein to predict that the mean response for favorable events would be above average (a number higher than 7), and the mean response for unfavorable events would be below average (a number less than 7).

Weinstein first conducted his experiment with undergraduate students. I administered Question D3 to undergraduate finance majors, as well as to the same professionals described in earlier sections. With one exception, the responses are robust across groups. For all groups, mean responses for unfavorable events are below 7. For all groups except finance professionals, mean responses for favorable events are above 7. See Table D.7. As for the one anomaly, I suspect that it stems from conditions in European financial markets after the financial crisis. Prior to 2008, the mean responses for this group were 6.3 for unfavorable events and 7.0 for favorable events.

Notice that undergraduate finance majors, almost all in their early twenties, exhibit excessive optimism the most strongly. Roughly speaking excessive

Table D.7 This table summarizes the responses of four different groups to Question D3

	UG Fin Majors	Exec MBA	Risk Managers	Finance Professionals
Unfavorable	5.98	6.27	6.07	6.39
Favorable	7.68	7.54	7.19	6.78

optimism bias is 10% for unfavorable events and 7% for favorable events. Being older, in most cases by at least ten years, the other groups exhibit the bias less strongly.

Risk managers appear to be excessively optimistic, just like everyone else. Of course, there are interpersonal differences within all groups. As for Beth and Larry, their responses were both average in respect to unfavorable events. However, for favorable events, Beth's response was 10.3, and Larry's response was 5.1.

In his experiment, Weinstein probed his subjects for the determinants of their optimism. He focused on four possible drivers: controllability, desirability, familiarity, and representativeness. Weinstein's hypothesis was that excessive optimism would be positively related to each of these determinants. I administered the following question in order to identify which, if any, of these variables were correlated with subjects' responses to Question D3.

Question D4: Question D3 pertains to a series of possible life events. Please assess each of these events on the following four criteria:

1. For each of the life events, assign one of the following controllability category numbers (1 through 5):
   1. There is nothing one can do that will change the likelihood that the event will take place.
   2. There are things one can do to have a small effect on the chances that the event will occur.
   3. There are things one can do to have a moderate effect on the chances that the event will occur.
   4. There are things one can do to have a large effect on the chances that the event will occur.
   5. The event is completely controllable.
2. For each of the life events, assign a desirability number on a scale of 1 to 9, where
   1 = extremely undesirable
   3 = undesirable
   5 = neutral
   7 = desirable
   9 = extremely desirable

3. For each of the life events, assign a category number for familiarity, where the categories are the following:
   1. The event has not happened to anyone I know.
   2. The event has happened to acquaintances.
   3. The event has happened to friends or close relatives.
   4. The event happened to me once.
   5. The event has happened to me more than once.
4. For each of the life events, assign a category number for mental imaging, where the categories are the following:
   1. No particular person with a high chance comes to mind.
   2. When I think about the event, a type of person comes to mind to whom it is likely to happen, but this image is not very clear.
   3. When I think about the event, a clear picture comes to mind of a particular type of person to whom it is likely to happen.

Weinstein found evidence that all four variables influenced the degree of optimism bias. I computed the correlation coefficients of responses to Question D3 and the four parts of Question D4, and found that some correlations were much stronger than others. Moreover, the high correlations varied across groups, were different for favorable events than for unfavorable events, and some (familiarity in particular) had the opposite sign from what I expected. See Table D.8.

As for Beth and Larry, the strongest determinant of Beth's optimism was desirability, and for Larry was familiarity. The correlations of both for favorable events were about 60%.

In Chapters 2 and 5, I discussed the connection between dispositional optimism and choice. Dispositional optimism pertains to how rosy an outlook people have on life's outcomes, and is measured differently than unrealistic optimism above. I was able to compare the two constructs for three

Table D.8 This table summarizes the responses of four different groups to Question D4

	UG Fin Majors	Exec MBA	Risk Managers	Finance Professionals
Unfavorable events				
Controllability	−47.6%	−24.8%	−61.4%	−0.6%
Desirability	−4.0%	−15.5%	−25.6%	27.8%
Familiarity	40.7%	20.7%	20.5%	53.4%
Representativeness	−58.8%	−13.9%	−20.8%	−4.0%
Favorable events				
Controllability	63.7%	78.7%	40.9%	−23.0%
Desirability	50.2%	76.8%	30.4%	−17.5%
Familiarity	−3.5%	2.2%	−17.4%	80.5%
Representativeness	94.1%	82.7%	67.5%	−17.0%

groups, and found that in all cases, the two are positively correlated. For undergraduates, the correlation coefficient is 0.34, for business professionals it is 0.33, and for risk managers it is 0.27. As for Beth and Larry, mean dispositional optimism for those having a risk management focus was 0.75, and Beth's score was 0.8, while Larry's score was 0.7. Nevertheless, although all three correlation coefficients are statistically significant, it is clear that the relationships are far from being tight.

OVERCONFIDENCE

Psychologists can test for overconfidence about knowledge by using a survey that elicits confidence intervals as responses. Here is an example discussed by Russo and Schoemaker in their book *Decision Traps*.

Question D5: Below you will find a trivia test consisting of ten questions for you to answer from memory alone. In addition to giving your best guess, consider a range: a low guess and a high guess so that you feel 90% confident that the right answer will lie between your low guess and your high guess. Try not to make the range between your low guess and high guess too narrow. Otherwise, you will appear overconfident. At the same time, try not to make the range between your low guess and high guess too wide. This will make you appear underconfident. If you are well calibrated, you should expect that only one out of the ten correct answers you provide does not lie between your low guess and your high guess.

1. How old was Martin Luther King when he died?
2. How long, in miles, is the Nile River?
3. How many countries were members of OPEC in 1989?
4. According to the conventional canon, how many books are there in the Hebrew Bible?
5. What is the diameter, in miles, of the moon?
6. What is the weight, in pounds, of an empty Boeing 747?
7. In what year was Wolfgang Amadeus Mozart born?
8. How long, in days, is the gestation period of an Asian elephant?
9. What is the air distance, in miles, from London to Tokyo?
10. How deep, in feet, is the deepest known point in the ocean?

Feel free to give Question D5 a try. Remember that for each item, you are to give three answers, a best guess, a low guess and a high guess. When the true answer falls between your low guess and high guess, you score a hit. Otherwise, you score a miss. For each item, the risk you face in setting your low and high guesses too narrowly is that you will score a miss. Because you are asked to set 90% confidence intervals, being well calibrated means that for all ten items, you should expect to score nine out of ten hits.[2]

Psychologists test for overconfidence about ability using a question such as the following:

Question D6: Relative to all people who are the same general age and gender as you, how would you rate yourself as a driver? (1) Above average? (2) Average? (3) Below average? Here average is defined as the median. Recall that by definition, the median splits a sample into two parts, half greater or equal to the median, and half less than or equal to the median.

According to Question D5, our protagonists, Beth and Larry, are overconfident about knowledge. Beth's hit rate was 60%, and Larry's hit rate was 40%, both of which are well below 90%. These rates are typical. For the group of 150 subjects that included Beth and Larry, all focused on risk management, the mean hit rate was 38%.

The responses to Question D5 are robust across groups. For my sample of 120 executive MBA students, the mean hit rate was 48%. For my sample of 207 European financial professionals, the mean rate was 43%. For a sample of 245 undergraduate finance majors, the mean hit rate was 46%. Figure D.3 displays the histogram response rates for all four groups.

Overconfidence can be circumstantial. Hit rates systematically differ across the ten questions. See Figure D.4. For Americans, hit rates are highest for the Martin Luther King question. For Europeans, hit rates are highest for the Mozart question. The questions pertaining to Boeing and the Asian elephant tend to feature the lowest hit rates. Generally, people tend to be overconfident about difficult tasks. However, there is some evidence that they are actually underconfident about relatively easy tasks.

According to Question D6, a group is overconfident when the relative frequency of those who judge themselves to be above average is substantially

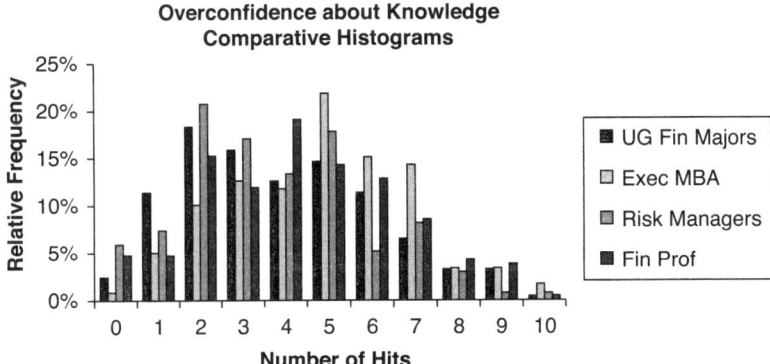

Figure D.3 This figure displays the histogram response rates, for the aggregate of four groups, to the Russo-Schoemaker overconfidence trivia quiz (Question D5). The four groups are undergraduate finance majors, executive MBA students, risk managers, and European financial professionals.

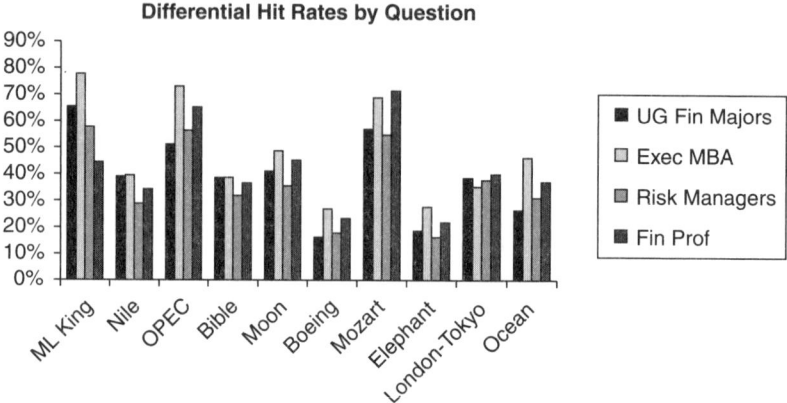

Figure D.4 This figure displays hit rates, for the aggregate of four groups, for each of the ten questions in the Russo-Schoemaker overconfidence trivia quiz (Question D5). The four groups are undergraduate finance majors, executive MBA students, risk managers, and European financial professionals.

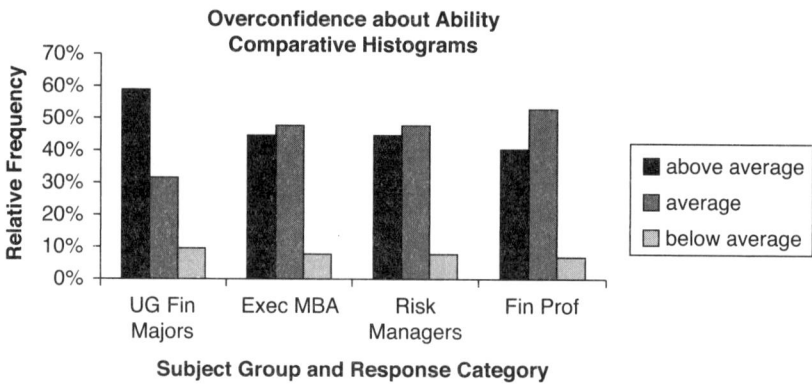

Figure D.5 This figure displays the histogram response rates for Question D6 in Appendix D for the aggregate of the following four groups: undergraduate finance majors, executive MBA students, risk managers, and European financial professionals.

higher than the relative frequency of those who judge themselves to be below average. For my sample of executive MBA students, the above-average relative frequency was 54%, and the below-average relative frequency was 5%. In this regard, there is reason to suspect that Beth and Larry are both overconfident about their driving abilities, in that both responded that they are above-average drivers.

For my sample of European financial professionals, the above/below frequencies were respectively 40%/7%. For a sample of undergraduate finance majors, the above/below frequencies were respectively 59%/10%. Figure D.5 displays the histogram response rates for all four groups.

Overconfidence bias is tenacious. After presenting these results to experimental subjects, I often repeat the exercise with a different set of ten items, explicitly urging people to widen their confidence intervals. Although most people claim to have understood the lesson from the first task, mean hit rates for the second round tend to be similar to the first round.

Overconfidence leads people to be surprised more often they anticipated. This is especially important in respect to risk, in that overconfidence can lead people to take riskier positions than they realize.

CONFIRMATION BIAS

For executive MBAs who answered Question 6 in Chapter 4, the Wason experiment, 15% chose correctly, and 51% chose "a&2." For a group of 56 European finance professionals, 9% chose correctly, and 32% chose "a&2." For undergraduate finance majors, 7% chose correctly, and 61% chose "a&2."

Risk managers will encounter confirmation bias routinely. For many, confirmation bias is almost set in stone. Even after participating in the Wason experiment and having the issue explained to them, some subjects will continue to insist that their response of "a&2" is correct. Therefore, here is a practice question that is similar in form, but different in detail. Why don't you try it, particularly if you were in the majority of people who exhibited confirmation bias when answering Question 6 in Chapter 4?

Question D7: Five cards are placed in front of you as shown. All cards are either green-backed or red-backed. Cards 1 and 5 are face down, and the other three are face up.

	Card 1	Card 2	Card 3	Card 4	Card 5
	Red Back	☺ Joker	☺ Joker	♥ Four of Hearts ♥	**Green** Back

Suppose you are asked to test the following hypothesis about these four cards: "Each card that has a green back on one side has a joker on the other side." In particular, select those cards, and only those cards, that will determine whether the statement is true. That is, select the *minimum number of cards* that will enable you to determine whether or not the statement is true. Of the four cards, which would you turn over? After answering this question, read on.

I conducted this version of Wason's experiment with two groups, one a group of 95 European finance professionals, and the second a group of 55 European PhD students in finance. The correct answer for this problem is to turn over the four of hearts and the card with the green back: these are the only two cards capable of producing a guilty verdict. For the finance professionals, 32% answered correctly, and 25% exhibited confirmation bias by turning over a card with a green back or a joker. For the PhD students, 14% answered correctly, and 34% exhibited confirmation bias. I would point out that the bias associated with Question D7 appears to be somewhat less than with Question 6 in Chapter 4, which is interesting and suggestive. Research on confirmation bias does show that it is context dependent.

ILLUSION OF CONTROL

In running Langer's experiment described in Chapter 4, I assign participants to the two versions by whether the day of their birthday is even or odd. The evens play the first version. My findings running the experiment with undergraduate finance majors broadly agree with Langer's original study. In a sample of 272, the median response for version 1 is $5, while the median response for version 2 is $4. The mean valuations were much more extreme, $29 for version 1 and $16 for version 2. My findings with a sample of 90 MBA students, most of whom were working professionals, feature the same general pattern, with the median amount for version 1 being $2 and the median amount for version 2 being $1. As with undergraduate finance majors, mean valuations were larger: $13 for version 1 and $5 for version 2.

Although my subjects behaved similarly to those in Langer's original study, my findings with other groups have led me to be less confident in the robustness of these results. In a sample of 150 subjects with a strong interest in risk management, a group that included Beth and Larry, the median valuations for both versions were $2. As for the mean valuations, the results actually went the other way, $25 for version 2 and $8 for version 1. Notably, Beth and Larry set the same valuation, $5, even though Beth participated in version 2, and Larry participated in version 1. With experienced business professionals, the results appear to be more mixed than with students. Therefore, risk managers need to be cautious when applying the lessons from Langer's illusion of control experiment.

Intuitively, there is reason to expect a relationship between illusion of control and desire for control. Although there is some evidence for this effect in the group that included Beth and Larry, it is weak and not robust across groups. Here again, the message is to proceed with caution: when focusing on different aspects of control, be wary of relying on intuition.

To explain the connection for sake of completeness, divide the group into two: one half for whom desire for control (DC) is at or above the group mean, and the other half for whom DC is below the group mean. If we focus on version 2 in the experiment that included Beth and Larry, where subjects were handed their cards, WTA valuations were almost the same in the low-DC subgroup as the high-DC subgroup. However, for version 1, where subjects chose their own cards, the mean WTA valuation for the high-DC subgroup was 87% higher than for the low-DC subgroup. In contrast, when we divide the group on the basis of dispositional optimism instead of desire for control, the results are different: WTA was much higher for the above-average subgroup, regardless of whether subjects selected their cards or were handed their cards.

Bayesian Avoidance

Below you will find a series of questions, all of which relate to the application of Bayes' rule. After the questions, you will find a discussion about how people generally respond.

Question D8: Consider a geographic area that is served by two taxi companies, one large and the other small. Eighty-five (85) percent of the taxis are operated by the larger company, which uses yellow cabs. The smaller company uses red cabs. Suppose that there is a hit-and-run accident involving a taxi one evening, and an eyewitness reports that the taxi was red. In testing the accuracy of the eyewitness, the police determine that in circumstances similar to those in which the accident occurred, the witness correctly identifies the color of the taxi 80% of the time.

Consider the following two questions about the hit-and-run accident.

   a. A major risk associated with the eyewitness report is that the eyewitness is mistaken. Taking into account the eyewitness report, what probability would you assign to the color of the taxi involved in the accident truly being red?
   b. In addition to giving your best probability estimate, specify a low estimate and a high estimate so that you feel 90% confident that the right answer will lie between your low estimate and your high estimate.

Question D9: Consider breast cancer screening using mammography, which is conducted in your region. You know the following information about women in this region:

- The probability that a woman has breast cancer is 1%.
- If a woman has breast cancer, the probability that she tests positive is 90%.
- If a woman does not have breast cancer, the probability that she nevertheless tests positive is 9%.

A woman tests positive. She wants to know from you what the chances are she has breast cancer. In light of the test result, what would you tell her about her risk of having breast cancer?

Question D10: Imagine 100 book bags, each of which contains 1,000 poker chips. Forty-five bags contain 700 black chips and 300 red chips. The other 55 bags contain 300 black chips and 700 red chips. You cannot see inside any of the bags. One of the bags is selected at random by means of a coin toss.

Consider the following three questions about the book bag:

a. What probability would you assign to the event that the selected bag contains predominantly black chips?
b. Now imagine that 12 chips are drawn, with replacement, from the selected bag. These 12 draws produce 8 blacks and 4 reds. Would you use the new information about the drawing of chips to revise your probability that the selected bag contains predominantly black chips? If so, what new probability would you assign?
c. In addition to giving your best probability estimate, consider a range: a low estimate and a high estimate so that you feel 90% confident that the right answer will lie between your low estimate and your high estimate. Try not to make the range between your low estimate and high estimate too narrow. Otherwise, you will appear overconfident. At the same time, try not to make the range between your low estimate and high estimate too wide. This will make you appear underconfident. If you are well calibrated, you should expect the true probability to lie outside the range between your low estimate and your high estimate one time in ten.

Question D11: A company uses a first-pass quality assurance test to address the risk of defect in its products as they come off the production line. Below are data relevant to the testing process.

- Ten out of every 1,000 items are defective.
- Of these 10 items, the test indicates that 9 are defective.
- Of the 990 items that are free of defects, the test indicates that about 89 are defective.

If the test identifies an item as defective, a more detailed (second-pass) screening test is used to ascertain with certainty whether the item is indeed defective. Suppose that the first pass test identifies a particular item as defective. Identify a whole number "X" in connection with the sentence "About 1 in X items that are identified as defective by the first pass test actually turn out to be defective."

All four preceding questions involve straightforward applications of Bayes' rule. To describe Bayes' rule formally, imagine two events, denoted D and F. Think of F as an event whose occurrence constitutes a risk, and D as an event in which we receive a signal about F warning us that F is likely. In the absence of a signal, Pr{F} is the probability we attach to the occurrence of F, and we call this the "prior probability." After a warning signal D, Pr{F|D} is the probability we attach to the occurrence of F, and we call this the "posterior probability." When all probabilities are strictly positive, Bayes' rule is an equation for the posterior probability, and is written

Pr{F|D} = Pr{F} × Pr{D|F} /Pr{D}.

In the Bayes' rule equation, the term Pr{D|F} / Pr{D} is called the "likelihood ratio." Think of the likelihood ratio as measuring the strength of the allegorical "smoking gun." In the allegory, we see a dead body, we see a smoking gun lying on the floor nearby, and although we did not observe the gun being used as the weapon in question, the fact that it is still smoking sure looks suspicious.

The likelihood ratio measures how likely it is to receive a warning signal when the risk F materializes, relative to the general likelihood of receiving the warning signal, whether F materializes or not. In the special case, when D occurs only in conjunction with F, then the likelihood ratio will be higher than unity. In the special case where F is irrelevant to the occurrence of D, the likelihood ratio is unity. Of course, if D never occurs in conjunction with F, then the likelihood ratio is zero.

The principle behind Bayes' rule is simple. Begin with the prior probability, and then scale it by the likelihood ratio. The likelihood ratio measures the strength of the signal as a smoking gun. If D is an effective warning signal, then the adjustment is a significant increase in the probability attached to F.

In Question D8, the taxicab problem, F is the event in which the taxi involved in the accident was red. D is the event in which the witness describes the taxi involved in the accident as having been red. The prior probability is 15%. The numerator of the likelihood ratio is 80%, the accuracy rate of the witness. The denominator of the likelihood ratio is 29%, and is computed as follows. There are two ways in which D can occur. First, the taxi involved in the accident was yellow, but the witness is mistaken: this conjunction of events occurs with probability 0.85 × 0.2 = 17%. Second, the taxi involved in the accident was red, and the witness correctly identified it: this conjunction of events occurs with probability 0.15 × 0.8 = 12%. Adding 17% and 12% gives us 29%. Therefore the likelihood ratio is 2.76 = 0.8 /0.29. To apply Bayes' rule, we have to multiply the base rate Pr{F} = 0.15 by 2.76 to arrive at Pr{F|D} = 41%.

In Question D9, the mammogram problem—which is the same as Question 8 in Chapter 4—F is the event in which the woman has breast cancer, and D is having a positive mammogram test. The logic is exactly the same as in the taxicab problem, with the prior probability being 1%, the likelihood ratio being 9.2, and Pr{F|D} therefore being 9.2%.

In Question D10, the bag of chips problem, F is the event in which the book bag contains predominantly black chips, and D is the event in which we draw 12 chips, with 8 being black. The prior probability is 45%, and the likelihood ratio is 2.1. Computing the likelihood ratio is not easily done by hand because it involves using the binomial probability distribution to find the probability of drawing 8 black chips in 12 independent draws when the probability of drawing black is 30% in one case and 70% in the other. Because the probability of drawing 8 blacks in 12 draws is nearly zero when only 30% of the chips are black, but not when 70% of the chips are black, the signal is strong. As a result, the likelihood ratio Pr{D|F} / Pr{D} is approximately 1.0/0.45 = 2.2.

Question D11, the quality assurance problem, is numerically equivalent to the mammogram problem. However it is stated in terms of natural frequencies instead of probabilities. Psychologist Gerd Gigerenzer argues that people can use information more easily if it is described in terms of natural frequencies instead of probabilities. Here the thought process is a little different than applying Bayes' rule. In 1,000 items, 10 are truly defective, of which 9 are identified by the first pass test as being defective. These are true positives. Of the 990 that are not defective, the first pass test identifies 89 as being defective. These are false positives. The total number of positives is the sum, 98 = 89 + 9. The fraction of this total that are true positives is 9/98 = 9.2%, corresponding to 1 in 11.

How well do people do at solving these four problems?

For the group having a risk management focus, the mean judgment in Question D8, the taxi cab problem was 51%, with more than 55% providing judgments above 70%. Daniel Kahneman and Amos Tversky, who designed this problem, suggested that people are inclined to overfocus on the 80% accuracy rate in the description of the problem, and therefore to underfocus on the prior probability. This question also elicits 90% confidence intervals. The mean hit rate for this question was 3%, which tells us not only that most of the subjects do not know how to apply Bayes' rule but that they also are overconfident about their ability to form an accurate judgment.

For Question D9, the mammogram problem, the mean judgment was 53%, and the median judgment was 81%. Both are very far from the 9.2% correct answer. Only 18% of subjects provide responses that are close to 9%.

For Question D10, the bag of chips problem, the mean hit rate for the group with a risk management focus was 8%. Figure D.6 displays the histogram of responses for both the prior probability and posterior probability.

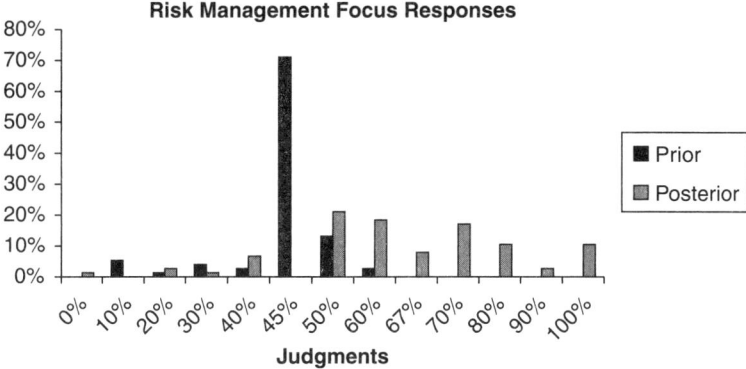

Figure D.6 This figure displays the histogram of responses for both the prior probability and posterior probability for Question D10, the bag of chips problem, associated with the responses of a group of risk managers.

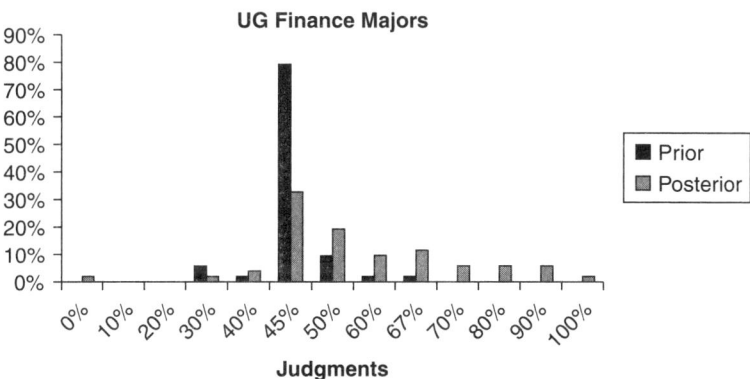

Figure D.7 This figure displays the histogram of responses for both the prior probability and posterior probability for Question D10, the bag of chips problem, associated with the responses of a group of undergraduate finance majors.

Notice that most subjects correctly perceived the prior probability to be 95%. However, there was wide variation in the posterior probabilities. Clearly, most subjects adjusted their probabilities in light of the signal. However, not knowing how to apply Bayes' rule, they did not adjust sufficiently. As with the taxicab problem, most were also overconfident about their ability to make an accurate judgment.

For Question D11, the quality assurance problem, the mean response was 305, and the median response was 10.5. For this particular group, natural frequencies appear to have led to more accurate judgments. However, only 32% came close to having the correct judgment.

The responses of the finance professionals and the undergraduate finance majors were similar to those of the risk management group, but with some differences. In the taxi problem, the finance professionals were relatively more prone to choose 80% as their response: 62% did so. However, they were less overconfident: their mean hit rate was 16%. In the bag of chips problem, both the finance professionals and the undergraduate business majors were more prone to choosing 45% as their posterior probability, as well as their prior probability. Subjects making this judgment completely ignored the information content in the smoking gun. See Figure D.7 for the histogram of undergraduate finance major responses.

APPENDIX E: A FORMAL MODEL OF ORGANIZATIONAL RISK

THIS APPENDIX DESCRIBES THE FORMAL FRAMEWORK SHAPIRA USES TO describe balancing risks and rewards in project selection, and related principal-agent issues. The informal framework is developed in Chapter 6.

FORMAL FRAMEWORK

The probabilistic structure underlying Shapira's risk-taking model is depicted in Figure E.1, which displays an area bounded by an ellipse not centered at the origin. Statistical theory implies that if x and y are random variables which are jointly distributed as a bivariate normal, then the isodensity curves will be elliptical.[1] In this case, the area in Figure E.1 represents a confidence region. Let $h1$ be the height of ellipse along the vertical axis, and $h2$ be the height of the ellipse at the mean of x. The correlation coefficient r_{xy} between x and y is approximately equal to $(1 - (h2/h1)^2)^{1/2}$. When the ellipse is circular, $h1=h2$, and $r_{xy}=0$. When the ellipse approximates (collapses to) a positively sloped straight line, $h2<<h1$, and $r_{xy}=1$. When x and y are positively correlated and jointly distributed uniformly, the isodensity curves will be approximately elliptical, and the above approximating formula for the correlation coefficient r_{xy} will continue to hold.

In Figure E.1, the horizontal axis is interpreted to depict possible values of x, the assessment or figure of merit. The vertical axis is interpreted to depict possible values of y, the outcome of the project. For sake of exposition, consider the bivariate uniform case. That is, for any value of x, say x', y is assumed to take on any value, with equal probability, along a vertical line from x' that lies within the ellipse depicted in the figure. In this respect, the expected value of y, given any x, lies along the line with positive slope.

In the Shapira framework, the variable $yCrit$ denotes the "aspiration" level that defines whether a project turns out to have been a success or a failure.

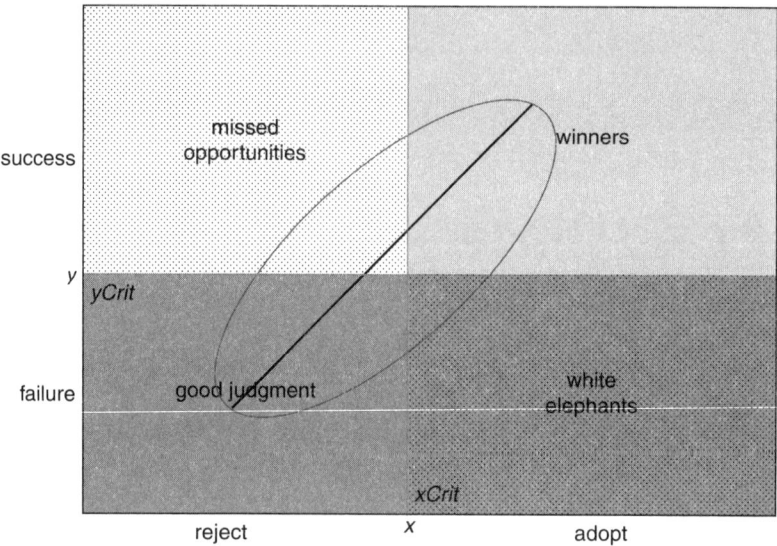

Figure E.1 This figure depicts the elliptical confidence region for a bivariate distribution for random variables x and y, where x is a figure of merit and y represents the ex post value of the project. Here $xCrit$ denotes the lowest value of x associated with project adoption and $yCrit$ is the lowest value of y associated with success. The elliptical confidence region is partitioned into four regions by the values of $xCrit$ and $yCrit$.

That is, if the project generates an outcome y that is at least $yCrit$, the organization will judge the project to have been a success. Otherwise, it will be judged a failure. Likewise, managers will adopt a project when their judgment x of its value is at least $xCrit$, representing the project "hurdle rate."[2]

Assume that the probability associated with the confidence region depicted in Figure E.1 is almost unity, so that only very rare events are excluded. In this case, Figure E.1 displays four possibilities. Projects that are adopted have values of x that lie to the right of $xCrit$. Successful projects are projects with values of y that lie above $yCrit$. The two inequalities combine to generate four regions within the ellipse.

In the upper-right quadrant is the region that defines winners, projects that are adopted and turn out successful. Below the region of winners is the region of white elephants, projects that are adopted and turn out to be failures. In the bottom-left quadrant is the region associated with good judgment, projects that are rejected and in hindsight would have been failures. Finally, in the top-left quadrant are missed opportunities, projects that were rejected but would have been winners if adopted.

In Figure E.1, extreme values of x appear to be associated with low risk projects. This is because the vertical range of y within the ellipse narrows as x approaches the extremes. However, the narrowing simply reflects the low joint probability of x and y both taking on extreme values, not that the risk attached to extreme values of x is low. To analyze the risk associated with extreme values of x, we would focus on the conditional probabilities associated with those extreme values, which would require consideration of a much larger ellipse. Visually, this would be akin to focusing on an intermediate value of x.

A type 1 error occurs when a good project is rejected, which would typically show up as a missed opportunity. A type 2 error occurs when a bad project is adopted, which would typically show up as a white elephant.

To illustrate how to apply this conceptual framework, consider the Ebola epidemic of 2014, and the WHO's decision task about how to respond to the early indications of outbreak. The decision to deploy resources is modeled as a project.

In the context of the Ebola outbreak, interpret x as the variable measuring the WHO's assessment of the severity of the outbreak, and y as the number of lives saved. A project being considered in April 2014 might entail mobilization: making expenditures quickly in the three affected countries, and expending resources on isolation centers with sufficient beds and trained healthcare staff, all in an effort to house and if necessary treat people suspected of having Ebola, or who have contracted Ebola.

The critical value of x would then correspond to how severe the WHO would judge the outbreak to be before committing major resources to its containment. The critical value of y would represent the number of lives saved that would qualify the effort as a success. Every project is taken to have an associated value of x, and so the firm adopts all projects whose values of x are at least as great as the threshold value $xCrit$.

To facilitate the discussion of how to model the structuring of incentives, we are assuming that all the points within the ellipse occur with uniform probability. Therefore, the probability of an event within the ellipse is effectively given by its area. In this regard, the probability of a type 1 error is the area of the ellipse associated with missed opportunities.

How type 1 and type 2 errors are weighted relative to each other impacts managerial choices about the critical values $xCrit$ and $yCrit$. Managers will have a natural preference to have the success criterion $yCrit$ be as low as possible. In making this statement, there is an implicit assumption that managers are rewarded for winners, and are fearful of being penalized for white elephants but not missed opportunities. This incentive structure will also induce managers to favor high threshold values $xCrit$. High threshold values increase the likelihood that projects that are adopted turn out to be successful.

Shapira points out that a side effect of increasing the threshold value $xCrit$ is an increased probability associated with missed opportunities, the Type 1 errors. In Figure E.2, the arrow at the top of the figure indicates that the value of $xCrit$ is being increased. Notice that as the vertical $xCrit$

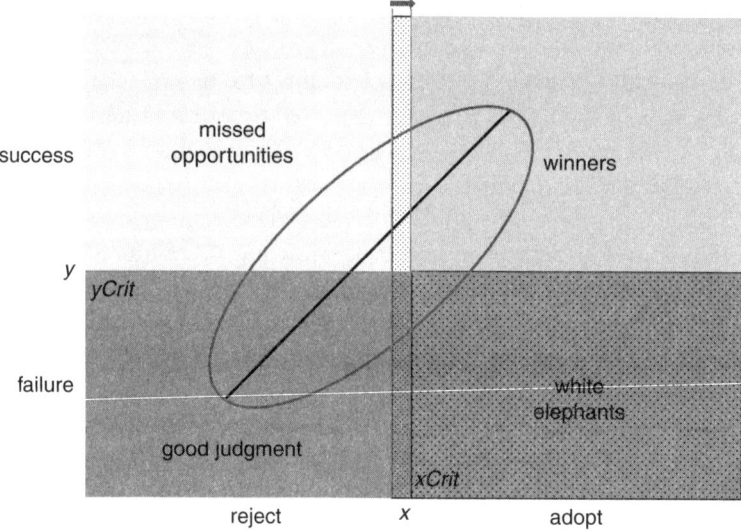

Figure E.2 This figure shows the impact associated with increasing the value of *xCrit*. As the vertical *xCrit* line moves right, the areas indicating the probabilities attached to missed opportunities and good judgment increase, while the probabilities attached to winners and white elephants decrease.

line moves right, the areas indicating the probabilities attached to missed opportunities and good judgment increase, while the probabilities attached to winners and white elephants decrease.

Suppose that *yCrit* is fixed, and consider a simple example to describe how to find the optimal value of *xCrit*. In the example, the firm receives a payoff of $1 if the project turns out to be a success and –$1 if the project turns out to be a failure.[3]

If the firm were to set the value of *xCrit* at the far left of the ellipse, then every project is selected, and the firm's expected payoff would be the probability of success minus the probability of failure. Graphically, this probability difference is the area in the ellipse above the *yCrit*-line minus the area of the ellipse below the *yCrit*-line.

Notice that moving *xCrit* ever so slightly to the right so that it intersects a bit of the ellipse increases the probability of good judgment, but leaves the probability of missed opportunities equal to zero. Therefore, shifting *xCrit* to the right increases value.

By the same token, if the firm were to set the value of *xCrit* to the far right of the ellipse, then no project would be selected. Notice that moving *xCrit* ever so slightly to the left so that it intersects a bit of the ellipse increases the probability of winners, but leaves the probability of white elephants equal to zero. Therefore, shifting *xCrit* to the left increases value.

The optimal value of *xCrit* lies somewhere in the middle and involves a balancing act: a small rightward shift in the value of *xCrit* increases the probability of winners and white elephants by the exact same amount, and so the change in expected payoff from such a shift is zero. Another way of putting this is that the rightward shift in *xCrit* increases the probability of white elephants by the same amount as it decreases the probability of missed opportunities. That is, the marginal increase in the probability of a type 2 error is just offset by the increase in the probability of a type 1 error.

Figure E.2 displays the impact of a marginal shift in *xCrit* to the right. Would this shift be desirable? The way to tell is to compare two areas in the hatched region within the ellipsis, the area above the *yCrit* line and the area below the *yCrit* line. At the optimal value of *xCrit*, the two areas are equal. Are they equal in Figure E.2? They are not. The top area is larger than the bottom, which indicates that the marginal cost of increased missed opportunities is larger than the marginal benefit of reducing white elephants. Therefore, the value of *xCrit* should be moved back to the left.

Incentive systems that reward managers handsomely for winners, but impose low penalties for white elephants induce these managers to set too low a bar for *xCrit*.[4] As a result, managers take on unnecessary risk and adopt value-reducing projects. By the same token, incentive systems that excessively penalize managers for white elephants induce these managers to set too high a bar for *xCrit*. As a result, managers take on too little risk and avoid some projects that would increase firm value. These managers are excessively timid, and end up with too many missed opportunities.

In applying the model to shed some understanding about the WHO's decisions about Ebola, we might ask whether the WHO had been using a value of *yCrit* that was too low or a value of *xCrit* that was too high? We might ask whether in March and April 2014 their incentive structures overweighted concern about funding white elephants or underweighted the probability of missed opportunities?

Contracts in the Presence of Principal-Agent Conflicts

Consider the question of how to design efficient contracts when a principal engages an agent to perform work on behalf of the principal. At the core of principal-agent contract issues are two concepts, known respectively as "the participation constraint" and "the incentive compatibility constraint." The participation constraint is about offering a sufficiently attractive compensation package to induce people to join a company and stay. The incentive compatibility constraint is about the principal appropriately paying the agent for performance.[5]

Theoretical discussions about incentive contracts often begin with sharecropping. There are two good reasons why this is the case. First, sharecropping provides a real-world example of an incentive contract between a principal and an agent. Second, and perhaps even more important, sharecropping serves as a powerful metaphor for incentive contracts in general.

Sharecroppers live as tenant farmers, growing crops on land owned by a principal, the landowner. In this respect, the sharecropper serves as the agent of the landowner. As compensation, sharecroppers get to keep a portion of the total crops as their "share."

Consider two alternative ways in which the landowner can compensate the sharecropper. The first way is for the landowner to agree to pay the sharecropper a fixed amount of the total as a wage, and to keep what remains from the total crop as profit. The second way is for the landowner to agree to accept a fixed amount of the crop produced as rent, and for the sharecropper to keep what remains from the total crop as profit.

In the typical sharecropping arrangement, it is the landowner who receives the fixed amount, and the sharecropper who keeps any residual. Why this way rather than the other way around? The answer involves incentives.

Farming is hard work. It takes effort. Moreover, there is risk in what crop yields will turn out to be. A contract that promises the sharecropper a fixed amount offers less of an incentive to expend effort than a contract that lets the sharecropper keep the entire surplus, once the landowner has been paid. Letting the sharecropper keep the entire surplus features pay for performance, and is incentive compatible.

There is no social loafing here, since the sharecropper alone captures the full benefit of going the extra mile beyond what is minimally acceptable to remain employed. In contrast, paying the sharecropper a fixed amount, regardless of the amount produced, is not incentive compatible. This is because the sharecropper would not capture the entire benefit of additional effort, and so would be inclined not to go the extra mile.

There is still the issue of the magnitude of the fixed amount the landowner is to receive. Naturally, landowners want the amount to be more, and sharecroppers want it to be less. It is the participation constraint that effectively determines this amount. In a functioning labor market, landlords and sharecroppers are in search of each other. Landowners who ask for too large an amount will fail to attract sharecroppers to work their land. Sharecroppers who insist on too low a share for the landowner's amount will fail to be engaged.

The risk dimension associated with incentive compatibility is very important. Because crop yields feature risk, an incentive-compatible contract imposes a great deal of risk on the sharecropper. The sharecropper bears 100% of the cost of production. In a bad year, the size of the crop might not even cover the fixed amount that is due the landowner, in which case the sharecropper is due nothing.

Risk can be expensive, both for the sharecropper and the landowner alike. The cost to the sharecropper is obvious. The cost to the landowner is less obvious. If sharecroppers cannot easily tolerate risk, then landowners will have to pay more for performance than otherwise, and this means landowners having to accept lower rents.

Sometimes, there are ways around the risk issue, especially when the landowner can tolerate more risk than the sharecropper. Keep in mind that the landowner would be happy to pay the sharecropper a fixed wage if the landowner could be assured that the sharecropper would exert the appropriate effort. And how might the landowner find such reassurance? One answer is monitoring.

If the landowner can directly observe how much effort the sharecropper exerts, then the compensation contract can be "pay for effort" instead of "pay for performance." In this case, direct monitoring allows for a contract in which the sharecropper either puts in the requisite effort or, if not, gets fired, the job loss outcome.

Being fired is a stick. Paying for performance is a carrot. Depending on the situation, incentives can be carrots, sticks, or some combination. Indeed, there are laws against the use of some sticks. Civilized countries do not allow their citizens to be executed for being lazy. This makes paying for performance that much more important.

Suppose that monitoring is expensive, sticks are limited in scope, and sharecroppers are very averse to risk. In this case, landowners might find that they will have to accept living in an imperfect world. This might mean offering very weak or nonexistent incentives in the knowledge that crop yields are bound to be small. In the days of the Soviet Union, Soviet workers would joke about this, saying, "They pretend to pay us, and we pretend to work!"

Of course, there is a middle ground between the two extremes, having the sharecropper face all the risk and none of the risk. That middle ground involves risk sharing. In a risk-sharing arrangement, the sharecropper receives a small fixed payment (base wage) and is entitled to a share of the total crop above some mutually agreed threshold. This share is more than zero, but less than 100 percent. The payment above the base wage is akin to a bonus.

The sharecropping situation serves to highlight the key issues about effective compensation plans in general. Effort is a surrogate for job quality. Compensation plans need to be attractive enough to recruit and retain executives and employees. If there are motivational issues involving differential interests between principals and agents, compensation plans need to feature appropriate incentives that bring the interests of principals and agents into closer alignment. Incentives can be a combination of carrots and sticks.

If monitoring is expensive, or infeasible because of the need for decentralized decision-making, then agents need to be paid for performance. However, paying for performance might subject agents to considerable risk, and risk is expensive for both agents and principals.

In financial firms, the principals are the firms' owners, and the sharecroppers are the traders and risk managers. If board members, as fiduciaries of owners, are able to provide complete oversight of traders and risk managers, then they need not pay bonuses. All they need to do is fire anyone whose effort is insufficient.

Of course, monitoring is expensive, particularly for traders. Therefore, traders are likely to be offered risk-sharing contracts with bonuses. When the principal's interests are best served by the trader taking highly risky positions, and incentive compatibility requires that the trader share in the risk, then the trader's compensation contract will need to feature a substantial expected bonus in order that the participation constraint be satisfied. This is why efficient risk-sharing contracts might feature a great deal of upside exposure, but limited downside exposure. Of course, this feature can be taken too far, with poorly designed contracts inducing traders to take on risk that the principal would deem excessive.

In terms of Figures E.1 and E.2, the principal would ideally like to select *xCrit* in such a way as to maximize the expected value of the projects that are adopted, meaning those projects for which $x \geq xCrit$. If the trader is insufficiently compensated for bearing risk, then he or she chooses a value of *xCrit* that is too high. Doing so generates too many missed opportunities and not enough white elephants, because the penalty for white elephants is excessive. Therefore, contracts need to be structured to soften the penalty for white elephants in order to address the issue. Of course, doing so will provide asymmetric rewards to traders.

From the perspective of SP/A theory, hope and aspiration on the part of traders can lead them to take on excessive risk, meaning too low a value for *xCrit*. Extreme trigger-happy traders might be willing to set the value of *xCrit* so low that all trading opportunities (that is, projects) are selected. One way to remedy this state of affairs is to reduce the size of the bonus in the compensation contract. This will work if traders are able to assess the risks in question. However, because risk assessment is a special skill, it might be that the services of risk managers are needed in order to identify the underlying risks and associated value for *xCrit*.

Risk management can improve traders' knowledge about risk. However, knowledge alone might not align the principal's interests with traders' interests. After all, their psychological profiles might be different, with traders setting higher aspirations and greater importance to achieving those aspirations. As a result, traders' compensation contracts might need to feature rewards for using and complying with the input from risk managers. Contracts might also need to feature penalties for using manipulative practices for failing to comply appropriately with whatever risk management practices are in place.

Risk managers have a different job than traders. The risk manager identifies the risk in various trading opportunities, communicates those risks, and seeks to persuade others in the firm to take proper account of those risks. However, risk managers are also agents. They too choose how much effort to exert in terms of the service they provide to the principal. Some aspects of their efforts are observable, and some not.

The efforts of traders lead to trading profits for the principal, which are either winners or white elephants. The effort of risk managers produces a characterization that can be described in terms of Figure E.2. If the risk manager makes a mistake, for example, by erring in identifying the ellipse in Figure E.2, then the result can feature incorrect risk exposure by the firm. A serious risk management mistake is to underestimate the probability of white elephants with an estimate of the location of the ellipse that is too high. This type of mistake leads the principal, who relies on risk managers' estimates, to experience excessive optimism (too high a value for the expected value of y) and overconfidence (too narrow a range for the lower and upper bounds of y for the portion of the ellipse associated with trades (that is, projects) that have been adopted.

Contracts for risk managers need to provide incentives for properly identifying risks, such as the probability of white elephants, or the probabilities of white elephants of a particular size. These contracts take the form of a base salary and bonus with a penalty (clawback) for white elephants of a particular magnitude that occur too frequently.[6]

Consider a stylized framework in which a principal hires both a trader and a risk manager. The risk manager's task is to assess the maximizing value of *xCrit*. The trader's task is to expend effort to monitor markets, and trade when it is profitable to do so. Because identifying trading opportunities is costly in terms of effort, the principal needs to compensate the trader for trading, as opposed to not trading. Therefore, the trader's compensation will feature a base salary plus bonus tied to his trading frequency. A trader will only expend the effort to trade if his expected reward from trading warrants the cost of his effort. Notably, infrequent trading will require that the trader's trading bonus (per trade) be larger than when trading is frequent.

A trader might well engage in frequent trading, even without risk management. In our conceptual framework, this is akin to trading being worthwhile even when *xCrit* is set at its minimum value. What risk management does is to restrict trading frequency, by setting a higher bar for *xCrit*. If traders have discretion about whether or not to comply with the prescriptions of risk management, then they need to be incentivized to do so. This means that in the presence of a risk management option, traders need to have a second bonus for invoking risk management.

Because risk managers might invoke risk management to receive the second bonus, but then fail to comply, then some form of valuation control such as an audit will be required, which has the potential to detect compliance failure. Detection needs to be backed up with teeth, which means some form of clawback or related penalty. Termination is a possibility. Parenthetically, the higher the detection rate from valuation control, the lower the required second bonus need be.

Trading opportunities are typically time sensitive. Performing risk management can take time, thereby delaying traders from moving ahead. As a result, there are often tensions between traders and risk managers. A principal needs to be aware of the subtleties associated with compensating both traders and risk managers. The greater the time pressure facing traders, the more they need to be compensated with a bonus for engaging with risk management.

In this stylized framework, trader compensation consists of a base salary with two bonuses, one tied to trading frequency and one tied to the engagement of risk management, along with a penalty for engaging but not complying with the prescriptions offered by risk management.

Appendix F: Modelling FIH Issues

Hyman Minsky did not develop a mathematical model of his ideas. Most economists use models, and I believe that Minsky's failure to do so was a major obstacle in having those ideas gain acceptance by economists at large. Nevertheless, he did engage in some modeling, and other economists sympathetic to his perspective have built Minsky models. In this Appendix, I discuss three types of Minsky models, and a related behavioral model that pertains to the impact of sentiment on the term structure of interest rates. Taken together, these models help sharpen our understanding of Minsky's perspective, and I suggest that risk managers would do well to become familiar with them or at least their general structure.

Keynes-Godley Models[1]

The first Minsky-type model features is the traditional textbook Keynesian structure and is based on the macroeconomic equation

$$C + I + G + (X-M) = Y$$

which states that national income Y, which we pay ourselves for what we produce in goods and services, must equal the amount spent on consumption C, investment I, government expenditure G, and the net difference between what we export X and what we import M.[2] For simplicity, call this the $C+I+G$ equation.

Macroeconomic models feature behavioral equations to explain the determinants of the components of aggregate demand, C, I, G, and $X-M$. Notably, consumption C (and saving S) are behaviorally related to income Y. In the simplest version of the theory, consumers save a fraction called the marginal propensity to save (MPS) out of every extra dollar of national income Y, and consume the remainder.

I imagine that most readers will already be familiar with these concepts. Nevertheless, I will provide a quick review of the highlights, in order to make clear how they reflect the issues Minsky highlighted.

The behavioral equations for C, I, G, and X-M provide a basis for an equilibrium approach for the determination of Y, and therefore overall economic activity. The central feature of this equilibrium approach is the concept of a Keynesian multiplier in which an exogenous change in some driver of aggregate demand leads to an amplified or multiplied effect on the equilibrium level of Y. In the simplest version of the theory, the multiplier is the ratio $1/MPS$, where MPS is the marginal propensity to save. For example, should government spending increase by $1 billion, and the marginal propensity to save is 1/3, then the equilibrium level of economic activity will increase by $3 billion.

In the theory, the level of national income does not instantaneously jump between equilibria, but moves iteratively. This movement comes about because of changes to exogenous variables such as government spending G, private investment I, the autonomous component of consumption, or demand for exports by the rest of the world.

Minsky speaks of the euphoria that develops during the boom phase of an economic cycle. In the context of the model, this euphoria leads the private sector to increase private investment I and to finance that investment largely with increased debt. The associated Keynesian multiplier effect results in increased economic activity, higher levels of employment, and increased national income Y. In turn, the higher levels of Y generate higher levels of consumption C.

In the Minsky dynamic, euphoria leads economic agents to take on levels of debt that are irrationally high and too concentrated in speculative and Ponzi finance. For this reason, there arrives a point in time when the hoped-for cash flows to service the debt do not materialize, and the exogenous variables decline instead of increase. In turn, private investment declines. Quite possibly, the autonomous portion of consumption also declines. The multiplier effect begins to operate in reverse.

Minsky's point is that the euphoria leads dangerous balances to develop. Minsky used what is known as the Kalecki equation to emphasize the interdependencies among private sector investment, saving, the government deficit, and the export surplus.[3] In doing so, he pointed out how changes in some components, which we might call imbalances, induce imbalances elsewhere in the economy that ultimately generate instability.

A modified version of the Kalecki equation is known as "the three balances equation." The derivation of the three balances equation is straightforward. Governments pay for G by collecting taxes T, so that what is left over from national income after consumption is what we save and what we pay in taxes. This relationship, in combination with the $C+I+G$ equation implies that

$$I + G + (X-M) = Y - C = S + T$$

Now a little algebraic manipulation gives us the three balances equation.

$$(S-I) = (G-T) + (X-M)$$

Think about what the three balances equation tells us. It tells that the private surplus $S-I$ must be just sufficient to fund the government deficit plus the current account deficits of our trading partners. Here the private surplus is how much output is leftover from S after filling claims by I, which is available to cover the public sector deficit and the deficits of our trading partners.

In applying the three balances equation, consider dividing both sides by Y and ask how $(S-I)/Y$ would behave over time as the government deficit $(G-T)/Y$ changed and the trade balance ratio $(X-M)/Y$ changed. In this respect, consider an example, based on insights developed by economists Wynne Godley and Randall Wray. They point out that during the Clinton years, the US government ran a surplus (so $G-T$ was negative), and a trade deficit (so $X-M$ was negative). By the three balances equation, it must be the case that $S-I$ was also negative, which means American saving was low. In terms of numbers, during the late 1990s, $(G-T)/Y$ was approximately -2.5%, and $(X-M)/Y$ was approximately -4%. This meant that $(S-I)/Y$ had to be approximately -6.5%. Effectively, the US private sector was spending $106.50 for every $100 of income, and it did so by using debt. This was a case of a structural imbalance.

Economic agents who engage in debt finance and pay interest at a higher rate than the growth of their income eventually lose all their wealth. For US consumers in the 1990s, this meant that at some stage they would stop financing so much of their consumption with debt, and begin to retrench. The structural imbalance could not continue to grow, and would not stabilize; rather, it would reverse. Autonomous consumption would have to fall, and would contribute to a negative multiplier. The only question would be when would this happen.

Deleveraging can involve a complicated dynamic, and in extreme cases Fisher debt deflation, as occurred during the Great Depression. This deflation occurs as part of a chain reaction, which begins as follows. In the absence of cash flows to pay debt obligations, firms begin to sell assets. Defaults rise, and with them home foreclosures. As a result, asset prices decline more broadly. Business failures mount. Loan demand falls, and with it the money supply. Interest rates decline. Deflation occurs, thereby inducing lower consumption, which accentuates the downward spiral in economic activity.

Goodwin-Keen Models[4]

Building on what is known as a Goodwin growth cycle model, economist Steve Keen developed a dynamic model to capture Minsky's insights about excessive debt. The model features a set of chained relationships that begin with the economy's capital stock K. Investment leads K to increase, although capital is assumed to depreciate naturally at a rate δ. In the chain, K determines output or equivalently income Y through the relationship $Y = K/v$. The production level Y requires labor L as well as capital K, and so L is determined. In this regard, labor productivity Y/L is assumed to grow at constant rate α. Given overall population N, which is assumed to grow at a constant rate β, the labor participation rate $\lambda = L/N$ induces the rate of change of the wage rate. The wage bill at a given time t is thereby determined as the product of the wage rate and the level of employment. Profit is simultaneously determined as output minus the wage bill.

Keen's starting point is Goodwin's model, expressed as two coupled differential equations, one for the employment rate (λ) and the other for wages as a share of output (ω), where $\lambda_{fn}(\lambda)$ is a Phillips-curve relation and $I_{fn}(\pi_r)$ is an investment function depending on the rate of profit $\pi_r = \Pi/Y$. Here the subscript "fn" denotes function, to distinguish it from the variable itself. The equations for λ and ω are:

$$\frac{d\lambda}{dt} = \lambda \cdot \left(\frac{I_{fn}(\pi_r)}{v} - (\alpha + \beta + \delta) \right)$$

$$\frac{d\omega}{dt} = \omega \cdot \left(\lambda_{fn}(\lambda) - \alpha \right)$$

In the original Goodwin model, investment I is set equal to profit Π. In keeping with Minsky's perspective, Keen modified this assumption so that investment exceeded profit at high rates of profit, and was below profit at low rates. He then added an equation to represent debt-financed investment, and redefined profit to be net of interest payments ($\Pi = Y - W - r \cdot D$):

$$\frac{d}{dt} D = I - \Pi$$

Doing so transformed Goodwin's model into a three-state model to capture Minsky's perspective, with the third equation describing the dynamics of $d = D/Y$, the private debt-to-output ratio.

In both the original Goodwin model and Keen's extension, a stable economy is impossible. This is because the three equations cannot equate to zero simultaneously. Something must always be moving. For instance, in the original

Goodwin model, when the combination of λ and ω produce a stable high employment rate λ, wage inflation is still underway, and so the subsequent increase in ω leads the employment rate λ to fall. In Keen's extension, high stable employment also occurs in conjunction with continued growth in debt (D/Y), and investment (I/Y). However, declining profitability eventually leads the growth rates of D/Y and I/Y to fall to zero. When the combination of λ, ω, and D produce this state of affairs, λ and ω are still in motion, and the economy can move into a debt deflation. That said, one of the most intriguing aspects of Keen's model is that the economy can hover around stability for long periods of time, but then move abruptly into a period of profound instability.

EGGERTON-KRUGMAN MODEL[5]

The two models discussed above are built from the top down, by focusing on behavioral equations for sectors. The third Minsky-type model is built from the bottom up and features the optimizing decisions of heterogeneous economic agents. This model was developed by Eggerton and Krugman (2012).

Eggerton and Krugman set out a flexible-price endowment model in which "impatient" agents can borrow from "patient" agents, but only up to some limit. The simple version of the model features two representative agents, each of whom begins each period with a constant endowment (1/2)Y. Both agents possess log-utility functions and are assumed to maximize the expected discounted utility $E(\Sigma\ \zeta^t \log(c_t))$, where c denotes consumption, ζ is a discount factor, and the range of summation is $t=0$ to ∞. In every period, each agent faces a budget constraint, making a choice about consumption and debt so that the value of current consumption and the beginning portfolio coincide with the value of the ending portfolio and current income Y/2. The patient agent will not be constrained, and therefore their maximizing solution will satisfy the regular first-order conditions. However, the impatient agent, when constrained, would choose to consume more if possible, but is prevented by virtue of being rationed by the debt constraint.

As in the deleveraging scenarios described above, if the debt limit is suddenly reduced, then impatient agents are required to reduce their expenditures. When debt takes the form of nominal obligations, then Fisher debt deflation magnifies the impact generated by the initial shock. In the extreme, output can fall to zero, even as economic agents are making rational decisions at the individual level.

Notably this type of model has features similar to the traditional Keynesian framework. In respect to monetary and fiscal policy, additional public debt can be the solution to a debt-induced slump induced by excessive private debt. Moreover, because some economic agents are debt constrained, Keynesian-type multipliers operate.

IMPLICATIONS FOR RISK MANAGERS

Despite the insights offered by these models, there is something missing from all of them. That something is risk. All of these models are deterministic, and yet the world is stochastic. The Eggerton-Krugman model is stylized, and the "expectation operator" in "expected utility" is totally misleading.

The models developed by Godley, especially with Marc Lavoie, are closer to being the kind of large-scale empirical macroeconomic model that captures essential real-world features. However, keep in mind that Godley predicted a financial crisis at the end of the Clinton era when one did not materialize. He did not anticipate the continued increase in household debt made possible through the mortgage market.

Keen has built a large simulation model, which he named *Minsky*, that allows him to investigate the kind of economic trajectories that are likely to arise as a result of particular behavioral assumptions. However, Keen's model is also deterministic, and does not feature the categorization of financing into hedge, speculative, and Ponzi.

To be sure, none of the models provides comprehensive theoretical coverage of all the components making up Minsky's perspective. However, they are useful in spite of their incompleteness. The models are aids to help us understand complex economic interactions in our efforts to manage the risks lying at the heart of what makes financial systems fragile and what takes economies from being stable to being unstable. We want to use them judiciously, and seek to avoid being overconfident about interpreting the results or succumbing to confirmation bias because we do not care for the results they suggest.

XIONG-YAN BEHAVIORAL MODEL

Minsky expressed concern about rollover risk associated with speculative and Ponzi finance, as a positively sloped yield curve leads financial institutions to borrow at short-term rates in order to lend at higher long-term rates. According to the "expectations hypothesis of interest rates," market expectations about future increases in long-term yields should counter this tendency. The reasoning is that, when the yield curve is positively sloped and fixed income investors expect yields on long-term bonds to fall or remain steady, investors expect to earn higher returns by shunning if not selling, short-term bonds and purchasing long-term bonds.

An insightful equation was developed in Campbell and Shiller (1991) and formalizes the point.[6] Let $Y_t(n)$ be the annual yield of a bond that matures n periods time t, for general t and n. The Campbell-Shiller equation is

$$Y_{t+1}(n-1) - Y_t(n) = \alpha_n + \beta_n (Y_t(n) - Y_t(1))/n - 1.$$

Notably, if the expectations hypothesis holds, then $\beta = 1$. This is because when $Y_t(n) - Y_t(1) > 0$, the average yield advantage per period to the long bond (maturing n periods hence) must be offset by a fall in the price of the long bond, and therefore a rise in its yield over the next period (from t to $t+1$).

Nevertheless, the empirical evidence indicates that the magnitude of β_n is close to zero, but positive, for a maturity of two months, and declines for longer maturities, with the magnitude being about −4 for a maturity of ten years. Hence, in practice, when the yield spread is positive, the prices of long-term bonds rise on average rather than fall. This historical pattern reinforces rather than mitigates the tendency to borrow short term in order to lend long term.

Consider a behavioral explanation for the historical finding that was advanced by Xiong and Yan (2010).[7] Suppose that the market's forecast of future short rates is too high. This bias will lead the market to excessively discount the payoffs from long bonds, thereby unduly driving down their prices. As a result, yields on current long-term bonds will be lower than they would in the case of a fully rational market, meaning that the long-term bond is underpriced relative to fundamentals. Therefore over time, because in the long run prices revert to fundamental values, the price of long-term bonds can be expected to rise, thereby driving down future yields.

Cochrane and Piazzesi (2005) find that a tent-shaped function of three forward rates corresponding to maturities of one, three and five years appears to forecast holding period bond returns of all maturities better than the maturity specific forward spreads.[8] Xiong and Yan use their model to advance an interesting explanation for the tent-shaped factor that is consistent with the behavioral dynamics described in the preceding paragraph.

Appendix G: Empirical Proxies of Sentiment

This Appendix provides additional details about the empirical series and theoretical concepts used in Chapter 12. The key empirical series are the Baker-Wurgler (BW) sentiment index and the Investor Behavior Project (IBP) series pertaining to investor confidence. The theoretical concepts pertain to estimating sentiment from derivative prices.

Empirical Series

The BW is based on six specific sentiment proxies: turnover on the NYSE; dividend premium; closed-end fund discount; number and first-day returns on IPOs; and the equity share in new issues.

Baker and Wurgler based their sentiment measure BW on a series of studies that appeared over a 20-year period showing different manifestations of sentiment. These studies find that when investors become more euphoric, turnover on the NYSE rises. The studies find that increased euphoria leads investors to place less importance on dividends and more on capital gains; therefore, the premium to dividend-paying stocks declines. Closed-end funds tend to trade at market prices that differ from net asset value (NAV), and usually at discounts. The studies find that increased euphoria leads these discounts to decline. IPO activity features what has come to be known as "hot issue" markets. The studies find that increased euphoria leads to more IPOs, and higher first-day returns. CEOs and CFOs do not like to issue new stock when stock prices are falling. The studies find that increased euphoria leads to an increase in the number of new share issues.

Baker and Wurgler constructed their BW measure of sentiment to identify the common, or system-wide, component in the different manifestations of sentiment. To do so, they applied a principal component analysis to extract a common factor, using data from July 1965 through December 2010. They then normalized the resulting series, BW, to have a mean of zero and a standard deviation of one over their sample period.

The IBP US data is based on a survey of two samples of investors. The first is a sample of wealthy individual investors, and the second is a sample of institutional investors. In the recent past, the data on individual investors consisted of a random sample of high-income Americans from Survey Sampling, Inc. The investment managers in the sample are taken from the *Money Market Directory of Pension Funds and Their Investment Managers*.

The IBP confidence indexes consist of monthly six-month averages of monthly survey results. For example, an index value for January 2002 is an average of results from surveys between August 2001 and January 2002. Sample size has averaged a little over one hundred per six-month interval since the beginnings of the surveys. This means that standard errors are typically plus or minus five percentage points.

The valuation index provides a judgmental overlay to CAPE, while the crash confidence provides an indication of investors' judgments of left-tail risk. The other two IBP confidence indexes measure judgments about short and intermediate stock market movements. All are informative, but for the purpose of Chapter 12, I focus only on crash confidence.

THEORETICAL CONCEPTS

This section provides an overview of the basic framework used to obtain estimates of sentiment from historical price data for derivatives, their underlying assets, and interest rates. The discussion is only intended to provide the intuition behind the approach, not the formal model per se.

The subtext for this discussion is the importance for risk managers of understanding that there are formal frameworks for analyzing the sentiment embodied within the prices of derivatives, the assets underlying the derivatives, and interest rates. Risk managers use sophisticated theories to model volatility. Some frameworks are designed to study smile and smirk patterns in the prices of derivatives. Smile and smirks naturally occur in the presence of sentiment. Therefore, because volatility reflects both fundamental risk and sentiment risk, it is in risk managers' interests to disentangle the manner in which risk decomposes into a fundamental component and a sentiment component. The discussion below describes a general approach for doing so.

Imagine that a risk manager is interested in estimating sentiment associated with a broad market such as the market for US equities. Figure G.1 displays three pdfs associated with the future gross returns for the market at some specific date, conditional on information currently available. The density function P_{obj} represents the objective (physical) pdf for this future value. Because of market sentiment, investors' errors might lead current prices to be established as if the market believed that the pdf was given by P_{sub}, which is subjective rather than objective. In the absence of sentiment, P_{sub} coincides with P_{obj}. In

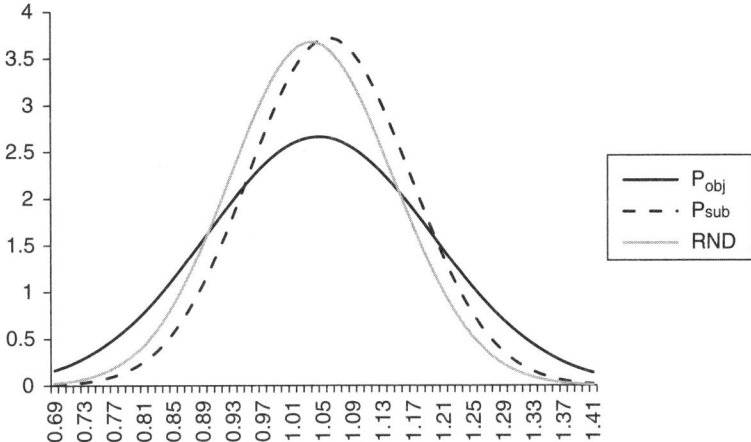

Figure G.1 This figure displays three pdfs associated with the future gross returns for the market at some specific date, conditional on information currently available. The density function P_{obj} represents the objective (physical) pdf for this future value. The pdf P_{sub} reflects the market's subjective pdf which might differ from the objective pdf. In the absence of pure arbitrage opportunities, the prices for derivatives such as index options, generate a risk neutral density function (RND), which gives the future value of contingent state prices compounded at the risk-free rate.

the absence of pure arbitrage opportunities, the prices for derivatives such as index options, generate a risk neutral density function (RND), which gives the future value of contingent state prices compounded at the risk-free rate. Notably, RND reflects the market's beliefs P_{sub}, which might differ from P_{obj}.

When P_{sub} coincides with P_{obj}, there is no mispricing in the market. Conversely, when P_{sub} differs from P_{obj}, there are some assets that are mispriced and therefore reflect sentiment. In Figure G.1, P_{sub} will have higher first moment and a lower second moment than P_{obj}. This means that relative to what is objectively the case, the market's estimate of expected return is too high, and its estimate of volatility too low. In other words, the market is excessively optimistic and overconfident. These two manifestations of sentiment will be embodied in RND.

As was mentioned above, the RND encapsulates the future value of contingent state prices. By dividing a contingent state price, discounted at the risk-free rate, by the probability attached to the occurrence of a state, we obtain a pricing kernel, or more correctly, the value of the pricing kernel for that state. Notably, there will be a different pricing kernel for each selection of pdf. In other words, dividing the discounted RND by P_{obj} leads to one pricing kernel, and dividing by P_{sub} leads to a different pricing kernel.

Figure G.2 illustrates two different pricing kernels, one objective and one subjective. The objective pricing kernel in the figure is monotone declining,

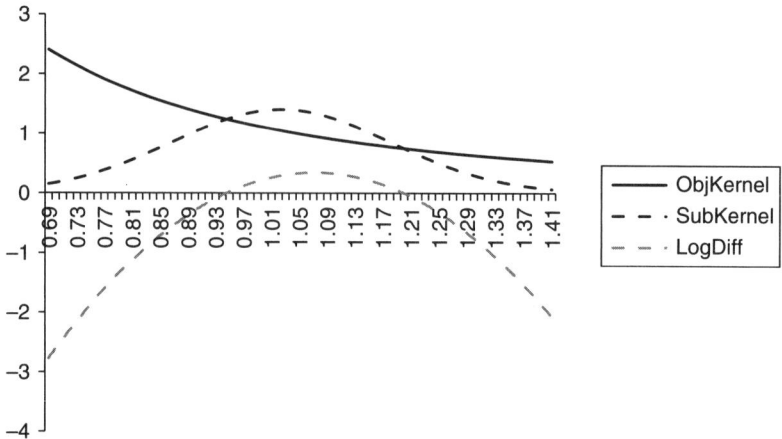

Figure G.2 This figure illustrates two different pricing kernels, one objective and one subjective. The objective pricing kernel in the figure is monotone declining, reflecting the idea that when sentiment is zero, state prices are higher for states with low returns than for states with high returns. However, the subjective pricing kernel in this figure is not monotone declining. The non-monotonicity reflects investors' biases such as excessive optimism and overconfidence.

reflecting the idea that when sentiment is zero, state prices are higher for states with low returns than for states with high returns. However, the subjective pricing kernel in Figure G.2 is not monotone declining. The nonmonotonicity reflects investors' biases such as excessive optimism and overconfidence.

The nonmonotonic pricing kernel results from dividing the RND, which is based on P_{sub}, by the probabilities associated with P_{obj}. It is the contrast in pdfs associated with the numerator and denominator respectively that allows for the expression of sentiment in the shape of the pricing kernel. The monotonically declining pricing kernel is associated with the division of RND by P_{sub}.

In Figure G.2, we interpret the objective pricing kernel as the pricing kernel that would prevail if sentiment were zero. That is, if P_{sub} coincides with P_{obj}, then the two pricing kernels will be identical. Therefore, any difference between the subjective pricing kernel that we observe and the objective pricing kernel reflects sentiment. Behavioral asset-pricing theory tells us that the log-difference between the two pricing kernels is a scaled change of measure, which transforms the subjective pdf into the objective pdf.[1]

Expressed differently, the subjective pricing kernel that underlies market prices decomposes into two components, a fundamental objective component and a sentiment component. This is an important point for risk managers, as the framework provides an approach for doing the decomposition in practice. Moreover, a risk manager with a change of measure in hand will be able to impute the magnitude of biases such as excessive optimism, overconfidence, and left-tail sentiment.

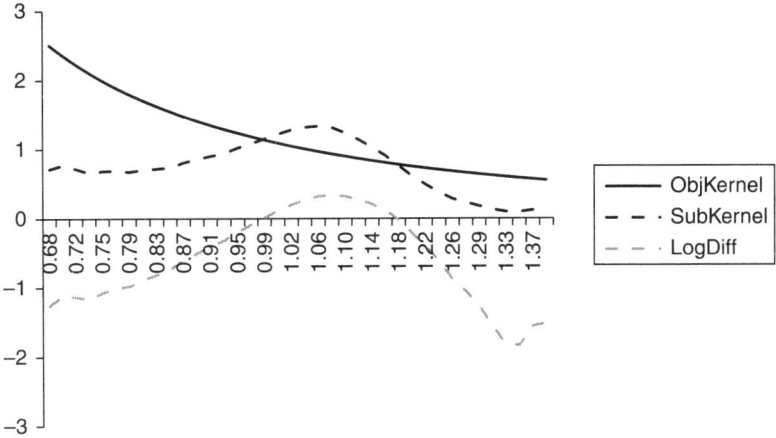

Figure G.3 This figure illustrates output from the application of the theoretical concepts to market data from December 12, 2005. Depicted in Figure A12.3 are an objective pricing kernel, a subjective pricing kernel, and the log-difference function, which embodies the associated change of measure.

Figure G.3 illustrates output from the application of the theoretical concepts to market data from December 12, 2005. Depicted in Figure G.3 are an objective pricing kernel, a subjective pricing kernel, and the log-difference function, which embodies the associated change of measure. Here P_{obj} was estimated from the time series of returns on the S&P 500 index, using a GARCH model. The RND was estimated using a technique known as filtered historical simulation (FHS), applied to index options on the S&P 500. The subjective pricing kernel was then determined by dividing the discounted value of the RND by P_{obj}, return by return.

In practice, the estimated RND is not quite as uniform as its theoretical counterpart, as can be seen by comparing Figures G.3 and G.2. However, the same general shape emerges. The negative values for the log-difference function at the extremes imply that the market underestimates the probabilities of extreme events, which gives rise to overconfidence.

Notably, there are many empirical ways to estimate risk neutral density functions and the properties of the stochastic process for the evolution governing the underlying asset. In this respect, the theory allows for a wide variety of empirical techniques.

Appendix H: A Formal Model for Identifying Failing Banks

THE DISCUSSION BELOW PROVIDES A FORMAL FRAMEWORK FOR IDEAS developed in Chapter 13, which extend the model developed in Appendix E.

Figure H.1 is the analogue of Figure E.2 in Appendix E. In Figure H.1, the hit rate and false alarm rate are established by choosing the critical value of x. In this figure, x represents the parameter values used in a classification heuristic such as those depicted in Figure 13.5. Notice that shifting the critical

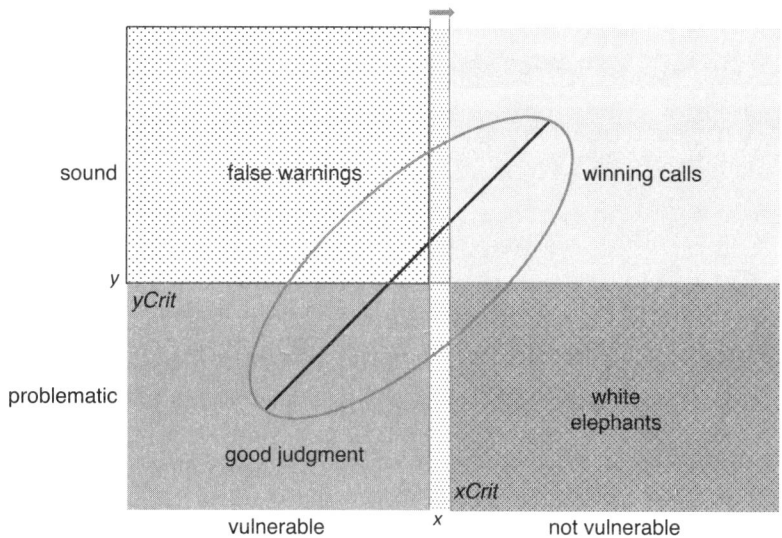

Figure H.1 This figure is the analogue of Figure E.2 in Appendix E. In this figure (H.1), the hit rate and false alarm rate are established by choosing the critical value of x. Here, x represents the parameter values used in a classification heuristic such as those depicted in Figure 13.5. Notice that shifting the critical value to the right increases both "good judgment" and "false warnings," thereby increasing the hit rate (in the darker bottom region of this figure) and the false alarm rate (in the lighter top region of this figure).

value to the right increases both "good judgment" and "false warnings," thereby increasing the hit rate (in the darker bottom region of Figure H.1) and the false alarm rate (in the lighter top region of Figure H.1).

Appendix E also discusses an example to illustrate how best to choose the value of x based on the probabilities of the two types of errors, white elephants and missed opportunities. That discussion is consistent with the criterion that the Bank of England used to assess classification heuristics, namely the difference (hit rate—α false alarm rate). Here, α is a nonnegative parameter that weights the importance of the false alarm rate relative to the hit rate. Notably, the hit rate is the flip side of the white elephant rate, and so the approaches in the two chapters are effectively the same in broad structure.

Appendix I: FIH Issues in China and Europe

SOME YEARS AFTER THE GLOBAL FINANCIAL CRISIS ERUPTED, THE FIH DYNAMIC was clearly discernable in events that took place in China and Europe. Future manifestations of the FIH are likely to take place against the backdrop of a shifting global financial landscape, and for this reason it is important to understand FIH dynamics in these two parts of the world.

FIH Issues in China Post–Financial Crisis

China's importance in global economic affairs keeps on growing. In 2015, Britain, Germany, Italy, and France joined a Chinese-led initiative to change the institutional financial structure underlying the international financial system. A newly created institution, the Asian Infrastructure Investment Bank (AIIB), will compete with the World Bank and the Asian Development Bank, and to a lesser extent the International Monetary Fund (IMF).[1]

Consider economic events in China, where the majority of banks, industries, and stock exchanges are government entities.[2] Between 2004 and 2010, the annual growth rate of China's economy exceeded 10%, with the exception of the period around the Lehman bankruptcy when growth slowed to about 6%. Notably, the global economic downturn eventually reduced the demand for Chinese exports. This decline, in combination with structural imbalances such as low consumption-to-investment, a shifting rural-urban mix in the labor market, and a fall in the marginal efficiency of investment, led the country's growth rate to slow, reaching 7.7% at the end of 2014, with the consensus forecast for 2015 being below 7%. In consequence, the Chinese government looked for ways to stimulate aggregate demand in an effort to maintain the country's growth. In this regard, China did many of the FIH don'ts and avoided many of the FIH dos.

Consider excessive leverage and shadow banking, the first two components of the FIH. At the beginning of 2015, China's ratio of debt-to-GDP was 250%, which was the highest for emerging economies. In China, shadow banking typically involves trust companies. The role of these trust companies has been to allow China's major banks to finance, off-balance sheet, highly risky projects that were being undertaken by real estate developers and local governments. In July 2013, shadow banking comprised almost 70% of China's financial sector.

The riskiness of the loans banks made off their balance sheets did not meet regulatory compliance standards, which is why banks funneled the associated transactions though trusts. The source of the money used to fund these loans was obtained by trust companies selling short-term fixed-income financial products at high interest rates. In this regard, investors were being told that principal was guaranteed, but with no clause asserting such a guarantee in the contract. These financial products paid interest rates of 6% and higher, in contrast to regular savings deposit rates, which were capped by bank regulators at 3.3%. The developers and local governments were paying 9% and more for their loans.

A lack of transparency in these transactions, in conjunction with the risks, led some to ask whether the arrangements amounted to a Ponzi scheme, with investors receiving cash flows from the inflows of other investors rather than the cash flows being generated by the projects being financed.[3] In terms of the FIH, the shadow banking structure just described is replete with don'ts: excessive leverage by risky borrowers, the shift to speculative and Ponzi finance, short term liabilities being used to fund long term assets with attendant rollover risk, and weak regulatory oversight.

Notably, this type of institutional structure brings to mind a series of past catastrophes in the United States mentioned in Chapters 7 and 8. Parallels include the structured investment vehicles associated with ABCP in the period leading up to the global financial crisis; the savings and loan crisis in the United States in the 1980s, with its cap on deposit rates and funding of risky construction loans; and the run on REIT commercial paper in the severe recession of 1974.

In the period after 2010, China experienced two major bubbles, one in real estate and the other in stocks. At the beginning of 2014, housing prices in China were growing at the rate of 10%. However, throughout the first half of the year, the rate of price increases steadily declined, and in September 2014 turned negative. By April 2014, housing prices were falling at the rate of 5% a year. Developers faced increasing unsold inventory, with the 2014 ratio of unsold property to annual sales exceeding 50%—compared to about 25% in 2011—and a 2014 debt-to-asset ratio of 75%, which is high. With respect to the FIH, what makes these figures especially noteworthy is "too big to fail:" property serves as collateral for approximately one-half of China's bank lending.

China's 2015 stock market bubble occurred against the following backdrop. China has two main stock exchanges, one in Shanghai and the other in Shenzhen, which taken together are second largest in the world.[4] However, these exchanges are not international institutions, but instead are almost completely closed to foreign investors. Retail investors generate most of the trading, which is four times as large as that on the NYSE. Notably, China's 2015 stock market bubble occurred at a time when the country's economic growth was slowing, its real estate prices were falling, and the amount of nonperforming loans on the books of its banks was rising.

In respect to a shift in speculative and Ponzi finance, the 2015 stock market bubble featured high-margin trading. As an indication of the degree of euphoria, investors borrowed five times more than they had the previous year to purchase stocks. Over a nine-month period ending in June, the Shanghai stock market rose 135%. At its peak, the price-to-earnings ratio was over 37, much higher than the historical average of about 10. The corresponding P/E ratio on the Shenzhen market, on which small stocks are traded, was almost 80. Trading volume was frenetic, sometimes exceeding the combined volume on all the world's other stock markets.

In the three and a half weeks that followed the bursting of the bubble, the Shanghai index lost 32% of its value. The Chinese government, which had actually encouraged the bubble to stimulate innovation and start-ups, established a $20 billion fund to support prices.[5] This fund complemented other means of support. Unlike stock markets in other parts of the world, companies in China can simply suspend trading in their shares, and many companies with falling prices did so. The government pressured, if not prevented large shareholders from selling shares. State-run institutions repurchased shares.[6]

These measures appeared to have an effect, at least temporarily. Between July 8 and July 24, the Shanghai gauge rebounded 16%. However, on July 27 the Shanghai Composite Index plunged 8.5%, the largest one-day drop since 2007.[7] In line with the FIH dynamic, the Chinese financial system was becoming more fragile, with an increased probability of experiencing a crisis with its attendant runs and the need to rescue firms that are too big to fail.

FIH Issues in Europe Post–Financial Crisis

For Europe, FIH issues lay at the heart of the sovereign debt crisis in the eurozone, which began with the threat of default by Greece. Greece's difficulties focused attention on other countries with fragile finances, such as Portugal, Spain, Ireland, and Italy. MF Global's risky investment strategy, which is discussed in Chapter 16, focused on the sovereign debts of these countries.

Between 2010 and 2015, Greece's situation was especially salient, and for this reason I discuss Greece's experience as part of the eurozone through the lens of the FIH.[8]

When Greece adopted the euro as its currency, it found itself able to borrow at much more attractive rates than previously. As a result, the Greek government took on high leverage in the period of euphoria that preceded the global financial crisis. In 2006, the ratio of Greece's debt to GDP was 100%, almost twice the average for the European Union.

No doubt excessive optimism and overconfidence were factors that encouraged Greece's excessive leverage. However, the Greek government's lack of self-control was a major issue in at least two ways. First, was "borrow and buy now, pay later" behavior featuring immediate benefits and much larger delayed costs. Second was cheating behavior: although reforming its public finances was a requirement for Greece to join the euro, the Greek government masked the true (and very high) value of its budget deficit.

Once the global financial crisis erupted, Greek economic activity plunged along with the rest of the world, and Greece's debt-to-GDP ratio rose to about 175%. In the aftermath of an election, a new government disclosed that its predecessors had hidden the magnitudes of its deficits. In 2010 and 2012, eurozone countries and the IMF assembled a series of rescue plans, totaling approximately €240 billion, which came with conditions involving reform through austerity. Austerity had the effect of driving the Greek economy into depression, with the unemployment rate rising to 25%, similar to those experienced during the Great Depression.

Much of the drama in 2015 involved whether Greek's creditors, notably Germany, would agree to the Greek government's request to write down a large portion of the debt as part of a new wave of rescue financing. The Germans were reluctant to do so, despite the very low probability that Greece would be able to pay off its debts in full.[9]

Were the Germans behaving as if they were averse to accepting a sure loss? While possible, a more likely explanation involves a German-Greek values clash pertaining to risk management culture. The Germans place a high value on discipline, process, and the respecting of rules. The Greeks occupy a different portion of the spectrum.

Historically, France has been the champion for establishing the euro, and Germany had gone along after being assured that they would not have to foot the bill for shoring up financial fragility associated with undisciplined economic behavior of the kind exhibited by Greece. For its part, the IMF urged that part of the rescue plan feature debt relief. The Germans did not disguise their frustration. Indeed, in at least one stage of the 2015 negotiations, the German finance minister suggested that Greece might consider exiting from having the euro as its currency, a so-called Grexit.

Risk management is a core issue for Europe to have a common currency like the euro, a lesson learned the hard way in the aftermath of the global financial crisis. Countries on a common currency such as the euro lack the ability to devalue, exposing them to the risk that financial fragility will severely reduce economic activity, making it more difficult to meet their debt obligations. Recall that the FIH list of do's includes a fiscal stimulus response to economic downturn, not austerity, in an effort to reduce unemployment. To be sure, the threat of austerity certainly provides an incentive to counteract moral hazard, but the incentive is much stronger when decision makers are fully rational, rather than driven by psychological factors such as euphoria, excessive optimism, overconfidence, and limited self-control.

Most of the funds associated with the Greek rescue have actually been used to service the Greek debt, not to stimulate Greece's economy. With respect to the FIH, keep in mind that hedge finance involves debt that is repaid from cash flows generated by the asset being financed, not capital appreciation. The rescue loans from Greece's European neighbors and the IMF do not qualify as hedge finance. Greece's debt is so large, that it is unlikely to be repaid in full.

There is a natural tendency to do the FIHs don'ts and to avoid doing the FIH do's. China's economy is now the second largest in the world, and the euro is the world's second-most important currency. The FIH predicts and past events support the notion that the global economy is vulnerable to financial fragility stemming from psychological forces. These forces present a major challenge for risk managers to understand, analyze, and address.

Final Thoughts: Ignore Sentiment at Your Peril

FIH issues in China and Europe dominated financial markets during the summer of 2015. As I mentioned earlier, in a keynote presentation at ICBI's 2015 Global Derivatives & Risk Management conference, which took place in May, I reminded risk managers about one of my key messages: Ignore sentiment at their peril. The presentation itself was based on material pertaining to the FIH which appears in Chapters 7 and 12.

Discussion during the question and answer period of my presentation focused on identifying the locus of sentiment at the time. I pointed out that although the high value of CAPE for US equity markets which prevailed at the time is always a cause for concern, and that the European sovereign debt issues were still with us as fallout from the global financial crisis, the main locus of sentiment and concerns associated with the FIH lay in China.

With these remarks in mind, consider how the summer of 2015 unfolded. The early part featured the major drama of negotiations between Greece and her creditors who were engaged in a game of chicken around a series of thorny issues. As mentioned above, the issues involved whether a new rescue package for Greece would feature significant debt relief as requested by the Greek government, or instead further austerity moves by Greece in combination with efforts to liberalize its economy. With Greek banks closed to almost all activity except small withdrawals by depositors, and on the verge of collapse, the Greek government blinked. The acceptance by the Greek government of the conditions laid down by Greek's creditors, especially Germany, came against the background of the Greeks holding a referendum in which the majority of voters rejected the terms demanded by their creditors. Shortly thereafter, the Greek prime minister who had called the referendum actually urging Greeks to reject the conditions, instead accepted them and then resigned. The creditors responded by agreeing to yet a third rescue package, this one totaling 86 billion euros.[10]

Later in the summer of 2015, FIH issues in China came to the fore. The Chinese cabinet decided that in order to address the decline in the country's growth rate, devaluation of its currency was in order. In early August, it did devalue, allowing the renminbi to fall by about 4.4% against the US dollar. Equity markets around the world reacted by falling sharply.

As mentioned above, earlier in the summer, the Chinese government had been taking actions to prevent the bubble in the country's stock market from bursting. However, in mid-August, it appeared to change course by withdrawing support, and on Monday August 24, Chinese stocks fell by 8.5%. Again, equity markets around the world reacted to events in China by falling sharply. In the US, the Dow Jones Industrial Average opened the day down by 7.8% and closed the day down 3.5%, a clear systemic event. The S&P 500 declined by 4.2% over the day.[11] In May when I spoke at the ICBI Global Derivatives conference, I said that high values of CAPE, especially above 25, always heralded danger. Between November 2014 and July 2015, CAPE had been above 26.

When euphoria has been high and begins to wane, some investors come to hold beliefs that reflect the bimodal pattern discussed in Chapter 2, with the possibility of both very high and very low subsequent returns featuring high probability. In this case, nervous investors look for information to signal which direction markets will move, with the result being increased volatility.

August was a very volatile month for global equity markets, including China. Stock market rallies occurred in the last week of the month after China's central bank reduced its benchmark interest rate and also freed banks to increase lending.[12] For the volatile week of August 24, the S&P fluctuated in value by almost 5% and closed the week up 1.2%. Still, as shown by Figure 12.6, at the end of August CAPE remained above 25. Figure 12.7 shows that for individual investors, crash confidence fell by about five points during the summer of 2015. However, for institutional investors, it remained at about 35. The VIX, which had been below 11 at the beginning of August rose above 30 by month end. See Figure 12.1.

Investors, who experienced the market volatility of summer 2015 learned from experience that they ignore sentiment at their peril. I think that Minksy, the author of the FIH, would not have been surprised by the increased financial fragility in China and Europe.

As this book goes to press in the autumn of 2015, the events in question are still a tale half told. China's financial system has experienced the first six components of the FIH, from excessive leverage through regulatory failure.[13] Whether the remaining components of the FIH dynamic play out, especially a full scale financial crisis with bank runs and the rescue of firms too big to fail, remains to be seen. Certainly the turbulence in global equity markets in the second half of the summer of 2015 reflected concerns about a decline in Chinese economic activity if not outright economic instability.

As for Europe, Greece's debt is simply too high to be repaid in full, and the austerity measures have reduced its ability to service its debt. Whether the reforms insisted by Greece's creditors produce their intended effect remains to be seen. And while Greece gets most of the attention, and there has been improvement in other parts of Europe, the European Union's financial system remains fragile. An unstable Chinese economy would only exacerbate that fragility.

Notes

Preface

1. See Marcia Carruthers (2013), "Behavioral Risk Management: Recognizing the Elephant in the Room," *IMRI*, February. http://www.irmi.com/expert/articles/2013/carruthers02-workers-compensation-disability-insurance.aspx.
2. http://www.automatedtrader.net/headlines/153811/gdtrm15-latest-on-derivatives-markets-risk-and-regulation.
3. In Yiddish, the words for "think" and "laugh" rhyme, making the statement a bit sharper.
4. The last chapter discusses the concept of "safety factors" and illustrates how the "fence" concept applies in practice.
5. "Richard Barfield interviews Hersh Shefrin at RiskMinds 2011," [n.d.], video clip, accessed July 21, 2015, YouTube, https://www.youtube.com/watch?v=xyupMtzwcUE.

1 Introduction

1. The psychological issues discussed in this book apply to many historical episodes, not just recent events. For example, the operational risks that the Captain of the Titanic took in trying to achieve a new record for crossing the Atlantic, in the face of warnings about sightings of nearby icebergs by other ships, can be analyzed in terms of the aspiration framework developed in Chapter 2 and the bias framework of Chapter 4. Similarly, in the Battle of Gettysburg, which many regard as the turning point of the Americn Civil War, the concept of "sunk cost" inherent within ideas developed in Chapter 3 can be used to analyze the decision by General Robert E. Lee when he ordered Pickett's Charge.
2. The part of our brain is known as the locus ceruleus.
3. See Julie Makinen (2015), "4 years after Fukushima, Japan Considers Restarting Nuclear Facilities," *Los Angeles Times*, March 30.
4. Jonathan Soble and Dickie Mure (2011), "How Fukushima Failed," *Financial Times*, May 6, http://www.ft.com/cms/s/2/5207d550-76b9-11e0-bd5d-00144 feabdc0.html#axzz3WILJyKBt.

5. James M. Acton and Mark Hibbs (2012), "Why Fukushima Was Preventable," *The Carnegie Papers*, http://carnegieendowment.org/2012/03/06/why-fukushima-was-preventable.
6. See p. 28 of the report.
7. The event occurred in December 1999, when a storm surge at high tide caused flooding at two units at the Blayais Nuclear Power Station in France, along with a partial loss of power. The surge exceeded the design-basis flood scenario for the plant.
8. See John Coates (2012), *The Hour between Dog and Wolf: How Risk Taking Transforms Us, Body, and Mind* (New York: Penguin).
9. See Ye Cai and Hersh Shefrin (2013), "Bad Corporate Marriages: Waking Up in Bed the Morning After," ssrn.com, http://papers.ssrn.com/sol3/papers.cfm?abstract_id=2372248.
10. According to authorities in the United Kingdom, 25 traders at 16 banks collaborated to manipulate Libor rates. The Serious Fraud Office identified Tom Hayes, who had worked for both Citgroup and UBS, as the ringleader, and in August 2015 he was convicted on eight counts in a UK court for misconduct that took place between 2006 and 2010. Hayes described the manipulative practices as "widespread" and "blatant," so much so that he thought he had been open about his behavior. See Chad Bray (2015). "Former Citigroup and UBS Trader Convicted in Libor Case," *New York Times*, August 3. http://www.nytimes.com/2015/08/04/business/dealbook/former-citigroup-and-ubs-trader-convicted-in-libor-case.html?hp&action=click&pgtype=Homepage&module=second-column-region&region=top-news&WT.nav=top-news&_r=0
11. See the article "Libor Scandal: The Most Outrageous Exchanges between Traders" (2013), *Huffington Post*, posted: June 2, http://www.huffingtonpost.co.uk/2013/02/06/libor-scandal-outrageous-traders-exchanges_n_2630945.html?just_reloaded=1.
12. See Michael Corkery and Ben Protess (2015). "Rigging of Foreign Exchange Market Makes Felons of Top Banks," *New York Times*, May 20. http://www.nytimes.com/2015/05/21/business/dealbook/5-big-banks-to-pay-billions-and-plead-guilty-in-currency-and-interest-rate-cases.html
13. See Sebastian Chrispin (2015). "Forex Scandal: How to Rig the Market," *BBC News*, May 20. http://www.bbc.com/news/business-26526905.
14. The Forex manipulators referred to themselves using macho pseudonyms such as "The players," "the A team," and "the three musketeers." Not surprisingly, they also used colorful language in their communications with each other, such as, "how can I make free money with no fcking heads up." See Claer Barrett and John Aglionby (2014). "Traders' Forex Chatroom Banter Exposed," *Financial Times*, November 12. http://www.ft.com/intl/cms/s/2/47c32ec4-6a34-11e4-8fca-00144feabdc0.html#slide0.
15. See Simon Hansen (2014), "The China-US Climate Change Agreement Is a Step Forward for Green Power Relations," *The Guardian*, November 14, http://www.theguardian.com/commentisfree/2014/nov/14/the-china-us-climate-change-agreement-is-a-step-forward-for-green-power-relations. See

also Mark Landler (2014), "U.S. and China Reach Climate Accord after Months of Talks, *New York Times*, November 11.
16. See Brian Kahn (2014), "What You Need to Know about U.S.-China Climate Pact," http://www.climatecentral.org/news/details-behind-u.s.-china-climate-pact-18317.
17. The consensus among climate scientists about global warming contrasts with the lack of consensus about social policy, at what rate to discount future outcomes, and how to assess the probabilities associated with new technologies that will counter greenhouse gas emissions. See Robert Pindyck (2013). "Climate Change Policy: What Do the Models Tell Us?" *Journal of Economic Literature*, 51(3), 860–872; and Richard Tol (2013), "Targets for Global Climate Policy: An Overview." *Journal of Economic Dynamics and Control*, 37 (5), 911–928. The moral dimension of the climate change debate took on a new complexion with the publication of Pope Francis's encyclical on the issue: see Pope Francis (2015). *Laudato Si': On Care of Our Common Home.*" Encyclical Letter, Vatican: Vatican Press. The encyclical only briefly touches on the role played by human population growth, which is controversial in light of Church doctrine concerning that topic. Indeed, concerns about population growth that were expressed during the second half of the twentieth century turned out to be much exaggerated. See Andrew Revkin (2015), "The Population Bomb, Then and Now," *New York Times*, June 1. http://dotearth.blogs.nytimes.com/2015/06/01/the-population-bomb-then-and-now/.
18. In August 2015, the Obama administration announced a set of environmental regulations that featured stronger standards than in previous drafts from the Environmental Protection Agency, released in 2012 and 2014. Notably, the new regulations establish a requirement that by 2030, power plant carbon emissions need to be 32% less than 2005 levels, which is 2% more than the the 30% target in previous drafts. The new regulations seek a major replacement of coal-based electricity generation with renewable technology such as solar and wind power. Given the existence of strong vested interests, especially in coal-producing states such as West Virginia and Wyoming, subsequent legal battles are likely to be hard fought. See Coral Davenport and Gardiner Harrisaug (2105). "Obama to Unveil Tougher Climate Plan With His Legacy in Mind," *New York Times*, August 2. http://www.nytimes.com/2015/08/02/us/obama-to-unveil-tougher-climate-plan-with-his-legacy-in-mind.html?hp&action=click&pgtype=Homepage&module=first-column-region&region=top-news&WT.nav=top-news.
19. See http://environment.yale.edu/climate-communication/.
20. The three biases mentioned in the text are not exhaustive. According to the Yale project, an important reason underlying the stability is availability bias, a phenomenon explained in Chapter 4. At this stage, let me simply reiterate the comments in the Yale Project report. The report indicates that most Americans were not hearing about or speaking about global warming. Their survey found that only 40% of Americans indicated that they heard about global warming in the media at the rate of once a month or more. At the weekly frequency, only

19% heard about global warming in the media at least once. In addition, only 16% indicated that they heard other people who they know talk about global warming at least once a month, and only 4% reported that they heard other people talking about global warming at least once a week.
21. Confirmation bias plays an important role in public perceptions and public debates about climate change and climate policy. There are genuine debates that need to take place about climate change issues, although psychological issues sometimes make dispassionate debate difficult. See Bjørn Lomborg (2015), "The Honor of Being Mugged by Climate Censors," *Wall Street Journal*, May 13, 2015, http://www.wsj.com/articles/the-honor-of-being-mugged-by-climate-censors-1431558936. Some of the psychological issues can be seen in Lomborg's article "The Alarming Thing About Climate Alarmism," which appeared in the *Wall Street Journal* on February 1, 2015, http://www.wsj.com/articles/bjorn-lomborg-the-alarming-thing-about-climate-alarmism-1422832462, and in "Bjørn Lomborg Sings WSJ's Same Old Climate Change Song: Don't Worry, Be Happy," desmogblog.com, http://www.desmogblog.com/2015/02/02/lomborg-sings-wsj-s-same-old-climate-change-song-don-t-worry-be-happy.
22. See James Hug (2015), "Loyola-Chicago Conference Finds a 'Perfect Storm' of Mental Barriers to Climate Action," ncronline.org, March 31, 2015. http://ncronline.org/blogs/eco-catholic/loyola-chicago-conference-finds-perfect-storm-mental-barriers-climate-action.
23. See the 2004 report by the Committee of Sponsoring Organizations of the Treadway Commission (COSO), 2004. *Enterprise Risk Management Integrated Framework*. In May 2013, COSO released an updated version of its Internal Control-Integrated Framework. See the COSO of the Treadway Commission (2013), *Internal Control-Integrated Framework*. For a discussion of the update, see J. Stephen McNally (2013), "The 2013 COSO Framework & SOX Compliance," *Strategic Finance*, June, 1–8.

For references that cover enterprise risk management from a variety of perspectives, see the following: John Fraser and Betty Simkins, eds. (2010), *Enterprise Risk Management: Today's Leading Research and Best Practices for Tomorrow's Executives* (Hoboken, NJ: Wiley); John Fraser, Betty Simkins, and Kristina Narvaez, eds. (2014), *Implementing Enterprise Risk Management: Case Studies and Best Practices*, Robert W. Kolb Series. Edited by (Hoboken, NJ: Wiley).
24. Bob Hirth (2015), "COSO 2013: What Happened?" in *COSO Lessons Learned: The Evolution of Controls Assurance*, Webinar by Blackline, FEI, August 11.
25. For a discussion of the COSO ERM approach, see COSO (2004), *Enterprise Risk Management—Integrated Framework: Executive Summary*, http://www.coso.org/documents/COSO_ERM_ExecutiveSummary.pdf. While not stressing psychological issues, there is certainly an awareness of psychological issues within COSO. See Steven Glover and Douglas Prawitt (2012), "Enhancing Board Oversight, Avoiding Judgment Traps and Biases," http://www.coso.org/documents/COSO-EnhancingBoardOversight_r8_Web-ready%20(2).pdf.

2 SP/A THEORY'S FOCUS ON THREE KEY EMOTIONS

1. In a private communication, Luca Celati provided the following important comment to me: "Context dependence is a key finding of textbook behavioral finance, and no force beats compensation at establishing and reinforcing a given contextual perspective on business and trades inside a financial institution, irrespective of size. These powerful compensation dynamics get even more magnified as an executive moves up the corporate ladder, thereby providing more reinforcement for these differences."
2. Lola Lopes (1987), "Between Hope and Fear: The Psychology of Risk," *Advances in Experimental Social Psychology* 20: 255–295. The emotions of hope and fear can be identified with particular regions in the brain, such as the nucleus accumbens whose activation is associated with, and generally leads to, increased risk taking. See Brian Knutson, G. Elliott Wimmer, Camelia M. Kuhnen and Piotr Winkielman (2008), "Nucleus accumbens activation mediates the influence of reward cues on financial risk taking," *NeuroReport* 19(5): 509–513. Weather and amount of daylight can also influence risk appetite. See Mark Kamstra, Lisa Kramer, and Maurice Levi (2003), "Winter Blues: Seasonal Affective Disorder (SAD) and Stock Market Returns," *American Economic Review* 93(1): 324–343. A recurrent theme in this book is that circumstances impact risk appetite. There is an academic literature documenting that professional traders are willing to take riskier positions in the second part of the day after a morning of inferior returns. See Hersh Shefrin (2007), "How the Disposition Effect and Momentum Impact Investment Professionals," *Monitor and Journal of Investment Consulting* 8(2): 68–79.
3. She called the comments "verbal protocols" as they were written transcription of remarks made orally.
4. This type of comment from subjects is fairly common and is not confined to undergraduate finance majors. The following comment is from an executive named Tom, whose job title is director of information technology, and who participated in an experiment for business professionals. Tom explained how he compared alternatives and ranked PK over RF, stating: "I added probabilities to earn more than $1,100, calculated the probability to earn less than $500, and made a ranking to avoid a high risk of no gain at all while keeping good chances of earning significantly more than $1,000."
5. Daniel Kahneman, Jack L. Knetsch, and Richard H. Thaler (1990), "Experimental Tests of the Endowment Effect and the Coase Theorem," *Journal of Political Economy* 98 (6): 1325–1348.

3 PROSPECT THEORY'S FOCUS ON GAINS, LOSSES, AND FRAMING

1. See Daniel Kahneman and Amos Tversky (1979), "Prospect Theory: An Analysis of Decision Making under Risk," *Econometrica*, 5(2): 263–291; Amos Tversky and Daniel Kahneman (1992), "Advances in Prospect Theory: Cumulative Representation of Uncertainty," *Journal of Risk and Uncertainty* 5: 297–323.

2. In these two tasks, B and D involve risk, while A and C do not involve risk. This alone does not make A the risk-averse choice and D the risk-seeking choice, as expected payoffs are also part of the story. The expected payoff to the risky alternative B is $2,500, (obtained as the product of 25% × $10,000 + 75% × $0). The expected payoff from the risky alternative D is a $7,500 loss (obtained as the product of 75% × $10,000 + 25% × $0). Of course, the expected payoffs for A and C are just their respective certain payoffs, $2,400 and −$7,500 respectively.
3. Kahneman and Tversky developed the main ideas for prospect theory in the 1970s when they were on faculty at The Hebrew University in Jerusalem, where they used Israeli university students as subjects. To round out the discussion, let me report the results from a group of 20 Israeli graduate business students from 2010. The median coefficient of loss aversion was 4.0: 77% chose A, 71% chose D, and 58% chose the combination A&D.
4. Richard H. Thaler and Eric J. Johnson (1990), "Gambling with the House Money and Trying to Break Even: The Effects of Prior Outcomes on Risky Choice," *Management Science* 36 (6): 643–660.
5. For more general groups of financial professionals, the figure is closer to 12%. Of course, these percentages are all greater than the 6.25% associated with the random assignment, but they are still much smaller relative to 100%, which applies when everyone behaves in accordance with prospect theory.
6. See Daniel Kahneman (2002), "Maps of Bounded Rationality: A Perspective on Intuitive Judgment and Choice," nobelprize.org, http://www.nobelprize.org/nobel_prizes/economic-sciences/laureates/2002/kahnemann-lecture.pdf.
7. I replicated the revised experiment, with the size of stakes higher than in the original version, and, with the exception of PhD students in finance, obtained comparable results in respect to reversal of ranking.

4 BIASES AND RISK

1. Luca Celati (2004), *The Dark Side of Risk Management: How People Frame Decisions in Financial Markets* (London: Prentice-Hall: Financial Times); Riccardo Rebonato (2010) *Plight of the Fortune Tellers: Why We Need to Manage Financial Risk Differently* (Princeton: Princeton University Press).
2. Amos Tversky and Daniel Kahneman (1973), "Availability: A Heuristic for Judging Frequency and Probability," *Cognitive Psychology* 5, 207–232.
3. Tracy Keller (2012), "Why Do 90% of Restaurants Fail in the First Year," Concordia St. Paul Blog & News Updates, posted June 18, csp.edu, http://online.csp.edu/blog/business/why-do-90-of-restaurants-fail-in-the-first-year.
4. H. G. Parsa, John T. Self, David Njite, and Tiffany King (2005), "Why Restaurants Fail," *Cornell Hotel and Restaurant Administration Quarterly* 46 (3): 304–322.
5. Paul Slovic (1987), "Perception of Risk," *Science*, New Series, 236 (4799): 280–285.
6. See http://www.world-nuclear.org/info/Safety-and-Security/Safety-of-Plants/Safety-of-Nuclear-Power-Reactors/.

7. See http://uspirg.org/issues/usp/campaign-safe-energy.
8. Judy Dempsey and Jack Ewing (2011), "Germany, in Reversal, Will Close Nuclear Plants by 2022," *New York Times*, May 30. http://www.nytimes.com/2011/05/31/world/europe/31germany.html.
9. Melissa Finucane, Paul Slovic, C. K. Mertz, James Flynn, and Teresa Satterfield (2000), "Gender, Race, and Perceived Risk: The 'White Male' Effect," *Healthy Risk & Society* 2 (2): 159–172.
10. Amos Tversky and Daniel Kahneman (1974), "Judgment under Uncertainty: Heuristics and Biases," *Science*, New Series, 185 (4157): 1124–1131.
11. Thomas Gilovich, Robert Vallone, and Amos Tversky (1985), "The Hot Hand in Basketball: On the Misperception of Random Sequences," *Cognitive Psychology* 17: 295–314.
12. Andrew Bocskocsky, John Ezekowitz, and Carolyn Stein (2014), "The Hot Hand: A New Approach to an Old 'Fallacy'," Working paper: Harvard University.
13. Neil D. Weinstein (1980), "Unrealistic Optimism about Future Life Events," *Journal of Personality and Social Psychology* 39 (5): 806–820.
14. Stuart Oskamp (1965), "Overconfidence in Case-Study Judgments," *Journal of Consulting Psychology* 29 (3): 261–265.
15. For the sake of this discussion, the Colorado River is 1,450 miles long.
16. Peter C. Wason (1966), "Reasoning," in *New Horizons in Psychology*, ed. B. Foss (Harmondsworth: Penguin Books), 135–151.
17. This issue involves how people react to authority, and is discussed further in Chapter 16 on MF Global.
18. See Solomon Asch (1951), "Effects of Group Pressure on the Modification and Distortion of Judgments," in *Groups, Leadership and Men*, ed. H. Guetzkow (Pittsburgh: Carnegie Press), 177–190. Asch conducted an experiment that posed a length of line judgment task to groups composed of eight, with seven being confederates and one being the true subject. A single task consisted of being presented with two cards, one with a single line and a second with three lines of varying length. The group was charged with making a collective judgment about which of the three lines on the second card exactly matched the first card. Group members announced their judgments, with the true subject always going last. In some trials, the confederates made judgments that were clearly erroneous, thereby presenting the true subject with a quandary about whether or not to conform. Asch found significant individual variation among true subjects. Many succumbed to their urge to conform, while others did not, and instead acted with independence, although some independents were uncomfortable doing so. Many of those who conformed reported that they did so out of a lack of confidence in their own judgments, despite those judgments being at odds with those of the majority. With all the focus on overconfidence, it is nonetheless important to identify the implications of underconfidence.
19. Ellen J. Langer (1975), "The Illusion of Control," *Journal of Personality and Social Psychology* 32 (2): 311–328.
20. Gerd Gigerenzer, Wolfgang Gaissmaier, and Elke Kurz-Milcke (2007), "Helping Doctors and Patients Make Sense of Health Statistics," *Psychological Science in the Public Interest* 8 (2): 53–96.

5 PERSONALITY AND RISK

1. David Ingram and Elijah Bush (2013), "Collective Approaches to Risk in Business: An Introduction to Plural Rationality Theory," *North American Actuarial Journal* 17 (4): 297–305.
2. See Barbara Fredrickson (2009), *Positivity: Top-Notch Research Reveals the Upward Spiral That Will Change Your Life*, New York: Crown.
3. For academic references, see the following: optimism (Scheier, 1985), desirability of control (Burger and Cooper, 1979), social anxiousness (Leary, 1983), self-monitoring behavior (Snyder, 1974; Lennox and Wolfe, 1984), life satisfaction (Diener, Emmons, Larsen, and Griffin, 1985), and affect (Watson and Clark, 1988). The complete references mentioned are as follows:
    Michael Scheier (1985), Optimism, Coping, and Health: Assessment and Implications of Generalized Outcome Expectancies, *Health Psychology* 4 (3): 219–247.
    Jerry Burger and Harris Cooper (1979), "The Desirability of Control," *Motivation and Emotion* 3 (4): 381–393.
    Mark Leary (1983), "Social Anxiousness: The Construct and Its Measurement," *Journal of Personality Assessment* 47 (1): 66–75.
    Richard D. Lennox and Raymond N. Wolfe (1984), "Revision of the Self-Monitoring Scale," *Journal of Personality and Social Psychology* 46 (6): 1349–1364.
    Mark Snyder (1974), "Self-Monitoring of Expressive Behavior," *Journal of Personality and Social Psychology* 30 (4): 526–537.
    Ed Diener, Robert Emmons, Randy Larsen, and Sharon Griffin (1985), "The Satisfaction with Life Scale, *Journal of Personality Assessment* 49 (1): 71–75.
    David Watson and Lee Anna Clark (1988), "Development and Validation of Brief Measures of Positive and Negative Affect: The PANAS Scales," *Journal of Personality and Social Psychology* 54 (6): 1063–1070.
4. Hersh Shefrin (2010), "Insights into the Psychological Profiles of Entrepreneurs," in R. Yazdipour (ed.) *Advances in Entrepreneurial Finance* (New York: Springer).
5. Risk managers, take note. If this result is robust, and it derives from a sample of about 825 respondents, then it can provide risk managers with important information about when to expect deviations from the prototypical behavior pattern. Notably, the general pattern for gains applied to all groups, with one exception. That exception involved a group of 22 European risk managers. Recall that Beth's inferred coefficient of loss aversion was 5 and Larry's was 2. However, Beth and Larry both selected the combination A&D. In this regard, for the group that included Beth and Larry, mean loss aversion was 4.2 for those who took the sure gain and 0.9 for those who took the risk.
6. Here those accepting a sure loss have a coefficient of loss aversion of 5.3, while those taking the risk have a corresponding coefficient of 4.7.
7. That said, my data indicate that this finding does not apply as evenly across groups for losses as it does for gains. It does apply to business professionals

in executive risk management degree programs, executive MBA students in the United States, financial executives, and undergraduate finance majors. However, it does not apply to regular MBA students in the United States, executive MBA students outside the United States, and risk managers enrolled in executive training programs.

8. Here are the numbers for this paragraph. In respect to undergraduate finance majors, mean loss aversion for those who conform to the prototypical pattern is 4.2, while for all others it is 6.3. In respect to business professionals, where I have only a small sample, mean loss aversion for those who conform to the prototypical pattern is 6.1, while for all others it is 5.0.

9. Here are the numbers for this paragraph. In respect to undergraduate finance majors, mean levels for cautious hope and for establishing target outcomes (5.1 and 5.8 respectively) are higher for those who conform to the prototypical pattern than for others (4.4 and 5.4 respectively). To this point, those who conform also feel the pain of missing a goal much less acutely than others (4.4 vs. 4.8). Moreover, those who switch contend that they are much more willing to take risks if meeting a goal is not an issue, either because achieving the goal is guaranteed (6.0 vs. 5.3) or because achieving the goal is impossible (3.4 vs. 2.3).

10. Here are the numbers. When comparing those undergraduate finance majors who conform to the prototypical quasi-hedonic pattern, loss aversion is lower (4.2 vs. 4.9) for those who switch from accepting a sure gain to taking a risk (after a prior gain) and higher (5.9 vs. 4.2) for those who switch from taking a risk in the domain of losses to accepting a sure loss (after a prior loss).

11. The complete response scale is as follows:
    1. The statement does not apply to me at all.
    2. The statement usually does not apply to me.
    3. Most often, the statement does not apply.
    4. I am unsure about whether or not the statement applies to me or it applies to me about half the time.
    5. The statement applies more often than not.
    6. The statement usually applies to me.
    7. The statement always applies to me.

12. Notably, for the rest of the group, the difference in conditional means was smaller (4.2 vs. 3.9).

6 PROCESS, PITFALLS, AND CULTURE

1. See Jack Stack, with Bo Burlingham (2013), *The Great Game of Business, Expanded and Updated: The Only Sensible Way to Run a Company* (New York: Crown Business). For coverage by PBS, see http://www.pbs.org/newshour/bb/;business/jan-june10/makingsense_04-28.html; http://www.pbs.org/newshour/businessdesk/2010/04/making-use-of-employees-talent.html; http://www.pbs.org/newshour/bb/business/jan-june10/makingsense_06-21.html.

2. See Stack and Burlingham, *The Great Game of Business.*

3. James March and Zur Shapira (1987), "Managerial Perspectives on Risk and Risk Taking," *Management Science* 33 (11): 1404–1418.
4. Unless otherwise indicated, the historical information about the 2014 Ebola outbreak is taken from Jen Christensen (2014), "'Out of Control': How the World Reacted as Ebola Spread," *CNN*, http://www.cnn.com/interactive/2014/11/health/ebola-outbreak-timeline/index.html?hpt=hp_t2, and Kevin Sack, Sheri Fink, Pam Belluck, and Adam Nossiter (2014), "How Ebola Roared Back," *New York Times,* December 29, http://www.nytimes.com/2014/12/30/health/how-ebola-roared-back.html?hp&action=click&pgtype=Homepage&module=a-lede-package-region&region=top-news&WT.nav=top-news.
5. See Sack et al., "How Ebola Roared Back."
6. Somini Sengupta (2015), "Effort on Ebola Hurt W.H.O. Chief," *New York Times,* January 6, http://www.nytimes.com/2015/01/07/world/leader-of-world-health-organization-defends-ebola-response.html.
7. See Sack et al., "How Ebola Roared Back."
8. See Sack et al., "How Ebola Roared Back."
9. Sarah Boseley (2014), "World Health Organisation Admits Botching Response to Ebola Outbreak," *Guardian*, October 17, http://www.theguardian.com/world/2014/oct/17/world-health-organisation-botched-ebola-outbreak.
10. See http://apps.who.int/ebola/ebola-situation-reports.
11. Elizabeth Sheedy and Barbara Griffin (2014), "Empirical Analysis of Risk Culture in Financial Institutions: Interim Report," Working paper: MacQuarie University. Although this paper focuses on financial firms, the methodology is actually based on the literature about industrial accidents and safety. The COSO ERM framework discussed in Chapter 1 provides a detailed perspective on analyzing how risk issues are addressed within organizations. See Douglas Anderson and Gina Eubanks (2015), "Leveraging COSO Across the Three Lines of Defense," http://www.coso.org/documents/COSO-2015-3LOD-PDF.pdf.
12. See Gerd Gigerenzer (2014), *Risk Savvy* (New York: Penguin Group, USA). Gigerenzer contrasts the practices in the airline industry, which has actively worked to improve crash safety over the last several decades, to the practices in the health-care industry, the safety record of which is much worse.
13. Their approach uses a survey that they administer to a sample drawn from multiple business units in five specific business lines. The survey consists of 22 questions about risk culture and another 45 questions that relate to demographics, personal attitude to risk management, personal risk tolerance, and perceptions about risk management and behavior within the bank for which they work. Respondents are asked to provide responses on a 6-point scale where a "1" means "strongly disagree" and a "6" means "strongly agree."
14. Christopher Vaughan (2011), "Interview with Jack Stack," *Ethics and Entrepreneurship*, April 11, http://www.ethicsandentrepreneurship.org/20110411/interview-with-jack-stack/.
15. Robert S. Kaplan and Anette Mikes (2012), "Managing Risks: A New Framework," *Harvard Business Review*, 6 (June). https://hbr.org/2012/06/managing-risks-a-new-framework.

16. Robert Simons (1999), "How Risky Is Your Company?" *Harvard Business Review*, 77, no. 1 (January–February): 85–94. https://hbr.org/1999/05/how-risky-is-your-company.
17. However, reasonable minds can differ: Beth might perceive her ranking of RF over PK as reflecting preventable risk. After all, nobody is saying that eliminating preventable risks is necessarily without cost: RF does not stochastically dominate PK. However, RF does offer the same expected payoff as PK, and safer downside exposure.
18. K. C. Green (2005), "Game Theory, Simulated Interaction, and Unaided Judgement for Forecasting Decisions In Conflicts: Further Evidence," *International Journal of Forecasting* 21: 463–472; K. C. Green (2002), "Forecasting Decisions in Conflict Situations: A Comparison of Game Theory, Role-Playing, and Unaided Judgement," *International Journal of Forecasting* 18: 321–344.
19. Robert Simons' approach, described in the *Harvard Business Review* was mentioned in a previous footnote.
20. Zur Shapiro (1997), *Risk Taking: A Managerial Perspective* (New York: Russell Sage Foundation).
21. Christopher DiGiorgio and Jeanne G. Harris (2013), "If Venture Capital Falters, Will Job Creation Fade?" *Accenture Research* report, August. The authors of this report used the July 28, 2012, issue of *The Economist* to contrast company creation in the eurozone with company creation in California.
22. Edward L. Deci and Richard M. Ryan (2000), "The 'What' and 'Why' of Goal Pursuits: Human Needs and the Self-Determination of Behavior," *Psychological Inquiry* 11: 227–268.
23. Chris Nicholson (2010), "Kerviel: Bosses Never Said a Thing," *New York Times*, November 17, http://dealbook.nytimes.com/2010/11/17/kerviels-comeback-they-never-said-a-thing/?_r=0. Additional details about the psychological features of the Kerviel case can be found in my book *Ending the Management Illusion*.
24. See Norma Onishia (2015), "Empty Ebola Clinics in Liberia Are Seen as Misstep in U.S. Relief Effort," *New York Times*, April 11, http://www.nytimes.com/2015/04/12/world/africa/idle-ebola-clinics-in-liberia-are-seen-as-misstep-in-us-relief-effort.html?_r=0. This article documents the US response to helping Liberia deal with its Ebola outbreak in 2014 by using US troops to construct treatment centers. The response began in mid-September, but by the time the centers were complete, the measures Liberian residents took on their own had been quite effective, with the result that the beds in these centers ended up largely being empty.

7   MINSKY, THE FINANCIAL INSTABILITY HYPOTHESIS, AND RISK MANAGEMENT

1. See Hyman Minsky (1986), reprinted in 2008. *Stabilizing an Unstable Economy* (New York: McGraw-Hill). The original publication date for this book occurred as a financial crisis was developing in the savings and loan

(S&L) industry, which evolved according to the dynamic which Minsky articulated. See Chapter 8.

2. PIMCO economist Paul McCulley coined the phrase "Minsky moment" in reference to the Asian debt crisis of 1997. The term appears in a *Wall Street Journal* quote on the cover of Minsky's 1986 book, which was reprinted after the financial crisis erupted.

3. This chapter draws from my previous writings. See Hersh Shefrin and Meir Statman (2012), "Behavioral Finance in the Financial Crisis: Market Efficiency, Minsky, and Keynes," in *Rethinking the Financial Crisis*, ed. Alan Blinder, Andrew Lo, and Robert Solow (New York: Sage Foundation/Century Foundation), 99–135. Also see Hersh Shefrin (forthcoming), "Assessing Hyman Minsky's Insights," in *The Global Financial Crisis: Economics, Psychology, and Values*, ed. A. G. Malliaris, L. Shaw, and H. Shefrin (New York: Oxford University Press).

4. For information about the financial crisis, I draw on several sources. See *Financial Crisis Inquiry Report*, 2011. Washington, DC: US Government Printing Office, available at http://fcic.law.stanford.edu/ and Martin Wolf (2014), *The Shifts and the Shocks* (London: Penguin Press HC).

5. See John Coates (2012), *The Hour between Dog and Wolf: How Risk Taking Transforms Us, Body, and Mind* (New York: Penguin).

6. Social psychologists Amy Cuddy, Caroline Wilmuth, and Dana Carney emphasize that, relatively speaking, leaders are higher in testosterone and lower in cortisol. As a result, leaders tend to be aggressive about moving forward, but cool under pressure. They also find that it is possible to manipulate levels of testosterone and cortisol for short periods through the use of power postures. High power postures elevate testosterone and cortisol, while low power postures reduce them. They report that willingness to take risk is significantly greater after adopting a high power pose. See Amy J. C. Cuddy, Caroline A. Wilmuth, and Dana R. Carney (2012), "The Benefit of Power Posing Before a High-Stakes Social Evaluation," Harvard Business School Working Paper, No. 13–027, September. See also Cuddy's TED talk at http://www.ted.com/talks/amy_cuddy_your_body_language_shapes_who_you_are.

7. See Susan Greenfield (2015), *Mind Change: How Digital Technologies Are Leaving Their Mark on Our Brains* (New York: Random House).

8. Paul McCulley (2009), "The Shadow Banking System and Hyman Minsky's Economic Journey," in *Insights into the Global Financial Crisis*, ed. Laurence B. Siegel. (Charlottesville: Research Foundation of CFA Institute), 224–256.

9. Scott Lanman and Steve Matthews (2013), "Greenspan Concedes to 'Flaw' in His Market Ideology," *Bloomberg*, October 23, http://www.bloomberg.com/apps/news?pid=newsarchive&sid=ah5qh9Up4rIg.

10. See Alan Blinder (2013). *After the Music Stopped: The Financial Crisis, the Response, and the Work Ahead*. (New York: Penguin). The discussion about "Mr. Bailout" appears on p. 123. In his book and in later writings, Blinder is unequivocal in his view that Minsky was right. See Alan Blinder (2015), "Can Economists Learn? The Right Lessons From the Financial Crisis," *Foreign Affairs* March-April. https://www.foreignaffairs.com/reviews/review

-essay/2015-02-16/can-economists-learn. Additional insight into the faulty decision to allow Lehman to fail can be found in James Stewart and Peter Eavis (2014), "Revisiting the Lehman Brothers Bailout That Never Was," *New York Times*, September 29. http://www.nytimes.com/2014/09/30 /business/revisiting-the-lehman-brothers-bailout-that-never-was.html? hp&action=click&pgtype=Homepage&version=HpSumSmallMediaHigh &module=second-column-region&region=top-news&WT.nav=top -news&_r=0. As this book goes to press, Bernanke published a new book in which he articulates his position for why Lehman's low net worth made the firm impossible to rescue at taxpayer expense. In this regard, Lehman's creditors subsequently lost $200 billion. He also points out that Paulson's comments were not germane to the decision, as it was the Fed that would have provided the funds needed for a rescue. I would ask whether rescuing Lehman might have avoided the tipping point of the financial crisis, thereby avoiding the need to rescue AIG and some of the other financial institutions and the subsequent reductions in employment and output. If so, then $200 billion to rescue Lehman might have been well spent. See Ben Bernanke (2015). *The Courage to Act: A Memoir of a Crisis and Its Aftermath*. New York, New York: W. W. Norton & Company. Also see Andrew Ross Sorkin (2015), "In Ben Bernanke's Memoir, a Candid Look at Lehman Brothers' Collapse," *New York Times*, October 5, http://www.nytimes.com/2015/10/06/business /dealbook/in-ben-bernankes-memoir-a-candid-look-at-lehman-brothers -collapse.html?_r=0. Sorkin discusses why deliberately vague communication by Bernanke and Paulson in the wake of the Lehman failure created confusion about whether or not they had intentionally let Lehman fail. Bernanke contends not.

11. See Paul Krugman (2010), "How Did We Know the Stimulus Was Too Small?" *New York Times*, July 28, http://krugman.blogs.nytimes.com/2010/07/28 /how-did-we-know-the-stimulus-was-too-small/?_r=0.
12. See Paul Krugman (2014), "Secular Stagnation, Coalmines, Bubbles, and Larry Summers," *New York Times*, November 16, http://krugman.blogs .nytimes.com/2013/11/16/secular-stagnation-coalmines-bubbles-and-larry -summers/. Also see Philip Pilkington (2014), "Paul Krugman Does Not Understand the Liquidity Trap," nakedcapitalism.com, http://www.naked capitalism.com/2014/07/philip-pilkington-paul-krugman-understand -liquidity-trap.html.
13. See Charles Riley (2012), "Sandy Weill: Break Up the Big Banks," CNNMoney, July 25. http://money.cnn.com/2012/07/25/news/economy /sandy-weill-banks/index.htm?hpt=hp_t3.
14. See Julie L. Stackhouse (2013), "Central View: On the 'Too Big To Fail' Debate: Implications of the Dodd-Frank Act," *St. Louis Fed*, https://www .stlouisfed.org/publications/central-banker/summer-2013/on-the-too-big-to -fail-debate-implications-of-the-doddfrank-act. Stackhouse mentions that both Dodd-Frank and Basel III have provisions to curtail bailouts.
15. See Lydia Wheeler (2015), "GOP Bill Would Abolish Dodd-Frank 'Too Big to Fail' Provision," *thehill.com*, July 21, http://thehill.com/regulation

/finance/248666-gop-bill-would-abolish-dodd-frank-too-big-to-fail-provision. The proposed legislation seeks to eliminate Title II of Dodd-Frank, which provides for orderly liquidation, and replace it with a bankruptcy provision.

16. See Leslie Scism (2015), "Former AIG Chief Hank Greenberg Wins Moral Victory in Bailout Trial," *Wall Street Journal*, June 15, http://www.wsj.com/articles/judge-rules-in-former-aig-chief-greenbergs-favor-in-bailout-trial-1434384756.

17. Ben S. Bernanke, Ben (2012), "Some Reflections on the Crisis and the Policy Response," at the Russell Sage Foundation and The Century Foundation Conference on "Rethinking Finance," New York, April 13, federalreserve.gov, http://www.federalreserve.gov/newsevents/speech/bernanke20120413a.htm.

18. In 2014, the president of the New York Fed, William Dudley, publicly stated that problematic behavior on Wall Street continued to occur. Based on survey data, a study conducted at the University of Notre Dame reached the same conclusion. See Andrew Ross Sorkin (2015), "Many on Wall Street Say It Remains Untamed," *New York Times*, May 18, http://www.nytimes.com/2015/05/19/business/dealbook/many-on-wall-street-say-it-remains-untamed.html?ref=dealbook&_r=0.

19. L. Randall Wray (2012), "Global Financial Crisis: A Minskyan Interpretation of the Causes, the Fed's Bailout, and the Future," Working paper number 711, Levy Economics Institute of Bard College.

20. Janet Yellen (2009) "A Minsky Meltdown: Lessons for Central Bankers," *FRBSF Economic Letter*, May.

8 Aspirational Pitfalls at UBS and Merrill Lynch

1. This chapter draws from my previous writings. See Hersh Shefrin (2009a), "Ending the Management Illusion: Preventing Another Financial Crisis," *Ivey Business Journal*, January/February, http://www.iveybusinessjournal.com/article.asp?intArticle_ID=805. See also Hersh Shefrin (2009b), "How Psychological Pitfalls Generated the Global Financial Crisis," in *Insights into the Global Financial Crisis*, ed. Laurence B. Siegel (Charlottesville: Research Foundation of CFA), Institute, 2009. http://papers.ssrn.com/sol3/papers.cfm?abstract_id=1523931.

2. UBS (2007), "Shareholder Report on UBS Writedowns," ubs.com, www.ubs.com/1/ShowMedia/investors/agm?contentId=140333&name=080418ShareholderReport.pdf, accessed on July 16, 2008.

3. To be fair, the evidence is mixed. The President's Working Group on Financial Markets (2008) concluded, "The turmoil in financial markets was triggered by a dramatic weakening of underwriting standards for U.S. subprime mortgages, beginning in late 2004, and extending into early 2007." In contrast, studies by Bhardwaj and Sengupta (2008a, 2008b) from the Federal Reserve Bank of St. Louis suggest that subprime mortgage quality did not deteriorate after 2004 because FICO scores improved at the same

time that the other indicators of credit quality worsened. The authors also pointed out that adjustable-rate subprime mortgages are designed as bridge loans, with the view that they be prepaid when interest rates reset as homeowners refinance. They attributed the subprime meltdown to the decline in housing prices that began at the end of 2006 rather than to a lowering of lending standards. See *President's Working Group on Financial Markets* 2008, ustreas.gov, March, www.ustreas.gov/press/releases/reports/pwgpolicystatemktturmoil_03122008.pdf, and Geetesh Bhardwajand and Rajdeep Sengupta (2008a), "Where's the Smoking Gun? A Study of Underwriting Standards for US Subprime Mortgages," Federal Reserve Bank of St. Louis, Working Paper 2008–036B.
4. Ponzi finance is defined in Chapter 7.
5. Bethany McLean and Joe Nocera (2010), *All the Devils Are Here: The Hidden History of the Financial Crisis* (New York: Penguin).
6. Dow Jones News Service (2004), "Lehman Brothers Reports Record 1Q Earnings Of $670M," March 16; Dow Jones Business News (2004), "Merrill Lynch's Earnings Rose 10%; Revenue Nearly Flat," July 13.
7. See Gretchen Morgenson (2008), "The Reckoning: How the Thundering Herd Faltered and Fell," *New York Times*, November 9. Also see the transcript of Gretchen Morgenson's interview on NPR: *Fresh Air* (2008), "Merrill Lynch and the Mortgage Crisis," November 13, and Floyd Norris (2008), "Another Crisis, Another Guarantee," November 25.
8. According to McLean and Nocera, *All the Devils Are Here*.
9. According to McLean and Nocera, *All the Devils Are Here*.
10. According to McLean and Nocera, *All the Devils Are Here*.
11. According to the FCIC, former employees expressed this view in a complaint filed against Merrill Lynch.
12. See McClean and Nocera, *All the Devils Are Here*, p. 67.
13. See McClean and Nocera, *All the Devils Are Here*, p. 203.
14. See McClean and Nocera, *All the Devils Are Here*, p. 237.
15. See citation above.
16. See McLean and Nocera, *All the Devils Are Here*.
17. See McClean and Nocera, *All the Devils Are Here*, p. 237.
18. G. Akerlof, P. Romer, R. Hall, and N. G. Mankiw (1993) "Looting: The Economic Underworld of Bankruptcy for Profit," *Brookings Papers on Economic Activity*, No. 2: 1–73.
19. Willian Black (2005), "Control Fraud as an Explanation for White-collar Crime Waves: The Case of the Savings & Loan Debacle," *Crime, Law and Social Change* 43; 1–29. See also William Black (2005), *The Best Way to Rob a Bank Is to Own One: How Corporate Executives and Politicians Looted the S&L Industry* (Austin: University of Texas Press).
20. See McClean and Nocera, *All the Devils Are Here*, pp. 318–319.
21. See Marian Wang (2011), "Why No Financial Crisis Prosecutions? Ex-Justice Official Says It's Just too Hard," *ProPublica*, December 6. http://www.propublica.org/article/why-no-financial-crisis-prosecutions-official-says-its-just-too-hard.

9 CHEATING ISSUES AT S&P AND MOODY'S

1. This chapter draws from my previous writings. See Hersh Shefrin (2009), "How Psychological Pitfalls Generated the Global Financial Crisis," in *Insights into the Global Financial Crisis*, ed. Laurence B. Siegel (Charlottesville: Research Foundation of CFA Institute, 2010, 224, 256.
2. Ponzi finance is defined in Chapter 7.
3. See Lawrence J. White (2013), "Credit Rating Agencies: An Overview," in *Annual Review of Financial Economics*, Stern School of Business, New York University. White provides the context to understand the institutional structure within which rating firms operate.
4. *United States of America v. McGraw-Hill Companies, Inc. and Standard and Poor's Financial Services, LLC.*
5. See John Carney (2013), "A Flaw in the Heart of the Justice Department's Case against Standard & Poor's," CNBC.com, February 5. http://www.cnbc.com/id/100436608. The attorney representing S&P was Floyd Abrams, from the law firm Cahill Gordon & Reindel, who was interviewed by CNBC correspondent David Faber. Faber reports that Abrams indicated to him that the Justice Department would have to prove that S&P analysts knew one thing but said another. During the portion of the interview that was aired, Abrams pointed out that the investigation into S&P intensified after S&P downgraded US government debt in the summer of 2011, which suggests that the suit was retaliatory in nature.
6. Aruna Viswanatha and Luciana Lopez (2013), "Justice Department, States Weigh Action Against Moody's," Reuters, February 7, http://www.reuters.com/article/2013/02/08/us-moodys-investigation-idUSBRE91618520130208.
7. Elliot Blair Smith (2008), "'Race to Bottom' at Moody's, S&P Secured Subprime's Boom, Bust," Bloomberg, September 28, http://www.bloomberg.com/apps/news?pid=newsarchive&sid=ax3vfya_Vtdo.
8. Quoted by Smith, "'Race to Bottom.'"
9. Aaron Lucchetti (2008a), "McGraw Scion Grapples with S&P's Woes—Chairman Helped Set Tone in Profit Push as Ratings Firms Feasted on New Products," *Wall Street Journal* (2 August 2), B1. Aaron Lucchetti (2008b), "S&P Email: 'We Should Not Be Rating It'," *Wall Street Journal*, August 2, B1.
10. See FCIC report, p. 121.
11. See FCIC report, p. 121.
12. See FCIC report, p. 121.
13. See FCIC report, p. 210.
14. Chen-Bo Zhong, Vanessa K. Bohns, and Francesca Gino (2010), "Good Lamps Are the Best Police: Darkness Increases Dishonesty and Self-Interested Behavior," *Psychological Science* 21 (3): 311–4.
15. Francesca Gino, Maurice E. Schweitzer, Nicole L. Mead, and Dan Ariely (2011), "Unable to Resist Temptation: How Self-control Depletion Promotes Unethical Behavior," *Organizational Behavior and Human Decision Processes* 115 (2): 191–203.

16. Walter Mischel (2014), *The Marshmallow Test: Mastering Self-Control* (New York: Little, Brown and Company).
17. Todd Hare, Colin Camerer, and Antonio Rangel (2009), "Self-Control in Decision-Making Involves Modulation of the vmPFC Valuation System," *Science 12*, 324 (5927): 646–648.
18. Stefano Pagliaro, Naomi Ellemers, and Manuela Barreto (2011), "Sharing Moral Values: Anticipated Ingroup Respect as a Determinant of Adherence to Morality-based (But Not Competence-based) Group Norms," *Personality and Social Psychology Bulletin* 37: 1117–1129.
19. Francesca Gino, Shahar Ayal, and Dan Ariely (2009), "Contagion and Differentiation in Unethical Behavior," *Psychological Science* 20 (3): 393–398.
20. Marko Pitesa and Stefan Thau (2013), "Masters of the Universe: How Power and Accountability Influence Self-serving Decisions under Moral Hazard," *Journal of Applied Psychology* 98(3): 550–558.
21. Francesca Gino and Lamar Pierce (2009), "The Abundance Effect: Unethical Behavior in the Presence of Wealth," *Organizational Behavior and Human Decision Processes* 109 (2): 142–155.
22. J. Jordan, E. Mullen, and J. K. Murnighan (2011), "Striving for the Moral Self: The Effects of Recalling Past Moral Actions on Future Moral Behavior," *Personality and Social Psychology Bulletin* 37: 701–713.
23. Sally Simpson, M. Lyn Exum, and N. Craig Smith (2000), "The Social Control of Corporate Criminals," in *Of Crime and Criminality: The Use of Theory in Everyday Life*, ed. Sally Simpson (New York: Sage), 141–158.
24. Biography of Louis D. Brandeis, Brandeis University, http://www.brandeis.edu/legacyfund/bio.html.

10 GROUPTHINK AT FANNIE, FREDDIE, AND AIG

1. Most of the information presented in this chapter is taken from the FCIC report. Endnotes indicate when other sources are used.
2. Ginnie Mae is a mnemonic for GNMA, the acronym for Government National Mortgage Association. Ginnie Mae was a wholly owned government corporation that provided special assistance and managed government loan portfolios. When Fannie Mae became a GSE in 1968, Ginnie Mae remained part of the Department of Housing and Urban Development (HUD). With Fannie Mae and Freddie Mac entering the conventional mortgage market in 1970, Ginnie Mae assumed their role as the leading secondary market organization that provided liquidity for federally insured FHA and VA mortgages. Ginnie Mae's role was to guarantee MBS backed by pools of federally insured mortgages. It neither participated in the market for conventional mortgages nor held a portfolio.
3. FCIC (2010), Preliminary Staff Report. "Government Sponsored Enterprises and the Financial Crisis," April 10.
4. FCIC report, p. 178.
5. FCIC report, p. 178.

6. FCIC report, p. 178.
7. FCIC report, p. 182.
8. In the next two sections, I draw in part from "The Rise and Fall of AIG's Financial Products Unit," March 20, 2009, talkingpointsmemo.com, http://talkingpointsmemo.com/muckraker/the-rise-and-fall-of-aig-s-financial-products-unit.
9. FCIC Report, p. 200.
10. Michael Lewis (2009), "The Man Who Crashed the World," *Vanity Fair*, June 30, http://www.vanityfair.com/online/daily/2009/06/the-man-who-crashed-the-world.
11. See Lewis, "The Man Who Crashed the World."
12. See "The Rise and Fall of AIG's Financial Products Unit."
13. David Stout and Brian Knowlton (2009), "Fed Chief Says Insurance Giant Acted Irresponsibly," *New York Times*, March 3, http://www.nytimes.com/2009/03/04/business/economy/04webecon.html?pagewanted=all&_r=0.
14. Indeed, the FCIC tells us that in the lead up to the financial crisis, there was an internal debate within Lehman Brothers about excessive risk appetite. On one side of the debate were the head of fixed income, Michael Gelband, and the firm's chief risk officer Madelyn Antoncic. Both warned Lehman's senior management against the firm taking on excessive risk in order to compete aggressively against other investment banks. As a result of the conflict, Antoncic was reassigned within the firm, and Gelband left due to what the bank called "philosophical differences." See FCIC report, pp. 18–19.

11 THE WINNER'S CURSE STRIKES AT RBS, FORTIS, AND ABN AMRO

1. See "New RBS Chairman Calls for End to 'Public Flogging' of Its Bankers" (2009), *Guardian*, April 3.
2. See Financial Services Authority Board (2011), *The Failure of the Royal Bank of Scotland: Financial Services Authority Board Report*. This report provides most of the information about the chronology of the acquisition of ABN AMRO by the consortium, including the data depicted in the tables. Additional information is taken from Jeroen Smit (2010), *The Perfect Prey: The Fall of Abn Amro, Or What Went Wrong in the Banking Industry* (London: Quercus).
3. Phillip Inman (2007), "Losing Out on ABN Amro Could Prove a Winner for Barclays," *Guardian*, October 3, http://www.theguardian.com/business/2007/oct/04/3.
4. See Gwen Robinson (2009), "RBS Admits ABN Buy 'a Mistake'," *Financial Times*. February 11, http://ftalphaville.ft.com/tag/abn-amro/.
5. Richard Lambert (2011), "Unchecked Excess: The Lessons of RBS Failure" *Financial Times*, December 12, http://www.ft.com/intl/cms/s/0/c91ca412-24b6-11e1-ac4b-00144feabdc0.html#axzz3LdsXo1lw.

6. See John Coates (2012), *The Hour between Dog and Wolf: How Risk Taking Transforms Us, Body, and Mind* (New York: Penguin).
7. In a press interview, Groenink mentioned that the bank would consider offers. Negative news continued to flow. That August, shares of ABN AMRO declined by 20%. Analyst recommendations were moving from hold to sell. The share price drop made ABN AMRO appear more appealing as an acquisition, and ING's chair, Michel Tilmant, began considering it as a target. In October, RBS and ABN AMRO set January 2007 as a time to begin a dialogue. In November, Barclays's governors decided that ABN AMRO would be an attractive acquisition.

    Of its possible suitors, ING was particularly interesting. Tilmant managed to convince the head of ING's Supervisory board that ING should bid for ABN AMRO. Notably, ING is a Dutch bank, and a merger would require the approval of the DNB. Tilmant applied for and received the green light from DNB president Nout Wellink, who saw the combination as producing a top five bank in Europe that was Dutch. Tilmant and Groenink met to explore a bid from ING. However, Groenink indicated that he was in no hurry, as he wanted to explore other possibilities.
8. A second measure was to prohibit future acquisition activity. Of course, this measure would rule out merging with ING.
9. TCI's letter created a thorny problem for DNB, which had already approved and welcomed ING acquiring ABN AMRO. As it happened, the Dutch prime minister was not anxious to be active in saving a breakup of ABN AMRO, having lectured the government of Italy about the importance of free markets when ABN AMRO was pursuing Antonveneta
10. The announcement also led to lower prices for shares of ING. Nevertheless, ING lost interest in the acquisition and withdrew.
11. See Chad Bray (2015), "Britain Expects Initial Losses as It Prepares to Sell Its R.B.S. Stake," *New York Times*, June 10. http://www.nytimes.com /2015/06/11/business/dealbook/britain-expects-initial-losses-as-it-prepares -to-sell-royal-bank-of-scotland-holdings.html?ref=dealbook.

12 Behavioral Dimension of Systemic Risk

1. See page 334 of *Financial Crisis Inquiry Report*, 2011. Washington, DC: US Government Printing Office, available at http://fcic.law.stanford.edu/.
2. See FCIC report, page xviii.
3. http://vlab.stern.nyu.edu/.
4. There are several ways to measure the systemic risk of an individual firm. Some of the most prominent are: Delta Conditional Value-at-Risk, Multi-Conditional-VaR, Component Expected Shortfall (CES), Marginal Expected Shortfall (MES), and the Systemic RISK measure (SRISK). Notably, different measures can give rise to different systemic risk rankings of financial institutions. A good resource for following updates about different perspectives on systemic risk is the Systemic Risk Hub found at the website of the *Global*

Risk Institute, http://globalriskinstitute.org/. The Global Risk Institute (GRI) was founded by the public and private sectors in Canada. The GRI website describes the Systemic Risk Hub as an independent and collaborative initiative that is sponsored by the Global Risk Institute in Financial Services, and supported by various partners such as the Louis Bachelier Institute and ABN AMRO Advisors.
5. V. Acharya, L. Pedersen, T. Philippon, and M. Richardson (2010), "Measuring Systemic Risk," Technical Report, Department of Finance, New York University.
6. C. Brownlees and R. Engle (2010), "Volatility, Correlation and Tails for Systemic Risk Management," Working paper, New York University.
7. Eight percent is the default for the Americas, and can be changed at the V-Lab website. The default for Europe is 5%.
8. Much of the material in this chapter is drawn from Giovanni Barone-Adesi, Loriano Mancini, and Hersh Shefrin (2013), "Systemic Risk and Sentiment," in *Handbook on Systemic Risk*, ed. Jean-Pierre Fouque and Joe Langsam (Cambridge: Cambridge University Press), 714–741.
9. The data are from OptionMetrics.
10. Malcolm Baker and Jeffrey Wurgler (2006), "Investor Sentiment and the Cross-section of Stock Returns," *Journal of Finance* 61: 1645–1680; Malcolm Baker and Jeffrey Wurgler (2007), "Investor Sentiment in the Stock Market," *Journal of Economic Perspectives* 21: 129–151.
11. See Baker and Wurgler, "Investor Sentiment in the Stock Market," 132.
12. J. Campbell and R. Shiller (1998), "Valuation Ratios and the Long Run Market Outlook," *Journal of Portfolio Management* 24: 11–26.
13. Updated data is available at http://www.econ.yale.edu/~shiller/data.htm.
14. The survey question that is used to elicit the index reads as follows: "What do you think is the probability of a catastrophic stock market crash in the U. S., like that of October 28, 1929, or October 19, 1987, in the next six months, including the case that a crash occurred in the other countries and spreads to the U. S.? (An answer of 0% means that it cannot happen, an answer of 100% means it is sure to happen.)."
15. Leverage data prior to 2007 is not displayed. However, interested readers can find these data on the V-Lab website.
16. Speech 2005–107, OCC, given by John Dugan. In his speech, Dugan also said, "Thus, it should come as no surprise that, of the least creditworthy holders of payment-option ARMs, nearly 50 percent have current balances above their original loan amount.... Some have suggested that payment option ARMs are inherently unsafe and unsound, and that regulators should banish them from reputable banking practice. I would characterize them differently, in this way: They have a legitimate use in the right hands, but they need to be handled with extreme care."
17. During 2006, after housing prices peaked, MES for both Bear Stearns and Lehman did actually rise above previous historical levels, but in 2007 reverted to the historical range that prevailed during the period 2000–2005, ending 2007 in this range.

18. Citigroup was number 6, and JPMorgan Chase was number 8.
19. See FCIC report, pp. 477–478.
20. The correlation coefficients are respectively 0.88, 0.69, and 0.73.
21. Indeed, with the exception of Citibank, the seven firms topping this list are no longer in existence as independent firms. As for Fannie Mae and Freddie Mac, in 2015, they were still in conservatorship.
22. Wachovia's MES in August was actually 70, which is not shown in Figure 12.10, as it dwarfs the other values.
23. Correlations of MES with overconfidence were much lower than for optimism, and also varied in sign. Correlations of leverage with optimism tended to be large and negative, in the range of 70% and below. Goldman Sachs was an exception, at -35%. However, the correlations of leverage with overconfidence were closer to zero, and mixed in sign.

13   FINANCIAL REGULATION AND PSYCHOLOGY

1. See William Black (2005), *The Best Way to Rob a Bank is to Own One: How Corporate Executives and Politicians Looted the S&L Industry* (Austin: University of Texas at Austin Press).
2. Jake Bernstein (2014), "Inside the New York Fed: Secret Recordings and a Culture Clash," *ProPublica*, September 26, http://www.propublica.org/article/carmen-segarras-secret-recordings-from-inside-new-york-fed.
3. Michiyo Nakamoto and David Wighton (2007), "Citigroup Chief Stays Bullish on Buy-Outs," *Financial Times*, July 9, http://www.ft.com/intl/cms/s/0/80e2987a-2e50-11dc-821c-0000779fd2ac.html#axzz3PbLcPFql.
4. Mattieu Bouvard and Samuel Lee (2014), "Risk Management Failures." Working paper, McGill University, New York University.
5. The logic is similar for earnings per share, which is defined as $EPS = [(EBIT - iD)(1-t)]/n$, where n denotes the number of shares. The formula for EPS is linear in $EBIT$ with a slope of $(1-t)/n$ and an intercept of $-iD(1-t)/n$.
6. Ricardo Rebonato (2008), "Robust Risk Management Tools: Insights from Interest Rates," Royal Bank of Scotland.
7. The data underlying this figure is from Moody's and was analyzed by the Bank of England in David Aikman, Mirta Galesic, Gerd Gigerenzer, Sujit Kapadia, Konstantinos Katsikopoulos, Amit Kothiyal, Emma Murphy, and Tobias Neumann (2014), "Taking Uncertainty Seriously: Simplicity Versus Complexity in Financial Regulation," Financial Stability Paper No. 28, May.
8. The liquidity coverage ratio requires a financial firm to hold sufficient high-quality liquid assets to cover its total net cash flows over 30 days. The net stable funding ratio requires the available amount of stable funding to exceed the required amount of stable funding over a one-year period of extended stress.
9. The stressed VaR measure is designed to force financial firms to consider the impact of a period of stress on their trading books.
10. Mark Pengelly (2010), "Challenging Change: Banks Struggle with Basel 2.5," *Risk Magazine*, September 3.

11. Anat Admati and Martin Hellwig (2013), *The Bankers' New Clothes: What's Wrong with Banking and What to Do about It* (Princeton: Princeton University Press).
12. In the United States, Dodd-Frank sought to limit wealth transfers from taxpayers to the shareholders of financial institutions with provisions such as the so-called "push-out" rule. This rule required that the largest banks conduct a portion of their riskiest derivatives' transactions in subsidiaries lying outside federally insured institutions. However, in December 2014 during a lame duck session of Congress, the push-out rule was repealed. See Teresa Tritch (2014), "No Surprise: Wall Street Got Its Way in Spending Bill," *New York Times*, December 12, http://takingnote.blogs.nytimes.com/2014/12/12/no-surprise-wall-street-got-its-way-in-spending-bill/?hp&action=click&pgtype=Homepage&module=c-column-top-span-region&region=c-column-top-span-region&WT.nav=c-column-top-span-region.
13. Ranjit Lall (2009), "Why Basel II Failed and Why Any Basel III Is Doomed to Fail," Global Economic Governance (GEG) Working Paper 2009/52, University College, Oxford.
14. Andrew Haldane and Vasileios Madouros (2012), "The Dog and the Frisbee," Paper presented at Federal Reserve Bank of Kansas City's 36th economic policy symposium, "The Changing Policy Landscape", Jackson Hole, WY, August 31.
15. Robyn Dawes (1979), "The Robust Beauty of Improper Linear Models in Decision Making," *American Psychologist* 34 (7): 571–582.
16. See Jonathan Bendor (2010), *Bounded Rationality and Politics* (Berkeley: University of California Press) for a good discussion of the application of heuristics in organizations.
17. See Aikman et al., "Taking Uncertainty Seriously."
18. For sake of comparison, the NYU V-Lab assessment for year-end 2006 lists UBS as the seventh ranked European bank by systemic risk, with an MES of 2.48. Wachovia's V-Lab rank in the U.S. was 83, and its MES was 3.00. Neither the heuristic under discussion nor the V-Lab metrics incorporate sentiment or exposure to Ponzi finance.
19. The cues are the balance sheet leverage ratio, the market based capital ratio, the wholesale funding level, the loan to deposit ratio, total asset growth, the balance sheet risk-based capital ratio, the market-based leverage ratio, the wholesale funding ratio, the core funding ratio, the net stable funding ratio, the and liquid asset ratio.
20. See *Independent* (2013), "Andy Haldane: The Coming Man of British Banking," December 10. http://www.independent.co.uk/news/people/profiles/andy-haldane-the-coming-man-of-british-banking-8975109.html.
21. See the discussion in Chapter 7 about limiting the ability of governments to rescue financial firms. In a rational world, doing so reduces the propensity for excessive leverage and risk related to moral hazard. However, in the past, bailouts have prevented financial crises from accelerating into collapses of the financial system.

14 RISK OF FRAUD, MADOFF, AND THE SEC

1. In this respect, Basel II classifies fraud events by category. Internal fraud pertains to events that involve complicity within the financial institution itself, while external fraud pertains to events that do not involve complicity.
2. The loss in principal from the Ponzi scheme appears to be in the range $17.5 to $20 billion. See "A Message from SIPA Trustee Irving H. Picard," madofftrustee.com, http://www.madofftrustee.com/trustee-message-02.html.
3. See http://www.madofftrustee.com/.
4. This chapter draws from my previous writings. See Hersh Shefrin (2009), "How Psychological Pitfalls Generated the Global Financial Crisis," in *Insights into the Global Financial Crisis*, ed. Laurence B. Siegel (Charlottesville: Research Foundation of CFA Institute), 224–256.
5. "Wife, Son Give Texture to 'the Way Madoff Kept Them in the Dark'," (2011), PBS, October 31, http://www.pbs.org/newshour/bb/business/july-dec11/madoff_10-31.html.
6. Sital Pateo (2013), "My Interview with Madoff: Prison? This Is as Good as It Gets.' His Whistleblower? 'Idiot.' Fed Stimulus? 'Greatest Manipulation' He's Ever Seen," *Wall Street Journal*, December 8.
7. Erin Arvedlund (2001), "Don't Ask, Don't Tell: Bernie Madoff Attracts Skeptics in 2001: Bernie Madoff Is So Secretive, He Even Asks Investors to Keep Mum," *Barron's*, May 7. http://online.barrons.com/articles/SB989019667829349012.
8. See Harry Markopolous (2009), Letter to the SEC 2005, against Madoff, January 7, made available by A.B. Dada, Filed under Featured, Money, http://www.unanimocracy.com/featured/harry-markopolous-markopolos-letter-to-the-sec-2005-against-madoff/. Markopolos writes that the put options Markopolos used would have involved trading costs of at least 8%, and that the revenue he might have earned from stock dividends and call option premiums would have been at most 4%.
9. Thomas Catan and Cassell Bryan-Low (2008), "The Madoff Fraud Case: European Clients Were Cultivated within Social Networks by Word of Mouth," *Wall Street Journal*, December 16, A19.
10. Michael Ocrant (2001), "Madoff Tops Charts; Skeptics Ask How," *MARHedge* (RIP), No. 89, May.
11. Robert Frank, Peter Lattman, Dionne Searcey, and Aaron Lucchetti (2008), "Fund Fraud Hits Big Names—Madoff's Clients Included Mets Owner, GMAC Chairman, Country-Club Recruits," *Wall Street Journal*, December 13.
12. Nevertheless, the statement is still a stretch. This is because there are commission costs associated with trading the puts and calls, and premiums as well, the net value of which is dependent on the structure of the collar. Moreover, Madoff's strategy involved selecting about 35 stocks, not the entire index. Consistently outperforming the S&P 500 over a long period of time requires stock-picking skill, as reducing systematic risk through the use of a collar serves to reduce expected return.

13. Carole Bernard and Phelim Boyle (2009), "Mr. Madoff's Amazing Returns: An Analysis of the Split-Strike Conversion Strategy," *The Journal of Derivatives*, 17(1): 62–76.
14. See Ocrant, "Madoff Tops Charts." Ocrant wrote for *MARHedge*, which was a semimonthly financial newsletter that covered the hedge fund industry. Euromoney Institutional Investor's acquired *MARHedge*, and publication ceased in November 2006.
15. "The Madoff Affair" (2009), *Frontline*, PBS, May 12, http://www.pbs.org/wgbh/pages/frontline/madoff/.
16. Madoff's responses appear in the *MARHedge* article.
17. Pateo, "My Interview with Madoff."
18. US Securities and Exchange Commission Office of Investigations (2009), "Investigation of Failure of the SEC to Uncover Bernard Madoff's Ponzi Scheme," August 31, Report No. OIG-509.
19. OIG report, p. 228.
20. OIG report, p. 167.
21. OIG report, p. 256.
22. OIG report, p. 261.
23. Pateo, "My Interview with Madoff."
24. The Office of Compliance Inspections and Examinations.
25. OIG report, p. 223. As noted below, OCIE is the SEC's Office of Compliance Inspections and Examinations in Washington, DC.
26. OIG report, pp. 363–364.
27. OIG report, p. 257.
28. OIG report, p. 387.
29. The OIG report states, "In addition, while the Enforcement investigators acknowledged becoming aware of Madoff's stature during the investigation, they denied that his prominence impacted the investigation, except to the extent that they were less likely to believe that Bernie Madoff had engaged in a Ponzi scheme," p. 388.

15 Risk, Return, and Individual Stocks

1. This chapter draws from my previous writings. See Hersh Shefrin (2015), "Investors' Judgments, Asset Pricing Factors, and Sentiment," *European Financial Management*, 21 (2), 205–227.
2. Michael Solt and Meir Statman (1989), "Good Companies, Bad Stocks," *Journal of Portfolio Management* 15 (4): 39–44. The representativeness heuristic applies here because good stocks are viewed as being representative, or fitting the stereotype, of stocks of good companies.
3. Malcolm Baker and Jeffrey Wurgler (2006), "Investor Sentiment and the Cross-section of Stock Returns," *Journal of Finance* 61: 1645–1680. Malcolm Baker and Jeffrey Wurgler (2007), "Investor Sentiment in the Stock Market," *Journal of Economic Perspectives* 21: 129–151.
4. See Baker and Wurgler, "Investor Sentiment in the Stock Market," p. 132.
5. ($t = 2.7$, $p = 0.017$).

6. (t = −0.36, p = 0.72).
7. Figure 15.4a,b. Time series of Baker-Wurgler sentiment and mean expected stock return from workshop data, 1999–2010. This figure displays the comovement of the Baker-Wurgler sentiment index BW and the mean expected return from workshop participants for the period 1999 through 2010. For some years, more than one workshop took place, in which case the workshops are broken out separately and the year designation followed by a number for the workshop. For example, 2004.1 denotes the first workshop conducted in 2004, and 2004.2 denotes the second workshop conducted in 2004. Figure 15.4a displays the evolution of the two time series. Mean expected return for a given workshop date is computed by first forming the expected return for each stock as the mean of the expected returns of the workshop participants, and then forming the unweighted average across stocks, as for an equally weighted portfolio.
8. I lack the data to test for the U-shaped patterns, and inverse U-shaped patterns identified by Baker and Wurgler (2006). I also note that Baker and Wurgler find evidence of a negative relationship between total risk and realized returns in periods following positive sentiment, with the relationship being positive after negative sentiment. I find no significant correlation between BW and the mean correlation between judgments of risk and expected return. Likewise, Baker and Wurgler find that the relationship between realized returns and ROE is generally positive following periods of positive sentiment and negative following periods of negative sentiment. I do not find such an effect for perceived risk and ROE, but instead find a negative relationship regardless of whether sentiment has recently been positive or negative.
9. Consider a possible momentum interaction in respect to the conditional size effect. Recall the finding from Table 15.3 that following periods of positive sentiment, investors judge recent winners to be less risky and to have higher expected returns than recent losers. However, following periods of negative sentiment, the signs reverse: investors judge recent winners to be more risky than recent losers, and to have lower subsequent returns. Therefore, following periods of positive sentiment, if recent winners are more concentrated in small-cap stocks, then the impact of past returns would lead to upward pressure on the prices of small-cap stocks, thereby lowering subsequent returns and dampening the size effect conditional on BW being positive.

16 How Psychology Brought Down MF Global

1. See Jacob Bunge (2011), "MF Global: History from IPO to Bankruptcy," *Wall Street Journal*, October 31. http://blogs.wsj.com/deals/2011/10/31/mf-global-history-from-ipo-to-bankruptcy/.
2. This history is described by Michael Roseman in his statement on February 2, 2012, before the US House of Representatives Committee on Financial Services Oversight and Investigations Subcommittee.

3. See Bryan Burrough, William Cohan, and Bethany McLean (2012), "Jon Corzine's Riskiest Business," *Vanity Fair*, February, 94–153. This article is available online, and in this form the listed authors are Burrough and McLean. See http://www.vanityfair.com/news/business/2012/02/jon-corzine-201202. Unless otherwise indicated, this article and Roseman's testimony mentioned above form the source of the information discussed in this section.
4. Richard A. Brealey, Stewart C. Myers, and Franklin Allen (2007), *Principles of Corporate Finance* (Burr Ridge: McGraw-Hill Irwin).
5. Paulson later became Secretary of the Treasury, following in the footsteps of Robert Rubin, another senior Goldman partner. This history might be irrelevant, but for the possibility raised by Burrough, Cohan, and McLean, "Jon Corzine's Riskiest Business," that Corzine could have seen himself as a candidate for Treasury Secretary in President Barack Obama's second term.
6. This information is taken from the account in Burrough, Cohan, and McLean, "Jon Corzine's Riskiest Business."
7. This information comes from Roseman's testimony cited above.
8. James Stewart (2013), "COMMON SENSE: "Boss's Remark, Employee's Deed and Moral Quandary," *New York Times*, July 5, http://www.nytimes.com/2013/07/06/business/moral-quandaries-at-mf-global.html.
9. Ben Walsh (2012), "Jon Corzine Replaced 'Risk Officer' with an 'Everything Is OK' Officer." *Business Insider*, February 3, http://www.businessinsider.com/jon-corzine-replaced-mf-globals-risk-officer-with-an-everything-is-ok-officer-2012-2.
10. Ben Protess (2012), "MF Global's Former Risk Officers Defend Their Tenures," *New York Times*, February 2, http://dealbook.nytimes.com/2012/02/02/mf-globals-former-risk-officers-defend-their-tenures/?_php=true&_type=blogs&_r=0.
11. See Joe Herbert and John Coates (2008), "Endogenous Steroids and Financial Risk Taking on a London Trading Floor," *PNAS* 105 (16): 6167–6172.
12. Daniel Kahneman (2011), *Thinking, Fast and Slow* (New York: Farrar, Straus, and Giroux).
13. See Sarah Lynch and Karey Wutkowski (2012), "MF Global Risk Officer Says Ousted after Warnings," *Reuters*, February 2, http://www.reuters.com/article/2012/02/02/us-mfglobal-hearing-idUSTRE8111RM20120202.

17 JPMorgan's Whale of a Risk Management Failure

1. Robert Kaplan and Anette Mikes (2012), "JP Morgan's Loss: Bigger than 'Risk Management,'" hbr.org, May 23, http://blogs.hbr.org/cs/2012/05/jp_morgans_loss_bigger_than_ri.html.
2. See Kaplan and Mikes, "JP Morgan's Loss."
3. In this chapter, the acronym CIO is used for Chief Investment Office. Elsewhere in the book, the acronym CIO is used for chief investment officer.
4. See US Senate Subcommittee Report, 2013. "JPMorgan Whale Trades: A Case History of Derivatives Risks and Abuses," Majority and Minority Staff Report. This report provides the core material for the chapter.

5. See Susan Dominus (2012), "The Woman Who Took the Fall for JPMorgan Chase," *New York Times*, October 7.
6. Dominus, "The Woman Who Took the Fall," reports that the New York group was run by Althea Duersten. One colleague described her as excessively risk averse. In contrast, a colleague of Macris described him as a gunslinger who was willing to take large positions when he liked a particular trade.
7. US Senate Subcommittee Report, p. 63.
8. See US Senate Subcommittee report, p. 62. JPMorgan Chase's CFO at the time was Douglas Braunstein, and John Wilmot was the CIO's CFO.
9. US Senate Subcommittee report, p. 78.
10. According to Martin-Artajo, who later described the situation to a JPMorgan Chase Task Force investigation of the issue. See US Senate report, p. 67.
11. US Senate Subcommittee report, p. 52.
12. This is akin to an investor buying a house in a neighborhood one month, and then a month later buying a lot more houses in the same neighborhood. The more recent buying activities serve to increase the market prices of the houses purchased during the previous month. A more apt analogy might be a real estate developer who sells new homes before they are built. The selling activity decreases the price per unit, and ultimately the developer finds that he cannot build all the houses he has sold in advance. Therefore, he stops selling claims to new homes, which leads prices to stop declining and begin to rise. In addition, he finds that he must now buy completed homes to make good on his prior obligations, and needs to do so at higher prices than he sold for initially. The developer is akin to the CIO, and the contracts for houses yet to be built are akin to the IG.
13. The positions included a variety of IG on- and off-the-run holdings.
14. US Senate subcommittee report, p. 84.
15. Remember that quasi-hedonic editing predicts that people will be risk averse in the domain of losses once they have incurred prior losses.
16. Statement by Jamie Dimon, quoted by Chairman Tim Johnson in "A Breakdown in Risk Management: What Went Wrong at JPMorgan Chase?" before the US Senate Committee on Banking, Housing, and Urban Affairs, S.Hrg. 112–715 (June 13, 2012). See US Senate report, p. 93.
17. Erik Schatzker, Dawn Kopecki, Bradley Keoun, and Christine Harper (2012), "Jamie Dimon's Risky Business," *Bloomberg*, June 14, http://www.businessweek.com/articles/2012-06-14/jamie-dimons-risky-business. The Bloomberg article opened with a section entitled "The Hubris of Jamie Dimon." Much of the material in this section is taken from this article and the US Senate report cited earlier.
18. See Dominus, "The Woman Who Took the Fall."
19. US Senate Subcommittee report, p. 164.
20. US Senate Subcommittee report, p. 203.
21. In February 2012, Drew hired Irvin Goldman to be the CRO of the CIO. Goldman was a former Credit Suisse First Boston executive, and also a longtime professional friend. A month later, he was also new to the position and in learning mode. In this regard, he did not respond vigorously to CIO

breaches of various risk metrics. When he was informed of limit breaches, bank documents indicate that his reaction was to challenge the metrics, not the CIO traders. The same was true of the CIO's top risk quantitative analyst, Patrick Hagan.

22. See US Senate Subcommittee report, p. 157.
23. See Schatzker et al., "Jamie Dimon's Risky Business."
24. In a recorded telephone conversation, Grout told Iksil, "I am not marking at mids as per a previous conversation." The next day, Iksil expressed to Grout his concerns about the growing discrepancy between the marks they were reporting versus those called for by marking at the midpoint prices: "I can't keep this going...I think what he's [their supervisor, Javier Martin-Artajo] expecting is a re-marking at the end of the month...I don't know where he wants to stop, but it's getting idiotic."
25. US Senate Subcommitee Report, p. 96.
26. The total losses would have amounted to $593 million.
27. Martin-Artajo is Spanish, and after leaving JPMorgan Chase, he returned to Spain. The United States requested that Spain extradite him in order that he be tried in the United States In March 2015, Martin-Artajo professed his innocence to the Spanish court, contending that he did not, could not, and had no motive to engage in the behavior alleged in the complaint. Moreover, he pointed out that he did not work in the department in which the complaint alleges that abuses occurred. Martin-Artajo also argued the events in question occurred in the United Kingdom, not in the United States, and noted that he is a Spanish citizen. Additionally, he pointed out that the penalties demanded by the US authorities were disproportionately high. See Macarena Munoz Montijano and Charles Penty (2015), "Ex-JPMorgan's Martin-Artajo Tells Madrid Court He's Innocent," *Bloomberg*, March 5, http://www.bloomberg.com/news/articles/2015-03-05/ex-jpmorgan-s-martin-artajo-tells-madrid-court-he-is-innocent. In April 2015, a Spanish court rejected a US request for the extradition of Martin-Artajo, although an appeal of the decision is possible. The Spanish court also allowed for the possibility that Martin-Artajo be tried in Spain. See Macarena Munoz Montijano and Patricia Hurtado (2015), "Spain Rejects U.S. Extradition of London Whale Case Banker," *Bloomberg*, April 23, http://www.bloomberg.com/news/articles/2015-04-23/spain-rejects-u-s-extradition-of-banker-in-london-whale-case.
28. Lindsay Fortado (2014), "Ex-JPMorgan Executive Macris Wins London Whale Report Case," *Bloomberg*, April 11, http://www.bloomberg.com/news/2014-04-11/ex-jpmorgan-executive-macris-wins-case-over-london-whale-report.html.
29. US Senate Subcommittee Report, p. 214.
30. As this book goes to press, there is little to suggest that prosecutions of CIO personnel will result. See James Stewart (2015), "Convictions Prove Elusive in 'London Whale' Trading Case," *New York Times*, July 16. http://www.nytimes.com/2015/07/17/business/figures-in-london-whale-trading-case-escape-the-authorities-nets.html?hp&action=click&pgtype=Homepage

&module=first-column-region&region=top-news&WT.nav=top-news. Stewart writes that in July 2015, the FCA announced that it was dropping its case against Iksil, whom the United States Justice Deparment agreed not to prosecute. Stewart also notes that the probability is small for Spain to extradite Martin-Artajo and for France to extradite Grout (where he resides and is a citizen).

18 RISK MANAGEMENT PROFILES: CON ED, BP, AND MMS

1. Bryan Walsh (2012), "Outsmarting the Surge," *Time* magazine, November 12, http://www.time.com/time/magazine/article/0,9171,2128304,00.html.
2. Michael W. Dominowski (2013), "U.S. Weather Agency Looks for Lessons from Baffling Hurricane Sandy," *Staten Island Advance*, silive.com, http://www.silive.com/news/index.ssf/2013/03/us_weather_agency_looks_for_le.html, March 17, updated March 18; Eric S. Blake, Todd B. Kimberlain, Robert J. Berg, John P. Cangialosi, and John L. Beven II (2013), "Tropical Cyclone Report: Hurricane Sandy (AL182012), 22–29 October 2012," National Hurricane Center, February 12. http://www.nhc.noaa.gov/data/tcr/AL182012_Sandy.pdf.
3. Paul Barrett (2012), "Weather on Steroids Is Global Warming, Stupid," *Bloomberg*, November 1, http://www.bloomberg.com/news/2012-11-01/weather-on-steroids-is-global-warming-stupid-paul-barrett.html.
4. Tina Moore (2012), "Bloomberg Defends ConEd against Hurricane Sandy Criticisms," *New York Daily News*, November 30, http://www.nydailynews.com/new-york/bloomberg-defends-coned-sandy-criticisms-article-1.1211026. While Con Ed serves New York City and Westchester County, O&R's service territory encompasses all of Rockland County and parts of Sullivan and Orange County.
5. Consolidated Edison, "Superstorm Sandy 2013: State of the Company," http://www.conedison.com/ehs/2012-sustainability-report/engaging-stakeholders/reliability/superstorm-sandy/index.html#gsc.tab=0.
6. Stephen Gandel (2012), "How Con Ed Turned New York City's Lights Back On," *Fortune*, November 12, http://fortune.com/2012/11/12/how-con-ed-turned-new-york-citys-lights-back-on/.
7. As described by Gandel, "How Con Ed."
8. *Moreland Commission on Utility Storm Preparation and Response*, June 22, 2013.
9. The older device was "a plastic disconnect boot," while the newer device was "a green adapter plate."
10. Con Edison Media Relations (2013), "Sandy 1-Year Update: Con Edison Investing $1 Billion to Help Protect New Yorkers From Major Storms," coned.com, October 21, http://www.coned.com/newsroom/news/pr20131021.asp.
11. "Con Edison's Plan to Get New York Ready for the Next Storm of the Century," coned.com, http://www.coned.com/fortifying-the-future/index.html.

12. "Superstorm Sandy 2013: State of the Company," coned.com, http://www.conedison.com/ehs/2012-sustainability-report/engaging-stakeholders/reliability/superstorm-sandy/index.html#gsc.tab=0.
13. John Schwartzian (2015), "Judge's Ruling on Gulf Oil Spill Lowers Ceiling on the Fine BP Is Facing," *New York Times*, January 15, http://www.nytimes.com/2015/01/16/business/energy-environment/judge-sets-top-penalty-for-bp-in-deepwater-horizon-spill-at-nearly-14-billion.html?_r=0. In July 2015, BP achieved a $18.7b settlement with the US government. See Tom Huddleston, Jr. (2015), "BP May Have Billions More to Pay, Even After Its $19 Billion Settlement," *Fortune* July 13, http://time.com/3955864/bp-billions-compensation-claims/. At the time, the company announced that as of early July 2015, it had paid $53.8b thus far in connection with the Gulf oil spill.
14. Report to the President (2011), *National Commission on the BP Deepwater Horizon Oil Spill and Offshore Drilling*, p. ix.
15. Hersh Shefrin (2008), *Ending the Management Illusion* (New York: McGraw-Hill), p. 95. In this book, I characterized BP as a problematic firm that was engaged in excessive cost-cutting and excessive risk taking, with environmental consequences that were unfavorable.
16. Much of the material in the remainder of this chapter is drawn from Hersh Shefrin and Enrico Cervelatti (2011), "BP's Failure to Debias: Underscoring the Importance of Behavioral Corporate Finance," *Quarterly Journal of Finance* 1 (1): 127–168.
17. The report is entitled "Review of Operational Technical Concerns at Prudhoe Bay," and is available at http://www.propublica.org/documents/item/2001-bp-operational-integrity-report. The report is mentioned in a *Frontline* documentary, whose website is http://www.pbs.org/wgbh/pages/frontline/the-spill/bp-troubled-past/.
18. See Abrahm Lustgarten and Ryan Knutson (2010), "Years of Internal BP Probes Warned That Neglect Could Lead to Accidents," *ProPublica*, June 7.
19. In Shefrin, *Ending the Management Illusion*, I report that the company that operates and maintains Trans Alaska Pipeline System, Alyeska Pipeline Service, checks its pipelines with intelligent pigs every three years, and it also uses cleaning pigs at least twice a month.
20. See Lustgarten and Knutson, "Years of Internal BP Probes."
21. See Sarah Lyall (2010), "In BP's Record, a History of Boldness and Costly Blunders," *New York Times*, July 2, http://www.nytimes.com/2010/07/13/business/energy-environment/13bprisk.html?pagewanted=1&_r=1&ref=todayspaper.
22. See Andy Rowell (2010), "BP: Boldness and Blunders with no Hand on the Brake," *Oil Change International*. [http://priceofoil.org/2010/07/13/bp-boldness-and-blunders-with-no-hand-on-the-brake/]
23. See Lyall, "In BP's Record."
24. See Lyall, "In BP's Record."
25. Josua Frank (2010), "Safety Violations and Fines Did Not Deter BP and Massey Disasters," *Truthout*, June 2, http://truth-out.org/archive/component/k2/item/89849:safety-violations-and-fines-did-not-deter-bp-and-massey-disasters.

26. See Rowell, "BP: Boldness and Blunders."
27. Ed Crooks (2010), "BP: The Inside Story," *FT.com*, July, 2. Although Macondo was almost 900 feet deeper than Tiber, it was only 13,000 feet below the sea bed, in contrast to 31,000 feet for the larger field.
28. Scott Bronstein and Wayne Drash (2010), "Rig Survivors: BP Ordered Shortcut on Day of Blast," CNN Online, June 9.
29. Stanley Reed (2009) "What BP's New Oil Strike Means," *Bloomberg*, August 31. http://www.bloomberg.com/bw/stories/2009-08-31/what-bps-new-oil-strike-means.
30. The report was authored by Fred Lucas and is dated March 3, 2010.
31. Russell Gold and Ben Casselman (2010), "Deeper Trouble: On Doomed Rig's Last Day, A Divisive Change of Plan," *Wall Street Journal*, August 26.
32. See Gold and Casselman, "Deeper Trouble."
33. See Gold and Casselman, "Deeper Trouble."
34. National Commission report, pp. 77–78.
35. Mark Thompson (2010), "Washington's Revolving Door: How Oil Oversight Failed," *Time* magazine, June 9, http://www.time.com/time/nation/article/0,8599,1995137,00.html.
36. The source of the information in the remainder of this document is the report of the National Commission.
37. National Commission report, pp. 73–74.
38. National Commission report, pp. vii, ix, 76.
39. Coral Davenport (2015), "New Sea Drilling Rule Planned, 5 Years after BP Oil Spill," *New York Times*, April 10, http://www.nytimes.com/2015/04/11/us/new-sea-drilling-rule-planned-5-years-after-bp-oil-spill.html?_r=0.

19 Information Sharing Failures at Southwest Airlines, General Motors, and the Agencies that Regulate Them

1. Data on commercial airline crashes available at http://www.planecrashinfo.com/cause.htm.
2. NHTSA 32–13 (2013), "NHTSA Data Confirms Traffic Fatalities Increased in 2012," nhtsa.gov, November 14, http://www.nhtsa.gov/About+NHTSA/Press+Releases/NHTSA+Data+Confirms+Traffic+Fatalities+Increased+In+2012.
3. That said, current law makes criminal prosecution more difficult in the automotive industry than other regulated industries, such as energy. See Danielle Ivory and Ben Protess (2015), "Laws Hinder Prosecutors in Charging G.M. Employees in Ignition Defect," *New York Times*, July 19, http://www.nytimes.com/2015/07/20/business/laws-hinder-prosecutors-in-charging-gm-employees-in-ignition-defect.html?hp&action=click&pgtype=Homepage&module=photo-spot-region&region=top-news&WT.nav=top-news&_r=0.
4. The discussion about Southwest Airlines in this chapter draws from my previous writings. See Hersh Shefrin (2008), *Ending the Management Illusion* (New York: McGraw-Hill). The present book updates the history

of Southwest's maintenance lapse, an event that was just unfolding when *Ending the Management Illusion* went to press.
5. Dawn Gilbertson (2014) "JetBlue, Southwest Top Airline Customer Satisfaction Survey," *The Arizona Republic*, April 22, http://www.azcentral.com/story/nowdeparting/2014/04/22/jetblue-and-southwest-airlines-tops-in-airline-satisfaction/8013587/.
6. See Shefrin, *Ending the Management Illusion*.
7. The source material for the chronology comes from a *CNN* story, "FAA Inspectors: Bosses Tried to Suppress Reports On Inspections," that appeared on April 3, 2008; Andy Pasztor (2008), "Very Friendly Skies: Southwest's Cozy Ties Triggered FAA Tumult—Airline's Interference Led to Wider Probe; Job Favors at Issue," *Wall Street Journal*, April 3.
8. The Valukas report is available at http://www.nytimes.com/interactive/2014/06/05/business/06gm-report-doc.html?_r=0.
9. For example, see Jeff Bennett and Joann S. Lublin (2014), "GM Report to Cite Cultural Failings—Recall Inquiry to Highlight Poor Communications But Clear Top Executives; Dismissals Are Expected," *Wall Street Journal*, June 5, B1; and Hilary Stout, Rebecca Ruiz, and Danielle Ivory (2014). "G.M. Response to a Fatal Flaw Was to Shrug," *New York Times*, June 6, A.
10. The source material for this section is Bill Vlasic (2014), "A Fatally Flawed Switch, and a Burdened G.M. Engineer," *New York Times*, November 13, http://www.nytimes.com/2014/11/14/business/a-fatally-flawed-switch-and-a-burdened-engineer.html.
11. Aversion to a sure loss is a typical explanation for why people generally withhold information that is negative, and it is worth pondering whether this was the case here. Recall that aversion to a sure loss often leads people to take bets that are unlikely to turn out well. It is a key pitfall, just as information sharing is a key process. In the case at hand, by withholding information from GM's internal investigators, DeGiorgio prolonged the company's ability to react to the safety switch issue, once they had begun to address it. His denials under oath about having authorized the change led attorneys for the Melton family to file a suit alleging possible perjury on his part. For his part, DeGiorgio contends that he had no recollection of having signed a form authorizing the change in part as well as the maintenance of the same part number. See Matthew Wald and Bill Vlasic (2014), "'Upset' G.M. Engineer Spoke in House Inquiry," *New York Times*, May 28, http://www.nytimes.com/2014/05/29/business/upset-gm-engineer-spoke-in-house-inquiry.html.
12. In September 2013, GM settled the suit for $5 million. However, attorneys for Brooke Melton's family later filed a second suit, alleging that that GM knew more about the ignition switch defect than it had disclosed in the prior case. See the previous footnote. The suit also alleged that in the original proceedings GM had committed fraud. GM settled the second suit in March 2015. See Joseph White (2015), "GM Settles High-Profile Ignition-Switch Case with Georgia Family," *Reuters*, March 13, http://www.reuters.com/article/2015/03/13/us-gm-recall-settlement-idUSKBN0M922D20150313.

13. Bill Vlasic and Aaron Kessler (2014), "At Hearing on G.M. Recall, Mary Barra Gives Little Ground," *New York Times*, July 17, http://www.nytimes.com/2014/07/18/business/senate-hearing-on-general-motors.html.
14. In contrast to Southwest's nimble open-book approach, GM operated as a large cumbersome bureaucracy that reacted slowly to changing circumstances. For example, as the financial crisis began to unfold and demand for automobiles declined, GM maintained production levels for a long time, which resulted in growing inventories of unsold cars that dealers could not move. Its chief competitor, Ford, responded much more quickly in reducing production and inventory. Ford was the only one of the Big Three automobile manufacturers to decline government assistance and not to declare bankruptcy.
15. See Jack Stack (1992, 2013), *The Great Game of Business: The Only Sensible Way to Run a Company* (New York: Crown/Random House).
16. Darren Dahl (2009), "Open-Book Management's Lessons for Detroit," *New York Times*, May 20, http://www.nytimes.com/2009/05/21/business/smallbusiness/21open.html.
17. Chris Isidore and Katie Lobosco (2014), "GM CEO Barra: 'I am deeply sorry,'" *CNNMoney*, April 1, http://money.cnn.com/2014/04/01/news/companies/barra-congress-testimony/.
18. Bill Vlasic and Aaron Kessler (2014), "At Hearing on G.M. Recall, Mary Barra Gives Little Ground," *New York Times*, July 17, http://www.nytimes.com/2014/07/18/business/senate-hearing-on-general-motors.html.
19. Rebecca Ruiz and Danielle Ivory (2014), "Documents Show General Motors Kept Silent on Fatal Crashes," *New York Times*, July 15, http://www.nytimes.com/2014/07/16/business/documents-show-general-motors-kept-silent-on-fatal-crashes.html?_r=0.
20. See Bill Vlasic (2015). "Fiat Chrysler Faces Record $105 Million Fine for Safety Issues," *New York Times*, July 26. http://www.nytimes.com/2015/07/27/business/fiat-chrysler-faces-record-105-million-fine-for-safety-issues.html?hp&action=click&pgtype=Homepage&module=second-column-region&region=top-news&WT.nav=top-news&_r=0.
21. In 2015 another automaker scandal came to light when US regulators discovered that Volkswagen had deliberately installed deceptive software in its diesel vehicles. The software induced emission control technology only when vehicles were being tested, but not when they were regularly being driven. An article in the New York Times described this behavior as cheating on emission tests, thereby providing yet one more instance of cheating. See Guilbert Gates, Josh Keller, Karl Russell, and Derek Watkins (2015). "How Volkswagen Got Away With Diesel Deception," *New York Times*, October 2, http://www.nytimes.com/interactive/2015/09/22/business/international/vw-volkswagen-emissions-explainer.html.

20 CONCLUSION

1. See René Stulz (2009), "Six Ways Companies Mismanage Risk," *Harvard Business Review* 87 (3): 86–94, https://hbr.org/2009/03/six-ways-companies

-mismanage-risk. This article identifies six important sources of risk management failure. However, Stulz makes no reference to behavioral psychology, which lies at the root of the issue. One, "failing to communicate" corresponds to poor information sharing, a topic discussed throughout the book. I suggest that the route from "mismanaging" to "effective managing" will be smoother if done with an understanding of the biases in need of debiasing.
2. People do many tasks automatically, relying on System 1. On pages 6 and 7 of his book *The Hour between the Dog and the Wolf*, cited in chapter 1, former trader turned neuroscientist John Coates writes that traders viewing complex displays of financial data rely on their gut instinct while trading, subconsciously recognizing changing patterns without being consciously aware of the information they are processing. This is an example of educated gut instinct.
3. See Chip Heath and Dan Heath (2010), *Switch: How to Change Things When Change is Hard* (New York: Broadway Books).
4. See Edith Orenstein (2015), "The Color of Risk," *Financial Executive* 3 (1): 30–36. Also see the PwC series *Get Up to Speed on Risk Management Issues* with its ten-step "How to Tackle It" risk management framework written by Bob Semple.
5. See Derek Atkins, Anthony Fitzsimmons, Christopher Parsons, and Alan Punter (2011), "Roads to Ruin: A Study of Major Risk Events." This report was written by the Cass Business School in London for the Association of Insurance and Risk Managers in Industry and Commerce. The report analyzes more than 20 major corporate crises that occurred between 2000 and 2011. Notably, the report considers three of the firms discussed in this volume, namely BP, Société Générale, and AIG. Explicit discussion of psychology appears in just two places, one when mentioning groupthink, and the second in connection with rogue trading.
6. For example, risk issues associated with data breaches are growing in frequency and importance. These issues are complex, but one aspect certainly involves the failure of health firms and government bodies to make necessary investments in data encryption. Cases discussed in the book, such as BP and Southwest Airlines, which deal with the psychological factors underlying failures to make investments for mitigating risk, can serve as analogues. For cases involving data breaches, see the following: Mark Hosenball (2015), "U.S. Has Yet to Notify 21.5 Million Data Breach Victims: Officials," *Reuters*, July 14, https://www.yahoo.com/tech/s/u-yet-notify-21-5-million-data-breach-225745853.html; Mike Segar (2014), "JPMorgan Data Breach Entry Point Identified," *Reuters*, December 22, http://www.reuters.com/article/2014/12/23/us-jpmorgan-cybersecurity-idUSKBN0K105R20141223; Sarah Halzack (2015), "Target Data Breach Victims Could Get Up To $10,000 Each From Court Settlement," *Washington Post*, March 19, http://www.washingtonpost.com/news/business/wp/2015/03/19/target-data-breach-victims-could-get-up-10000-each-from-court-settlement/; Marianne Kolbasuk McGee

(2014), "Sutter Health Breach Suit DismissedCourt Decision Follows Similar Rulings in Other Cases," *HealthInfoSec*, July 22, http://www.databreachtoday.com/sutter-health-breach-suit-dismissed-a-7095. For a discussion of how the COSO framework applies to cybersecurity risk, see Mary Galligan and Kelly Rau (2015), "COSO in the Cyber Age," http://www.coso.org/documents/COSO%20in%20the%20Cyber%20Age_FULL_r11.pdf.

7. Some might wonder whether representativeness is at work here. Typically representativeness applies to excessive optimism about an event to the extent that people view themselves as representative of those to whom the event happens. My own view is that the WHO might have judged the 2014 outbreak of Ebola as fitting the stereotype with which they were familiar, but that familiarity is the more likely driver.
8. See Kevin Sack, Sheri Fink, Pam Belluck, and Adam Nossiter (2014), "How Ebola Roared Back," *New York Times* December 29, http://www.nytimes.com/2014/12/30/health/how-ebola-roared-back.html?hp&action=click&pgtype=Homepage&module=a-lede-package-region&region=top-news&WT.nav=top-news.
9. Shann Turnbull (2012), "Discovering the 'Natural Laws' Of Governance," *The Corporate Board*, March/April, 1–5.
10. See the Carnegie Foundation report discussed in Chapter 1, pp. 11, 12, and 28. James M. Acton and Mark Hibbs (2012), "Why Fukushima Was Preventable," *The Carnegie Papers*, http://carnegieendowment.org/2012/03/06/why-fukushima-was-preventable.
11. See the discussion about a fault tree experiment and availability bias, which appears in Appendix D.
12. See Chip Heath, Richard Larrick, and Joshua Klayman (1998), "Cognitive Repairs: How Organizational Practices Can Compensate for Individual Shortcomings," *Research in Organizational Behavior* 20: 1–37.

Appendix A: A Deeper Dive into SP/A Theory

1. See Lola Lopes and Gregory Oden (1999), "The Role of Aspiration Level in Risk Choice: A Comparison of Cumulative Prospect Theory and SP/A theory," *Journal of Mathematical Psychology* 43: 286–313.
2. Eduard Gerd Gigerenzer Brandstätter and Ralph Hertwig (2006), "The Priority Heuristic: Making Choices without Trade-Offs," *Psychological Review*, 113 (2): 409–432.

Appendix B: A Deeper Dive into Prospect Theory

1. Richard H. Thaler and Eric J. Johnson (1990), "Gambling with the House Money and Trying to Break Even: The Effects of Prior Outcomes on Risky Choice," *Management Science*, 36 (6): 643–660.
2. Daniel Kahneman and Amos Tversky (1979), "Prospect Theory: An Analysis of Decision Making under Risk," *Econometrica*, 5(2): 263–291.

APPENDIX C: INTEGRATING SP/A THEORY AND PROSPECT THEORY

1. Shlomo Benartzi and Richard H. Thaler (1995), "Myopic Loss Aversion and the Equity Premium Puzzle," *The Quarterly Journal of Economics*, 110 (1): 73–92.
2. See Itzhak Gilboa and David Schmeidler (1989), "Maxmin Expected Utility with a Non-Unique Prior," *Journal of Mathematical Economics* 18: 141–153; Itzhak Gilboa and David Schmeidler (1993), "Updating Ambiguous Beliefs," *Journal of Economic Theory* 59: 33–49. For some, ambiguity is formally identical to facing a uniform probability distribution. For others, ambiguity is conceptually different. Decision-makers who are Bayesians might model uncertainty by means of a prior distribution on possible probability distributions. When there is an option to delay committing to a decision, Bayesian techniques can be used to assess the relative benefits of delaying in order to obtain new information that will produce sharper posteriors.

APPENDIX D: A DEEPER DIVE INTO HEURISTICS AND BIASES

1. J. Edward Russo and Paul J. H. Schoemaker (1990), *Decision Traps: Ten Barriers to Brilliant Decision-Making and How to Overcome Them* (New York: Simon & Schuster).
2. The "correct" answers to Question D5 are as follows: 1. 39 years. 2. 4,187 miles. 3. 13 countries. 4. 24 books. 5. 2,160 miles. 6. 390,000 lbs. 7. 1756. 8. 645 days. 9. 5,959 miles. 10. 36,198 feet. In addition, the answer to the length of the Colorado river question in Chapter 4 is 1,450 miles.

APPENDIX E: A FORMAL MODEL OF ORGANIZATIONAL RISK

1. See Joseph Lee Rodgers and W. Alan Nicewander (1988), "Thirteen Ways to Look at the Correlation Coefficient," *The American Statistician*, 42(1), 59–66. The equation for a nonrotated ellipse is $(x-h)^2/a^2 + (y-k)^2/b^2 = 1$. In the equation, x is centered at h and y is centered at k. The parameters a and b are the radii for x and y respectively.
2. In theory, managers typically assess projects using some numerical criterion x such as net present value (NPV) or internal rate of return (IRR). The typical adoption criterion for a project involves adopting the project if the assessed value exceeds some threshold known as a "hurdle rate."
3. This type of simplifying assumption appears in a paper about risk management by Mattieu Bouvard and Samuel Lee. See Mattieu Bouvard and Samuel Lee (2014), "Risk Management Failures," Working paper, McGill University and New York University.
4. Luca Celati emphasizes this point in his fine book about the behavioral approach to risk management. The associated reward asymmetry might be induced through the compensation system, or it might be psychological, as is the case with the prospect theory S-shaped value function. See Luca Celati

(2004), *The Dark Side of Risk Management: How People Frame Decisions in Financial Markets* (London: Financial Times/Prentice Hall).
5. This material is adapted from Chapter 6 of my book *Ending the Management Illusion*.
6. See Bouvard and Lee, "Risk Management Failures."

APPENDIX F: MODELLING FIH ISSUES

1. See John Maynard Keynes (1936), reprinted in 1967. *The General Theory of Employment, Interest, and Money* (London: McMillan). A good exposition of Godley's model can be found in Wynne Godley and Marc Lavoie (2007), *Monetary Economics: An Integrated Approach to Credit, Money, Income, Production and Wealth* (New York: Palgrave MacMillan).
2. In respect to foreign trade, if we export goods this year, but do not import goods, then we still need to pay ourselves for producing the goods we ship abroad.
3. In chapter 7 of his book *Stabilizing an Unstable Economy Minsky*, titled "Prices and Profits in a Capitalist Economy," Minsky does present a formal model of investment based largely on the ideas of Kalecki. See Michael Kalecki (1933–1970), *Selected Essays on the Dynamics of the Capitalist Economy*, Cambridge: Cambridge University Press. A presentation by Alexander Lipton, titled "Improved Monetary Circuit Theory, Interconnected Banking Networks, and Behavior of Individual Banks," traces the various contributions to the associated stream of literature. Lipton gave this presentation at the ICBI Global Derivatives & Risk Management Conference held in Amsterdam in May 2015.
4. See Steve Keen (2013), "Predicting the 'Global Financial Crisis': Post-Keynesian Macroeconomics," *Economic Record* 89: 228–254.
5. See Gauti Eggertsson and Paul Krugman (2012), "Debt, Deleveraging, and the Liquidity Trap: A Fisher-Minsky-Koo Approach," *The Quarterly Journal of Economics* 127 (3): 1469–1513.
6. See John Campbell and Robert. Shiller (1991), "Yield Spreads and Interest Rate Movements: A Bird's Eye View," *Review of Economic Studies* 58, 495–514.
7. See Wei Xiong, and Hongjun Yan (2010), "Heterogeneous Expectations and Bond Markets," *Review of Financial Studies* 23 (4): 1433–1466.
8. See John Cochrane and Monika Piazzesi (2005), "Bond Risk Premia," *American Economic Review* 95, 138–160. In a presentation entitled "Modelling Bond Risk Premia Empirical and Theoretical Developments," made at the ICBI Global Derivatives & Risk Management Conference held in Amsterdam in May 2015, Ricardo Rebonato described the implications of the Cochrane-Piazzesi findings for risk management.

APPENDIX G: EMPIRICAL PROXIES OF SENTIMENT

1. See Hersh Shefrin (2008), *A Behavioral Approach to Asset Pricing Theory* (Boston: Elsevier).

APPENDIX I: FIH ISSUES IN CHINA AND EUROPE

1. See Andrew Higgins and David E. Sanger (2015), "3 European Powers Say They Will Join China-Led Bank," *New York Times*, March 17, http://www.nytimes.com/2015/03/18/business/france-germany-and-italy-join-asian-infrastructure-investment-bank.html.
2. Material for this part of the discussion comes from the following sources:
   David Barboza (2013), "Loan Practices of China's Banks Raising Concern," *New York Times*, July 2, http://www.nytimes.com/2013/07/02/business/global/loan-practices-of-chinas-banks-raising-concern.html.
   David Barboza (2015), "In China, a Building Frenzy's Fault Lines, *New York Times*, March 13, http://www.nytimes.com/2015/03/15/business/dealbook/in-china-a-building-frenzys-fault-lines.html?&hp&action=click&pgtype=Homepage&module=first-column-region&region=top-news&WT.nav=top-news&_r=0.
   Forbes magazine (2015), "The China Syndrome: Is China Headed For A Financial Meltdown?" April 23, http://www.forbes.com/sites/mikepatton/2015/04/23/the-china-syndrome-is-china-headed-for-a-financial-meltdown/.
   Craig Stephen (2015), "Opinion: China Scrambles to Defuse Property Bubble," *MarketWatch*, April 8, http://www.marketwatch.com/story/china-scrambles-to-defuse-property-bubble-2015-04-08.
   Minxin Pei (2015), "China's Slowing Economy: The Worst Has Yet to Come," *Fortune* magazine, January 21, http://fortune.com/2015/01/21/china-economy-growth-slowdown/.
3. See Barboza (2013), "Loan Practices Of China's Banks Raising Concern."
4. Material for this part of the discussion comes from the following sources:
   Gregor Stuart Hunter and Jacky Wong (2015), "Everything You Need to Know about China's Stock Markets," *Dow Jones Institutional News*, July 10, http://www.wsj.com/articles/everything-you-need-to-know-about-chinas-stock-markets-1436534913.
   Edward Wong and Chris Buckley (2015), "Stock Market Plunge in China Dents Communist Party's Stature," *New York Times*, July 9, http://www.nytimes.com/2015/07/10/world/asia/china-stock-market-crash-communist-xi-jinping.html?hpw&rref=world&action=click&pgtype=Homepage&module=well-region&region=bottom-well&WT.nav=bottom-well.
   James Stewart (2015), "Why China's Stock Market Bailout Just Might Work," *New York Times*, July 9, http://www.nytimes.com/2015/07/10/business/international/why-chinas-stock-market-bailout-just-might-work.html.
   David Barboza (2015), "China's Incendiary Market Is Fanned by Borrowers and Manipulation," *New York Times*, July 12, http://www.nytimes.com/2015/07/13/business/dealbook/chinas-incendiary-market-is-fanned-by-borrowers-and-manipulation.html?hp&action=click&pgtype=Homepage&module=first-column-region&region=top-news&WT.nav=top-news.

5. That the Chinese government actively encouraged the bubble suggests aspiration-based risk seeking, or aversion to a sure loss, in an environment of declining economic growth.
6. See Paul Krugman (2015), "China's Naked Emperors," *New York Times*, July 31, http://www.nytimes.com/2015/07/31/opinion/paul-krugman-chinas-naked-emperors.html.
7. See Kyoungwha Kim (2015), "China Has Biggest One-Day Stock Crash Since 2007," *Bloomberg*, July 26, updated July 27. http://www.bloomberg.com/news/articles/2015-07-27/chinese-stock-index-futures-drop-before-industrial-profits.
8. Material for this part of the discussion comes from the following sources:
    New York Times (2015), "Greece's Debt Crisis Explained," July 5, http://www.nytimes.com/interactive/2015/business/international/greece-debt-crisis-euro.html.
    Steven Erlanger (2015), "Deal on Greek Debt Crisis Exposes Europe's Deepening Fissures, *New York Times*, July 13, http://www.nytimes.com/2015/07/14/world/europe/greece-debt-deal.html?hp&action=click&pgtype=Homepage&module=b-lede-package-region&region=top-news&WT.nav=top-news.
    Jack Ewing (2015), "I.M.F. Demands Debt Relief as Condition for Greek Bailout," *New York Times*, July 14, http://www.nytimes.com/2015/07/15/business/international/international-monetary-fund-proposed-greek-debt-relief.html?hp&action=click&pgtype=Homepage&module=first-column-region&region=top-news&WT.nav=top-news.
9. Political negotiations introduce another complex dimension to risk analysis. See
    The Economist (2011), "Game theory in Practice: Computing: Software That Models Human Behaviour Can Make Forecasts, Outfox Rivals and Transform Negotiations," September 3, http://www.economist.com/node/21527025.
    Hersh Shefrin and Shabnam Mousavi (2010), "Prediction Tools: Financial Market Regulation, Politics and Psychology," *Journal of Risk Management in Financial Institutions* 3 (4): 318–333.
10. See Liz Alderman (2015), "Greece Says It Has Reached a Deal for a Third Bailout," *New York Times*, August 11. http://www.nytimes.com/2015/08/12/business/international/greece-third-bailout-deal.html?hp&action=click&pgtype=Homepage&module=first-column-region&region=top-news&WT.nav=top-news. This article describes the main conditions demanded by Greece's creditors as well as concessions won by the Greek government. See also Huw Jones (2015), "Greece deal points to flexible approach to bank rescues in EU," *Reuters*, August 26. http://www.reuters.com/article/2015/08/26/us-eurozone-greece-bailout-idUSKCN0QV1FN20150826.
11. See Nathaniel Popper and Neil Gough (2015), "A Plunge in China Rattles Markets Across the Globe," *New York Times*, August 23. http://www.nytimes.com/2015/08/25/business/dealbook/daily-stock-market-activity.html.

12. See Neil Gough and Chris Buckley (2015), "China Again Cuts Interest Rates as Concerns Mount Over Economy," *New York Times*, August 25. http://www.nytimes.com/2015/08/26/business/international/china-interest-rates-stock-market-distress.html.
13. A major difference in China's experience with the Ponzi finance induced bubble under discussion and the past experience of the West relates to the use of police. In addition to imposing restrictions, such as prohibiting short sales, which are aimed at preventing sharp declines in securities prices, Chinese authorities have also used the police to harass investment firms they suspect of betting on price declines. See Edward Wong, Neil Gough, and Alexandra Stevenson (2015), "China's Response to Stock Plunge Rattles Traders," *New York Times*, September 9, http://www.nytimes.com/2015/09/10/world/asia/in-china-a-forceful-crackdown-in-response-to-stock-market-crisis.html.

INDEX

ABN AMRO
    acquisition and male competition, 185–9
    background on, 174
    FSA and, 178–84
    RBS post-acquisition, 177–8
    RBS's pursuit of, 174–7
Adaptive Behavior and Cognition (ABC Group), 223–4
Admati, Anat, 222, 228
affect and well-being, 77
AIG (American International Group)
    background on, 166
    bailout, 120, 123, 207
    CDSs and, 166
    financial products division (AIGFP), 166–70, 339
    global financial crisis and, 166–7, 191, 202–8
    groupthink and, 339
    housing bubble and, 166–70
    insurance of CDOs, 136
    leverage, 207–8
    subprime crisis and, 201
    "too big to fail," 120
Allais, Maurice, 24, 37, 395
Altman, Ed, xvi
Amazon, 73–4
American Airlines, 285–6, 320, 325
Amsterdam Institute of Finance (AIF), xvi, xx
Anderson, Candice, 328, 330, 332
Anderson, Cathy, 330
Anderson, Jason, 312–13
Antoncic, Madelyn, 486n14

Apple, 102
Asian Development Bank, 461
Asian Infrastructure Investment Bank (AIIB), 461
aspiration
    directly testing importance of, 388–92
    impact on valuation, 358–61
    relative importance of, 357–8
asset-backed commercial paper (ABCP), 119, 176, 179, 204, 462
availability bias, 54–6, 409–14
aversion to sure loss
    busts and, 114
    China and, 506n5
    explained, 50–2
    Fannie Mae and, 340–1
    Iksil and, 285, 287–9
    JPMorgan Chase and, 290–1, 340–1
    loss aversion vs., 51
    managing strategy risk and, 97, 278, 506n5
    mitigating, 341
    open-book companies and, 88
    Ponzi financing and, 230
    process-pitfall framework and, 336
    risk-seeking and, 88, 97
    rogue trading and, 103
    withholding of information and, 500n11
    see also loss aversion

Bacon, Asley, 296
Baker-Wurgler (BW) sentiment index, 261–5, 453
Bank of America, 133, 175–7, 188–9, 191, 205–6, 208

Bank of England, 178, 213, 222, 224, 227–8, 338, 460
Bankers Trust, 221
Barclays, 10–11, 174–5, 177, 186–9
Barone-Adesi, Giovanni, 195
Basel Accords
  2.5, 221
  I, 179–80, 183, 219–20, 222
  II, 180, 182–3, 220–2
  III, 179, 221–2
  heuristics, 219–21
  RWA and, 228
  shortcomings, 225
  UBS and, 338
Bayesian avoidance, 67–8, 429–34
Bayesian models, 53–4, 150, 219, 429–34
Bear Sterns, 119–20, 133, 148, 167, 192, 202–6, 208, 219, 281
Beim report, 212–13, 340
Belgian Generale Bank (GB), 185–6
Bergen Brunswig, 4, 7–9, 14
Bernanke, Ben, 117, 120, 123–4, 170, 344
Bezos, Jeff, 73–4
biases and risk
  availability bias, 54–6
  Bayesian avoidance, 67–8
  confirmation bias, 63–4
  groupthink, 64–6
  illusion of control, 66–7
  optimism, 61–2
  overconfidence, 62–3
  overview, 53–4
  perceived risks, 56–9
  representativeness, 59–61
Botin, Emilio, 239
BP (British Petroleum)
  Alaskan oil spills, 305–7
  culture and, 304–5
  Macondo well, 308–11
  regulators and, 314–16
  risk management, 311–14
  Texas city explosion, 307–8
  U.S. government and, 309–11
  see also Deepwater Horizon

British Bankers' Association (BBA), 10
Budnick, Adam, 167
Bureau of Ocean Energy Management, Regulation and Enforcement (BOEMRE), 314
Bush, Elijah, 72

capital cushions, 107, 114, 177, 180, 182, 192, 206, 211, 214–16, 219–20, 222, 225–6
Cassano, Joseph, 168–70, 339
Celati, Luca, xiv, xix, 53, 472n1, 504n4
Chernobyl disaster, 57–8
Chester, Beth, 20, 268
Cheung, Meaghan, 242–4
Cisneros, Henry, 117
Citigroup, 10–11, 120, 122, 136, 161–2, 192, 202, 204–9, 213
Citizens, 175, 177
Clinton, Bill, 447, 449
Coates, John, 106–7, 184–6, 189, 277
collateralized debt obligations (CDOs)
  ABN AMRO and, 179
  AIG and, 167–8
  Basel II and, 221
  housing market and, 143
  innovation and, 115
  market crash and, 339
  Merrill Lynch and, 132–6, 138, 201
  Moody's and, 150–2
  mortgage-backed securities, 115, 125
  S&P and, 144–50
  UBS and, 125, 127–9, 131, 201, 338
Comeau, Paul, 324, 326
Con Ed (Consolidated Edison)
  Hurricane Sandy and, 301–4
  risk management at, 300–1
confirmation bias, 63–5, 427–8
control
  desire for, 76
  illusion of, 66–7, 428–9
Corzine, Jon, 267–74, 276–9, 339
COSO, xx, 14–15
Countrywide Financial, 161, 165, 205
credit default swaps (CDSs), 166–70, 201, 270, 283–4

Credit Rating Agency Reform Act (CRARA) of 2006, 143
cumulative prospect theory (CPT), 377–80, 383–400, 405
cyclically adjusted price-earnings ratio (CAPE), 198–9, 454, 465–6

Dark Side of Risk Management, The (Celati), xiv, 53
Dawes, Robyn, 223
De Nederlandsche Bank (DNB), 182–3
Deepwater Horizon, 14, 299, 304–5, 308–14, 316–17, 342
  see also BP
Delta Airlines, 320
Deutsche Bank, 10
Devaney, Earl, 314–15
Dillon Read Capital Management, 128
Dimon, Jamie, 112, 281–3, 289–92, 295, 297
dispositional optimism, 76
Dodd-Frank Act, 123, 281
dread risk, 57–8, 415
Drew, Ina, 282–3, 286, 289–91, 293, 296–7
Dudley, William, 212
Dugan, John, 201–2

Eastman Kodak, 286
Ebola outbreak of 2014, 85, 89–93, 95, 99–100, 336–7, 437, 439
emotions
  overview, 25–7
  SP/A and, 29–30
Enron, 143
Erikson, Gene, 328
euphoria, 5, 108, 115, 124, 139, 168, 191–2, 208–9, 343, 446, 453, 463–6
  hormones and, 106–7
  waxing and waning of, 200–4
excessive optimism
  Bergen Brunswig and, 9
  BP and, 306
  BW sentiment index and, 262
  decision-making and, 101, 343
  disappointment and, 130, 326
  factors driving, 5
  global financial crisis and, 171
  Greek financial crisis and, 464–5
  IPCC and, 13
  loss aversion and, 345
  Merrill Lynch and, 138–9
  new era thinking and, 115
  open-book organizations and, 88
  perceived control and, 343
  planning fallacy and, 337
  Ponzi finance and, 237
  process-pitfall framework and, 336
  rating firms and, 155
  risk management and, 278, 338, 443
  sentiment and, 191, 194–6, 198, 208, 262, 456–7
  strategy risk and, 97
  Weinstein's study of, 420–4
expected utility, 369–71
external risks, 98–100

Fair Isaac Corporation (FICO) scores, 129, 159, 162
Fairfield Greenwich Group, 230–1, 233–8
Fannie Mae/Freddie Mac
  background on, 157–9
  housing bubble and, 159–65
Fanning, Pat, 312
Federal Open Market Committee (FOMC), 117
Federal Reserve Bank, 108–9, 117, 120, 124, 167, 205, 208, 212, 340
financial instability hypothesis (FIH)
  ABM AMRO acquisition and, 173, 189
  capital cushions and, 222, 228
  China and, 461–3, 465–7
  Europe and, 463–7
  global financial crisis and, 343–4
  Minsky and, 105–6, 124
  Ponzi finance and, 129, 139, 141, 168, 202
  regulation and, 202, 222
  risk and, 124, 126
  S&P and, 155

financial instability
    hypothesis—*Continued*
  subprime crisis and, 129
  systemic risk and, 191–2, 209
  too big to fail and, 171
  V-Lab and, 201
financial regulation, psychology and
  assets, liabilities, and value-at-risk in practice, 216–19
  assets, liabilities, and value-at-risk in theory, 214–16
  Basel Accord heuristics, 219–21
  complexity and vested interests, 221–3
  fast and frugal heuristics, 223–4
  overview, 211–13
  regulating financial firms, 224–8
Financial Safety and Soundness Act, 159
foreign currency manipulation, 9–11
  see also Libor
foreign exchange rates (Forex), 10–11, 14
Fortis, 124, 175, 184–6, 188–9, 191–2
framing, 42–5
fraud
  Barron's investigation of, 230–1
  culture issues at SEC, 245–7
  Fairfield Greenwich and, 233–7
  Madoff, Bernard, 230–1, 237–44
  overview, 229–30
  spilt-strike conversion strategy, 231–3
Friedman, David, 333
Friedman, Milton, 24, 37
Froeba, Mark, 152
Frost, Alan, 167–8
Fukushima Daiichi power plant, 1, 4–7, 13–14, 57–9, 341–2, 344, 417
  see also Tokyo Electric Power Company

Geithner, Timothy, 120
Gelband, Michael, 486n14
General Motors (GM)
  culture and Barra's testimony, 331–2
  internal response to faulty ignition switch, 328–31
  NHTSA and, 332–3
  wrong choice of ignition switch, 326–8

Gigerenzer, Gerd, 94, 223, 355, 432
Gilchrist, Simon, 199
Gillis, Thomas, 146–7, 149
Global Association of Risk Professionals (GARP), xvi–xvii
Global Banking and Markets (GBM), 174, 180, 184
global financial crisis, 105–6, 108, 118, 120, 124, 125, 139, 141, 157, 166, 170–1, 184, 189, 191–2, 194–5, 209, 212, 227, 247, 269, 338, 343–4, 462, 464
global warming, 12–14
Godley, Wynne, 447, 449
Goodwin, Fred, 175, 177–8, 187, 189
Goodwin-Keen models, 447–9
Gorton, Gary, 167
Great Depression, 108, 120, 122–3, 157, 447, 464
Greenberg, Maurice (Hank), 166, 169–70
Greenfield, Susan, 107
greenhouse gas (GHG) emissions, 12
Greenspan, Alan, 117
Groenink, Rijkman, 174, 185–8
Group of Thirty, 222
groupthink, 64–6, 87, 95, 97, 131, 139, 150, 155, 168, 171, 178, 189, 191, 212, 243, 276–7, 279, 288, 314, 330, 336, 339–40
Grout, Julien, 295–6
Gugliada, Richard, 146–8

Haldane, Andrew, 222–3, 228
Hayward, Tony, 308, 310–11, 317
hedge funds, 115, 119, 128, 135, 188, 231, 234, 237–8, 251–4, 257, 265–8, 272, 290
Hellwig, Martin, 222, 228
hormones, 2, 5–6, 10, 153, 189
  euphoria and, 106–7
  male competition and, 184–5
  self-control and, 277–8
Housing and Urban Development (HUD), 159
HSBC, 174, 187

Iksil, Bruno, 283–90, 292–3, 295–6
incentives and risk taking, 100–3
individual stocks
    Baker-Wurgler sentiment, 261–5
    dissonance at hedge fund workshop, 251–4
    general findings from data, 254–7
    integrated approach, 265–6
    overview, 249–50
    return and risk, 257–61
    textbook approach to, 250–1
IndyMac Bank, 165
Inglis, Andy, 311, 342
Ingram, David, 72
Institute of International Finance (IIF), 222
Intergovernmental Panel on Climate Change (IPCC), 12–13
International Monetary Fund (IMF), 221, 461–2, 465
International Swaps and Derivatives Association (ISDA), 222
Investor Behavior Project (IBP) series, 453–4

JPMorgan, risk management and
    Drew, Ina and, 289–91
    hiding losses with skewed statistics, 295–6
    limit breaches, 291–5
    OCC and, 296–7
    overview, 281–2
    playing out of complex objectives, 286–9
    trading at CIO, 282–5

Kahneman, Daniel, 24, 37–8, 47–8, 51, 54, 59–60, 130, 250, 278, 371–2, 374, 376–8, 380–1, 383–6, 392–4, 396, 398, 405, 418, 432
Kaluza, Robert, 312–13
Kaplan, Robert, 96–9, 281–2, 296–7
Kaplan-Mikes risk typology framework, 96–100
    external risks, 98–100
    preventable risks, 96–7
    strategy risks, 97–8

Kerviel, Jérôme, xv, 103
key performance indicators (KPIs), 94, 131, 138
key risk indicators (KRIs), 94
Keynes-Godley models, 445–7
Kimball, Andrew, 152
Krivanek, Bill, 323, 326
Kronthal, Jeff, 134–5
Krugman, Paul, 121–2, 449

LaSalle bankm, 174–7, 181, 188–9
Lehman Brothers, 1, 119–20, 123, 125, 133–5, 166, 178, 192, 202–7, 229, 339, 344, 461
Levin, Robert, 163, 165
Libor, 4, 9–11, 14
Lippens, Maurice, 185, 189
Lloyds Banking, 10
Loan Evaluation & Estimate of Loss System (LEVELS), 144, 147–8
London Whale, 281–3, 290, 296, 341
long shots (LS), 28, 32, 35, 51, 347, 350, 357–64, 366, 386–8, 400, 403–4, 407
Long Term Capital Management (LTCM), 128–9
Lopes, Lola, 24–9, 31, 297, 347, 350–7, 362, 385–8, 397, 400, 406
    see also SP/A (security, potential, and aspiration) theory
loss aversion
    aversion to sure loss vs., 51
    CPT and, 392, 396, 398, 404–7
    decision-making and, 101
    excessive optimism and, 345
    explained, 38–40
    framing and, 42, 44, 48
    Merrill Lynch and, 134
    myopic loss aversion, 392
    prospect theory and, 373–4, 378, 380, 385
    risk management and, 72, 80, 134
    SP/A theory and, 78–80, 404–7
    see also aversion to sure loss
lottery, 28, 37, 79
Lucas, Douglas, 145

Madoff, Bernard
  background, 229
  Barron's 2001 story on, 230–1
  Fairfield Sentry and, 233–7
  psychological issues associated with fraud of, 229–30
  response to issues raised, 237–9
  SEC and, 239–44, 339
  SEC culture issues and, 245–7
  split-strike conversion strategy and, 231–3
  see also Ponzi finance
Madouros, Vasileios, 222–3
Mancini, Loriano, 195
Manzke, Sandra, 238–9
marginal expected shortfall (MES), 192–4, 201–2, 205–8
MARHedge, 234, 237–8, 245
Markopolos, Harry, 240–3, 245, 339
Markowitz, Harry, 24, 37, 398–9
Martin-Artajo, Javier, 283, 287–90, 296
McCulley, Paul, 108
McDonald's, 409
McDougall, Cameron, 252–4, 265
McGraw-Hill, 142–3, 145–6
McKinsey, 126
McLean, Bethany, 137–8, 273
Merrill Lynch
  incentives at, 137–9
  information sharing, 136–7
  overview, 132–3
  planning at, 133–4
  standards for risk at, 134–6
MF Global
  financial crisis and, 268–74
  groupthink at, 276–7
  hormones and self-control, 277–8
  Milgram's experiment and, 274–6
  overview, 267–8
  risk management and, 278–9
Mikes, Annette, 96–9, 281–2, 296–7
Milgram, Stanley, 274–6
Minerals Management Service (MMS), 314–16

Minsky, Hyman, Financial Instability Hypothesis
  euphoria and hormones, 106–7
  financial innovation and asset values, 112–15
  fringe finance, 108–9
  leverage, 107–8
  new era thinking, 115–16
  overview, 105–6
  policy recommendations, 120–4
  Ponzi schemes, 109–12
  regulatory failure, 116–17
  runs on financial institutions and markets, 118–19
  too big to fail, 119–20
Moody's
  AIG and, 168
  background, 141–4
  CDOs and, 150–2
  MF Global and, 270, 272
  mortgage defaults and, 124, 150–2
  psychology and cheating, 153
  psychology and competitive bidding, 152
  race to the bottom, 145, 147–8, 159, 339
  risk management and, 14, 128, 170
  sentiment and, 194
Morgan Stanley, 133, 135, 202, 204, 207–8
Mudd, Dan, 162–3, 165

nationally recognized statistical rating organizations (NRSRO), 143
NatWest, 175, 177
Neue Privat Bank, 235
Nocera, Joe, 137–8
Nomura, 235
Northeast Regional Office (NERO), 240–2, 244–6
  see also Securities and Exchange Commission

Obama, Barack, 12, 121, 305, 316
Oden, Greg, 385–8, 397

Office of Inspector General (OIG), 240–1, 243–7
  see also Securities and Exchange Commission
Office of the Federal Housing Enterprise Oversight (OFHEO), 117, 160, 162–3
O'Neal, Stanley, 133–5, 137–8, 339
open-book management (OBM)
  Ebola outbreak of 2014, 89–92
  incentives and risk taking, 100–3
  Kaplan-Mikes risk typology framework, 96–100
  overview, 85–6
  pitfalls and processes, 92–3
  process and culture, 86–9
  risk management structure and culture, 93–6
optimism, 61–2
Ospel, Marcel, 125
overconfidence, 62–3, 424–7

Paulsen, Hank, 120, 271, 273
perceived risks, 56–9, 414–18
personality, risk and
  affect and well-being, 77
  Bezos, Jeff and, 73–4
  desire for control, 76
  dimensions of personality, 75–7
  dispositional optimism, 76
  loss aversion, SP/A, and risk taking, 78–80
  optimism and entrepreneurial risk taking, 74–5
  overview, 71
  risk management styles, 72–3
  social anxiousness and self-monitoring, 76–7
  SP/A theory and, 77–8
  survey questions to probe for style, 80–2
Petra Plan, 187–8
PharMerica, 4, 7–9, 14
Plight of the Fortune Tellers, The (Rebonato), xiv, 53, 173
plural risk management (PRM), 72–4, 77–8

Ponzi finance, 109–16, 118, 123–4, 129, 139, 141, 155, 157, 168, 171, 192, 201–2, 209, 227, 229–30, 232, 239–47, 339, 344, 446, 450, 462–3
  see also Madoff, Bernard
positive psychology, 75
preventable risks, 96–7
price fixing, 10, 155
Prince, Charles, 213
priority heuristic, 355–7
private mortgage-backed securities (PMBS), 203–4
probability density functions (pdfs), 347–51
probability magnitudes, 45–7
Professional Risk Managers' Association (PRMIA), xvi
prospect theory
  aversion to a sure loss, 50–2
  framing and concurrent choice, 42–3
  loss aversion, 38–40
  modeling, 372–9
  overview, 37–8
  probability magnitudes, 45–7
  psychological principles underlying, 47–8
  quasi-hedonic editing, 44–5
  stake size and individual differences, 49–50
  varying risk attitude according to circumstances, 40–2
psychology
  principles underlying prospect theory, 47–8
  of risk, 23–5
  valuation, 30–5
Puri, Manju, 74–7

quasi-hedonic editing, 379–84

Raiter, Frank, 146–8
rating firms
  adjustment, limitation, and delay in RMBs and CDOs ratings, 147–50

rating firms—*Continued*
  decision-making in structured finance, 146–7
  history and context, 142–4
  Moody's, 150–2
  psychology and cheating, 153–5
  psychology and competitive bidding, 152–3
  race to the bottom, 145–6
  S&P, 144–50
rationality, violations of, 371–2
Rebonato, Riccardo, xiv, xix, 53, 173, 216–19, 221
Representative Concentration Pathways (RCPs), 12–13
representativeness, 59–61, 418–20
repurchase agreements (repos), 203
residential mortgage-backed securities (RMBS), 143–7, 149, 152, 155, 179, 339
risk
  example of, 20–3
  overview, 19–20
  psychology of, 23–5
  risk managers, 29–30
  SP/A theory and, 27–30
  styles of risk management, 72–3
  three key emotions, 25–7
  valuation psychology and, 30–5
Risk and Insurance Management Society (RIMS), xiii
risk management behavior (RMB), 94, 133, 135, 293
risk management culture (RMC), 94, 133, 135, 293
risk management structure (RMS), 94, 100, 131, 133, 135, 293, 308
Ri$k Minds conference, xiv–xvi, xx
Risk Savvy (Gigerenzer), 94
Risk Taking: A Managerial Perspective (Shapira), 100
Robinson, David, 74–7
Rohner, Marcel, 125
Rose, Amber, 330
Rose, Joanne, 146–8

Roseman, Michael, 268–72, 274, 276, 278–9, 339
Royal Bank of Scotland (RBS)
  Basel II and, 182–3
  capital position, liquidity risk, and risk exposure, 179–81
  FIH and, 343
  FSA's take on risk management of, 178–84
  Libor and, 9–11
  male competition and, 187–9
  overconfidence and, 342
  postacquisition of ABN AMRO, 177–8
  pursuit of ABN AMRO, 14, 173–7, 187
  Rebonato, Riccardo and, xiv
  risks generated by decision to lead consortium, 183–4
  short-term debt and, 181–2
Russo, J. Edward, 411, 414, 424

Santa Clara University, 418
Santander, 10, 175, 188–9, 238–9
Savage, Leonard J., 37
Savage, Tom, 168
Schoemaker, Paul, 411, 414, 424
Securities and Exchange Commission (SEC)
  see also Northeast Regional Office; Office of Inspector General
Sepulvado, Ronald, 311, 314
Shapira, Zur, 88, 100–1, 435, 437
skewed statistics, hiding losses with, 295–6
Slovic, Paul, 56
Smith, Adam, 116
social anxiousness and self-monitoring, 76–7
Société Générale (SocGen), xv, 10, 103, 186, 502n5
Southwest Airlines
  failures, 322–6
  risk management, 320–2
SP/A (security, potential, and aspiration) theory
  ABN AMRO acquisition and, 185

applying to ranking and valuation, 364–7
aspiration and, 360, 442
aversion to loss and, 50–1
dual focal point framework and, 88, 127, 139
explained, 25, 351
long shots/short shots and, 28–9
loss aversion and risk taking, 78–80
mathematical structure, 352–5
modeling prospect theory and, 377–8
Moody's and, 141
personality and key emotions, 77–8
prospect theory and, 385–400, 405–6
psychological issues and, 33, 88
questions to probe for style, 80–2
risk management and, 72–4, 274, 306
S&P and, 141, 146
valuation psychology and, 33
see also Lopes, Lola
Spitzer, Eliot, 166
split-strike conversion strategy, 231–3
Stack, Jack, 96, 329
stake size, 49–50
Standard and Poor's (S&P)
  AIG and, 168
  background, 141–4
  Bergen Brunswig and, 8–9
  CDOs and, 144–50
  CPT and, 392–4
  decision-making in structured finance at, 146–7
  Fairfield Sentry and, 233–6
  Madoff, Bernard and, 231, 237
  MF Global and, 270
  mortgage defaults and, 124
  operating framework at, 144–5
  psychology and cheating, 153, 155
  psychology and competitive bidding, 152
  race to the bottom, 145–6, 159, 339
  risk management and, 14, 128, 170
  RMBS and, 147–8, 339
  sentiment and, 194–6, 203–5
  split-strike conversion strategy and, 232

Starr, Cornelius Vander, 166
  see also AIG
Stephan, Larry, 20, 268
strategy risks, 97–8
Stupak, Bart, 310
Suh, Simona, 242–3, 247
Sullivan, Martin, 166, 169
System 1/System 2 thinking, 250, 254, 265, 278, 335, 506n2
systemic risk (SRISK)
  indicators of sentiment, 197–201
  measuring risk of financial firms, 192–5
  measuring sentiment, 194–7
  overview, 191–2
  sentiment and (2008–2009), 205–8
  trajectories of sentiment and, 201–4

Tesher, David, 146–7
Three Mile Island, 57–9
Tokyo Electric Power Company (TEPCO), 4–7, 14, 341–3
  see also Fukushima Daiichi power plant
Turnbull, Shann, xvi
Tversky, Amos, 24, 37–8, 48, 51, 54, 59–61, 130, 371–4, 376–8, 380–1, 383–6, 392–4, 396, 398, 405, 418, 432

UBS
  CDOs and, 125, 127–9, 131
  compensation systems, 138
  Forex rates and, 11
  global financial crisis and, 124, 191, 338
  housing market and, 194, 201–2
  incentives and governance, 131–2
  information sharing at, 130–1
  leverage and, 226–7
  Merrill Lynch and, 132–3
  overview, 126
  planning at, 126–7
  risk management, 125–6, 155
  senior executives, 170
  standards for risk at, 127–30
Unicredito, 186, 188

Varley, John, 174, 187
varying risk attitude according to circumstances, 40–2
Vijayvergiya, Amit, 233
VIX, 194–5, 467
V-Lab (NY University's Volatility Lab), 193, 201–2, 205, 208
Votron, Jean-Paul, 185, 189

Wachovia, 192, 203–4, 206–7, 227
Wall Street Journal, 145, 239, 243, 290, 326, 329
Wallace (experiment participant), 274–6
Washington Mutual, 192
Weill, Sandy, 122–3
Wells Fargo, 207
Wheeler, Wyman, 312
Winer, Mark, 164–5

Wolf, Martin, 108
World Bank, 461
World Health Organization (WHO), 89–93, 95, 99–100, 336–7, 437, 439
Wray, Randall, 447
Wuffli, Peter, 126
Wyman, Oliver, 126–8, 338

Xiong-Yan behavioral model, 450–1

Yarish, Allan, xv
Yellen, Janet, 124

Zagat, 321
Zakrajšek, Egon, 199
Zeisberger, Stefan, 388–9, 391
Zuckerman, Mortimer, 230